FIFTH EDITION

SOCIOLOGY

Exploring the Architecture of Everyday Life
READINGS

TITLES OF RELATED INTEREST FROM PINE FORGE PRESS

Sociology: Exploring The Architecture of Everyday Life, Fifth Edition by David M. Newman

The Globalization of Nothing by George Ritzer

The McDonaldization of Society, Revised New Century Edition by George Ritzer

McDonaldization: The Reader edited by George Ritzer

Second Thoughts: Seeing Conventional Wisdom Through the Sociological Eye, Third Edition by Janet M. Ruane and Karen A. Cerulo

Sociological Snapshots 4 by Jack Levin

Key Ideas in Sociology, Second Edition by Peter Kivisto

This Book Is Not Required, Revised Edition by Inge Bell and Bernard McGrane

Sociology Through Active Learning: Student Exercises by Kathleen McKinney, Frank Beck, and Barbara Heyl

Sociology in Action: Cases for Critical and Sociological Thinking by David Hachen

Women and Men at Work, Second Edition by Irene Padavic and Barbara Reskin

Race, Ethnicity, Gender, and Class: The Sociology of Group Conflict and Change, Third Edition by Joseph F. Healey

Diversity and Society: Race, Ethnicity, and Gender by Joseph F. Healey

Race, Ethnicity, and Gender: Selected Readings edited by Joseph F. Healey and Eileen O'Brien

Illuminating Social Life: Classical and Contemporary Theory, Second Edition by Peter Kivsito

Sociology of Families, Second Edition by David M. Newman and Liz Grauerholz

The Production of Reality: Essays and Readings on Social Interaction, Third Edition, edited by Jodi O'Brien and Peter Kollock

FIFTH EDITION

SOCIOLOGY

Exploring the Architecture of Everyday Life
READINGS

EDITORS
DAVID M. NEWMAN
DePauw University
JODI O'BRIEN
Seattle University

PINE FORGE PRESS
An Imprint of Sage Publications, Inc.
Thousand Oaks • London • New Delhi

For information:

Pine Forge Press
An imprint of Sage Publications, Inc.
2455, Teller Road
Thousand Oaks, California 91320
E-mail: order@sagepub.com

Sage Publications Ltd.
1 Oliver's Yard
55 City Road
London EC1Y 1SP
United Kingdom

Sage Publications India Pvt. Ltd.
B-42, Panchsheel Enclave
Post Box 4109
New Delhi 110 017 India

Printed in the United States of America

Library of Congress Cataloging-in-Publication Data

Sociology: Exploring the architecture of everyday life: Readings / David M. Newman, Jodi O'Brien, editors.—5th ed.
     p. cm.
Includes bibliographical references and index.
ISBN 0-7619-8827-0 (Paper)
   1. Sociology. I. Newman, David M., 1958- II. O'Brien, Jodi. HM585 .N48 2004 301—dc22

                              2003022062

   05 06 07 08 09 7 6 5 4 3

Acquiring Editor:	Jerry Westby
Editorial Assistant:	Vonessa Vondera
Production Editor:	Diana E. Axelsen
Typesetter:	C&M Digitals (P) Ltd.
Cover Designer:	Michelle Lee Kenny

Contents

PART II
THE CONSTRUCTION OF SELF AND SOCIETY   77

Preface

One of the greatest challenges we face as teachers of sociology is getting our students to see the relevance of the course material to their own lives and to appreciate fully its connection to the larger society. We teach our students to see that sociology is all around us. It's in our families, our careers, our media, our goals, our interests, our desires, even our minds. Sociology can be found at the neighborhood pub, the maintenance bay at the local gas station, and the highest offices of government. It's with us when we're alone and when we're in a mob of people. Sociology can answer questions of global as well as private significance—from how some countries create and maintain dominance over others to why we find some people attractive and not others; from why poverty, discrimination, crime, and homelessness exist to why many Americans eat scrambled eggs rather than rice for breakfast.

With these ideas in mind we set out to compile this collection of short articles, chapters, and excerpts designed to help introduce you to sociology. Instructors and students alike responded quite positively to the readings in the first four editions of this book. It would have been easy simply to include those same readings in this fifth edition. But we very much wanted the book to be fresh and contemporary. And we especially wanted to emphasize the importance of race, social class, and gender in people's everyday lives. In addition, we've streamlined this collection by reducing the number of readings from 38 to 32. Of these selections, 9 are new to this edition. Most of these were written within the past few years.

As in the first four editions, these selections are intended to be vivid, provocative, and eye-opening examples of the practice of sociology. Many of the readings are drawn from carefully conducted social research. They provide important illustrations of how sociologists support their theories, insights, and ideas with empirical evidence. Others are personal narratives that put human faces on matters of sociological relevance. In addition to accurately representing the sociological perspective and providing rigorous coverage of the discipline, we hope the selections are thought-provoking and enjoyable to read.

The readings represent a variety of styles. Some use common, everyday experiences and phenomena (such as sadness, drug use, disability, employment, webcam Internet sites, intimacy, parenthood) to illustrate the relationship between the individual and society. Others focus on important social issues and problems (crime, definitions of race, poverty, educational inequalities, sexuality, immigration, global economics, environmental degradation, political extremism) or on historical events (massacres during war, drug scares, early movements for women's rights). You need not be a trained sociologist to see the world sociologically. So this book includes articles written by psychologists, anthropologists, social commentators, and journalists as well as by sociologists.

To help you get the most out of these selections we've written brief introductions to each chapter that provide the sociological context for the readings. For those of you who are also reading the accompanying textbook, these introductions will furnish a quick intellectual link between the readings and information in the textbook. After each selection you will find a set of discussion questions to ponder. Many of these questions ask you to apply a specific author's conclusions to some contemporary issue in society or to your own life experiences. It is our hope that these questions will generate a lot of classroom debate and help you see the sociological merit of the readings.

Books like these are enormous projects. We would like to thank Jerry Westby, Denise Simon, Diana Axelsen, Vonessa Vondera, and Kristin Snow and the rest of the staff at Pine Forge Press for their useful advice and assistance in putting this reader together. We are also grateful to the following people for their helpful suggestions regarding the various readings that are new to this edition: Michele Berger, Wendy Chapkis, Judy Howard, Val Jenness, Townsand Price-Spratlen, Nicole Raeburn, Barbara Trepagnier, France Winddance Twine, and David Yamane. Finally, a heartfelt thanks to Samm Lindsey for continuously inspiring me to stretch.

Enjoy!

David M. Newman
Department of Sociology/Anthropology
DePauw University
Greencastle, IN 46135
E-Mail: DNEWMAN@DEPAUW.EDU

Jodi O'Brien
Department of Sociology
Seattle University
Seattle, WA 98122
E-mail: JOBRIEN@SEATTLEU.EDU

Acknowledgments

We appreciate to the many helpful comments offered by the reviewers of the four editions of this book:

Sharon Abbott, Fairfield University

Deborah Abowitz, Bucknell University

Stephen Adair, Central Connecticut State University

Rebecca Adams, University of North Carolina, Greensboro

Ron Aminzade, University of Minnesota

Afroza Anwary, Carleton College

George Arquitt, Oklahoma State University

Carol Auster, Franklin and Marshall College

Ellen C. Baird, Arizona State University

David Bogen, Emerson College

Frances A. Boudreau, Connecticut College

Todd Campbell, Loyola University, Chicago

Wanda Clark, South Plains College

Thomas Conroy, St. Peter's College

Norman Conti, Cleveland State University

Doug Currivan, University of Massachusetts, Boston

Jeff Davidson, University of Delaware

Kimberly Davies, Augusta State University

Tricia Davis, North Carolina State University

James J. Dowd, University of Georgia

Charlotte Chorn Dunham, Texas Tech University

Charles Edgley, Oklahoma State University

Rachel Einwohner, Purdue University

Shalom Endleman, Quinnipiac College

Rebecca Erickson, University of Akron

Kimberly Faust, Fitchburg State University

Patrick Fontane, St. Louis College of Pharmacy

Michael J. Fraleigh, Bryant College

Barry Goetz, University of Dayton

Lorie Schabo Grabowski, University of Minnesota

Valerie Gunter, University of New Orleans

Roger Guy, Texas Lutheran University

Charles Harper, Creighton University

Doug Harper, Duquesne University

Peter Hennen, University of Minnesota

Max Herman, Oberlin College

Susan Hoerbelt, University of South Florida

Gary Hytreck, Georgia Southern University

Valerie Jenness, University of California, Irvine

Kathryn Johnson, Barat College

Richard Jones, Marquette University

Tom Kando, California State University, Sacramento

Steve Keto, Kent State University

Peter Kivisto, Augustana College

Marc LaFountain, State University of West Georgia

Melissa Latimer, West Virginia University

Joseph Lengermann, University of Maryland, College Park

Lynda A. Litteral, Clark State Community College

Fred Maher

Kristen Marcussen, University of Iowa

Benjamin Mariante, Stonehill College

Joseph Marolla, Virginia Commonwealth University

Michallene McDaniel, University of Georgia

James R. McIntosh, Lehigh University

Jerome McKibben, Fitchburg State University

Ted P. McNeilsmith, Adams State College

Melinda J. Milligan, Tulane Univeristy

Susannne Monahan, Montana State University

Kelly Murphy, University of Pittsburgh

Daniel Myers, University of Notre Dame

Elizabeth Ehrhardt Mustaine, University of Central Florida

Anne Nurse, College of Wooster

Marjukka Ollilainen, Weber State University

Toska Olson, University of Washington

Larry Perkins

Bernice Pescosolido, Indiana University, Bloomington

Mike Plummer, Boston College

Edward Ponczek, William Rainey Harper College

Tanya Poteet, Capitol University

Sharon E. Preves, Grand Valley State University

Judith Richlin-Klonsky, University of California, Los Angeles

Robert Robinson, Indiana University, Bloomington

Mary Rogers, University of West Florida

Sally S. Rogers, Montgomery College

Michael Ryan, Upper Iowa University

Mark Shibley, Southern Oregon University

Thomas Shriver, Oklahoma State University

Katherine Slevin, College of William and Mary

Lisa White Smith, Christopher Newport University

Eldon Snyder, Bowling Green State University

Nicholas Sofios, Providence College

Kandi Stinson, Xavier University

Richard Tardanico, Florida International University

Robert Tellander, Sonoma State University

Kathleen Tiemann, University of North Dakota

Steven Vallas, Georgia Institute of Technology

Tom Vander Ven, Hofstra University

John Walsh, University of Illinois, Chicago

Gregory Weiss, Roanoke College

Marty Wenglinsky, Quinnipiac College

Stephan Werba, Catonsville Community College

Cheryl E. Whitley, Marist College

Norma Williams, University of North Texas

Janelle Wilson, University of Minnesota, Duluth

Mark Winton, University of Central Florida

Cynthia A. Woolever, Lexington Theological Seminary

Ashraf Zahedi, Santa Clara University

Stephen Zehr, University of Southern Indiana

About the Editors

David M. Newman (Ph.D., University of Washington) is Professor of Sociology at DePauw University. In addition to the introductory course in sociology, he teaches courses on research methods, family, social psychology, and deviance. He has won teaching awards at both the University of Washington and DePauw University. His other books include the companion textbook for this reader, *Sociology: Exploring the Architecture of Everyday Life, Fifth Edition*, and *Sociology of Families, Second Edition* (with coauthor Elizabeth Grauerholz).

Jodi O'Brien (Ph.D., University of Washington) is Associate Professor of Sociology at Seattle University. She teaches courses in social psychology, sexuality, inequality, and classical and contemporary theory. She writes and lectures on the cultural politics of transgressive identities and communities. Her other books include *Everyday Inequalities* (Basil Blackwell), *Social Prisms: Reflections on Everyday Myths and Paradoxes* (Pine Forge Press), and (with coeditor Peter Kollock) *The Production of Reality: Essays and Readings on Social Interaction, Third Edition* (Pine Forge Press).

PART I

The Individual and Society

Taking a New Look at a Familiar World

The primary theme of sociology is that our everyday thoughts and actions are the product of a complex interplay between massive social forces and personal characteristics. We can't understand the relationship between individuals and their societies without understanding both. The sociological imagination is the ability to see the impact of social forces on our private lives. It is an awareness that our lives lie at the intersection of personal biography and societal history. The sociological imagination encourages us to move beyond individualistic explanations of human experiences to an understanding of the mutual influence that individuals and society have on one another. So, rather than study what goes on within people, sociologists study what goes on between and among people, as individuals, groups, organizations, or entire societies. Sociology forces us to look outside the tight confines of our individual personalities to understand the social phenomena that shape us.

Consider illegal drug use. Why do some people merely experiment with drugs while others become habitual users? Howard Becker addresses this question in "Becoming a Marihuana User," a piece he wrote in the early 1950s. He concludes that those who continue smoking marijuana do so not because they have become physically dependent on the drug but because they have "learned" to think of the experience and the effects as enjoyable. People "learn" to respond to events and experiences through their interactions with others. They learn how to engage with things (in this case how to actually smoke marijuana to produce effects) and how to recognize experiences (knowing whether you're high). And when they introduce the drug to friends, they pass along this positive information. By explaining habitual drug use in such a way, Becker helps introduce us to the sociological perspective on understanding social life: Behavior commonly attributed to individual personality traits or even physiological processes can be better understood by examining the broader social context within which it takes place.

Becoming a Marihuana User

Howard S. Becker

(1953)

The use of marihuana is and has been the focus of a good deal of attention on the part of both scientists and laymen. One of the major problems students of the practice have addressed themselves to has been the identification of those individual psychological traits which differentiate marihuana users from nonusers and which are assumed to account for the use of the drug. That approach, common in the study of behavior categorized as deviant, is based on the premise that the presence of a given kind of behavior in an individual can best be explained as the result of some trait which predisposes or motivates him to engage in the behavior.[1]

This study is likewise concerned with accounting for the presence or absence of marihuana use in an individual's behavior. It starts, however, from a different premise: that the presence of a given kind of behavior is the result of a sequence of social experiences during which the person acquires a conception of the meaning of the behavior, and perceptions and judgments of objects and situations, all of which make the activity possible and desirable. Thus, the motivation or disposition to engage in the activity is built up in the course of learning to engage in it and does not antedate this learning process. For such a view it is not necessary to identify those "traits" which "cause" the behavior. Instead, the problem becomes one of describing the set of changes in the person's conception of the activity and of the experience it provides for him.[2]

This paper seeks to describe the sequence of changes in attitude and experience which lead to *the use of marihuana for pleasure.* Marihuana does not produce addiction, as do alcohol and the opiate drugs; there is no withdrawal sickness and no ineradicable craving for the drug.[3] The most frequent pattern of use might be termed "recreational." The drug is used occasionally for the pleasure the user finds in it, a relatively casual kind of behavior in comparison with the connected use of addicting drugs. The term "use for pleasure" is meant to emphasize the noncompulsive and casual character of the behavior. It is also meant to eliminate from consideration here those few cases in which marihuana is used for its prestige value only, as a symbol that one is a certain kind of person, with no pleasure at all being derived from its use.

The analysis presented here is conceived of as demonstrating the greater explanatory usefulness of the kind of theory outlined above as opposed to the predispositional theories now current. This may be seen in two ways: (1) predispositional theories cannot account for that group of users (whose existence is admitted)[4] who do not exhibit the trait or traits considered to cause the behavior and (2) such theories cannot account for the great variability over time of a given individual's behavior with reference to the drug. The same person will at one stage be unable to use the drug for pleasure, at a later stage be able and willing to do so, and still later, again be unable to use it in this way. These changes, difficult to explain from a predispositional or motivational theory, are readily understandable in terms of changes in the individual's conception of the drug as is the existence of "normal" users.

The study attempted to arrive at a general statement of the sequence of changes in individual attitude and experience which have always occurred when the individual has become willing and able to use marihuana for pleasure and which have not occurred or not been permanently maintained when this is not the case. This generalization is stated in universal terms in order that negative cases may be discovered and used to revise the explanatory hypothesis.[5]

Fifty interviews with marihuana users from a variety of social backgrounds and present positions in society constitute the data from which the generalization was constructed and against which it was tested.[6] The interviews focused on the history of the person's experience with the drug, seeking major changes in his attitude toward it and in his actual use of it, and the reasons for these changes. The final generalization is a statement of that sequence of changes in attitude which occurred in every case known to me in which the person came to use marihuana for pleasure. Until a negative case is found, it may be considered as an explanation of all cases of marihuana use for pleasure. In addition, changes from use to non-use are shown to be related to similar changes in conception, and in each case it is possible to explain variations in the individual's behavior in these terms.

This paper covers only a portion of the natural history of an individual's use of marihuana,[7] starting with the person having arrived at the point of willingness to try marihuana. He knows that others use it to "get high," but he does not know what this means in concrete terms. He is curious about the experience, ignorant of what it may turn out to be, and afraid that it may be more than he has bargained for. The steps outlined below, if he undergoes them all and maintains the attitudes developed in them, leave him willing and able to use the drug for pleasure when the opportunity presents itself.

I

The novice does not ordinarily get high the first time he smokes marihuana, and several attempts are usually necessary to induce this state. One explanation of this may be that the drug is not smoked "properly," that is, in a way that ensures sufficient dosage to produce real symptoms of intoxication. Most users agree that it cannot be smoked like tobacco if one is to get high:

> Take in a lot of air, you know, and . . . I don't know how to describe it, you don't smoke it like a cigarette, you draw in a lot of air and get it deep down in your system and then keep it there. Keep it there as long as you can.

Without the use of some such technique[8] the drug will produce no effects, and the user will be unable to get high:

> The trouble with people like that [who are not able to get high] is that they're just not smoking it right, that's all there is to it. Either they're not holding it down long enough, or they're getting too much air and not enough smoke, or the other way around or something like that. A lot of people just don't smoke it right, so naturally nothing's gonna happen.

If nothing happens, it is manifestly impossible for the user to develop a conception of the drug as an object which can be used for pleasure, and use will therefore not continue. The first step in the sequence of events that must occur if the person is to become a user is that he must learn to use the proper smoking technique in order that his use of the drug will produce some effects in terms of which his conception of it can change.

Such a change is, as might be expected, a result of the individual's participation in groups in which marihuana is used. In them the individual learns the proper way to smoke the drug. This may occur through direct learning:

> I was smoking like I did an ordinary cigarette. He said, "No, don't do it like that." He said, "Suck it, you know, draw in and hold it in your lungs till you . . . for a period of time."
>
> I said, "Is there any limit of time to hold it?"
>
> He said, "No, just till you feel that you want to let it out, let it out." So I did that three or four times.

Many new users are ashamed to admit ignorance and, pretending to know already, must learn through the more indirect means of observation and imitation:

> I came on like I had turned on [smoked mari-huana] many times before, you know. I didn't want to seem like a punk to this cat. See, like I didn't know the first thing about it—how to smoke it, or what was going to happen, or what. I just watched him like a hawk—I didn't take my eyes off him for a second, because I wanted to do everything just as he did it. I watched how he held it, how he smoked it, and everything. Then when he gave it to me I just came on cool, as though I knew exactly what the score was. I held it like he did and took a poke just the way he did.

No person continued marihuana use for pleasure without learning a technique that supplied sufficient dosage for the effects of the drug to appear. Only when this was learned was it possible for a conception of the drug as an object which could be used for pleasure to emerge. Without such a conception marihuana use was considered meaningless and did not continue.

‖

Even after he learns the proper smoking technique, the new user may not get high and thus not form a conception of the drug as something which can be used for pleasure. A remark made by a user suggested the reason

for this difficulty in getting high and pointed to the next necessary step on the road to being a user:

> I was told during an interview, "As a matter of fact, I've seen a guy who was high out of his mind and didn't know it."
>
> I expressed disbelief: "How can that be, man?"
>
> The interviewee said, "Well, it's pretty strange, I'll grant you that, but I've seen it. This guy got on with me, claiming that he'd never got high, one of those guys, and he got completely stoned. And he kept insisting that he wasn't high. So I had to prove to him that he was."

What does this mean? It suggests that being high consists of two elements: the presence of symptoms caused by marihuana use and the recognition of these symptoms and their connection by the user with his use of the drug. It is not enough, that is, that the effects be present; they alone do not automatically provide the experience of being high. The user must be able to point them out to himself and consciously connect them with his having smoked marihuana before he can have this experience. Otherwise, regardless of the actual effects produced, he considers that the drug has had no effect on him: "I figured it either had no effect on me or other people were exaggerating its effect on them, you know. I thought it was probably psychological, see." Such persons believe that the whole thing is an illusion and that the wish to be high leads the user to deceive himself into believing that something is happening when, in fact, nothing is. They do not continue marihuana use, feeling that "it does nothing" for them.

Typically, however, the novice has faith (developed from his observation of users who do get high) that the drug actually will produce some new experience and continues to experiment with it until it does. His failure to get high worries him, and he is likely to ask more experienced users or provoke comments from them about it. In such conversations he is made aware of specific details of his experience which he may not have noticed or may have noticed but failed to identify as symptoms of being high.

> I didn't get high the first time . . . I don't think I held it in long enough. I probably let it out, you know, you're a little afraid. The second time I wasn't sure, and he [smoking companion] told me, like I asked him for some of the symptoms or something, how would I know, you know. . . . So he told me to sit on a stool. I sat on—I think I sat on a bar stool—and he said. "Let your feet hang," and then when I got down my feet were real cold, you know.
>
> And I started feeling it, you know. That was the first time. And then about a week after that, sometime pretty close to it, I really got on. That was the first time I got on a big laughing kick, you know. Then I really knew I was on.

One symptom of being high is an intense hunger. In the next case the novice becomes aware of this and gets high for the first time:

> They were just laughing the hell out of me because like I was eating so much. I just scoffed [ate] so much food, and they were just laughing at me, you know. Sometimes I'd be looking at them, you know, wondering why they're laughing, you know, not knowing what I was doing. [Well, did they tell you why they were laughing eventually?] Yeah, yeah, I come back, "Hey, man, what's happening?" Like, you know, like I'd ask, "What's happening?" and all of a sudden I feel weird, you know. "Man, you're on you know. You're on pot [high on marihuana]." I said, "No, am I?" Like I don't know what's happening.

The learning may occur in more indirect ways:

> I heard little remarks that were made by other people. Somebody said, "My legs are rubbery," and I can't remember all the remarks that were

made because I was very attentively listening for all these cues for what I was supposed to feel like.

The novice, then, eager to have this feeling, picks up from other users some concrete referents of the term "high" and applies these notions to his own experience. The new concepts make it possible for him to locate these symptoms among his own sensations and to point out to himself a "something different" in his experience that he connects with drug use. It is only when he can do this that he is high. In the next case, the contrast between two successive experiences of a user makes clear the crucial importance of the awareness of the symptoms in being high and re-emphasizes the important role of interaction with other users in acquiring the concepts that make this awareness possible:

> [Did you get high the first time you turned on?] Yeah, sure. Although, come to think of it, I guess I really didn't. I mean, like that first time it was more or less of a mild drunk. I was happy, I guess, you know what I mean. But I didn't really know I was high, you know what I mean. It was only after the second time I got high that I realized I was high the first time. Then I knew that something different was happening.
>
> [How did you know that?] How did I know? If what happened to me that night would of happened to you, you would've known, believe me. We played the first tune for almost two hours—one tune! Imagine, man! We got on the stand and played this one tune, we started at nine o'clock. When we got finished I looked at my watch, it's a quarter to eleven. Almost two hours on one tune. And it didn't seem like anything. I mean, you know, it does that to you. It's like you have much more time or something. Anyway, when I saw that, man, it was too much. I knew I must really be high or something if anything like that could happen. See, and then they explained to me that that's what it did to you, you had a different sense of time and everything. So I realized that that's

what it was. I knew then. Like the first time, I probably felt that way, you know, but I didn't know what's happening.

It is only when the novice becomes able to get high in this sense that he will continue to use marihuana for pleasure. In every case in which use continued, the user had acquired the necessary concepts with which to express to himself the fact that he was experiencing new sensations caused by the drug. That is, for use to continue, it is necessary not only to use the drug so as to produce effects but also to learn to perceive these effects when they occur. In this way marihuana acquires meaning for the user as an object which can be used for pleasure.

With increasing experience the user develops a greater appreciation of the drug's effects; he continues to learn to get high. He examines succeeding experiences closely, looking for new effects, making sure the old ones are still there. Out of this there grows a stable set of categories for experiencing the drug's effects whose presence enables the user to get high with ease.

The ability to perceive the drug's effects must be maintained if use is to continue; if it is lost, marihuana use ceases. Two kinds of evidence support this statement. First, people who become heavy users of alcohol, barbiturates, or opiates do not continue to smoke marihuana, largely because they lose the ability to distinguish between its effects and those of the other drugs.[9] They no longer know whether the marihuana gets them high. Second, in those few cases in which an individual uses marihuana in such quantities that he is always high, he is apt to get this same feeling that the drug has no effect on him, since the essential element of a noticeable difference between feeling high and feeling normal is missing. In such a situation, use is likely to be given up completely, but temporarily, in order that the user may once again be able to perceive the difference.

III

One more step is necessary if the user who has now learned to get high is to continue use. He must learn to enjoy the effects he has just learned to experience. Marihuana-produced sensations are not automatically or necessarily pleasurable. The taste for such experience is a socially acquired one, not different in kind from acquired tastes for oysters or dry martinis. The user feels dizzy, thirsty; his scalp tingles; he misjudges time and distances; and so on. Are these things pleasurable? He isn't sure. If he is to continue marihuana use, he must decide that they are. Otherwise, getting high, while a real enough experience, will be an unpleasant one he would rather avoid.

The effects of the drug, when first perceived, may be physically unpleasant or at least ambiguous:

> It started taking effect, and I didn't know what was happening, you know, what it was, and I was very sick. I walked around the room, walking around the room trying to get off, you know; it just scared me at first, you know. I wasn't used to that kind of feeling.

In addition, the novice's naïve interpretation of what is happening to him may further confuse and frighten him, particularly if he decides, as many do, that he is going insane:

> I felt I was insane, you know. Everything people done to me just wigged me. I couldn't hold a conversation, and my mind would be wandering, and I was always thinking, oh, I don't know, weird things, like hearing music different. . . . I get the feeling that I can't talk to anyone. I'll goof completely.

Given these typically frightening and unpleasant first experiences, the beginner will not continue use unless he learns to redefine the sensations as pleasurable:

> It was offered to me, and I tried it. I'll tell you one thing. I never did enjoy it at all. I mean it

was just nothing that I could enjoy. [Well, did you get high when you turned on?] Oh, yeah, I got definite feelings from it. But I didn't enjoy them. I mean I got plenty of reactions, but they were mostly reactions of fear. [You were frightened?] Yes, I didn't enjoy it. I couldn't seem to relax with it, you know. If you can't relax with a thing, you can't enjoy it, I don't think.

In other cases the first experiences were also definitely unpleasant, but the person did become a marihuana user. This occurred, however, only after a later experience enabled him to redefine the sensations as pleasurable:

[This man's first experience was extremely unpleasant, involving distortion of spatial relationships and sounds, violent thirst, and panic produced by these symptoms.] After the first time I didn't turn on for about, I'd say, ten months to a year. . . . It wasn't a moral thing; it was because I'd gotten so frightened, bein' so high. An' I didn't want to go through that again, I mean, my reaction was, "Well, if this is what they call bein' high, I don't dig [like] it." . . . So I didn't turn on for a year almost, accounta that. . . .

Well, my friends started, an' consequently I started again. But I didn't have any more, I didn't have that same initial reaction, after I started turning on again.

[In interaction with his friends he became able to find pleasure in the effects of the drug and eventually became a regular user.]

In no case will use continue without such a redefinition of the effects as enjoyable.

This redefinition occurs, typically, in interaction with more experienced users who, in a number of ways, teach the novice to find pleasure in this experience which is at first so frightening.[10] They may reassure him as to the temporary character of the unpleasant sensations and minimize their seriousness, at the same time calling attention to the more enjoyable aspects. An experienced user describes how he handles newcomers to marihuana use:

Well, they get pretty high sometimes. The average person isn't ready for that, and it is a little frightening to them sometimes. I mean, they've been high on lush [alcohol], and they get higher that way than they've ever been before, and they don't know what's happening to them. Because they think they're going to keep going up, up, up till they lose their minds or begin doing weird things or something. You have to like reassure them, explain to them that they're not really flipping or anything, that they're gonna be all right. You have to just talk them out of being afraid. Keep talking to them, reassuring, telling them it's all right. And come on with your own story, you know: "The same thing happened to me. You'll get to like that after awhile." Keep coming on like that; pretty soon you talk them out of being scared. And besides they see you doing it and nothing horrible is happening to you, so that gives them more confidence.

The more experienced user may also teach the novice to regulate the amount he smokes more carefully, so as to avoid any severely uncomfortable symptoms while retaining the pleasant ones. Finally, he teaches the new user that he can "get to like it after awhile." He teaches him to regard those ambiguous experiences formerly defined as unpleasant as enjoyable. The older user in the following incident is a person whose tastes have shifted in this way, and his remarks have the effect of helping others to make a similar redefinition:

A new user had her first experience of the effects of marihuana and became frightened and hysterical. She "felt like she was half in and half out of the room" and experienced a number of alarming physical symptoms. One of the more experienced users present said, "She's dragged because she's high like that. I'd give anything to get that high myself. I haven't been that high in years."

In short, what was once frightening and distasteful becomes, after a taste for it is built up, pleasant, desired, and sought after. Enjoyment is introduced by the favorable definition of the experience that one acquires from others. Without this, use will not continue, for marihuana will not be for the user an object he can use for pleasure.

In addition to being a necessary step in becoming a user, this represents an important condition for continued use. It is quite common for experienced users suddenly to have an unpleasant or frightening experience, which they cannot define as pleasurable, either because they have used a larger amount of marihuana than usual or because it turns out to be a higher-quality marihuana than they expected. The user has sensations which go beyond any conception he has of what being high is and is in much the same situation as the novice, uncomfortable and frightened. He may blame it on an overdose and simply be more careful in the future. But he may make this the occasion for a rethinking of his attitude toward the drug and decide that it no longer can give him pleasure. When this occurs and is not followed by a redefinition of the drug as capable of producing pleasure, use will cease.

The likelihood of such a redefinition occurring depends on the degree of the individual's participation with other users. Where this participation is intensive, the individual is quickly talked out of his feeling against marihuana use. In the next case, on the other hand, the experience was very disturbing, and the aftermath of the incident cut the person's participation with other users to almost zero. Use stopped for three years and began again only when a combination of circumstances, important among which was a resumption of ties with users, made possible a redefinition of the nature of the drug:

It was too much, like I only made about four pokes, and I couldn't even get it out of my mouth, I was so high, I got real flipped. In the basement, you know, I just couldn't stay in

there anymore. My heart was pounding real hard, you know, and I was going out of my mind; I thought I was losing my mind completely. So I cut out of this basement, and this other guy, he's out of his mind, told me, "Don't, don't leave me, man. Stay here." And I couldn't.

I walked outside, and it was five below zero, and I thought I was dying, and I had my coat open; I was sweating. I was perspiring. My whole insides were all . . . , and I walked about two blocks away, and I fainted behind a bush. I don't know how long I laid there. I woke up, and I was feeling the worst, I can't describe it at all, so I made it to a bowling alley, man, and I was trying to act normal, I was trying to shoot pool, you know, trying to act real normal, and I couldn't lay and I couldn't stand up and I couldn't sit down, and I went up and laid down where some guys that spot pins lay down, and that didn't help me, and I went down to a doctor's office. I was going to go in there and tell the doctor to put me out of my misery . . . because my heart was pounding so hard, you know. . . . So then all weekend I started flipping, seeing things there and going through hell, you know, all kinds of abnormal things. . . . I just quit for a long time then.

[He went to a doctor who defined the symptoms for him as those of a nervous breakdown caused by "nerves" and "worries." Although he was no longer using marihuana, he had some recurrences of the symptoms which led him to suspect that "it was all his nerves."] So I just stopped worrying, you know; so it was about thirty-six months later I started making it again. I'd just take a few pokes, you know. [He first resumed use in the company of the same user-friend with whom he had been involved in the original incident.]

A person, then, cannot begin to use marihuana for pleasure, or continue its use for pleasure, unless he learns to define its effects as enjoyable, unless it becomes and remains an object which he conceived of as capable of producing pleasure.

IV

In summary, an individual will be able to use marihuana for pleasure only when he goes through a process of learning to conceive of it as an object which can be used in this way. No one becomes a user without (1) learning to smoke the drug in a way which will produce real effects; (2) learning to recognize the effects and connect them with drug use (learning, in other words, to get high); and (3) learning to enjoy the sensations he perceives. In the course of this process he develops a disposition or motivation to use marihuana which was not and could not have been present when he began use, for it involves and depends on conceptions of the drug which could only grow out of the kind of actual experience detailed above. On completion of this process he is willing and able to use marihuana for pleasure.

He has learned, in short, to answer "Yes" to the question: "Is it fun?" The direction his further use of the drug takes depends on his being able to continue to answer "Yes" to this question and, in addition, on his being able to answer "Yes" to other questions which arise as he becomes aware of the implications of the fact that the society as a whole disapproves of the practice: "Is it expedient?" "Is it moral?" Once he has acquired the ability to get enjoyment out of the drug, use will continue to be possible for him. Considerations of morality and expediency, occasioned by the reactions of society, may interfere and inhibit use, but use continues to be a possibility in terms of his conception of the drug. The act becomes impossible only when the ability to enjoy the experience of being high is lost, through a change in the user's conception of the drug occasioned by certain kinds of experience with it.

In comparing this theory with those which ascribe marihuana use to motives or predispositions rooted deep in individual behavior, the evidence makes it clear that marihuana use for pleasure can occur only when the process described above is undergone and cannot occur without it. This is apparently so without reference to the nature of the individual's personal makeup, or psychic problems. Such theories assume that people have stable modes of response which predetermine the way they will act in relation to any particular situation or object and that, when they come in contact with the given object or situation, they act in the way in which their makeup predisposes them.

This analysis of the genesis of marihuana use shows that the individuals who come in contact with a given object may respond to it at first in a great variety of ways. If a stable form of new behavior toward the object is to emerge, a transformation of meanings must occur, in which the person develops a new conception of the nature of the object.[11] This happens in a series of communicative acts in which others point out new aspects of his experience to him, present him with new interpretations of events, and help him achieve a new conceptual organization of his world, without which the new behavior is not possible. Persons who do not achieve the proper kind of conceptualization are unable to engage in the given behavior and turn off in the direction of some other relationship to the object or activity.

This suggests that behavior of any kind might fruitfully be studied developmentally, in terms of changes in meanings and concepts, their organization and reorganization, and the way they channel behavior, making some acts possible while excluding others.

NOTES

1. See, as examples of this approach, the following: E. Marcovitz & H. J. Meyers (1944, December), "The marihuana addict in the army," *War Medicine, 6,* 382–391; H. S. Gaskill (1945, September), "Marihuana, an intoxicant," *American*

Journal of Psychiatry, 102, 202–204; S. Charen & L. Perelman (1946, March), "Personality studies of marihuana addicts," *American Journal of Psychiatry, 102,* 674–682.

2. This approach stems from George Herbert Mead's (1934) discussion of objects in *Mind, self, and society,* Chicago: University of Chicago Press, pp. 277–280.

3. Cf. R. Adams (1942, November), "Marihuana," *Bulletin of the New York Academy of Medicine, 18,* 705–730.

4. Cf. L. Kolb (1938, July), "Marihuana," *Federal Probation, 2,* 22–25; and W. Bromberg (1939, July 1), "Marihuana: A psychiatric study," *Journal of the American Medical Association, 113,* 11.

5. The method used is that described in A. R. Lindesmith (1947), *Opiate addiction,* Bloomington, IN: Principia, chap. i. I would like also to acknowledge the important role Lindesmith's work played in shaping my thinking about the genesis of marihuana use.

6. Most of the interviews were done by the author. I am grateful to Solomon Kobrin and Harold Finestone for allowing me to make use of interviews done by them.

7. I hope to discuss elsewhere other stages in this natural history.

8. A pharmacologist notes that this ritual is in fact an extremely efficient way of getting the drug into the blood stream. R. P. Walton (1938), *Marihuana: America's new drug problem,* Philadelphia: J. B. Lippincott, p. 48.

9. "Smokers have repeatedly stated that the consumption of whiskey while smoking negates the potency of the drug. They find it very difficult to get 'high' while drinking whiskey and because of that smokers will not drink while using the 'weed.'" Cf. New York City Mayor's Committee on Marihuana (1944), *The marihuana problem in the city of New York,* Lancaster, PA: Jacques Cattel, p. 13.

10. Charen & Perelman (1946), p. 679.

11. Cf. A. Strauss (1952, June), "The development and transformation of monetary meanings in the child," *American Sociological Review, 17,* 275–286.

THINKING ABOUT THE READING

This article illustrates that our responses to things are based on the social meaning they hold for us and highlights the power of social groups in teaching us what to enjoy. Is Becker's argument applicable only to illegal drug use or can it be applied to the process by which we learn to enjoy more mundane activities, such as eating certain foods and drinking certain beverages? Can his argument also be used to explain how we come to fear certain activities? What are some things that you are afraid of? Think about whether you have had a direct experience that has created these fears or whether you learned them from others. Likewise, consider also some of the routines you engage in at work, school, and home. How did you learn these routines? Can you recall specific individuals or groups from whom you learned them? What about your beliefs and ideals? Can you trace these to their various social sources?

2 Seeing and Thinking Sociologically

Although society exists as an objective entity, it is also a social construction that is created, reaffirmed, and altered through the day-to-day interactions of the very people it influences and controls. Humans are social beings. We constantly look to others to help define and interpret the situations in which we find ourselves. Other people can influence what we see, feel, think, and do. But it's not just other people who influence us. We also live in a *society*, which consists of socially recognizable combinations of individuals—relationships, groups, and organizations—as well as the products of human action—statuses, roles, culture, and institutions.

The influence of social structure on our personal actions is often felt most forcefully when we are compelled to obey the commands of someone who is in a position of authority. In "The My Lai Massacre: A Military Crime of Obedience," Herbert Kelman and Lee Hamilton describe a specific example of a crime in which the individuals involved attempted to deny responsibility for their actions by claiming that they were following the orders of a military officer who had the legitimate right to command them. This incident occurred in the midst of the Vietnam War. Arguably, people do things under such trying conditions that they wouldn't ordinarily do, even—as in this case—kill defenseless people. Kelman and Hamilton make a key sociological point by showing that these soldiers were not necessarily psychological misfits who were especially mean or violent. Instead, the researchers argue, they were ordinary people caught up in tense circumstances that made obeying the brutal commands of an authority seem like the normatively and morally acceptable thing to do.

The influence society has on our everyday lives is often obscured by our culture's tendency to see people's problems in individualistic terms. In his article "Speaking of Sadness," David Karp shows us how the private experience of depression is shaped by social processes and cultural expectations. Karp, a sufferer of clinical depression himself, observes that our society's emphasis on individual achievement and self-fulfillment, not to mention Americans' ever-increasing sense of social isolation, conspires to create an environment in which more and more people suffer from debilitating depression. Karp's observations illustrate the profound power of the sociological imagination by showing that even such an apparently private "illness" as depression cannot be fully understood without seeing its relationship to the culture and the economy.

The My Lai Massacre

A Military Crime of Obedience

Herbert Kelman and V. Lee Hamilton

(1989)

March 16, 1968, was a busy day in U.S. history. Stateside, Robert F. Kennedy announced his presidential candidacy, challenging a sitting president from his own party—in part out of opposition to an undeclared and disastrous war. In Vietnam, the war continued. In many ways, March 16 may have been a typical day in that war. We will probably never know. But we do know that on that day a typical company went on a mission—which may or may not have been typical—to a village called Son (or Song) My. Most of what is remembered from that mission occurred in the subhamlet known to Americans as My Lai 4.

The My Lai massacre was investigated and charges were brought in 1969 and 1970. Trials and disciplinary actions lasted into 1971. Entire books have been written about the army's year-long cover-up of the massacre (for example, Hersh, 1972), and the cover-up was a major focus of the army's own investigation of the incident. Our central concern here is the massacre itself—a crime of obedience—and public reactions to such crimes, rather than the lengths to which many went to deny the event. Therefore this account concentrates on one day: March 16, 1968.

Many verbal testimonials to the horrors that occurred at My Lai were available. More unusual was the fact that an army photographer, Ronald Haeberle, was assigned the task of documenting the anticipated military engagement at My Lai—and documented a massacre instead. Later, as the story of the massacre emerged, his photographs were

widely distributed and seared the public conscience. What might have been dismissed as unreal or exaggerated was depicted in photographs of demonstrable authenticity. The dominant image appeared on the cover of *Life:* piles of bodies jumbled together in a ditch along a trail—the dead all apparently unarmed. All were Oriental, and all appeared to be children, women, or old men. Clearly there had been a mass execution, one whose image would not quickly fade.

So many bodies (over twenty in the cover photo alone) are hard to imagine as the handi-work of one killer. These were not. They were the product of what we call a crime of obedience. Crimes of obedience begin with orders. But orders are often vague and rarely survive with any clarity the transition from one authority down a chain of subordinates to the ultimate actors. The operation at Son My was no exception.

"Charlie" Company, Company C, under Lt. Col. Frank Barker's command, arrived in Vietnam in December 1967. As the army's investigative unit, directed by Lt. Gen. William R. Peers, characterized the personnel, they "contained no significant deviation from the average" for the time. Seymour S. Hersh (1970) described the "average" more explicitly: "Most of the men in Charlie Company had volunteered for the draft; only a few had gone to college for even one year. Nearly half were black, with a few Mexican-Americans. Most were eighteen to twenty-two years old. The favorite reading matter of Charlie Company, like that of other line infantry units in Vietnam, was comic books" (p. 18). The action at My Lai, like that throughout Vietnam, was fought by a cross-section of those Americans who either believed in the war or lacked the social resources to avoid participating in it. Charlie Company was indeed average for that time, that place, and that war.

Two key figures in Charlie Company were more unusual. The company's commander, Capt. Ernest Medina, was an upwardly mobile Mexican-American who wanted to make the army his career, although he feared that he might never advance beyond captain because of his lack of formal education. His eagerness had earned him a nickname among his men: "Mad Dog Medina." One of his admirers was the platoon leader Second Lt. William L. Calley, Jr., an undistinguished, five-foot-three-inch junior-college dropout who had failed four of the seven courses in which he had enrolled his first year. Many viewed him as one of those "instant officers" made possible only by the army's then-desperate need for manpower. Whatever the cause, he was an insecure leader whose frequent claim was "I'm the boss." His nickname among some of the troops was "Surfside 5½," a reference to the swashbuckling heroes of a popular television show, "Surfside 6."

The Son My operation was planned by Lieutenant Colonel Barker and his staff as a search-and-destroy mission with the objective of rooting out the Forty-eighth Viet Cong Battalion from their base area of Son My village. Apparently no written orders were ever issued. Barker's superior, Col. Oran Henderson, arrived at the staging point the day before. Among the issues he reviewed with the assembled officers were some of the weaknesses of prior operations by their units, including their failure to be appropriately aggressive in pursuit of the enemy. Later briefings by Lieutenant Colonel Barker and his staff asserted that no one except Viet Cong was expected to be in the village after 7 A.M. on the following day. The "innocent" would all be at the market. Those present at the briefings gave conflicting accounts of Barker's exact orders, but he conveyed at least a strong suggestion that the Son My area was to be obliterated. As the army's inquiry reported: "While there is some conflict in the testimony as to whether LTC Barker ordered the destruction of houses, dwellings, livestock, and other foodstuffs in the Song My area, the preponderance of the evidence indicates that such destruction was implied, if not specifically directed, by his orders of 15 March" (Peers Report, in Goldstein et al., 1976, p. 94).

Evidence that Barker ordered the killing of civilians is even more murky. What does seem clear, however, is that—having asserted that civilians would be away at the market—he did not specify what was to be done with any who might nevertheless be found on the scene. The Peers Report therefore considered it "reasonable to conclude that LTC Barker's minimal or nonexistent instructions concerning the handling of noncombatants created the potential for grave misunderstandings as to his intentions and for interpretation of his orders as authority to fire, without restriction, on all persons found in target area" (Goldstein et al., 1976, p. 95). Since Barker was killed in action in June 1968, his own formal version of the truth was never available.

Charlie Company's Captain Medina was briefed for the operation by Barker and his staff. He then transmitted the already vague orders to his own men. Charlie Company was spoiling for a fight, having been totally frustrated during its months in Vietnam—first by waiting for battles that never came, then by incompetent forays led by inexperienced commanders, and finally by mines and booby traps. In fact, the emotion-laden funeral of a sergeant killed by a booby trap was held on March 15, the day before My Lai. Captain Medina gave the orders for the next day's action at the close of that funeral. Many were in a mood for revenge.

It is again unclear what was ordered. Although all participants were alive by the time of the trials for the massacre, they were either on trial or probably felt under threat of trial. Memories are often flawed and self-serving at such times. It is apparent that Medina relayed to the men at least some of Barker's general message—to expect Viet Cong resistance, to burn, and to kill livestock. It is not clear that he ordered the slaughter of the inhabitants, but some of the men who heard him thought he had. One of those who claimed to have heard such orders was Lt. William Calley.

As March 16 dawned, much was expected of the operation by those who had set it into motion. Therefore a full complement of "brass" was present in helicopters overhead, including Barker, Colonel Henderson, and their superior, Major General Koster (who went on to become commandant of West Point before the story of My Lai broke). On the ground, the troops were to carry with them one reporter and one photographer to immortalize the anticipated battle.

The action for Company C began at 7:30 as their first wave of helicopters touched down near the subhamlet of My Lai 4. By 7:47 all of Company C was present and set to fight. But instead of the Viet Cong Forty-eighth Battalion, My Lai was filled with the old men, women, and children who were supposed to have gone to market. By this time, in their version of the war, and with whatever orders they thought they had heard, the men from Company C were nevertheless ready to find Viet Cong everywhere. By nightfall, the official tally was 128 VC killed and three weapons captured, although later, unofficial body counts ran as high as 500. The operation at Son My was over. And by nightfall, as Hersh reported: "the Viet Cong were back in My Lai 4, helping the survivors bury the dead. It took five days.

Most of the funeral speeches were made by the Communist guerrillas. Nguyen Bat was not a Communist at the time of the massacre, but the incident changed his mind. 'After the shooting,' he said, 'all the villagers became Communists'" (1970, p. 74). To this day, the memory of the massacre is kept alive by markers and plaques designating the spots where groups of villagers were killed, by a large statue, and by the My Lai Museum, established in 1975 (Williams, 1985).

But what could have happened to leave American troops reporting a victory over Viet Cong when in fact they had killed hundreds of noncombatants? It is not hard to explain the report of victory; that is the essence of a cover-up. It is harder to understand how the killings came to be committed in the first place, making a cover-up necessary.

Mass Executions and the Defense of Superior Orders

Some of the atrocities on March 16, 1968, were evidently unofficial, spontaneous acts: rapes, tortures, killings. For example, Hersh (1970) describes Charlie Company's Second Platoon as entering "My Lai 4 with guns blazing" (p. 50); more graphically, Lieutenant "Brooks and his men in the second platoon to the north had begun to systematically ransack the hamlet and slaughter the people, kill the livestock, and destroy the crops. Men poured rifle and machine-gun fire into huts without knowing—or seemingly caring—who was inside" (pp. 49–50).

Some atrocities toward the end of the action were part of an almost casual "mopping-up," much of which was the responsibility of Lieutenant LaCross's Third Platoon of Charlie Company. The Peers Report states: "The entire 3rd Platoon then began moving into the western edge of My Lai (4), for the mop-up operation. . . . The squad . . . began to burn the houses in the southwestern portion of the hamlet" (Goldstein et al., 1976, p. 133). They became mingled with other platoons during a series of rapes and killings of survivors for which it was impossible to fix responsibility. Certainly to a Vietnamese all GIs would by this point look alike: "Nineteen-year-old Nguyen Thi Ngoc Tuyet watched a baby trying to open her slain mother's blouse to nurse. A soldier shot the infant while it was struggling with the blouse, and then slashed it with his bayonet." Tuyet also said she saw another baby hacked to death by GIs wielding their bayonets. "Le Tong, a twenty-eight-year-old rice farmer, reported seeing one woman raped after GIs killed her children. Nguyen Khoa, a thirty-seven-year-old peasant, told of a thirteen-year-old girl who was raped before being killed. GIs then attacked Khoa's wife, tearing off her clothes. Before they could rape her, however, Khoa said, their six-year-old son, riddled with bullets, fell and saturated her with blood. The GIs left her alone" (Hersh, 1970, p. 72). All of Company C was implicated in a pattern of death and destruction throughout the hamlet, much of which seemingly lacked rhyme or reason.

But a substantial amount of the killing was *organized* and traceable to one authority: the First Platoon's Lt. William Calley. Calley was originally charged with 109 killings, almost all of them mass executions at the trail and other locations. He stood trial for 102 of these killings, was convicted of 22 in 1971, and at first received a life sentence. Though others—both superior and subordinate to Calley—were brought to trial, he was the only one convicted for the My Lai crimes. Thus, the only actions of My Lai for which *anyone* was ever convicted were mass executions, ordered and committed. We suspect that there are commonsense reasons why this one type of killing was singled out. In the midst of rapidly moving events with people running about, an execution of stationary targets is literally a still life that stands out and whose participants

are clearly visible. It can be proven that specific people committed specific deeds. An execution, in contrast to the shooting of someone on the run, is also more likely to meet the legal definition of an act resulting from intent—with malice aforethought. Moreover, American military law specifically forbids the killing of unarmed civilians or military prisoners, as does the Geneva Convention between nations. Thus common sense, legal standards, and explicit doctrine all made such actions the likeliest target for prosecution.

When Lieutenant Calley was charged under military law it was for violation of the Uniform Code of Military Justice (UCMJ) Article 118 (murder). This article is similar to civilian codes in that it provides for conviction if an accused:

> without justification or excuse, unlawfully kills a human being, when he—
>
> 1. has a premeditated design to kill;
> 2. intends to kill or inflict great bodily harm;
> 3. is engaged in an act which is inherently dangerous to others and evinces a wanton disregard of human life; or
> 4. is engaged in the perpetration or attempted perpetration of burglary, sodomy, rape, robbery, or aggravated arson. (Goldstein et al., 1976, p. 507)

For a soldier, one legal justification for killing is warfare; but warfare is subject to many legal limits and restrictions, including, of course, the inadmissibility of killing unarmed noncombatants or prisoners whom one has disarmed. The pictures of the trail victims at My Lai certainly portrayed one or the other of these. Such an action would be illegal under military law; ordering another to commit such an action would be illegal; and following such an order would be illegal.

But following an order may provide a second and pivotal justification for an act that would be murder when committed by a civilian. American military law assumes that the subordinate is inclined to follow orders, as that is the normal obligation of the role. Hence, legally, obedient subordinates are protected from unreasonable expectations regarding their capacity to evaluate those orders:

> An order requiring the performance of a military duty may be inferred to be legal. An act performed manifestly beyond the scope of authority, or pursuant to an order that a man of ordinary sense and understanding would know to be illegal, or in a wanton manner in the discharge of a lawful duty, is not excusable. (Par. 216, Subpar. *d*, Manual for Courts Martial, United States, 1969 Rev.)

Thus what *may* be excusable is the good-faith carrying out of an order, as long as that order appears to the ordinary soldier to be a legal one. In military law, invoking superior orders moves the question from one of the action's consequences—the body count—to one of evaluating the actor's motives and good sense.

In sum, if anyone is to be brought to justice for a massacre, common sense and legal codes decree that the most appropriate targets are those who make themselves executioners. This is the kind of target the government selected in prosecuting Lieutenant Calley with the greatest fervor. And in a military context, the most promising way in which one can redefine one's undeniable deeds into acceptability is to invoke superior orders. This is what Calley did in attempting to avoid conviction. Since the core legal issues involved points of mass execution—the ditches and trail where America's image of My Lai was formed—we review these events in greater detail.

The day's quiet beginning has already been noted. Troops landed and swept unopposed into the village. The three weapons eventually reported as the haul from the operation were picked up from three apparent Viet Cong who fled the village when the troops arrived

and were pursued and killed by helicopter gunships. Obviously the Viet Cong did frequent the area. But it appears that by about 8:00 A.M. no one who met the troops was aggressive, and no one was armed. By the laws of war Charlie Company had no argument with such people.

As they moved into the village, the soldiers began to gather its inhabitants together. Shortly after 8:00 A.M. Lieutenant Calley told Pfc. Paul Meadlo that "you know what to do with" a group of villagers Meadlo was guarding. Estimates of the numbers in the group ranged as high as eighty women, children, and old men, and Meadlo's own estimate under oath was thirty to fifty people. As Meadlo later testified, Calley returned after ten or fifteen minutes: "He [Calley] said, 'How come they're not dead?' I said, 'I didn't know we were supposed to kill them.' He said, 'I want them dead.' He backed off twenty or thirty feet and started shooting into the people—the Viet Cong—shooting automatic. He was beside me. He burned four or five magazines. I burned off a few, about three. I helped shoot 'em" (Hammer, 1971, p. 155). Meadlo himself and others testified that Meadlo cried as he fired; others reported him later to be sobbing and "all broke up." It would appear that to Lieutenant Calley's subordinates something was unusual, and stressful, in these orders.

At the trial, the first specification in the murder charge against Calley was for this incident; he was accused of premeditated murder of "an unknown number, not less than 30, Oriental human beings, males and females of various ages, whose names are unknown, occupants of the village of My Lai 4, by means of shooting them with a rifle" (Goldstein et al., 1976, p. 497).

Among the helicopters flying reconnaissance above Son My was that of CWO Hugh Thompson. By 9:00 or soon after, Thompson had noticed some horrifying events from his perch. As he spotted wounded civilians, he sent down smoke markers so that soldiers on the ground could treat them. They killed them instead. He reported to headquarters, trying to persuade someone to stop what was going on. Barker, hearing the message, called down to Captain Medina. Medina, in turn, later claimed to have told Calley that it was "enough for today." But it was not yet enough.

At Calley's orders, his men began gathering the remaining villagers—roughly seventy-five individuals, mostly women and children—and herding them toward a drainage ditch. Accompanied by three or four enlisted men, Lieutenant Calley executed several batches of civilians who had been gathered into ditches. Some of the details of the process were entered into testimony in such accounts as Pfc. Dennis Conti's: "A lot of them, the people, were trying to get up and mostly they was just screaming and pretty bad shot up. . . . I seen a woman tried to get up. I seen Lieutenant Calley fire. He hit the side of her head and blew it off" (Hammer, 1971, p. 125).

Testimony by other soldiers presented the shooting's aftermath. Specialist Four Charles Hall, asked by Prosecutor Aubrey Daniel how he knew the people in the ditch were dead, said: "There was blood coming from them. They were just scattered all over the ground in the ditch, some in piles and some scattered out 20, 25 meters perhaps up the ditch. . . . They were very old people, very young children, and mothers. . . . There was blood all over them" (Goldstein et al., 1976, pp. 501–502). And Pfc. Gregory Olsen corroborated the general picture of the victims: "They were—the majority were women and children, some babies. I distinctly remember one middle-aged Vietnamese male dressed in white right at my feet as I crossed. None of the bodies were mangled in any way. There was blood. Some appeared to be dead, others followed me with their eyes as I walked across the ditch" (Goldstein et al., 1976, p. 502).

The second specification in the murder charge stated that Calley did "with

premeditation, murder an unknown number of Oriental human beings, not less than seventy, males and females of various ages, whose names are unknown, occupants of the village of My Lai 4, by means of shooting them with a rifle" (Goldstein et al., 1976, p. 497). Calley was also charged with and tried for shootings of individuals (an old man and a child); these charges were clearly supplemental to the main issue at trial—the mass killings and how they came about.

It is noteworthy that during these executions more than one enlisted man avoided carrying out Calley's orders, and more than one, by sworn oath, directly refused to obey them. For example, Pfc. James Joseph Dursi testified, when asked if he fired when Lieutenant Calley ordered him to: "No I just stood there. Meadlo turned to me after a couple of minutes and said 'Shoot! Why don't you shoot! Why don't you fire!' He was crying and yelling. I said, 'I can't! I won't!' And the people were screaming and crying and yelling. They kept firing for a couple of minutes, mostly automatic and semi-automatic" (Hammer, 1971, p. 143). . . .

Disobedience of Lieutenant Calley's own orders to kill represented a serious legal and moral threat to a defense *based* on superior orders, such as Calley was attempting. This defense had to assert that the orders seemed reasonable enough to carry out; that they appeared to be legal orders. Even if the orders in question were not legal, the defense had to assert that an ordinary individual could not and should not be expected to see the distinction. In short, if what happened was "business as usual," even though it might be bad business, then the defendant stood a chance of acquittal. But under direct command from "Surfside 5½," some ordinary enlisted men managed to refuse, to avoid, or at least to stop doing what they were ordered to do. As "reasonable men" of "ordinary sense and understanding," they had apparently found something awry that morning; and it would have been hard for an officer to plead successfully that he was more ordinary than his men in his capacity to evaluate the reasonableness of orders.

Even those who obeyed Calley's orders showed great stress. For example, Meadlo eventually began to argue and cry directly in front of Calley. Pfc. Herbert Carter shot himself in the foot, possibly because he could no longer take what he was doing. We were not destined to hear a sworn version of the incident, since neither side at the Calley trial called him to testify.

The most unusual instance of resistance to authority came from the skies. CWO Hugh Thompson, who had protested the apparent carnage of civilians, was Calley's inferior in rank but was not in his line of command. He was also watching the ditch from his helicopter and noticed some people moving after the first round of slaughter—chiefly children who had been shielded by their mothers' bodies. Landing to rescue the wounded, he also found some villagers hiding in a nearby bunker. Protecting the Vietnamese with his own body, Thompson ordered his men to train their guns on the Americans and to open fire if the Americans fired on the Vietnamese. He then radioed for additional rescue helicopters and stood between the Vietnamese and the Americans under Calley's command until the Vietnamese could be evacuated. He later returned to the ditch to unearth a child buried, unharmed, beneath layers of bodies. In October 1969, Thompson was awarded the Distinguished Flying Cross for heroism at My Lai, specifically (albeit inaccurately) for the rescue of children hiding in a bunker "between Viet Cong forces and advancing friendly forces" and for the rescue of a wounded child "caught in the intense crossfire" (Hersh, 1970, p. 119). Four months earlier, at the Pentagon, Thompson had identified Calley as having been at the ditch.

By about 10:00 A.M., the massacre was winding down. The remaining actions consisted largely of isolated rapes and killings, "clean-up" shootings of the wounded, and the destruction of the village by fire. We have already seen some examples of these more indiscriminate and possibly less premeditated acts. By the 11:00 A.M. lunch break, when the exhausted men of Company C were relaxing, two young girls wandered back from a hiding place only to be invited to share lunch. This surrealist touch illustrates the extent to which the soldiers' action had become dissociated from its meaning. An hour earlier, some of these men were making sure that not even a child would escape the executioner's bullet. But now the job was done and it was time for lunch—and in this new context it seemed only natural to ask the children who had managed to escape execution to join them. The massacre had ended. It remained only for the Viet Cong to reap the political rewards among the survivors in hiding.

The army command in the area knew that something had gone wrong. Direct commanders, including Lieutenant Colonel Barker, had firsthand reports, such as Thompson's complaints. Others had such odd bits of evidence as the claim of 128 Viet Cong dead with a booty of only three weapons. But the cover-up of My Lai began at once. The operation was reported as a victory over a stronghold of the Viet Cong Forty-eighth. . . .

William Calley was not the only man tried for the event at My Lai. The actions of over thirty soldiers and civilians were scrutinized by investigators; over half of these had to face charges or disciplinary action of some sort. Targets of investigation included Captain Medina, who was tried, and various higher-ups, including General Koster. But Lieutenant Calley was the only person convicted, the only person to serve time.

The core of Lieutenant Calley's defense was superior orders. What this meant to him—in contrast to what it meant to the judge and jury—can be gleaned from his responses to a series of questions from his defense attorney, George Latimer, in which Calley sketched out his understanding of the laws of war and the actions that constitute doing one's duty within those laws:

Latimer: Did you receive any training which had to do with the obedience to orders?

Calley: Yes, sir.

Latimer: . . . what were you informed [were] the principles involved in that field?

Calley: That all orders were to be assumed legal, that the soldier's job was to carry out any order given him to the best of his ability.

Latimer: . . . what might occur if you disobeyed an order by a senior officer?

Calley: You could be court-martialed for refusing an order and refusing an order in the face of the enemy, you could be sent to death, sir.

Latimer: [I am asking] whether you were required in any way, shape or form to make a determination of the legality or illegality of an order?

Calley: No, sir. I was never told that I had the choice, sir.

Latimer: If you had a doubt about the order, what were you supposed to do?

Calley: . . . I was supposed to carry the order out and then come back and make my complaint. (Hammer, 1971, pp. 240–241)

Lieutenant Calley steadfastly maintained that his actions within My Lai had constituted, in his mind, carrying out orders from Captain Medina. Both his own actions and the orders he gave to others (such as the instruction to Meadlo to "waste 'em") were entirely in response to superior orders. He denied any intent to kill individuals and any but the most passing awareness of distinctions among the individuals: "I was ordered to go in there and destroy the enemy. That was my job on that day. That was the mission I was given. I did not sit down and think in terms of men, women, and children. They were all classified the same, and that was the classification that we dealt with, just as enemy soldiers." When Latimer asked if in his own opinion Calley had acted "rightly and according to your understanding of your directions and orders," Calley replied, "I felt then and I still do that I acted as I was directed, and I carried out the orders that I was given, and I do not feel wrong in doing so, sir" (Hammer, 1971, p. 257).

His court-martial did not accept Calley's defense of superior orders and clearly did not share his interpretation of his duty. The jury evidently reasoned that, even if there had been orders to destroy everything in sight and to "waste the Vietnamese," any reasonable person would have realized that such orders were illegal and should have refused to carry them out. The defense of superior orders under such conditions is inadmissible under international and military law. The U.S. Army's *Law of Land Warfare* (Dept. of the Army, 1956), for example, states that "the fact that the law of war has been violated pursuant to an order of a superior authority, whether military or civil, does not deprive the act in question of its character of a war crime, nor does it constitute a defense in the trial of an accused individual, unless he did not know and could not reasonably have been expected to know that the act was unlawful" and that "members of the armed forces are bound to obey only lawful orders" (in Falk et al., 1971, pp. 71–72).

The disagreement between Calley and the court-martial seems to have revolved around the definition of the responsibilities of a subordinate to obey, on the one hand, and to evaluate, on the other. This tension . . . can best be captured via the charge to the jury in the Calley court-martial, made by the trial judge, Col. Reid Kennedy. The forty-one pages of the charge include the following:

Both combatants captured by and noncombatants detained by the opposing force . . . have the right to be treated as prisoners. . . . Summary execution of detainees or prisoners is forbidden by law. . . . I therefore instruct you . . . that if unresisting human beings were killed at My Lai (4) while within the effective custody and control of our military forces, their deaths cannot be considered justified. . . . Thus if you find that Lieutenant Calley received an order directing him to kill unresisting Vietnamese within his control or within the control of his troops, *that order would be an illegal order.*

A determination that an order is illegal does not, of itself, assign criminal responsibility to the person following the order for acts done in compliance with it. Soldiers are taught to follow orders, and special attention is given to obedience of orders on the battlefield. Military effectiveness depends on obedience to orders. On the other hand, the obedience of a soldier is not the obedience of an automaton. A soldier is a reasoning agent, obliged to respond, not as a machine, but as a person. The law takes these factors into account in assessing criminal responsibility for acts done in compliance with illegal orders.

> The acts of a subordinate done in compliance with an unlawful order given him by his superior are excused and impose no criminal liability upon him unless the superior's order is one which a man of *ordinary sense and understanding* would, under the circumstances, know to be unlawful, or if the order in question is actually known to the accused to be unlawful. (Goldstein et al., 1976, pp. 525–526; emphasis added)

By this definition, subordinates take part in a balancing act, one tipped toward obedience but tempered by "ordinary sense and understanding."

A jury of combat veterans proceeded to convict William Calley of the premeditated murder of no less than twenty-two human beings. (The army, realizing some unfortunate connotations in referring to the victims as "Oriental human beings," eventually referred to them as "human beings.") Regarding the first specification in the murder charge, the bodies on the trail, [Calley] was convicted of premeditated murder of not less than one person. (Medical testimony had been able to pinpoint only one person whose wounds as revealed in Haeberle's photos were sure to be immediately fatal.) Regarding the second specification, the bodies in the ditch, Calley was convicted of the premeditated murder of not less than twenty human beings. Regarding additional specifications that he had killed an old man and a child, Calley was convicted of premeditated murder in the first case and of assault with intent to commit murder in the second.

Lieutenant Calley was initially sentenced to life imprisonment. That sentence was reduced: first to twenty years, eventually to ten (the latter by Secretary of Defense Callaway in 1974). Calley served three years before being released on bond. The time was spent under house arrest in his apartment, where he was able to receive visits from his girlfriend. He was granted parole on September 10, 1975.

Sanctioned Massacres

The slaughter at My Lai is an instance of a class of violent acts that can be described as sanctioned massacres (Kelman, 1973): acts of indiscriminate, ruthless, and often systematic mass violence, carried out by military or paramilitary personnel while engaged in officially sanctioned campaigns, the victims of which are defenseless and unresisting civilians, including old men, women, and children. Sanctioned massacres have occurred throughout history. Within American history, My Lai had its precursors in the Philippine war around the turn of the century (Schirmer, 1971) and in the massacres of American Indians. Elsewhere in the world, one recalls the

Nazis' "final solution" for European Jews, the massacres and deportations of Armenians by Turks, the liquidation of the kulaks and the great purges in the Soviet Union, and more recently the massacres in Indonesia and Bangladesh, in Biafra and Burundi, in South Africa and Mozambique, in Cambodia and Afghanistan, in Syria and Lebanon. . . .

The occurrence of sanctioned massacres cannot be adequately explained by the existence of psychological forces—whether these be characterological dispositions to engage in murderous violence or profound hostility against the target—so powerful that they must find expression in violent acts unhampered by moral restraints. Instead, the major instigators for this class of violence derive from the policy process. The question that really calls for psychological analysis is why so many people are willing to formulate, participate in, and condone policies that call for the mass killings of defenseless civilians. Thus it is more instructive to look not at the motives for violence but at the conditions under which the usual moral inhibitions against violence become weakened. Three social processes that tend to create such conditions can be identified: authorization, routinization, and dehumanization. Through authorization, the situation becomes so defined that the individual is absolved of the responsibility to make personal moral choices. Through routinization, the action becomes so organized that there is no opportunity for raising moral questions. Through dehumanization, the actors' attitudes toward the target and toward themselves become so structured that it is neither necessary nor possible for them to view the relationship in moral terms.

Authorization

Sanctioned massacres by definition occur in the context of an authority situation, a situation in which, at least for many of the participants, the moral principles that generally govern human

relationships do not apply. Thus, when acts of violence are explicitly ordered, implicitly encouraged, tacitly approved, or at least permitted by legitimate authorities, people's readiness to commit or condone them is enhanced. That such acts are authorized seems to carry automatic justification for them. Behaviorally, authorization obviates the necessity of making judgments or choices. Not only do normal moral principles become inoperative, but—particularly when the actions are explicitly ordered—a different kind of morality, linked to the duty to obey superior orders, tends to take over.

In an authority situation, individuals characteristically feel obligated to obey the orders of the authorities, whether or not these correspond with their personal preferences. They see themselves as having no choice as long as they accept the legitimacy of the orders and of the authorities who give them. Individuals differ considerably in the degree to which—and the conditions under which—they are prepared to challenge the legitimacy of an order on the grounds that the order itself is illegal, or that those giving it have overstepped their authority, or that it stems from a policy that violates fundamental societal values. Regardless of such individual differences, however, the basic structure of a situation of legitimate authority requires subordinates to respond in terms of their role obligations rather than their personal preferences; they can openly disobey only by challenging the legitimacy of the authority. Often people obey without question even though the behavior they engage in may entail great personal sacrifice or great harm to others.

An important corollary of the basic structure of the authority situation is that actors often do not see themselves as personally responsible for the consequences of their actions. Again, there are individual differences, depending on actors' capacity and readiness to evaluate the legitimacy of orders received. Insofar as they see themselves as having had no choice in their actions, however, they do not feel personally responsible for them. They were not personal agents, but merely extensions of the authority. Thus, when their actions cause harm to others, they can feel relatively free of guilt. A similar mechanism operates when a person engages in antisocial behavior that was not ordered by the authorities but was tacitly encouraged and approved by them—even if only by making it clear that such behavior will not be punished. In this situation, behavior that was formerly illegitimate is legitimized by the authorities' acquiescence.

In the My Lai massacre, it is likely that the structure of the authority situation contributed to the massive violence in both ways—that is, by conveying the message that acts of violence against Vietnamese villagers were *required,* as well as the message that such acts, even if not ordered, were *permitted* by the authorities in charge. The actions at My Lai represented, at least in some respects, responses to explicit or implicit orders. Lieutenant Calley indicated, by orders and by example, that he wanted large numbers of villagers killed. Whether Calley himself had been ordered by his superiors to "waste" the whole area, as he claimed, remains a matter of controversy. Even if we assume, however, that he was not explicitly ordered to wipe out the village, he had reason to believe that such actions were expected by his superior officers. Indeed, the very nature of the war conveyed this expectation. The principal measure of military success was the "body count"—the number of enemy soldiers killed—and any Vietnamese killed by the U.S. military was commonly defined as a "Viet Cong." Thus, it was not totally bizarre for Calley to believe that what he was doing at My Lai was to increase his body count, as any good officer was expected to do.

Even to the extent that the actions at My Lai occurred spontaneously, without reference to superior orders, those committing them had

reason to assume that such actions might be tacitly approved of by the military authorities. Not only had they failed to punish such acts in most cases, but the very strategies and tactics that the authorities consistently devised were based on the proposition that the civilian population of South Vietnam—whether "hostile" or "friendly"—was expendable. Such policies as search-and-destroy missions, the establishment of free-shooting zones, the use of antipersonnel weapons, the bombing of entire villages if they were suspected of harboring guerrillas, the forced migration of masses of the rural population, and the defoliation of vast forest areas helped legitimize acts of massive violence of the kind occurring at My Lai.

Some of the actions at My Lai suggest an orientation to authority based on unquestioning obedience to superior orders, no matter how destructive the actions these orders call for. Such obedience is specifically fostered in the course of military training and reinforced by the structure of the military authority situation. It also reflects, however, an ideological orientation that may be more widespread in the general population. . . .

Routinization

Authorization processes create a situation in which people become involved in an action without considering its implications and without really making a decision. Once they have taken the initial step, they are in a new psychological and social situation in which the pressures to continue are powerful. As Lewin (1947) has pointed out, many forces that might originally have kept people out of a situation reverse direction once they have made a commitment (once they have gone through the "gate region") and now serve to keep them in the situation. For example, concern about the criminal nature of an action, which might originally have inhibited a person from becoming involved, may now lead to deeper involvement in efforts to justify the action and to avoid negative consequences.

Despite these forces, however, given the nature of the actions involved in sanctioned massacres, one might still expect moral scruples to intervene; but the likelihood of moral resistance is greatly reduced by transforming the action into routine, mechanical, highly programmed operations. Routinization fulfills two functions. First, it reduces the necessity of making decisions, thus minimizing the occasions in which moral questions may arise. Second, it makes it easier to avoid the implications of the action, since the actor focuses on the details of the job rather than on its meaning. The latter effect is more readily achieved among those who participate in sanctioned massacres from a distance—from their desks or even from the cockpits of their bombers.

Routinization operates both at the level of the individual actor and at the organizational level. Individual job performance is broken down into a series of discrete steps, most of them carried out in automatic, regularized fashion. It becomes easy to forget the nature of the product that emerges from this process. When Lieutenant Calley said of My Lai that it was "no great deal," he probably implied that it was all in a day's work. Organizationally, the task is divided among different offices, each of which has responsibility for a small portion of it. This arrangement diffuses responsibility and limits the amount and scope of decision making that is necessary. There is no expectation that the moral implications will be considered at any of these points, nor is there any opportunity to do so. The organizational processes also help further legitimize the actions of each participant. By proceeding in routine fashion—processing papers, exchanging memos, diligently carrying out their assigned tasks—the different units mutually reinforce each other in the view that what is going on must be perfectly normal, correct, and legitimate. The shared illusion that they are engaged in a legitimate enterprise helps the participants assimilate their activities to other purposes, such as the efficiency of their performance, the productivity of their unit, or the cohesiveness of their group (see Janis, 1972).

Normalization of atrocities is more difficult to the extent that there are constant reminders of the true meaning of the enterprise. Bureaucratic inventiveness in the use of language helps to cover up such meaning. For example, the SS had a set of *Sprachregelungen*, or "language rules," to govern descriptions of their extermination program. As Arendt (1964) points out, the term *language rule* in itself was "a code name; it meant what in ordinary language would be called a lie" (p. 85). The code names for killing and liquidation were "final solution," "evacuation," and "special treatment." The war in Indochina produced its own set of euphemisms, such as "protective reaction," "pacification," and "forced-draft urbanization and modernization." The use of euphemisms allows participants in sanctioned massacres to differentiate their actions from ordinary killing and destruction and thus to avoid confronting their true meaning.

Dehumanization

Authorization processes override standard moral considerations; routinization processes reduce the likelihood that such considerations will arise. Still, the inhibitions against murdering one's fellow human beings are generally so strong that the victims must also be stripped of their human status if they are to be subjected to systematic killing. Insofar as they are dehumanized, the usual principles of morality no longer apply to them.

Sanctioned massacres become possible to the extent that the victims are deprived in the perpetrators' eyes of the two qualities essential to being perceived as fully human and included in the moral compact that governs human relationships: *identity*—standing as independent, distinctive individuals, capable of making choices and entitled to live their own lives—and *community*—fellow membership in an interconnected network of individuals who care for each other and respect each other's individuality and rights (Kelman, 1973; see also Bakan, 1966, for a related distinction between "agency" and "communion"). Thus, when a group of people is defined entirely in terms of a category to which they belong, and when this category is excluded from the human family, moral restraints against killing them are more readily overcome.

Dehumanization of the enemy is a common phenomenon in any war situation. Sanctioned massacres, however, presuppose a more extreme degree of dehumanization, insofar as the killing is not in direct response to the target's threats or provocations. It is not what they have done that marks such victims for death but who they are—the category to which they happen to belong. They are the victims of policies that regard their systematic destruction as a desirable end or an acceptable means. Such extreme dehumanization becomes possible when the target group can readily be identified as a separate category of people who have historically been stigmatized and excluded by the victimizers; often the victims belong to a distinct racial, religious, ethnic, or political group regarded as inferior or sinister. The traditions, the habits, the images, and the vocabularies for dehumanizing such groups are already well established and can be drawn upon when the groups are selected for massacre. Labels help deprive the victims of identity and community, as in the epithet "gooks" that was commonly used to refer to Vietnamese and other Indochinese peoples.

The dynamics of the massacre process itself further increase the participants' tendency to dehumanize their victims. Those who participate as part of the bureaucratic apparatus increasingly come to see their victims as bodies to be counted and entered into their reports, as faceless figures that will determine their productivity rates and promotions. Those who participate in the massacre directly—in the field, as it were—are reinforced in their perception of the victims as less than human by observing their very victimization. The only way they can justify what is being done to these people—both by others and by themselves—and the only way they can extract some degree of meaning out of the absurd events in which they find themselves participating (see Lifton, 1971, 1973) is by coming to believe that the victims are subhuman and deserve to be rooted out. And thus the process of dehumanization feeds on itself.

REFERENCES

Arendt, H. (1964). *Eichmann in Jerusalem: A report on the banality of evil.* New York: Viking Press.

Bakan, D. (1966). *The duality of human existence.* Chicago: Rand McNally.

Department of the Army. (1956). *The law of land warfare* (Field Manual, No. 27-10). Washington, DC: U.S. Government Printing Office.

Falk, R. A.; Kolko, G.; & Lifton, R. J. (Eds.). (1971). *Crimes of war.* New York: Vintage Books.

French, P. (Ed.). (1972). *Individual and collective responsibility: The massacre at My Lai.* Cambridge, MA: Schenkman.

Goldstein, J.; Marshall, B.; & Schwartz, J. (Eds.). (1976). *The My Lai massacre and its cover-up: Beyond the reach of law?* (The Peers report with a supplement and introductory essay on the limits of law). New York: Free Press.

Hammer, R. (1971). *The court-martial of Lt. Calley.* New York: Coward, McCann, & Geoghegan.

Hersh, S. (1970). *My Lai 4: A report on the massacre and its aftermath.* New York: Vintage Books.

_____. (1972). *Cover-up.* New York: Random House.

Janis, I. L. (1972). *Victims of groupthink: A psychological study of foreign-policy decisions and fiascoes.* Boston: Houghton Mifflin.

Kelman, H. C. (1973). Violence without moral restraint: Reflections on the dehumanization of victims and victimizers. *Journal of Social Issues,* 29(4), 25–61.

Lewin, K. (1947). Group decision and social change. In T. M. Newcomb & E. L. Hartley (Eds.), *Readings in social psychology.* New York: Holt.

Lifton, R. J. (1971). Existential evil. In N. Sanford, C. Comstock, & Associates, *Sanctions for evil: Sources of social destructiveness.* San Francisco: Jossey-Bass.

_____. (1973). *Home from the war—Vietnam veterans: Neither victims nor executioners.* New York: Simon & Schuster.

Manual for courts martial, United States (rev. ed.). (1969). Washington, DC: U.S. Government Printing Office.

Schirmer, D. B. (1971, April 24). My Lai was not the first time. *New Republic,* pp. 18–21.

Williams, B. (1985, April 14–15). "I will never forgive," says My Lai survivor. *Jordan Times* (Amman), p. 4.

THINKING ABOUT THE READING

According to Kelman and Hamilton, social processes can create conditions under which usual restraints against violence are weakened. What social processes were in evidence during the My Lai massacre? The incident they describe provides us with an uncomfortable picture of human nature. Do you think most people would have reacted the way the soldiers at My Lai did? Are we all potential massacrers? Does the phenomenon of obedience to authority go beyond the tightly structured environment of the military? Can you think of incidents in your own life when you've done something—perhaps harmed or humiliated another person—because of the powerful influence of others? How might Kelman and Hamilton explain the actions of the individuals who carried out the hijackings and attacks of September 11, 2001?

Speaking of Sadness

Depression, Disconnection, and the Meanings of Illness

David A. Karp

(1996)

Living With Depression

In greater or lesser degree I have grappled with depression for almost 20 years. I suppose that even as a child my experience of life was as much characterized by anxiety as by joy and pleasure. And as I look back, there were lots of tip-offs that things weren't right. I find it difficult to remember much of my early years, but throughout high school and college I felt uncertain of myself, feared that I could not accomplish what was expected of me, and had plenty of sleepless nights. At college one of my roommates nicknamed me "weak heart," after a character-type in Dostoyevsky novels, because I often seemed a bit of a lost soul. During all those years, though, I had no real baseline for evaluating the "normalcy" of my feelings. At most, I had defined myself as more anxious than other people and as a "worrier." None of this seemed to warrant treatment of any sort. Even though I was muddling along emotionally, probably like having a constant low-grade fever, I was achieving well enough in school to presume that underneath it all I was okay. It wasn't until my early thirties that I was forced to conclude that something was "really wrong" with me.

People who have lived with depression can often vividly remember the situations that forced them to have a new consciousness as a troubled person. One such occasion for me was a 1974 professional meeting of sociologists in Montreal. By any objective standards I should have been feeling pretty good. I had a

solid academic job at Boston College, had just signed my first book contract, and I had a great wife, beautiful son, and a new baby daughter at home. From the outside my life looked pretty good.

During the week I was in Montreal I got virtually no sleep. It's true, I was staying in a strange city and in a borrowed apartment—maybe this was the problem. But I had done a fair amount of traveling and never had sleeping difficulties quite as bad. Then, I thought, "Maybe I'm physically ill. It must be the flu." But again, it was unlike any flu I'd ever had. I wasn't just tired and achy. Each sleepless night my head was filled with disturbing ruminations and during the day I felt a sense of intolerable grief as though somebody close to me had died. I was agitated and sensed a melancholy qualitatively different from anything in the past. I couldn't concentrate because the top of my head felt as if it would blow off, and the excitement of having received the book contract was replaced by the dread and certainty that I wasn't up to the task of writing it. It truly was a miserable week and the start of what I now know was an extended episode of depression. It was also the beginning of a long pilgrimage to figure out what was wrong with me, what to name it, what to do about it, and how to live with it. It has been a bewildering, frustrating, often deeply painful journey.

Despite a progressive worsening of the feelings I first experienced in Montreal, it took me quite a while before I fully connected the word depression to my situation. Being depressed was not yet part of my self-description or identity. It was another prolonged and even more debilitating period of insomnia, compounded with anxiety and sadness, that pushed me to a doctor's office (an internist, not a psychiatrist). For the first time, I heard someone tell me that I was clinically depressed and that I needed "antidepressant medications." This too was a decisive moment in my growing self-definition as a troubled person. . . .

Like everyone who suffers with depression, I [have] spent a lot of time . . . considering its causes. Throughout the early 1970s I thought I had a pretty good explanation. I was a young assistant professor struggling to do enough publishing so that I would not lose my job. As they say in the academic business, 1977 was to be my "up or out year"; I would either be promoted or "terminated." In short, I was under enormous pressure for six years, juggling the tasks of teaching, counseling students, serving on departmental and university committees, presenting papers at professional meetings, and writing two books that had to be done before I was evaluated for tenure.

I thought for sure that my depression was rooted in these situational demands and that once I got tenure it would go away. I was promoted in 1977 and found that the depression actually deepened. Of course, this meant that my "tenure theory" was wrong and I needed to construct a new one. However, discarding it was no easy thing. The theory's failure suggested a wholly new and more frightening interpretation of depression's locus. Now I had to confront the possibility that my sickness might not arise from social situations, but somehow from my self.

By 1980 my sleeping, which has always been the key barometer of my psychic state, had become just awful. . . . Sometimes I might get to sleep, but even on my best nights I was up every hour or so. On my worst nights I got no sleep. I remember those nights

especially well because they were so distinctly horrible. . . .

The two central feelings typifying my depression were frantic anxiety and a sense of grief. These feelings coupled to generate a sort of catastrophic thinking about events in my life as concrete as the next day's lecture and as amorphous as the quality of my relationships. None of these thoughts were productive. They were just insistently there, looping endlessly in my brain. Sometimes, as though God were serving up a particularly ironic punishment, I would drift off to sleep only shortly before I had to begin my day. The day did follow, filled with obligations that seemed burdensome and often impossible. Each day was spent struggling to appear competent, constantly feeling amazed that I had gotten through the last test and that I would certainly "shut down" in the face of the next. . . .

During all of this I felt deeply alone. Everyone else seemed to be moving through their days peacefully, laughing and having fun. I resented them because they were experiencing such an easy time of it; I felt utterly cut off from them emotionally. I was angry because there was no way they could understand what I was going through. Their very presence seemed to magnify my sense of isolation. I never felt seriously suicidal, but the combination of those days and nights often led me to feel that my life was not worth living. Although some days were far better than others, raising the elusive hope that I might be emerging from my difficulty, I basically dragged along, feeling barely alive. . . .

Given the pervasiveness of depression, it is not surprising that both medical and social scientists have tried to understand its causes and suggest ways of dealing with it. When I first considered writing about depression I did a computer search that turned up nearly 500 social science studies done in just the last few years. Researchers have tried to link the incidence of depression to every imaginable social factor. For example, since the rate of depression is twice as great for women than for men, studies have been conducted seeking to relate depression with gender roles, family structure, powerlessness, child rearing, and the like. Studies can also be found trying to link depression with, among other things, age (especially during adolescence and old age), unemployment, physical illness, disability, child abuse, ethnicity, race, and social class. . . .

Sickness, Self, and Society

. . . All human beings . . . think about the world in causal terms. All of us use cause and effect inferences in trying to understand important features of our lives. . . . Efforts to come to grips with depression turn on its presumed causes. . . . In this way, everyone suffering from depression inevitably becomes a theorist as they try to give order and coherence to their situation. With rare exceptions, the theories they generate locate the cause(s) of depression somewhere either in their biographies or their biologies. Occasionally, [people] spin out more complex theories that see depression as resulting from the subtle interplay of personal history, recent life events, and chemical imbalances. However, even those who name situational causes for their emotional problems typically restrict their conceptual vision to the immediate and local circumstances of their lives. Only rarely do sufferers of depression relate their condition to the kinds of broad cultural trends that, I believe, influence our consciousness about everything.

The reach of sociological thinking extends well beyond the immediate milieus of daily life. In fact, exercise of the sociological imagination *requires* analysis of the connections between daily life and larger cultural arrangements. . . . The abiding theoretical questions of sociology flow from consideration of the individual-society connection. Sociologists presume an ongoing intersection of personal biographies and the larger arenas of history and social structure. A sociological angle of vision sees an inseparability between the character of culture and even our innermost thoughts and feelings, including, of course, the deeply troubling thoughts and feelings we label as depression. As George Herbert Mead expressed it with the title of his famous book, an adequate *social* psychology of human experience must consider the ways in which *Mind, Self and Society*[1] mutually transform each other. [Next I will focus] on how the structure of contemporary American society may be implicated in the production of increasingly larger numbers of people who complain of and are diagnosed as having diseased minds and selves.

Like many sociologists, one of my favorite examples to illustrate the cultural roots of what initially appears to be an exclusively personal disorder is Émile Durkheim's classic study of suicide[2] that is generally seen as a sociological *tour de force*. Aside from the intrinsic importance of the topic, Durkheim presumably chose to study suicide because, at first glance, it appears explicable *only* in individualistic, psychological terms. However, by testing a series of logically produced, deductive hypotheses linking suicide to such variables as religion, marital status, and membership in the military, Durkheim convincingly demonstrated the connection between suicide *rates* and degrees of *social integration*. Specifically, he argued that modernizing societies, like his own nineteenth century France, were less successful than earlier agrarian societies in providing sources of integration for their members. Such societies were characterized by what Durkheim termed *anomie*—a state of relative normlessness. His brilliant work verified that anomic societies that fail to integrate their members adequately also fail to insulate them from suicide. Suicide, in short, is as much a social as it is a psychological phenomenon.

Another first-rate sociologist, Kai Erikson, provides a valuable example for illustrating how a sociological perspective is necessary to see social patterns that would be missed if we only look at things "up close and personal," as they say on *Wide World of Sports*.[3] He has us imagine that we are walking along 42nd Street near Times Square. At the street level we can clearly see the faces of the thousands of people who pass us. We can see their individual expressions, their particular body idioms, their apparent ages, and so on. At this range, they normally seem to take no notice of anyone around them. Each stranger appears as a solitary atom, buzzing along in a wholly independent way.

Were we, however, to climb to the roof of a nearby 12-story building and look down on the flow of sidewalk traffic, we would see an extraordinary thing. It is true that from this vantage point we miss the particularities of each individual. However, we would instead witness a miraculous pattern—thousands of people moving along the street in an incredibly well-organized, efficient, and cooperative fashion. Moreover, each person on the street would likely be wholly unaware of their contribution to the web of behavior necessary to sustain such an enormously complex social order. It is as if each pedestrian is guided by an invisible social force, a kind of social gravity, about which they have only the vaguest awareness. I am proposing that most people suffering from depression, like street pedestrians, are only dimly aware of how the constitution of culture might be contributing to their depressed condition.

Although estimates of the number of Americans suffering from depression vary, there is general consensus that the number is in the vicinity of 11 million people and that economic losses from poor productivity, lost work days, hospitalization, outpatient care, and so on, is a staggering $43.7 billion dollars a year.[4] More important to my concerns are the data from a range of studies showing tremendous increases in the rates of depression. For example: (1) The incidence of depression among those born after World War II is much higher and the age of onset much earlier than in earlier population cohorts.[5] (2) In recent decades, there has been a continuing rise in depression among young women, but a disproportionate increase of depression among men has been closing the depression gender gap.[6] (3) There has been an absolute explosion of depression among "baby boomers."[7] These and similar findings warrant the conclusion that America is in the grip of a depression epidemic; that we have entered an "age of melancholy."[8]

. . . While any search for patterns necessarily suggests cause, I prefer to think about the link between cultural dimensions and depression in probabilistic terms. Epidemiologists, for example, describe poverty as a "risk factor" for a range of health problems. Poverty provides a context that makes individuals more vulnerable to disease. The notion of risk factors implies likelihoods rather than direct causal relationships. In Durkheimian fashion, [I will detail] the cultural dimensions of contemporary American society that provide the context for our collective vulnerability to emotional distress.[9] In particular, my thesis can be expressed as a theoretical equation. It is:

$$\text{MEDICALIZATION} + \text{DISCONNECTION} + \text{POSTMODERNIZATION} = \text{PERSONAL DISLOCATION}$$

. . . I will define what I have in mind as each is discussed. Immediately, though, my argument is best advanced by showing how fundamentally the idea of depression is connected to culture. If the features of a particular culture truly influence what is even recognized as an illness, we should expect wide cultural variation in the labeling of particular physical and emotional experiences as health or illness.

Culture, Health, and Emotion

In a classic article written [over] 50 years ago, the medical historian Erwin H. Ackerknecht argued against the view that disease is a strictly physical phenomenon. Citing the important role played by social factors in the definition and treatment of illness, Ackerknecht maintained that "medicine's practical goal is not primarily a biological one, but that of social adjustment in a given society. . . . Even the notion of disease depends rather on the decisions of society than on objective facts."[10] As the following examples illustrate, societies differ dramatically in their response to the same physical symptoms:

> Pinto (dyschromic spirochetosis), a skin disease, is so common among many South American tribes that the few *healthy* men that *are not* suffering from pinto are regarded as *pathological* to the point of being excluded from marriage. The crippled feet of the traditional Chinese woman, diseased to us, were, of course, normal to the Chinese. Intestinal worms among the African Thongas are not at all regarded as pathological. They are thought to be necessary for digestion.[11]

Not only is the definition of what constitutes an illness or pathological condition subject to cultural variations, but, in an even more far-reaching sense, one's *experience* of bodily symptoms is shaped by social processes and expectations as well. In a now famous study, Mark Zborowski illustrated how responses to pain varied by the respondent's ethnicity.[12] Jewish-American patients, for example, evidenced substantial philosophical concern and anxiety about their condition and were pessimistic about the future course of their illness. Protestant patients felt optimistic about their prospects for recovery while viewing doctors as experts to whom one went for "mending," much like bringing a car to an auto mechanic for repairs. Italian-Americans, by contrast, wanted immediate pain relief, and, unlike Jewish respondents, had little concern about the larger "meanings" of the pain.

We should expect that the same principles apply to emotional pain and there is, indeed, substantial evidence that depression carries quite different meanings in different cultures. In a series of books and articles,[13] Arthur Kleinman, who is both an anthropologist and a physician, has written with eloquence and power on the value of looking at a range of emotional disorders cross culturally. Although he does not posit a particular theory as underlying his inquiries, Kleinman's analysis bears a striking resemblance to "symbolic interaction." . . . I say this because the underlying motif of his work is the *socially generated meanings of illness*, the importance of appreciating the dialectics of body and culture, symptom and society. In fact, Kleinman's mission seems nothing short of reforming the teaching and practice of medicine. By dismissing how illness carries very different symbolic meanings in different cultural settings, Western medicine, based nearly exclusively on a biomedical model, falls short in both its modes of diagnosis and treatment.

Like other medical anthropologists, Kleinman's thinking rests on the fundamental distinction between *illness* and *disease*. . . . Distinguishing the two words helps to make plain the difference between the subjective experience of bodily or emotional distress (illness) and the presumed biological cause of the distress (disease).

When first becoming sick we begin an interpretive process about the meaning of symptoms. We make assessments about the severity of our discomfort, and, usually in consultation with family and friends, assess the significance of our trouble, deciding what to name it and how to respond to it. The point here is that these interpretations can be rooted in widely varying normative orders and cultural symbol systems. Such culturally induced interpretations, moreover, "orient us to how to act when ill, how to communicate distress, how to diagnose and treat, how to regard and manage the life problems illness creates, how to negotiate this social reality and interpret its meaning for ourselves and for others."[14] Disease, in contrast to illness, is "what the practitioner creates in the recasting of illness in terms of theories of disorder."[15] In Western medicine this typically means identifying the biological dysfunction presumably giving rise to the symptoms described by the patient.

Once we recognize the critical importance of cultural meanings in how symptoms are experienced and dealt with, we can also pinpoint a fundamental difficulty with the practice of Western medicine. American medicine is primarily concerned with disease and pays little attention to the patient's illness. The nearly single-minded efforts of physicians to quickly locate the presumed biological dysfunctions associated with symptoms leads to a problematic disjunction between what patients want from doctors and what they get. Evidence from a recent poll on dissatisfaction with conventional medicine[16] suggests that patients want to be heard by physicians and feel alienated when the full context of their illness experience is defined as irrelevant to their treatment. As a result, patients are seeking treatment from "alternative" healers in ever increasing numbers. Not incidentally, anxiety and depression rank one and two among the problems for which alternative help is sought.

Because of bureaucratic time imperatives[17] and physicians' felt need to quickly diagnose the patient's disease, most doctor/patient encounters in the United States are very short. While initial visits to a doctor might range up to 30 minutes, the average length of doctor/patient encounters is typically between 5 and 10 minutes. In a recent *Newsweek* story,[18] it was reported that patients' average time spent with psychiatrists in some clinics is an astonishing 3 minutes! Whether the figure is as low as 3 or

as high as the 17 minutes reported in another study,[19] one thing is plain: Doctors are normally uninterested in hearing patients' illness experience—they listen only insofar as the information provided helps them to make a diagnosis. In fact, to let the patient "go on" about their symptoms and feelings is often seen as an obstacle to "good" medicine.[20] . . .

An anthropologically informed view sees diagnosis and treatment in very different terms. Illness narratives are deemed critical for appreciating precisely what physicians typically leave out of the picture—namely, how culturally prescribed meanings shape illness realities and, therefore, patients' likely responses to different modes of treatment. just as patients' experiences of symptoms arise out of particular symbol systems, so also must the likely efficacy of treatments be understood in cultural context. Nowhere is this line of thinking more apparently true than in psychiatry where emotional feelings define the problem and where the discovery of a clear disease entity is most elusive. Kleinman and his colleague Byron Good state with wonderful clarity what a crosscultural perspective on depression teaches us. Based on a range of investigations, they say

> It is simply not tenable . . . to argue that dysphoric emotion and depressive illness are invariant across cultures. When culture is treated as a constant . . . it is relatively easy to view depression as [exclusively] a biological disorder. . . . From this perspective, culture appears epiphenomenal; cultural differences may exist, but they are not considered essential to the phenomenon itself. However, when culture is treated as a significant variable . . . many of our assumptions about the nature of emotions and illness are cast into sharp relief. Dramatic differences are found across cultures in the social organization, personal experience, and consequences of such emotions as sadness, grief, and anger, of behaviors such as withdrawal or aggression, and of psychological characteristics such as passivity and

helplessness. . . . Dysphoria, even the pervasive loss of pleasure . . . is associated with quite different symptoms of distress and has widely varied consequences for the sufferer. . . . Depressive illness and dysphoria are thus not only interpreted differently in non-Western societies and across cultures; they are constituted as fundamentally different forms of social reality.[21]

The essential finding of Kleinman's work and a number of other anthropologically oriented investigations on depression is that biological, psychological, and social processes are intricately woven together in creating the depression phenomenon. While there does appear to be a core syndrome of depression that can be observed universally across cultures, the equally clear findings of comparative research show wide variation in the experience of depression. Depressive disorders, in other words, display both universal and culture-specific properties.

Psychiatric medicine in the United States, with its heavily scientific bias, largely presumes biochemical pathology as the ultimate source of depressive disorders everywhere. Such a view is sustained despite the existence of "impressive data that there is no such thing as depression that occurs solely from biological causes."[22] To be sure, it would be equally plausible to say that real-world experiences produce depression by altering biochemistry and thus stand first in the hierarchy of depression's causes. Right now, though, it would be as presumptuous to make this claim as it is of American medicine to claim biology as the absolute foundation of depressive disorders. The truth is that there is no way to untangle the intersection of cultural and biological factors and, consequently, no sure way to claim the greater significance of either nature or nurture in causing depression. Despite this epistemological problem, the role of culture and the contributions of social science in understanding the course of illness remain

very much at the margins of American medical training and practice.

This discussion asserts wide cultural variation in the incidence, meaning, and experience of psychiatric disorders, but is not grounded with concrete examples. To get specific, I can report that historically the best predictor of rates of admission to mental hospitals and suicides in North America is the health of the economy (the worse the economy the greater the rates); that the incidence and course of schizophrenia is tied to a society's level of technology (the more modernized a society the greater is the incidence of intractable schizophrenia); that a diagnostic category such as "narcissistic personality disorder," increasingly common in the United States, is virtually unheard of elsewhere; that in certain Asian societies "semen loss" resulting from nocturnal discharge is viewed with great alarm and anguish because sperm contains "qi" (vital energy), seen as absolutely necessary for health; that eating disorders such as anorexia and bulimia are most thoroughly characteristic of capitalist economies; that lack of joy, a central criterion for defining someone as depressed in the United States, would never be mentioned as a problem in Buddhist cultures such as Sri Lanka; that it is considered perfectly normal for American Indians grieving the loss of a spouse literally to hear the voices of the dead, and that the linguistic equivalents of anxiety and depression simply do not exist in many languages.[23]

In several of his books, Kleinman singles out China to illustrate how cultural sentiments influence the way doctors and their patients respond to the complex of feelings American doctors would unmistakably call depression. In contrast to the United States, depression is an infrequent diagnosis in China. Instead, patients suffering from a combination of such symptoms as anxiety, general debility, headaches, backaches, sadness, irritability, insomnia, poor appetite, and sexual dysfunction are diagnosed as suffering from "neurasthenia." Ironically, neurasthenia as a diagnostic category originated in the United States and was once thought of as "the American disease." Now, it is virtually never used in this country, just as the depression diagnosis is very rarely used in China. The choice of the neurasthenia diagnosis turns on cultural preferences. In China, where mental illness is deeply stigmatizing for both sick individuals and their families, doctors and patients find congenial a diagnosis—neurasthenia—that traces the disease to a neurological weakness rather than a mental disorder. In other words, the same symptoms are labeled, interpreted, responded to, and experienced quite differently in the two cultures. It would be proper to say that, although suffering from nominally the same symptoms, the illness realities of Chinese and Americans are truly worlds apart.

Medicalization

The foregoing discussion implies that a necessary condition for widespread depressive illness is a culturally induced readiness to view emotional pain as a disease requiring medical intervention. The grounds for interpreting pain as an abnormal medical condition have been largely established through the increasing incursion of medical and other therapeutic experts into literally every aspect of our lives. Doctors in particular have become explorers, discovering every conceivable aspect of the human condition as potentially problematic and warranting their intervention. Such a "medicalization" process[24] has dramatically increased the number of uncomfortable or disliked feelings and behaviors that we now see as illnesses.

The so-called medical model is based on two apparently unassailable premises: (1) Normalcy is preferable to abnormalcy, and (2) normalcy is a synonym for health and abnormalcy a synonym for pathology. Definitions of health and pathology, in turn, are derived from laboratory research that is presumed to be thoroughly objective. In this way, medical definitions of health gain the status of scientific facts instead of merely collectively agreed on cultural designations.

Because it is better to be healthy than to be sick, the medical model legitimizes physicians' intervention, whether requested or not, to determine one's health status. No other profession provides for the extensive access to a person's body, mind, and self as do physical and psychiatric medicine. By defining certain features of the human condition as illnesses to be cured, physicians give themselves the right to explore every part of the human anatomy, to prescribe a myriad of curative agents, and even to compel treatment.

The term *healthy,* as used in the medical model, can be equated with *conformity.* In societies where it predominates, the medical model often supersedes legal or religious commandments in regulating behavior. "Peculiar" individuals who were once viewed as possessed or as agents of the devil are now classified as emotionally ill. In the name of science, the advice of medical experts is used in the courts to determine whether certain actions should be defined as crimes. Medicine, especially psychiatric medicine, is often used to "treat" individuals whose behaviors do not conform to the expectations of the powerful or impinge on their moral sensitivities.

There can be little dispute that behavior in today's "postindustrial" society is dominated by "experts." Experts follow us through the life course, advising us on virtually every aspect of existence. They are there when we are born and accompany us each step along the way until we die. Among other things, we rely on experts to tell us how to maintain health, how to become educated, how to make love, how to raise children, and how to age correctly. Most relevant here is that experts now tell us when our "selves" need repair and the proper procedures for doing it. . . .

You might also understand that this dependence on therapeutic experts arises out of the distinctive problems posed by modern life. Every generation, because of its unique historical situation, experiences the world differently than its predecessors. Whatever the historical conditions into which people are born, however, one problem remains constant: Human beings need a coherent framework for comprehending life and death. In some historical periods the traditional meanings transmitted from one generation to the next adequately perform this function. In other epochs, meaning coherence is not so easily established. As Peter Berger and Thomas Luckmann note, the current moment in the Western world appears to be one in which many individuals experience particular difficulty in understanding themselves. They say that "In societies with a very simple division of labor . . . there is . . . no problem of identity. The question 'Who am I?' is unlikely to arise in consciousness, since the socially defined answer is massively real subjectively and consistently confirmed in all significant social interaction."[25]

When people come together and collectively act on their definitions of injustice, a social movement is born. In Ralph Turner's words, "The phenomenon of a man crying out with indignation because his society has not supplied him with a sense of personal worth and identity is the distinctive new feature of our era. The idea that a man who does not feel worthy and cannot find his proper place in life is to be pitied is an old one. The notion that he is indeed a victim of injustice is the new idea."[26] Today, alienation, previously seen as only a work-related phenomenon, has a much broader connotation. In the present era, alienation refers to a psychological condition in which people are unable to locate a clear conception of self and feel a sense of wholeness. In the context of such alienation, the "therapeutic state" has triumphed.[27]

As a more personalized conception of alienation has been taking root in American society, popular writings by psychiatrists, psychologists, and advice columnists have become increasingly influential. Television appearances have made "mind-tinkerers" such as Leo Buscaglia, "Dr. Ruth," Marianne Williamson, and John Bradshaw national celebrities. Their appeal attests to a pervasive anxiety about questions of identity and psychological well-being in the society. Such experts are constantly dispensing prescriptions for happiness, sexual fulfillment, and mental health.

The movement toward an all-embracing concern with psychological health and personal identity has been accompanied by a corresponding transformation in our explanations of human behavior. When people act in a way we consider deviant, our first impulse is to question their mental health and to probe their psychological makeup. Are they normal? Why are they doing that? What is wrong with them? Because of the medicalization process, such behaviors as alcoholism that years ago were viewed as evidence of sinfulness or moral degeneracy are now explained as illness. A "sickness vocabulary" has replaced a "sin vocabulary." For instance, the so-called "abuse excuse" as used in the celebrated trials of Erik and Lyle Menendez for murdering their parents has resulted in two hung juries. I would guess the same result would be virtually impossible had the Menendez brothers committed their crime 20 years ago.

Preoccupied with their dis-ease, huge numbers of Americans purchase the time and expertise of professionals in order to discover more about themselves. . . . We are in an era that has been characterized as the *age of narcissism*[28] and Americans are said to have constructed a "me, myself, and I" society. The availability of thousands of self-help books alone suggests that ours is a culture intensively absorbed with questions of self-fulfillment and self-realization.

The transformation in our self-conceptions has not been accomplished by mental health experts alone. Their orientation toward life is complemented by other self-oriented, self-discovery groups and movements. For example, large numbers of Americans continue to be involved in various fundamentalist and Eastern religious groups, as well as quasi-religious "personal growth" movements like Scientology and Transcendental Meditation.[29] Groups of this sort provide guidance for self-searching pilgrims, often by supplying absolutely definitive answers to the questions "Who am I and where do I fit in?" "New" religions thrive by providing world views alternative to the kind of scientific and bureaucratic rationality that insinuates even the innermost preserves of our everyday lives. The widespread interest in astrology, dianetics, and the paranormal is explicable as a reaction to a world in which science and technology have portrayed the universe as barren and bereft of meaning.

Yet another "revolution" directed toward the search for and repair of broken selves has been occurring in the last decade or so. In many ways, the springing up of self-help and support groups for dealing with almost every imaginable human trouble represents a combination of many of the elements I have been describing. The self-help revolution reflects the full flowering of a therapeutic culture in America. In self-help groups people turn to others afflicted with the same personal troubles and try, through conversation, to "heal" themselves of what they perceive to be their shared illness. An illness rhetoric (often implying biological causation) is sometimes joined with a spiritual vocabulary (as in programs like Alcoholics Anonymous) positing that "recovery" requires surrendering to a higher power. The self-help phenomenon thus derives its allure by combining elements of therapy with elements of religion and science. It is a powerful brew that has drawn the faith of millions.[30]

. . . As might be expected, the response of mental health professionals to the self-help phenomenon has been lukewarm.[31] While many mental health professionals are legitimately concerned about the wisdom of laypersons treating themselves, we should not miss the point that the self-help idea threatens their own claim to exclusive expertise about a number of mental health problems.

Recently a self-help backlash has developed. While people may individually feel better through participation in them, critics say that their collective effect may be the production of a national mentality in which virtually everyone perceives themselves as suffering from some sort of illness and as the "victim" of circumstances beyond their control. Dissidents wonder whether claims such as the one made by John Bradshaw, a leader of the "recovery movement," that 96 percent of American families are "dysfunctional," trivializes such real abuses as incest by grouping them with an enormous range of experiences that are somehow deemed as damaging people. Critics worry that the underlying illness ideology of support groups furthers the view—distinctly a product of the modern world—that individuals do not bear ultimate responsibility for their life problems and personal behaviors. Along these lines, the sociologist Edwin Shur pointed out several years ago that increased personal consciousness is too often achieved at the expense of a diminished social consciousness.[32]

As a final observation about the emergence of a therapeutic culture, I would add that self-absorption is consistent with the emphasis on self-satisfaction fostered by capitalism in general and advertising in particular. In the industrial age, society was primarily organized around the world of work. A person who did not work, for any reason other than physical disability, was defined as immoral, lazy, and worthless. This perspective on work was beautifully captured in Max Weber's notion of the Protestant Ethic which defines work as intrinsically valuable.[33] It appears, however, that the moral restraints of the work ethic have fundamentally been undermined by a consumption ethic. If workers imbued with the Protestant Ethic lived to work, now most of us work to consume.

The shift toward the social production of consumer-oriented selves has had far-reaching consequences. Since material possessions alone cannot ensure feelings of meaningfulness and satisfaction, many today find themselves caught up in an endless quest for personal significance; a quest made even more illusive by the built-in obsolescence of the products produced. There is always a "better" product in the works, and so the flames of advertising are always nearby heating the cauldron of contemporary anxiety.[34] In advanced capitalist societies virtually anything can be made into a commodity for sale, including our selves. . . .

. . . The experience of depression occurs within a cultural context that has enormously expanded the range of emotions defined as abnormal. Authors like Martin Gross have been skeptical about the legitimacy of such redefinitions. He comments, for example, that "what the psychological society has done is to redefine normality. It has taken the painful reactions to the normal vicissitudes of life . . . despair, anger, frustration—and labeled them as maladjustments. The semantic trick is in equating happiness with normality. By permitting this, we have given up our simple right to be normal and suffering at the same time."[35] While my sense is that such brush stroke observations about the "diseasing of America"[36] are unfair to millions of people whose suffering far exceeds what human beings ought to endure, they do properly sensitize us to an enormously increased readiness to interpret emotional discomfort as disease. Such a cultural mind-set has made it possible for medicine to "discover" depression and for millions of Americans to realize that they suffer from it.

The underlying metaphor . . . is of a cultural chemistry that catalyzes depression. Thus far I have outlined one piece of the mix that foments depression, a culturally induced readiness to interpret emotional pain as illness. Like any chemical mix, the elements involved cannot create a particular reaction until they are brought together. A second factor that really gets the depression reaction going is the increasing disconnection that appears to characterize Americans' relations with each other and with society. An elaboration of the social forces diminishing human connection extends my argument . . . that depression, at its root, is a disease of disconnection.

Disconnection

Sigmund Freud was once asked what people needed to be happy. The questioner no doubt expected a long, complicated answer reflecting Freud's years of deep reflection on the matter. His simple response, however, was "arbeiten und lieben,"—work and love. Happy people feel connected to others at work and through their intimate relationships. When those connections are threatened, diminished, or broken, people suffer. Today, millions of Americans are suffering from what my colleague Charles Derber calls "double trouble."[37] Those in double trouble have neither meaningful work nor sustaining intimate ties. The withering of community life in both domains fosters a rootlessness and social disintegration that unquestionably contributes to the growth of emotional disorders.[38]

. . . These ideas have a rich history. Classical sociological theorists (such as Émile Durkheim, Max Weber, and Ferdinand Toennies) fundamentally agreed that the bond between individuals and society had been dangerously weakened in "modern" society.[39] They were unanimous in their view that people were less morally constrained in urban societies because their relationships and commitments to communities of all sorts had become far more tenuous. These nineteenth century writers feared that the eclipse of community would foreshadow the demise of the family and would, in turn, precipitate an increase in all sorts of human pathologies—from crime to suicide.

Although these sociologists could not have had America in mind when they wrote, their analysis appears prophetic. Even the most optimistic among us must acknowledge that America has extraordinary problems. Each day the newspaper assails us with more bad news about rates of homelessness, poverty, suicide, drug addiction, AIDS, teenage pregnancy, illiteracy, and unemployment. In the midst of great wealth we are increasingly becoming two nations, the haves and the have nots, one nation black and the other white, one comfortable and the other destitute.[40] Racism, sexism, and ageism characterize ever-increasing antagonisms between groups that perceive each other only as adversaries. The focus here is more limited, however. My analysis turns on the question: "How do the increasingly loose human connections at work and at home contribute to the staggering and growing number of Americans who have fallen sick with depression?" Although any analytical separation of work and home is artificial since these life areas extensively affect each other,[41] I choose for simplicity's sake to discuss them one at a time.

The Work Disconnection. A well-established tradition of sociological literature illustrates the centrality of work to personal identity.[42] Occupational status may be the central yardstick by which we assess our own and others' "social value." In a very fundamental way, we *are* what we *do*. Our feelings of self-esteem and personal well-being are wrapped up in our work. Therefore, it is perfectly predictable that a legion of studies demonstrate how unemployment deprives individuals of much more than a regular paycheck. Loss of work bears a

consistent relationship with serious family and psychiatric problems.[43] Our mental health unquestionably depends on being able to provide a satisfactory answer to the ubiquitous question "What kind of work do you do?" Without work, people feel lifeless, rootless, and marginal.

The disastrous consequences of joblessness for those at the bottom of the American class structure is an old story. If there is any news here it is, unfortunately, that things have gotten worse for the poorest and most marginalized populations in America's dying inner cities. Perhaps the outstanding fact bearing on this issue is the increasing concentration of nonwhites in central city areas. While there has been some modest movement of blacks to the suburbs since 1970, it has largely been the middle-class segment of the black population that has moved, leaving behind an increasing concentration of poor blacks within urban ghettoes. Blacks have been greatly overrepresented in inner-city areas since their initial migration from the rural South to the urban North beginning in the 1950s. However, according to William Julius Wilson,[44] poor blacks are experiencing ever increasing *social isolation* within central cities.

Such profoundly important demographic transformations in American society cannot be understood apart from the imperatives of corporate capitalism. We have entered into a new round of capitalist accumulation in which older, industrial cities are no longer favorable sites for the accumulation of profit. Corporations, free to move wherever there is cheaper labor and fewer legal restrictions, have largely fled the rustbelt cities of the midwest and the frostbelt cities of the northeast in favor of cities in the south and southwest. In yet another round of moves, corporations are now leaving the country altogether to "exploit" the cheap labor in Third World countries. These processes are part of the general "deindustrialization of America"[45] that has removed almost all meaningful job opportunities for the hyperghettoized minorities trapped in America's once great cities.

Without work, black men become less desirable marriage partners and are unable to support the families they do have. Poor black families are then increasingly headed by young women dependent on welfare or the few available jobs that provide less than bare subsistence wages. As a result, "children are being raised in an institutionless community, where everyone is poor, instability is the norm, and the social and psychological role of fatherhood is nonexistent.[46] Such a situation breeds depression that spreads easily from one generation to the next. The mechanism of transmission acts like this: (1) Unemployed women caring for children at home suffer from rates of depression as high as 40 percent.[47] (2) Depressed mothers simply cannot provide the care, nurturance, and empathy that is necessary for children to grow up with good emotional health. Understandably, (3) children whose primary caretaker is depressed are themselves at enormously high risk for becoming depressed.[48] (4) Depressed children become depressed adults who pass on their disease to their own children. And so on and on. So, we have another of the vicious cycles associated with depression. This one, however, is pushed along by an obviously dysfunctional *social* rather than biological system.[49]

The poor in America have always lived with occupational instability and its fallout. In contrast, middle-class workers have historically been immune from occupational insecurity. Indeed, achieving the American Dream of middle-class life has until recently been synonymous with tremendous occupational stability. In decades past, middle- to upper-middle-class workers in large organizations could count on being taken care of from "Womb to tomb." No more. Today, the catchwords "downsizing" and "reengineering" keep the fear of job loss at the forefront of middle-class workers' collective consciousness. Once

again the logic of capitalist accumulation is creating a revolution. This one is qualitatively different than earlier economic restructurings because it directly touches the middle classes in hurtful ways. Instead of the strong bond of commitment and loyalty that organizations and middle-class workers previously felt toward each other, the new economic rules of corporate life emphasize efficiency, whatever the human cost. Knowing that they could be here today, but gone tomorrow, middle-class workers are constantly in "fear of falling.[50]

Along with those middle-class workers who continue to hold full-time jobs, however tenuously, is a growing army of well-educated "contingent workers" who are occupational nomads often working for "temp agencies." By 1988 one quarter of the American workforce worked on a contingent basis and the numbers are growing so rapidly that they will likely outnumber full-time workers by the turn of the century.[51] . . . Middle-class contingent workers *feel* contingent for good reason. They are disconnected from work in a way never before witnessed in the United States.

All social life involves a tension between freedom and constraint. Living in a society inevitably involves a trade-off between personal liberty and commitment to others. We judge some societies as immoral because they allow virtually no personal freedoms and others because they seem unable to constrain their members. For much of its history, the glory of American democracy seemed to be that it provided a healthy balance between commitment and freedom. For a long time, the pursuit of personal happiness and individual goals seemed compatible with a set of cultural values that Americans willingly embraced and held them together as a nation.

In the world of work, at least for "white collar" workers, there has been, until recently, a kind of *quid pro quo*. Organizations provided long-term security and received, in turn, worker loyalty, commitment, and responsibility.

Loyalty, responsibility, security, commitment. These are the binding features of social systems, the glue that sustains the bond between individuals and social institutions. Unhappily, America's emerging "post-industrial" economy seems to have fundamentally altered the meaning of work for many by eroding loyalty, commitment, and mutual responsibility between organizations and workers.[52] Because emotional well-being is so unquestionably related to social attachment, the millions of Americans who are becoming occupationally marginal are at increasingly greater risk for being victimized by diseases of disconnection.

This section has sustained attention on how work is being reshaped in America's post-industrial, advanced capitalist society. Critics of capitalism, however, would maintain that the negative effects of capitalism on human relationships are far more inclusive than those in the workplace. In a more general way, the values underpinning capitalism are evident in a large variety of face-to-face encounters.

Competition, for example, is one of the cornerstones of capitalism. Advocates of capitalism maintain that competition is a necessary ingredient in both maintaining organizational efficiency and motivating individuals. On the negative side, however, competition pits individuals against each other, diminishes trust, and generally dehumanizes relationships. As the earlier discussion of advertising also intimates, capitalism contributes to a culture of inauthenticity. In a society where everything and everyone is evaluated by their profit potential, individuals are aware that they are constantly being manipulated, seduced, and conned by those who want to sell them or "take them." In a world held together by appearances and a tissue of illusions and deceptions, everyone becomes an enemy of sorts whose motives cannot be accepted at face value. In short, the abstract values of capitalism "trickle down" to everyday consciousness in a way that induces human beings to distrust and withdraw

from each other. Withdrawal and increased isolation ... are important features of the social dialectics of depression.

The Love Disconnection. Another underlying theme of nineteenth-century theory was the parallel development of capitalism and unbridled individualism. Although each of the classical theorists focused on somewhat different features of the social order, they agreed that while the central unit of earlier societies had been the larger collectivities of family and community, the central unit in their contemporary society had become the individual. Further, as the pursuit of financial gain and personal mobility became ascendant social values, relationships became more rational, impersonal, and contractual. Whereas people in earlier agrarian societies related to each other emotionally, with their hearts, those in the new social order related rationally, with their heads.

While the sociological analysis of individualism extends to the origins of the discipline, the conversation about its significance in understanding American character and social structure has recently been reinvigorated through the writings of Robert Bellah and his colleagues.[53] In 1985 they published a book entitled *Habits of the Heart* that details how individualism fosters self-absorption and guarantees a collective sense of strangeness, isolation, and loneliness. This book has been widely praised as providing lucid, penetrating insights into our current cultural condition and has stimulated multiple responses to its ideas.

Bellah and his co-authors distinguish two forms of individualism, *instrumental individualism* and *expressive individualism*. Instrumental individualism refers to the freedom to pursue financial and career success. This is the kind of individualism celebrated in the maxims of Ben Franklin's "Poor Richard" and in the Horatio Alger "rags to riches" stories. Expressive individualism, in contrast, refers to the deep and abiding concerns that Americans have with personal self-fulfillment, with the idea that one of life's missions is to maximize personal happiness by discovering who you "really" are. This second form of individualism is thoroughly consistent with the "therapeutic culture" described earlier.

The essential problem posed by "excessive" individualism is that it privatizes the goals and pursuits of persons and thereby erodes the social attachments that provide society's moral anchor. Individualism undermines commitment to community since membership in any community (from the family to local community to nation) implies behavioral constraints that people perceive as inconsistent with personal fulfillment. The dilemma posed by the need both for attachment and freedom is beautifully captured in Bellah's analysis of romantic love in America. Americans believe deeply in romantic love as a necessary requirement for self satisfaction. At the same time, love and marriage, which are based on the free giving of self to another, pose the problem that in sharing too completely with another one might lose oneself. The difficulties that Americans have in maintaining intimate relationships stems in part from the uneasy balance between sharing and being separate. . . .

Among the many groups that have emerged as part of the self-help phenomenon, one deserves special mention in the context of this discussion. Across the country these days thousands flock to a group called "Co-Dependents Anonymous," a relatively new "12-stepper." Co-dependency is "a popular new disease, blamed for such diverse disorders as drug abuse, alcoholism, anorexia, child abuse, compulsive gambling, chronic lateness, fear of intimacy, and low self esteem."[54] I find the idea of co-dependence interesting because this newly discovered disorder arises out of widespread confusion about the permissible limits of human closeness. Members come to these groups because they see themselves as unable

to sustain reasonable intimacy boundaries and feel overwhelmed by certain relationships. As previously, it would be unfair to minimize the real pain that pushes individuals to cure themselves of overinvolvement. It nevertheless seems clear that codependency can arise as a pathological condition only in a society that fosters deep ambivalence about the value of extensive ties.

That Americans have problems with intimacy and commitment is surely reflected in the failure of half the marriages made in the country. Of course, marital problems and failures cannot be linked exclusively to patterns of self-absorption intrinsic to a cultural ethic of individualism. Failed relationships, as I indicated earlier, are also a result of the long-term, institutionalized poverty of some groups and the declining economic fortunes of others. Such difficult circumstances are hardly conducive to maintaining strong family and communal ties. Still, the passionate belief in individualism itself takes its toll. Americans feel incredibly ambivalent about all forms of social attachments. Like moths to the proverbial flame, they are drawn to sources of connection for the comfort they provide, but equally fear what they perceive as the stifling features of all sorts of intimacies. Many are afraid that supportive social bonds will evolve into bondage. They continuously flirt with intimacy and commitment, but in the end often choose a life style that maximizes both freedom and loneliness.

For a time the prevailing wisdom in America was that, on balance, children were better off when poor marriages split up. Yes, certainly there is substantial trauma when a marriage first ends, but children, the thinking went, are enormously resilient and eventually adapt in an emotionally healthy way. Whatever lingering problems they might have would surely have been worse if they too had to endure the bad marriage. Since the divorce revolution did not really begin until the 1970s, only now are we able to learn about the long-term emotional effects of broken marriages on children.

Immediately, let's recognize that children most usually live with their mothers after a divorce. This fact, coupled with compelling data on the "feminization of poverty"[55] post divorce, suggest the possible initiation of the same type of depression cycle earlier described as existing among poor inner-city, female-headed households. In addition, recent data on the long-term effects of divorce debunk the notion that the negative emotional effects of divorce on children are short-lived. The 50 percent divorce rate seems instead to have produced an adult population with persistent and severe emotional problems, depression among them.[56] Among the few issues that political conservatives and liberals agree on these days is that the disintegration of the traditional family across all social classes may be producing just the kinds of problems nineteenth-century theorists presciently imagined.

It is said that when people on their death beds review their lives they rarely say they should have worked harder in order to own even more things than they do. Presumably, most regrets center on relationships that could have been better nurtured and more fulfilling. However, as Bellah's analysis maintains, to live a life that truly centers on the quality of relations with others is exceedingly difficult for many, maybe most, Americans. The cultural pull away from others is often too powerful to resist. A culture that prizes individual self-realization above all else becomes a world held together by only the barest and most tenuous social connections. More and more Americans, identifying individual achievement as the primary medium for personal fulfillment, join the "lonely crowd" identified years ago by David Riesman.[57] To be part of the lonely crowd means being connected to many in general and few in particular. Having opted for loose intimate connections, increasing numbers of people then wonder why they feel the stirrings

of emotional discontent that often evolves into the more dramatic malaise of depression.

NOTES

1. George Herbert Mead, *Mind, Self and Society* (Chicago: University of Chicago, 1934).

2. E. Durkheim, *Suicide* (New York: The Free Press, 1951).

3. K. Erikson, "On sociological prose," *The Yale Review* 78 (1989): 525–538.

4. M. Miller, "Dark days, the staggering cost of depression," *The Wall Street Journal*, Thursday, December 2, 1993, pp. B1, 6.

5. G. Klerman, "Evidence for increases in rates of depression in North America and Western Europe in recent decades." In H. Hippius, G. Klerman, and N. Matusssek (eds.), *New Results in Depression Research* (Berlin, Germany: Springer Verlag, 1986).

6. J. Brody, "Recognizing demons of depression, in either sex," *New York Times*, Wednesday, December 18, 1991, p. C21.

7. See, G. Klerman, et. al., *Interpersonal Psychotherapy of Depression* (New York: Basic Books, 1984); B. Felton, "Cohort variation in happiness," *International Journal of Aging and Human Development* 25 (1987): 27–42; D. Regier, et al., "One month prevalence of mental disorders in the United States," *Archives of General Psychiatry* 45 (1988): 977–986.

8. T. Maher, "The withering of community life and the growth of emotional disorders." *Journal of Sociology and Social Welfare* 19 (1992), p. 138.

9. Although the context of the discussion here, as throughout the book, is on the ways social context shapes the depression experience, the broad social and cultural arrangements described in this chapter do not relate exclusively to depression. As indicated in the text, to pin generic features of American culture to depression alone would be like relating poverty in America to one social problem only. Just as poverty bears a strong relationship to a whole host of human difficulties, the features of American society that foster loneliness, depersonalization, distrust, inauthenticity, mutual indifference, and social disconnection are associated with multiple emotional illnesses. A whole range of disorders from anxiety to depression to paranoia to schizophrenia

flourish in societies and situations that maximize the kinds of personal dislocations arising out of social disattachment.

10. E. Ackernecht, "The role of medical history in medical education," *Bulletin of the History of Medicine* 21 (1947): 142–143.

11. Ibid., p. 143.

12. M. Zborowski, "Cultural components in responses to pain." In C. Clark and H. Robboy (eds.), *Social Interaction* (New York: St. Martin's, 1992).

13. Among his work demonstrating cross-cultural variation in the meanings of affective disorders, see A. Kleinman and B. Good (eds.), *Culture and Depression* (Berkeley: University of California Press, 1986), *Social Origins of Distress and Disease* (New Haven, CT: Yale University Press, 1986), *Rethinking Psychiatry* (New York: Free Press, 1988), and *The Illness Narratives* (New York: Basic Books, 1988).

14. A. Kleinman, *Social Origins of Distress and Disease*, op. cit., p. 145.

15. A. Kleinman, *The Illness Narratives*, op. cit., p. 5.

16. The results of this survey were reported in the Boston Globe on Thursday, January 28, 1993, p. 11.

17. See W. Yoels and J. Clair, 1994. "Never enough time: How medical residents manage a scarce resource," *The Journal of Contemporary Ethnography* 23 (1994): 185–213.

18. Newsweek (February 1, 1994).

19. H. Waitzkin, *The Politics of Medical Encounters: How Patients and Doctors Deal with Social Problems* (New Haven, CT: Yale University Press, 1991).

20. W. Yoels and W. Clair, op. cit.

21. A. Kleinman, The Illness Narratives (New York, Basic Books, 1988, p. 5).

22. A. Kleinman, Rethinking Psychiatry, op. cit., p. 73.

23. These and similar examples are found throughout the works of Arthur Kleinman noted above.

24. For a complete discussion of the medicalization process and particularly the medicalization of deviance, see P. Conrad and J. Schneider, *Deviance and Medicalization* (St. Louis: C. V. Mosby, 1980).

25. P. Berger and T. Luckmann, *The Social Construction of Reality* (New York: Doubleday Anchor, 1967), p. 164.

26. R. Turner, "The theme of contemporary social movements," *British Journal of Sociology* 20 (1969), p. 395.

27. See P. Rieff, *Triumph of the Therapeutic State* (New York: Harper & Row, 1966).

28. C. Lasch, *The Culture of Narcissism* (New York: W. W. Norton, 1978).

29. For a broadly based discussion of such groups, see R. Wuthnow, "Religious movements and counter-movements in North America." In J. Beckford (ed.), *New Religious Movements and Rapid Social Change* (London: Sage, 1986).

30. In his recent book entitled *Sharing the Journey Together: Support Groups and America's New Quest for Community* (New York: The Free Press, 1994), Robert Wuthnow argues that the ever-proliferating range of support groups now constitute the primary mechanism through which Americans achieve a sense of community and connection.

31. See T. Powell, *Self Help Organizations and Professional Practice* (Silver Spring, MD: National Association of Social Workers, 1987) and T. Powell (ed.), *Working with Self Help* (Silver Spring, MD: National Association of Social Workers, 1990).

32. E. Schur, *The Awareness Trap* (New York: McGraw-Hill, 1976).

33. M. Weber, *The Protestant Ethic and the Spirit of Capitalism,* translated by T. Parsons (New York: Scribner's, 1930).

34. Among those who have written about the relationship between capitalism and advertising, the work of Stewart Ewen is particularly cogent. See Ewen's two books entitled *Captains of Consciousness* (New York: McGraw-Hill, 1976) and *All Consuming Images* (New York: Basic Books, 1988).

35. M. Gross, *The Psychological Society* (New York: Random House, 1978), p. 6.

36. S. Peele, *Diseasing of America: Addiction Treatment Out of Control* (Lexington, MA: Lexington Books, 1989).

37. Personal conversation.

38. See T. Maher, "The withering of community life and the growth of emotional disorders," *Journal of Sociology and Social Welfare* 19 (1992): 125–143.

39. For a discussion of how nineteenth-century theorists considered the changing nature of the social bond with the advent of urban industrialization, see D. Karp, G. Stone, and W. Yoels,

Being Urban: A Sociology of City Life (New York: Praeger, 1991).

40. A. Hacker, *Two Nations: Black and White, Separate, Hostile, Unequal* (New York: Scribner's, 1992).

41. R. Sennett and J. Cobb demonstrate, as an example, how the powerlessness of working-class men on their jobs helps to explain the widely observed pattern of male authoritarianism in working-class homes. This analysis is found in their book *The Hidden Injuries of Class* (New York: Random House, 1973).

42. See, for example, H. Becker and A. Strauss, "Careers, personality, and adult socialization," *American Journal of Sociology* 62 (1956): 253–263, and E. Hughes, *Men and Their Work* (New York: The Free Press, 1958).

43. See, R. Cohn, "The effects of employment status change on self attitudes," *Social Psychology* 41 (1978): 81–93; R. Coles, "Work and self respect." In E. Erikson (ed.), *Adulthood* (New York: W. W. Norton, 1978); R. Rothman, *Working: Sociological Perspectives* (Englewood Cliffs, NJ: Prentice Hall, 1987).

44. W. Wilson, *The Truly Disadvantaged* (Chicago: University of Chicago Press, 1987).

45. B. Bluestone and B. Harrison, *The Deindustrialization of America* (New York: Basic Books, 1982).

46. T. Maher, op. cit., p. 134.

47. Reported in T. Maher, op. cit.

48. Reported in T. Maher, op. cit.

49. If anything, the rate of severe depression among America's underclass is probably underestimated since this population segment is the most invisible, has the least access to information about depression, and has effectively been abandoned by the health care system.

50. B. Ehrenreich, *Fear of Falling: The Inner Life of the Middle Class* (New York: HarperCollins, 1989).

51. *Time,* "The temping of America," March 29, 1993.

52. See, for example, C. Davies, "The throwaway culture: Job detachment and depression," *The Gerontologist* 25 (1985): 228–231.

53. R. Bellah, R. Madson, W. M. Sullivan, A. Swidler, and S. M. Tipton, *Habits of the Heart: Individualism and Commitment in American Life* (Berkeley: University of California Press, 1985).

54. W. Kaminer, "Chances are you're co-dependent too," *New York Times Book Review* (February 11, 1990): 1, 26ff.

55. L. Weitzman, *The Divorce Revolution: The Unexpected Social and Economic Consequences in America* (New York: Free Press, 1985).

56. J. Wallerstein and S. Blakeulee, *Second Chances: Men, Women and Children: A Decade After Divorce* (New York: Ticknor and Fields, 1989).

57. D. Riesman, *The Lonely Crowd* (New Haven, CT: Yale University Press, 1950).

THINKING ABOUT THE READING

What does Karp mean when he says that depression is not an exclusively personal, biochemical disorder? What evidence does he provide to support his argument that this ailment is shaped by cultural and social processes? Why is depression so pervasive in technologically complex, postindustrial societies? Pay particular attention to the impact of individualism, occupational instability, and economic competition on people's emotions. If we take this argument one step further, it would imply that simple, preindustrial societies are somewhat inoculated against depression. Do you agree? Using Karp's argument as a starting point, discuss the effectiveness of drug therapy as the dominant treatment for depression. If it's true that people in different cultures experience depression differently, can the same antidepressant drug have similar effects across cultures?

Building Reality

The Social Construction of Knowledge

Sociologists often talk about reality as a *social construction*. What they mean is that truth, knowledge, and so on, are discovered, made known, reinforced, and changed by members of society. As social beings, we respond to our interpretations and definitions of situations, not to the situations themselves, thereby shaping reality. How we distinguish fact from fantasy, truth from fiction, myth from reality are not merely abstract philosophical questions but are very much tied to interpersonal inter-action, group membership, culture, history, power, economics, and politics. But not all of us possess the same ability to define reality. Individuals and groups in positions of power have the ability to control information, define values, create myths, manipulate events, and ultimately influence what others take for granted. The mass media are especially influential in shaping perceptions of reality.

In "The Crack Attack," Craig Reinarman and Harry Levine show us how the news media function to *create* a reality that the public comes to take for granted. They focus, in particular, on the emergence of "the crack problem" in American society. In the late 1980s, crack, a cocaine derivative, came to be seen as one of the most evil scourges on the social landscape. Even today we hear it described with terms like *plague* and *epidemic*. We hear horror stories about crack babies—children born addicted to the drug—whose lives are marked by emotional, intellectual, and behavioral suffering. But Reinarman and Levine point out that the terrified public concern over crack—the reality of the crack problem—is as much a function of media publicity, political opportunism, and the class, race, and ethnicity of crack users as it is a consequence of the actual chemical power and physical danger of the substance itself. In this sense, media representations don't merely *reflect* some "objective" reality, they actually help create it.

Discovering truth and amassing useful knowledge lie at the heart of any academic discipline. The purpose of a field such as sociology is to provide the public with useful and accurate information about how society works. This task is typically accomplished through systematic social research—experiments, field research, unobtrusive research, and surveys. But gathering trustworthy data from people can be difficult. People some-times lie or have difficulty recalling past events in their lives. Sometimes the simple fact of observing people's behavior changes that behavior. And sometimes the information needed to answer questions about important, controversial issues is hard to obtain without raising ethical issues.

Patricia Adler provides an interesting example of how sociologists do research on controversial topics in "Researching Dealers and Smugglers." To many people, the sellers and users of illegal drugs are a dangerous scourge on American society. Adler was interested in understanding the upper echelons of the illicit drug trade—a small, secretive group of people condemned by most members of society but understood by few. Given the illegal and potentially dangerous activities involved, it is unlikely that drug smugglers would willingly answer questions about their trade on a survey or in an interview. So Adler and her husband established close friendships with dealers and smugglers and used a research technique called participant observation to collect inside information about their activities. Putting oneself in the world of one's research subjects can provide rich information, but it can also create serious potential dangers.

The Crack Attack

Politics and Media in the Crack Scare

Craig Reinarman and Harry G. Levine

(1997)

America discovered crack and overdosed on oratory.

—*New York Times*
(Editorial, October 4, 1988)

This *New York Times* editorial had a certain unintended irony, for "America's paper of record" itself had long been one of the leading orators, supplying a steady stream of the stuff on which the nation had, as they put it, "overdosed." Irony aside, the editorial hit the mark. The use of powder cocaine by affluent people in music, film, sports, and business had been common since the 1970s. According to surveys by the National Institute on Drug Abuse (NIDA), by 1985, more than twenty-two million Americans in all social classes and occupations had reported at least trying cocaine. Cocaine smoking originated with "freebasing," which began increasing by the late 1970s (see Inciardi, 1987; Siegel, 1982). Then (as now) most cocaine users bought cocaine hydrochloride (powder) for intranasal use (snorting). But by the end of the 1970s, some users had begun to "cook" powder cocaine down to crystalline or "base" form for smoking. All phases of freebasing, from selling to smoking, took place most often in the privacy of homes and offices of middle-class or well-to-do users. They typically purchased cocaine in units of a gram or more costing $80 to $100 a gram. These relatively affluent "basers" had been discovering the intense rush of smoking cocaine, as well as the risks, for a number of years before the term "crack" was coined. But most such users had a stake in conventional life. Therefore, when they felt their cocaine use was too heavy or out of control, they had the incentives and resources to cut down, quit, or get private treatment.

There was no orgy of media and political attention in the late 1970s when the prevalence of cocaine use jumped sharply, or even after middle-class and upper-class users began to use heavily, especially when freebasing. Like the crack users who followed them, basers had found that this mode of ingesting cocaine produced a much more intense and far shorter "high" because it delivered more pure cocaine into the brain far more directly and rapidly than by snorting. Many basers had found that crack's intense, brutally brief rush, combined with the painful "low" or "down" that immediately followed, produced a powerful desire immediately to repeat use—to binge (Waldorf et al., 1991).

Crack's pharmacological power alone does not explain the attention it received. In 1986, politicians and the media focused on crack—and the drug scare began—when cocaine smoking became visible among a "dangerous" group. Crack attracted the attention of politicians and the media because of its downward mobility to and increased visibility in ghettos and barrios. The new users were a different social class, race, and status (Duster, 1970; Washton and Gold, 1987). Crack was sold in smaller, cheaper, precooked units, on ghetto streets, to poorer, younger buyers who were already seen as a threat (e.g., *New York Times,* August 30, 1987; *Newsweek,* November 23, 1987; *Boston Globe,* May 18, 1988). Crack spread cocaine smoking into poor populations already beset with a cornucopia of troubles (Wilson, 1987). These people tended to have fewer bonds to conventional society, less to lose, and far fewer resources to cope with or shield themselves from drug-related problems.

The earliest mass media reference to the new form of cocaine may have been a *Los Angeles Times* article in late 1984 (November 25, p. cc1) on the use of cocaine "rocks" in ghettos and barrios in Los Angeles. By late 1985, the *New York Times* made the national media's first specific reference to "crack" in a story about three teenagers seeking treatment for cocaine abuse (November 17, p. B12). At the start of 1986, crack was known only in a few impoverished neighborhoods in Los Angeles, New York, Miami, and perhaps a few other large cities. . . .

The Frenzy: Cocaine and Crack in the Public Eye

When two celebrity athletes died in what news stories called "crack-related deaths" in the spring of 1986, the media seemed to sense a potential bonanza. Coverage skyrocketed and crack became widely known. "Dramatic footage" of black and Latino men being carted off in chains, or of police breaking down crack house doors, became a near nightly news event. In July 1986 alone, the three major TV networks offered seventy-four evening news segments on drugs, half of these about crack (Diamond et al., 1987; Reeves and Campbell, 1994). In the months leading up to the November elections, a handful of national newspapers and magazines produced roughly

a thousand stories discussing crack (Inciardi, 1987, p. 481; Trebach, 1987, pp. 6–16). Like the TV networks, leading news magazines such as *Time* and *Newsweek* seemed determined not to be outdone; each devoted five cover stories to crack and the "drug crisis" in 1986 alone.

In the fall of 1986, the CBS news show *48 Hours* aired a heavily promoted documentary called "48 Hours on Crack Street," which Dan Rather previewed on his evening news show: "Tonight, CBS News takes you to the streets, to the war zone, for an unusual two hours of hands-on horror." Among many shots from hidden cameras was one of New York Senator Alphonse D'Amato and then-U.S. Attorney Rudolf Guiliani, incognito, purchasing crack to dramatize the brazenness of street corner sales in the ghetto. All this was good business for CBS: the program earned the highest Nielsen rating of any similar news show in the previous five years—fifteen million viewers (Diamond et al., 1987, p. 10). Three years later, after poor ratings nearly killed *48 Hours,* the show kicked off its season with a three-hour special, "Return to Crack Street."

The intense media competition for audience shares and advertising dollars spawned many similar shows. Three days after "48 Hours on Crack Street," NBC ran its own prime-time special, "Cocaine Country," which suggested that cocaine and crack use had become pandemic. This was one of dozens of separate stories on crack and cocaine produced by NBC alone—an unprecedented fifteen hours of air time—in the seven months leading up to the 1986 elections (Diamond et al., 1987; Hoffman, 1987). By mid-1986, *Newsweek* claimed that crack was the biggest story since Vietnam and Watergate (June 15, p. 15), and *Time* soon followed by calling crack "the Issue of the Year" (September 22, 1986, p. 25). The words "plague," "epidemic," and "crisis" had become routine. The *New York Times,* for example, did a three-part, front-page series called "The Crack Plague" (June 24, 1988, p. A1).

The crack scare began in 1986, but it waned somewhat in 1987 (a nonelection year). In 1988, drugs returned to the national stage as stories about the "crack epidemic" again appeared regularly on front pages and TV screens (Reeves and Campbell, 1994). One politician after another reenlisted in the War on Drugs. In that election year, as in 1986, overwhelming majorities of both houses of Congress voted for new antidrug laws with long mandatory prison terms, death sentences, and large increases in funding for police and prisons. The annual federal budget for antidrug efforts surged from less than $2 billion in 1981 to more than $12 billion in 1993. The budget for the Drug Enforcement Administration (DEA) quadrupled between 1981 and 1992 (Massing, 1993). The Bush administration alone spent $45 billion—more than all other presidents since Nixon combined—mostly for law enforcement (Horgan, 1993; Office of National Drug Control Policy, 1992). . . .

An April 1988 ABC News special report termed crack "a plague" that was "eating away at the fabric of America." According to this documentary, Americans spend "$20 billion a year on cocaine," American businesses lose "$60 billion" a year in productivity because their workers use drugs, "the educational system is being undermined" by student drug use, and "the family" is "disintegrating" in the face of this "epidemic." This program did not give its millions of viewers any evidence to support such dramatic claims, but it did give them a powerful *vocabulary of attribution:* "drugs," especially crack, threatened all the central institutions in American life—families, communities, schools, businesses, law enforcement, even national sovereignty.

This media frenzy continued into 1989. Between October 1988 and October 1989, for example, the *Washington Post* alone ran 1,565 stories—28,476 column inches—about the drug crisis. Even Richard Harwood (1989), the *Post*'s own ombudsman, editorialized against what he called the loss of "a proper sense of perspective" due to such a "hyperbole epidemic." He said that "politicians are doing a number on people's heads." In the fall of 1989, another major new federal antidrug bill to further increase drug war funding (S-1233) began winding its way through Congress. In September, President Bush's "drug czar," William Bennett, unveiled his comprehensive battle plan, the *National Drug Control Strategy.* His introduction asks, "What . . . accounts for the intensifying drug-related chaos that we see every day in our newspapers and on television? One word explains much of it. That word is *crack.* . . . Crack is responsible for the fact that vast patches of the American urban landscape are rapidly deteriorating" (The White House, 1989, p. 3, original emphasis). . . .

On September 5, 1989, President Bush, speaking from the presidential desk in the Oval Office, announced his plan for achieving "victory over drugs" in his first major prime-time address to the nation, broadcast on all three national television networks. We want to focus on this incident as an example of the way politicians and the media systematically misinformed and deceived the public in order to promote the War on Drugs. During the address, Bush held up to the cameras a clear plastic bag of crack labeled "EVIDENCE." He announced that it was "seized a few days ago in a park across the street from the White House" (*Washington Post*, September 22, 1989, p. A1). Its contents, Bush said, were "turning our cities into battle zones and murdering our children." The president proclaimed that, because of crack and other drugs, he would "more than double" federal assistance to state and local law enforcement (*New York Times*, September 6, 1989, p. A11). The next morning the picture of the president holding a bag of crack was on the front pages of newspapers across America.

About two weeks later, the *Washington Post,* and then National Public Radio and other newspapers, discovered how the president of the United States had obtained his bag of crack. According to White House and DEA officials, "the idea of the President holding up crack was [first] included in some drafts" of his speech. Bush enthusiastically approved. A White House aide told the *Post* that the president "liked the prop. . . . It drove the point home." Bush and his advisors also decided that the crack should be seized in Lafayette Park across from the White House so the president could say that crack had become so pervasive that it was being sold "in front of the White House" (Isikoff, 1989).

This decision set up a complex chain of events. White House Communications Director David Demarst asked Cabinet Affairs Secretary David Bates to instruct the Justice Department "to find some crack that fit the description in the speech." Bates called Richard Weatherbee, special assistant to Attorney General Dick Thornburgh, who then called James Milford, executive assistant to the DEA chief. Finally, Milford phoned William McMullen, special agent in charge of the DEA's Washington office, and told him to arrange an undercover crack buy near the White House because "evidently, the President wants to show it could be bought anywhere" (Isikoff, 1989).

Despite their best efforts, the top federal drug agents were not able to find anyone selling crack (or any other drug) in Lafayette Park, or anywhere else in the vicinity of the White House. Therefore, in order to carry out their assignment, DEA agents had to entice someone to come to the park to make the sale. Apparently, the only person the DEA could convince was Keith Jackson, an eighteen-year-old African-American high school senior. McMullan reported that it was difficult because Jackson "did not even know where the White House was." The DEA's secret tape recording of the conversation revealed that the

teenager seemed baffled by the request: "Where the [expletive deleted] is the White House?" he asked. Therefore, McMullan told the *Post,* "we had to manipulate him to get him down there. It wasn't easy" (Isikoff, 1989).

The undesirability of selling crack in Lafayette Park was confirmed by men from Washington, D.C., imprisoned for drug selling, and interviewed by National Public Radio. All agreed that nobody would sell crack there because, among other reasons, there would be no customers. The crack-using population was in Washington's poor African-American neighborhoods some distance from the White House. The *Washington Post* and other papers also reported that the undercover DEA agents had not, after all, actually seized the crack, as Bush had claimed in his speech. Rather, the DEA agents purchased it from Jackson for $2,400 and then let him go.

This incident illustrates how a drug scare distorts and perverts public knowledge and policy. The claim that crack was threatening every neighborhood in America was not based on evidence; after three years of the scare, crack remained predominantly in the inner cities where it began. Instead, this claim appears to have been based on the symbolic political value seen by Bush's speech writers. When they sought, after the fact, to purchase their own crack to prove this point, they found that reality did not match their script. Instead of changing the script to reflect reality, a series of high-level officials instructed federal drug agents to *create* a reality that would fit the script. Finally, the president of the United States displayed the procured prop on national television. Yet, when all this was revealed, neither politicians nor the media were led to question the president's policies or his claims about crack's pervasiveness.

As a result of Bush's performance and all the other antidrug publicity and propaganda, in 1988 and 1989, the drug war commanded more public attention than any other issue.

The media and politicians' antidrug crusade succeeded in making many Americans even more fearful of crack and other illicit drugs. A *New York Times/CBS News* poll has periodically asked Americans to identify "the most important problem facing this country today." In January 1985, 23% answered war or nuclear war; less than 1% believed the most important problem was drugs. In September 1989, shortly after the president's speech and the blizzard of drug stories that followed, 64% of those polled believed that drugs were now the most important problem, and only 1% thought that war or nuclear war was most important. Even the *New York Times* declared in a lead editorial that this reversal was "incredible" and then gently suggested that problems like war, "homelessness and the need to give poor children a chance in life" should perhaps be given more attention (September 28, 1989, p. A26).

A year later, during a lull in antidrug speeches and coverage, the percentage citing "drugs" as the nation's top problem had dropped to 10%. Noting this "precipitous fall from a remarkable height," the *Times* observed that an "alliance of Presidents and news directors" shaped public opinion about drugs. Indeed, once the White House let it be known that the president would be giving a prime-time address on the subject, all three networks tripled their coverage of drugs in the two weeks prior to his speech and quadrupled it for a week afterward (*New York Times*, September 6, 1990, p. A11; see also Reeves and Campbell, 1994). All this occurred while nearly every index of drug use was dropping.

The crack scare continued in 1990 and 1991, although with somewhat less media and political attention. By the beginning of 1992—the last year of the Bush administration—the War on Drugs in general, and the crack scare in particular, had begun to decline significantly in prominence and importance. However, even as the drug war was receiving less notice from politicians and the media, it remained institutionalized, bureaucratically powerful, and extremely well funded (especially police, military, and education/propaganda activities).

From the opening shots in 1986 to President Bush's national address in 1989, and through all the stories about "crack babies" in 1990 and 1991, politicians and the media depicted crack as supremely evil—*the* most important cause of America's problems. As recently as February of 1994, a prominent *New York Times* journalist repeated the claim that "An entire generation is being sacrificed to [crack]" (Staples, 1994). As in all drug scares since the nineteenth-century crusade against alcohol, a core feature of drug war discourse is the *routinization of caricature*—worst cases framed as typical cases, the episodic rhetorically recrafted into the epidemic.

Official Government Evidence

On those rare occasions when politicians and journalists cited statistical evidence to support their claims about the prevalence of crack and other drug use, they usually relied on two basic sources, both funded by the National Institute on Drug Abuse. One was the Drug Abuse Warning Network (DAWN), a monitoring project set up to survey a sample of hospitals, crisis and treatment centers, and coroners across the country about drug-related emergencies and deaths. The other was the National Household Survey on Drug Abuse among general population households and among young people. Other data sources existed, but these usually were either anecdotal, specific to a particular location, or based on a skewed sample. Therefore, we review what these two NIDA data sources had to say about crack because they were the only national data and because they are still considered by experts and claims makers to be the most reliable form of evidence available.

The Drug Abuse Warning Network

DAWN collects data on a whole series of drugs—from amphetamine to aspirin—that might be present in emergencies or fatalities. These data take the form of "mentions." A drug mention is produced when a patient, or someone with a patient, tells attending medical personnel that the patient recently used the drug, or occasionally, if a blood test shows the presence of the drug. These data provided perhaps the only piece of statistical support for the crack scare. They indicated that cocaine was "mentioned" in an increasing number of emergency room episodes in the 1980s. During 1986, as the scare moved into full swing, there were an estimated 51,600 emergency room episodes in which cocaine was mentioned (NIDA, 1993a). In subsequent years, the estimated number of such mentions continued to rise, providing clear cause for concern. By 1989, for example, the estimated number of emergency room episodes in which cocaine was mentioned had more than doubled to 110,000. Although the estimate dropped sharply in 1990 to 80,400, by 1992, it had risen again to 119,800 (NIDA, 1993a).

Unfortunately, the meaning of a mention is ambiguous. In many of these cases, cocaine was probably incidental to the emergency room visit. Such episodes included routine cases in which people went to emergency rooms, for example, after being injured as passengers in auto accidents and in home accidents. Moreover, in most cases, cocaine was only one of the drugs in the person's system; most people had also been drinking alcohol. Finally, the DAWN data do not include information about preexisting medical or mental health conditions that make any drug use, legal or illegal, more risky. For all these reasons, one cannot properly infer direct cause from the estimates of emergency room mentions. Cocaine did play a causal role in many of these emergency cases, but no one knows how many or what proportion of the total they were.

The DAWN data on deaths in which cocaine was mentioned by medical examiners also must be closely examined. When the crack scare got under way in 1986, coroners coded 1,092 deaths as "cocaine related" (NIDA, 1986a), and as crack spread, this number, too, increased substantially. In 1989, the secretary of health and human services reported a 20% decline in both deaths and emergency room episodes in which cocaine was mentioned, but both indices rose again in 1991 and 1992. The 1992 DAWN figures showed 3,020 deaths in which cocaine was mentioned (NIDA, 1992).

But cocaine *alone* was mentioned in only a fraction of these deaths; in 1986, for example, in less than one in five (NIDA, 1986a). In most of these cases, cocaine had been used with other drugs, again, most often alcohol. Although any death is tragic, cocaine's role in such fatalities remains ambiguous. "Cocaine related" is not the same as "cocaine caused," and "cocaine-related deaths" does not mean "deaths *due to* cocaine." There is little doubt that cocaine contributes to some significant (but unknown) percentage of such deaths. But journalists, politicians, and most of the experts on whom they relied never acknowledged the ambiguities in the data. Nor did they commonly provide any comparative perspective. For example, for every *one* cocaine-related death in the U.S., there have been approximately two hundred tobacco-related deaths and at least fifty alcohol-related deaths. Seen in this light, cocaine's role in mortality and morbidity was substantially less than media accounts and political rhetoric implied.

More serious interpretive and empirical difficulties appeared when the DAWN data were used to support claims about crack. Despite all the attention paid to the crack "plague" in 1986, when crack was allegedly "killing a whole generation," the DAWN data contained *no specific information on crack* as distinct from cocaine. In fact, the DAWN data show that in the vast majority of both emergencies and deaths in which cocaine received a mention, the mode of ingestion of cocaine was *not* "smoking" and therefore could not have been caused by crack. Thus, although it is likely that crack played a role in some of the emergencies and deaths in which cocaine was "mentioned," the data necessary to attribute them accurately to crack did not exist.

NIDA Surveys

The NIDA-sponsored surveys of drug use produce the data that are the statistical basis of all estimates of the prevalence of cocaine and other drug use. One of the core claims in the crack scare was that drug use among teenagers and young adults was already high and that it was growing at an alarming rate. Although politicians and the media often referred to teen drug use as an "epidemic" or "plague," the best official evidence available at the time did not support such claims. The National Household Survey on Drug Abuse surveys over eight thousand randomly selected households each year. These surveys show that the number of Americans who had used any illegal drug in the previous month began to decline in 1979, and in the early years of the crack scare, use of drugs, including cocaine, continued to decline (*New York Times,* September 24, 1989, p. A1; *Newsweek,* February 19, 1990, p. 74). Lifetime prevalence of cocaine use among young people (the percentage of those twelve through twenty-five years old who had "ever" tried it) peaked in 1982, *four years before the scare began,* and continued to decline after that (NIDA, 1991, p. 14). The sharpest rise in lifetime prevalence among young adults had taken place between 1972 and 1979; it produced no claims of an epidemic or plague by politicians and journalists (Johnston et al., 1988; NIDA, 1986b).

In February 1987, NIDA released the results of its 1986 annual survey of high school seniors. The *New York Times* handling of the

story shows how even the most respectable media institutions sometimes skew facts about drug use to fit a story line. In the article's "lead," the *Times* announced a rise in the percentage of high school seniors reporting "daily" use of cocaine. Only later did one learn that this had risen very slightly and, more important for evaluating claims of a "plague," that daily use among seniors had now reached 0.4%. Daily crack use, even by this fraction of 1% of high school seniors, is surely troubling, but it hardly constituted a new drug epidemic or plague. Still later in the story, the *Times* presented a table showing other declines in cocaine use by young adults and high school seniors. Indeed, as the *Times* noted toward the end of its piece, virtually all forms of teenage drug use (including marijuana, LSD, and heroin) had declined—as they had in previous years (*New York Times,* February 24, 1987, p. A21; cf. Johnston et al., 1988; NIDA, 1991).

Two leading NIDA scholars, reporting in 1986 on the results of the household survey in *Science* magazine, wrote that "both annual prevalence and current prevalence [of all drug use] among college students and the total sample up to four years after high school has been relatively stable between 1980 and 1985" (Kozel and Adams, 1986, p. 973). The director of NIDA's high school surveys, Dr. Lloyd Johnston, made a similar point in 1987: "To some degree the fad quality of drugs has worn off" (*New York Times,* February 24, 1987, p. A21). When the findings of the high school senior survey for 1987 were released, the survey's director reported that "the most important" finding was that cocaine had again "showed a significant drop in use." He even reported a decline in the use of crack (Johnston et al., 1988).

These reported declines were in keeping with the general downward trend in drug use. In the early 1980s, according to the NIDA surveys, about one in six young Americans had tried cocaine powder. But between 1986 and

1987, the proportion of both high school seniors and young adults who had used cocaine in any form in the previous year dropped by 20% (Johnston et al., 1988). Further, two-thirds of those who had ever tried cocaine had not used it in the previous month. Although a significant minority of young people had tried cocaine powder at some point, the great majority of them did not continue to use it.

There had been a few signs of increasing cocaine use. The proportion of youngsters who reported using cocaine at least once in the previous month had increased slightly over the years, although it never exceeded 2% of all teens in the seven national household surveys between 1972 and 1985. The 1988 NIDA household survey found an increase in the number of adult daily users of cocaine, presumably the group that included crack addicts. But this group constituted only about 1.3% of those adults who had ever used cocaine. NIDA also estimated that about 0.5% of the total U.S. adult population had used cocaine in the week prior to the survey (NIDA, 1988).

But aside from these few slight increases, almost all other measures showed that the trends in official drug use statistics had been down even before the scare began. . . . The figures for cocaine use in particular were dropping just as crisis claims were reaching a crescendo, and had dropped still further precisely when the Bush/Bennett battle plan was being announced with such fanfare in 1989. Indeed, as White House officials anonymously admitted a few weeks after the president's "bag of crack" speech, the new plan's "true goals" were far more modest than its rhetoric: the Bush plan was "simply to move the nation 'a little bit' beyond where current trends would put it anyway" (*New York Times*, September 24, 1989, p. A1).

National Survey Data on Crack

Tom Brokaw reported on *NBC Nightly News* in 1986 (May 23) that crack was "flooding America" and that it had become "America's drug of choice." His colleagues at the other networks and in the print media had made similar claims. An ordinarily competent news consumer might well have gathered the impression that crack could be found in the lockers of most high school students. Yet, at the time of these press reports, *there were no prevalence statistics at all on crack* and no evidence of any sort showing that smoking crack had become the preferred mode even of cocaine use, much less of drug use.

When NIDA released the first official data on crack a few months later, they still did not support claims about widespread crack use. On the contrary, the NIDA survey found that most cocaine use could not have been crack because the preferred mode of use for 90% of cocaine users was "sniffing" rather than smoking (NIDA, 1986a; see also Inciardi, 1987). An all-but-ignored Drug Enforcement Administration press release issued in August 1986, during the first hysterical summer of the crack scare, sought to correct the misperception that crack use was now the major drug problem in America. The DEA said, "Crack is currently the subject of considerable media attention. . . . The result has been a distortion of the public perception of the extent of crack use as compared to the use of other drugs. . . . [Crack] presently appears to be a secondary rather than primary problem in most areas" (Drug Enforcement Administration, cited in Diamond et al., 1987, p. 10; Inciardi, 1987, p. 482).

The first official measures of the prevalence of teenage crack use began with NIDA's 1986 high school survey. It found that 4.1% of high school seniors reported having *tried* crack (at least once) in the previous year. This figure dropped to 3.9% in 1987 and to 3.1% in 1988, a 25% decline (Johnston et al., 1988; *National Report on Substance Abuse*, 1994, p. 3). This means that at the peak of crack use, 96% of America's high school seniors had never tried crack, much less gone on to more regular use, abuse, or addiction. Any drug use among the young is certainly worrisome, particularly when in such an intense form as crack. However, at the start of the crusade to save "a whole generation" of children from death by crack in the spring of 1986, the latest official data showed a national total of eight "cocaine-related" deaths of young people age eighteen and under for the preceding year (Trebach, 1987, p. 11). There was no way to determine whether any of these deaths involved crack use or even if cocaine was in fact the direct cause.

In general, the government's national surveys indicate that a substantial minority of teenagers and young adults experiment with illicit drugs. But as with other forms of youthful deviance, most tend to abandon such behavior as they assume adult roles. Politicians, the media, and antidrug advertisements often claimed that cocaine is inevitably addicting but that crack is still worse because it is "instantaneously addicting." However, according to the official national surveys, two-thirds of Americans of all ages who had ever tried cocaine had not used it in the month prior to the surveys. It is clear that the vast majority of the more than twenty-two million Americans who have tried cocaine do not use it in crack form, do not escalate to regular use, and do not end up addicted. . . .

In sum, the official evidence on cocaine and crack available during the crack scare gave a rather different picture than Americans received from the media and politicians. The sharp rise in mentions of cocaine in emergency room episodes and coroners' reports did offer cause for concern. But the best official evidence of drug use never supported the claims about an "epidemic" or "plague" throughout America or about "instantaneous addiction." Moreover, as media attention to crack was burgeoning, the actual extent of crack use was virtually unknown, and most other official measures of cocaine use were actually decreasing. Once crack use was actually measured, its

prevalence turned out to be low to start with and to have declined throughout the scare (*National Report on Substance Abuse*, 1994, p. 3).

Crack as an Epidemic and Plague

The empirical evidence on crack use suggests that politicians and journalists have routinely used the words "epidemic" and "plague" imprecisely and rhetorically as words of warning, alarm, and danger. Therefore, on the basis of press reports, it is difficult to determine if there was any legitimacy at all in the description of crack use as an epidemic or plague. Like most other drug researchers and epidemiologists, we have concluded that crack addiction has never been anything but relatively rare across the great middle strata of the U.S. population. If the word "epidemic" is used to mean a disease or diseaselike condition that is "widespread" or "prevalent," then there has never been an epidemic of crack addiction (or even crack use) among the vast majority of Americans. Among the urban poor, however, especially African-American and Latino youth, heavy crack use has been more common. An "epidemic of crack *use*" might be a description of what happened among a distinct minority of teenagers and young adults from impoverished urban neighborhoods in the mid to late 1980s. However, many more people use tobacco and alcohol heavily than use cocaine in any form. Alcohol drinking and tobacco smoking each kills far more people than all forms of cocaine and heroin use combined. Therefore, "epidemic" would be more appropriate to describe tobacco and alcohol use. But politicians and the media have not talked about tobacco and alcohol use as epidemics or plagues. The word "epidemic" also can mean a rapidly spreading disease. In this precise sense as well, in inner-city neighborhoods, crack use may have been epidemic (spreading rapidly) for a few years among impoverished young African-Americans and

Latinos. However, crack use was never spreading fast or far enough among the general population to be termed an epidemic there.

"Plague" is even a stronger word than epidemic. Plague can mean a "deadly contagious disease," an epidemic "with great mortality," or it can refer to a "pestilence," an "infestation of a pest, [e.g.,] a plague of caterpillars." Crack is a central nervous system stimulant. Continuous and frequent use of crack often burns people out and does them substantial psychological and physical harm. But even very heavy use does not usually directly kill users. In this sense, crack use is not a plague. One could say that drug dealers were "infesting" some blocks of some poor neighborhoods in some cities, that there were pockets of plague in some specific areas; but that was not how "crack plague" was used.

When evaluating whether the extent and dangers of crack use match the claims of politicians and the media, it is instructive to compare how other drug use patterns are discussed. For example, an unusually balanced *New York Times* story (October 7, 1989, p. 26) compared crack and alcohol use among suburban teenagers and focused on the middle class. The *Times* reported that, except for a few "urban pockets" in suburban counties, "crack and other narcotics are rarely seen in the suburbs, whether modest or wealthy." . . .

The *Times* also reported that high school seniors were outdrinking the general adult population. Compared to 64% of teenagers, only 55% of adults had consumed alcohol in the last month. Furthermore, teenagers have been drinking more than adults since at least 1972, when the surveys began. Even more significant is the *kind* of drinking teenagers do—what the *Times* called "excessive 'binge' drinking": "More than a third of the high school seniors had said that in the last two weeks they had had five or more drinks in a row." Drinking is, of course, the most widespread form of illicit drug use

among high school students. As the *Times* explained, on the weekend, "practically every town has at least one underage party, indoors or out" and that "fake identification cards, older siblings, friends, and even parents all help teenagers obtain" alcohol.

The point we wish to emphasize is that even though illicit alcohol use was far more prevalent than cocaine or crack use, and even though it held substantial risk for alcohol dependence, addiction, drinking-driving deaths, and other alcohol-related problems, the media and politicians have not campaigned against teen drunkenness. Used as a descriptive term meaning "prevalent," the word "epidemic" fits teenage drinking far better than it does teenage crack use. Although many organizations have campaigned against drinking and driving by teenagers, the politicians and media have not used terms like "epidemic" or "plague" to call attention to illicit teenage drinking and drunkenness. Unlike the *Times* articles on crack, often on the front page, this article on teen drunkenness was placed in the second section on a Saturday.

It is also worth noting the unintentionally ironic mixing of metaphors, or of diagnoses and remedies, when advocates for the War on Drugs described crack use as an epidemic or plague. Although such disease terminology was used to call attention to the consequences of crack use, most of the federal government's domestic responses have centered on using police to arrest users. Treatment and prevention have always received a far smaller proportion of total federal antidrug funding than police and prisons do as a means of handling the "epidemic." If crack use is primarily a crime problem, then terms like "wave" (as in crime wave) would be more fitting. But if this truly is an "epidemic"—a widespread disease—then police and prisons are the wrong remedy, and the victims of the epidemic should be offered treatment, public health programs, and social services. . . .

The Political Context of the "Crack Crisis"

If the many claims about an "epidemic" or "plague" endangering "a whole generation" of youth were at odds with the best official data, then what else was animating the new War on Drugs? In fact, even if all the exaggerated claims about crack had been true, it would not explain all the attention crack received. Poverty, homelessness, auto accidents, handgun deaths, and environmental hazards are also widespread, costly, even deadly, but most politicians and journalists never speak of them in terms of crisis or plague. Indeed, far more people were (and still are) injured and killed every year by domestic violence than by illicit drugs, but one would never know this from media reports or political speeches. The existence of government studies suggesting that crack contributed to the deaths of a small proportion of its users, that an unknown but somewhat larger minority of users became addicted to it, that its use was related to some forms of crime, and so on were neither necessary nor sufficient conditions for all the attention crack received (Spector and Kitsuse, 1977).

Like other sociologists, historians, and students of drug law and public policy, we suggest that understanding antidrug campaigns requires more than evidence of drug abuse and drug-related problems, which can be found in almost any period. It requires analyzing these crusades and scares as phenomena in their own right and understanding the broader social, political, and economic circumstances under which they occur (see, e.g., Bakalar and Grinspoon, 1984; Brecher, 1972; Duster, 1970; Gusfield, 1963, 1981; Lindesmith, 1965; Morgan, 1978; Musto, 1973; Rumbarger, 1989). The crack scare also must be understood in terms of its political context and its appeal to important groups within American society. The mass media and politicians, however, did not talk about drugs this way. Rather, they decontextualized the drama, making it appear as if the story had no authors aside from dealers and addicts. Their writing of the crack drama kept abusers, dealers, crimes, and casualties under spotlights while hiding other important factors in the shadows. We suggest that over and above the very real problems some users suffered with crack, the rise of the New Right and the competition between political parties in a conservative context contributed significantly to the making of the crack scare.

The New Right and Its Moral Ideology

During the post-Watergate rebuilding of the Republican Party, far right wing political organizations and fundamentalist Christian groups set about to impose what they called "traditional family values" on public policy. This self-proclaimed "New Right" felt increasingly threatened by the diffusion of modernist values, behaviors, and cultural practices—particularly by what they saw as the interconnected forms of 1960s hedonism involved in sex outside (heterosexual) marriage and consciousness alteration with (illicit) drugs. The New Right formed a core constituency for Ronald Reagan, an extreme conservative who had come to prominence as governor of California in part by taking a hard line against the new political movements and cultural practices of the 1960s.

Once he became president in 1981, Reagan and his appointees attempted to restructure public policy according to a radically conservative ideology. Through the lens of this ideology, most social problems appeared to be simply the consequences of *individual moral choices* (Ryan, 1976). Programs and research that had for many years been directed at the social and structural sources of social problems were systematically defunded in budgets and delegitimated in discourse. Unemployment, poverty, urban decay, school crises, crime, and all their attendant forms of human troubles were spoken of and acted upon as if they were the result of *individual* deviance, immorality, or weakness. The most basic premise of social science—that individual choices are influenced by social circumstances—was rejected as left-wing ideology. Reagan and the New Right constricted the aperture of attribution for America's ills so that only the lone deviant came into focus. They conceptualized people *in* trouble as people who *make* trouble (Gusfield, 1985); they made social control rather than social welfare the organizing axis of public policy (Reinarman, 1988).

With regard to drug problems, this conservative ideology is a form of *sociological denial.* For the New Right, people did not so much abuse drugs because they were jobless, homeless, poor, depressed, or alienated; they were jobless, homeless, poor, depressed, or alienated because they were weak, immoral, or foolish enough to use illicit drugs. For the right wing, American business productivity was not lagging because investors spent their capital on mergers and stock speculation instead of on new plants and equipment, or for any number of other economic reasons routinely mentioned in the *Wall Street Journal* or *Business Week.* Rather, conservatives claimed that businesses had difficulty competing partly because many workers were using drugs. In this view, U.S. education was in trouble not because it had suffered demoralizing budget cuts, but because a "generation" of students was "on drugs" and their teachers did not "get tough" with them. The new drug warriors did not see crime plaguing the ghettos and barrios for all the reasons it always has, but because of the influence of a new chemical bogeyman. Crack was a godsend to the Right. They used it and the drug issue as an ideological fig leaf to place over the unsightly urban ills that had increased markedly under Reagan administration social and economic policies. "The drug problem" served conservative politicians as an all-purpose scapegoat. They could blame an array of

problems on the deviant individuals and then expand the nets of social control to imprison those people for causing the problems.

The crack crisis had other, more specific political uses. Nancy Reagan was a highly visible antidrug crusader, crisscrossing the nation to urge schoolchildren to "Just Say No" to drugs. Mrs. Reagan's crusade began in 1983 (before crack came into existence) when her "p.r.-conscious operatives," as *Time* magazine called them, convinced her that "serious-minded displays" of "social consciousness" would "make her appear more caring and less frivolous." Such a public relations strategy was important to Mrs. Reagan. The press had often criticized her for spending hundreds of thousands of dollars on new china for the White House, lavish galas for wealthy friends, and high-fashion evening gowns at a time when her husband's economic policies had induced a sharp recession, raised joblessness to near Depression-era levels, and cut funding for virtually all programs for the poor. *Time* explained that "the timing and destinations of her antidrug excursions last year were coordinated with the Reagan-Bush campaign officials to satisfy their particular political needs" (*Time,* January 14, 1985, p. 30). . . .

Political Party Competition

The primary political task facing liberals in the 1980s was to recapture some of the electorate that had gone over to the Right. Reagan's shrewdness in symbolically colonizing "middle American" fears put Democrats on the defensive. Most Democrats responded by moving to the right and pouncing upon the drug issue. Part of the early energy for the drug scare in the spring and summer of 1986 came from Democratic candidates trading charges with their Republican opponents about being "soft on drugs." Many candidates challenged each other to take urine tests as a symbol of their commitment to a "drug-free America."

One Southern politician even proposed that candidates' spouses be tested. A California senatorial candidate charged his opponent with being "a noncombatant in the war on drugs" *(San Francisco Chronicle,* August 12, 1986, p. 9). By the fall of 1986, increasingly strident calls for a drug war became so much a part of candidates' standard stump speeches that even conservative columnist William Safire complained of antidrug "hysteria" and "narcomania" (*New York Times,* September 11, 1986, p. A27). Politicians demanded everything from death penalties in North America to bombing raids in South America.

Crack could not have appeared at a more opportune political moment. After years of dull debates on budget balancing, a "hot" issue had arrived just in time for a crucial election. In an age of fiscal constraint, when most problems were seen as intractable and most solutions costly, the crack crisis was the one "safe" issue on which all politicians could take "tough stands" without losing a single vote or campaign contribution. The legislative results of the competition to "get tough" included a $2 billion law in 1986, the so-called "Drug-Free America Act," which whizzed through the House (392 to 16) just in time for members of Congress to go home and tell their constituents about it. In the heat of the preelection, antidrug hysteria, the symbolic value of such spending seemed to dwarf the deficit worries that had hamstrung other legislation. According to *Newsweek,* what occurred was "a can-you-top-this competition" among "election-bound members of both parties" seeking tough antidrug amendments. The 1986 drug bill, as Representative David McCurdy (D-Okla) put it, was "out of control," adding through a wry smile, "but of course I'm for it" (September 22, 1986, p. 39).

The prominence of the drug issue dropped sharply in both political speeches and media coverage after the 1986 election, but returned during the 1988 primaries. Once again the crack issue had political utility. One common observation about the 1988 presidential election campaigns was that there were no domestic or foreign policy crises looming on which the two parties could differentiate themselves. As a *New York Times* headline put it: "Drugs as 1988 Issue: Filling a Vacuum" (May 24, 1988, p. A14). In the 1988 primary season, candidates of both parties moved to fill this vacuum in part by drug-baiting their opponents and attacking them as "soft on drugs." In the fall, both Democrats Dukakis and Bentsen and Republicans Bush and Quayle claimed that their opponents were soft on drugs while asserting that their side would wage a "*real* War on Drugs." And, just as they did before the 1986 election, members of Congress from both parties overwhelmingly passed a new, even more strict and costly antidrug bill.

The antidrug speeches favoring such expenditures became increasingly transparent as posturing, even to many of the speakers. For example, Senator Christopher Dodd (D-Conn) called the flurry of antidrug amendments a "feeding frenzy" (*New York Times,* May 22, 1988, p. E4). An aide to another senator admitted that "everybody was scrambling to get a piece of the action" (*New York Times,* May 24, 1988, p. A14). Even President Reagan's spokesperson, Marlin Fitzwater, told the White House press corps that "everybody wants to out-drug each other in terms of political rhetoric" (*Boston Globe,* May 18, 1988, p. 4). But however transparent, such election-year posturing—magnified by a media hungry for the readers and ratings that dramatic drug stories bring—enhanced the viability of claims about the menace of crack far more than any available empirical evidence could. In the fall of 1989, Congress finalized yet another major antidrug bill costing more than the other two combined. According to research by the Government Accounting Office, the federal government spent more than $23 billion on the drug war during the Reagan era, three-fourths of it for law enforcement *(Alcoholism and Drug Abuse Week,* 1989, p. 3). . . .

Politicians and the media were *forging,* not following, public opinion. The speeches and stories *led* the oft-cited poll results, not the other way around. In 1987, between elections—when drug problems persisted in the ghettos and barrios but when the drug scare was not so enflamed by election rhetoric and media coverage—only 3 to 5% of those surveyed picked drugs as our most important problem *(New York Times,* May 24, 1988, p. A14). But then again in 1989, immediately following President Bush's speech escalating the drug war, nearly two-thirds of the people polled identified drugs as America's most important problem. When the media and politicians invoked "public opinion" as the driving force behind their actions against crack, they inverted the actual causal sequence (Edelman, 1964, p. 172).

We argued in the previous section that the New Right and other conservatives found ideological utility in the crack scare. In this section, we have suggested that conservatives were not the only political group in America to help foment the scare and to benefit from it. Liberals and Democrats, too, found in crack and drugs a means of recapturing Democratic defectors by appearing more conservative. And they too found drugs to be a convenient scapegoat for the worsening conditions in the inner cities. All this happened at a historical moment when the Right successfully stigmatized the liberals' traditional solutions to the problems of the poor as ineffective and costly. Thus, in addition to the political capital to be gained by waging the war, the new chemical bogeyman afforded politicians across the ideological spectrum both an explanation for pressing public problems and an excuse for not proposing the unpopular taxing, spending, or redistributing needed to do something about them.

The End of the Crack Scare

In the 1980s, the conservative drive to reduce social spending exacerbated the enduring problems of impoverished African-American and Latino city residents. Partly in response, a minority of the young urban poor turned either to crack sales as their best shot at the American Dream and/or to the crack high as their best shot at a fleeting moment of pleasure. Inner-city churches, community organizations, and parent groups then tried to defend their children and neighborhoods from drug dealing and use on the one hand and to lobby for services and jobs on the other hand. But the crack scare did not inspire politicians of either party to address the worsening conditions and growing needs of the inner-city poor and working class or to launch a "Marshall Plan for cities." In the meantime, the white middle-class majority viewed with alarm the growing numbers, visibility, and desperation of the urban poor. And for years many Americans believed the central fiction of the crack scare: that drug use was not a symptom of urban decay but one of its most important causes.

All this gave federal and local authorities justification for widening the nets of social control. Of course, the new drug squads did not reduce the dangerousness of impoverished urban neighborhoods. But the crack scare did increase criminal justice system supervision of the underclass. By 1992, one in four young African-American males was in jail or prison or on probation or parole—more than were in higher education. . . . During the crack scare, the prison population more than doubled, largely because of the arrests of drug users and small dealers. This gave the U.S. the highest incarceration rate in the world (Currie, 1985; Irwin and Austin, 1994).

By the end of 1992, however, the crack scare seemed spent. There are a number of overlapping reasons for this. Most important was the failure of the War on Drugs itself.

Democrats as well as Republicans supported the War on Drugs, but the Reagan and Bush administrations initiated and led it, and the drug war required support from the White House. George Bush appointed William Bennett to be a "tough" and extremely high profile "drug czar" to lead the campaign against drugs. But Bennett, criticized for his bombastic style, quit after only eighteen months (some press accounts referred to it as the "czar's abdication"). After that, the Bush administration downplayed the drug war, and it hardly figured at all in the presidential primaries or campaign in 1992. Bill Clinton said during the campaign that there were no easy solutions to drug problems and that programs that work only on reducing supply were doomed to fail. The Clinton administration eschewed the phrase "War on Drugs," and Lee Brown, Clinton's first top drug official, explicitly rejected the title of drug czar (Reinarman, 1994). After billions of tax dollars had been spent and millions of young Americans had been imprisoned, hard-core drug problems remained. With so little to show for years of drug war, politicians seemed to discover the limits of the drug issue as a political weapon. Moreover, with both parties firmly in favor of the "get tough" approach, there was no longer any partisan political advantage to be had.

The news media probably would have written dramatic stories about the appearance of smokeable cocaine in poor neighborhoods at any time. Television producers have found that drug stories, especially timely, well-advertised, dramatic ones, often receive high ratings. But the context of the Reagan-led drug war encouraged the media to write such pieces. Conservatives had long complained that the media had a liberal bias; in the mid-1980s, drug coverage allowed the media to rebut such criticism and to establish conservative credentials (Reeves and Campbell, 1994). As we have suggested, news coverage of drugs rose and fell with political initiatives, especially those coming from the president. Therefore, as the White House withdrew from the drug issue, so did the press.

After about 1989, it became increasingly difficult to sustain the exaggerated claims of the beginning of the crack scare. The mainstream media began to publish stories critical of earlier news coverage (though usually not their own). . . . . *Newsweek* finally admitted in 1990 what it called the "dirty little secret" about crack that it had concealed in all of its earlier scare stories: "A lot of people use it without getting addicted," and that the anonymous "media" had "hyped instant and total addiction" (February 19, 1990, pp. 74–75). As early as 1988, it was clear that crack was not "destroying a whole generation"; it was not even spreading beyond the same poverty context that had long given rise to hard-core heroin addiction. Moreover, because of the obvious destructive effects of heavy use, people in ghettos and barrios had come to view "crack heads" as even lower in status than winos or junkies. Even crack dealers preferred powder cocaine and routinely disparaged crack heads (Williams, 1989). All of this meant that drugs in general, and crack in particular, declined in newsworthiness. Media competition had fueled the crack scare in its early years, and the same scramble for dramatic stories guaranteed that the media would move on to other stories. By 1992, the crack scare had faded beyond the media's horizon of hot new issues.

Finally, the crack scare could recede into the background partly because it had been *institutionalized.* Between 1986 and 1992, Congress passed and two presidents signed a series of increasingly harsh antidrug laws. Federal antidrug funding increased for seven successive years, and an array of prison and police programs was established or expanded. All levels of government, from schools to cities, counties, and states, established agencies to warn about crack and other drug problems. And multimillion-dollar, corporate-sponsored, private organizations such as the Partnership for a Drug-Free America had been established to continue the crusade.

Conclusion

Smoking crack *is* a risky way to use an already potent drug. Despite all the exaggerations, heavy use of it *has* made life more difficult for many people—most of them from impoverished urban neighborhoods. If we agree that too many families have been touched by drug-related tragedies, why have we bothered criticizing the crack scare and the War on Drugs? If even a few people are saved from crack addiction, why should anyone care if this latest drug scare was in some measure concocted by the press, politicians, and moral entrepreneurs to serve their other agendas? Given the damage that drug abuse can do, what's the harm in a little hysteria? . . .

First, we suspect that drug scares do not work very well to reduce drug problems and that they may well promote the behavior they claim to be preventing. For all the repression successive drug wars have wrought (primarily upon the poor and the powerless), they have yet to make a measurable dent in our drug *problems.* For example, prompted by the crack crisis and inspired by the success of patriotic propaganda in World War II, the Partnership for a Drug-Free America ran a massive advertising campaign to "unsell drugs." From 1987 to 1993, the Partnership placed over $1 billion worth of advertising donated by corporations and the advertising industry. The Partnership claims to have had a "measurable impact" by "accelerating intolerance" to drugs and drug users. The Partnership claims it "can legitimately take some of the credit for the 25% decline in illicit drug usage since our program was launched" (Hedrick, 1990). However, the association between the Partnership's antidrug advertising and the declines in drug use appears to be spurious. Drug use was declining

well before the Partnership's founding; taking credit for what was already happening is a bit like jumping in front of a parade and then claiming to have been leading it all along. More important, drug *use* increased in the mid 1990s among precisely those age groups that had been targeted by Partnership ads, while drug *problems* continued throughout their campaign. Furthermore, Partnership ads scrupulously avoided any mention of the two forms of drug use most prevalent among youth: smoking and drinking. This may have something to do with the fact that the Partnership for a Drug-Free America is a partnership between the media and advertising industries, which make millions from alcohol and tobacco advertising each year, and with the fact that alcohol and tobacco companies contribute financially to the Partnership's campaign against illicit drugs. Surely public health education is important, but there is no evidence that selective antidrug propaganda and scare tactics have significantly reduced drug problems.

Indeed, hysterical and exaggerated antidrug campaigns may have increased drug-related harm in the U.S. There is the risk that all of the exaggerated claims made to mobilize the population for war actually arouse interest in drug use. In 1986, the *New England Journal of Medicine* reported that the frequency of teenage suicides increases after lurid news reports and TV shows about them (Gould and Shaffer, 1986; Phillips and Carstensen, 1986). Reports about drugs, especially of new and exotic drugs like crack, may work the same way. In his classic chapter, "How To Launch a Nationwide Drug Menace," Brecher (1972) shows how exaggerated newspaper reports of dramatic police raids in 1960 functioned as advertising for glue sniffing. The arrests of a handful of sniffers led to anti–glue sniffing hysteria that actually spread this hitherto unknown practice across the U.S. In 1986, the media's desire for dramatic drug stories interacted with politicians' desire for partisan advantage and safe election-year issues, so news about crack spread to every nook and cranny of the nation far faster than dealers could have spread word on the street. When the media and politicians claimed that crack is "the most addictive substance known to man," there was some commonsense obligation to explain why. Therefore, alongside all the statements about "instant addiction," the media also reported some very intriguing things about crack: "whole body orgasm," "better than sex," and "cheaper than cocaine." For TV-raised young people in the inner city, faced with a dismal social environment and little economic opportunity, news about such a substance in their neighborhoods may have functioned as a massive advertising campaign for crack.

Further, advocates of the crack scare and the War on Drugs explicitly rejected public health approaches to drug problems that conflicted with their ideology. The most striking and devastating example of this was the total rejection of syringe distribution programs by the Reagan and Bush administrations and by drug warriors such as Congressman Charles Rangel. People can and do recover from drug addiction, but no one recovers from AIDS. By the end of the 1980s, the fastest growing AIDS population was intravenous drug users. Because syringes were hard to get, or their possession criminalized, injectors shared their syringes and infected each other and their sexual partners with AIDS. In the early 1980s, activists in a number of other Western countries had developed syringe distribution and exchange programs to prevent AIDS, and there is by now an enormous body of evidence that such programs are effective. But the U.S. government has consistently rejected such "harm reduction" programs on the grounds that they conflict with the policy of "zero tolerance" for drug use or "send the wrong message." As a result, cities such as Amsterdam, Liverpool, and Sydney, which have needle exchange programs, have very low or almost no transmission of AIDS by intravenous

drug users. In New York City, however, roughly half the hundreds of thousands of injection drug users are HIV positive or already have AIDS. In short, the crack scare and the drug war policies it fueled will ultimately contribute to the deaths of tens of thousands of Americans, including the families, children, and sexual partners of the infected drug users.

Another important harm resulting from American drug scares is they have routinely blamed individual immorality and personal behavior for endemic social and structural problems. In so doing, they diverted attention and resources away from the underlying sources of drug abuse and the array of other social ills of which they are part. One necessary condition for the emergence of the crack scare (as in previous drug scares) was the linking of drug use with the problems faced by racial minorities, the poor, and youth. In the logic of the scare, whatever economic and social troubles these people have suffered were due largely to their drug use. Obscured or forgotten during the crack scare were all the social and economic problems that underlie crack abuse—and that are much more widespread—especially poverty, unemployment, racism, and the prospects of life in the permanent underclass.

Democrats denounced the Reagan and Bush administrations' hypocrisy in proclaiming "War on Drugs" while cutting the budgets for drug treatment, prevention, and research. However, the Democrats often neglected to mention an equally important but more politically popular development: the "Just Say No to Drugs" administrations had, with the help of many Democrats in Congress, also "just said no" to virtually every social program aimed at creating alternatives for and improving the lawful life chances of inner-city youth. These black and Latino young people were and are the group with the highest rate of crack abuse. Although most inner-city youth have always steered clear of drug abuse, they could not "just say no" to poverty and unemployment. Dealing drugs, after all, was (and still is) accurately perceived by many poor city kids as the highest-paying job—straight or criminal—that they are likely to get.

The crack scare, like previous drug scares and antidrug campaigns, promoted misunderstandings of drug use and abuse, blinded people to the social sources of many social problems (including drug problems), and constrained the social policies that might reduce those problems. It routinely used inflated, misleading rhetoric and falsehoods such as Bush's televised account of how he came into possession of a bag of crack. At best, the crack scare was not good for public health. At worst, by manipulating and misinforming citizens about drug use and effects, it perverted social policy and political democracy.

REFERENCES

Alcoholism and Drug Abuse Week, "$23 Billion Spent on Federal Drug Effort Since 1981." July 5, 1989, pp. 3–4.

Anderson, Jack, and Michael Binstein, "Drug Informants Beating the System." *Washington Post,* September 10, 1992, p. D23.

Bakalar, James B., and Lester Grinspoon, *Drug Control in a Free Society.* Cambridge: Cambridge University Press, 1984.

Belenko, Steven, and Jeffrey Fagan, "Crack and the Criminal Justice System." New York: New York City Criminal Justice Agency, 1987.

Brecher, Edward M., *Licit and Illicit Drugs.* Boston: Little, Brown, 1972.

Chin K.-L, "Special Event Codes for Crack Arrests." Internal memorandum, New York City Criminal Justice Agency, 1988.

Currie, Elliott, *Confronting Crime.* New York: Pantheon, 1985.

Diamond, Edwin, Frank Accosta, and Leslie-Jean Thornton, "Is TV News Hyping America's Cocaine Problem?" *TV Guide,* February 7, 1987, pp. 4–10.

Drug Enforcement Administration, "Special Report: The Crack Situation in the U.S." Unpublished, Strategic Intelligence Section. Washington, DC: DEA, August 22, 1986.

Duster, Troy, *The Legislation of Morality.* New York: Free Press, 1970.

Edelman, Murray, *The Symbolic Uses of Politics.* Urbana: University of Illinois Press, 1964.

Gould, Madelyn S., and David Shaffer, "The Impact of Suicide in Television Movies: Evidence of Imitation." *New England Journal of Medicine* 315:690–694 (1986).

Grinspoon, Lester, and James B. Bakalar, *Cocaine: A Drug and Its Social Evolution.* New York: Basic Books, 1976.

Gusfield, Joseph R., *Symbolic Crusade.* Urbana: University of Illinois Press, 1963.

———, *The Culture of Public Problems.* Chicago: University of Chicago Press, 1981.

———, "Alcohol Problems—An Interactionist View," in J. P. von Wartburg et al., eds., *Currents in Alcohol Research and the Prevention of Alcohol Problems.* Berne, Switzerland: Hans Huber, 1985.

Harwood, Richard, "Hyperbole Epidemic." *Washington Post,* October 1, 1989, p. D6.

Hedrick, Thomas A., Jr., "Pro Bono Anti-Drug Ad Campaign Is Working." *Advertising Age,* June 25, 1990, p. 22.

Himmelstein, Jerome, *The Strange Career of Marijuana.* Westport, CT: Greenwood Press, 1983.

Hoffman, Abbie, *Steal This Urine Test: Fighting Drug Hysteria in America.* New York: Penguin Books, 1987.

Horgan, John, "A Kinder War." *Scientific American,* July 25, 1993, p. 6.

Inciardi, James, "Beyond Cocaine: Basuco, Crack, and Other Coca Products." *Contemporary Drug Problems* 14:461–492 (1987).

Irwin, John, and James Austin, *It's About Time: America's Imprisonment Binge.* Belmont, CA: Wadsworth, 1994.

Isikoff, Michael, "Drug Buy Set Up for Bush Speech: DEA Lured Seller to Lafayette Park." *Washington Post,* September 22, 1989, p. A1.

Johnson, Bruce D., et al., *Taking Care of Business: The Economics of Crime by Heroin Abusers.* Lexington, MA: Lexington Books, 1985.

Johnston, Lloyd D., Patrick M. O'Malley, and Jerald G. Bachman, *Illicit Drug Use, Smoking, and Drinking by America's High School Students, College Students, and Young Adults, 1975–1987.*

Washington, DC: National Institute on Drug Abuse, 1988.

Kitsuse, John I., and Aaron V. Cicourel, "A Note on the Use of Official Statistics." *Social Problems* 11:131–139 (1963).

Kozel, Nicholas, and Edgar Adams, "Epidemiology of Drug Abuse: An Overview." *Science* 234: 970–974 (1986).

Lindesmith, Alfred R., *The Addict and the Law.* Bloomington: Indiana University Press, 1965.

Massing, Michael, Review essay on "Swordfish," *New York Review of Books,* July 15, 1993, pp. 30–32.

Morgan, Patricia, "The Legislation of Drug Law: Economic Crisis and Social Control," *Journal of Drug Issues* 8:53–62 (1978).

Musto, David, *The American Disease: Origins of Narcotic Control.* New Haven, CT: Yale University Press, 1973.

National Institute on Drug Abuse, *Data from the Drug Abuse Warning Network: Annual Data 1985.* Statistical Series 1, #5. Washington, DC: National Institute on Drug Abuse, 1986a.

———, *National Household Survey on Drug Abuse, 1985.* Washington, DC: Division of Epidemiology and Statistical Analysis, National Institute on Drug Abuse, 1986b.

———, *National Household Survey on Drug Abuse: 1988 Population Estimates.* Washington, DC: Division of Epidemiology and Prevention Research, National Institute on Drug Abuse, 1988.

———, *National Household Survey on Drug Abuse: Main Findings 1990.* Washington, DC: Epidemiology and Prevention Research, National Institute on Drug Abuse, 1990.

———, *Annual Medical Examiner Data, 1991: Data from the Drug Abuse Warning Network.* Washington, DC: Division of Epidemiology and Prevention Research, National Institute on Drug Abuse, 1992.

———, *Estimates from the Drug Abuse Warning Network: 1992 Estimates of Drug-Related Emergency Room Episodes.* Washington, DC: Substance Abuse and Mental Health Services Administration, U.S. Dept. of Health and Human Services, 1993a.

———, *National Household Survey on Drug Abuse: Population Estimates 1992.* Washington, DC:

Substance Abuse and Mental Health Services Administration, U.S. Dept. of Health and Human Services, 1993b.

National Report on Substance Abuse, "Federal Officials Express Alarm at Youth's Rising Illicit Drug Use." February 11, 1994, p. 2.

Office of National Drug Control Policy, *National Drug Control Strategy: Budget Summary.* Washington, DC: U.S. Government Printing Office, 1992.

Phillips, David P., and Lundie L. Carstensen, "Clustering of Teenage Suicides After Television News Stories About Suicide." *New England Journal of Medicine* 315:685–689 (1986).

Reeves, Jimmie L., and Richard Campbell, *Cracked Coverage: Television News, the Anti-Cocaine Crusade, and the Reagan Legacy.* Durham, NC: Duke University Press, 1994.

Reinarman, Craig, "The Social Construction of an Alcohol Problem: The Case of Mothers Against Drunk Drivers and Social Control in the 1980s." *Theory and Society* 17:91–119 (1988).

———, "Glasnost in U.S. Drug Policy?: Clinton Constrained." *International Journal of Drug Policy* 5:42–49 (1994).

Rogin, Michael Paul, *Ronald Reagan, the Movie: and Other Episodes in Political Demonology.* Berkeley: University of California Press, 1987.

Rumbarger, John, *Profits, Power, and Prohibition,* Albany: State University of New York Press, 1989.

Ryan, William, *Blaming the Victim.* New York: Vintage, 1976.

Schneider, Joseph, and John I. Kitsuse, eds., *Studies in the Sociology of Social Problems.* Norwood, NJ: Ablex, 1984.

Siegel, Ronald, "Cocaine Smoking." *Journal of Psychoactive Drugs* 14:271–359 (1982).

Spector, Malcolm, and John Kitsuse, *Constructing Social Problems.* Menlo Park, CA: Cummings, 1977.

Staples, Brent, "Coke Wars." *New York Times Book Review,* February 6, 1994, p. 11.

Trebach, Arnold, *The Great Drug War.* New York: Macmillan, 1987.

University of Michigan, "Drug Use Rises Among American Teen-Agers." News and Information Services, January 27, 1994.

Waldorf, Dan, Craig Reinarman, and Sheigla Murphy, *Cocaine Changes*. Philadelphia: Temple University Press, 1991.

Washton, Arnold, and Mark Gold, "Recent Trends in Cocaine Abuse," *Advances in Alcohol and Substance Abuse* 6:31–47 (1987).

The White House, *National Drug Control Strategy*. Washington, DC: U.S. Government Printing Office, 1989.

Williams, Terry, *The Cocaine Kids*. Reading, MA: Addison-Wesley, 1989.

Wilson, William Julius, *The Truly Disadvantaged*. Chicago: University of Chicago Press, 1987.

Zinberg, Norman E., *Drug, Set, and Setting: The Basis for Controlled Drug Use*. New Haven, CT: Yale University Press, 1984.

THINKING ABOUT THE READING

How does Reinarman and Levine's article support the contention that reality is a social construction? Consider the broader implications of their argument: The use of certain substances becomes a serious social problem *not* because it is an objectively dangerous activity but because it receives sufficient media and political attention. What does this contention suggest about the way social problems and public fears are created and maintained in society? What does it tell us about our collective need to identify a scapegoat for our social problems? Why are there such vastly different public attitudes and legal responses to crack cocaine versus powder cocaine? Can you think of other situations in which heightened media coverage and political attention have created widespread public concern and moral outrage where none was warranted? How has this article affected your views about the "War on Drugs" and the decriminalization of illegal drugs?

Researching Dealers and Smugglers

Patricia A. Adler

(1985)

I strongly believe that investigative field research (Douglas 1976), with emphasis on direct personal observation, interaction, and experience, is the only way to acquire accurate knowledge about deviant behavior. Investigative techniques are especially necessary for studying groups such as drug dealers and smugglers because the highly illegal nature of their occupation makes them secretive, deceitful, mistrustful, and paranoid. To insulate themselves from the straight world, they construct multiple false fronts, offer lies and misinformation, and withdraw into their group. In fact, detailed, scientific information about upper-level drug dealers and smugglers is lacking precisely because of the difficulty sociological researchers have had in penetrating into their midst. As a result, the only way I could possibly get close enough to these individuals to discover what they were doing and to understand their world from their perspectives (Blumer 1969) was to take a membership role in the setting. While my different values and goals precluded my becoming converted to complete membership in the sub-culture, and my fears prevented my ever becoming "actively" involved in their trafficking activities, I was able to assume a "peripheral" membership role. I became a member of the dealers' and smugglers' social world and participated in their daily activities on that basis. . . .

Getting In

When I moved to Southwest County [California] in the summer of 1974, I had no idea that I would soon be swept up in a subculture of vast drug trafficking and unending partying, mixed with occasional cloak-and-dagger subterfuge. I had moved to California with my husband, Peter, to attend graduate school in sociology. We rented a condominium townhouse near the beach and started taking classes in the fall. We had always felt that socializing exclusively with academicians left us nowhere to escape from our work, so we tried to meet people in the nearby community. One of the first friends we made was our closest neighbor, a fellow in his late twenties with a tall, hulking frame and gentle expression. Dave, as he introduced himself, was always dressed rather casually, if not sloppily, in T-shirts and jeans. He spent most of his time hanging out or walking on the beach with a variety of friends who visited his house, and taking care of his two young boys, who lived alternately with him and his estranged wife. He also went out of town a lot. We started spending much of our free time over at his house, talking, playing board games late into the night, and smoking marijuana together. We were glad to find someone from whom we could buy marijuana in this new place, since we did not know too many people. He also began treating us to a fairly regular supply of cocaine, which was a thrill because this was a drug we could rarely afford on our student budgets. We noticed right away, however, that there was something unusual about his use and knowledge of drugs: while he always had a plentiful supply and was fairly expert about marijuana and cocaine, when we tried to buy a small bag of marijuana from him he had little idea of the going price. This incongruity piqued our curiosity and raised suspicion. We wondered if he might be dealing in larger quantities.

Keeping our suspicions to ourselves, we began observing Dave's activities a little more closely. Most of his friends were in their late twenties and early thirties and, judging by their lifestyles and automobiles, rather wealthy. They came and left his house at all hours, occasionally extending their parties through the night and the next day into the following night. Yet throughout this time we never saw Dave or any of his friends engage in any activity that resembled a legitimate job. In most places this might have evoked community suspicion, but few of the people we encountered in Southwest County seemed to hold traditionally structured jobs. Dave, in fact, had no visible means of financial support. When we asked him what he did for a living, he said something vague about being a real estate speculator, and we let it go at that. We never voiced our suspicions directly since he chose not to broach the subject with us.

We did discuss the subject with our mentor, Jack Douglas, however. He was excited by the prospect that we might be living among a group of big dealers, and urged us to follow our instincts and develop leads into the group. He knew that the local area was rife with drug trafficking, since he had begun a life history case study of two drug dealers with another graduate student several years previously. That earlier study was aborted when the graduate student quit school, but Jack still had many hours of taped interviews he had conducted with them, as well as an interview that he had done with an undergraduate student who had known the two dealers independently, to serve as a cross-check on their accounts. He therefore encouraged us to become friendlier with Dave and his friends. We decided that if anything did develop out of our observations of Dave, it might make a nice paper for a field methods class or independent study. . . .

We thus watched Dave and continued to develop our friendship with him. We also watched his friends and got to know a few of his more regular visitors. We continued to build friendly relations by doing, quite naturally, what Becker (1963), Polsky (1969), and Douglas (1972) had advocated for the early stages of field research: we gave them a chance to know us and form judgments about our trustworthiness by jointly pursuing those interests and activities which we had in common.

Then one day something happened which forced a breakthrough in the research. Dave had two guys visiting him from out of town and, after snorting quite a bit of cocaine, they turned their conversation to a trip they had just made from Mexico, where they piloted a load of marijuana back across the border in a small plane. Dave made a few efforts to shift the conversation to another subject, telling them to "button their lips," but they apparently thought that he was joking. They thought that anybody as close to Dave as we seemed to be undoubtedly knew the nature of his business. They made further allusions to his involvement in the operation and discussed the outcome of the sale. We could feel the wave of tension and awkwardness from Dave when this conversation began, as he looked toward us to see if we understood the implications of what was being said, but then he just shrugged it off as done. Later, after the two guys left, he discussed with us what happened. He admitted to us that he was a member of a smuggling crew and a major marijuana dealer on the side. He said that he knew he could trust us, but that it was his practice to say as little as possible to outsiders about his activities. This inadvertent slip, and Dave's subsequent opening up, were highly significant in forging our entry into Southwest County's drug world. From then on he was open in discussing the nature of his dealing and smuggling activities with us.

He was, it turned out, a member of a smuggling crew that was importing a ton of marijuana weekly and 40 kilos of cocaine every few months. During that first winter and spring, we observed Dave at work and also got to know the other members of his crew, including Ben, the smuggler himself. Ben was also very tall and broad shouldered, but his long black hair, now flecked with gray, bespoke his earlier membership in the hippie subculture. A large physical stature, we observed, was common to most of the male participants involved in this drug community. The women also had a unifying physical trait: they were extremely attractive and stylishly dressed. This included Dave's ex-wife, Jean, with whom he reconciled during the spring. We therefore became friendly with Jean and through her met a number of women ("dope chicks") who hung around the dealers and smugglers. As we continued to gain the friendship of Dave and Jean's associates we were progressively admitted into their inner circle and apprised of each person's dealing or smuggling role.

Once we realized the scope of Ben's and his associates' activities, we saw the enormous research potential in studying them. This scene was different from any analysis of drug trafficking that we had read in the sociological literature because of the amounts they were dealing and the fact that they were importing it themselves. We decided that, if it was at all possible, we would capitalize on this situation, to "opportunistically" (Riemer 1977) take advantage of our prior expertise and of the knowledge, entree, and rapport we had already developed with several key people in this setting. We therefore discussed the idea of doing a study of the general subculture with Dave and several of his closest friends (now becoming our friends). We assured them of the anonymity, confidentiality, and innocuousness of our work. They were happy to reciprocate our friendship by being of help to our professional careers. In fact, they basked in the subsequent attention we gave their lives.

We began by turning first Dave, then others, into key informants and collecting their life histories in detail. We conducted a series of taped, in-depth interviews with an unstructured, open-ended format. We questioned them about such topics as their backgrounds, their recruitment into the occupation, the stages of their dealing careers, their relations with others, their motivations, their lifestyle, and their general impressions about the community as a whole.

We continued to do taped interviews with key informants for the next six years until 1980, when we moved away from the area. After that, we occasionally did follow-up interviews when we returned for vacation visits. These later interviews focused on recording the continuing unfolding of events and included detailed probing into specific conceptual areas, such as dealing networks, types of dealers, secrecy, trust, paranoia, reputation, the law, occupational mobility, and occupational stratification. The number of taped interviews we did with each key informant varied, ranging between 10 and 30 hours of discussion.

Our relationship with Dave and the others thus took on an added dimension—the research relationship. As Douglas (1976), Henslin (1972), and Wax (1952) have noted, research relationships involve some form of mutual exchange. In our case, we offered everything that friendship could entail. We did routine favors for them in the course of our everyday lives, offered them insights and advice about their lives from the perspective of our more respectable position, wrote letters on their behalf to the authorities when they got in trouble, testified as character witnesses at their non-drug-related trials, and loaned them money when they were down and out. When Dave was arrested and brought to trial for check-kiting, we helped Jean organize his defense and raise the money to pay his fines. We spelled her in taking care of the children so that she could work on his behalf. When he was eventually sent to the state prison we maintained close ties with her and discussed our mutual efforts to buoy Dave up and secure his release. We also visited him in jail. During Dave's incarceration, however, Jean was courted by an old boyfriend and gave up her reconciliation with Dave. This proved to be another significant turning point in our research because, desperate for money, Jean looked up Dave's old dealing connections and went into the business herself. She did not stay with these marijuana dealers and smugglers for long, but soon moved into the cocaine business. Over the next several years her experiences in the world of cocaine dealing brought us into contact with a different group of people. While these people knew Dave and his associates (this was very common in the Southwest County dealing and smuggling community), they did not deal with them directly. We were thus able to gain access to a much wider and more diverse range of subjects than we would have had she not branched out on her own.

Dave's eventual release from prison three months later brought our involvement in the research to an even deeper level. He was broke and had nowhere to go. When he showed up on our doorstep, we took him in. We offered to let him stay with us until he was back on his feet again and could afford a place of his own. He lived with us for seven months, intimately sharing his daily experiences with us. During this time we witnessed, firsthand, his transformation from a scared ex-con who would never break the law again to a hard-working legitimate employee who only dealt to get money for his children's Christmas presents, to a full-time dealer with no pretensions at legitimate work. Both his process of changing attitudes and the community's gradual reacceptance of him proved very revealing.

We socialized with Dave, Jean, and other members of Southwest County's dealing and smuggling community on a near-daily basis, especially during the first four years of the research (before we had a child). We worked in their legitimate businesses, vacationed together, attended their weddings, and cared for their children. Throughout their relationship with us, several participants became co-opted to the

researcher's perspective and actively sought out instances of behavior which filled holes in the conceptualizations we were developing. Dave, for one, became so intrigued by our conceptual dilemmas that he undertook a "natural experiment" entirely on his own, offering an unlimited supply of drugs to a lower-level dealer to see if he could work up to higher levels of dealing, and what factors would enhance or impinge upon his upward mobility.

In addition to helping us directly through their own experiences, our key informants aided us in widening our circle of contacts. For instance, they let us know when someone in whom we might be interested was planning on dropping by, vouching for our trustworthiness and reliability as friends who could be included in business conversations. Several times we were even awakened in the night by phone calls informing us that someone had dropped by for a visit, should we want to "casually" drop over too. We rubbed the sleep from our eyes, dressed, and walked or drove over, feeling like sleuths out of a television series. We thus were able to snowball, through the active efforts of our key informants, into an expanded study population. This was supplemented by our own efforts to cast a research net and befriend other dealers, moving from contact to contact slowly and carefully through the domino effect.

The Covert Role

The highly illegal nature of dealing in illicit drugs and dealers' and smugglers' general level of suspicion made the adoption of an overt research role highly sensitive and problematic. In discussing this issue with our key informants, they all agreed that we should be extremely discreet (for both our sakes and theirs). We carefully approached new individuals before we admitted that we were studying them. With many of these people, then, we took a covert posture in the research setting.

As nonparticipants in the business activities which bound members together into the group, it was difficult to become fully accepted as peers. We therefore tried to establish some sort of peripheral, social membership in the general crowd, where we could be accepted as "wise" (Goffman 1963) individuals and granted a courtesy membership. This seemed an attainable goal, since we had begun our involvement by forming such relationships with our key informants. By being introduced to others in this wise rather than overt role, we were able to interact with people who would otherwise have shied away from us. Adopting a courtesy membership caused us to bear a courtesy stigma, however, and we suffered since we, at times, had to disguise the nature of our research from both lay outsiders and academicians.

In our overt posture we showed interest in dealers' and smugglers' activities, encouraged them to talk about themselves (within limits, so as to avoid acting like narcs), and ran home to write field notes. This role offered us the advantage of gaining access to unapproachable people while avoiding researcher effects, but it prevented us from asking some necessary, probing questions and from tape recording conversations. We therefore sought, at all times, to build toward a conversion to the overt role. We did this by working to develop their trust.

Developing Trust

Like achieving entree, the process of developing trust with members of unorganized deviant groups can be slow and difficult. In the absence of a formal structure separating members from outsiders, each individual must form his or her own judgment about whether new persons can be admitted to their confidence. No gatekeeper existed to smooth our path to being trusted, although our key informants acted in this role whenever they could by providing introductions and references. In addition, the unorganized

nature of this group meant that we met people at different times and were constantly at different levels in our developing relationships with them. We were thus trusted more by some people than by others, in part because of their greater familiarity with us. But as Douglas (1976) has noted, just because someone knew us or even liked us did not automatically guarantee that they would trust us.

We actively tried to cultivate the trust of our respondents by tying them to us with favors. Small things, like offering the use of our phone, were followed with bigger favors, like offering the use of our car, and finally really meaningful favors, like offering the use of our home. Here we often trod a thin line, trying to ensure our personal safety while putting ourselves in enough of a risk position, along with our research subjects, so that they would trust us. While we were able to build a "web of trust" (Douglas 1976) with some members, we found that trust, in large part, was not a simple status to attain in the drug world. Johnson (1975) has pointed out that trust is not a one-time phenomenon, but an ongoing developmental process. From my experiences in this research I would add that it cannot be simply assumed to be a one-way process either, for it can be diminished, withdrawn, reinstated to varying degrees, and requestioned at any point. Carey (1972) and Douglas (1972) have remarked on this waxing and waning process, but it was especially pronounced for us because our subjects used large amounts of cocaine over an extended period of time. This tended to make them alternately warm and cold to us. We thus lived through a series of ups and downs with the people we were trying to cultivate as research informants.

The Overt Role

After this initial covert phase, we began to feel that some new people trusted us. We tried to intuitively feel when the time was right to approach them and go overt. We used two means of approaching people to inform them that we were involved in a study of dealing and smuggling: direct and indirect. In some cases our key informants approached their friends or connections and, after vouching for our absolute trustworthiness, convinced these associates to talk to us. In other instances, we approached people directly, asking for their help with our project. We worked our way through a progression with these secondary contacts, first discussing the dealing scene overtly and later moving to taped life history interviews. Some people reacted well to us, but others responded skittishly, making appointments to do taped interviews only to break them as the day drew near, and going through fluctuating stages of being honest with us or putting up fronts about their dealing activities. This varied, for some, with their degree of active involvement in the business. During the times when they had quit dealing, they would tell us about their present and past activities, but when they became actively involved again, they would hide it from us.

This progression of covert to overt roles generated a number of tactical difficulties. The first was the problem of *coming on too fast* and blowing it. Early in the research we had a dealer's old lady (we thought) all set up for the direct approach. We knew many dealers in common and had discussed many things tangential to dealing with her without actually mentioning the subject. When we asked her to do a taped interview of her bohemian lifestyle, she agreed without hesitation. When the interview began, though, and she found out why we were interested in her, she balked, gave us a lot of incoherent jumble, and ended the session as quickly as possible. Even though she lived only three houses away we never saw her again. We tried to move more slowly after that.

A second problem involved simultaneously *juggling our overt and covert roles* with different people. This created the danger of getting our cover blown with people who did

not know about our research (Henslin 1972). It was very confusing to separate the people who knew about our study from those who did not, especially in the minds of our informants. They would make occasional veiled references in front of people, especially when loosened by intoxicants, that made us extremely uncomfortable. We also frequently worried that our snooping would someday be mistaken for police tactics. Fortunately, this never happened. . . .

Problems and Issues

Reflecting on the research process, I have isolated a number of issues which I believe merit additional discussion. These are rooted in experiences which have the potential for greater generic applicability.

The first is the *effect of drugs on the data-gathering process.* Carey (1972) has elaborated on some of the problems he encountered when trying to interview respondents who used amphetamines, while Wax (1952, 1957) has mentioned the difficulty of trying to record field notes while drinking sake. I found that marijuana and cocaine had nearly opposite effects from each other. The latter helped the interview process, while the former hindered it. Our attempts to interview respondents who were stoned on marijuana were unproductive for a number of reasons. The primary obstacle was the effects of the drug. Often, people became confused, sleepy, or involved in eating to varying degrees. This distracted them from our purpose. At times, people even simulated overreactions to marijuana to hide behind the drug's supposed disorienting influence and thereby avoid divulging information. Cocaine, in contrast, proved to be a research aid. The drug's warming and sociable influence opened people up, diminished their inhibitions, and generally increased their enthusiasm for both the interview experience and us.

A second problem I encountered involved *assuming risks while doing research.* As I noted earlier, dangerous situations are often generic to research on deviant behavior. We were most afraid of the people we studied. As Carey (1972), Henslin (1972), and Whyte (1955) have stated, members of deviant groups can become hostile toward a researcher if they think that they are being treated wrongfully. This could have happened at any time from a simple occurrence, such as a misunderstanding, or from something more serious, such as our covert posture being exposed. Because of the inordinate amount of drugs they consumed, drug dealers and smugglers were particularly volatile, capable of becoming malicious toward each other or us with little warning. They were also likely to behave erratically owing to the great risks they faced from the police and other dealers. These factors made them moody, and they vacillated between trusting us and being suspicious of us.

At various times we also had to protect our research tapes. We encountered several threats to our collection of taped interviews from people who had granted us these interviews. This made us anxious, since we had taken great pains to acquire these tapes and felt strongly about maintaining confidences entrusted to us by our informants. When threatened, we became extremely frightened and shifted the tapes between different hiding places. We even ventured forth one rainy night with our tapes packed in a suitcase to meet a person who was uninvolved in the research at a secret rendezvous so that he could guard the tapes for us.

We were fearful, lastly, of the police. We often worried about local police or drug agents discovering the nature of our study and confiscating or subpoenaing our tapes and field notes. Sociologists have no privileged relationship with their subjects that would enable us legally to withhold evidence from the authorities should they subpoena it. For this reason we studiously avoided any publicity about the research, even holding back on publishing articles in scholarly journals until we were nearly ready to move out of the setting. The closest we came to being

publicly exposed as drug researchers came when a former sociology graduate student (turned dealer, we had heard from inside sources) was arrested at the scene of a cocaine deal. His lawyer wanted us to testify about the dangers of doing drug-related research, since he was using his research status as his defense. Fortunately, the crisis was averted when his lawyer succeeded in suppressing evidence and had the case dismissed before the trial was to have begun. Had we been exposed, however, our respondents would have acquired guilt by association through their friendship with us.

Our fear of the police went beyond our concern for protecting our research subjects, however. We risked the danger of arrest ourselves through our own violations of the law. Many sociologists (Becker 1963; Carey 1972; Polsky 1969; Whyte 1955) have remarked that field researchers studying deviance must inevitably break the law in order to acquire valid participant observation data. This occurs in its most innocuous form from having "guilty knowledge": information about crimes that are committed. Being aware of major dealing and smuggling operations made us an accessory to their commission, since we failed to notify the police. We broke the law, secondly, through our "guilty observations," by being present at the scene of a crime and witnessing its occurrence (see also Carey 1972). We knew it was possible to get caught in a bust involving others, yet buying and selling was so pervasive that to leave every time it occurred would have been unnatural and highly suspicious. Sometimes drug transactions even occurred in our home, especially when Dave was living there, but we finally had to put a stop to that because we could not handle the anxiety. Lastly, we broke the law through our "guilty actions," by taking part in illegal behavior ourselves. Although we never dealt drugs (we were too scared to be seriously tempted), we consumed drugs and possessed them in small quantities. Quite frankly, it would have been impossible for a nonuser to have gained access to this group to gather the data presented here. This was the minimum involvement necessary to obtain even the courtesy membership we achieved. Some kind of illegal action was also found to be a necessary or helpful component of the research by Becker (1963), Carey (1972), Johnson (1975), Polsky (1969), and Whyte (1955).

Another methodological issue arose from the *cultural clash between our research subjects and ourselves*. While other sociologists have alluded to these kinds of differences (Humphreys 1970, Whyte 1955), few have discussed how the research relationships affected them. Relationships with research subjects are unique because they involve a bond of intimacy between persons who might not ordinarily associate together, or who might otherwise be no more than casual friends. When fieldworkers undertake a major project, they commit themselves to maintaining a long-term relationship with the people they study. However, as researchers try to get depth involvement, they are apt to come across fundamental differences in character, values, and attitudes between their subjects and themselves. In our case, we were most strongly confronted by differences in present versus future orientations, a desire for risk versus security, and feelings of spontaneity versus self-discipline. These differences often caused us great frustration. We repeatedly saw dealers act irrationally, setting themselves up for failure. We wrestled with our desire to point out their patterns of foolhardy behavior and offer advice, feeling competing pulls between our detached, observer role which advised us not to influence the natural setting, and our involved, participant role which called for us to offer friendly help whenever possible. . . .

The final issue I will discuss involved the various *ethical problems* which arose during this research. Many fieldworkers have encountered ethical dilemmas or pangs of guilt during the course of their research experiences (Carey 1972;

Douglas 1976; Humphreys 1970; Johnson 1975; Klockars 1977, 1979; Rochford 1985). The researchers' role in the field makes this necessary because they can never fully align themselves with their subjects while maintaining their identity and personal commitment to the scientific community. Ethical dilemmas, then, are directly related to the amount of deception researchers use in gathering the data, and the degree to which they have accepted such acts as necessary and therefore neutralized them.

Throughout the research, we suffered from the burden of intimacies and confidences. Guarding secrets which had been told to us during taped interviews was not always easy or pleasant. Dealers occasionally revealed things about themselves or others that we had to pretend not to know when interacting with their close associates. This sometimes meant that we had to lie or build elaborate stories to cover for some people. Their fronts therefore became our fronts, and we had to weave our own web of deception to guard their performances. This became especially disturbing during the writing of the research report, as I was torn by conflicts between using details to enrich the data and glossing over descriptions to guard confidences.

Using the covert research role generated feelings of guilt, despite the fact that our key informants deemed it necessary, and thereby condoned it. Their own covert experiences were far more deeply entrenched than ours, being a part of their daily existence with non-drug world members. Despite the universal presence of covert behavior throughout the setting, we still felt a sense of betrayal every time we ran home to write research notes on observations we had made under the guise of innocent participants. . . .

Conclusions

The aggressive research strategy I employed was vital to this study. I could not just walk up to strangers and start hanging out with them as Liebow (1967) did, or be sponsored to a member of this group by a social service or reform organization as Whyte (1955) was, and expect to be accepted, let alone welcomed. Perhaps such a strategy might have worked with a group that had nothing to hide, but I doubt it. Our modern, pluralistic society is so filled with diverse subcultures whose interests compete or conflict with each other that each subculture has a set of knowledge which is reserved exclusively for insiders. In order to survive and prosper, they do not ordinarily show this side to just anyone. To obtain the kind of depth insight and information I needed, I had to become like the members in certain ways. They dealt only with people they knew and trusted, so l had to become known and trusted before I could reveal my true self and my research interests. Confronted with secrecy, danger, hidden alliances, misrepresentations, and unpredictable changes of intent, I had to use a delicate combination of overt and covert roles. Throughout, my deliberate cultivation of the norm of reciprocal exchange enabled me to trade my friendship for their knowledge, rather than waiting for the highly unlikely event that information would be delivered into my lap. I thus actively built a web of research contacts, used them to obtain highly sensitive data, and carefully checked them out to ensure validity. . . .

Finally, I feel strongly that to ensure accuracy, research on deviant groups must be conducted in the settings where it naturally occurs. As Polsky (1969:115–16) has forcefully asserted:

> This means—there is no getting away from it—the study of career criminals *au natural,* in the field, the study of such criminals as they normally go about their work and play, the study of "uncaught" criminals and the study of others who in the past have been caught but are not caught at the time you study them.

. . . Obviously we can no longer afford the convenient fiction that in studying criminals in their natural habitat, we would discover nothing really important that could not be discovered from criminals behind bars.

By studying criminals in their natural habitat I was able to see them in the full variability and complexity of their surrounding subculture, rather than within the artificial environment of a prison. I was thus able to learn about otherwise inaccessible dimensions of their lives, observing and analyzing firsthand the nature of their social organization, social stratification, lifestyle, and motivation.

REFERENCES

Becker, Howard. 1963. *Outsiders.* New York: Free Press.

Blumer, Herbert. 1969. *Symbolic Interactionism.* Englewood Cliffs, NJ: Prentice-Hall.

Carey, James T. 1972. "Problems of access and risk in observing drug scenes." In Jack D. Douglas, ed., *Research on Deviance*, pp. 71–92. New York: Random House.

Douglas, Jack D. 1972. "Observing deviance." In Jack D. Douglas, ed., *Research on Deviance*, pp. 3–34. New York: Random House.

———. 1976. *Investigative Social Research.* Beverly Hills, CA: Sage.

Goffman, Erving. 1963. *Stigma.* Englewood Cliffs, NJ: Prentice-Hall.

Henslin, James M. 1972. "Studying deviance in four settings: research experiences with cabbies, suicides, drug users and abortionees." In Jack D. Douglas, ed., *Research on Deviance*, pp. 35–70. New York: Random House.

Humphreys, Laud. 1970. *Tearoom Trade.* Chicago: Aldine.

Johnson, John M. 1975. *Doing Field Research.* New York: Free Press.

Klockars, Carl B. 1977. "Field ethics for the life history." In Robert Weppner, ed., *Street Ethnography*, pp. 201–26. Beverly Hills, CA: Sage.

———. 1979. "Dirty hands and deviant subjects." In Carl B. Klockars and Finnbarr W. O'Connor, eds., *Deviance and Decency*, pp. 261–82. Beverly Hills, CA: Sage.

Liebow, Elliot. 1967. *Tally's Corner.* Boston: Little, Brown.

Polsky, Ned. 1969. *Hustlers, Beats, and Others.* New York: Doubleday.

Riemer, Jeffrey W. 1977. "Varieties of opportunistic research." *Urban Life* 5:467–77.

Rochford, E. Burke, Jr. 1985. *Hare Krishna in America.* New Brunswick, NJ: Rutgers University Press.

Wax, Rosalie. 1952. "Reciprocity as a field technique." *Human Organization* 11:34–37.

_____. 1957. "Twelve years later: an analysis of a field experience." *American Journal of Sociology* 63: 133–42.

Whyte, William F. 1955. *Street Corner Society.* Chicago: University of Chicago Press.

THINKING ABOUT THE READING

Many of the issues sociologists try to understand are phenomena that occur under highly secretive circumstances. Patricia Adler chose a research method that brought her and her husband face to face with people involved in serious criminal activities. Only from this vantage point could they fully understand the social forces at play. What does she mean when she says researchers want to understand the world of criminals from their own perspective (p. 67)? Do you think their tactic was ethically justifiable? Should social researchers be obligated to report criminal activity to the proper authorities, or is it appropriate to conceal such information in the name of scientific inquiry? Can you think of a better way to acquire accurate information about drug dealers and smugglers?

PART II

The Construction of Self and Society

4 Building Order

Culture and History

Culture provides members of a society with a common bond, a sense that they see certain facets of society in similar ways. That members of a society can live together at all depends on the fact that they share a certain amount of cultural knowledge. Social norms—the rules and standards that govern all social encounters—provide order in our day-to-day lives. Norms reflect commonly held assumptions about conventional behavior. They tell us what to expect from others and what others can expect from us. Violations of norms mark the boundaries of acceptable behavior and symbolically reaffirm what a particular society defines as right and wrong.

Sociology tells us that virtually every aspect of our lives is influenced by culture. When we examine these influences, things that were once familiar and taken for granted suddenly become unfamiliar and curious. During the course of our lives we are rarely forced to examine *why* we do the common things we do, we just do them. But if we take a step back and examine our common customs and behaviors they begin to look as strange as the "mystical" rituals of some far off, exotic land. It is for this reason that Horace Miner's article, "Body Ritual Among the Nacirema" has become a classic in sociology and anthropology.

Norms, of course, vary greatly across cultures. Indeed, the more ethnically and culturally diverse a society is, the greater the likelihood of normative clashes between groups. We can see clear evidence of the power of cultural norms when we examine how members of a different society handle some taken-for-granted aspect of everyday life. Take, for instance, the experience of time. If you've ever traveled abroad you know that people perceive the importance of time differently. In some places everyday life is incredibly fast-paced; in others it seems frustratingly slow and lethargic. In the industrialized world, events are often meticulously timed and scheduled. But in less developed parts of the world, time is much less restrictive and events occur more spontaneously.

We don't have to travel to a foreign country, though, to see the clash of different cultural beliefs and expectations. Such clashes can be quite confusing and painful for newly arrived immigrants from countries with vastly different cultural traditions. In the article "The Melting Pot," Anne Fadiman examines the experiences of Hmong refugees in the United States. Hundreds of thousands of Hmong people have fled Laos since that country fell to communist forces in 1975. Most have settled in the United States. Virtually every element of Hmong culture and tradition lies in stark contrast to the standard assumptions of American life. They have been described in the American media as simplistic, primitive, and throwbacks to the Stone Age. This article vividly portrays the everyday conflicts immigrants face as they straddle two vastly different cultures.

Body Ritual Among the Nacirema

Horace Miner

(1956)

The anthropologist has become so familiar with the diversity of ways in which different peoples behave in similar situations that he is not apt to be surprised by even the most exotic customs. In fact, if all of the logically possible combinations of behavior have not been found somewhere in the world, he is apt to suspect that they must be present in some yet undescribed tribe. This point has, in fact, been expressed with respect to clan organization by Murdock (1949, p. 71). In this light, the magical beliefs and practices of the Nacirema present such unusual aspects that it seems desirable to describe them as an example of the extremes to which human behavior can go.

Professor Linton first brought the ritual of the Nacirema to the attention of anthropologists twenty years ago (1936, p. 326), but the culture of this people is still very poorly understood. They are a North American group living in the territory between the Canadian Cree, the Yaqui and Tarahumara of Mexico, and the Carib and Arawak of the Antilles. Little is known of their origin, although tradition states that they came from the east. According to Nacirema mythology, their nation was originated by a culture hero, Notgnihsaw, who is otherwise known for two great feats of strength—the throwing of a piece of wampum across the river Pa-To-Mac and the chopping down of a cherry tree in which the Spirit of Truth resided.

Nacirema culture is characterized by a highly developed market economy which has evolved in a rich natural habitat. While much of the people's time is devoted to economic pursuits, a large part of the fruits of these labors and a considerable portion of the day are spent in ritual activity. The focus of this activity is the human body, the appearance and health of which loom as a dominant concern in the ethos of the people. While such a concern is certainly not unusual, its ceremonial aspects and associated philosophy are unique.

The fundamental belief underlying the whole system appears to be that the human body is ugly and that its natural tendency is to debility and disease. Incarcerated in such a body, man's only hope is to avert these characteristics through the use of the powerful influences of ritual and ceremony. Every household has one or more shrines devoted to this purpose. The more powerful individuals in this society have several shrines in their houses and, in fact, the opulence of a house is often referred to in terms of the number of such ritual centers it possesses. Most houses are of wattle and daub construction, but the shrine rooms of the more wealthy are walled with stone. Poorer families imitate the rich by applying pottery plaques to their shrine walls.

While each family has at least one such shrine, the rituals associated with it are not family ceremonies but are private and secret. The rites are normally only discussed with children, and then only during the period when they are being initiated into these mysteries. I was able, however, to establish sufficient rapport with the natives to examine these shrines and to have the rituals described to me.

The focal point of the shrine is a box or chest which is built into the wall. In this chest are kept the many charms and magical potions without which no native believes he could live. These preparations are secured from a variety of specialized practitioners. The most powerful of these are the medicine men, whose assistance must be rewarded with substantial gifts. However, the medicine men do not provide the curative potions for their clients, but decide what the ingredients should be and then write them down in an ancient and secret language. This writing is understood only by the medicine men and by the herbalists who, for another gift, provide the required charm.

The charm is not disposed of after it has served its purpose, but is placed in the charm-box of the household shrine. As these magical materials are specific for certain ills, and the real or imagined maladies of the people are many, the charm-box is usually full to overflowing. The magical packets are so numerous that people forget what their purposes were and fear to use them again. While the natives are very vague on this point, we can only assume that the idea in retaining all the old magical materials is that their presence in the charm-box, before which the body rituals are conducted, will in some way protect the worshipper.

Beneath the charm-box is a small font. Each day every member of the family, in succession, enters the shrine room, bows his head before the charm-box, mingles different sorts of holy water in the font, and proceeds with a brief rite of ablution. The holy waters are secured from the Water Temple of the community, where the priests conduct elaborate ceremonies to make the liquid ritually pure.

In the hierarchy of magical practitioners, and below the medicine men in prestige, are specialists whose designation is best translated "holy-mouth-men." The Nacirema have an almost pathological horror of and fascination with the mouth, the condition of which is believed to have a supernatural influence on all

social relationships. Were it not for the rituals of the mouth, they believe that their teeth would fall out, their gums bleed, their jaws shrink, their friends desert them, and their lovers reject them. They also believe that a strong relationship exists between oral and moral characteristics. For example, there is a ritual ablution of the mouth for children which is supposed to improve their moral fiber.

The daily body ritual performed by everyone includes a mouth-rite. Despite the fact that these people are so punctilious about care of the mouth, this rite involves a practice which strikes the uninitiated stranger as revolting. It was reported to me that the ritual consists of inserting a small bundle of hog hairs into the mouth, along with certain magical powders, and then moving the bundle in a highly formalized series of gestures.

In addition to the private mouth-rite, the people seek out a holy-mouth-man once or twice a year. These practitioners have an impressive set of paraphernalia, consisting of a variety of augers, awls, probes, and prods. The use of these objects in the exorcism of the evils of the mouth involves almost unbelievable ritual torture of the client. The holy-mouth-man opens the client's mouth and, using the above-mentioned tools, enlarges any holes which decay may have created in the teeth. Magical materials are put into these holes. If there are no naturally occurring holes in the teeth, large sections of one or more teeth are gouged out so that the supernatural substance can be applied. In the client's view, the purpose of these ministrations is to arrest decay and to draw friends. The extremely sacred and traditional character of the rite is evident in the fact that the natives return to the holy-mouth-man year after year, despite the fact that their teeth continue to decay.

It is to be hoped that, when a thorough study of the Nacirema is made, there will be careful inquiry into the personality structure of these people. One has but to watch the gleam in the eye of a holy-mouth-man, as he jabs an awl into an exposed nerve, to suspect that a certain amount of sadism is involved. If this can be established, a very interesting pattern emerges, for most of the population shows definite masochistic tendencies. It was to these that Professor Linton referred in discussing a distinctive part of the daily body ritual which is performed only by men. This part of the rite involves scraping and lacerating the surface of the face with a sharp instrument. Special women's rites are performed only four times during each lunar month, but what they lack in frequency is made up in barbarity. As part of this ceremony, women bake their heads in small ovens for about an hour. The theoretically interesting point is that what seems to be a preponderantly masochistic people have developed sadistic specialists.

The medicine men have an imposing temple, or *latipso,* in every community of any size. The more elaborate ceremonies required to treat very sick patients can only be performed at this temple. These ceremonies involve not only the thaumaturge but a permanent group of vestal maidens who move sedately about the temple chambers in distinctive costume and headdress.

The *latipso* ceremonies are so harsh that it is phenomenal that a fair proportion of the really sick natives who enter the temple ever recover. Small children whose indoctrination is still incomplete have been known to resist attempts to take them to the temple because "that is where you go to die." Despite this fact, sick adults are not only willing but eager to undergo the protracted ritual purification, if they can afford to do so. No matter how ill the supplicant or how grave the emergency, the guardians of many temples will not admit a client if he cannot give a rich gift to the custodian. Even after one has gained admission and survived the ceremonies, the guardians will not permit the neophyte to leave until he makes still another gift.

The supplicant entering the temple is first stripped of all his or her clothes. In everyday life the Nacirema avoids exposure of his body and its natural functions. Bathing and excretory acts are performed only in the secrecy of the household shrine, where they are ritualized as part of the body-rites. Psychological shock results from the fact that body secrecy is suddenly lost upon entry into the *latipso.* A man, whose own wife has never seen him in an excretory act, suddenly finds himself naked and assisted by a vestal maiden while he performs his natural functions into a sacred vessel. This sort of ceremonial treatment is necessitated by the fact that the excreta are used by a diviner to ascertain the course and nature of the client's sickness. Female clients, on the other hand, find their naked bodies are subjected to the scrutiny, manipulation, and prodding of the medicine men.

Few supplicants in the temple are well enough to do anything but lie on their hard beds. The daily ceremonies, like the rites of the holy-mouth-men, involve discomfort and torture. With ritual precision, the vestals awaken their miserable charges each dawn and roll them about on their beds of pain while performing ablutions, in the formal movements of which the maidens are highly trained. At other times they insert magic wands in the supplicant's mouth or force him to eat substances which are supposed to be healing. From time to time the medicine men come to their clients and jab magically treated needles into their flesh. The fact that these temple ceremonies may not cure, and may even kill the neophyte, in no way decreases the people's faith in the medicine men.

There remains one other kind of practitioner, known as a "listener." This witch-doctor has the power to exorcise the devils that lodge in the heads of people who have been bewitched. The Nacirema believe that parents bewitch their own children. Mothers are particularly suspected of putting a curse on children while teaching them the secret body rituals. The counter-magic of the witch-doctor is unusual in its lack of ritual. The patient simply tells the "listener" all his troubles and fears, beginning with the earliest difficulties he can remember. The memory displayed by the Nacirema in these exorcism sessions is truly remarkable. It is not uncommon for the patient to bemoan the rejection he felt upon being weaned as a babe, and a few individuals even see their troubles going back to the traumatic effects of their own birth.

In conclusion, mention must be made of certain practices which have their base in native esthetics but which depend upon the pervasive aversion to the natural body and its functions. There are ritual fasts to make fat people thin and ceremonial feasts to make thin people fat. Still other rites are used to make women's breasts larger if they are small, and smaller if they are large. General dissatisfaction with breast shape is symbolized in the fact that the ideal form is virtually outside the range of human variation. A few women afflicted with almost inhuman hypermammary development are so idolized that they make a handsome living by simply going from village to village and permitting the natives to stare at them for a fee.

Reference has already been made to the fact that excretory functions are ritualized, routinized, and relegated to secrecy. Natural reproductive functions are similarly distorted. Intercourse is taboo as a topic and scheduled as an act. Efforts are made to avoid pregnancy by the use of magical materials or by limiting intercourse to certain phases of the moon. Conception is actually very infrequent. When pregnant, women dress so as to hide their condition. Parturition takes place in secret, without friends or relatives to assist, and the majority of women do not nurse their infants.

Our review of the ritual life of the Nacirema has certainly shown them to be a magic-ridden people. It is hard to understand how they have managed to exist so long under the burdens which they have imposed upon themselves. But even such exotic customs as these take on real meaning when they are viewed with the insight provided by Malinowski when he wrote (1948, p. 70):

> Looking from far and above, from our high places of safety in the developed civilization, it is easy to see all the crudity and irrelevance of magic. But without its power and guidance early man could not have mastered his practical difficulties as he has done, nor could man have advanced to the higher stages of civilization.

REFERENCES

Linton, R. (1936). *The study of man.* New York: Appleton-Century.

Malinowski, B. (1948). *Magic, science, and religion.* Glencoe, IL: Free Press.

Murdock, G. P. (1949). *Social structure.* New York: Macmillan.

THINKING ABOUT THE READING

What do you think of this culture? Do their ways seem very foreign or are there some things that seem familiar? This article was written over 40 years ago and, of course, much has changed since then.

How might you update this description of the "Nacirema" to account for current values and rituals? Imagine you are an anthropologist from a culture completely unfamiliar with Western traditions. Using your own life as a starting point, think of common patterns of work, leisure, learning, intimacy, eating, sleeping, and so forth. Are there some customs that distinguish your group (religious, racial, ethnic, friendship, and so on) from others? See if you can find the reasons why these customs exist. Which customs serve an obvious purpose (for example, health)? Which might seem arbitrary and silly to an outside observer?

The Melting Pot

Anne Fadiman

(1997)

The Lee family—Nao Kao, Foua, Chong, Zoua, Cheng, May, Yer, and True—arrived in the United States on December 18, 1980. Their luggage consisted of a few clothes, a blue blanket, and a wooden mortar and pestle that Foua had chiseled from a block of wood in Houaysouy. They flew from Bangkok to Honolulu, and then to Portland, Oregon, where they were to spend two years before moving to Merced. Other refugees told me that their airplane flights—a mode of travel that strained the limits of the familiar Hmong concept of migration—had been fraught with anxiety and shame: they got airsick, they didn't know how to use the bathroom but were afraid to soil themselves, they thought they had to pay for their food but had no money, they tried to eat the Wash'n Dris. The Lees, though perplexed, took the novelties of the trip in stride. Nao Kao remembers the airplane as being "just like a big house."

Their first week in Portland, however, was miserably disorienting. Before being placed by a local refugee agency in a small rented house, they spent a week with relatives, sleeping on the floor. "We didn't know anything so our relatives had to show us everything," Foua said. "They knew because they had lived in America for three or four months already. Our relatives told us about electricity and said the children shouldn't touch those plugs in the wall because they could get hurt. They told us that the refrigerator is a cold box where you put meat. They showed us how to open the TV so we could see it. We had never seen a toilet before and we thought maybe the water in it was to drink or cook with. Then our relatives told us what it was, but we didn't know whether we should sit or whether we should stand on it. Our relatives took us to the store but we didn't know that the cans and packages had food in them. We could tell what the meat was, but the chickens and cows and pigs were all cut up in little pieces and had plastic on them. Our relatives told us the stove is for cooking the food, but I was afraid to use it because it might explode. Our relatives said in America the food you don't eat you just throw away. In Laos we always fed it to the animals and it was strange to waste it like that. In this country there were a lot of strange things and even now I don't know a lot of things and my children have to help me, and it still seems like a strange country."

Seventeen years later, Foua and Nao Kao use American appliances, but they still speak only Hmong, celebrate only Hmong holidays, practice only the Hmong religion, cook only Hmong dishes, sing only Hmong songs, play only Hmong musical instruments, tell only Hmong stories, and know far more about current political events in Laos and Thailand than about those in the United States. When I first met them, during their eighth year in this country, only one American adult, Jeanine Hilt, had ever been invited to their home as a guest. It would be hard to imagine anything further from the vaunted American ideal of assimilation, in which immigrants are expected to submerge their cultural differences in order to embrace a shared national identity. *E pluribus unum:* from many, one.

During the late 1910s and early 1920s, immigrant workers at the Ford automotive plant in Dearborn, Michigan, were given free, compulsory "Americanization" classes. In addition to English lessons, there were lectures on work habits, personal hygiene, and table manners. The first sentence they memorized was "I am a good American." During their graduation ceremony they gathered next to a gigantic wooden pot, which their teachers stirred with ten-foot ladles. The students walked through a door into the pot, wearing traditional costumes from their countries of origin and singing songs in their native languages. A few minutes later, the door in the pot opened, and the students walked out again, wearing suits and ties, waving American flags, and singing "The Star-Spangled Banner."

The European immigrants who emerged from the Ford Motor Company melting pot came to the United States because they hoped to assimilate into mainstream American society. The Hmong came to the United States for the same reason they had left China in the nineteenth century: because they were trying to *resist* assimilation. As the anthropologist Jacques Lemoine has observed, "they did not come to our countries only to save their lives, they rather came to save their selves, that is, their Hmong ethnicity." If their Hmong ethnicity had been safe in Laos, they would have preferred to remain there, just as their ancestors—for whom migration had always been a problem-solving strategy, not a footloose impulse—would have preferred to remain in China. Unlike the Ford workers who enthusiastically, or at least uncomplainingly, belted out the "The Star-Spangled Banner" (of which Foua and Nao Kao know not a single word), the Hmong are what sociologists call "involuntary migrants." It is well known that involuntary migrants, no matter what pot they are thrown into, tend not to melt.

What the Hmong wanted here was to be left alone to be Hmong: clustered in all-Hmong enclaves, protected from government interference, self-sufficient, and agrarian. Some brought hoes in their luggage. General Vang Pao has said, "For many years, right from the start, I tell the American government that we need a little bit of land where we can grow vegetables and build homes like in Laos. . . . I tell them it does not have to be the best land, just a little land where we can live." This proposal was never seriously considered. "It was just out of the question," said a spokesman for the State Department's refugee program. "It would cost too much, it would be impractical, but most of all it would set off wild protests from [other Americans] and from other refugees who weren't getting land for themselves." . . .

Just as newly arrived immigrants in earlier eras had been called "FOBs"—Fresh Off the Boat—some social workers nicknamed the incoming Hmong, along with the other Southeast Asian refugees who entered the United States after the Vietnamese War, "JOJs": Just Off the Jet. Unlike the first waves of Vietnamese and Cambodian refugees, most of whom received several months of vocational and language training at regional "reception centers," the Hmong JOJs, who arrived after the centers had closed, were all sent directly to their new homes. (Later on, some were given "cultural orientation" training in Thailand before flying to the United States. Their classes covered such topics as how to distinguish a one-dollar bill from a ten-dollar bill and how to use a peephole.) The logistical details of their resettlement were contracted by the federal government to private nonprofit groups known as VOLAGs, or national voluntary resettlement agencies, which found local sponsors. Within their first few weeks in this country, newly arrived families were likely to deal with VOLAG officials, immigration officials, public health officials, social service officials, employment officials, and public assistance officials. The Hmong are not known for holding bureaucrats in high esteem. As one proverb puts it, "To see a tiger is to die; to see an official is to become destitute." In a study of adaptation problems among Indochinese refugees, Hmong respondents rated "Difficulty with American Agencies" as a more serious problem than either "War Memories" or "Separation from Family." Because many of the VOLAGs had religious affiliations, the JOJs also often found themselves dealing with Christian ministers, who, not surprisingly, took a dim view of shamanistic animism. A sponsoring pastor in Minnesota told a local newspaper, "It would be wicked to just bring them over and feed and clothe them and let them go to hell. The God who made us wants them to be converted. If anyone thinks that a gospel-preaching church would bring them over and not tell them about the Lord, they're out of their mind." The proselytizing backfired. According to a study of Hmong mental health problems, refugees sponsored by this pastor's religious organization were significantly more likely, when compared to other refugees, to require psychiatric treatment.

The Hmong were accustomed to living in the mountains, and most of them had never seen snow. Almost all their resettlement sites had flat topography and freezing winters. The majority were sent to cities, including Minneapolis, Chicago, Milwaukee, Detroit, Hartford, and Providence, because that was where refugee services—health care, language classes, job training, public housing—were concentrated. To encourage assimilation, and to avoid burdening any one community with more than its "fair share" of refugees, the Immigration and Naturalization Service adopted a policy of dispersal rather than clustering. Newly arrived Hmong were assigned to fifty-three cities in twenty-five different states: stirred into the melting pot in tiny, manageable portions, or, as John Finck, who worked with Hmong at the Rhode Island Office of Refugee Resettlement, put it, "spread like a thin layer

of butter throughout the country so they'd disappear." In some places, clans were broken up. In others, members of only one clan were resettled, making it impossible for young people, who were forbidden by cultural taboo from marrying within their own clan, to find local marriage partners. Group solidarity, the cornerstone of Hmong social organization for more than two thousand years, was completely ignored.

Although most Hmong were resettled in cities, some nuclear families, unaccompanied by any of their extended relations, were placed in isolated rural areas. Disconnected from traditional supports, these families exhibited unusually high levels of anxiety, depression, and paranoia. In one such case, the distraught and delusional father of the Yang family—the only Hmong family sponsored by the First Baptist Church of Fairfield, Iowa—attempted to hang himself in the basement of his wooden bungalow along with his wife and four children. His wife changed her mind at the last minute and cut the family down, but she acted too late to save their only son. An Iowa grand jury declined to indict either parent, on the grounds that the father was suffering from Post-Traumatic Stress Disorder, and the mother, cut off from all sources of information except her husband, had no way to develop an independent version of reality.

Reviewing the initial resettlement of the Hmong with a decade's hindsight, Lionel Rosenblatt, the former United States Refugee Coordinator in Thailand, conceded that it had been catastrophically mishandled. "We knew at the start their situation was different, but we just couldn't make any special provisions for them," he said. "I still feel it was no mistake to bring the Hmong here, but you look back now and say, 'How could we have done it so shoddily?'" Eugene Douglas, President Reagan's ambassador-at-large for refugee affairs, stated flatly, "It was a kind of hell they landed into. Really, it couldn't have been done much worse."

The Hmong who sought asylum in the United States were, of course, not a homogeneous lump. A small percentage, mostly the high-ranking military officers who were admitted first, were multilingual and cosmopolitan, and a larger percentage had been exposed in a desultory fashion to some aspects of American culture and technology during the war or while living in Thai refugee camps. But the experience of tens of thousands of Hmong was much like the Lees.' It is possible to get some idea of how monumental the task of adjustment was likely to be by glancing at some of the pamphlets, audiotapes, and videos that refugee agencies produced for Southeast Asian JOJs. For example, "Your New Life in the United States," a handbook published by the Language and Orientation Resource Center in Washington, D.C., included the following tips:

Learn the meaning of "WALK"–"DON'T WALK" signs when crossing the street.

To send mail, you must use stamps.

To use the phone:

1) Pick up the receiver
2) Listen for dial tone
3) Dial each number separately
4) Wait for person to answer after it rings
5) Speak.

The door of the refrigerator must be shut.

Never put your hand in the garbage disposal.

Do not stand or squat on the toilet since it may break.

Never put rocks or other hard objects in the tub or sink since this will damage them.

Always ask before picking your neighbor's flowers, fruit, or vegetables.

In colder areas you must wear shoes, socks, and appropriate outerwear. Otherwise, you may become ill.

Always use a handkerchief or a kleenex to blow your nose in public places or inside a public building.

Never urinate in the street. This creates a smell that is offensive to Americans. They also believe that it causes disease.

Spitting in public is considered impolite and unhealthy. Use a kleenex or handkerchief.

Picking your nose or your ears in public is frowned upon in the United States.

The customs they were expected to follow seemed so peculiar, the rules and regulations so numerous, the language so hard to learn, and the emphasis on literacy and the decoding of other unfamiliar symbols so strong, that many Hmong were overwhelmed. Jonas Vangay told me, "In America, we are blind because even though we have eyes, we cannot see. We are deaf because even though we have ears, we cannot hear." Some newcomers wore pajamas as street clothes; poured water on electric stoves to extinguish them; lit charcoal fires in their living rooms; stored blankets in their refrigerators; washed rice in their toilets; washed their clothes in swimming pools; washed their hair with Lestoil; cooked with motor oil and furniture polish; drank Clorox; ate cat food; planted crops in public parks; shot and ate skunks, porcupines, woodpeckers, robins, egrets, sparrows, and a bald eagle; and hunted pigeons with crossbows in the streets of Philadelphia.

If the United States seemed incomprehensible to the Hmong, the Hmong seemed equally incomprehensible to the United States. Journalists seized excitedly on a label that is still trotted out at regular intervals: "the most primitive refugee group in America." (In an angry letter to the *New York Times,* in which that phrase had appeared in a 1990 news article, a Hmong computer specialist observed, "Evidently, we were not too primitive to fight as proxies for United States troops in the war in Laos.") Typical phrases from newspaper and magazine stories in the late seventies and eighties included "low-caste hill tribe," "Stone Age," "emerging from the mists of time," "like Alice falling down a rabbit hole." Inaccuracies were in no short supply. A 1981 article in the *Christian Science Monitor* called the Hmong language "extremely simplistic"; declared that the Hmong, who have been sewing *paj ntaub* [embroidered cloth] with organic motifs for centuries, make "no connection between a picture of a tree and a real tree"; and noted that "the Hmong have no oral tradition of literature. . . . Apparently no folk tales exist." Some journalists seemed to shed all inhibition, and much of their good sense as well, when they were loosed on the Hmong. My favorite passage is a 1981 *New York Times* editorial about the large number of Hmong men who had died unexpectedly in their sleep, killed—or so it was widely believed at the time—by their own nightmares.[1] After explaining that the Hmong "attributed conscious life to natural objects," the writer asked,

> What were these nightmares? Did a palm tree's fronds turn into threatening fingers? Did a forest move and march with the implacability of the tide? Did a rose stretch on its stalk and throttle the sleeper?
>
> Or did a gasoline hose curl and crush like a python? Was one of the dreamers pinned by a perambulating postbox? Or stabbed by scissors run amok?

("Or did the editorial writer drop acid?" I wrote in the newspaper margin when I first read this.)

Timothy Dunnigan, a linguistic anthropologist who has taught a seminar at the University of Minnesota on the media presentation of Hmong and Native Americans, once remarked to me, "The kinds of metaphorical language that we use to describe the Hmong say far more about us, and our attachment to our own frame of reference, than they do about the Hmong." So much for the Perambulating

Postbox Theory. Dunnigan's comment resonates with Dwight Conquergood's observation about the uneasiness Westerners feel when confronted with the Other—for who could be more Other than the Hmong? Not only did they squat on toilets and eat skunks, not only did they bang gongs and sacrifice cows, but they also displayed what struck many people as an offensively selective interest in adopting the customs of the majority culture. For example, many Hmong quickly learned how to use telephones and drive cars, because those skills fit their own agenda of communicating with other Hmong, but failed to learn English. In 1987, when Senator Alan Simpson, then the ranking minority member of the Senate Subcommittee on Immigration and Refugee Affairs, called the Hmong "the most indigestible group in society," he sounded much like the authorities in China long ago, who were grievously insulted when the Hmong refused to speak Chinese or eat with chopsticks.

It could not be denied that the Hmong were genuinely mysterious—far more so, for instance, than the Vietnamese and Cambodians who were streaming into the United States at the same time. Hardly anyone knew how to pronounce the word "Hmong." Hardly anyone—except the anthropology graduate students who suddenly realized they could write dissertations on patrilineal exogamous clan structures without leaving their hometowns—knew what role the Hmong had played during the war, or even what war it had been, since our government had succeeded all too well in keeping the Quiet War quiet. Hardly anyone knew they had a rich history, a complex culture, an efficient social system, and enviable family values. They were therefore an ideal blank surface on which to project xenophobic fantasies.

The most expedient mode of projection has always been the rumor, and the Hmong attracted more than their share. This was to be expected. After all, the Hmong of China had had wings under their armpits and small tails. In prevalence and nastiness, American rumors about the Hmong are at least an even match for the Hmong rumors about America that circulated in the refugee camps of Thailand. Some samples: The Hmong run a white slave trade. The Hmong are given cars by the government. The Hmong force their children to run in front of cars in order to get big insurance settlements. The Hmong sell their daughters and buy their wives. Hmong women think speed bumps are washboards for scrubbing clothes, and they get run over by eighteen-wheelers. The Hmong eat dogs.[2] (That one comes complete with its own set of racist jokes. "What's the name of the Hmong cookbook? *101 Ways to Wok Your Dog.*") The dog-eating rumor has joined the national pantheon of deathless urban legends, right up there with alligators in the sewers and worms in the Big Macs. . . .

Not everyone who wanted to make the Hmong feel unwelcome stopped at slander. In the words of the president of a youth center in Minneapolis, his Hmong neighbors in the mid-eighties were "prime meat for predators." In Laos, Hmong houses had no locks. Sometimes they had no doors. Cultural taboos against theft and intra-community violence were poor preparation for life in the high-crime, inner-city neighborhoods in which most Hmong were placed. Some of the violence directed against them had nothing to do with their ethnicity; they were simply easy marks. But a good deal of it was motivated by resentment, particularly in urban areas, for what was perceived as preferential welfare treatment.[3]

In Minneapolis, tires were slashed and windows smashed. A high school student getting off a bus was hit in the face and told to "go back to China." A woman was kicked in the thighs, face, and kidneys, and her purse, which contained the family's entire savings of $400, was stolen; afterwards, she forbade her

children to play outdoors, and her husband, who had once commanded a fifty-man unit in the Armée Clandestine, stayed home to guard the family's belongings. In Providence, children were beaten walking home from school. In Missoula, teenagers were stoned. In Milwaukee, garden plots were vandalized and a car was set on fire. In Eureka, California, two burning crosses were placed on a family's front lawn. In a random act of violence near Springfield, Illinois, a twelve-year-old boy was shot and killed by three men who forced his family's car off Interstate 55 and demanded money. His father told a reporter, "In a war, you know who your enemies are. Here, you don't know if the person walking up to you will hurt you."

In Philadelphia, anti-Hmong muggings, robberies, beatings, stonings, and vandalism were so commonplace during the early eighties that the city's Commission on Human Relations held public hearings to investigate the violence. One source of discord seemed to be a $100,000 federal grant for Hmong employment assistance that had incensed local residents, who were mostly unemployed themselves and believed the money should have been allocated to American citizens, not resident aliens. In one of the most grievous incidents, Seng Vang, a Hmong resident of Quebec who was visiting his mother, brothers, and sisters in west Philadelphia, was beaten with steel rods and a large rock, and left on the street with two broken legs and a brain injury. Later that day, a rifle shot was fired into his mother's apartment, breaking a window near the spot where she stood washing dishes. When Vang was treated at the University of Pennsylvania hospital, he was given a blood transfusion that was probably tainted. He was gravely ill for months with a rare form of hepatitis, and, seized by justifiable paranoia, became convinced that his doctors, too, had tried to kill him.

One thing stands out in all these accounts: the Hmong didn't fight back. I pondered that fact one day as I was thumbing through the index of Charles Johnson's *Dab Neeg Hmoob: Myths, Legends and Folk Tales from the Hmong of Laos*, which contained the following entries:

Fighting

Enemies fighting . . . 29–46, 52–58, 198, 227, 470–471

Revenge

Murdered man reincarnated to revenge his death . . . 308–309

Cruel 9-tongued eagle has tongues cut out . . . 330

Ngao Njua boils king who sent away her husband . . . 362

Family kills tiger murderer of daughter, husband & children . . . 403

. . .

Vengeance

Punishment of evil-doers by lightning . . . 11, 20

Wildcat tortured & killed to avenge murder of woman . . . 436–437

To quote from the last folktale cited: "Quickly, the rooster came down, seized the cat, threw him into the mortar of the rice mill, and started in immediately pounding him with the heavy pestle: DA DUH NDUH! DA DUH NDUH! He kept pounding until all the wildcat's bones were completely broken. And that's how the wildcat died, and that's how the story ends." It was clear that the Hmong were hardly the docile, passive, mild-mannered Asians of popular stereotype. Why hadn't the Americans who tormented the Hmong ended up like that wildcat?

Charles Johnson's background notes to another tale in *Dab Neeg Hmoob* provide a partial explanation:

Our interviews indicate that the Hmong do not fight very much. When they do, it is with fists and feet. (In contrast with some neighboring peoples [in Laos] who tend to fight a lot, seem to take it lightly, and can be friends later, if two Hmong fight once, they are likely to take it very seriously, as a big issue which they do not forget, and may remain enemies forever.) . . . The Hmong do have an ideal of patience and stoical self-control, alluded to in the idiomatic expression often used by the Hmong to admonish someone who is acting impatiently or impulsively, or by parents in teaching good behavior to their children: "Ua siab ntev" (literally, Make, do, or act with a long liver, that is, a spirit or attitude of long-suffering, patient endurance of wrongs or difficulties).

Although on the battlefield the Hmong were known more for their fierceness than for their long livers, in the United States many were too proud to lower themselves to the level of the petty criminals they encountered, or even to admit they had been victims. An anthropologist named George M. Scott, Jr., once asked a group of Hmong in San Diego, all victims of property damage or assault, why they had not defended themselves or taken revenge. Scott wrote, "several Hmong victims of such abuse, both young and old, answered that to have done so, besides inviting further, retaliatory, abuse, would have made them feel 'embarrassed' or ashamed. . . . In addition, the current president of Lao Family [a Hmong mutual assistance organization], when asked why his people did not 'fight back' when attacked here as they did in Laos, replied simply, 'because nothing here is worth defending to us.'"

There were exceptions, of course. If he was threatened with what he perceived as unbearable *poob ntsej muag* (loss of face), a Hmong sometimes decided that his shame and embarrassment would be even greater if he didn't fight back than if he did. Several Hmong in Fresno, hearing rumors that their welfare grants might be terminated because they owned cars, sent death threats ("You take away my grant and I'm going to blow your head off") to the county Social Services Department. As visual aids, they enclosed bullets and pictures of swords in their envelopes. (The grants were not terminated, and the bullets and swords were never used.) In Chicago, an elderly Hmong man and his son, insulted because an American driver had honked at them loudly and persistently, hit the American over the head with a steering-wheel locking device. The injury required thirteen stitches. When the men, Ching and Bravo Xiong, were brought to trial for aggravated battery, they asked the judge to allow each party to tell his side of the story and then drink a mixture of water and the blood of a sacrificed rooster. According to Hmong tradition, anyone who drinks rooster blood after telling a lie is destined to die within a year, so if a man partakes willingly, he is recognized as a truthteller. The judge denied this request. Instead, he sentenced the younger Xiong to two weekends in jail and six hundred hours of community service. He also ordered both men to learn English and study American culture.

Such incidents were rare. Most Hmong kept an apprehensive distance from the American penal system, which was radically different from their own. There were no prisons in their villages in Laos. The Hmong sense of justice was pragmatic and personal: how would incarceration benefit the victim? Corporal punishment was also unknown. Instead, various forms of public humiliation— a powerful deterrent in a society where loss of face was considered a worse fate than death— were employed. For example, a thief who had stolen four bars of silver might be forced to repay five bars to the victim and then be hauled off to the village chief with his hands tied, while the entire community jeered. The victim ended up enriched, the criminal suffered the shame he deserved, the criminal's innocent family kept its primary provider in the household, and any would-be thieves in the village were discouraged from potential crimes by witnessing the disgraceful spectacle. The Hmong who came to this country had heard that if they hurt someone, for whatever the reason, they would be sent to an American prison, and most of them were willing to do almost anything to avoid such an unimaginable calamity. Chao Wang Vang, a Fresno resident who had been charged with misdemeanor manslaughter after a fatal traffic accident, hanged himself in the county jail before his case came to court, not knowing he had the right to a trial and believing he would be imprisoned for the rest of his life.

In any case, Hmong who were persecuted by their neighbors could exercise a time-honored alternative to violence: flight. . . . Between 1982 and 1984, three quarters of the Hmong population of Philadelphia simply left town and joined relatives in other cities. During approximately the same period, one third of all the Hmong in the United States moved from one city to another. When they decided to relocate, Hmong families often lit off without notifying their sponsors, who were invariably offended. If they couldn't fit one of their possessions, such as a television set, in a car or bus or U-Haul, they left it behind, seemingly without so much as a backward glance. Some families traveled alone, but more often they moved in groups. When there was an exodus from Portland, Oregon, a long caravan of overloaded cars motored together down Interstate 5, bound for the Central Valley of California. With this "secondary migration," as sociologists termed it, the government's attempt to stir the Hmong evenly into the melting pot was definitively sabotaged.

Although local violence was often the triggering factor, there were also other reasons for migrating. In 1982, when all refugees who had lived in the United States for more than eighteen months stopped receiving Refugee Cash Assistance—the period of eligibility had previously been three years—many Hmong who had no jobs and no prospects moved to states that provided welfare benefits to two-parent families. Their original host states were often glad to get rid of them. For a time, the Oregon Human Resources Department, strapped by a tight state budget, sent refugees letters that pointedly detailed the levels of welfare benefits available in several other states. California's were among the highest. Thousands of Hmong also moved to California because they had heard it was an agricultural state where they might be able to farm. But by far the most important reason for relocating was reunification with other members of one's clan. Hmong clans are sometimes at odds with each other, but within a clan, whose thousands of members are regarded as siblings, one can always count on support and sympathy. A Hmong who tries to gain acceptance to a kin group other than his own is called a *puav*, or bat. He is rejected by the birds because he has fur and by the mice because he has wings. Only when a Hmong lives among his own subspecies can he stop flitting restlessly from group to group, haunted by the shame of not belonging.

The Hmong may have been following their venerable proverb, "There's always another mountain," but in the past, each new mountain had yielded a living. Unfortunately, the most popular areas of secondary resettlement all had high unemployment rates, and they got higher. For example, in the Central Valley—which had no Hmong in 1980 and more than 20,000 three years later—the economic recession of 1982 shut down dozens of factories and other businesses, driving up local unemployment and forcing the Hmong to compete with out-of-work Americans for even the most unskilled jobs. The dream of farming quickly fizzled for all but a few hundred. Hmong farmers knew a great deal about torching fields for slash-and-burn agriculture, planting mountain rice with dibble sticks, and tapping opium pods, but they had much to learn (to quote from the course plan for a not-very-successful Hmong training program) about

> crop varieties, soil preparation, machinery and equipment, timing and succession of planting, seeds and transplants, fertilizer, pest and weed management, disease control, irrigation, erosion control, record-keeping, harvesting, washing and handling, grading and size selection, packing, conditioning, market selection, product planning, pricing strategies, shipping and receiving, advertising, merchandising, verbal and non-verbal communication skills for dealing with consumers, etc.

By 1985, at least eighty percent of the Hmong in Merced, Fresno, and San Joaquin counties were on welfare.

That didn't halt the migration. Family reunification tends to have a snowball effect. The more Thaos or Xiongs there were in one place, the more mutual assistance they could provide, the more cultural traditions they could practice together, and the more stable their community would be. Americans, however, tended to view secondary migration as an indication of instability and dependence. . . .

Seeing that the Hmong were redistributing themselves as they saw fit, and that they were becoming an economic burden on the places to which they chose to move, the federal Office of Refugee Resettlement tried to slow the migratory tide. The 1983 Highland Lao Initiative, a three-million-dollar "emergency effort" to bolster employment and community stability in Hmong communities outside California, offered vocational training, English classes, and other enticements for the Hmong to stay put. Though the initiative claimed a handful of modest local successes, the California migration was essentially unstoppable. By this time, most Hmong JOJs were being sponsored by relatives in America rather than by voluntary organizations, so the government no longer had geographic control over their placements. The influx therefore came—and, in smaller increments, is still coming—from Thailand as well as from other parts of America. Therefore, in addition to trying to prevent the Hmong from moving to high-welfare states, the Office of Refugee Resettlement started trying to encourage the ones who were already there to leave. Spending an average of $7,000 per family on moving expenses, job placement, and a month or two of rent and food subsidies, the Planned Secondary Resettlement Program, which was phased out in 1994, relocated about 800 unemployed Hmong families from what it called "congested areas" to communities with "favorable employment opportunities"—i.e., unskilled jobs with wages too low to attract a full complement of local American workers.

Within the economic limitations of blue-collar labor, those 800 families have fared well. Ninety-five percent have become self-sufficient. They work in manufacturing plants in Dallas, on electronics assembly lines in Atlanta, in furniture and textile factories in Morganton, North Carolina. More than a quarter of them have saved enough money to buy their own houses, as have three quarters of the Hmong families who live in Lancaster County, Pennsylvania, where the men farm or work in food-processing plants, and the women work for the Amish, sewing quilts that are truthfully advertised as "locally made." Elsewhere, Hmong are employed as grocers, carpenters, poultry processors, machinists, welders, auto mechanics, tool and die makers, teachers, nurses, interpreters, and community liaisons. In a survey of Minnesota employers, the respondents were asked "What do you think of the Hmong as workers?" Eighty-six percent rated them "very good." . . .

Some younger Hmong have become lawyers, doctors, dentists, engineers, computer programmers, accountants, and public administrators. Hmong National Development, an association that promotes Hmong self-sufficiency, encourages this small corps of professionals to serve as mentors and sponsors for other Hmong who might thereby be induced to follow suit. The cultural legacy of mutual assistance has been remarkably adaptive. Hundreds of Hmong students converse electronically, trading gossip and information—opinions on the relevance of traditional customs, advice on college admissions, personal ads—via the Hmong Channel on the Internet Relay Chat system. . . . There is also a Hmong Homepage on the World Wide Web (http://www.stolaf.edu/people/cdr/hmong/) and several burgeoning Hmong electronic mailing lists, including Hmongnet, Hmongforum, and Hmong Language Users Group.[4]

The M.D.s and J.D.s and digital sophisticates constitute a small, though growing, minority. Although younger, English-speaking Hmong who have been educated in the United States have better employment records than their elders, they still lag behind most other Asian-Americans. As for Hmong workers over thirty-five, the majority are immovably wedged at or near entry level. They can't get jobs that require better English, and they can't learn English on their current jobs. The federal *Hmong Resettlement Study* cited, as an example, a Hmong worker in Dallas who after three years on the job was unable to name the machine he operated. He stated that he never expected a promotion or a pay raise other than cost-of-living increases. Other Hmong have been thwarted by placing a higher value on group solidarity than on individual initiative. In San Diego, the manager of an electronics plant was so enthusiastic about one Hmong assembly worker that he tried to promote him to supervisor. The man quit, ashamed to accept a job that would place him above his Hmong coworkers.

For the many Hmong who live in high-unemployment areas, questions of advancement are often moot. They have no jobs at all. This is the reason the Hmong are routinely called this country's "least successful refugees." It is worth noting that the standard American tests of success that they have flunked are almost exclusively economic. If one applied social indices instead—such as rates of crime, child abuse, illegitimacy, and divorce—the Hmong would probably score better than most refugee groups (and also better than most Americans), but those are not the forms of success to which our culture assigns its highest priority. Instead, we have trained the spotlight on our best-loved index of failure, the welfare rolls. In California, Minnesota, and Wisconsin, where, not coincidentally, benefits tend to be relatively generous and eligibility requirements relatively loose, the percentages of Hmong on welfare are approximately forty-five, forty, and thirty-five (an improvement over five years ago, when they were approximately sixty-five, seventy, and sixty). The cycle of dependence that began with rice drops in Laos and reinforced with daily handouts at Thai refugee camps has been completed here in the United States. The conflicting structures of the Hmong culture and the American welfare system make it almost impossible for the average family to become independent. In California, for example, a man with seven children—a typical Hmong family size—would have to make $10.60 an hour, working forty hours a week, to equal his welfare stipend and food stamp allowance. But with few marketable skills and little English, he would probably be ineligible for most jobs that paid more than minimum wage, at which, even at the newly elevated rate of $5.15 an hour, he would have to work an improbable eighty-two hours a week in order to equal his welfare allotment. In addition, until the mid-nineties in most states, if he worked more than one hundred hours a month—as a part-time worker trying to acquire job skills, for example, or a farmer in the start-up phase—his family would lose their entire welfare grant, all their food stamps, and their health insurance.[5]

The 1996 welfare reform bill, which in its present form promises to deny benefits to legal immigrants, has stirred up monumental waves of anxiety among the Hmong. Faced with the possibility of having their assistance cut off, some have applied for citizenship, although many middle-aged Hmong find the English language requirement an insuperable obstacle. (The hurdles are lower for older Hmong who came to the United States shortly after the end of the war in Laos. The language rule is waived for "lawful permanent residents" age fifty or older who have been in this country for at least twenty years, and for those age fifty-five or older who have been here at least fifteen years. The Lees, who are considering applying for citizenship, would qualify for this waiver.) Some Hmong have moved, or are planning to move, to states with better job markets. Some will become dependent on their relatives. Because a few states will probably elect to use their own funds to assist legal immigrants, some will simply continue to depend on welfare in altered, reduced, and more precarious forms.

Few things gall the Hmong more than to be criticized for accepting public assistance. For one thing, they feel they deserve the money. Every Hmong has a different version of what is commonly called "The Promise": a written or verbal contract, made by CIA personnel in Laos, that if they fought for the Americans, the Americans would aid them if the Pathet Lao won the war. After risking their lives to rescue downed American pilots, seeing their villages flattened by incidental American bombs, and being forced to flee their country because they had supported the "American War," the Hmong expected a hero's welcome here. According to many of them, the first betrayal came when the American airlifts rescued only the officers from Long Tieng, leaving nearly everyone else behind. The second betrayal came in the Thai camps, when the Hmong who wanted to come to the United States were not all automatically admitted. The third betrayal came when they arrived here and found they were ineligible for veterans' benefits. The fourth betrayal came when Americans condemned them for what the Hmong call "eating welfare." The fifth betrayal came when the Americans announced that the welfare would stop.

Aside from some older people who consider welfare a retirement benefit, most Hmong would prefer almost any other option—if other options existed. What right-thinking Hmong would choose to be yoked to one of the most bureaucratic institutions in America? (A tip from "Your New Life in the United States," on applying for cash assistance: "You should have as many of the following documents available as possible: I-94—take the original, if you can; rent bill or lease; Social Security card; any pay stubs; bank account statement or savings passbook; utility bills; medical bills or proof of medical disability; employment registration card.") What Hmong would choose to become addicted to a way of life that some clan leaders have likened to opium? And what Hmong would choose the disgrace of being *dev mus nuam yaj,* a dog waiting for scraps? Dang Moua, the Merced businessman who had kept his family alive en route to Thailand by shooting birds with a homemade crossbow, once told me, "One time when I am first in America, a Korean man tell me that if someone is lazy and doesn't work, the government still pay them. I say, you crazy! That doesn't ring my bell at all! I am not afraid of working! My parents raised me as a man! I work till the last day I leave this earth!" And indeed, Dang held three concurrent nearly full-time jobs, as a grocer, an interpreter, and a pig farmer. He was once a clerk-typist in the American Embassy in Vientiane and speaks five languages, so his success is not one most Hmong could reasonably be expected to emulate. More typical are two middle-aged men who were interviewed in San Diego for a survey on refugee adaptation. The first said:

> I used to be a real man like any other man, but not now any longer. . . . We only live day by day, just like the baby birds who are only staying in the nest opening their mouths and waiting for the mother bird to bring the worms.

The second said:

> We are not born to earth to have somebody give us feed; we are so ashamed to depend on somebody like this. When we were in our country, we never ask anybody for help like this. . . . I've been trying very hard to learn English and at the same time looking for a job. No matter what kind of job, even the job to clean people's toilets; but still people don't even trust you or offer you such work. I'm looking at me that I'm not even worth as much as a dog's stool. Talking about this, I want to die right here so I won't see my future.

These men were both suffering from a global despair to which their economic dependence was only one of many contributing factors. In the survey for which they were interviewed, part of a longitudinal study of Hmong, Cambodians, Vietnamese, and Chinese-Vietnamese refugees, the Hmong respondents scored lowest in "happiness" and "life satisfaction." In a study of Indochinese refugees in Illinois, the Hmong exhibited the highest degree of "alienation from their environment." According to a Minnesota study, Hmong refugees who had lived in the United States for a year and a half had "very high levels of depression, anxiety, hostility, phobia, paranoid ideation, obsessive compulsiveness and feelings of inadequacy." (Over the next decade, some of these symptoms moderated, but the refugees' levels of anxiety, hostility, and paranoia showed little or no improvement.) The study that I found most disheartening was the 1987 California Southeast Asian Mental Health Needs Assessment, a statewide epidemiological survey funded by the Office of Refugee Resettlement and the National Institute of Mental Health. It was shocking to look at the bar graphs comparing the Hmong with the Vietnamese, the Chinese-Vietnamese, the Cambodians, and the Lao—all of whom, particularly the Cambodians, fared poorly compared to the general population—and see how the Hmong stacked up: Most depressed. Most psychosocially dysfunctional. Most likely to be severely in need of mental health treatment. Least educated. Least literate. Smallest percentage in labor force. Most likely to cite "fear" as a reason for immigration and least likely to cite "a better life."

The same bleak ground was covered from the Hmong point of view by Bruce Thowpaou Bliatout, a public health administrator in Portland, Oregon. Dr. Bliatout, who is Hmong, explained in an article on mental health concepts that such issues as job adjustment and family happiness are regarded by the Hmong as problems of the liver. If patience, as Charles Johnson noted in *Dab Neeg Hmoob,* is attributed to a long—that is, a robust and healthy— liver, what Americans would call mental illness is attributed to a liver that has become diseased or damaged through soul loss. According to Bliatout, who provided case histories for each one, some illnesses common among Hmong in the United States are:

Nyuab Siab

Translation: Difficult liver.

Causes: Loss of family, status, home, country, or any important item that has a high emotional value.

Symptoms: Excessive worry; crying; confusion; disjointed speech; loss of sleep and appetite; delusions.

Tu Siab

Translation: Broken liver.

Causes: Loss of family member; quarrel between family members; break of family unity.

Symptoms: Grief; worry; loneliness; guilt; feeling of loss; insecurity.

Lwj Siab

Translation: Rotten liver.

Causes: Stressful family relations; constant unfulfillment of goals.

Symptoms: Loss of memory; short temper; delusions.

Before I came to Merced, Bill Selvidge described to me the first Hmong patient he had ever seen. Bruce Thowpaou Bliatout would have diagnosed this patient as having a difficult liver; Bill thought of it, not so differently, as a broken heart. "Mr. Thao was a man in his fifties," said Bill. "He told me through an interpreter that he had a bad back, but after I listened for a while I realized that he'd really come in because of depression. It turned out he was an agoraphobe. He was afraid to leave his house because he thought if he walked more than a couple of blocks he'd get lost and never find his way home again. What a metaphor! He'd seen his entire immediate family die in Laos, he'd seen his country collapse, and he never *was* going to find his way home again. All I could do was prescribe antidepressants."

Mr. Thao turned out to be the first of a long procession of depressed Hmong patients whom Bill was to treat over the next three years. Bill cut to the nub of the matter when he described the man's profound loss of "home." For the Hmong in America—where not only the social mores but also the sound of every birdsong, the shape of every tree and flower, the smell of the air, and the very texture of the earth are unfamiliar—the ache of homesickness can be incapacitating. . . .

The home to which the older Hmong dream of returning—which they call *peb lub tebchaws,* "our fields and our lands"—is prewar Laos. Their memories of wartime Laos are almost unrelievedly traumatic: a "bereavement overload" that critically magnifies all their other stresses. Richard Mollica, a psychiatrist who helped found the IndoChinese Psychiatry Clinic in Boston, found that during the war and its aftermath, Hmong refugees had experienced an average of fifteen "major trauma events," such as witnessing killings and torture. Mollica has observed of his patients, "Their psychological reality is both full and empty. They are 'full' of the past; they are 'empty' of new ideas and life experiences."

"Full" of both past trauma and past longing, the Hmong have found it especially hard to deal with present threats to their old identities. I once went to a conference on Southeast Asian mental health at which a psychologist named Evelyn Lee, who was born in Macao, invited six members of the audience to come to the front of the auditorium for a role-playing exercise. She cast them as a grandfather, a father, a mother, an eighteen-year-old son, a sixteen-year-old daughter, and a twelve-year-old daughter. "Okay," she told them, "line up according to your status in your old country." Ranking themselves by traditional notions of age and gender, they queued up in the order I've just mentioned, with the grandfather standing proudly at the head of the line. "Now they come to America," said Dr. Lee. "Grandfather has no job. Father can only chop vegetables. Mother didn't work in the old country, but here she gets a job in a garment factory. Oldest daughter works there too. Son drops out of high school because he can't learn English. Youngest daughter learns the best English in the family and ends up at U.C. Berkeley. Now you line up again." As the family reshuffled, I realized that its power structure had turned completely upside down, with the twelve-year-old girl now occupying the head of the line and the grandfather standing forlornly at the tail.

Dr. Lee's exercise was an eloquent demonstration of what sociologists call "role loss." Of all the stresses in the Hmong community, role loss . . . may be the most corrosive to the ego. Every Hmong can tell stories about colonels who became janitors, military communications specialists who became chicken processors, flight crewmen who found no work at all. Dang Moua's cousin Moua Kee, a former judge, worked first in a box factory and then on the night shift in a machine shop. "When you have no country, no land, no house, no power, everyone is the same," he said with a shrug. Major Wang Seng Khang, a former battalion commander who served as leader for 10,000 Hmong in his refugee camp, took five years to find a job as a part-time church liaison. Even then, he depended on his wife's wages from a jewelry factory to pay the rent and on his children to translate for him. Of himself and his fellow leaders, he said, "We have become children in this country."

And in this country the real children have assumed some of the power that used to belong to their elders. The status conferred by speaking English and understanding American conventions is a phenomenon familiar to most immigrant groups, but the Hmong, whose identity has always hinged on tradition, have taken it particularly hard. "Animals are responsible to their masters, and children to their parents," advised a Hmong proverb that survived unquestioned for countless generations. In prewar Laos, where families worked in the fields all day and shared a single room at night, it was not uncommon for children and their parents to be together around the clock. Remoteness and altitude insulated their villages from the majority culture. Hmong children here spend six hours in school and often several more at large in their communities, soaking up America. "My sisters don't feel they're Hmong at all," my interpreter, May Ying Xiong, once told me. "One of them has spiked hair. The youngest one speaks mostly English. I don't see the respect I gave elders at that age." Lia's sister May said, "I know how to do *paj ntaub,* but I hate sewing. My mom says, why aren't you doing *paj ntaub?* I say, Mom, this is America."

Although Americanization may bring certain benefits—more job opportunities, more money, less cultural dislocation—Hmong parents are likely to view any earmarks of assimilation as an insult and a threat. "In our families, the kids eat hamburger and bread," said Dang Moua sadly, "whereas the parents prefer hot soup with vegetables, rice, and meat like tripes or liver or kidney that the young ones don't want. The old ones may have no driver's licenses and they ask the young ones to take them some place. Sometimes the kid say I'm too busy. That is a serious situation when the kid will not obey us. The old ones are really upset." Rebellious young Hmong sometimes go beyond refusing to chauffeur their parents, and tangle with drugs or violence. In 1994, Xou Yang, a nineteen-year-old high-school dropout from Banning, California, robbed and murdered a German tourist. His father, a veteran of the war in Laos, told a reporter, "We have lost all control. Our children do not respect us. One of the hardest things for me is when I tell my children things and they say, 'I already know that.' When my wife and I try to tell my son about Hmong culture, he tells me people here are different, and he will not listen to me."

Sukey Waller, Merced's maverick psychologist, once recalled a Hmong community meeting she had attended. "An old man of seventy or eighty stood up in the front row," she said, "and he asked one of the most poignant questions I have ever heard: 'Why, when what we did worked so well for two hundred years, is everything breaking down?'" When Sukey told me this, I understood why the man had asked the question, but I thought he was wrong. Much has broken down, but not everything. Jacques Lemoine's analysis of the postwar hegira—that the Hmong came to the West to save not only their lives but their ethnicity—has been at least partially confirmed in the

United States. I can think of no other group of immigrants whose culture, in its most essential aspects, has been so little eroded by assimilation. Virtually all Hmong still marry other Hmong, marry young, obey the taboo against marrying within their own clans, pay brideprices, and have large families. Clan and lineage structures are intact, as is the ethic of group solidarity and mutual assistance. On most weekends in Merced, it is possible to hear a death drum beating at a Hmong funeral or a *txiv neeb's* gong and rattle sounding at a healing ceremony. Babies wear strings on their wrists to protect their souls from abduction by *dabs.* People divine their fortunes by interpreting their dreams. (If you dream of opium, you will have bad luck; if you dream you are covered with excrement, you will have good luck; if you dream you have a snake on your lap, you will become pregnant.) Animal sacrifices are common, even among Christian converts, a fact I first learned when May Ying Xiong told me that she would be unavailable to interpret one weekend because her family was sacrificing a cow to safeguard her niece during an upcoming open-heart operation. When I said, "I didn't know your family was so religious," she replied, "Oh yes, we're Mormon."

Even more crucially, the essential Hmong temperament—independent, insular, antiauthoritarian, suspicious, stubborn, proud, choleric, energetic, vehement, loquacious, humorous, hospitable, generous—has so far been ineradicable. Indeed, as George M. Scott, Jr., has observed, the Hmong have responded to the hardships of life in the United States "by becoming *more* Hmong, rather than less so." Summing up his impressions of the Hmong in 1924, François Marie Savina, the French missionary, attributed their ethnic durability to six factors: religion; love of liberty; traditional customs; refusal to marry outside their race; life in cold, dry, mountainous areas; and the toughening effects of war. Even though their experience here has been suffused with despair and loss, the 180,000 Hmong who live in the United States are doing passably or better on the first four counts.[6]

I was able to see the whole cycle of adjustment to American life start all over again during one of my visits to Merced. When I arrived at the Lees' apartment, I was surprised to find it crammed with people I'd never met before. These turned out to be a cousin of Nao Kao's named Joua Chai Lee, his wife, Yeng Lor, and their nine children, who ranged in age from eight months to twenty-five years. They had arrived from Thailand two weeks earlier, carrying one piece of luggage for all eleven of them. In it were packed some clothes, a bag of rice, and, because Joua is a *txiv neeb's* assistant, a set of rattles, a drum, and a pair of divinatory water-buffalo horns. The cousins were staying with Foua and Nao Kao until they found a place of their own. The two families had not seen each other in more than a decade, and there was a festive atmosphere in the little apartment, with small children dashing around in their new American sneakers and the four barefooted adults frequently throwing back their heads and laughing. Joua said to me, via May Ying's translation, "Even though there are a lot of us, you can spend the night here too." May Ying explained to me later that Joua didn't really expect me to lie down on the floor with twenty of his relatives. It was simply his way, even though he was in a strange country where he owned almost nothing, of extending a face-saving bit of Hmong hospitality.

I asked Joua what he thought of America. "It is really nice but it is different," he said, "It is very flat. You cannot tell one place from another. There are many things I have not seen before, like that"—a light switch—"and that"—a telephone—"and that"—an air conditioner. "Yesterday our relatives took us somewhere in a car and I saw a lady and I thought she was real but she was fake." This turned out to have been a mannequin at the Merced Mall. "I couldn't stop laughing all the way home," he

said. And remembering how funny his mistake had been, he started to laugh again.

Then I asked Joua what he hoped for his family's future here. "I will work if I can," he said, "but I think I probably cannot. As old as I am, I think I will not be able to learn one word of English. If my children put a heart to it, they will be able to learn English and get really smart. But as for myself, I have no hope."

NOTES

1. Sudden Unexpected Death Syndrome, which until the early 1980s was the leading cause of death among young Hmong males in the United States, is triggered by cardiac failure, often during or after a bad dream. No one has been able to explain what produces the cardiac irregularity, although theories over the years have included potassium deficiency, thiamine deficiency, sleep apnea, depression, culture shock, and survivor guilt. Many Hmong have attributed the deaths to attacks by an incubuslike *dab* [spirit] who sits on the victim's chest and presses the breath out of him.

2. Like most false rumors, these all grew from germs of truth. The white-slavery rumor originated in press accounts of Vietnamese crimes in California, most of which were themselves probably unfounded. The car rumor originated in the Hmong custom of pooling the savings of several families to buy cars and other items too expensive for one family to afford. The insurance rumor originated in the $78,000 that a Hmong family in Wisconsin was awarded after their fourteen-year-old son was killed after being hit by a car. The daughter-selling rumor originated in the Hmong custom of brideprice, or "nurturing charge," as it is now sometimes called in the United States in order to avoid just such misinterpretations. The speed-bump rumor originated in the many nonlethal domestic faux pas the Hmong have actually committed. The dog-eating rumor, which, as I've mentioned elsewhere, is current in Merced, originated in Hmong ritual sacrifices.

3. Like all low-income refugees, newly arrived Hmong were automatically eligible for Refugee Cash Assistance. The RCA program enabled Hmong who would otherwise have been ineligible

for welfare in some states—for instance, because an able-bodied male was present in the home—to receive benefits. But it did not enable Hmong families to receive more money than American families. In a given state, Refugee Cash Assistance payments were always identical to benefits from AFDC (Aid to Families with Dependent Children, the form of public assistance most people mean by the word "welfare").

4. The Hmong Channel is accessed almost exclusively by Hmong users. The Hmong Homepage and the electronic mailing lists also have an audience of Americans with an academic or professional interest in Hmong culture, as well as a number of Mormon elders who have been assigned missionary work in Hmong communities.

5. At the request of local public assistance agencies, the infamous "100-Hour Rule," which prevented so many Hmong from becoming economically self-sufficient, was waived in the majority of states, starting with California, between 1994 and 1996. "Basically, it required people not to work," explained John Cullen, who directed Merced's Human Services Agency during the last years of the rule's sway. The 100-Hour Rule was replaced by a formula of gradually decreasing benefits based on earnings.

6. About 150,000 Hmong—some of whom resettled in countries other than the United States, and some of whom are still in Thailand—fled Laos. The Hmong now living in the United States exceed that number because of their high birthrate.

THINKING ABOUT THE READING

Why has it been so difficult for Hmong refugees to adjust to the American way of life? How do the experiences of younger Hmong compare to those of their elders? Why are the Hmong such a popular target of anti-immigrant violence and persecution? Why is American society so unwilling to grant the Hmong their wish to be "left alone"? In other words, why is there such a strong desire to assimilate them into American culture? On a more general level, why is there such distaste in this society when certain ethnic groups desire to retain their traditional way of life?

5 Building Identity

Socialization

ociology teaches us that humans don't develop in a social vacuum. Other people, cultural practices, historical events, and social institutions can determine not only what we do and say but what we value and who we become. Our self-concept, identity, and sense of self-worth are derived from the reactions, real or imagined, of other people.

The fundamental task of any society is to reproduce itself—to create members whose behaviors, desires, and goals correspond to those defined as appropriate by that particular society. *Socialization* is the process by which individuals learn their culture and learn to live according to the norms of their society. It is how we learn to perceive our world, gain a sense of our own identity, and interact appropriately with others. This learning process occurs within the context of several social institutions—schools, religious institutions, the mass media, and the family—and it extends beyond childhood. Adults must be resocialized into a new galaxy of norms, values, and expectations each time they leave or abandon old roles and enter new ones.

The socialization process is also strongly influenced by race and social class. In "Life as the Maid's Daughter," sociologist Mary Romero describes a research interview with a young Chicana regarding her recollections of growing up as the daughter of a live-in maid for white, upper-class families living in Los Angeles. Romero describes the many ways in which this girl learns to move between different social settings, adapting to different expectations and occupying different roles. This girl must constantly negotiate the boundaries of inclusion and exclusion, as she struggles between the socializing influence of her ethnic group and that of the white, middle-class employers she and her mother live with. In so doing, she illustrates the sociological contention that we take on different identities in different situations.

One of the key products of socialization is an understanding of gender, both as a cultural construct and as a personal attribute. In "Sisyphus in a Wheelchair," Tom Gerschick focuses on some of the ways in which perceptions of masculinity are based on assumptions of able-bodiedness. In particular, the men in his study find that the identities other impose on them are strongly connected to impressions regarding the physical body. Men with disabilities struggle to be seen as whole persons, but sometimes this means reconsidering their own social ideals regarding masculinity.

Life as the Maid's Daughter

An Exploration of the Everyday Boundaries of Race, Class, and Gender

Mary Romero

(1995)

Introduction

... My current research attempts to expand the sociological understanding of the dynamics of race, class, and gender in the everyday routines of family life and reproductive labor. ... I am lured to the unique setting presented by domestic service ... and I turn to the realities experienced by the children of private household workers. This focus is not entirely voluntary. While presenting my research on Chicana private household workers, I was approached repeatedly by Latina/os and African Americans who wanted to share their knowledge about domestic service—knowledge they obtained as the daughters and sons of household workers. Listening to their accounts about their mothers' employment presents another reality to understanding paid and unpaid reproductive labor and the way in which persons of color are socialized into a class-based, gendered, racist social structure. The following discussion explores issues of stratification in everyday life by analyzing the life story of a maid's daughter. This life story illustrates the potential of the standpoint of the maid's daughter for generating knowledge about race, class, and gender. ...

Social Boundaries Presented in the Life Story

The first interview with Teresa,[1] the daughter of a live-in maid, eventually led to a life history

project. I am intrigued by Teresa's experiences with her mother's white, upper-middle-class employers while maintaining close ties to her relatives in Juarez, Mexico, and Mexican friends in Los Angeles. While some may view Teresa's life as a freak accident, living a life of "rags to riches," and certainly not a common Chicana/o experience, her story represents a microcosm of power relationships in the larger society. Life as the maid's daughter in an upper-middle-class neighborhood exemplifies many aspects of the Chicano/Mexicano experience as "racial ethnics" in the United States, whereby the boundaries of inclusion and exclusion are constantly changing as we move from one social setting and one social role to another.

Teresa's narrative contains descriptive accounts of negotiating boundaries in the employers' homes and in their community. As the maid's daughter, the old adage "Just like one of the family" is a reality, and Teresa has to learn when she must act like the employer's child and when she must assume the appropriate behavior as the maid's daughter. She has to recognize all the social cues and interpret social settings correctly—when to expect the same rights and privileges as the employer's children and when to fulfill the expectations and obligations as the maid's daughter. Unlike the employers' families, Teresa and her mother rely on different ways of obtaining knowledge. The taken-for-granted reality of the employers' families do not contain conscious experiences of negotiating race and class status, particularly not in the intimate setting of the home. Teresa's status is constantly changing in response to the wide range of social settings she encounters—from employers' dinner parties with movie stars and corporate executives to Sunday dinners with Mexican garment workers in Los Angeles and factory workers in El Paso. Since Teresa remains bilingual and bicultural throughout her life, her story reflects the constant struggle and resistance to maintain her Mexican identity, claiming a reality that is neither rewarded nor acknowledged as valid.

Teresa's account of her life as the maid's daughter is symbolic of the way that racial ethnics participate in the United States; sometimes we are included and other times excluded or ignored. Teresa's story captures the reality of social stratification in the United States, that is, a racist, sexist, and class-structured society upheld by an ideology of equality. I will analyze the experiences of the maid's daughter in an upper-middle-class neighborhood in Los Angeles to investigate the ways that boundaries of race, class, and gender are maintained or diffused in everyday life. I have selected various excerpts from the transcripts that illustrate how knowledge about a class-based and gendered, racist social order is learned, the type of information that is conveyed, and how the boundaries between systems of domination impact everyday life. I begin with a brief history of Teresa and her mother, Carmen.

Learning Social Boundaries: Background

Teresa's mother was born in Piedras Negras, a small town in Aguas Calientes in Mexico. After her father was seriously injured in a railroad accident, the family moved to a small town outside Ciudad Juarez. Teresa's mother soon became involved in a variety of activities to earn money. She sold food and trinkets at the railroad station and during train stops boarded the trains seeking customers. By the time [Carmen] was fifteen she moved to Juarez and took a job as a domestic, making about eight dollars a week. She soon crossed the border and began working for Anglo families in the country club area in El Paso. Like other domestics in El Paso, Teresa's mother returned to Mexico on weekends and helped support her mother and sisters. In her late twenties she joined several of her friends in their search for better-paying jobs in Los Angeles. The women immediately found jobs in the garment industry. Yet, after six months in the sweatshops, Teresa's mother went to an agency in search of domestic work. She was placed in a very exclusive Los Angeles neighborhood. Several years later Teresa was born. Her friends took care of the baby while Carmen continued working; childcare became a burden, however, and she eventually returned to Mexico. At the age of thirty-six Teresa's mother returned to Mexico with her newborn baby. Leaving Teresa with her grandmother and aunts, her mother sought work in the country club area. Three years later Teresa and her mother returned to Los Angeles.

Over the next fifteen years Teresa lived with her mother in the employer's (Smith) home, usually the two sharing the maid's room located off the kitchen. From the age of three until Teresa started school, she accompanied her mother to work. She continued to live in the Smiths' home until she left for college. All of Teresa's live-in years were spent in one employer's household. The Smiths were unable to afford a full-time maid, however, so Teresa's mother began doing day work throughout the neighborhood. After school Teresa went to whatever house her mother was cleaning and waited until her mother finished working, around 4 or 6 P.M., and then returned to the Smiths' home with her mother. Many prominent families in the neighborhood knew Teresa as the maid's daughter and treated her accordingly. While Teresa wanted the relationship with the employers to cease when she went to college and left the neighborhood, her mother continued to work as a live-in maid with no residence other than the room in the employer's home; consequently, Teresa's social status as the maid's daughter continued.

Entrance into the Employers' World

Having spent her first three years in a female-dominated and monolingual, Spanish-speaking household in Juarez and in a Mexican immigrant community in Los Angeles, Teresa had a great deal to learn about the foreign environment presented by her mother's working conditions as a live-in maid. As a pre-schooler, Teresa began to learn that her social status reflected her mother's social position. In Mexico her mother was the primary wage earner for her grandmother and aunts. In this Mexican household dominated by women, Teresa received special attention and privileges as Carmen's daughter. Teresa recalled very vivid memories about entering the employers' world and being forced to learn an entirely new set of rules and beliefs of a Euro-American social order that consisted of a white, monolingual, male-dominated, and upper-middle-class family life. Teresa's account of her early years in the employers' homes is clearly from the perspective of the maid's daughter. She was an outsider and had to learn the appropriate behavior for each setting.

Rules were a major theme in Teresa's recollections of growing up in the employers' homes. She was very much aware of different rules operating in each home and of the need to act accordingly. In one of her mother's work sites, she was expected to play with the employer's children, in another she was allowed to play with their toys in specific areas of the house, and in other workplaces she sat quietly and was not allowed to touch the things around her. From the beginning she was socialized by the employers and their children, who emphasized conformity and change to their culture. The employers did not make any attempt to create a bicultural or multicultural environment in their homes or community. Teresa was expected to conform to their linguistic norms and acquiesce to becoming "the other"—the little Spanish-speaking Mexican girl among the English-speaking white children.

In the following excerpt Teresa describes her first encounter with the boundaries she confronted in the employers' homes. The excerpt is typical of her observances and recollections about her daily life, in which she is constantly assessing the practices and routines and reading signs in order to determine her position in each social setting and, thus, select the appropriate behavior. While the demands to conform and change were repeated throughout her experiences, Teresa did not embrace the opportunity to assimilate. Her resistance and struggle against assimilation is evident throughout her account, as indicated by her attempt to leave the employer's home and her refusal to speak English:

> I started to realize that every day I went to somebody else's house. Everybody's house had different rules.... My mother says that she constantly had to watch me, because she tried to get me to sit still and I'd be really depressed and I cried or I wanted to go see things, and my mother was afraid I was going to break something and she told me not to touch anything. The kids wanted to play with me. To them, I was a novelty and they wanted to play with the little Mexican girl....
>
> I think I just had an attitude problem as I describe it now. I didn't want to play with them, they were different. My mother would tell me to go play with them, and in a little while later I'd come back and say: "Mama no me quieren aguntar"—obviously it was the communication problem. We couldn't communicate. I got really mad one day at these girls, because "no me quieran aguntar," and

they did not understand what I was trying to say. They couldn't, we couldn't play, so I decided that I was going to go home, and that I didn't like this anymore. So I just opened the door and I walked out. I went around the block and I was going to walk home, to the apartment where we lived. I went out of the house, and walked around and went the opposite direction around the block. The little girls came to my mom and said: "Carmen your little daughter she left!" So my mom dropped everything and was hysterical and one of the older daughters drove my mom around and she found me on the corner. My mom was crying and crying, upset, and she asked me where I was going and I said: "Well, I was going to go home, porque no me quieran aguntar," and I didn't want to be there anymore, and I was gonna walk home. So my mother had to really keep an eye on me.

I would go to the Jones' [employers], and they had kids, and I would just mostly sit and play with their toys, but I wouldn't try to interact with them. Then they tried to teach me English. I really resented that. They had an aquarium and fishes and they would say: "Teresa, can you say Fiishh?" and I would just glare at them, just really upset. Then I would say "Fish, no, es pescado." You know, like trying to change me, and I did not want to speak their language, or play with their kids, or do anything with them. At the Smiths they tried to teach me English. There were different rules there. I couldn't touch anything. The first things I learned were "No touch, no touch," and "Don't do this, don't do that."

At different houses, I started picking up different things. I remember that my mother used to also work for a Jewish family, when I was about five, the Altman's. We had to walk to their house. Things were different at the Altman's. At the Altman's they were really nice to me. They had this little metal stove that they let me play with. I would play with that. That was like the one thing I could play with, in the house. I immediately—I'd get there and sit down in my designated area that I could be in, and I'd play there. Sometimes, Ms. Altman would take me to the park and I'd play there.

She would try to talk to me. Sometimes I would talk and sometimes I would just sit there.

Teresa's account of going to work with her mother as a toddler was not a story of a child running freely and exploring the world around her; instead, her story was shaped by the need to learn the rules set by white, monolingual, English-speaking adults and children. The emphasis in her socialization within employers' homes was quite different than that given to the employers' male children; rather than advocating independence, individuality, and adventure, Teresa was socialized to conform to female sex roles, restricting her movement and playing with gendered toys. Learning the restrictions that limit her behavior—"No touch. Don't do this"—served to educate Teresa about her social status in the employers' homes. She was clearly different from the other children, "a novelty," and was bound by rules regulating her use of social space and linguistic behavior. Teresa's resistance against changing her language points to the strong self-esteem and pride in her culture and Mexican identity that she obtained from her experience in a Mexican household. Teresa's early memories were dominated by pressure to assimilate and to restrain her movement and activity to fit into a white, male-dominated, upper-middle-class household.

The context in which Teresa learned English was very significant in acquiring knowledge about the social order. English was introduced into her life as a means of control and to restrict her movement within employers' homes. The employers' children were involved in teaching Teresa English, and they exerted pressure that she conform to the linguistic norms governing their households. Teresa was not praised or rewarded for ability to speak Spanish, and her racial and cultural differences were only perceived positively when they served a function for the employer's family, such as a curiosity, entertainment, or a cross-cultural experience. While her mother continued to talk to Teresa in Spanish when they were alone, Carmen was not able to defend her daughter's right to decide which language to speak in the presence of the employers' families. Furthermore, Teresa observed her mother serving and waiting on the employers' families, taking orders, and being treated in a familiar manner. While Teresa referred to the employers formally, by their last names, the employers' children called Teresa's mother by her first name. The circumstances created an environment whereby all monolingual, Spanish-speaking women, including her mother, were in powerless positions. The experiences provided Teresa with knowledge about social stratification—that is, the negative value placed on the Spanish language and Mexican culture—as well as about the social status of Spanish-speaking Mexican immigrant women.

One of the Family

As Teresa got older, the boundaries between insider and outsider became more complicated, as employers referred to her and Carmen as "one of the family." Entering into an employer's world as the maid's daughter, Teresa was not only subjected to the rules of an outsider but also had to recognize when the rules changed, making her momentarily an insider. While the boundaries dictating Carmen's work became blurred between the obligations of an employee and that of a friend or family member, Teresa was forced into situations in which she was expected to be just like one of the employer's children, and yet she remained the maid's daughter. . . .

Living under conditions established by the employers made Teresa and her mother's efforts to maintain a distinction between their family life and an employer's family very difficult. Analyzing incidents in which the boundaries between the worker's family and employer's family were blurred highlights the issues that complicate the mother-daughter relationship. Teresa's account of her mother's hospitalization was the first of numerous conflicts between the two that stemmed from the live-in situation and their relationships with the employer's family. The following excerpt demonstrates the difficulty in interacting as a family unit and the degree of influence and power employers exerted over their daily lives:

When I was about ten my mother got real sick. That summer, instead of sleeping downstairs in my mother's room when my mother wasn't there, one of the kids was gone away to college, so it was just Rosalyn, David and myself that were home. The other two were gone, so I was gonna sleep upstairs in one of the rooms. I was around eight or nine, ten I guess. I lived in the back room. It was a really neat room because Rosalyn was allowed to paint it. She got her friend who was real good, painted a big tree and clouds and all this stuff on the walls. So I really loved it and I had my own room. I was with the Smiths all the time, as my parents, for about two months. My mother was in the hospital for about a month. Then when she came home, she really couldn't do anything. We would all have dinner, the Smiths were really, really supportive. I went to summer school and I took math and English and stuff like that. I was in this drama class and I did drama and I got to do the leading role. Everybody really liked me and Ms. Smith would come and see my play. So things started to change when I got a lot closer to them and I was with them alone. I would go see my mother every day, and my cousin was there. I think that my cousin kind of resented all the time that the Smiths spent with me. I think my mother was really afraid that now that she wasn't there that they were going to steal me from her. I went to see her, but I could only stay a couple of hours and it was really weird. I didn't like seeing my mother in pain and she was in a lot of pain. I remember before she came home the Smiths said that they thought it would be a really good idea if

I stayed upstairs and I had my own room now that my mother was going to be sick and I couldn't sleep in the same bed 'cause I might hurt her. It was important for my mother to be alone. And how did I feel about that? I was really excited about that [having her own room]—you know. They said, "Your mom she is probably not going to like it and she might get upset about it, but I think that we can convince her that it is ok." When my mom came home, she understood that she couldn't be touched and that she had to be really careful, but she wanted it [having her own room] to be temporary. Then my mother was really upset. She got into it with them and said, "No, I don't want it that way." She would tell me, "No, I want you to be down here. ¿Qué crees que eres hija de ellos? You're gonna be with me all the time, you can't do that." So I would tell Ms. Smith. She would ask me when we would go to the market together, "How does your mom seem, what does she feel, what does she say?" She would get me to relay that. I would say, "I think my mom is really upset about me moving upstairs. She doesn't like it and she just says no." I wouldn't tell her everything. They would talk to her and finally they convinced her, but my mom really, really resented it and was really angry about it. She was just generally afraid. All these times that my mother wasn't there, things happened and they would take me places with them, go out to dinner with them and their friends. So that was a real big change, in that I slept upstairs and had different rules. Everything changed. I was more independent. I did my own homework; they would open the back door and yell that dinner was ready— you know. Things were just real different.

The account illustrates how assuming the role of insider was an illusion because neither the worker's daughter nor the worker ever became a member of the white, middle-class family. Teresa was only allowed to move out of the maid's quarter, where she shared a bed with her mother, when two of the employer's children were leaving home, vacating two bedrooms. This was not the first time that "space"

determined whether Teresa was included in the employer's family activities. Her description of Thanksgiving dinner illustrates that she did not decide when to be included but, rather, the decision was based on the available space at the table:

> I never wanted to eat with them, I wanted to eat with my mom. Like Thanksgiving, it was always an awkward situation, because I never knew, up until dinnertime, where I was going to sit, every single time. It depended on how many guests they had, and how much room there was at the table. Sometimes, when they invited all their friends, the Carters and the Richmans, who had kids, the adults would all eat dinner in one room and then the kids would have dinner in another room. Then I could go eat dinner with the kids or sometimes I'd eat with my mom in the kitchen. It really depended.

Since Teresa preferred to eat with her mother, the inclusion was burdensome and unwanted. In the case of moving upstairs, however, Teresa wanted to have her "own" bedroom. The conflict arising from Teresa's move upstairs points to the way in which the employer's actions threatened the bonds between mother and daughter.

Teresa and Carmen did not experience the boundaries of insider and outsider in the same way. Teresa was in a position to assume a more active family role when employers made certain requests. Unlike her mother, she was not an employee and was not expected to clean and serve the employer. Carmen's responsibility for the housework never ceased, however, regardless of the emotional ties existing between employee and employers. She and her employers understood that, whatever family activity she might be participating in, if the situation called for someone to clean, pick up, or serve, that was Carmen's job. When the Smiths requested Teresa to sit at the dinner table with the family, they placed Teresa in a different class position than her mother, who was now expected to serve her daughter alongside her employer. Moving Teresa upstairs in a bedroom alongside the employer and their children was bound to drive a wedge between Teresa and Carmen. There is a long history of spatial deference in domestic service, including separate entrances, staircases, and eating and sleeping arrangements. Carmen's room reflected her position in the household. As the maid's quarter, the room was separated from the rest of the bedrooms and was located near the maid's central work area, the kitchen. The room was obviously not large enough for two beds because Carmen and Teresa shared a bed. Once Teresa was moved upstairs, she no longer shared the same social space in the employer's home as her mother. Weakening the bonds between the maid and her daughter permitted the employers to broaden their range of relationships and interaction with Teresa.

Carmen's feelings of betrayal and loss underline how threatening the employers' actions were. She understood that the employers were in a position to buy her child's love. They had already attempted to socialize Teresa into Euro-American ideals by planning Teresa's education and deciding what courses she would take. Guided by the importance they place on European culture, the employers defined the Mexican Spanish spoken by Teresa and her mother as inadequate and classified Castillan Spanish as "proper" Spanish. As a Mexican immigrant woman working as a live-in maid, Carmen was able to experience certain middle-class privileges, but her only access to these privileges was through her relationship with employers. Therefore, without the employers' assistance, she did not have the necessary connections to enroll Teresa in private schools or provide her with upper-middle-class experiences to help her develop the skills needed to survive in elite schools. Carmen only gained these privileges for her daughter at a price; she relinquished many of

her parental rights to her employers. To a large degree the Smiths determined Carmen's role as a parent, and the other employers restricted the time she had to attend school functions and the amount of energy left at the end of the day to mother her own child.

Carmen pointed to the myth of "being like one of the family" in her comment, "¿Qué crees que eres hija de ellos? You're gonna be with me all the time, you can't do that." The statement underlines the fact that the bond between mother and daughter is for life, whereas the pseudofamily relationship with employers is temporary and conditional. Carmen wanted her daughter to understand that taking on the role of being one of the employer's family did not relinquish her from the responsibility of fulfilling her "real" family obligations. The resentment Teresa felt from her cousin who was keeping vigil at his aunt's hospital bed indicated that she had not been a dutiful daughter. The outside pressure from an employer did not remove her own family obligations and responsibilities. Teresa's relatives expected a daughter to be at her mother's side providing any assistance possible as a caretaker, even if it was limited to companionship. The employer determined Teresa's activity, however, and shaped her behavior into that of a middle-class child; consequently, she was kept away from the hospital and protected from the realities of her mother's illness. Furthermore, she was submerged into the employer's world, dining at the country club and interacting with their friends.

Her mother's accusation that Teresa wanted to be the Smiths' daughter signifies the feelings of betrayal or loss and the degree to which Carmen was threatened by the employer's power and authority. Yet Teresa also felt betrayal and loss and viewed herself in competition with the employers for her mother's time, attention, and love. In this excerpt Teresa accuses her mother of wanting to be part of employers' families and community:

I couldn't understand it—you know—until I was about eighteen and then I said, "It is your fault. If I treat the Smiths differently, it is your fault. You chose to have me live in this situation. It was your decision to let me have two parents, and for me to balance things off, so you can't tell me that I said this. You are the one who wanted this." When I was about eighteen we got into a huge fight on Christmas. I hated the holidays because I hated spending them with the Smiths. My mother always worked. She worked on every holiday. She loved to work on the holidays! She would look forward to working. My mother just worked all the time! I think that part of it was that she wanted to have power and control over this community, and she wanted the network, and she wanted to go to different people's houses.

As employers, Mr. and Mrs. Smith were able to exert an enormous amount of power over the relationship between Teresa and her mother. Carmen was employed in an occupation in which the way to improve working conditions, pay, and benefits was through the manipulation of personal relationships with employers. Carmen obviously tried to take advantage of her relationship with the Smiths in order to provide the best for her daughter. The more intimate and interpersonal the relationship, the more likely employers were to give gifts, do favors, and provide financial assistance. Although speaking in anger and filled with hurt, Teresa accused her mother of choosing to be with employers and their families rather than with her own daughter. Underneath Teresa's accusation was the understanding that the only influence and status her mother had as a domestic was gained through her personal relationships with employers. Although her mother had limited power in rejecting the Smiths' demands, Teresa held her responsible for giving them too much control. Teresa argued that the positive relationship with the Smiths was done out of obedience to her mother and denied any familial feelings toward the employers. The web between employee and employers' families affected both mother and daughter, who were unable to separate the boundaries of work and family.

Maintaining Cultural Identity

A major theme in Teresa's narrative was her struggle to retain her Mexican culture and her political commitment to social justice. Rather than internalizing meaning attached to Euro-American practices and redefining Mexican culture and bilingualism as negative social traits, Teresa learned to be a competent social actor in both white, upper-middle-class environments and in working- and middle-class Chicano and Mexicano environments. To survive as a stranger in so many social settings, Teresa developed an acute skill for assessing the rules governing a particular social setting and acting accordingly. Her ability to be competent in diverse social settings was only possible, however, because of her life with the employers' children. Teresa and her mother maintained another life—one that was guarded and protected against any employer intrusion. Their other life was Mexican, not white, was Spanish speaking, not English speaking, was female dominated rather than male dominated, and was poor and working-class, not upper-middle-class. During the week Teresa and her mother visited the other Mexican maids in the neighborhoods, on weekends they occasionally took a bus into the Mexican barrio in Los Angeles to have dinner with friends, and every summer they spent a month in Ciudad Juarez with their family. . . .

Teresa's description of evening activity with the Mexican maids in the neighborhood provides insight into her daily socialization and explains how she learned to live in the employer's home without internalizing all their negative attitudes toward Mexican and working-class culture. Within the white, upper-class neighborhood in which they worked, the

Mexican maids got together on a regular basis and cooked Mexican food, listened to Mexican music, and gossiped in Spanish about their employers. Treated as invisible or as confidants, the maids were frequently exposed to the intimate details of their employers' marriages and family life. The Mexican maids voiced their disapproval of the lenient child-rearing practices and parental decisions, particularly surrounding drug usage and the importance of material possessions:

> Raquel was the only one [maid] in the neighborhood who had her own room and own TV set. So everybody would go over to Raquel's. . . . This was my mother's support system. After hours, they would go to different people's [maid's] rooms depending on what their rooms had. Some of them had kitchens and they would go and cook all together, or do things like play cards and talk all the time. I remember that in those situations they would sit, and my mother would talk about the Smiths, what they were like. When they were going to negotiate for raises, when they didn't like certain things, I would listen and hear all the different discussions about what was going on in different houses. And they would talk, also, about the family relationships. The way they interacted, the kids did this and that. At the time some of the kids were smoking pot and they would talk about who was smoking marijuana. How weird it was that the parents didn't care. They would talk about what they saw as being wrong. The marriage relationship, or how weird it was they would go off to the beauty shop and spend all this money, go shopping and do all these weird things and the effect that it had on the kids.

The interaction among the maids points to the existence of another culture operating invisibly within a Euro-American and male-dominated community. The workers' support system did not include employers and addressed their concerns as mothers, immigrants, workers, and women. They created a Mexican-dominated domain for themselves. Here they ate Mexican food, spoke Spanish, listened to the Spanish radio station, and watched novellas on TV. Here Teresa was not a cultural artifact but, instead, a member of the Mexican community.

In exchanging gossip and voicing their opinions about the employers' lifestyles, the maids rejected many of the employers' priorities in life. Sharing stories about the employers' families allowed the Mexican immigrant women to be critical of white, upper-middle-class families and to affirm and enhance their own cultural practices and beliefs. The regular evening sessions with other working-class Mexican immigrant women were essential in preserving Teresa and her mother's cultural values and were an important agency of socialization for Teresa. For instance, the maids had a much higher regard for their duties and responsibilities as mothers than as wives or lovers. In comparison to their mistresses, they were not financially dependent on men, nor did they engage in the expensive and time-consuming activity of being an ideal wife, such as dieting, exercising, and maintaining a certain standard of beauty in their dress, makeup, and hairdos. Unlike the employers' daughters, who attended cotillions and were socialized to acquire success through marriage, Teresa was constantly pushed to succeed academically in order to pursue a career. The gender identity cultivated among the maids did not include dependence on men or the learned helplessness that was enforced in the employers' homes but, rather, promoted self-sufficiency. However, both white women employers and Mexican women employees were expected to be nurturing and caring. These traits were further reinforced when employers asked Teresa to babysit for their children or to provide them with companionship during their husbands' absences.

So, while Teresa observed her mother adapting to the employers' standards in her interaction with their children, she learned that her mother did not approve of their lifestyle and understood that she had another set of expectations to adhere to. Teresa attended the same schools as employers' children, wore similar clothes, and conducted most of her social life within the same socioeconomic class, but she remained the maid's daughter— and learned the limitations of that position. Teresa watched her mother uphold higher standards for her and apply a different set of standards to the employers' children; most of the time, however, it appeared to Teresa as if they had no rules at all.

Sharing stories about the Smiths and other employers in a female, Mexican, and worker-dominated social setting provided Teresa with a clear image of the people she lived with as employers rather than as family members. Seeing the employers through the eyes of the employees forced Teresa to question their kindness and benevolence and to recognize their use of manipulation to obtain additional physical and emotional labor from the employees. She became aware of the workers' struggles and the long list of grievances, including no annual raises, no paid vacations, no social security or health benefits, little if any privacy, and sexual harassment. Teresa was also exposed to the price that working-class immigrant women employed as live-in maids paid in maintaining white, middle-class, patriarchal communities. Employers' careers and lifestyles, particularly the everyday rituals affirming male privilege, were made possible through the labor women provided for men's physical, social, and emotional needs. Female employers depended on the maid's labor to assist in the reproduction of their gendered class status. Household labor was expanded in order to accommodate the male members of the employers' families and to preserve their privilege. Additional work was created by rearranging meals around men's work and recreation schedules and by waiting on

them and serving them. Teresa's mother was frequently called upon to provide emotional labor for the wife, husband, mother, and father within an employer's family, thus freeing members to work or increase their leisure time.

Discussion

Teresa's account offers insight into the ways racial ethnic women gain knowledge about the social order and use the knowledge to develop survival strategies. As the college-educated daughter of an immigrant Mexican woman employed as a live-in maid, Teresa's experiences in the employers' homes, neighborhood, and school and her experiences in the homes of working-class Mexicano families and barrios provided her with the skills to cross the class and cultural boundaries separating the two worlds. The process of negotiating social boundaries involved an evaluation of Euro-American culture and its belief system in light of an intimate knowledge of white, middle-class families. Being in the position to compare and contrast behavior within different communities, Teresa debunked notions of "American family values" and resisted efforts toward assimilation. Learning to function in the employers' world was accomplished without internalizing its belief system, which defined ethnic culture as inferior. Unlike the employers' families, Teresa's was not able to assume the taken-for-granted reality of her mother's employers because her experiences provided a different kind of knowledge about the social order.

While the employers' children were surrounded by positive images of their race and class status, Teresa faced negative sanctions against her culture and powerless images of her race. Among employers' families she quickly learned that her "mother tongue" was not valued and that her culture was denied. All the Mexican adults in the neighborhood were in subordinate positions to the white adults and were responsible for caring for and nurturing white children. Most of the female employers were full-time homemakers who enjoyed the financial security provided by their husbands, whereas the Mexican immigrant women in the neighborhood all worked as maids and were financially independent; in many cases they were supporting children, husbands, and other family members. By directly observing her mother serve, pick up after, and nurture employers and their families, Teresa learned about white, middleclass privileges. Her experiences with other working-class Mexicans were dominated by women's responsibility for their children and extended families. Here the major responsibility of mothering was financial; caring and nurturing were secondary and were provided by the extended family or children did without. Confronted with a working mother who was too tired to spend time with her, Teresa learned about the racial, class, and gender parameters of parenthood, including its privileges, rights, responsibilities, and obligations. She also learned that the role of a daughter included helping her mother with everyday household tasks and, eventually, with the financial needs of the extended family. Unlike her uncles and male cousins, Teresa was not exempt from cooking and housework, regardless of her financial contributions. Within the extended family Teresa was subjected to standards of beauty strongly weighted by male definitions of women as modest beings, many times restricted in her dress and physical movements. Her social worlds became clearly marked by race, ethnic, class, and gender differences.

Successfully negotiating movement from a white, male, and middle-class setting to one dominated by working-class, immigrant, Mexican women involved a socialization process that provided Teresa with the skills to be bicultural. Since neither setting was bicultural,

Teresa had to become that in order to be a competent social actor in each. Being bicultural included having the ability to assess the rules governing each setting and to understand her ethnic, class, and gender position. Her early socialization in the employers' households was not guided by principles of creativity, independence, and leadership but, rather, was based on conformity and accommodation. Teresa's experiences in two different cultural groups allowed her to separate each and to fulfill the employers' expectations without necessarily internalizing the meaning attached to the act. Therefore, she was able to learn English without internalizing the idea that English is superior to Spanish or that monolingualism is normal. The existence of a Mexican community within the employers' neighborhood provided Teresa with a collective experience of class-based racism, and the maids' support system affirmed and enhanced their own belief system and culture. As Philomena Essed (1991, 294) points out, "The problem is not only how knowledge of racism is acquired but also what kind of knowledge is being transmitted."

Teresa's life story lends itself to a complex set of analyses because the pressures to assimilate were challenged by the positive interactions she experienced within her ethnic community. Like other bilingual persons in the United States, Teresa's linguistic abilities were shaped by the linguistic practices of the social settings she had access to. Teresa learned the appropriate behavior for each social setting, each marked by different class and cultural dynamics and in which women's economic roles and relationships to men were distinct. An overview of Teresa's socialization illustrates the process of biculturalism—a process that included different sets of standards and rules governing her actions as a woman, as a Chicana, and as the maid's daughter. . . .

NOTES

This essay was originally presented as a paper at the University of Michigan, "Feminist Scholarship: Thinking through the Disciplines," 30 January 1992. I want to thank Abigail J. Stewart and Donna Stanton for their insightful comments and suggestions.

1. The names are pseudonyms.

REFERENCE

Essed, Philomena. 1991. *Understanding Everyday Racism.* Newbury Park, Calif.: Sage Publications.

THINKING ABOUT THE READING

Teresa's childhood is unique in that she and her mother lived in several employers' homes, requiring her to learn different sets of rules and to adjust her behavior to these new expectations each time they moved. Unlike most children who are free to explore the world around them, her childhood was shaped by the need to read signals from others to determine her position in each social setting. What were some of the different influences in Teresa's early socialization? Did she accept people's attempts to mold her, or did she resist? How did she react to her mother's employers referring to her as "one of the family"? Teresa came from a poor family, but she spent her childhood in affluent households. With respect to socialization, what advantages do you think these experiences provided her? What were the disadvantages? How do you think these experiences would have changed if she was a *son* of a live-in maid rather than a daughter? If she was a poor *white* girl rather than Latina?

Sisyphus in a Wheelchair

Physical Disabilities and Masculinity

Thomas J. Gerschick

(1998)

Sisyphus, the King of Corinth in Greek mythology, has been condemned for all eternity by the Judges of the Dead to roll a large boulder up a mountain. Each time he approaches the summit, after much bitter toil, he inevitably loses control and the rock returns to the plains below. He repeatedly retrieves it and wearily begins the climb anew. The myth of Sisyphus captures the struggle and frustration men with physical disabilities experience as they seek to create and maintain masculine gender identities in a culture that views them as "not men." . . .

This article focuses specifically on the ways in which men with physical disabilities experience gender domination by the temporarily-able-bodied[1] in the United States.[2] This domination depends upon a double-bind: men with physical disabilities are judged according to the standards of hegemonic masculinity which are difficult to achieve due to the limitations of their bodies. Simultaneously, these men are blocked in everyday interactions from opportunities to achieve this form of masculinity. The most significant barriers they face occur in the key domains of hegemonic masculinity: work, the body, athletics, sexuality, and independence and control.[3] Because men with physical disabilities cannot enact hegemonic standards in these realms, they are denied recognition as men. As "failed" men, they are marginalized and occupy a position in the gender order similar to gay men, men of color, and women. Successfully creating and maintaining self-satisfactory masculine

gender identities under these circumstances is an almost Sisyphean task. Men with physical disabilities, at times, act complicit in their domination by internalizing the dominant group's stereotypes and images of them. Hence these men's struggle against gender domination occurs not only with others, but also with themselves. The effort to resist gender domination has led some men with physical disabilities to develop counter-hegemonic gender identities.

In order to explore the struggle that men with physical disabilities undergo to create a realistic and positive self-image as men, I address the following three questions. First, how are men with physical disabilities dominated due to their inability to meet the demands of hegemonic masculinity? Second, how do they act complicit with, or resist, hegemonic masculinity? Third, what can be learned from the struggles of men with physical disabilities, especially from the alternative gender identities that some men with physical disabilities develop as a result of these struggles?

Data to address these questions come from two sources. First, an associate and I conducted in-depth, semi-structured interviews with 11 men with physical disabilities. Initial interviews lasted an average of an hour. We provided informants with their transcripts and asked them to read them carefully to ensure that they were accurately represented. We then conducted follow-up interviews with most of these men to clarify statements and to ask questions which were stimulated in the first round of interviews. All of the interviews were tape recorded and transcribed verbatim. Correspondence with several informants continues and has been added, with permission, to the transcripts. Most of the informants had paraplegia and sustained their disabilities through either accidents or disease. None of the men we interviewed has a congenital disability. Their ages ranged from 16 to 72. Nine of these men were white, two were Black. Seven were professionally employed, one was a retired business-owner, two were full-time students, and one was a service-sector worker. The second source of data is ten autobiographies, semi-autobiographies, and collections of essays.[4] None of these books were expressly about masculinity and disability, however, all of them addressed issues related to these topics at least implicitly. Extensive notes were taken from these accounts which were then treated as fieldnotes. . . .

The lives of men with physical disabilities provide an instructive arena in which to study gender domination for three reasons. First, men with physical disabilities contravene many of the beliefs associated with being a man. Studying their gender identity struggles provides valuable insight into the struggles that all men experience in this realm. Second, men with physical disabilities occupy a unique subject position in what Patricia Hill Collins (1990: 225–7) calls the matrix of domination and privilege.[5] These men have gender privilege by virtue of being men, yet this privilege is significantly eroded due to their disability, which leaves them subject to domination and marginalization. Their marginal position in the gender order provides access to knowledge that is obscured from those in the mainstream (Beisser 1989; Janeway 1980). One of the goals of this article is to elucidate their "fugitive information," as writer Kay Hagan (1993) calls the knowledge of the marginalized, and how it can be used to construct counter-hegemonic masculine gender identities. Third, little has been written about the intersection of disability and gender. Where gender has been explored with reference to disability, the research has primarily focused on women. Consequently, this research addresses a lacuna in the literature.

Life at the Crossroads: Physical Disability and Masculinity

In order to contextualize the gender domination that men with physical disabilities experience, three sets of social dynamics need to be woven together. The first involves the stigma associated with having a physical disability, the second concerns gender as an interactional process, and the third is the hegemonic gender standard to which men with physical disabilities are held.

To have a disability is not only a physical or mental condition, it is also a social and stigmatized one (Goffman 1963; Kriegel 1991; Zola 1982). As anthropologist Robert Murphy (1990: 113) observed:

> Whatever the physically impaired person may think of himself [sic], he is attributed a negative identity by society, and much of his social life is a struggle against this imposed image. It is for this reason that we can say that stigmatization is less a by-product of disability than its substance. The greatest impediment to a person's taking full part in this society are not his physical flaws, but rather the tissue of myths, fears, and misunderstandings that society attaches to them.

This stigma is embodied in the popular stereotypes of people with disabilities; they are perceived to be weak, passive, and dependent (Shapiro 1993). Our language exemplifies this stigmatization: people with disabilities are de-formed, dis-eased, dis-abled, dis-ordered, ab-normal, and in-valid (Zola 1982: 206).

This stigma is also embedded in the daily interactions between people with disabilities and the temporarily-able-bodied. People with disabilities are evaluated in terms of normative expectations and are, because of their disability, frequently found wanting. As a consequence, they experience a range of reactions from those without disabilities from subtle indignities and slights to overt hostility and outright cruelty. More commonly people with disabilities are avoided, ignored, and marginalized (Fine and Asch 1988; Shapiro 1993). This treatment creates formidable physical, economic, psychological, architectural, and social obstacles to their participation in all aspects of social life. Having a disability also becomes a primary identity which overshadows almost all other aspects of one's identity. As a consequence, it influences all interactions with the temporarily-able-bodied, including gendered interactions.

In order to accomplish gender, each person in a social situation needs to be recognized by others as appropriately masculine or feminine. Those with whom we interact continuously assess our gender performance and decide whether we are "doing gender" appropriately in that situation. Our "audience" or interaction partners then hold us accountable and sanction us in a variety of ways in order to encourage compliance (West and Zimmerman 1987). Our need for social approval and validation as gendered beings further encourages conformity. Much is at stake in this process, as one's sense of self rests precariously upon the audience's decision to validate or reject one's gender performance. Successful enactment bestows status and acceptance, failure invites embarrassment and humiliation (West and Zimmerman 1987).

In the contemporary United States, men's gender performance tends to be judged using the standard of hegemonic masculinity which represents the optimal attributes, activities, behaviors, and values expected of men in a culture (Connell 1990). Social scientists have identified career-orientation, activeness, athleticism, sexual desirability and virility,

independence, and self-reliance as exalted masculine attributes in the United States (Connell 1995; Gerschick and Miller 1994; Kimmel 1994). Consequently, the body is central to the attainment of hegemonic masculinity. Men whose bodies allow them to evidence the identified characteristics are differentially rewarded in U.S. dominant culture over those who cannot. Despite the fact that attaining these attributes is often unrealistic and more based in fantasy than reality, men continue to internalize them as ideals and strive to demonstrate them as well as judge themselves and other men using them. Women also tend to judge men using these standards. . . .

Arenas of Gender Domination, Complicity and Resistance

Work

The prejudice and discrimination that many men with physical disabilities face in the labor market threaten to undermine an important measure of self-determination and a key component of their masculine gender identity. Despite being qualified, these men report being discriminated against in hiring, work-place accommodations, retention, and promotion. They encounter a particular form of double-bind. Due to the actions of the temporarily-able-bodied, men with physical disabilities are discouraged or prevented from competing for highly remunerated or prestigious jobs and are then devalued as men because they do not have them. Given the importance of work to a masculine identity, this situation reinforces their marginalized status as men.

Many men with physical disabilities have internalized the importance of work to enacting masculinity, realizing that in our culture the type of job a man has and the income he earns contribute significantly to his status and power. For instance, after contracting polio as a teenager, Leo realized "I didn't want to be weak. I wanted to be strong. I wanted to have a regular job, bring in income, be a success." When asked what being a man meant to him, Michael, an Independent Living Skills Specialist who has paraplegia, replied, "being able to work, to ay my own way. . . . It [having a job] enhances my self image."

Due to ignorance and prejudice, many temporarily-able-bodied people do not perceive men with physical disabilities as valuable employees; instead they are perceived to have high rates of absenteeism, to have low rates of productivity, and to be expensive to accommodate and insure (Shapiro 1993). . . . Brent, an administrator of a university's disability program who has paraplegia, observed that:

> In this culture there is a quite a bit of stereotypical attitudes about people with disabilities, about who we are, what we can do, why we do what we do, and I think that makes it difficult for me to be, to have job flexibility. I don't think that I have the same access to jobs that other people do. I don't think I have the same access to promotions that other people do.

Having tired of being tracked into jobs which lacked recognition and opportunities for advancement, Brent recently took early retirement. Another of my informants, Jerry, a high school junior with Juvenile Rheumatoid Arthritis, lamented, "I know I have had a hard time finding part-time jobs, just because it seems like people are really intimidated and sort of afraid." Attitudes like these on the part of the temporarily-able-bodied contribute significantly to the 41 percent unemployment rate for men with physical disabilities (McNeil 1993, table 24: 62).

Men with physical disabilities are frequently steered into low-status, low-paying, low-prestige white collar or service sector jobs. Generally these involve some type of social service work, most frequently disability-related, which is deemed more culturally appropriate. Harold, for instance, noted that people who are temporarily-able-bodied "want to pigeonhole you. They see a disabled guy and they go, oh, the only thing you can write about is, you know, covering the disability scene. But that's not always true." Harold's example reveals how the temporarily-able-bodied subtly attach conditions to the employment of men with physical disabilities which impede their ability to compete for higher-status jobs, which in turn hinders their ability to be recognized as "real" men. The segregation in the labor force that many of these men face is similar to that experienced by people of color and women (Amott and Matthaei 1991) and gay men (Levine 1992) and demonstrates the similarity of their subject positions.

Several of my informants report cooperating in their labor force segregation. Of the eight informants who held jobs at the time of their interviews, six worked in disability-related occupations. Three noted that they gravitated to their occupations because they "knew it would be easier to find work" or it "seemed appropriate." Perhaps unconsciously they turned to disability-related jobs because they knew they would face less prejudice and discrimination.

Given their generally low-status and low-power position in society, men with physical disabilities do not control how they are perceived among the temporarily-able-bodied. As a consequence, they face formidable barriers in the labor market. The prejudice and discrimination they face make it difficult for them to achieve economic success, which is a key characteristic of hegemonic masculinity. Consequently, their difficulties in the labor market contribute to their marginalized position within the hegemonic gender order.

The Body

Men with physical disabilities do not meet mainstream notions of what is athletic, physically attractive, or sexually desirable. Instead, because of their bodies, they "contravene all the values of youth, virility, activity, and physical beauty that Americans cherish" (Murphy 1990: 116). As a result, men with physical disabilities are significantly less likely than temporarily-able-bodied men to be publicly recognized as athletes and/or potential sexual partners. These are two of the bedrocks upon which masculine gender identities are built. Consequently, masculinity is threatened when corporeal appearance and performance are discordant with hegemonic expectations, such as in the case of having a physical disability (Connell 1995; Gerschick and Miller 1994).

Bodies are important in contemporary social life. One's body and relationship to it provide a way to apprehend the world and one's place in it (Gerschick and Miller 1994). When one is alienated from one's body, one is alienated from one's sense of self. Psychiatrist Arnold Beisser (1989: 166–7), who had polio, explains:

> I felt as though I were cut off from the elemental functions and activities which had grounded me. I was quite literally separated from the earth, for while I spent my time in an iron lung, in a bed, or in a wheelchair, my feet almost never touched the ground. But more important, I believe, was being separated from so many of the elemental routines that occupy people. Even if I would work, I did not have any experience of physical exertion. I could not, on my own, assume the familiar positions of standing, sitting, and lying down. I was even separated from my breathing, as it was done by a machine. I felt no longer connected with the familiar roles I had known in family, work, and sports. My place in the culture was gone.

Thus having a physical disability compromises men's connection to one of the key sources of their identity: their bodies.

In U.S. culture, bodies are simultaneously symbolic, kinetic, and social (Connell 1995). They are kinetic in that they allow us to move, to accomplish physical tasks, to perform. Bodies are also social; people respond to one another's bodies which initiates social processes such as validation and the assignment of status (Goffman 1963). Finally, bodies are symbolic. They are a form of self-presentation; one's body signifies one's worth. Bodies, then, are essential to the performance and achievement of gender. This becomes clear when one investigates men with physical disabilities' experiences with athletics, sexuality, and independence and control.

Athletics

In our sports-obsessed culture, ability, especially athletic ability, has become a key way for men to embody their masculinity. Sports provides men with an opportunity to exhibit key characteristics of hegemonic masculinity such as endurance, strength, and competitive spirit (Goffman 1977). The institutional organization of sports also embeds social relations such as competition, hierarchy, exclusion, and domination (Connell 1995: 54).

The athletic performances of men with physical disabilities tend not to be socially recognized and validated but instead are trivialized and devalued (Taub and Greer 1997). One of Taub and Greer's (1997: 13–4) informants, a 23-year-old student, described temporarily-able-bodied people's reactions to encountering him in the gym:

> It's people's perceptions [that] kill me . . . it doesn't seem like it's respect . . . it's just like a pat on the head type thing . . . "you're so courageous . . . you're overcoming all these boundaries . . . that's so good what you're doing." I wish people would . . . just look at wheelchair basketball as a sport . . . instead of just like a human interest story.

Because athletic performance embodies gender performance, not being taken seriously as an athlete symbolizes not being taken seriously as a man.

When men with physical disabilities are recognized as athletes, that recognition is conditional. This is represented by the qualifiers attached to titles such as "Special" Olympics, "wheelchair" basketball, and "disabled" athletes. Scott, a paraplegic, explained:

> Softball, I play it now from a wheelchair. I play in a regular city league, so it's able bodied, everyone else in the league is able-bodied. Um, I find that I do pretty well and everybody seems to think that. The guys I play with now have never seen me play before my disability, and so they are all impressed. For me sometimes, it bothers me because I know I'm not the player that I used to be, but I do still enjoy it, but occasionally I have those frustrated times where I feel like, you know, everybody is impressed that I'm a good player, for a gimp, where I just want to be a good player.

Qualifying men with physical disabilities' athletic performances is condescending and patronizing. The devaluation of these men's efforts reveals that social acceptance and recognition are based both on the ability to perform and on the quality of the performance. Men who cannot perform to the hegemonic standard, due to a disability for instance, are marginalized as feminine or sissies (Messner 1992). The lack of recognition of men with physical disabilities as athletes undermines their ability to establish and maintain self-satisfactory gender identities.

Sexuality

Similar to athletic marginalization, men with physical disabilities tend not to be perceived as sexually attractive. "What bothers me more than anything else is the stereotypes, and,

even more so, in terms of sexual desirability," Brent complained in his interview, "because I had a disability, I was less desirable than able bodied people and that I found very frustrating." Men with physical disabilities have a difficult time being recognized as potential life/sexual partners because they do not meet societal standards of beauty. Political scientist Harlan Hahn (1989: 54) explains:

> Much as they would prefer to deny it, the unavoidable reality is that men with disabilities are significantly devalued in modern society. This devaluation occurs not only in the labor force, where disabled men are often prevented from fulfilling the traditional role of "bread-winner," but also in the social marketplace, where they frequently are deprived of romantic partners and lasting companionship. Both forms of exclusion may result as much from aesthetic aversion to a different physical appearance as from limitations on functional capabilities.

One of my informants noted that the emphasis on the body is particularly costly for gay men with physical disabilities like himself because the body is so central to conceptions of beauty and sexuality in gay male culture.

Not only are men with physical disabilities frequently perceived as undesirable, they are also perceived to be asexual (Zola 1982). While there are exceptions, the sex lives of men with physical disabilities symbolize the passivity and dependency that is pervasive in their lives which contravenes what most men strive for: activity, initiative and control (Murphy 1990).

Like in other arenas of domination, men with physical disabilities act complicit in this one. In the following quote, Billy Golfus (1997: 420), who was disabled due to a motorcycle accident, illustrates the insidiousness of internalizing asexual stereotypes about people with disabilities when he discusses a potential relationship:

Even though she is attractive, I don't really think about her that way partly because the [wheel] chair makes me not even see her and because after so many years of being disabled you quit thinking about it as an option.

The woman in this illustration was as invisible to him as his own sexuality was. This example reveals how deeply some men with physical disabilities internalize hegemonic standards of desirability and sexuality which make them complicit in their own domination.

Similarly, many men with physical disabilities internalize the value associated with hegemonic masculinity that men's sexuality and sexual desirability determine their self-worth as men. Author and cartoonist John Callahan (1990: 121) explained:

I can remember looking at my body with loathing and thinking, Boy, if I ever get to heaven, I'm not going to ask for a new pair of legs like the average quad does. I'm going to ask for a dick I can feel. The idea promoted in rehab of the socially well-adjusted, happily married quad made me sick. This was the cruelest thing of all. Always, I felt humiliated. Surely a man with any self-respect would pull the plug on himself.

The lack of self-esteem in this crucial masculine arena leads men with physical disabilities to withdraw further into the margins as a form of self-protection, as the late sociologist Irving Zola (1982: 215) described: "We do not express or even show our wishes, because we have learned that in our condition of disablement or disfigurement, no one could (or should) find us sexually attractive."

Yet another strategy to deal with one's compromised sexuality is to enact hyper-sexuality as Michael attests:

My sexuality and being able to please my partner... is my most masculine, the thing most endearing to my masculinity... It's

probably the thing I feel most vulnerable about... I think that my compensation for my feelings of vulnerability is I overcompensate and trying to please my partner and leave little room to allow my partner to please me... Some of my greatest pleasure is exhausting my partner, while having sex.

Through his sexual behavior, Michael seeks validation of himself as a man. This is especially important to him because he has internalized the hegemonic standard and feels vulnerable that he will not be able to meet it. Michael's accordance with hegemonic masculinity in this example comes from sacrificing himself and his pleasure while pursuing an unobtainable ideal.

It is hard to be masculine if people restrict the opportunities to earn the recognition as a man. This is the difficulty that men with physical disabilities face in a culture where bodies are a type of social currency. Men's bodies become validated in two key arenas: athletics and sexuality. Due to temporarily-able-bodied people's stigmatization of men with physical disabilities, these arenas of self-expression and self-validation are largely closed to them. This situation further undermines men with physical disabilities' opportunities to establish and maintain satisfactory gender identities and reveals the pervasiveness of the domination they experience from the temporarily-able-bodied.

Independence and Control

Self-reliance is extremely important in the presentation of self to others in social interaction. As Jerry noted, this is especially true for men:

If I ever have to ask someone for help, it really makes me, like, feel like less of a man. I don't like asking for help at all. You know, like even if I could use some I'll usually not ask just because I can't, I just hate asking... [A man is] fairly self-sufficient in that you can sort of handle just about any situation, in that you can help other people, and that you don't need a lot of help.

The independence and control that most men take for granted is compromised for men with physical disabilities due to the response of temporarily-able-bodied people. In cultures like the United States where few accommodations are made for people with disabilities, dependency is synonymous with powerlessness and powerlessness is antithetical to masculinity. Arnold Beisser (1989: 21–2), paralyzed from the neck down and forced to rely on an iron lung after a bout of polio, describes how being dependent undermined his masculinity:

> I had been thrust backward in the developmental scale, and my dependence was now as profound as that of a newborn. Once again I had to deal with all of the overwhelming, degrading conditions of dependency that belong with infancy and childhood—at the same time that I considered myself a mature adult. I did not adjust easily to my new dependence, and despised giving up what I had won years ago in long-forgotten battles. The baby and the man were in conflict.

Through their actions, temporarily-able-bodied people subtly, and at times unconsciously, undermine the independence of men with physical disabilities and replace it with dependency. The following examples illustrate this process and the double-bind in which it places these men. The first example involves Irving Zola (1982: 52) who contracted polio at age 15, which weakened his back and legs. As a consequence, he utilized several braces. He described the change in his status when he took on the role of a wheelchair user in order to do participant observation:

> As soon as I sat in the wheelchair I was no longer seen as a person who could fend for himself. Although Metz had known me for

nine months, and had never before done anything physical for me without asking, now he took over without permission. Suddenly in his eyes I was no longer able to carry things, reach for objects, or even push myself around. Though I was perfectly capable of doing all of these things, I was being wheeled around, and things were brought to me—all without my asking. Most frightening was my own compliance, my alienation from myself and from the process.

Metz had worked closely with Zola and was cognizant of his use of braces and a cane. Interacting with Zola in a wheelchair, however, immediately transformed Metz's sense of Zola's capabilities and initiated a profound change in the status of their relationship. Zola was no longer an independent and accomplished man, but rather a dependent child.

One of my informants, Robert, who has paraplegia, helped explain Zola's compliance when he noted that having people do things you can do for yourself "kind of strips you of your independence. But it's a Catch-22 because a lot of times people do it with good intentions, you know, not recognizing that this guy really wants to [do it] by himself." This double-bind was felt most acutely by Jerry who provided the second example. He noted that his friends were "uncomfortable" about his disability and his use of a wheelchair. "They feel like you need to be sort of helped all the time, even when you don't," he said. This led to an unspoken social contract between he and his friends. When together socially, he would allow them to push him in his wheelchair, thereby making them feel more comfortable in the interaction, and they would in turn, hang around with him. Thus Jerry was forced to make a difficult decision: surrender his independence and remain in the group, or retain his autonomy at the expense of his friendships. Jerry acquiesced to his domination, but, given his lack of alternatives, one can clearly understand why.

These examples reveal the domination and complicity inherent in the social relations between the temporarily-able-bodied and men with physical disabilities. By doing something for men with physical disabilities that they could do for themselves, the temporarily-able-bodied deny these men of a sense of agency, independence, and control. Through this treatment, they infantilize men with disabilities.

In a similar way, the actions of the temporarily-able-bodied make it difficult for men with physical disabilities to control their public gender performance. For instance, Michael noted in his interview that:

> I'm confronted with my disability because someone blocks the curb and then I, um, try and get up over the curb and I end up, you know, not doing it with very much style. I look pretty awkward at it, and I don't like looking awkward, so I have a hard time.

By not being able to control his immediate physical environment, Michael was not able to control his public gender performance. According to the dictates of hegemonic masculinity, Michael should be in control of himself and his image at all times. But the carelessness of the temporarily-able-bodied can quickly and easily undercut these pretensions (Murphy 1990: 121).

Michael reveals the importance of control to many men with physical disabilities' sense of their masculinity in an additional example:

> If I fall in public, it's difficult, if not virtually impossible, for me to get back into my chair and I find it embarrassing. It makes me feel . . . if I am laying on the ground because I can't walk, I feel more disabled that way than I do if I'm just up and about in my chair. I feel crippled.

This helpless and dependent position is antithetical to hegemonic masculinity. To be a cripple, is not to be a man.

Philosopher Susan Wendell (1997: 273) has observed that "dependence on the help of others is humiliating in a society which prizes independence." Yet in U.S. culture, dependency and lack of control are thrust upon men with physical disabilities. Temporarily-able-bodied people infantilize these men through their attitudes and actions. This keeps men with physical disabilities marginalized and subordinated within the gender order.

Confronting Sisyphus: The Denial of Masculinity

When one considers the entire set of impediments: the stigmatization, marginalization, limited economic opportunities, rejection of athleticism, barriers to sexual expression and relations, and obstacles to cherished independence and control, it becomes apparent that the primary way that men with physical disabilities are dominated is through not being recognized or validated as men. As Jerry observed, they are figuratively emasculated: "I think you're not looked upon as much as a, you know, like you're, like I might be a really nice person, but not like a guy per se . . . you're sort of genderless to them." This lack of recognition occurs because the temporarily-able-bodied block access to the crucial arenas of masculine accomplishment.

The lack of recognition makes it difficult for men with physical disabilities to think of themselves as men. Jerry explained:

> I think it [others' definition of what it means to be a man] is very important because if they don't think of you as one, it is hard to think of yourself as one or it really doesn't matter if you think of yourself as one if no one else does . . . You're sort of still a boy even if you think of yourself as a man and you would be a man if you weren't disabled . . . It's so awful if no one else thinks of you as one, even if it doesn't affect how you think of yourself. It limits you so much to what you can do and how others

regard you as opposed to how they regard other people that it makes it hard. It doesn't really matter if you do as much as they do.

Despite Jerry's youth, he had already experienced and clearly understood how others invalidate his masculinity and the masculinity of other men with physical disabilities.

The denial of gender identity leads men with physical disabilities to experience what Robert Murphy (1990) calls embattled identities. They are not perceived as men and they know that they are not women. Yet they inhabit a similar social space, as the following quote illustrates:

> Whoever I was, whatever I had, there was always a sense that I should be grateful to someone for allowing it to happen, for like women, I, a handicapped person, was perceived as dependent on someone else's largesse for my happiness, or on someone else to *let* me achieve it for myself. (Zola 1982: 213)

This gender domination and resulting marginalization make it exceedingly difficult for men with physical disabilities to create and maintain self-satisfactory masculine gender identities. Because of the power of hegemonic masculinity, many men with physical disabilities act as modern day Sisyphi struggling with the social, economic, and physical barriers; the temporarily-able-bodied; and themselves to enact a form of masculinity which is recognized and validated.

Men with physical disabilities respond to their gender domination in a variety of ways. One response is to heed the siren call of hegemonic masculinity and to continually try to prove one's masculinity to oneself and to others. This leads to hyper-masculinity (Gerschick and Miller 1994) as Michael illustrates:

> I had just begun dating again after an eighteen month break while adjusting to being paralyzed. The girl I was dating lived on the second floor of an apartment complex without an elevator. I was so determined to see her and didn't want to ask for help that I tried to wheel myself up the stairs. I knew that it was impossible, but I tried anyway. I had been working out extensively since just after my accident and had good upper body strength. By popping the front wheels of my chair in the air while simultaneously rolling forward. I got up five stairs. It was hard work. By the time I reached the fifth stair, my strength gave out and my chair tipped back and I skidded back down the stairs on the back of my head. My girlfriend heard the noise and found me. I was never so embarrassed in all my life.

By trying to get up the stairs and maintain his independence and control, and thus his masculinity, all the while realizing the futility of it, Michael personified a modern day Sisyphus. As with Sisyphus, he was destined to fail. By taking hegemonic masculinity's demand for independence to an extreme, he resisted the limitations of his disability but he did so in a way that made him complicit with the demands of hegemonic masculinity to a point where he almost killed himself.

Escaping Sisyphus' Fate: Reconstructing Gender Identity

A resistant, and more healthy, response to gender domination comes from distancing oneself from hegemonic masculinity and the expectations of others while redefining masculinity for oneself. Ironically, for men with physical disabilities, being marginalized creates a social space where expectations are reduced, scrutiny is diminished, and there is more latitude for action. In this space counter-hegemonic masculine gender identities can be constructed, performed, and revised with minimum interference from the temporarily-able-bodied. In order for this reconstruction to occur, men with physical disabilities must resist the stigmatization associated with having a disability, change their primary reference group, and reject or redefine the hegemonic standards of career orientation, activeness, physical strength and athleticism, sexual desirability and virility, and independence and control.

Men with physical disabilities tend to internalize the hegemonic standard of career-orientation, however, they resist the labor market and workplace barriers associated with gender dominance. Rather than being governed by the prejudice and discrimination of others, they create work opportunities for themselves. Aaron, for instance, described how he begot his first job after a gunshot accident left him with paraplegia: "[I was] watching television one night and said, Wow! What a great vehicle for educating the public, and changing attitudes. I could do that . . . I think I will do that." The next day he arranged a meeting with a television station manager and convinced him that he should be hired as a reporter who focused on people's abilities, not their disabilities. Aaron later founded a social service agency dedicated to assisting people with disabilities. Three additional informants demonstrated a similar sense of vocation by working in disability-related positions. By defining their occupation for themselves, these men resisted the domination embodied in the prejudice and discrimination that steers others toward work that they would not otherwise do.

There are a variety of strategies that men with physical disabilities use to resist the activity and athletic ideals embodied in hegemonic masculinity. Some of these men reject temporarily-able-bodied persons' perceptions of them as non-athletes. Taub and Greer (1997), for instance, report that their informants did not internalize temporarily-able-bodied people's negative assessments of them because these men looked to alternative reference groups for their recognition. Other men with physical disabilities counter the hegemonic masculine ideal of physical strength and athleticism by rejecting it. Brent noted:

I think that I am probably insolent by the cultural norms that say that manhood is, that physical strength and physical well being is [*sic*] important. But, um, to me I don't think that's what makes me who I am, as how strong I am or how weak I am physically. . . . So physical strength is not, or ability is low down on the scale for me.

Yet others replace physical strength and athleticism with other forms of strength. For instance, Harold focused on his mental acuity: "I think the greatest thing a man can do is to develop his mind and think." Harold's conception of masculinity also privileged mental fortitude:

Strength is a very vague term . . . you can lack physical strength in the power sense or the soldier of fortune sense and you can be very strong in other areas . . . Disabled men can be very, very strong without even being able to, you know, do anything physically active, okay? It's the amount of crap that you can tolerate.

Attention to the mind as a place for demonstrating masculine strength leads to more emphasis on emotional connection to others. For some men with physical disabilities, this connection takes precedence over activity and ability. Brent explained:

Emotionally more than anything else, is the most important. You know, for me that is my measure of who I am as an individual and who I am as a man, is my ability to be able to be honest with my wife, be able to be close with her, to be able to ask for help, provide help, um, to have a commitment, to follow through and to do all those things that I think are important.

The attention to the emotional side of relationships reveals that some men with physical disabilities are incorporating traditional "feminine" characteristics into their counter-hegemonic masculine identities. For instance,

Aaron remarked that, "Manhood today means, um, being responsible for one's actions, being considerate of another's feelings, being sensitive to individuals who are more vulnerable than yourself to what their needs would be."

Resistance to hegemonic masculine sexuality is based on rejecting the ideal standards and replacing them with more realistic ones. Alex, a college student with quadriplegia, exemplifies this:

> There is a part of me that, you know, has been conditioned and acculturated and knows those [hegemonic] values, but my practical experience . . . keeps my common sense in order. You know, . . . because I may have to do something different or non-standard or difficult sexually, I don't think makes me less of a man, or even if I couldn't have sex at all, because I've learned that there's definitely a difference between fucking and making love and that even within the range of sexual behavior, there's a lot of different ways to give a partner that you care about pleasure and to receive pleasure.

While Alex demonstrates a willingness to enact his sexuality in a non-traditional way, his resistance is only successful if he can find a partner who shares his approach. This is possible, but difficult due to the cultural devaluation of men with physical disabilities.

In place of the unobtainable hegemonic demand for independence and control, some men with physical disabilities privilege interdependence and cooperation. Brent, for instance, shared that: "One of the values I have for myself, though, is to be more cooperative and to be able to help and to be helped in turn." This reflects a very different understanding of what it means to be a man.

The ramifications of rejecting the unobtainable ideals embodied in hegemonic masculinity and embracing new ways of performing gender are not limited solely to men with physical disabilities. The gender practices of men with physical disabilities who have developed counter-hegemonic identities provide viable models for new forms of masculinity for all men to practice. As a consequence, the struggles that men with physical disabilities experience have implications for all men regarding their masculinity and all people regarding gender relations.

Conclusion: Sisyphus in a Wheelchair

Returning to the metaphor with which I opened this article, for men with physical disabilities, Sisyphus' mountain represents hegemonic masculinity and his boulder their domination. The exertion of pushing the boulder to the summit represents the struggle that men with physical disabilities experience as they seek to gain recognition of themselves as men within the hostile hegemonic gender order that is largely controlled by the temporarily-able-bodied. Many men with physical disabilities act complicit with this domination and continue their Sisyphean struggle for acceptance according to the hegemonic standards.

There are limits, however, to this metaphor. While Sisyphus's struggle is futile and eternal, men with physical disabilities' exertions need not be. Despite the pervasive dominance that they face, they have an agency that Sisyphus lacks. They have the power to resist this domination. By rejecting hegemonic masculinity, changing their reference groups, and asserting their agency, it is possible for men with physical disabilities largely to escape their gender domination and to construct counter-hegemonic alternatives. In so doing, these men become models for all men who struggle with their masculinity.

NOTES

1. Among those who identify with the Disability Rights Movement, the use of this term acknowledges that almost everyone will experience

a disability before death. The term underscores the similarities between those who currently have a disability and those who are likely to have one in the future. For more on the importance of language in this context, see Zola 1993.

2. Relatively little research has been done comparing the experiences of men and women with disabilities. For accounts of the challenges that women with disabilities face, see Fine and Asch 1988.

3. The type and severity of a person's disability interact with other social characteristics to influence the kind and extent of domination they experience. As a consequence, the domination experienced by men with physical disabilities varies depending on their social class, race and ethnicity, age, and sexual orientation.

4. These are: Beisser 1989; Callahan 1989; Dubus 1992; Fries 1997; Hockenberry 1995; Kovic 1976; Kriegel 1991; Murphy 1990; Puller 1991; and Zola 1982.

5. The key axes of this matrix are race, social class, gender, ethnicity, sexual orientation, age, and ability/disability.

REFERENCES

Altman, Barbara M. and Sharon Barnartt. 1996. "Implications of Variations in Definitions of Disability Used in Policy Analysis: The Case of Labor Force Outcomes." Paper presented at the annual meeting of the Society for Disability Studies, June 13, Washington, DC.

Amott, Teresa and Julie A. Matthaei. 1991. *Race, Gender, and Work: A Multicultural Economic History of Women in the United States.* Boston, MA: Southend.

Beisser, Arnold. 1989. *Flying Without Wings: Personal Reflections on Being Disabled.* New York, NY: Doubleday.

Callahan, John. 1989. *Don't Worry, He Won't Get Far on Foot.* New York, NY: Vintage Books.

Connell, R. W. 1990. "An Iron Man: The Body and Some Contradictions of Hegemonic Masculinity," in *Sport, Men, and the Gender Order,* M. Messner and D. Sabo (eds). Champaign, IL: Human Kinetics, 83–96.

———. 1995. *Masculinities.* Berkeley, CA: University of California Press.

Denzin, Norman. 1989. *The Research Act: A Theoretical Introduction to Sociological Methods.* Englewood Cliffs, NJ: Prentice Hall.

Dubus, Andre. 1992. *Broken Vessels.* Boston, MA: David R. Godine.

Fine, Michelle and Adrienne Asch, (eds). 1988. *Women with Disabilities: Essays in Psychology, Culture, and Politics.* Philadelphia, PA: Temple University Press.

Fries, Kenny. 1997. *Body, Remember.* New York, NY: Dutton.

Gerschick, Thomas J. and Adam S. Miller. 1994. "Gender Identities at the Crossroads of Masculinity and Physical Disability." *Masculinities* 2(1):32–53.

Goffman, Erving. 1963. *Stigma: Notes on the Management of Spoiled Identity.* New York, NY: Simon and Schuster.

———. 1977. "The Arrangement Between the Sexes." *Theory and Society* 4(3):301–31.

Golfus, Billy. 1997. "Sex and the Single Gimp," in *The Disability Studies Reader,* L. J. Davis (ed.). New York: Routledge, 419–28.

Hagan, Kay Leigh. 1993. *Fugitive Information: Essays from a Feminist Hothead.* New York, NY: HarperCollins.

Hahn, Harlan. 1989. "Masculinity and Disability." *Disability Studies Quarterly* 9(1):54–6.

Hill Collins, Patricia. 1990. *Black Feminist Thought.* Boston, MA: Unwin Hyman.

Hockenberry, John. 1995. *Moving Violations: War Zones, Wheelchairs, and Declarations of Independence.* New York, NY: Hyperion.

Janeway, Elizabeth. 1980. *Powers of the Weak.* New York, NY: Alfred A. Knopf.

Kimmel, Michael S. 1994. "Consuming Manhood: The Feminization of American Culture and the Recreation of the Male Body, 1832–1920," in *The Male Body,* L. Goldstein (ed.). Ann Arbor, MI: The University of Michigan Press, 12–41.

Kovic, Ron. 1976. *Born on the Fourth of July.* New York, NY: Pocket Books.

Kriegel, Leonard. 1991. *Falling into Life.* San Francisco, CA: North Point Press.

Levine, Martin P. 1992. "The Status of Gay Men in the Workplace," in *Men's Lives,* 2nd ed., M. S. Kimmel and M. Messner (eds). New York, NY: Macmillan, 251–66.

McNeil, John M. 1993. *Americans with Disabilities 1991–92*. U.S. Bureau of the Census. Current Population Reports, P70–33. Washington, DC: U.S. Government Printing Office.

Messner, Michael A. 1992. *Power at Play: Sports and the Problem of Masculinity*. Boston, MA: Beacon Press.

Murphy, Robert F. 1990. *The Body Silent*. New York, NY: Norton.

Newby, Robert. 1992. "Review Symposium: Black Feminist Thought." *Gender and Society* 6(3): 508–11.

Puller, Lewis B. Jr. 1991. *Fortunate Son*. New York, NY: Bantam.

Shapiro, Joseph P. 1993. *No Pity: People with Disabilities Forging a New Civil Rights Movement*. New York, NY: Random House.

Taub, Diane E. and Kimberly R. Greer. 1997. "Sociology of Acceptance Revisited: Males with Physical Disabilities Participating in Sport and Physical Fitness Activity." Paper presented at the annual meeting of the Midwest Sociological Society, April 4, Des Moines, IA.

Wendell, Susan. 1997. "Toward a Feminist Theory of Disability," in *The Disability Studies Reader*, L. J. Davis (ed.). New York, NY: Routledge, 260–78.

West, Candace and Don H. Zimmerman. 1987. "Doing Gender." *Gender and Society* 1(2): 125–51.

Zola, Irving Kenneth. 1982. *Missing Pieces: A Chronicle of Living with a Disability*. Philadelphia, PA: Temple University Press.

———. 1993. "Self, Identity, and the Naming Question: Reflections on the Language of Disability," in *Perspectives on Disability*, 2nd ed., M. Nagler (ed.). Palo Alto, CA: Health Markets Research, 15–23.

THINKING ABOUT THE READING

Whether we're physically disabled or not, all of us have to "do gender." What are some of the culturally valued gender expectations women must live up to when they "do gender?" How might these expectations be affected by physical disabilities? In other words, is being in a wheelchair a threat to femininity in the same way that it's a threat to masculinity? Is it possible to disagree with these gender expectations and still act in ways that perpetuate them? This article illustrates one way in which the body is used as a form of self-presentation. Think of various messages conveyed by the body and how we work to shape this aspect of our identity. How important are the reactions of those around you in your efforts to shape a physical presentation that conforms to gender expectations? What are some ways in which men can enact "counter-hegemonic masculinities?" Are some of these techniques more or less culturally acceptable than others? Why?

Building Image:
The Presentation of Self

A significant portion of social life is influenced by the images we form of others. We typically form impressions of people based on an initial assessment of their social group membership (race, age, gender, and so on), their personal attributes (for example, physical attractiveness), and the verbal and nonverbal messages they provide. Such assessments are usually accompanied by a set of expectations we've learned to associate with members of certain social groups or people with certain attributes. Such judgments allow us to place people in broad categories and provide a degree of predictability to forthcoming interactions.

But while we are gathering information about others to form impressions of them, we are fully aware that they are doing the same thing with us. Early in life, most of us learn that it is to our advantage to have people think highly of us. Hence, through a process called *impression management*, we attempt to control and manipulate information about ourselves to influence the impressions others form of us. Impression management provides the link between the way we perceive ourselves and the way we want others to perceive us. We've all been in situations—a first date, a job interview, meeting a girlfriend's or boyfriend's family for the first time—in which we've felt compelled to "make a good impression." What we often fail to realize, however, is that personal impression management can often be influenced by larger organizational and institutional forces.

In "Frederick the Great or Frederick's of Hollywood?" sociologist Melissa S. Herbert shows us how impression management in some institutional settings is made especially difficult by conflicting expectations. She draws from her research interviews to explore the different impression management strategies of women in the military. These women are under constant pressure to present themselves as tough women who are capable of doing work that has been traditionally considered a "man's job." They must be able to prove to their fellow soldiers that they are up to the task and can be counted on in life-or-death situations. At the same time, they must take care to maintain the impression that they are still feminine. Military women use a variety of strategies to manage this double-bind, although their choice of strategy can have important implications regarding the perpetuation of gender stereotypes.

Sometimes our very survival requires astute impression management. In their article, "Suspended Identity," Thomas Schmid and Richard S. Jones show that whereas people are sometimes motivated to present an image of themselves as likable and sophisticated, other times identity transformations require more drastic impression management techniques. Through participant observation in a maximum security prison—one of the researchers was an inmate serving a year-long felony sentence—the authors show how inmates must suspend their preprison identities and construct an inauthentic and often fearsome prison identity to survive the rigors of prison life. Most inmates discover that they can never fully recover their preprison identity upon release. They cannot return to being the same person they were before imprisonment. Here, too, we see how institutional demands can dictate the types of impressions we want others to form of us.

Would you voluntarily place a camera in your home and invite strangers to view your most private daily (and nightly) activities? This is one of the questions raised in the article by Donald Snyder's "Webcam Women: Life on Your Screen." Snyder describes the live webcam sites of three women and discusses their varied reasons for displaying their intimate lives to strangers. This brief article brings up many questions about identity, performance and the relationship between individuals and their audiences.

Frederick the Great or Frederick's of Hollywood?

The Accomplishment of Gender Among Women in the Military

Melissa S. Herbert

(1998)

Introduction

In an article on military culture, Karen Dunivin writes, "the combat, masculine-warrior paradigm is the essence of military culture" (1994: 534). For military women, this may pose something of a contradiction. Women are often expected, by virtue of the perceived relationship between sex and gender, to display societal norms of femininity. What is expected when women fill an occupational role whose defining characteristics are inexorably linked with masculinity? While these women, by virtue of being in the military, fill a masculine work-role, it is quite possible that they are also penalized for being "too masculine," or, in essence, violating the societal expectations that they maintain some degree of femininity.

Masculinity in military men is not only rewarded, but is the primary construct around which resocialization as a soldier takes place. It is not surprising that femininity, or characteristics believed to be associated with femininity, would be discouraged. On the other hand, the military, reflecting the broader society, may find that women's femininity serves "to validate male identity and both individual and collective male power" (Lenskyj 1986: 56). This is, I believe, illustrated by the recently abandoned Marine Corps policy of requiring female Marines to undergo make-up and etiquette training and in current regulations that require women's hair not be cut "so short as to appear masculine." Additionally, the military is highly traditional, primarily conservative, institution in which we may expect the expression, "men are men and women are women" to be taken seriously. Exactly how are women in the military supposed to "be women?". . .

Perceptions of women and their "fit" with what is believed to be gender appropriate may be critical to the ability of women to become accepted as members of the military. The integration of women into an institution *defined* by its association with masculinity may pose an interesting dilemma for military women. Can one truly be a soldier[1] and a woman and not be viewed as deviating either from what it means to be a soldier, or from what it means to be a woman? I can recall being asked by a fellow soldier why I, and other women, didn't "dress up" when we were off duty. It struck me then, as it does now, that we were expected to do our jobs "like the men," and transform "into women" once we removed our flak jackets and helmets and turned in our rifles and ammunition. One respondent spoke to these contradictions when, addressing men's perceptions, she wrote, "If you're too feminine, then you're not strong enough to command respect and lead men into battle, but if you're strong and aggressive you're not being a woman."

Those in the military, but particularly women, must "do gender." In their article,

"Doing Gender," West and Zimmerman argue that gender is "a routine accomplishment embedded in everyday interaction" (1987: 125).... Gender is "the local management of conduct in relation to normative conceptions of appropriate attitudes and activities for particular sex categories" (West and Fenstermaker 1993: 156). Although women in the military are clearly recognized as women, that is, as belonging to both the female sex (i.e., physiologically female) and female sex category (i.e., perceived as physiologically female; what others might call gender), given their role as members of the military, these women must constantly create and manage their gendered identities. While all women must do so, it should be noted that men also "do gender," on a daily basis. As Ronnie Steinberg notes, men "actively recreate their dominance every day" (1992: 576).

The military, I believe, is a particularly good site in which to examine the "everyday" ways in which women negotiate a world in which they must simultaneously be recognized and accepted as women, but must perform a job that has been perceived by many as appropriate only for men. Not only has the "soldier" been constructed, both ideologically and historically, as male, but soldiering has been the very means by which men have "become" men. Thus, the masculinity of soldiering is not "just" masculinity, but hypermasculinity.... While women and men throughout society must "do gender," the increased salience of gender within the military makes it possible that it may be even more true within that setting, at least with regard to traditional conceptions of gender.

... [In this article I focus on the interactional processes related to the performance of gender in institutional settings.] "Interaction between individuals and groups is the medium for much institutional functioning, for decision making and image production" (Acker 1992: 568). It is through this process

that gender is created and re-created. Goffman, addressing the "interactional field" and the interactions themselves, argues that "these scenes do not so much allow for the expression of natural differences between the sexes as for the production of that difference itself" (1977: 324). Gender is not accomplished solely on the basis of specific actions (e.g., wearing a skirt instead of pants), but it requires that interactions occur in which the action is recognized as placing the actor in a particular gendered context. West and Zimmerman write:

> While it is individuals who do gender, the enterprise is fundamentally interactional and institutional in character, for accountability is a feature of social relationships and its idiom is drawn from the institutionalized arena in which those relationships are enacted (1987: 136–137).

... West and Zimmerman (1987) pose three central questions: "If, for example, individuals strive to achieve gender in encounters with others, how does a culture instill the need to achieve it? What is the relationship between the production of gender at the level of interaction and such institutional arrangements as the division of labor in society? And, perhaps most important, how does doing gender contribute to the subordination of women by men?" (140). In this [article] I respond to these questions by examining the place of gender in the lives of women in the United States military....

Methodology

The findings in this paper are based on 256 surveys collected from women who are veterans of, or currently serving in, the United States military. I used a variety of avenues to identify potential respondents including posting notices at women's bookstores, gay and lesbian community centers, on computer bulletin boards, in publications such as *Minerva's Bulletin Board, The Register* (the newsletter of the Women in Military Service for America Project), and at college and university veterans' program offices around the nation. The 15-page questionnaire contained seven sections with items in formats varying among yes/no questions, multiple choice questions, open-ended questions, check off items, and Likert-scale items. Each section has a different focus. The sections of the questionnaire assess the following: (1) personal information, (2) military service, (3) education, (4) personal assessment of military service, (5) personal resources, (6) gender, and (7) sexuality. The surveys were used to create a computerized data set as well as text files of the answers to open-ended questions. I should note that my own military service formed the basis for many of the questions. Though my experience is limited to the Army, I was able to formulate questions about uniforms, on-post and off-post activities, chain of command, etc., on the basis of not only familiarity with scholarship on women in the military, but with the aid of 15 years experience in both the active and reserve components of the U.S. Army as both enlisted and officer.

The women who answered the survey came from over 40 states, all branches, all ranks except flag officer (i.e., General/Admiral), and served as early as the 1950s. . . .

The survey asked respondents to indicate whether they believed that penalties exist for women who are perceived as "too feminine." In a separate question, it asked whether they believe that penalties exist for women who are perceived as "too masculine" and to provide examples of what the penalties might be. The results presented here are based on descriptive statistics and analyses of the open-ended responses about types of penalties.

The survey also included a list of 28 behaviors. Respondents were asked to "check any of the following that you believe applied to

yourself" (while on active duty). These items consisted of behaviors such as polishing one's fingernails, wearing cologne on duty, keeping one's hair trimmed above the collar, socializing with the men in the unit, and so on. Respondents were then asked, "Do you believe that any of those behaviors checked . . . were part of a conscious attempt to insure that others perceived you as feminine?" The survey also asked, "Do you believe that any of those behaviors checked . . . were part of a conscious attempt to insure that others perceived you as masculine?"

Respondents were asked the question: "Are there other things that you did that you believe were a conscious attempt to insure that others perceived you as feminine/masculine?" This question was included in the survey because it was impossible to identify a list of all possible strategies. Answers to questions, both closed-ended and open-ended, illuminate how women strategize about gender.

By examining if and/or how military women believe that gender is policed and what they do in response, we can begin to understand how women engage in the accomplishment of gender as opposed to simply "being" feminine or masculine. By "policed," I mean that their behaviors are monitored or censured by other members of the military, female and male and at all levels, to insure that women are not seen as violating norms of gender appropriateness. The strategies that women employ are both interactional and internal. . . . The strategies are interactional in that their existence, and perpetuation, is dependent upon the response that the individual receives from others. And, they are internal in that, to some degree, they become incorporated into the persona of the person deploying them.

. . . In this research . . . I wanted to see if women would recognize and acknowledge their consciously engaging in strategies to manage gender.

Perceptions of Femininity

Do women believe that they are penalized for being perceived as "too feminine" or "too masculine?" Findings indicate that there is very little latitude for women when it comes to perceptions of gender. Sixty-four percent believe there are penalties for being perceived as "too feminine," while 60 percent of respondents indicate that they believe there are penalties for being perceived as "too masculine." . . .

Those women who believed there are penalties were asked to describe what they believed such penalties to be. One-hundred and sixty-five women described penalties for femininity. One hundred and fifty-seven described penalties for masculinity. Rather than starting with expected categories and coding the answers for whether or not they "fit" a particular category, I conducted a content analysis on the responses to see what categories emerged. Some answers could be coded into more than one category, as some respondents provided numerous examples, sometimes just listing words (e.g., "being perceived as an airhead, bimbo, or slut"). . . .

Though the penalties for femininity were quite varied, six common themes emerged: (1) ostracism or disapproval from other women, (2) being viewed as a slut or sexually available, (3) being perceived as weak, (4) being perceived as incompetent or incapable, (5) not being taken seriously, and (6) career limitations. While some of these categories overlap and might even be perceived as one and the same (e.g., weak vs. incompetent), the specific words were used enough, and often within the same response, that it seemed as though they had different meanings for the respondents and should be coded accordingly.

The first five penalties are related to the sixth, and most frequently mentioned penalty: that of career limitations. This is true almost by definition, in that if there were no potentially negative impact on one's performance or career aspirations, one might question the way in which a given situation constituted a penalty. It is difficult to think of a situation in which a woman is penalized that does not carry with it the potential to damage one's work relationships and/or career.

"Career limitations" is actually a catch-all phrase for a number of career penalties. As illustrated by the respondents, they include, but are certainly not limited to, obvious limitations such as not being allowed to perform the job for which one was trained, not being promoted, not sent to a school needed for promotion, not getting choice assignments, etc. One woman wrote, "They are not assigned to 'career building' areas such as pilots, maintenance, security police—the generally thought of 'male jobs.'" Another woman wrote:

> I was a long haired blonde, outstanding figure, long beautiful nails (my own!) etc., etc. I was constantly told I couldn't do my job (working on aircraft) as I was a dumb blonde, I'd get my nails dirty, I was a danger to the guys working on aircraft because I distracted them, etc., etc. My first rating was not a favorable one even though I scored higher on the OJT [on-the-job-training] tests than anyone had ever scored in that shop!

Another indicated that "you don't get the tough jobs you need to be in good shape for promotion, and women who are too feminine usually get ignored or put in office jobs with no troops." Command positions, leading troops, are critical to the promotion of those in the officer ranks. Many women mentioned the penalty of being "removed from position[s] of authority and placed in somebody's office," or being "given more feminine jobs to do." Command positions are definitely not considered "feminine." One woman expressed her opinion on this issue:

It is a great privilege as an officer to be in a command position. Part of being a commander is having a "command presence." I greatly doubt that women who wear lots of perfume, make-up, speak softly, and/or make strong efforts to appear feminine are considered frequently as serious contenders for command positions.

The categories of penalties clearly overlap. Especially in a military that "has no place for weakness," it is difficult to discuss attributions of weakness without discussing incompetence as well. It is difficult to discuss perceptions of incompetence without noting its relationship to not being taken seriously and suffering career limitations. In sum, while about one-quarter of the respondents mentioned career limitations explicitly ("Not selected for schools, promotion."), virtually all the penalties discussed are related, whether directly or indirectly, to the ability of women to be treated equally with men and, therefore, to achieve the same degree of success as their male counterparts. While the penalties for being perceived as too feminine are varied, they do share a common theme. Whether at the informal (e.g., perceived as a slut by other members of the unit) or formal level (e.g., not selected to attend leadership training), each of these penalties serves as a mechanism for insuring that women remain "outsiders" to the boys' club of the military.

Perceptions of Masculinity

If women who are perceived as too feminine experience penalties, what happens to those women who are perceived as too masculine? Are they polar opposites on some scale of acceptability? One might argue that the best mechanism for combating penalties for being too feminine is to insure that one is perceived as masculine. Examination of the data reveals that this is not the case.

Of the 157 women who described the penalties for being perceived as too masculine,

over half indicated that such women would be labeled as lesbians. There were a number of responses that seemed as though that was what was being inferred, but because it wasn't stated explicitly I opted for a conservative approach and did not code them as such. Consider these examples: "Comments," "Many lewd remarks were made about 'masculine' type women," "I think they may have to prove themselves more especially if not married," and "'Too masculine' tends to be equated with 'man hating.'" If descriptions of this type were included, about two-thirds of the responses could be considered to address lesbianism.

Although the label "lesbian" emerges as a single category of penalty, it is illustrative to look at the different ways in which the issue is addressed. In many cases women stated very plainly, "Perceived as being a lesbian," "Perceived as lesbians," "Lesbo, dyke, etc.— Need I say more!" In other cases their descriptions were much more colorful or detailed. Consider the following description:

> Being teased by other service members... called "butch," "bitch," "dyke," a lesbian. If a female can't be told apart visually, at first glance, from a male she *will* be subjected to being called sir vs. ma'am and may be kicked out of a few female restrooms, at first glance.[2]

A number of respondents, as was the case when a woman is perceived as too feminine, indicated that penalties also came from other women. One woman wrote:

> If you go past gender neutral (the "ideal" woman officer), past masculine (conspicuous), to too masculine, you were courting being labeled a lesbian. Too masculine made men and women nervous. Me, too.

Another indicated that "they are often avoided by both male and female soldiers. They are the outcasts of the unit."

One of the most revealing findings regarding the penalty of being labeled a lesbian is the understanding that this label was often applied to women regardless of sexual orientation. This fact serves as a wonderful illustration of the way in which homophobia and perceptions of sexual orientation serve as mechanisms for the subjugation of all women. "I believe they are labeled as homosexuals, 'dykes,' whether they are or not." "Of course, they are tagged or stereotyped as lesbians, whether they are or not." The impact of such allegations can extend well beyond having to tolerate "talk." As one woman writes:

> One of the women in the unit who had a masculine appearance was accused of being a lesbian even though she wasn't. When her time was up she got out because of the accusations she was gay. She was a good soldier.

Being labeled a lesbian was the only category that clearly emerged from a content analysis of these items. Some answers occurred more frequently than others, but none so much as the penalty of being labeled a lesbian. Other penalties that respondents described included: (1) ostracism and ridicule and, (2) career limitations. Though they each constituted only about 10 percent of the descriptions, in these "non-sexualized" instances women are receiving social and career penalties for exhibiting behavior that is highly desirable in male soldiers. It is critical to understand that women are being penalized for exhibiting gendered behaviors that are consistent with the work-role of "soldier."

Bearing in mind that I am talking about the military, consider this description of how, and for what, women are penalized. "Women who were seen as too aggressive—too much focus on aggressive or violent activities were not seen as 'normal' or to be 'trusted.'" Exhibiting interests in activities that many would agree form the core of military ideology (i.e., aggression and violence) results in the

penalty of not being considered "normal" or "trustworthy." Another respondent indicated the "women were discouraged from being aggressive, displaying leadership skills, being self-assured and independent."

The ostracism that women describe is often, but not always, linked to the subject of lesbianism. While some women offered comments such as, "They are shunned, called names (e.g., dyke)," others were less specific in their remarks. "Rejected by both male and female peers," or "A woman who appears too masculine may be ridiculed for it." One woman wrote, "Yeah, everybody hates them." Whether explicitly related to sexual orientation or not, it seems apparent that women who violate gender norms of femininity are "outsiders" to the same degree, albeit in a different fashion, as are women who violate the masculine work-role of the military by being too feminine.

By understanding that women receive career penalties for being perceived as too masculine, as well as too feminine, we begin to understand the degree to which women are required to walk a fine line. One woman's comments capture this contradiction beautifully:

> [I] knew a female airman [sic] who could do her job on the flight line better than most of the guys in her unit. This convinced some people she was a "dyke"—just had to be a lesbian otherwise she wouldn't have been so good at a "man's job."

Although cast in the light of sexual orientation, such a description illustrates the difficulties women face when simply trying to do the job for which they were recruited. Another wrote:

> A female commander who does the exact same discipline as a male commander is probably seen as a bitch on a power trip. You're derided and not respected for playing tough by the rules. . . .You play by their rules but then you

lose because they didn't consider you part of their game.

In other instances, the examples described specific career penalties such as "not selected for 'high profile' jobs," "poor evaluations or less than deserved marks," and "overlooked for awards/promotions." As one woman described, "I believe it can affect performance reviews, assignments, and coaching or counseling which is provided for developmental growth." While the cynic might argue that women "just have to tough it out," it is clear that there are plenty of formal mechanisms by which women can be penalized if they are perceived as gender deviant, regardless of the direction of the alleged deviance. What, then, do women do?

Conscious Strategies— Femininity

. . . Forty-one percent, or close to half, of the sample indicated that they engaged in some form of gender management, or strategizing. . . .

Of those respondents who indicated employing strategies to be perceived as feminine, at least one-third chose each of the following strategies: wearing make-up on duty (40 percent), wearing long hair (38 percent), wearing earrings while in uniform when permitted (37 percent) (this figure may have been even higher if women had always been permitted to wear earrings; it was only in the 1980s that women were granted permission to wear earrings with certain dress uniforms), wearing cologne or perfume (35 percent), and wearing make-up off duty (34 percent). Slightly less than one-third indicated that they wore pumps instead of flat shoes (low quarters) with the dress uniform (32 percent) and that they wore skirt uniforms instead of pants uniforms (28 percent) as strategies to be perceived as feminine. The fact that these items focus on clothing is

primarily a function of the choices that were provided in the survey.

One of the most interesting aspects of clothing as a strategy for being perceived as feminine was the *way* in which clothing was often worn. This is of interest not only because it goes beyond the issue of clothing *choice*, but because the way in which an item was worn was often in violation of the regulations. Consider the following examples of strategies that women described: "My uniform skirt was always too short," "[I] did not wear a t-shirt under fatigues," and "I wore my BDU cap and Class A cap way back on my head to look more like a female." Such violations could lead to formal punishment, such as receiving a counseling statement, or to informal punishment, such as being the subject of negative comments. In my military experience, women were frequently ridiculed for not wearing their uniforms properly. Such women were viewed as not being serious soldiers and as being more concerned about their appearance than doing their job. Thus, women may highlight femininity as a means of being viewed more favorably, but to do so they may choose a strategy that has negative repercussions as well.

Women not only strategize with props such as clothing, jewelry, and make-up, but they also used their bodies to highlight femininity. One example of this is seen in the closed-ended item regarding hair length. As indicated above, 38 percent of those who indicated strategizing said that they wore their hair long as a strategy for being perceived as feminine. In the open-ended question, others referred to hair styling in general: "I tried to keep my hair in a feminine style that suited me. This involved getting a perm every 3–4 months."

Another strategy was the intentional avoidance of swearing. One woman wrote that she "never used bad language like many other women in [the] military do," while another wrote that she simply, "did not swear much." Other strategies that appeared repeatedly included home and office décor ("Flowers on my desk, my Noritake coffee cup, and picture frames on my desk"), and watching one's weight ("I kept a close watch on my weight because I was under the false assumption that 'thinness' and feminine were related"). In sum, conscious manipulation of one's appearance and engaging in behaviors traditionally marked as "female" were common strategies for managing the perceptions others had about one's status as feminine.

All of the strategies discussed thus far focus on appearance, personal space, and personal habits. None of these strategies are particularly surprising, nor can most immediately be labeled as detrimental to one's physical or emotional well-being. The same cannot be said of the last group of strategies.

It is evident from the data that both men and women not only shape ideas of femininity, but also mete out the penalties for gender violations. While men were not surveyed or interviewed, the women gave many examples of how both women and men let women know when they were seen as deviating from accepted norms of gender. Most strategies, while influenced by others, were engaged in on an individual basis. That is, they did not involve the active participation of another individual, but could be accomplished alone (e.g., wearing make-up or a knife). In the last group of strategies addressing femininity, discussed below, men play a key role. These strategies are those in which women intentionally engaged in social or sexual relations with men.

The closed-ended question revealed that anywhere from 6 to 10 percent of those who strategized either socialized with the men in their units (seven percent), dated men in their units (11 percent), or married while on active duty (six percent) as a conscious attempt to be perceived as feminine. Four percent indicated that, as a strategy for being perceived as feminine, when they had a boyfriend they "made

sure people knew it." These numbers may seem inconsequential until we realize that this means that people are intentionally engaging in personal relationships as strategies for altering or enhancing the perceptions that others have of them.

One woman wrote, "I believe I did a little 'indiscriminate' dating, more than I should have, maybe to feel more feminine." Another "Made up stories re: boyfriends, [heterosexual] sex, dates; even slept with man/men (when I was drunk) to cover for myself and the company." One woman said that she "tried to date civilian men," while another said, "I felt that I *had* to have a boyfriend." The relationship between femininity and heterosexuality is a key element to understanding why such social and sexual relations with men would serve as strategies. As one woman said, "I mostly made conscious attempts to appear heterosexual v. feminine." Another woman answered, "Hanging around with nothing but males and having sex with them to prove I wasn't a lesbian." Because of the obvious link to displays of heterosexuality, it is worth noting at this point that there was an entirely separate question, not analyzed here, about strategies to avoid being perceived as lesbian. The responses provided here are specifically in response to the question about being perceived as feminine. This is powerful evidence of the link between the ways gender and sexuality have been constructed.

Conscious Strategies— Masculinity

Although a majority of women who strategized did so toward femininity, this was not true for everyone. Twelve percent of those who employed strategies aimed some or all of their efforts at masculinity. Seventy-four percent of the respondents who indicated employing at least one masculine strategy said they wanted to be considered "one of the guys." Forty-one percent said that they "socialized with men" in their unit as a strategy. Thirty-one percent wore pants uniforms rather than skirt uniforms as a strategy and 30 percent indicated that their preference for work uniforms (e.g., camouflage uniforms) to dress uniforms was a strategy for being perceived as more masculine. Thus, clothing was also a strategy for being perceived as masculine, but not nearly as frequently as it was a strategy for being perceived as feminine. Clearly, being seen as "one of the guys" and/or socializing with men were key strategies for women wishing to be perceived as masculine.

Analysis of the open-ended items revealed strategies similar to those above. The four main strategies identified in the qualitative data are: swearing, drinking, working out, and doing other "guy things." In the findings concerning feminine strategies we saw that avoidance of swearing was considered by some to be a strategy for being perceived as feminine. In the results presented here we see the opposite approach. In answer to the open-ended question about strategies, one woman wrote, "My favorite cuss word is 'shit.' I cussed when I wanted to make a point." Other examples include: "Started cursing," "Swearing," "Perhaps a bit cruder, earthier way of talking," "Talk nasty like guys, swear and stuff," "Use foul language to the extent men did," and "Used profanity when around men." Clearly, the expression "the mouth of a sailor" held some meaning for these women, as a number of them put the cliché to work.

A number of women indicated that drinking also served as a strategy. One woman said that she drank more than she should have. Another said, "Drinking with the guys—trying to keep up." One woman, however, did not acknowledge employing strategies, but then wrote, "Maybe—I tried beer because all of the guys were drinking it." Yet another mentioned "the amount of substance abuse" as a strategy

for being perceived as masculine. As one woman wrote, "Foul language, smoking, drinking, joking—I am undeniably feminine—but I tried in many ways to 'compensate' (unfortunately)." While not all would agree, many would argue that swearing and drinking are more acceptable in men, relative to women, especially in the military.[3] Thus, it is not surprising that if women wished to emphasize masculinity, they would seize on these "available" behaviors as strategies for doing so.

A third strategy described by respondents was "working out" or concentrating on physical fitness. In the military, especially in recent years, we would expect this to be a "positive" strategy because of the military's emphasis on physical fitness. Additionally, if feminine women are perceived as weak, then it makes sense that some women might try to ensure that they are perceived as physically fit. As one woman described, "I made sure that I was physically fit to avoid being perceived as a weak female." Another wrote, "[I] Thought many other women were weak and pathetic. Made sure I was *very strong* physically." Several made specific mention of training in weight lifting, a stereotypically masculine mode of working out.

In a related vein, a number of women mentioned not allowing co-workers to help them with physical tasks. Typical responses included: "Not asking assistance of others when lifting heavy things" and [I] "lifted heavier things on the job than I should have." Another wrote:

> I did not let others (men) help me, unless a job normally required 2 people, and the guy was *assigned* to work with me. I only asked other women to help me, or went to great lengths to use leverage and improvise.

Demonstration of physical strength, whether through physical development or task accomplishment, is apparently one mechanism by which women try to be perceived as masculine and, as such, to fit in.

Though the last decade has led to significant change in this arena, the strategy of "working out," especially weight lifting, is viewed by some as "doing guy things." Some would say the same of swearing and drinking. If this weren't the case then it is unlikely that these would be identified as strategies for being perceived as masculine. Yet, the frequency with which these behaviors were mentioned warranted their being considered separate categories. The fourth strategy, "doing guy things," is distinct. Women mentioned a variety of behaviors, apart from those discussed above, that they exhibited as a means of being perceived as masculine. In some cases, these were specific behaviors (e.g., "learned to scuba and skydive"); in others they were general statements (e.g., "Go out with the guys and do the types of things they like to do"). The following comments illustrate these findings: "I drove a Pinto station wagon with a tool box in the back. I did my own oil changes." "Talked about stuff I did as a civilian—played in rock band, rode motorcycle, etc." "Auto hobby shop—fixed guys' cars—took flying lessons and mechanics with the guys." Again, certain behaviors, hobbies, etc., are culturally defined as masculine. If participation in these events is readily available then it is understandable that they would be part of the behavioral repertoire of those women who wish to be perceived as masculine.

"Demeanor" is another strategy of "doing guy things." One woman discussed "using the language and mannerisms of men," while another said she "became more assertive/aggressive." One woman said she "learned to be aggressive when necessary," while another said, "High assertiveness; low exhibited emotionality." As one woman described it, "Developed a tougher attitude and tried to hide my softer side at work."

Related to the strategy of "doing guy things" was the strategy of *not* doing "female things." One woman "attempted to downplay feminine 'traits' such as gossiping, flowers on desk, being emotional" while another wrote:

> Whenever I deployed, I reduced my attachment to "feminine" stuff; no contacts, no make-up, no complaints if I couldn't shower/wash hair, no perfume—made fun of women who continued these trappings while deployed.

In some instances, and as would be the case with some weight lifters, such behaviors involved physical change. One woman said, "I didn't wear make-up, I never swayed my hips, I strode along." Another said, "I kept my fingernails short and never polished them!" To some degree, the absence of the feminine may be seen, by default, as an approximation of the masculine. . . .

Results show that the types of strategies employed by women seeking to manage gender are numerous and diverse. Whether one is trying to be perceived as feminine or masculine there is an available repertoire of strategies from which one may choose. As I have shown, close to half of the women in this sample acknowledge the employment of strategies to manage gender. While most opt toward femininity, some do strategize toward masculinity. . . .

Doing Gender/Doing Sexuality

The first question posed by West and Zimmerman addressed the question of how a culture instills the need to achieve gender. . . . By establishing ideas about what is essentially female or male, what is "normal" or "natural" the culture instills within us a need to maintain these gendered identities. That is, we must continually create and recreate our identities as gendered beings.

I believe that this analysis is accurate, but fails to consider another important mechanism for insuring that we feel compelled to engage in the active accomplishment of gender. I argue that the link between gender and sexuality also serves to reinforce our need to "do gender." There are at least two ways in which sexuality functions to reinforce our need to do gender. First, notions of what types of sexual behavior are appropriate are used to insure that women work to be seen as "good women." For example, a woman who does not want to be viewed as a "whore," or a "tramp," must modify her appearance, and possibly demeanor, so that she fits "acceptable" ideas of how a "good woman" looks or acts. Similarly, men who have a certain "look" are assumed to possess, or not posses, a degree of sexual prowess. And, sexuality is viewed as being composed of the good vs. the bad. If all sexuality were viewed positively, there would be no negative connotations to labels such as whore or tramp. Homosexuality would not be viewed as bad; homophobia would not exist. If there were nothing "wrong" with being labeled a whore or a lesbian the labels would not be threatening.

Second, perceptions of gender are used to make assessments of one's sexual orientation. In women, femininity implies heterosexuality, masculinity implies homosexuality. And conversely, a woman known to be a lesbian may be assumed to possess more masculine traits than her heterosexual counterpart. Thus, perceptions about gender are used to make inferences about sexuality, and vice versa. This research provides ample evidence for the way that "masculinity" is used to "determine" that a woman is a lesbian.

Our culture instills the need to achieve gender not only by creating a sense of the "natural" or the "normal," but also by threatening social actors with penalties for violating prescribed notions of acceptable gendered behavior and acceptable sexual behavior. By linking the two together, we insure that violations in either arena result in penalties. Specifically, and because gendered behaviors are the more visible, the threat of being labeled sexually

deviant may function to insure that we "do gender" in the appropriate fashion. That is, women enact femininity, and men enact masculinity. West and Fenstermaker make clear that "doing gender does not always mean living up to normative conceptions of femininity or masculinity" (1993: 157). But, they also note that "To the extent that members of society know their actions are accountable, they will design their actions in relation to how they might be seen and described by others" (1993: 157). They write:

> First, and perhaps most important, conceiving of gender as an ongoing accomplishment, accountable to interaction, implies that we must locate its emergence in *social situations*, rather than within the individual or some ill-defined set of role expectations. . . . What it involves is crafting conduct that can be evaluated in relation to normative conceptions of manly and womanly natures (Fenstermaker and Berk 1985, p. 203), and assessing conduct in light of those conceptions—given the situation at hand (West and Zimmerman 1987, p. 139–140). (157)

Thus, it is not simply that women, for example, seek to enact femininity because it is expected of them, but also that situations call for such enactment. The social situation in which femininity serves as an indicator of heterosexuality can only compel one to enact femininity if there is some reason to want to insure that one is perceived to be heterosexual. Sociocultural attitudes toward homosexuality function to insure that this is the case. But, some situations are especially strongly marked, or call more strongly for gendered behavior. The military is one such situation.

The ban on lesbians, gay men, and bisexuals exacerbates this situation even further. As of this writing, military policy "allows" lesbians, gay men, and bisexuals to serve as long as they "don't tell." This, of course, requires that lesbians in the military do what they can to mask all potential "markers" of homosexuality. While the policymakers claim that they would not "ask" about sexual orientation and service-members could "be" homosexual as long as they didn't "tell" the military has not upheld their end of the bargain. People continue to be harassed, investigated, and discharged for being lesbian, gay, or bisexual. While there are many instances outside the military where this is so, there are few, if any, places where federal law supports such discrimination. Federal law may not *protect* civilians, but neither does it compel an employer to fire them if it is discovered that they are lesbian, gay, or bisexual.

As was addressed earlier, to be perceived as masculine may result in one being labeled a lesbian. Not only may women be "shunned," or lose the respect of their peers, but the institutional requirement that lesbians be discharged may result in investigation and, ultimately, discharge. One way of avoiding such charges is to insure that one is perceived as feminine, and thus, heterosexual. While I would not argue that this is the sole explanation for women enacting femininity, I do believe that it is a significant factor. As a number of women indicated, it was more important to be perceived as heterosexual than feminine, but the latter helps insure the former. Remember, one woman wrote, "I mostly made conscious attempts to appear heterosexual v. feminine." . . .

. . . For women in the military, women must "do femininity" to insure that they are perceived as heterosexual and, as such, are somewhat protected from potential stigma and/or expulsion.

Gender and the Institution

The second question posed by West and Zimmerman (1987) is: "What is the relationship between the production of gender at the level of interaction and such institutional arrangements as the division of labor in society?" In the case of the military, gender is produced at the level of interaction, but the result is the reinforcement of perceptions of women as unfit for military service. These perceptions are not merely micro-level assessments, but perceptions that permeate the broader institution. When the majority of women can be labeled "feminine," and anything feminine is viewed as inappropriate for military service, women, as a group, can become viewed as "inconsistent" with, or less than capable of performing, military service. Thus, by producing gender at the level of interaction (e.g., enacting femininity), a broader ideology, as well as institutional arrangements (e.g., job restrictions) in which women are perceived to be second class soldiers is maintained.

If women were aggressive they were seen as lesbians; if women were not aggressive enough they were seen as incapable of leading troops and could receive poor evaluation reviews. In either case, the ultimate penalty could be discharge. At the least, women as a group are subject to the label of "unfit." Women have to prove themselves the exception to the rule. One interesting example of this is the experience of the male sergeant who, together with a female flight surgeon, was captured by the Iraqis during Desert Storm. After their experience as prisoners of war, he acknowledged that she could go into battle with him anytime, but that he wasn't prepared to say the same for all women. SGT Troy Dunlap stated, "I was really amazed . . . I was overwhelmed by the way she handled herself. . . . She can go to combat with me anytime" (Pauley 1992). He made it clear that she was the exception. One woman had proven herself; women as a group remained questionable. As MAJ Rhonda Cronum said in response, "I don't think I'll ever change his mind that says that women as a category of people shouldn't go to combat, but I think I did change his mind that this one individual person who happens to be female can go" (Pauley 1992).

When women "produce enactments of their 'essential' femininity" (West and Zimmerman 1987: 144), they are not being good soldiers. When they are "good soldiers," they often risk being labeled as lesbians. As Navy Vice Admiral Joseph S. Donnell wrote in 1990, lesbian sailors are "generally hard-working, career-oriented, willing to put in long hours on the job and among the command's top performers" (Gross, 1990: 24). It is not difficult to imagine how women who fit this description, regardless of sexual orientation, may be labeled as lesbian (Shilts 1993). Thus, the enactment of gender at the interactional level has the potential to reinforce perceptions of women as inappropriate for military service for a number of reasons. Such a perception of women then reinforces the belief that men are somehow uniquely suited to serving in the nation's military. Thus, the production of gender at the interactional level reinforces both ideological and institutional arrangements that place women at the margins of military participation.

It should be noted that stereotypical gay men do not fit the model of "soldier," in that they are not seen as masculine "enough." If gay male soldiers, or *any* male soldier for that matter, were not seen as appropriately masculine they would risk censure. The paradox is that the stereotypical lesbian *does* fit the model of "soldier," and, yet, risks censure for being "gender appropriate" to the work role of soldier. While a gay man can "pass" by "doing masculinity" in the appropriate fashion, women are faced with the contradiction that "doing masculinity" results in being perceived as a lesbian.

Gender as a Tool of Male Dominance

The third question posed by West and Zimmerman (1987) is "how does doing gender contribute to the subordination of women by men?" If, as described above, women in the military are perceived as second class soldiers, or as less than capable, it is not farfetched to argue that women are being subordinated by men. It is important to reiterate that clearly not all women, as individuals, are seen as second rate or unsuccessful. There are thousands of women who have served admirably and have earned the respect of their male co-workers, peers and superiors alike.[4] The case I am making here is that military women *as a group* are viewed as second class and are subordinated by the male institution of the military. Whether women are sexually harassed, denied assignments, or prohibited from performing particular jobs, we must realize that it is not simply the case of a poor performing individual that allows such incidents to occur. The social and institutional arrangements (e.g., the prohibition of women from most combat jobs) which permit women to be viewed as poor substitutes for male soldiers subordinate women to men and limit their participation as full members of the military. In some cases, attributions of inadequacy have followed women to their deaths.

LT Kara Hultgreen was one of the first women to qualify to fly a Naval fighter jet, the F-14. LT Hultgreen died on October 25, 1994 when she crashed in the Pacific during a training exercise. The Navy rumor mill immediately spun into action with some going "so far as to send out false information in anonymous phone calls and faxes purporting that Hultgreen was unqualified and received special treatment by a politically correct Navy. In fact, Hultgreen was third out of seven flyers in her class" (*Minerva's Bulletin Board* Fall/Winter, 1994: 3). Subsequent investigation revealed that the aircraft had lost an engine and that even skilled pilots would have had a difficult time landing successfully. CDR Trish Beckman, president of Women Military Aviators, writes:

A combination of factors and limited time to recognize and correct them, put Kara in a "deep hole" which cost her life (and would have done the same to skilled Test Pilots in the same situation). What is different in this circumstance is that unnamed Navy men have attempted to slander and libel her reputation publicly (something that has never been done to a deceased male aviator, no matter how incompetent he was known to be or how many lives he took with him). (*Minerva's Bulletin Board* Fall/Winter, 1994: 3–4)

In contrast, when two Navy pilots flew their helicopter past the demilitarized zone into North Korea in December 1994, resulting in the death of one and the capture of the other, no mention was made of blame or incompetence. No one suggested that perhaps permitting men to fly was a mistake.

Does the above question address the issue of the relationship between doing gender in the military and the subordination of women to men? I believe so. When military women enact femininity, they are subject to accusations that they are not capable of performing tasks, etc., that have been labeled as "masculine." When military women enact masculinity, they are subject to accusations of lesbianism. Doing gender results in women being subjected to an endless range of accusations which together result in the subordination of women as a class of citizens. The question, however, remains, is it possible to avoid doing gender?

West and Zimmerman (1987) write:

If we do gender appropriately, we simultaneously sustain, reproduce, and render legitimate the institutional arrangements that are based on sex category. If we fail to do gender appropriately, we as individuals—not the institutional arrangements—may be called to account (for our character, motives, and predispositions). (146)

While it is unlikely, given the existing social order, that we can avoid doing gender, we can begin to tackle the resulting inequities in a number of ways. "Social change, then, must be pursued both at the institutional and cultural level of sex category and at the interactional level of gender" (West and Zimmerman 1987: 147). That is, we must challenge the institutional and cultural arrangements that perpetuate distinctions made on the basis of sex, or sex category. In the military, one way to accomplish this would be to eliminate prohibitions of women in combat. Another would be to eliminate the ban on lesbians, gay men, and bisexuals in the military. If we eliminate the importance of sex category in the "politics of sexual-object choice" (Connell 1985: 261) we eliminate the need for compulsory heterosexuality. That is, if whether a potential mate is female or male is irrelevant, heterosexuality loses it hegemonic stranglehold on society and its institutions. Thus, eliminating compulsory heterosexuality would do much to reduce the pressures women feel to be seen as feminine as well as the fear of being seen as too masculine, and not without significance, the fear men have of being seen as too feminine.

Conclusion

. . . There are some very real implications for women's day-to-day participation in the military. Women are likely to be subjected to a variety of unpleasantries ranging from sexual harassment to being shunned, from being denied access to schooling to being denied promotions. While the penalties are varied, they share one potential outcome. All of the penalties discussed in this research may lead to women being discharged or feeling compelled to leave the service. Thus, the major implication of this research is that the perpetuation of an ideology in which soldiering and masculinity are closely bound results in the perpetuation of a military which is not only ideologically, but numerically, male as well.

There are several mechanisms which function to keep the military "male." In addition to women leaving the service, whether by force or choice, perceptions of the military as male also limit the numbers of women who will consider the military as a career option. As of late 1993, the proportion of enlistees who were women was, in fact, on the rise (*Minerva's Bulletin Board* Spring, 1994: 1–2). As of this writing, the Army had experienced a slight drop in women recruits after widespread sexual harassment was exposed in late 1996. Whether this will have any long term effect on Army recruiting is not yet known. It is impossible, at this point, to determine if women are finding the military more attractive than has been true in the past, or whether smaller numbers of male recruits are inflating the proportion of female recruits.

In addition, the ideology of the "male military" and restrictions on the participation of women function together to limit the number of positions open to women. Thus, fewer women, compared to men, can enter the service. That is, even if huge numbers of women wished to enlist, their numbers would be suppressed by the comparatively fewer numbers of available positions, especially in the Army where large numbers of jobs are classified as combat arms and, as such, are off limits to women.

As long as the military is viewed as the domain of men, women will be outsiders and their participation will be challenged. Thus, a cycle of male dominance is perpetuated. The military is defined as male, a small proportion of women are allowed to participate, the participation of these women is challenged and penalized, the military remains ideologically and numerically male dominated, the numbers of women remain small. How can this cycle be broken? First, we can challenge cultural constructions of sex/gender. Second, we can challenge institutional arrangements which allow the perpetuation of distinctions on the basis of sex/sex category. That is, reduce the importance of being feminine or masculine and female or male.

The first of these institutional arrangements is the classification of military job eligibility by sex. That is, one is eligible for a particular job only if one is male. In the military this is the case for jobs coded as having a high likelihood of engaging the enemy. Women, as a group, are thus excluded from some specific occupations and some specific assignments. Barriers are being broken, but many remain. As long as women are eligible only for some jobs they will be viewed as second class soldiers (or sailors, "airmen," etc.). If we eliminate such barriers and assign individuals on the basis of their performance, ability, etc., it is highly likely that we will see a corresponding increase in the acceptance of women as participants in the military.

The second arrangement which will improve the ability of women to participate on equal terms with men is the repeal of the laws prohibiting the participation of lesbians, gay men, and bisexuals in the United States military. It is painfully apparent that this ban hurts many lesbians, gay men, and bisexuals. Many wish to serve in the military, but know that to do so is not without risk. Many do join the military only to have their careers ended prematurely. But, as I have indicated, the ban on lesbians, gay men, and bisexuals also impacts negatively on all women and men, regardless of sexual orientation. If the confirmation of heterosexuality were not imperative, women would be free to engage in a much wider range of behaviors, particularly those labeled as masculine. If women did not feel compelled to ensure that they are seen as heterosexual, there would be less pressure to enact femininity, a marker of heterosexuality.

By having to confirm heterosexuality, women enact femininity, thereby ensuring that they will be perceived as less capable than their male counterparts. The link between gender and sexuality, situated in an organization which has an institutional mandate for heterosexuality, ensures the subordination of women. To eliminate compulsory heterosexuality would greatly enhance the more equal participation of women. To be sure, eliminating the degree to and manner in which women deploy gender at the interactional level would also enhance equal participation. But, without corresponding changes at the institutional level such changes are unlikely to occur. By understanding: (1) how gender is produced at the interactional level, (2) how the interactional level is related to existing institutional arrangements, and (3) how the link between gender and sexuality empowers this relationship, we can offer a new vision for the equal participation of women and men in the military and, more importantly, throughout society.

NOTES

1. Members of the military are also referred to as airmen [*sic*], sailors, Marines, etc., depending upon their branch. For ease of discussion I use the term soldiers, as the Army is the largest branch and in common parlance many often refer to all members of the military as soldiers, regardless of branch.

2. For an interesting, non-military, account of the experiences of androgynous women see Holly Devor's *Gender Blending: Confronting the Limits of Duality,* Bloomington, IN: Indiana University Press, 1989.

3. In the past swearing was not viewed as inappropriate or unprofessional and drinking was not only tolerated, but encouraged. New policies on sexual harassment and alcohol abuse have led to significant changes in recent years.

4. Of course, one could argue as well that while women have to *earn* the respect of the men with whom they work, men begin with that respect and must do something to lose it.

REFERENCES

Acker, Joan. 1992. "Gendered Institutions." *Contemporary Sociology* 21(5): 565–569.

Connell, Robert W. 1985. "Theorizing Gender." *Sociology* 19(2) 260–272.

Dunivin, Karen. 1994. "Military Culture: Change and Continuity." *Armed Forces & Society* 20(4): 531–547.

"Freedom of Press Seen on Trial Now." 1942. *New York Times,* 17 April, 8.

Goffman, Erving. 1977. "The Arrangement Between the Sexes." *Theory and Society* 4(3): 301–331.

Gross, Jane, 1990. "Navy Is Urged to Root Out Lesbians Despite Abilities." *New York Times,* 2 September, 24.

Lenskyj, Helen. 1986. *Out of Bounds: Women, Sport and Sexuality.* Toronto: The Women's Press.

The MINERVA Center. Spring, 1994. "Proportion of Women Growing Among New Recruits." *Minerva's Bulletin Board,* 1–2.

———. Fall/Winter, 1994. "Second Woman to Qualify as F-14 Pilot Dies in Crash." *Minerva's Bulletin Board,* 3–4.

Pauley, Jane. 1992. *Dateline NBC:* Interview with MAJ Rhonda L. Cornum. New York.

Shilts, Randy. 1993. *Conduct Unbecoming: Lesbians and Gays in the U. S. Military Vietnam to the Persian Gulf.* New York, NY: St. Martin's Press.

Steinberg, Ronni. 1992. "Gender on the Agenda: Male Advantage in Organizations." *Contemporary Sociology* 21(5): 576–581.

Veterans Administration. 1985. *Survey of Female Veterans: A Study of the Needs, Attitudes, and Experiences of Women Veterans.* Office of Information Management and Statistics, IM & SM 70–85–7.

West, Candace and Sarah Fenstermaker. 1993. "Power, Inequality and the Accomplishment of Gender: An Ethnomethodological View," in *Theory on Gender/Feminism on Theory,* P. England (ed.). Hawthorne, NY: Aldine de Gruyter, 151–174.

West, Candace and Don H. Zimmerman. 1987. "Doing Gender." *Gender & Society* 1(2): 125–151.

THINKING ABOUT THE READING

Which do you think is worse for female soldiers: being perceived as "too masculine" or being perceived as "too feminine"? How is female soldiers' need to "walk a fine line" between masculinity and femininity related to impression management? Can you think of a comparable situation for men—one in which an occupation requires a certain degree of femininity, while at the same time demanding that they present an image of themselves as "real men"? Given the extreme, potentially life-and-death demands of military combat, do you think that female soldiers will ever be accepted as equals to male soldiers?

Suspended Identity

Identity Transformation in a Maximum Security Prison

Thomas J. Schmid and Richard S. Jones

(1991)

The extent to which people hide behind the masks of impression management in everyday life is a point of theoretical controversy (Goffman 1959; Gross and Stone 1964; Irwin 1977; Douglas et al. 1980; Douglas and Johnson 1977; Messinger et al. 1962; Blumer 1972, 1969). A variety of problematic circumstances can be identified, however, in which individuals find it necessary to accommodate a sudden but encompassing shift in social situations by establishing temporary identities. These circumstances, which can range from meteoric fame (Adler and Adler 1989) to confinement in total institutions, place new identity demands on the individual, while seriously challenging his or her prior identity bases.

A prison sentence constitutes a "massive assault" on the identity of those imprisoned (Berger 1963: 100–101). This assault is especially severe on first-time inmates, and we might expect radical identity changes to ensue from their imprisonment. At the same time, a prisoner's awareness of the challenge to his identity affords some measure of protection against it. . . .

Data for the study are derived principally from ten months of participant observation at a maximum security prison for men in the upper midwest of the United States. One of the authors was an inmate serving a felony sentence for one year and one day, while the other participated in the study as an outside observer. Relying on traditional ethnographic

data collection and analysis techniques, this approach offered us general observations of hundreds of prisoners, and extensive field-notes that were based on repeated, often daily, contacts with about fifty inmates, as well as on personal relationships established with a smaller number of inmates. We subsequently returned to the prison to conduct focused interviews with other prisoners; using information provided by prison officials, we were able to identify and interview twenty additional first-time inmates who were serving sentences of two years or less. . . .

Three interrelated research questions guided our analysis: How do first-time, short-term inmates define the prison world, and how do their definitions change during their prison careers? How do these inmates adapt to the prison world, and how do their adaptation strategies change during their prison careers? How do their self-definitions, change during their prison careers? . . .

Preprison Identity

Our data suggest that the inmates we studied have little in common before their arrival at prison, except their conventionality. Although convicted of felonies, most do not possess "criminal" identities (cf. Irwin 1970: 29–34). They begin their sentences with only a vague, incomplete image (Boulding 1961) of what prison is like, but an image that nonetheless stands in contrast to how they view their own social worlds. Their prison image is dominated by the theme of violence: they see prison inmates as violent, hostile, alien human beings, with whom they have nothing in common. They have several specific fears about what will happen to them in prison, including fears of assault, rape, and death. They are also concerned about their identities, fearing that—if they survive prison at all—they are in danger of changing in prison, either through the intentional efforts of rehabilitation personnel or through the unavoidable hardening effects of the prison environment. Acting on this imagery (Blumer 1969)—or, more precisely, on the inconsonance of their self-images with this prison image—they develop an anticipatory survival strategy . . . that consists primarily of protective resolutions: a resolve to avoid all hostilities; a resolve to avoid all nonessential contacts with inmates and guards; a resolve to defend themselves in any way possible; and a resolve not to change, or to be changed, in prison.

A felon's image and strategy are formulated through a running self-dialogue, a heightened state of reflexive awareness (Lewis 1979) through which he ruminates about his past behavior and motives, and imaginatively projects himself into the prison world. This self-dialogue begins shortly after his arrest, continues intermittently during his trial or court hearings, and becomes especially intense at the time of his transfer to prison. . . .

> My first night in the joint was spent mainly on kicking myself in the butt for putting myself in the joint. It was a very emotional evening. I thought a lot about all my friends and family, the good-byes, the things we did the last couple of months, how good they had been to me, sticking by me. I also thought about my fears: Am I going to go crazy? Will I end up fighting for my life? How am I going to survive in here for a year? Will I change? Will things be the same when I get out?

His self-dialogue is also typically the most extensive self-assessment he has ever conducted; thus, at the same time that he is resolving not to change, he is also initiating the kind of introspective analysis that is essential to any identity transformation process.

Self-Insulation

A felon's self-dialogue continues during the initial weeks and months of his sentence, and it remains a solitary activity, each inmate struggling to come to grips with the inconsonance of his established (preprison) identity and his present predicament. Despite the differences in their preprison identities, however, inmates now share a common situation that affects their identities. With few exceptions, their self-dialogues involve feelings of vulnerability, discontinuity, and differentiation from other inmates, emotions that reflect both the degradations and deprivations of institutional life (cf. Goffman 1961; Sykes 1958; and Garfinkel 1956) and their continuing outsiders' perspective on the prison world. These feelings are obviously the result of everything that has happened to the inmates, but they are something else as well: they are the conditions in which every first-time, short-term inmate finds himself. They might even be called the common attributes of the inmates' selves-in-prison, for the irrelevance of their preprison identities within the prison world reduces their self-definitions, temporarily, to the level of pure emotion. These feelings, and a consequent emphasis on the "physical self" (Zurcher 1977: 176), also constitute the essential motivation for the inmates' self-insulation strategies.

An inmate cannot remain wholly insulated within the prison world, for a number of reasons. He simply spends too much of his time in the presence of others to avoid all interaction with them. He also recognizes that his prison image is based on incomplete and inadequate information, and that he must interact with others in order to acquire first-hand information about the prison world. His behavior in prison, moreover, is guided not only by his prison image but by a fundamental ambivalence he feels about his situation, resulting from his marginality between the prison and outside social worlds (Schmid and Jones 1987). His ambivalence has several manifestations throughout his prison career, but the most important is his conflicting desires for self-insulation and for human communication.

Managing a Dualistic Self

An inmate is able to express both directions of his ambivalence (and to address his need for more information about the prison) by drawing a distinction between his "true" identity (i.e., his outside, preprison identity) and a "false" identity he creates for the prison world. For most of a new inmate's prison career, his preprison identity remains a "subjective" or "personal" identity while his prison identity serves as his "objective" or "social" basis for interaction in prison (see Weigert 1986; Goffman 1963). This bifurcation of his self . . . is not a conscious decision made at a single point in time, but it does represent two conscious and interdependent identity-preservation tactics, formulated through self-dialogue and refined through tentative interaction with others.

First, after coming to believe that he cannot "be himself" in prison because he would be too vulnerable, he decides to "suspend" his preprison identity for the duration of his sentence. He retains his resolve not to let prison change him, protecting himself by choosing not to reveal himself (his "true" self) to others. . . . An inmate's decision to suspend his preprison identity emanates directly from his feelings of vulnerability, discontinuity and differentiation from other inmates. These emotions foster something like a "proto-sociological attitude"

(Weigert 1986: 173; see also Zurcher 1977), in which new inmates find it necessary to step outside their taken-for-granted preprison identities. Rather than viewing these identities and the everyday life experience in which they are grounded as social constructions, however, inmates see the *prison* world as an artificial construction, and judge their "naturally occurring" preprison identities to be out of place within this construction. By attempting to suspend his preprison identity for the time that he spends in prison an inmate believes that he will again "be his old self" after his release.

While he is in confinement, an inmate's decision to suspend his identity leaves him with little or no basis for interaction. His second identity tactic, then, is the creation of an identity that allows him to interact, however cautiously, with others. This tactic consists of his increasingly sophisticated impression management skills (Goffman 1959; Schlenker 1980), which are initially designed simply to hide his vulnerability, but which gradually evolve into an alternative identity felt to be more suitable to the prison world. The character of the presented identity is remarkably similar from inmate to inmate:

> Well, I learned that you can't act like—you can't get the attitude where you are better than they are. Even where you might be better than them, you can't strut around like you are. Basically, you can't stick out. You don't stare at people and things like that. I knew a lot of these things from talking to people and I figured them out by myself. I sat down and figured out just what kind of attitude I'm going to have to take.
>
> Most people out here learn to be tough, whether they can back it up or not. If you don't learn to be tough, you will definitely pay for it. This toughness can be demonstrated through a mean look, tough language, or an extremely big build. . . . One important thing is never to let your guard down.

An inmate's prison identity, as an inauthentic presentation of self, is not in itself a form of identity transformation but is rather a form of identity construction. His prison identity is simply who he must pretend to be while he is in prison. It is a false identity created for survival in an artificial world. But this identity nonetheless emerges in the same manner as any other identity: it is learned from others, and it must be presented to, negotiated with, and validated by others. A new inmate arrives at prison with a general image of what prisoners are like, and he begins to flesh out this image from the day of his arrival, warily observing others just as they are observing him. Through watching others, through eavesdropping, through cautious conversation and selective interaction, a new inmate refines his understanding of what maximum security prisoners look like, how they talk, how they move, how they act. Despite his belief that he is different from these other prisoners, he knows that he cannot appear to be too different from them, if he is to hide his vulnerability. His initial image of other prisoners, his early observations, and his concern over how he appears to others thus provide a foundation for the identity he gradually creates through impression management.

Impression management skills, of course, are not exclusive to the prison world; a new inmate, like anyone else, has had experience in presenting a "front" to others, and he draws upon his experience in the creation of his prison identity. He has undoubtedly even had experience in projecting the very attributes—strength, stoicism, aplomb—required by his prison identity. Impression management in prison differs, however, in the totality with which it governs interactions and in the perceived costs of failure: humiliation, assault, or death. For these reasons the entire impression management process becomes a more highly conscious endeavor. When presenting himself before others, a new inmate pays close attention to such minute details of his front as eye contact, posture, and manner of walking:

[. . .]

The way you look seems to be very important. The feeling is you shouldn't smile, that a frown is much more appropriate. The eyes are very important. You should never look away; it is considered a sign of weakness. Either stare straight ahead, look around, or look the person dead in the eyes. The way you walk is important. You shouldn't walk too fast; they might think you were scared and in a hurry to get away.

To create an appropriate embodiment (Weigert 1986; Stone 1962) of their prison identities, some new intimates devote long hours to weightlifting or other body-building exercises, and virtually all of them relinquish their civilian clothes—which might express their preprison identities—in favor of the standard issue clothing that most inmates wear. Whenever a new inmate is open to the view of other inmates, in fact, he is likely to relinquish most overt symbols of his individuality, in favor of a standard issue "prison inmate" appearance.

By acting self-consciously, of course, a new inmate runs the risk of exposing the fact that he *is* acting. But he sees no alternative to playing his part better; he cannot "not act" because that too would expose the vulnerability of his "true" identity. He thus sees every new prison experience, every new territory that he is allowed to explore, as a test of his impression management skills. Every nonconfrontive encounter with another inmate symbolizes his success at these skills, but it is also a social validation of his prison identity. Eventually he comes to see that many, perhaps most, inmates are engaging in the same kind of inauthentic presentations of self (cf. Glaser and Strauss 1964). Their identities are as "false" as his, and their validations of his identity may be equally false. But he realizes that he is powerless to change this state of affairs, and that he must continue to present his prison identity for as long as he remains in prison. . . .

By the middle of his sentence, a new inmate comes to adopt what is essentially an insider's perspective on the prison world. His prison image has evolved to the point where it is dominated by the theme of boredom rather than violence. (The possibility of violence is still acknowledged and feared, but those violent incidents that do occur have been redefined as the consequences of prison norm violations rather than as random predatory acts; see Schmid and Jones 1990.) His survival strategy, although still extant, has been supplemented by such general adaptation techniques as legal and illegal diversionary activities and conscious efforts to suppress his thoughts about the outside world. . . . His impression management tactics have become second nature rather than self-conscious, as he routinely interacts with others in terms of his prison identity.

An inmate's suspension of his preprison identity, of course, is never absolute, and the separation between his suspended identity and his prison identity is never complete. He continues to interact with his visitors at least partially in terms of his preprison identity, and he is likely to have acquired at least one inmate "partner" with whom he interacts in terms of his preprison as well as his prison identity. During times of introspection, however—which take place less frequently but do not disappear—he generally continues to think of himself as being the same person he was before he came to prison. But it is also during these periods of self-dialogue that he begins to have doubts about his ability to revive his suspended identity. . . . At this point, both the inmate's suspended preprison identity and his created prison identity are part of his "performance consciousness" (Schechner 1985), although they are not given equal value. His

preprison identity is grounded primarily in the memory of his biography (Weigert 1986) rather than in self-performance. His concern, during the middle of his sentence, is that he has become so accustomed to dealing with others in terms of his prison identity—that he has been presenting and receiving affirmation of this identity for so long—that it is becoming his "true" identity.

An inmate's fear that he is becoming the character he has been presenting is not unfounded. All of his interactions within the prison world indicate the strong likelihood of a "role-person merger" (Turner 1978). An inmate views his presentation of his prison identity as a necessary expression of his inmate status. Unlike situational identities presented through impression management in the outside world, performance of the inmate role is transsituational and continuous. For a new inmate, prison consists almost exclusively of front regions, in which he must remain in character. As long as he is in the maximum security institution, he remains in at least partial view of the audience for which his prison identity is intended: other prison inmates. Moreover, because the stakes of his performance are so high, there is little room for self-mockery or other forms of role distance (Ungar 1984; Coser 1966) from his prison identity, and there is little possibility that an inmate's performance will be "punctured" (Adler and Adler 1989) by his partner or other prison acquaintances. And because his presentation of his prison identity is continuous, he also receives continuous affirmation of this identity from others—affirmation that becomes more significant in light of the fact that he also remains removed from day-to-day reaffirmation of his preprison identity by his associates in the outside world. The inauthenticity of the process is beside the point. Stone's (1962: 93) observation that "one's identity is established when others *place* him as a social object by assigning him the same words of identity that he appropriates for himself or *announces*" remains sound even when both the announcements and the placements are recognized as false. . . .

Identity Dialectic

When an inmate's concerns about his identity first emerge, there is little that he can do about them. He recognizes that he has no choice but to present his prison identity so, following the insider's perspective he has now adopted, he consciously attempts to suppress his concerns. Eventually, however, he must begin to consider seriously his capacity to revive his suspended identity; his identity concerns, and his belief that he must deal with them, become particularly acute if he is transferred to the minimum security unit of the prison for the final months of his sentence. At the conclusion of his prison career, an inmate shifts back toward an outsider's perspective on the prison world . . . ; this shift involves the dissipation of his maximum security adaptation strategy, further revision of his prison image, reconstruction of an image of the outside world, and the initial development of an outside plan. The inmate's efforts to revive his suspended identity are part of this shift in perspectives.

It is primarily through a renewed self-dialogue that the inmate struggles to revive his suspended identity—a struggle that amounts to a dialectic between his suspended identity and his prison identity. Through self-dialogue he recognizes, and tries to confront, the extent to which these two identities really do differ. He again tries to differentiate himself from maximum security inmates.

> There seems to be a concern with the inmates here to be able to distinguish . . . themselves from the other inmates. That is—they feel they are above the others. . . . Although they may associate with each other, it still seems important to degrade the majority here.

And he does have some success in freeing himself from his prison identity.

> Well, I think I am starting to soften up a little bit. I believe the identity I picked up in the prison is starting to leave me now that I have left the world of the [maximum security] joint. I find myself becoming more and more involved with the happenings of the outside world. I am even getting anxious to go out and see the sights, just to get away from this place.

But he recognizes that he *has* changed in prison, and that these changes run deeper than the mask he has been presenting to others. He has not returned to his "old self" simply because his impression management skills are used less frequently in minimum security. He raises the question—though he cannot answer it—of how permanent these changes are. He wonders how much his family and friends will see him as having changed. As stated by one of our interview respondents:

> I know I've changed a little bit. I just want to realize how the people I know are going to see it, because they [will] be able to see it more than I can see it. . . . Sometimes I just want to go somewhere and hide.

He speculates about how much the outside world—especially his own network of outside relationships—has changed in his absence. (It is his life, not those of his family and friends, that has been suspended during his prison sentence; he knows that changes have occurred in the outside world, and he suspects that some of these changes may have been withheld from him, intentionally or otherwise.) He has questions, if not serious doubts, about his ability to "make it" on the outside, especially concerning his relationships with others; he knows, in any case, that he cannot simply return to the outside world as if nothing has happened. Above all, he repeatedly confronts the question of who he is, and who he will be in the outside world.

An inmate's struggle with these questions, like his self-dialogue at the beginning of his prison career, is necessarily a solitary activity. The identity he claims at the time of his release, in contrast to his prison identity, cannot be learned from other inmates. Also like his earlier periods of self-dialogue, the questions he considers are not approached in a rational, systematic manner. The process is more one of rumination—of pondering one question until another replaces it, and then contemplating the new question until it is replaced by still another, or suppressed from his thoughts. There is, then, no final resolution to any of the inmate's identity questions. Each inmate confronts these questions in his own way, and each arrives at his own understanding of who he is, based on this unfinished, unresolved self-dialogue. In every case, however, an inmate's release identity is a synthesis of his suspended preprison identity and his prison identity.

Postprison Identity

Because each inmate's release identity is the outcome of his own identity dialectic, we cannot provide a profile of the "typical" release identity. But our data do allow us to specify some of the conditions that affect this outcome. Reaffirmations of his preprison identity by outsiders—visits and furloughs during which others interact with him as if he has not changed—provide powerful support for his efforts to revive his suspended identity. These efforts are also promoted by an inmate's recollection of his preprison identity (i.e., his attempts, through self-dialogue, to assess who he was before he came to prison), by his desire to abandon his prison identity, and by his general shift back toward an outsider's perspective. But there are also several factors that favor his prison identity, including his continued use of diversionary activities; his continued periodic efforts to suppress thoughts about the outside world; his continued ability

to use prison impression management skills; and his continuing sense of injustice about the treatment he has received. Strained or cautious interactions with outsiders, or unfulfilled furlough expectations, inhibit the revival of his preprison identity. And he faces direct, experiential evidence that he has changed: when a minimum security resident recognizes that he is now completely unaffected by reports of violent incidents in maximum security, he acknowledges that he is no longer the same person that he was when he entered prison. . . .

Just as we cannot define a typical release identity, we cannot predict these inmates' future, postprison identities, not only because we have restricted our analysis to their prison experiences but because each inmate's future identity is inherently unpredictable. What effect an ex-inmate's prison experience has on his identity depends on how he, in interaction with others, defines this experience. Some of the men we have studied will be returned to prison in the future; others will not. But all will have been changed by their prison experiences. They entered the prison world fearing for their lives; they depart with the knowledge that they have survived. On the one hand, these men are undoubtedly stronger persons by virtue of this accomplishment. On the other hand, the same tactics that enabled them to survive the prison world can be called upon, appropriately or not, in difficult situations in the outside world. To the extent that these men draw upon their prison survival tactics to cope with the hardships of the outside world—to the extent that their prison behavior becomes a meaningful part of their "role repertoire" (Turner 1978) in their everyday lives—their prison identities will have become inseparable from their "true" identities.

The Suspended Identity Model

As identity preservation tactics, an inmate's suspension of his preprison identity and development of a false prison identity are not, and cannot be, entirely successful. At the conclusion of his sentence, no inmate can ever fully revive his suspended identity; he cannot remain the same person he was before he came to prison. But his tactics do not fail entirely either. An inmate's resolve not to change, his decision to suspend his preprison identity, his belief that he will be able to revive this identity, and his subsequent struggle to revive this identity undoubtedly minimize the identity change that would otherwise have taken place. The inmate's tactics, leading up to his suspended identity dialectic, constitute an identity transformation process . . . that differs from both the gradual, sequential model of identity transformation and models of radical identity transformation (Strauss 1959). It also shares some characteristics with each of these models.

As in cases of brainwashing and conversion, there is an external change agency involved, the inmate does learn a new perspective (an insider's perspective) for evaluating himself and the world around him, and he does develop new group loyalties while his old loyalties are reduced. But unlike a radical identity transformation, the inmate does not interpret the changes that take place as changes in a *central* identity; the insider's perspective he learns and the new person he becomes in prison are viewed as a false front that he must present to others, but a front that does not affect who he really is. And while suspending his preprison identity necessarily entails a weakening of his outside loyalties, it does not, in most cases, destroy them. Because he never achieves more than a marginal status in the prison world, the inmate's ambivalence prevents him from accepting an insider's perspective too fully, and thus prevents him from fully severing his loyalties to the outside world (Schmid and Jones 1987). He retains a fundamental, if ambivalent, commitment to his outside world throughout his sentence, and he

expects to reestablish his outside relationships (just as he expects to revive his suspended identity) when his sentence is over.

Like a religious convert who later loses his faith, an inmate cannot simply return to his old self. The liminal conditions (Turner 1977) of the prison world have removed him, for too long, from his accustomed identity bearings in everyday life. He does change in prison, but his attempts to suspend and subsequently revive his preprison identity maintain a general sense of identity continuity for most of his prison career. As in the gradual identity transformation process delineated by Strauss (1959), he recognizes changes in his identity only at periodic "turning points," especially his mid-career doubts about his ability to revive his suspended identity and his self-dialogue at the end of his sentence. Also like a gradual identity transformation, the extent of his identity change depends on a balance between the situational adjustments he has made in prison and his continuing commitments to the outside world (Becker 1960, 1964). His identity depends, in other words, on the outcome of the dialectic between his prison identity and his suspended preprison identity.

The suspended identity model is one component of a holistic analysis of the experiences of first-time, short-term inmates at a specific maximum security prison. Like any holistic analysis, its usefulness lies primarily in its capacity to explain the particular case under study (Deising 1971). We nonetheless expect similar identity transformation processes to occur under similar circumstances: among individuals who desire to preserve their identities despite finding themselves involved in temporary but encompassing social worlds or social situations that subject them to new and disparate identity demands and render their prior identities inappropriate. The suspended identity model presented here provides a basis for further exploration of these circumstances.

REFERENCES

Adler, Patricia A. and Peter Adler. 1989. "The Gloried Self: The Aggrandizement and the Constriction of Self." *Social Psychology Quarterly* 52:299–310.

Becker, Howard S. 1960. "Notes on the Concept of Commitment." *American Journal of Sociology* 66:32–40.

———. 1964. "Personal Change in Adult Life." *Sociometry* 27:40–53.

Berger, Peter L. 1963. *Invitation to Sociology. A Humanistic Perspective.* Garden City, NY: Doubleday/Anchor Books.

Blumer, Herbert. 1972. "Action vs. Interaction: Review of *Relations in Public* by Erving Goffman." *Transaction* 9:50–53.

———. 1969. *Symbolic Interactionism: Perspective and Method.* Englewood Cliffs, NJ: Prentice Hall.

Boulding, Kenneth. 1961. *The Image.* Ann Arbor: University of Michigan Press.

Coser, R. 1966. "Role Distance, Sociological Ambivalence and Traditional Status Systems." *American Journal of Sociology* 72:173–187.

Deising, Paul. 1971. *Patterns of Discovery in the Social Sciences.* Chicago: Aldine-Atherton.

Douglas, Jack D., Patricia A. Adler, Peter Adler, Andrea Fontana, Robert C. Freeman, and Joseph A. Kotarba. 1980. *Introduction to the Sociologies of Everyday Life.* Boston: Allyn & Bacon.

Douglas, Jack D. and John M. Johnson. 1977. *Existential Sociology.* Cambridge: Cambridge University Press.

Garfinkel, Harold. 1956. "Conditions of Successful Degradation Ceremonies." *American Journal of Sociology* 61:420–424.

Glaser, Barney G. and Anselm L. Strauss. 1964. "Awareness Contexts and Social Interaction." *American Sociological Review* 29:269–279.

Goffman, Erving. 1961. *Asylums.* Garden City, NY: Doubleday/Anchor Books.

———. 1959. The *Presentation of Self in Everyday Life.* Garden City, NY: Doubleday/Anchor Books.

———. 1963. *Stigma: Notes on the Management of Spoiled Identity.* Englewood Cliffs, NJ: Prentice Hall.

Gross, Edward and Gregory P. Stone. 1964. "Embarrassment and the Analysis of Role Requirements." *American Journal of Sociology* 70:1–15.

Irwin, John. 1970. *The Felon.* Englewood Cliffs, NJ: Prentice Hall.

———. 1977. *Scenes.* Beverly Hills: Sage.

Lewis, David J. 1979. "A Social Behaviorist Interpretation of the Median I." *American Journal of Sociology* 84:261–287.

Messinger, Sheldon E., Harold Sampson, and Robert D. Towne. 1962. "Life as Theater: Some Notes on the Dramaturgic Approach to Social Reality." *Sociometry* 25: 98–111.

Schechner, Richard. 1985. *Between Theater and Anthropology.* Philadelphia. University of Pennsylvania Press.

Schlenker, B. 1980. *Impression Management. The Self Concept, Social Identity and Interpersonal Relations.* Belmont, CA: Wadsworth.

Schmid, Thomas and Richard Jones. 1987. "Ambivalent Actions: Prison Adaptation Strategies of New Inmates." American Society of Criminology, annual meetings, Montreal, Quebec.

Schmid, Thomas and Richard Jones. 1990. "Experiential Orientations to the Prison Experience: The Case of First-Time, Short-Term Inmates." Pp. 189–210 in *Perspectives on Social Problems,* edited by Gale Miller and James A. Holstein. Greenwich, CT: JAI Press.

Stone, Gregory P. 1962. "Appearance and the Self." Pp. 86–118 in *Human Behavior and Social Processes,* edited by Arnold Rose. Boston: Houghton Mifflin.

Strauss, Anselm L. 1959. *Mirrors and Masks: The Search for Identity,* Glencoe: Free Press.

Sykes, Gresham. 1958. *The Society of Captives: A Study of a Maximum Security Prison.* Princeton: Princeton University Press.

Turner, Ralph H. 1978. "The Role and the Person." *American Journal of Sociology* 84:1–23.

Turner, Victor. 1977. *The Ritual Process: Structure and Anti-Structure.* Ithaca, NY: Cornell University Press.

Ungar, Sheldon. 1984. "Self-Mockery: An Alternative Form of Self-Presentation." *Symbolic Interaction* 7:121–133.

Weigert, Andrew J. 1986. "The Social Production of Identity: Metatheoretical Foundations." *Sociological Quarterly* 27:165–183.

Zurcher, Louis A. 1977. *The Mutable Self.* Beverly Hills: Sage.

THINKING ABOUT THE READING

What happens to inmates' self-concepts in prison? Given the stigmatizing effects of being identified as an "ex-con," do you think it is ever possible for people to reclaim their normal, law-abiding identities once they get out of prison? How would the identity transformations described by Schmid and Jones differ for female prisoners? Consider another environment (for instance, military boot camp, a violent street gang, a religious sect) where such a dramatic shift in public identity must take place. How would the experiences of people in these situations differ and/or resemble those of the inmates described by Schmid and Jones? What does the process of identity transformation imply about the strength and permanence of identity?

Webcam Women

Life on Your Screen

Donald Snyder

(2000)

What if you could open a window at any time of the day and see into your next-door neighbour's bedroom? What do you think you would see: your neighbour doing a crossword puzzle, or in a compromising situation? Or maybe just an empty room? Would you want to look, especially if the neighbour had created the window for the *purpose* of you looking?

The World Wide Web is becoming populated by people who are providing windows into their lives for the purpose of your viewing pleasure. Over the last couple of years, a growing number of people have been hooking up digital cameras to their personal computers and broadcasting scenes from their lives out to the internet, for anyone with access to see. Webcams—live cameras which send continuously updated pictures of a subject over the internet—are becoming extremely popular, both for people using the technology to place their life on a screen and for people wanting to open those windows and see how other people live their lives.

A large percentage of the "webcam sites" on the internet feature women. How are these women being portrayed and how are they portraying themselves? Much has been written and discussed about the amount of pornography on the Web. Are these webcams only reflective of that trend, or are they offering potential spaces for other women—people who want to keep their clothes on and use the webcam for more philosophical, artistic or creative ends? In the same regard, are women able to take control over their own bodies, and over the economic gain assigned to those bodies, with the aid of

this new technology? What sort of power does the webcam offer to women who are interested in creating new kinds of art and exploring new ways of expressing their selves? Finally, who makes up the audience for these webcams, and what does the popularity of these sites say about that audience? It is necessary to examine several examples of this trend in order to find some answers to these questions.

Surveying some of the most popular websites of women running their own webcams, a pattern seems to emerge. Most of the webcams fit into one of three categories. In the first, the subject of the webcam—the site's "star"—operates her site as a hobby, with little interest in economic gain. One of the best examples of this is *JenniCam* (www.jennicam.org). In the second category, the webcam's subject operates the site as a source of personal expression and potential economic gain. *AnaCam* represents a very successful example of someone forging a career in art using this technology (www.anacam.com). In the final and probably most prevalent category, a woman has set up a webcam in order to represent herself sexually for the sole purpose of making money. One example of this is *CollegeCutie* (www.collegecutie.com). While all three women are using webcam technology, the way each is using it reflects their different reasons and goals attached to living their life on the screen.

The most famous woman using webcam technology to document her body, and life, is Jennifer Kaye Ringley. In 1996 Jennifer was a student at Dickinson College in Pennsylvania. She quickly became an internet legend by creating a website named *JenniCam*, which was one of the first 24-hour-a-day cameras displaying a person that existed on the Web. Since then, Jennifer has graduated from college and moved to the Washington DC area, continuing *JenniCam* along the way. Currently, Jennifer has several cameras located throughout her apartment. One of these cameras, depending upon where Jennifer is, takes a picture and uploads it to the internet every minute if you are a member, and a little less frequently if you are not. When Jennifer began *JenniCam*, she attempted to keep the site "private" by only telling a few of her friends. However, her friends told their friends, who told *their* friends, and after about 3 months of existence, 7,000 users were logged on to *JenniCam*. In 1998, Jennifer reported that her site was receiving over 100 million hits a week (Firth, 1998). To this day, *JenniCam* remains one of the most popular and interesting personal webcam sites on the internet.

To what extent is Jennifer presenting her real life on *JenniCam*, and to what extent is it a performance? In the very beginning of *JenniCam*, Jennifer was not aware that anyone was (necessarily) watching, so she easily ignored the camera. The camera was there to document her life and nothing more. After she learned of her success, Jennifer began to interact with the camera. Exploring her exhibitionist tendencies at the urging of her audience, she began putting on impromptu, and then planned, strip shows. Eventually, though, Jennifer decided to return *JenniCam* to the original idea of ignoring the camera. When accused of being an exhibitionist, Jennifer replied, "The definition of an exhibitionist is someone who gets off on having people watch them. And the whole point of *JenniCam* is that I ignore the fact that the camera is there. So by that definition, I am not an exhibitionist" (E! Television, 1998).

While Jennifer denies performing for an audience, she is still actively creating an image that attempts to counter the common image of women presented on screens. When asked about the success of *JenniCam*, Jennifer replied, "People enjoy seeing what other people do. And I think it makes other people feel better about themselves to know that they are not the only ones out there not living these glamorous lives" (1998). She presents to the internet not just the spectacular events of her life, but also—and much more often—the mundane. The camera captures her "normal" life, which might contain some nudity and sex, but more often than not captures a vision of a woman that is not only absent from the internet, but absent from all media. Jennifer attempts to show a vision of a "real" woman, and not the celluloid, glamorous image presented on television, in movies and over most of the Web. Nevertheless, Jenni has inevitably become a celebrity of sorts, and her site has correspondingly come to look more like a standard (self-) exploitation site. She is certainly not afraid to store some of the more revealing shots in her permanent online archive, and she includes on her site the photo shoots taken to accompany magazine features about *JenniCam*.

One woman that *JenniCam* inspired is Ana Voog, who created *AnaCam*. Ana explains her site as "a window into my house, into my life . . . sometimes I'll be surfing the net, sometimes I'll be dancing wildly about my house to some disco music . . . sometimes I might put on little skits for you or decide to cover myself in blue paint or something weird." Ana attempts to take more control over her image than Jennifer does. While Jennifer ignores the camera, Ana constantly interacts with the camera, pretending that the camera is her friend and her audience. Where Jennifer tries to replace the image of the spectacular sexualized woman on the internet with the image of the "normal" woman, Ana attempts to replace that same image with something *other* than woman. One of the reasons she does the site, she confesses, is to "push boundaries of what people think a woman is and isn't." Within *AnaCam*, Ana creates a cyberpunk image of herself. For example, in one series of shots she appears on the camera dressed in black leather, highlighted with metal. Her hair is spiked and dyed gold, while her eyebrows are dyed with silver sparkles. She is adorned with various piercings, and black face paint in the form of a cross. Unlike *JenniCam*, *AnaCam* challenges predictable representations of womanhood, and Ana's art questions the common perceptions of women's bodies. Her art commonly manipulates the female body with digital imaging or paint in a way that attempts to resist or manipulate sexist notions present in society and on the internet.

Where Jennifer's performance in the front of her camera is supposedly the very opposite of self-conscious "performance," Ana considers herself an artist, and *AnaCam* her art. In her FAQ section, in response to the question of what she does for a living, Ana replies, "I do *AnaCam* for a living . . . I am a singer/songwriter/performance artist. I am also a visual artist." She uses the camera in a very different way to Jennifer, while still using the camera to present an alternative image of a woman on the Web. Ana does performance art for the camera and distributes her music through her site; she has been able to utilize the technology of the Web in order to announce herself as an artist. She has made the webcam a new tool for the artists' palette, and turned her website into her own private gallery. *AnaCam* enabled Ana to bypass the traditional art world on her path to becoming a successful and economically viable artist.

When discussing *AnaCam* as a project with an economic gain in mind, one major point must be reinforced: like *JenniCam*, *AnaCam* is a free site. The difference between the two is that Jennifer has treated her site as a hobby, whilst Ana sees her site as a career maker. *AnaCam* has provided Ana with a way to advertise her consumer products, most importantly as a way to sell and distribute her music. Ana also allows companies to advertise on *AnaCam*, whereas Jennifer has maintained an organization (not for profit) status for

JenniCam. In addition, people can become members of both *JenniCam* and *AnaCam* and receive or gain access to added materials. In the case of *JenniCam*, for a small annual fee (US$15 in 2000, about £9), members are able to view a picture from the webcam at a more rapid rate than non-members. On *Ana2*, *AnaCam's* sister pay site, for a monthly fee almost equivalent to *JenniCam's* annual fee, members are able to view not just one cam every 5 minutes (the standard refresh time on *AnaCam*), but four cams every 30 seconds each. Ana occasionally uses one of these cams to document her life outside of her home, giving the viewer the ability to follow her throughout her day. Other features only members can access on *Ana2* include a picture archive, a members-only bulletin board system (BBS), and access to Ana's book while she is in the process of writing it. The appeal of these members-only benefits to Ana's audience has enabled her to use this new technology to build a successful business venture.

Much of Ana's success seems to be tied into how she has created a community of fans around her website. One way that Ana appeals to her audience is by including them as part of the artistic process that is *AnaCam*. The most successful aspect of this is apparent in the popularity of "Anapix." Anapix are digitally or artistically manipulated images of Ana from *AnaCam*; Ana's viewers download pictures of Ana from the webcam and create their own imaginative works of art, and then send them to Ana where they are displayed in a special section of the website. The inclusion of an exclusive BBS in *Ana2* also works to reinforce the community of true *AnaCam* fans, who Ana refers to as a "cool community of wonderful, creative and supportive people." Ana's life and art has become an important aspect of her fans' lives, and Ana uses the technology to foster this fascination.

Where Ana was inspired by Jennifer to use the webcam to create a new artistic community built around her life and image, Carlota was inspired by Jennifer to use the webcam to sell a sexualized vision of her own body. Carlota created her webcam site *CollegeCutie* in 1998 as a source of income for her education. She writes, "I got the idea for this from an article on (guess who) *JenniCam*. . . . I started grad school this fall and thought this would be a good way to help me out." Like most webcam sites, *CollegeCutie* offers a free image from the camera, in this case one picture every 15 minutes. In most pictures, she is nude or in various states of undress. *CollegeCutie* also offers a free gallery of nine pictures where Carlota is posing in various sexual positions. This page promises that a new similar one is added weekly for members. But for the majority, this site, unlike *JenniCam* and to a lesser extent *AnaCam*, is not intended to be a free site at all. If you are not a member, there is really little to do or see. Jennifer and Ana provide several options for the non-member to click and explore the site; Carlota, however, shows the non-member a sample of her merchandise and promises more only if the non-member joins for a monthly fee similar to Ana's. *CollegeCutie* is not an experiment in art or life, it is a way to make money.

Two of the most interesting aspects of *CollegeCutie* relate to how Carlota is using technology in order to enhance the effect of traditional pornography. First of all, she offers a real-time camera. Where most webcams refresh every 15 seconds at quickest, a real-time camera presents the image continuously. As Carlota explains, this type of camera caters to the experience desired by her audience: "You'll have access to my live webcam. . . . You'll be able to watch me shower, take a bath or just play around!" (In reality most personal computers do not have the capability to view the material in its intended quality; for the time being, most real-time cameras appear slow and disjointed.) The other way Carlota uses technology to appeal to her desired audience is that she provides a private chatroom. In this space, Carlota is able to interact with the people watching her,

chatting and "flirting" with them, or asking them what they would like her to do. She effectively builds a community around her website, using personal interaction to encourage her visitors to feel they are part of the experience (in line with Rheingold's community-building recommendations, 2000).

The fact that Carlota views *CollegeCutie* as a source of income and not as a hobby is reflected in the fact that it is not a 24-hour site. The picture only changes when Carlota is on, and Carlota posts a schedule, on the site, of times she will be on the webcam. While this is not always the case on webcams where the main goal is to offer sexualized bodies, in this case it seems to comment on the difference between Carlota's commitment and that of Jennifer or Ana. In essence, Carlota is able to use the webcam as a "convenient" and "safe" way of continually selling images of her body to those who desire to see it. She controls the economic gains in every way; there is no magazine, club or entertainment service exploiting her. *CollegeCutie* provides Carlota with a way of completely capitalizing on her own body. Although Carlota is not challenging the stereotype of women and pornography on the internet, she is using webcam technology to challenge successfully the traditional way in which women's sexual bodies have been controlled in economic terms.

In all three webcam sites, *JenniCam*, *AnaCam* and *CollegeCutie*, a woman is performing for the camera. That performance is dictated by the way that these women view their sites and their audiences. They each understand the needs of their target audience and use the technology in ways to appeal to those needs. Jennifer feels that her viewers want images of reality, and so her performance involves giving the impression that she is not performing (which often, we can suppose, she is not), and her exhibitionism becomes not exhibitionism but "real life." She refuses the "star" role and chooses not to romanticize her life. She becomes everywoman—a symbol of normalcy in a spectacular media-saturated world. Unlike Jennifer, Ana's appearances are self-styled performance art. Ana is appealing to those who are interested in seeing technology in extremely creative ways. Ana uses the webcam to turn the image of her body into a work of art. Whilst the site, by its nature, tends to position the viewer as voyeur and the artist as exhibitionist, these positions are challenged through the way Ana attempts to include her viewers in the creation of both the website and a strong community network of Ana fans. Once Ana's voyeurs begin to assist Ana in exhibiting the image of Ana, they too become exhibitionists of Ana's "body." Finally, Carlota uses the technology of the webcam to represent herself within the most traditional understanding of the exhibitionist-and-voyeur relationship. Because Carlota is interested in using the technology solely for economic gain, she offers what she feels most people seek and are willing to pay for: sex (or, more specifically, the digitized image of flesh). She exhibits her body for anyone willing to pay to view her. Her exhibitionism is a performance because a true exhibitionist would expose their body for the thrill, not for an income. Webcams are not always sites of exhibitionism, but if someone is watching, then they are always sites of voyeurism.

These three examples of women's webcams are interesting because of the ways they challenge the perceptions of what it means to be a woman on the World Wide Web. Webcams are an important trend on the internet and will continue to grow in popularity. There is a danger in writing off the webcam as only a new site for pornography; even when the subject is pornographic, there is much more being transmitted than pornography. With the recent popularity of reality television shows like *Cops*, and MTV's *The Real World* and *Road Rules*—an interest reflected in movies like *The Truman Show* and *EdTV*—"reality" is becoming a controversial but legitimate and successful source of entertainment. Webcams are a perfect site for examining why "reality" has become such an important subject for our culture and how this "reality" is constructed. In finding out how and why people want to live their lives on our screens, we can begin to understand our need and desire to watch them.

REFERENCE

Rheingold, Howard. 2000. "Community Development in the Cybersociety of the Future." In D. Gauntlett, *Web.Studies*, pp. 170-178. London: Arnold Press.

THINKING ABOUT THE READING

According to Snyder, Jennifer's main reason for creating *JenniCam* was to provide realistic images of women's lives, counter to the degrading images seen in the mainstream media. In what ways do you think she's been successful in achieving her objectives through her webcam? Some might question whether she is really being "herself" in the presence of the camera. What does it mean to say that we are never fully ourselves in the presence of others? To what extent are our actions shaped by the imagined reactions of others (the audience in our heads) even when we are completely alone? What are some of the similarities and differences between these live webcams and the many television "reality shows" that are so popular today? Why do you think people are so interested in viewing these shows?

7 Building Social Relationships

Intimacy and Family

In this culture, close, personal relationships are the standard by which we judge the quality and happiness of our everyday lives. Yet in a complex, individualistic society like ours, these relationships are becoming more difficult to establish and sustain. Although we like to think that the things we do in our relationships are completely private experiences, they are continually influenced by large-scale political interests and economic pressures. Like every other aspect of our lives, close relationships can be understood only within the broader social context. Laws, customs, and social institutions often regulate the way we form these relationships, how we act inside them, and how we dispose of them when they are no longer working. At a more fundamental level, societies determine which relationships can be considered "legitimate" and therefore entitled to cultural and institutional recognition. Those relationships that lack such societal validation are often scorned and stigmatized.

Such social validation is particularly difficult to obtain for homosexual couples, who are often portrayed by others as a threat to the institution of family. In "No Place Like Home," sociologist Christopher Carrington describes how lesbians and gay men construct and sustain a sense of family in their own lives. From his research, Carrington argues that *family* isn't necessarily determined by blood or law but by a consistent pattern of loving and caring. *Family* resides in the unremarkable, everyday things that partners do with and for each other. In that sense, same-sex couples establish extensive life-long bonds, just like those found in long-term heterosexual couples.

Questions about what constitutes a family are also raised in Helen Ragoné's article, "Chasing the Blood Tie: Surrogate Mothers, Adoptive Mothers, and Fathers." This article is a unique study of the relationship between surrogate mothers (women who, for a fee, become pregnant with and give birth to someone else's child), adoptive mothers, and fathers. Ragoné did fieldwork with three surrogate clinics and discovered some interesting, and sometimes counter-intuitive themes regarding the rationales that surrogate mothers have for performing this service and how these discourses play into existing ideals about motherhood, family, and women's work. Her work illustrates an interesting sociological paradox: the method surrogates use to achieve pregnancy can be considered quite unorthodox, but the motivation of all parties in this relationship—the desire to have a child—is very traditional.

No Place Like Home

Christopher Carrington

(1999)

This was a law developed for the purpose of ensuring that people can care for their families. It's inappropriate for a senator to cheapen the meaning of family by saying family is a "fill in the blank."

> —Kristi Hamrick, spokesperson for the
> Family Research Council, commenting on New Jersey Sen.
> Robert Torricelli's decision to voluntarily extend some of the
> provisions of the 1993 Family and Medical Leave Act to lesbian
> and gay members of his staff (www. glinn.com March 13, 1997)

As I write these words, a cultural debate in the United States rages over the status of lesbian and gay families, most notably in the struggles over lesbian and gay marriage, as well as in the struggles to gain "domestic partnership" benefits. Much of the current debate about lesbian and gay families stems from the threat that such families are perceived to pose to the dominant organization of family practices in contemporary Western societies (Mohr 1994; Stacey 1996). However, a pervasive sense of crisis in the American family has existed throughout much of American history (Skolnick 1991; Coontz 1992), and the national debate concerning lesbian and gay families is but the latest grist for the mill. This sense of family crisis pervades the political efforts to block lesbian and gay people from attaining legal marriage and benefits of domestic partnership. The sense of crisis, and the rhetorical overkill that accompanies it, not only makes it difficult for political debate to focus on the everyday realities of lesbian and gay families but insures that many people will both understand such families in stereotypical ways and impede efforts to improve the quality of lesbian and gay family life. The quotation at the beginning of this chapter from Ms. Hamrick denies the possibility that lesbian and gay families exist, much less acknowledges that they should enjoy any kind of cultural recognition.

. . . Actual lesbigay families, like most other American families, face the struggles of balancing work and family commitments, of managing the stresses and strains of waxing and waning sexual desires, of maintaining open and honest communication, of fighting over household responsibilities, and, most frequently, of simply trying to make ends meet. The latter point deserves much more attention, for if any phantom lurks in the lives of lesbian and gay families, it is their inability to achieve financial security, the foundation of a happy, communicative, and stable relationship (Voydanoff 1992).

This is a study of "family life" among a group of fifty-two lesbian and gay families (twenty-six female and twenty-six male). This study provides an ethnographic and empirical account of how lesbians and gay men actually construct, sustain, enhance, or undermine a sense of family in their lives. . . . I use the term *lesbigay,* which is coming into wider use, because it includes lesbians, bisexuals, and gay men, all of whom participate in the families I studied. Of the fifty-two adult women participants, two consider themselves bisexual, as does one of the fifty-three adult men.

In this study I reflect upon the *details* of everyday life in the households of the lesbigay families, and explore the relationship of such detail to the actual experience of and creation of family in the lives of lesbigay people. The participants in this research, similar to many other citizens, use the term *family* in diverse and often contradictory ways. At one moment a participant will conceive of family as a legal and biological category, a category that they reject, and might even define themselves as over and against. In a different place and time that same participant will conceive of family in favor of an understanding that emphasizes the labors involved and not the socially sanctioned roles. And at yet another place and time that same participant will embrace the legal and biological definitions of family with the hopes of achieving lesbigay inclusion into those categorizations (for example, advocating lesbigay legal marriage or attempting to secure custody of a child on the basis of biological linkage).

In my analysis the crucial element for defining what or who constitutes a family derives from whether the participants engage in a consistent and relatively reciprocal pattern of loving and caring activities and understand themselves to be bound to provide for, and entitled to partake of, the material and emotional needs and/or resources of other family members. I understand family as consisting of people who love and care for one another. This makes a couple a family. In other words, through their loving and caring activities, and their reflections upon them, people conceive

of, construct, and maintain social relationships that they come to recognize and treat as family (Schneider 1984). In this sense a family, any family, is a social construction, or set of relationships recognized, edified, and sustained through human initiative. People "do" family.

This research ponders the deceptively simple activities that constitute love and care, activities that frequently go unnoticed in most families, including most lesbigay families. These may entail trips to the store to pick up something special for dinner, phoning an order to a catalog company for someone's birthday, tallying the money owed to friends, sorting the daily mail, remembering a couple's anniversary, finishing up the laundry before one's spouse returns home, maintaining a photo album, remembering the vegetables that family members dislike, or attending to myriad other small, often hidden, seemingly insignificant matters. Decidedly not insignificant, these small matters form the fabric of our daily lives as participants in families. Moreover, the proliferation of these small matters produces a stronger and more pervasive sense of the relationship(s) as a family, both in the eyes of the participants and in the eyes of others. . . .

Kin Work Among Lesbigay Families

In recent years, scholars of family life have begun to document the forms of work that heterosexual women do in order to establish and sustain family relations. Some of this research reveals the forms of hidden and frequently unrecognized labor involved in maintaining kin relations (Rosenthal 1985; Di Leonardo 1987; Gerstel and Gallagher 1993 1994). Di Leonardo refers to these kinds of activities as "kin work":

> The conception, maintenance, and ritual celebration of cross-household kin ties, including visits, letters, telephone calls, presents and cards to kin; the organization of holiday

gatherings; the creation and maintenance of quasi-kin relations; decisions to neglect or to intensify particular ties; the mental work of reflection about all of these activities; and the creation and communication of altering images of family and kin vis-à-vis the images of others, both folk and mass media. (1987, 442–43)

The forms of kin work Di Leonardo delineates appear in lesbigay families as well, although much of the aforementioned empirical research fails to include such families. In writing letters, making phone calls, organizing holiday and social occasions, selecting and purchasing gifts, as well as the forethought and decisions about how to do these things, how much to do, and for whom to do them, lesbigay families engage in a great deal of kin work. In fact, engaging in kin work is essential to creating lesbigay family life.

Kith as Family

In most respects, lesbigay families engage in forms of kin work quite similar to heterosexual families, though many do so among intimate friends rather than among biolegally defined relatives (Weston 1991; Nardi 1992; Nardi and Sherrod 1994). In contrast to the traditional Anglo-Saxon distinction made between kith (friends and acquaintances) and kin (relatives), many lesbigay families operate with a different set of distinctions where kith become kin and, sometimes, kin become kith. For example, Mary Ann Callihan, a thirty-eight-year-old artist now living in Oakland, reflects:

> I do consider my close friends as my family. They are my real family, I mean, my other family lives back East, and I don't have much to do with them and they don't have much to do with me. They really aren't a family, not at least in how I think a family should be. The people who care for me, listen to me, and love me are right here. They are my kin.

And while Mary Ann's comments diminishing the importance of biolegally defined kin reflect the views of roughly a third of the sample, her

sentiments regarding the definition of family capture a common theme found in many lesbigay households: a normative sense of family as a voluntary association, as *chosen*. Sociologist Judith Stacey identifies this pattern of chosen kin and voluntary family ties as the "postmodern family" (Stacey 1990, 17, 270). Many lesbigay households operate with this postmodern conception of kin. Many respondents use the phrase "gay family" to designate their chosen family.

This conception of friends as family notwithstanding, lesbigay families make clear distinctions among friends. Anthropologist Kath Weston notes, "Although many gay families included friends, not just any friend would do" (1991, 109). Weston argues that "gay families differed from networks to the extent that they quite consciously incorporated symbolic demonstrations of love, shared history, material and emotional assistance and other signs of enduring solidarity" (109). Bringing the perspectives and findings of the literature on kin work to bear on Weston's findings raises a number of questions: What activities constitute symbolic demonstrations of love? What kind of work does material and emotional assistance involve and who performs that work? What activities/behaviors serve as signs of enduring solidarity and what forms of work come to play in those activities? Peter Nardi, describing the role of friendships in lives of gay people, points out that

> in addition to providing opportunities for expressions of intimacy and identity, friendships for gay men and lesbians serve as sources for various kinds of social support (ranging from the monetary to health care) and provide them with a network of people with whom they can share celebrations, holidays, and other transitional rituals. (1992, 112)

Nardi's delineation of activities crucial to friendship suggests the presence of kin work: planning, provisioning, and coordinating visits, celebrations, holidays, and transitional rituals; making phone calls and sending e-mail on a consistent basis; sending notes, cards, and flowers at the appropriate times; selecting, purchasing, and wrapping gifts; providing or arranging for the provision of healthcare (not a minor matter given the HIV/AIDS epidemic); and reflecting upon and strategizing about relationships. All of these activities constitute kin work, and performing these activities *creates* and sustains family.

When laying claim to the term *family* to describe lesbigay relationships, most respondents point to particular phenomena as evidence of family: sharing meals, sharing leisure, sharing holidays, sharing religious community, sharing resources, relying on someone for emotional or medical care, turning to someone in an emergency, and/or sharing a common history. For example, many lesbians and gay men point to the sharing of holiday meals as indicative of the presence of family in their lives. Susan Posner, reflecting on those people with whom she and her partner, Camille, spend their holidays, comments:

> Well, we have them over to eat or they have us over. We have been together through thick and thin for so long from when we first came out of the closet, through our commitment ceremony, and through buying this house. That makes us family. I have known one of them for a very long time, that's a lot of eating and sharing and crying and stuff.

Susan began to cry as she reflected on these events in her life. She then recounted several holiday gatherings where the joy that she experienced with her lesbigay family was so overwhelming that she began to cry during the events. Many lesbigay people can recount similar stories. In part, these are tears of exile from biolegal kin, but they are more than that. They are also tears of joy—joy in the discovery of a new home and a new family.

In addition to sharing holiday meals, other participants pointed to other kinds of kin work as evidence of family. Daniel Sen Yung, a twenty-eight-year-old accountant for a small nonprofit agency, offers another instance of kith becoming kin via various forms of kin work. Daniel, responding to my question about whether he considers his close friends as family, replies:

> Oh, yes, I know that I can depend on them for certain things that you would get from a family. If I were to get really ill, they would take care of me, house me, provide for me. We eat together, just like families should. I consider friends as family, especially as a gay person, I think that way. I definitely have a gay family. They look out for me and check in on me. They are the people who pay my bills when I go overseas for work, or who were with me when I had to take my cat to the veterinary hospital. They are the ones who came and visited me in the hospital, for God's sake.

Another participant, Raquel Rhodes, a thirty-one-year-old woman working as an assistant manger for a rental car agency, identified those who had loaned her money as central to her conception of family:

> I think you know who your real family is when you fall on hard times. My friends Rebecca and Sue, they came through for me when I lost my job. They lent me the money I needed to keep going. My own mother wouldn't because of all of her homophobic bullshit. That tells you who really counts and for me—Rebecca and Sue really count.

Loaning people money involves kin work. Managing and negotiating the feelings incumbent in such lending, particularly when a couple is doing the lending, as well as managing the money itself are both forms of kin work. Other forms of lesbigay kin work include all the efforts that people put into recognizing and celebrating their own and other people's relationships. The recent work by anthropologist

Ellen Lewin (1998) exploring the commitment ceremonies of lesbian and gay couples reveals the extensive work entailed in creating these ceremonies. Lewin chronicles the efforts these couples put into selecting invitations, attire, and locations for the ceremony, as well as making arrangements for out-of-town guests. She also reveals the extensive emotional labor that goes into deciding who to invite—a sometimes gut-wrenching and potentially combative enterprise. When we do these things, we create family.

The Lesbigay Family Kin Keepers

Quite frequently, relationships function as a center for extended kinship structures. To use an astronomical metaphor, these relationships become planets around whom a series of moons (frequently, single individuals) revolve. The planning, organization, and facilitation of social occasions (picnics, holiday gatherings, vacations, commitment ceremonies/holy unions, birthday parties, gay-pride celebrations, hiking trips) bring these individuals into an orbit around lesbigay relationships. These occasions often take place in the homes of couples, as contrasted with individuals, and one member of the couple often performs the work involved. In answering questions about holiday gatherings, lesbigay families frequently recount stories of shared Thanksgiving meals, Jewish Sedarim, gay-pride celebrations, and Christmas Eve gatherings. Many speak of the importance of making sure that everyone "has a place to go" on such occasions.

For example, Matthew Corrigan and his partner, Greg Fuss, have been together for thirteen years and live in San Francisco's Castro district. Matthew works as an administrator in a nearby hospital and Greg works as a salesperson for a large pharmaceutical company. Matthew responds to my question about how he decides whom to invite for holiday occasions by saying:

We have a lot of single friends. Many of them would like to be in couples, but they just haven't found Mr. or Mrs. Right yet. So, we are kind of their family. I mean, we will still be family after they find someone, but right now, they come here for holidays. I try to make sure that no one spends their Christmas alone. When we talk about who to invite, we always think about who doesn't have a place to go.

Matthew's comments capture a common dynamic where lesbigay families function as the center of kin relations for many single individuals. The lesbigay families can also function as a place where single individuals come into contact with one another and begin new relationships (Harry 1984, 143). These families become the center due to a number of socioeconomic factors. First, the formation of lesbigay families leads to pooling of resources. The shared resources of family groupings allow for larger residences, larger meal expenditures, and, interestingly, more time for kin work. Family status brings with it the possibility of at least one member in a family reducing the number of hours they work at paid labor and spending more time on family/household matters. Second, as lesbigay couples and threesomes come to perceive of their relationship in familial terms, they begin to act in familial ways: inviting others over for dinner, and creating holiday occasions, among other things. Third, it seems that unpartnered individuals view couples in familial ways and hold expectations that these individuals will act in familial terms. Angela DiVincenzo, a thirty-three-year-old elementary school teacher, felt this expectation from her lesbigay family:

I think that our friends have a stake in our relationship. A lot of them are single and they kind of view us as the ideal family. I mean, partly, I think, it's about their hopes of having their own relationship, but also, it's about the fact that we are their family. They look to us to act like a family. We all do things together, go on little trips or hiking or whatever. We are kind of a stabilizing influence in their lives. They know we are here and are interested in their lives, unlike many of their real families, that is, *supposedly* real families. We are the real family.

Moreover, in a number of the longer-term and more affluent lesbigay families, there emerges a person who becomes a family "kinkeeper" (Rosenthal 1985). This person functions as a sort of center for an extended lesbigay family. This individual actually coordinates some of the kin work across families. For example, Randy Ambert, a forty-two-year-old flight attendant, plans and coordinates many joint occasions for an extended kin group who he and his partner, Russ Pena, both consider their extended family. They include in this extended family a lesbian couple, another gay-male couple, a single lesbian, and two single gay men. In talking with Randy about these activities, he observes:

> I am sort of the family mom, if you get my drift. I tend to be the first person who thinks about what is coming up. I get everyone thinking about what we're going to do for summer travel, and I like to make sure that we don't forget anyone's birthday. With the other couples, that's not too much of an issue because they keep on top of each other's birthdays. But sometimes, the couples seem pretty busy and too worn out to make plans for things, you know, so I try to keep us all together. I plan a big celebration for Gay Pride each year that brings us all together.

In addition to planning these joint occasions, Randy reports making calls to gay family members who now live out of town and keeping them abreast of the news of the various people in the extended kin group. Randy's work sustains kinship; it makes real the claim of many lesbigay people, the claim to chosen family. Yet the work and the claim to family status occurs under a particular set of social conditions. Randy's relatively flexible work schedule and the relative affluence of his household allow Randy to invest more time in kin work, and to become a kinkeeper.

Arranging for such gatherings takes a great deal of kin work. In addition to the actual planning, provisioning and preparation of the food—all examples of feeding work—a number of other less observed labors make such family meals possible. Someone must envision such occasions and make decisions about whom to invite and when. Some people tend to think of the envisioning of such meals as a form of leisure, but in fact, this envisioning entails various hidden forms of labor. The envisioning of shared meals requires one to think and act in response to a number of different factors: individual, corporate, and societal calendars; whom to invite and how frequently; who gets along with whom and what mix of people would work; making phone calls or sending invitations; knowledge of social etiquette; and learning what foods guests like or dislike. Rich Niebuhr, a forty-one-year-old attorney working part-time, reveals the mental effort involved in deciding which people to invite to dinner:

> Well, it can be kind of awkward sometimes deciding whom to invite. Usually, I handle it because Joe doesn't like dealing with that kind of stuff. But, sometimes, I find myself torn because I know that we owe someone dinner, either we haven't seen them in a while and we run into them in Castro or at a movie, but I don't really feel like inviting them. Usually, I break down and invite them because I feel like a worm if I don't. I will think about whom to invite over at the same time—sort of to take the edge off, to make it a little less intense. It's okay. But, I kind of get mad that Joe just sort of expects me to negotiate all this stuff. Sometimes, I put my foot down, and make him call them. It can be real draining trying to stay on top of all this stuff.

Rich exemplifies the kinds of considerations that constitute kin work. Note how Rich bears responsibility for managing the interpersonal conflict and for strategizing the occasion because "Joe doesn't like dealing with that kind of stuff." Participant observation in Joe and Rich's home reveals that Rich performs much of the kin work, both in its visible forms (making calls and planning events), as well as in its invisible forms (thinking about whom they should call and planning when to make the calls).

Variations in Kin Work Patterns

Not surprisingly the character and extent of kin work varies dramatically depending on a number of different social factors. Class identities, . . . the presence or absence of children, gender identities, . . . and ethnic and racial identities all influence the context in which kin work happens and the character of that kin work.

Social class and lesbigay kin work. While most lesbigay families in this study fall into the middle and upper middle class, clear distinctions emerge between these groups in terms of kin work. More affluent, upper-middle-class lesbigay households engage in significantly more kin work and much more frequently conceive of friends as family than their middle-class counterparts. Those families earning more than the median annual household income ($61,500) report twice as many close friends (twelve per household) as those households earning below the median (five). This pattern conforms to other empirical research revealing that patterns of informal association become more extensive as one moves up the socio-economic hierarchy (Hodges 1964; Curtis and Jackson 1977). Among the ten most affluent households, all family members conceive of friends as family. In contrast, among the ten least affluent, only within four households

does even one family member conceive of friends as family. In part this pattern may reflect the relatively younger age of the less affluent families. It also appears that among the more affluent, friendship/family networks become more strongly lesbigay. Less affluent respondents' friendship/family networks, while smaller, consist of a greater proportion of straight people. Overall, more affluent households maintain larger family structures and they do family with other lesbigay people.

This means that the work of creating and sustaining such relationships becomes more extensive and requires more labor for more affluent lesbigay families. For instance, they invite others over for shared meals more often, entertain larger numbers of people at dinner parties and other occasions, and go out to dinner with others more consistently. These activities require extensive kin work in the form of planning for such occasions, deciding whom to invite, extending invitations, deciding where to go out to eat, and maintaining a record (mental or written) of previous engagements.

Lawrence Sing and Henry Goode, together as a family for over two decades, live in a restored Edwardian flat in a rapidly gentrifying neighborhood in San Francisco. Lawrence works part-time as a real estate agent, and Henry works as a physician. They both possess postgraduate degrees. Lawerence, who performs much of the kin-related work in the family, makes the following comments about some of that work:

> I'm the keeper of the social calendar. I decide whom to invite over and when. I keep a mental record of who came last and whom we would like to see. I ask Henry if there is anyone he would like to see, but generally, I know how he feels about certain people. I keep up our obligations. Some people we see once a year, but there is a core of twenty-five to thirty people who I maintain contact with and whom we see with some frequency.

Lawrence, speaking with great enthusiasm and affection for his family of gay friends, denotes other forms of kin work in the effort to maintain those family relationships:

> I write letters to our closest friends who live farther away, and we always send them birthday presents and cards and, of course, presents at Christmastime. We try to plan holiday travel and our vacations with some of them. I often call them on Sundays; that's the day I make many of the long-distance calls to everybody. It's a lot of effort to keep it all together, but I think it's worth it. They're our family.

Lawrence's observations reflect common forms of kin work among more affluent lesbigay households. In contrast to less affluent lesbigay families, the affluent ones engage in some forms of kin work much more frequently: writing letters; buying and mailing gifts for birthdays and holidays; sending flowers; sending birthday, anniversary, and get-well cards; and sending a larger number of holiday greeting cards. When dividing up the sample into thirds, the most affluent one-third sent an average of seventy-five cards; and the lower one-third, fifteen cards per household. The more affluent families keep in contact with out-of-town friends and biolegal relatives much more frequently than less affluent families. The affluent make more long-distance calls and spend more time talking. All of these efforts constitute kin work: deciding upon and purchasing gifts and cards, writing and mailing the gifts and cards, remembering to call and write and deciding for whom to do these things.

In like manner, the more affluent households report more extensive holiday celebrations, and they often point to the sharing of holidays together as evidence of the family status of their intimate friends. Kathy Atwood and Joan Kelsey live in the Oakland hills in an Arts and Crafts style cottage in a neighborhood with many other lesbian families. Kathy works as an accountant for a prominent bank headquartered in downtown San Francisco. Joan works part-time as a finance manager for a local savings and loan. Together they earn slightly over $100,000 per year. Joan has a master's degree in accounting from a prestigious college in the East and Kathy has a bachelor's degree from the University of California. Kathy expresses her conception of friends as constituting family:

> I consider my friends as family. I see them as often as I see my biolegal family. I discuss our relationship with them. They come here for holidays or we go to their house. Our shared holidays are symbolic of our familiness. We share personal experiences. I would want them here for significant events, like Christmas or our Holy Union or whatever.

Joan, who does much of the kin work in the family, engages in a great deal of effort to make the holidays pleasant and meaningful to her chosen family:

> I put quite a bit of effort into getting the house together for Christmas. We had a lot of people over at different times, and our chosen family over on Christmas Eve, and we went to their house on Christmas day. I mean, I planned out the meals, a very special one for Christmas Eve. I bought and mailed invitations for a Sunday afternoon holiday party. I went to the Flowermart in the city and bought greens and stuff like that. I bought a new tablecloth with a holiday theme. We chose presents for them together, but I had the time to wrap them and stuff like that.

Nearly a dozen individuals from more affluent families conceive of shared holidays as constitutive of family, while only two individuals from families earning below the median speak in these terms.

Conversely, in most cases, less affluent households more often conceive of family in biolegally defined terms, they engage in less kin work and to some extent they do different kinds of kin work. In terms of household income, most respondents perceiving of family as uniquely consisting of biolegal relatives fall below the median. I would characterize many of them as "minimal families" (Dizard and Gadlin 1990). They do not create and sustain large kin structures, either biolegally defined or lesbigay defined, and their conceptions of family emphasize biolegal links. Although these families afford less time and energy to maintaining kin relations, the efforts they do make often focus on biolegal relatives. These families often feel isolated and spend more time alone. Social researchers made the discovery long ago that the wealthy and the poor maintain stronger ties to kin for economic reasons than do middle-class Americans (Schneider and Smith 1973; Stack 1974). Most of those lesbigay families falling below the median income in this sample clearly fall into the middle or the lower middle class, as opposed to the working class or the poor. For instance, Amy Gilfoyle and Wendy Harper, a lesbian family living in a distant suburb north of San Francisco, a place where they could afford to buy a home, spend much of their time alone. They spend major holidays "alone together," without the presence of others. They both conceive of family as consisting of their own relationship and possibly Amy's biolegal parents. They report one close friend between the two of them, and both express disappointment about this. They would like more friends, but they seem conflicted. Wendy, a student and landscape gardener, feels somewhat threatened by new friends:

> I would worry about getting too close to a lot of other lesbians. There are always issues about falling in love with friends and that ruining your relationship. And, we live so far away from the places where we might meet friends. I suppose we could become friends with some gay men, but they don't live out here, or at least we don't have any way of finding those who do.

Wendy's comments point to issues partly beyond social class, to concerns about gender and sexuality. But the fact that Wendy and Amy live so far away from San Francisco speaks clearly of social class and the ability of more affluent families to buy and rent homes in the city. Interview questions focusing on the reasons for living in suburban communities almost always point to the cost of housing in the city as a factor in deciding where to live. Wendy and Amy bring in a household income of $35,000 per year. This places them somewhat below the Bay Area median household income of $41,459 (U.S. Census 1991). Like many other middle- and lower middle-class lesbigay families, they exert less effort in the maintenance of kinship structures than do more affluent families. They infrequently call friends or biolegal relatives. They rarely send cards of any sort. Together they sent eight holiday greeting cards in 1993. They rarely invite people over, though they actually have the space to entertain. Only once every few months do they go out to dinner, and then usually just the two of them go. They lead relatively isolated lives and feel ambiguous about changing this. . . .

In sum, social class appears to play a central role in the extent and the character of kin work among lesbigay families. As one ascends the social-class hierarchy of lesbigay families in this sample from lower middle class to upper middle class, the intensity of kin work increases. The character of kin work shifts from concerns about establishing kin relationships to managing and sustaining kin relationships. The flow of material exchange intensifies with affluent lesbigay families buying more gifts, throwing more parties, hosting more dinners, making more phone calls, and sending more cards. Explaining why more affluent households do more kin work than less affluent ones involves several interrelated influences. First, more affluent families live closer to the lesbigay enclaves due to the higher cost of living in the city. Proximity to other lesbigay people leads to larger kin networks. Yet, some lower middle-class lesbigay families live in the center of lesbigay enclaves and engage in significantly less kin work than their more affluent neighbors. Second, more affluent lesbigay families turn to the marketplace for other forms of domestic labor (for example, laundry and housekeeping) thus freeing these families to invest more energy in kin work. . . .

Lesbigay parenting and kin work. The presence of children diminishes the conception of friends as family in lesbian and gay households. In four of the five households with children present in this study, neither primary partner conceives of their close friends as family. Rather, these households limit family to the primary couple, the children, and to biolegal relatives. Emily Fortune and Alice Lauer, parents of two young infants, understand family in strongly biolegal terms. Emily states: "Some people use the term *family* very loosely. I don't call friends that. The kids and our relatives, they feel like family to me. To me, my family is my biolegal family. We have a natural bond to one another." Her partner, Alice:

> My concept of family has changed a great deal in the past few months. I think before the children were born I might have considered my friends as family. My relationship with my own sister has changed since the kids were born. I have more of a sense of this family right here. I have a new appreciation for my family of origin. We can turn to them in a crisis, even though they may not be that comfortable with our sexuality.

Gay and lesbian parents appear more vested in biolegal conceptions of family, perhaps for very concrete reasons. To establish biolegal links in the American kinship structure often also establishes and legitimates economic links. Three of the lesbian families, all with infants, report relying on biolegal kin for

resources, either in the form of providing housing, making loans, lending automobiles, or providing daycare. Anthropologist Ellen Lewin suggests that the pattern of intensifying relations to blood kin among lesbian parents expresses an attempt to legitimate the claim to family and to provide a stable socioeconomic environment for the children (1993, 91–94).

Moreover, the presence of children within some families distracts from the ability to maintain friends. Clarice Perry, a college professor who is also deaf, expresses her feelings about family:

> My experience with family is strange. It's not easy to draw the line since I have Cheryl's children. I share responsibility for the kids, that's my idea of family. As an individual, my close friends, mostly deaf, we can't share that much because of the kids. The kids have changed my relationship with my friends. I have mixed feelings about it. I resent the kids sometimes. They took my friends away. It was not my plan to have kids, but they are now my family and I love them.

The addition of children changes one's social circumstances, both for lesbigay people and for heterosexuals. However, given that relatively few lesbigay families have children, and that parents often befriend parents in American culture, lesbigay parents may find it quite difficult to establish social links. This further encourages lesbigay families with kids to establish stronger relations with biolegal kin. The possibility exists that lesbian and gay friends may also intentionally diminish relationships with friends who have children. Some scholars find a fairly strong sentiment against children, especially among some gay men (Newton 1993).

Gender identities and lesbigay kin work. Gender appears central to explaining kin work in many settings. For instance, Di Leonardo posits that kin work reflects the influence of gender much more strongly than the influence of social class in heterosexual families (1987, 449). I can make no such unilateral claim about gender within lesbigay families. I detect gender-related concerns in terms of how lesbians and gay men both portray and do kin work, but this is complicated by the impact of socioeconomic factors. Interestingly, in this study, gay men do significantly more kin work than lesbian women. This parallels the finding of Blumstein and Schwartz (1983, 149–50) and my own research that gay men do more housework than lesbian women do. Blumstein and Schwartz argue this emerges from an effort among lesbians to avoid the low-status role assigned to housework in American society. I think additional factors play a role here.

While Blumstein and Schwartz find lesbian women shunning domestic work to avoid the low-status stigma attached to it, in the case of kin work I find both patterns of avoidance and a significantly diminished rationale for the generally less affluent lesbian families to engage in extensive kin work. When considering the economic affluence, educational level, and occupational prestige of all lesbigay households, the more affluent the household, the more educated and the more prestigious the career, the more extensive the kin work becomes regardless of gender. Dividing the lesbian families on the basis of household income into three groups (high, medium, and low) shows that those with high income report twice as many friends as those with low incomes. The same holds for males. Affluent families, regardless of gender, engage in much more extensive kin work. Due to the persistence of gender inequality, and the barriers women face in achieving higher-status, higher-paid employment, the resources necessary to sustain larger kin structures do not exist for many lesbian households as much as they do for gay men. Nor does maintaining such a network provide any economic advantage, as it does for those in occupational categories where extensive networks provide business

and client contacts (lawyers, private-practice physicians, and psychologists).

Nonetheless, I am not suggesting that gender has no relevance here, but its relevance eludes easy classification. On the one hand, lesbian women may well avoid kin work activity in order to escape the devalued status associated with doing the work. After all, who wants to be "just a housewife" (Matthews 1987)? On the other hand, if one hopes to create and live within a family, then someone has to do this work. And in most lesbigay families these forms of work do occur. However, doing kin work, or failing to do it, carries different risks for gay men and lesbians. For the men, engaging in kin work produces threats to gender identity. Making calls to family, sending cards, buying presents, inviting dinner guests and worrying about soured relationships with family all carry the potential to become gender-producing phenomena (Berk 1985; West and Zimmerman 1987). A woman failing to engage in these nurturing/caring activities runs the risk of stigma. This "nurturing imperative" exists for women regardless of sexual orientation (Westkott 1986). I suspect that many lesbian women answering questions about kin work felt an obligation to do kin work. For instance, Melinda Rodriguez, a twenty-seven-year-old human resources administrator comments when I ask about making phone calls to biolegal relatives:

> Should I answer that the way I am supposed to or should I be more honest about it? *[Laughter]* I don't call too much. I feel guilty about it. But hey, my brothers don't call my parents. My mother complains to me about that, but not to my brothers. Why should I be judged differently? I guess it's not a very feminine attitude, but I don't care. Well, I do care, but I wish they would have more realistic expectations. You know, I work a lot, as much as my brothers do. So I don't have that much time. Not like my mother, who doesn't work. She has time to call people.

Meanwhile, men engaging in extensive kin work frequently struggle with even more intense concerns about gender identity. Lance Meyter and Mike Tuzin, both in their late twenties, together for three years, and both working in the healthcare field (one in clerical, the other in higher administration), illustrate the dilemma some male couples face in negotiating kin work. Mike does most of the limited amount of kin work for their relationship. Lance feels that because Mike works at a less stressful job and has more time at home, he should do more of the "arranging of the social life." Mike, while accepting Lance's calculus, comments:

> I feel kind of weird about doing this stuff sometimes. I mean, I work, basically, as a secretary because I can't decide what to do with my life. That's already kind of embarrassing and hard on my self-esteem. I like to do a lot of social-type stuff, like talking to our friends, and arranging for things, but you know, it's hard. I was talking to my mother recently, and she wanted to know what we were doing that weekend and I told her everything I had planned and she said: "My, aren't you the little housewife." She was just joshing me, but I sort of, I wanted to puke. I mean, I think it's important to do this stuff, but it's kind of embarrassing, you know? *I do go to the gym quite a bit, so I guess that sort of makes up for it* (emphasis added).

Here we see the potential for the stigmatization of men who do these activities. Mike, in attempting to manage both a feminine-defined occupation and responsibility for kin work (among other forms of domestic work), turns to the realm of athletics "to make up for it." Many gay-male families must manage the threatening character of domestic work (including kin work) to male gender identity. Let it suffice to say that there are many ways to resolve this issue, including constructing myths, using rhetorical strategies that hide the

true division of domestic labor, and, for a few, simply violating conventional expectations. . . .

Ethnic and racial distinctions and lesbigay kin work. The influence of ethnic and racial identity upon kin work eludes easy analysis. The confluence of class and race in American culture often conceals distinctions between race and class (Steinberg 1989). This study captures the diversity of lesbigay families in terms of ethnic/racial identity, with over 40 percent of the respondents identifying themselves as Latino-, African-, or Asian-American. However, comparisons are limited by the fact that many of these same respondents are middle class. I know from my attempts to identify lower middle-class and working-class respondents within these groups and among Euro-Americans that lesbigays with fewer economic resources are far more hesitant to participate in this kind of research due to concerns about exposure of sexual identity. That said, let me turn to some discussion of the possible influence of ethnic/racial identity upon the extent and character of kin work.

On the one hand, because most of these families' household earnings, education and occupational identities place them in the middle class, they exhibit kin work patterns similar to their Euro-American middle-class counterparts. Most live in what Dizard and Gadlin would characterize as "minimal families" (1990). Similar to many middle-class families, and in contrast to more affluent families, these families report fewer close friends, they invite nonbiolegal kin over less often, they send fewer cards, write fewer letters, make fewer visits, make fewer long-distance calls, buy, send and give fewer presents, and organize fewer social occasions. On the other hand, Latino/Asian/African-identified lesbigay families recurrently report more extensive connections to biolegal relatives than do Euro-American families, and further, they more often than not conceive of family in strongly biolegal terms. For instance, they report greater exchange of money and material goods with biolegal relatives. A number of factors help to explain these dynamics.

First, the wide majority of African-, Asian- and Latino-American lesbigays grew up in California. This contrasts markedly with the Euro-Americans, 90 percent of whom grew up elsewhere and relocated to California. This means that, because Asian-, African- and Latino-American biolegal kin live in the area, kin relations become more extensive and more pressing. This dynamic appears more strongly related to geographical proximity than to ethnic/racial distinction. Euro-Americans who grew up in this region also exhibit stronger ties to biolegal kin. However, many lesbigay people of color strongly link conceptions of racial/ethnic identity with conceptions of kinship, something not heard among Euro-Americans. Deborah James, an African-American woman, and her partner, Elsa Harding, also African-American, both speak of their connections to biolegal family as a component of their racial identity. Deborah, who works as a daycare provider, states:

> I think that Anglo-Americans don't value family as much as Black people do. I mean, I know some lesbians who think of each other as their family, but I really don't get that. I mean, I think you gotta love your family, even if they aren't that accepting of you. For us, part of being African-American is keeping your connections to your family and your church and stuff like that.

Barbara Cho, a thirty-eight-year-old Chinese-American woman working as a hotel clerk, holds a similar view: "I think of my family as my relatives. I love Barbara [her partner], but she is not really a part of my relatives. I don't want to say she isn't like family to me, but she's not my family. My mother and father, and my sisters, they are my family."

Although most Asian-, African-, and Latino-American lesbigay families conceive of

family in biolegal terms (many respondents use the phrase "blood is thicker than water"), not all share this conception. Ceasar Portes and Andy Yanez, together for seventeen years and living in San Francisco's Mission district, a predominantly Latino neighborhood, exhibit an alternative pattern. Ceasar comes from a large Mexican-American family, most of whom live within a half-day's drive. Andy comes from a somewhat smaller, though equally close, Filipino-American family. Ceasar, diminishing the distinction between biolegal and lesbigay kin, asserts:

> We try to include all of our family, I mean both our gay family and our blood family, who live in San Jose or in Pacifica, in our lives. We also have our religious family, you know, many brothers and sisters in the faith, who are a part of our community. We invite everyone to be here. At first, it was hard. I don't think my blood relatives really understood gay people. But they have really changed. My mother loves all of our gay family now, and so we are all family together.

Andy reports that his family, while less accepting of his sexual identity than Ceasar's family, remains strongly committed to "keeping the family together," and includes Ceasar in family activities. Ceasar says that one of his sisters thinks of Andy as a "padrino," or godfather, to her children and makes an effort to include him in family activities.

Derrick Harding and Andrew Joust, both African-American men, provide another counterexample to the notion that "blood is thicker than water." Derrick mentions two heterosexual couples at their local church whom he considers family. In response to a question as to why he considers them such, he reflects: "Why yes, without a doubt, they care about us. They are like our godparents. They adopted us. We are real close with them. They are our family." His partner, Andrew, comments on the same heterosexual couples: "They took us under their wing when we first got here. I think of them as our family, I don't know what else you would call them." These competing views of the importance of ethnic/racial distinctions upon family that exist among African-, Asian-, and Latino-American lesbigay families point to the influence of factors related to but different from ethnicity that play a role in conceptions and constructions of family life. In the case of Andrew and Derrick, they migrated to the Bay Area and established connections to a church community. Their biolegal relatives remain in the East and far away from their day-to-day lives. Andrew reports that he last spoke with a biolegal relative more than a year ago. What really seems to divide those African-, Asian-, and Latino-American lesbigay families who redefine family in non-biolegal terms from those who do is social class. All of those families who blur the distinctions between biolegal and chosen families possess bachelor's degrees, work in professional careers, and earn higher incomes. Ceasar and Derrick both work as social workers, Andrew works as a secondary education teacher, and Andy works in higher education administration.

Kin Work and the Creation of Family

In its extensiveness, its focused character, and its reflection of genuine bonds of love and affection, kin work contributes much to the creation and sustenance of lesbigay life. The family that results from this kin work is not, as many opponents of lesbigay people would have one believe, a rough approximation of the real thing or a sad substitute for genuine biolegal relations. Nor is it just a group of friends. Far from it. The bonds created within and among these families are far more extensive than what most middle-class Americans would conventionally view as friendship bonds (Rapp 1992). Middle-class Americans infrequently take in their friends and provide them housing, food, and medical care while they are dying. Moreover, any number of the lesbigay families in this study would not dream of sacrificing the lesbigay kin ties they have created in favor of some biolegally defined entity. Not to mention that many lesbigay families don't have to make that choice because their biolegal kin have not excluded them, and therein they have been able to integrate biolegal and lesbigay kin into a greater whole. Surely, many lesbigay families are struggling to create and sustain kin ties against socioeconomic conditions that deter them, but the effort is paradoxical and often threatening to the broader culture. These families are struggling to create and sustain kin relations with the qualities associated with family ideals in American culture, but not necessarily with the forms most citizens associate with family.

REFERENCES

Badgett, L., and M. King. 1997. Lesbian and gay occupational strategies. In A. Gluckman and B. Reed, eds., *Homo Economics: Capitalism, Community and Lesbian and Gay Life.* New York: Routledge.

Berk, S. Fenstermacher. 1985. *The Gender Factory: The Apportionment of Work in American Households.* New York: Plenum Press.

Blumstein, P., and P. Schwarz. 1983. *American Couples.* New York: Morrow.

Coontz, S. 1992. *The Way We Never Were: American Families and the Nostalgia Trap.* New York: Basic Books.

Curtis, R., and E. Jackson. 1977. *Inequality in American Communities.* New York: Academic Press.

D'Emilio, J. 1983. Capitalism and gay identity. In Ann Snitow, ed., *Powers of Desire: The Politics of Sexuality.* New York: Monthly Press Review.

Di Leonardo, M. 1987. The female world of cards and holidays: Women, families, and the work of kinship. *Signs* 12 (Summer): 440–52.

Dizard, J., and H. Gadlin. 1990. *The Minimal Family.* Amherst: University of Massachusetts Press.

Gerstel, N., and S. Gallagher. 1993. Kinkeeping and distress: Gender, recipients of care, and work-family conflict. *Journal of Marriage and the Family* 55 (Aug.): 598–607.

Gerstel, N., and S. Gallagher. 1994. Caring for kith and kin: Gender, employment, and privatization of care. *Social Problems* 41 (4): 519–39.

Harry, J. 1984. *Gay Couples.* New York: Praeger.

Hodges, H. 1964. *Social Stratification: Class in America.* Cambridge, Mass.: Schenkman.

Lewin, E. 1993. *Lesbian Mothers: Accounts of Gender in American Culture.* Ithaca, N.Y.: Cornell University Press.

———. 1998. *Recognizing Ourselves: Ceremonies of Lesbian and Gay Commitment.* New York: Columbia University Press.

Matthews, G. 1987. *Just a Housewife: The Rise and Fall of Domesticity in America.* New York: Oxford.

Mohr, R. 1994. *A More Perfect Union: Why Straight America Must Stand Up for Gay Rights.* Boston: Beacon.

Nardi, P. 1992. That's what friends are for: Friends as family in the gay and lesbian community. In K. Plummer, ed., *Modern Homosexualities.* London: Routledge.

Nardi, P., and D. Sherrod. 1994. Friendship in the lives of gay men and lesbians. *Journal of Social and Personal Relationships* 11:185–99.

Newton, E. 1993. *Cherry Grove, Fire Island: Sixty Years in America's First Gay and Lesbian Town.* Boston: Beacon.

Rosenthal, C. 1985. Kinkeeping in the family division of labor. *Journal of Marriage and the Family* 47 (4): 965–74.

Schneider, D. 1984. *A Critique of the Study of Kinship.* Ann Arbor: University of Michigan Press.

Schneider, D., and R. Smith. 1973. *Class Differences and Sex Roles in American Kinship and Family Structure.* Englewood Cliffs, N.J.: Prentice Hall.

Skolnick, A. 1991. *Embattled Paradise: The American Family in an Age of Uncertainty.* New York: Basic Books.

Stacey, J. 1990. *Brave New Families: Stories of Upheaval in the Late Twentieth Century.* New York: Basic Books.

———. 1996. *In the Name of the Family: Rethinking Family Values in the PostModern Age.* Boston: Beacon.

Stack, C. 1974. *All Our Kin: Strategies for Survival in a Black Community.* New York: Harper and Row.

Steinberg, Stephen. 1989. *The Ethnic Myth: Race, Ethnicity, and Class in America.* Boston: Beacon.

U.S. Bureau of the Census. 1991. *Money Income of Households, Families, and Persons in the United States: 1990.* Series P-60, no. 174. Washington, D.C: Author.

Voydanoff, P. 1992. Economic distress and family relations: A review of the eighties. *Journal of Marriage and the Family* 52: 1099–1115.

West, C., and D. Zimmerman. 1987. Doing gender. *Gender and Society* I (2): 125–51.

Westkott, M. 1986. *The Feminist Legacy of Karen Horney.* New Haven, Conn.: Yale University Press.

Weston, K. 1990. *Families We Choose: Lesbians, Gays, Kinship.* New York: Columbia University Press.

THINKING ABOUT THE READING

What is "kin work"? Do you agree that kin work is what creates and sustains families? Should two people who consistently love and care for each other and who engage in the day-to-day tasks necessary to maintain a household be considered a family and be eligible for all the benefits that legal families are entitled to? If, as Carrington argues, the family-defining activities that gay and lesbian couples engage in are no different from those that heterosexual couples engage in, why is there such strong public opposition to the legal recognition of gay couples as families? Carrington implies that individuals should have the freedom to define their own living arrangements as a family. Do you agree? Does society have an interest in controlling who can and can't be considered a family?

Chasing the Blood Tie

Surrogate Mothers, Adoptive Mothers, and Fathers

Helena Ragoné

(1996)

An election that's about ideas and values is also about philosophy, and I have one. At the bright center is the individual, and radiating out from him or her is the family, the essential unit of closeness and love. For it's the family that communicates to our children, to the 21st century, our culture, our religious faith, our traditions, and our history.

—George Bush, Presidential
Nomination Acceptance Speech, 1989

A couple, William and Elizabeth Stern, contracted with a surrogate, Mary Beth Whitehead, to bear a child for them because Elizabeth Stern suffered from multiple sclerosis, a condition that can be exacerbated by pregnancy. Once the child was born, however, Whitehead refused to relinquish the child to the Sterns, and in 1987, William Stern, the biological father, filed suit against Whitehead in an effort to enforce the terms of the surrogate contract. The decision of the lower court to award custody to the biological father and to permit his wife to adopt the child was overturned by the New Jersey Supreme Court, which then awarded custody to William Stern, prohibiting Elizabeth Stern from adopting the child while granting visitation rights to Mary Beth Whitehead.

. . . This case, known as The Baby M Case, raised many questions about what constitutes motherhood, fatherhood, family, reproduction, and kinship. Much of what has been written about surrogate motherhood has, however, been largely speculative or polemical in nature; it ranges from the view that surrogate motherhood is symptomatic of the dissolution of the American family and the sanctity of motherhood to charges that it reduces or assigns women to a breeder class structurally akin to prostitution (Dworkin 1978) or that it constitutes a form of commercial baby selling (Annas 1988; Neuhaus 1988). . . .

This article is based on fieldwork conducted at three different surrogate mother programs from 1988 to the present. . . .

Surrogate Motivations

When I began my field research in 1988, surrogate mother programs and directors had already become the subject of considerable media attention, a great deal of it sensationalized and negative in character. At that time there were ten established surrogate mother programs in the United States; in addition, there were also a number of small, part-time businesses (none of which were included in the study) in which lawyers, doctors, adoption agents, and others arranged occasional surrogate mother contracts.[1] In order to obtain as stable a sample as possible, I chose to include only firmly established programs in my study. The oldest of the programs was established in approximately 1980, and none of the programs included in my study had been in business for fewer than ten years as of 1994.

There are two types of surrogate mother programs: what I call "open" programs, in which surrogate and couple select one another and interact throughout the insemination and the pregnancy, and "closed" programs, in which couples select their surrogates from information—biographical and medical information and a photograph of the surrogate—provided to them by the programs. After the child is born in a "closed" program, the couple and surrogate meet only to finalize the stepparent adoption. I formally interviewed a total of 28 surrogates, from six different programs. Aside from these formal interviews I also engaged in countless conversations with surrogates, observing them as they interacted with their families, testified before legislative committees, worked in surrogate programs, and socialized at program gatherings with directors and others. Quite often I was an invited guest at the homes of program directors, a situation that provided me with a unique opportunity to observe directors interacting with their own spouses and children, with couples and surrogates, and with members of their staffs. The opportunity to observe the daily workings of the surrogate mother programs provided me with invaluable data on the day-to-day operations of the programs. At one program I attended staff meetings on a regular basis and observed consultations in which prospective couples and surrogates were interviewed singly by members of the staff such as the director, a psychologist, a medical coordinator, or the administrative coordinator.

A review of the literature on surrogate motherhood reveals that, until now, the primary research focus has been on the surrogate mother herself, and that there have been no ethnographic studies on surrogate mother programs and commissioning couples. Studies of the surrogate population tend to focus, at times exclusively, on surrogates' stated motivations for becoming surrogate mothers (Parker 1983). Their stated reasons include the desire to help an infertile couple start a family, financial remuneration, and a love of pregnancy (Parker 1983:140). As I began my own research I soon observed a remarkable degree of consistency or uniformity in surrogates' responses to questions about their initial motivations for becoming surrogates; it was as if they had all been given a script in which they espoused many of the motivations earlier catalogued by Parker, motivations that also, as I will show, reflect culturally accepted ideas about reproduction, motherhood, and family and are fully reinforced by the programs. I also began to uncover several areas of conflict between professed motivations and actual experiences, discovering, for example, that although surrogates claim to experience "easy pregnancies" and "problem-free labor," it was not unusual for surrogates to have experienced miscarriages, ectopic pregnancies, and related difficulties, as the following examples reveal. Jeannie, age 36, divorced with one child and employed in the entertainment industry, described the ectopic pregnancy she experienced while she was a surrogate in this manner: "I almost bled to death: I literally almost died for my couple." Nevertheless, she was again inseminating a second time for the same couple. As this and other examples demonstrate, even when their experiences are at odds with their stated motivations, surrogates tend not to acknowledge inconsistencies between their initially stated motivations and their subsequent experiences. This reformulation of motivation is seen in the following instance as well. Fran, age 27, divorced with one child and working as a dog trainer, described the difficulty of her delivery in this way: "I had a rough delivery, a C-section, and my lung collapsed because I had the flu, but it was worth every minute of it. If I were to die from childbirth, that's the best way to die. You died for a cause, a good one." As both these examples illustrate, some surrogates readily embrace the idea of meaningful suffering, heroism, or sacrifice, and although their stated motivations are of some interest they do not adequately account for the range of shifting motivations uncovered in my research.

One of the motivations most frequently assumed to be primary by the casual observer is remuneration, and I took considerable pains to try to evaluate its influence on surrogates. In the programs, surrogates receive between $10,000 and $15,000 (for three to four months of insemination and nine months of pregnancy, on average), a fee that has changed only nominally since the early 1980s.[2] As one program psychologist explained, the amount paid to surrogates is intentionally held at an artificially low rate by the programs so as to screen out women who might be motivated solely by monetary gain. One of the questions I sought to explore was whether surrogates were denying the importance of remuneration in order to cast their actions in a more culturally acceptable light, or whether they were motivated in part by remuneration and in part by other factors (with the importance of remuneration decreasing as the pregnancy progresses, the version of events put forth by both program staff and surrogates).

The opinion popular among both scholars and the general population, that surrogates are motivated primarily by financial gain, has tended to result in oversimplified analyses of surrogate motivations. The following are typical of surrogate explanations for the connection between the initial decision to become a surrogate and the remuneration they receive.

Dismissals of the idea that remuneration serves as a primary source of motivation for surrogates of the kind expressed by Fran were frequent: "it [surrogacy] sounded so interesting and fun. The money wasn't enough to be pregnant for nine months."

Andrea, age 29, was married with three children. A high school graduate who worked as a motel night auditor, she expressly denied the idea that remuneration motivates most surrogates. As she said here, "I'm not doing it for the money. Take the money: that wouldn't stop me. It wouldn't stop the majority."

Sara, age 27, who attended two years of college, was married with two children and worked part-time as a tax examiner. Here she explains her feelings about remuneration:

> What's 10,000 bucks? You can't even buy a car. If it was just for the money you will want the baby. Money wasn't important. I possibly would have done it just for expenses, especially for the people I did it for. My father would have given me the money not to do it.

The issue of remuneration proved to be of particular interest in that, although surrogates do accept monetary compensation for their reproductive work, its role is a multifaceted one. The surrogate pregnancy, unlike a traditional pregnancy, is viewed by the surrogate and her family as work; as such, it is informed by the belief that work is something that occurs only within the context of paid occupations (Ferree 1984:72). It is interesting to note that surrogates rarely spend the money they earn on themselves. Not one of the surrogates I interviewed spent the money she earned on herself alone; the majority spend it on their children—as a contribution to their college education funds, for example—while others spend it on home improvement, gifts for their husbands, a family vacation, or simply to pay off "family debts."

One of the primary reasons that most surrogates do not spend the money they earn on themselves alone appears to stem from the fact that the money serves as a buffer against and/or reward to their families—in particular to their husbands, who make a number of compromises as a result of the surrogate arrangement. One of these compromises is obligatory abstention from sexual intercourse with their wives from the time insemination begins until a pregnancy has been confirmed (a period of time that lasts on average from three to four months in length, but that may be extended for as long as one year). Surrogacy is viewed by surrogates as a part-time job in the sense that it allows a woman, especially a mother, to stay at home—to have, as one surrogate noted, "the luxury of staying home with my children," an idea that is also attractive to their husbands. The fact that a surrogate need not leave home on a routine basis or in any formalized way to earn money is perceived by the surrogate and her husband as a benefit; the surrogate, however, consequently spends less time with her family as a result of a new schedule that includes medical appointments, therapy sessions, [and] social engagements with the commissioning couple. Thus surrogates are able to use the monetary compensation they receive as a means of procuring their husbands' support when and if they become less available to the family because of their employment.

The devaluation of the amount of the surrogate payment by surrogates as insufficient to compensate for "nine months of pregnancy" serves several important purposes. First, this view is representative of the cultural belief that children are "priceless" (Zelizer 1985); in this sense surrogates are merely reiterating a widely held cultural belief when they devalue the amount of remuneration they receive. When, for example, the largest and one of the most well-established surrogate mother programs changed the wording of its advertising copy from "Help an Infertile Couple" to "Give the Gift of Life," the vastly increased volume of response revealed that the program had discovered a successful formula with which to reach the surrogate population. With surrogacy, the gift is conceptualized as a child, a formulation that is widely used in Euro-American culture—for example, in blood (Titmuss 1971) and organ donation (Fox and Swazey 1992).

The gift formulation holds particular appeal for surrogates because it reinforces the idea that having a child for someone is an act that cannot be compensated for monetarily. As I have already mentioned, the "gift of life" theme is further enhanced by some surrogates to embrace the near-sacrifice of their own lives in childbirth.

Fran, whose dismissal of the importance of payment I have already quoted, also offered another, more revealing account of her decision to become a surrogate mother: "I wanted to do the ultimate thing for somebody, to give them the ultimate gift. Nobody can beat that, nobody can do anything nicer for them." Stella, age 38, married with two children, noted that the commissioning couples "consider it [the baby] a gift and I consider it a gift." Carolyn, age 33, married with two children and the owner of a house-cleaning company, discussed her feelings about remuneration and having a surrogate child in these terms: "It's a gift of love. I have always been a really giving person, and it's the ultimate way to give. I've always had babies so easily. It's the ultimate gift of love."

As we can see, when surrogates characterize the child they reproduce for couples as a "gift," they are also suggesting tacitly that mere monetary compensation would never be sufficient to repay the debt incurred. Although this formulation may at first appear to be a reiteration of the belief that children are culturally priceless, it also suggests that surrogates recognize that they are creating a state of enduring solidarity between themselves and their couples . . . where the end result is "more profound than the result of other gift transactions, because the relationship established is not just one of reciprocity, but one of kinship" (Rubin 1975:172). . . .

Thus when surrogates frame the equation as one in which a gift is being proffered, the theme serves as a counterpoint to the business aspect of the arrangement, a reminder to them and to the commissioning couple that one of the symbolically central functions of money . . . may be insufficient to erase certain kinds of relationships, and that the relational element may continue to surface despite the monetary exchange.

This formulation of surrogacy as a matter of altruism versus remuneration has also proved to be a pivotal issue in legislative debates and discussions. Jan Sutton, the founder and spokeswoman of the National Association of Surrogate Mothers (a group of more than 100 surrogates who support legislation in favor of surrogacy), stated in her testimony before an information-gathering session of the California state legislature in 1989: "My organization and its members would all still be surrogates if no payment was involved" (Ragoné 1989). Her sentiment is not unrepresentative of those expressed by the surrogates interviewed for this study. Interestingly enough, once Sutton had informed the committee of that fact, several of the members of the panel who had previously voiced their opposition to surrogacy in its commercial form began to express praise for Sutton, indicating that her testimony had altered their opinion of surrogacy.

In direct response to her testimony, the committee began instead to discuss a proposal to ban commercial surrogacy but to allow for the practice of noncommercial surrogacy. In the latter practice the surrogate is barred from receiving financial compensation for her work, although the physicians and lawyers involved are allowed their usual compensation for services rendered. In Britain, where commercial surrogacy has been declared illegal, the issue was framed often in moral terms: "The symbol of the pure surrogate who creates a child for love was pitted against the symbol of the wicked surrogate who prostitutes her maternity" (Cannell 1990:683). This dichotomous rendering in which "pure" surrogates are set in opposition to "wicked" surrogates is predicated on the idea that altruism precludes remuneration. In the Baby M Case, for example, the most decisive issue was the one concerning payment to the surrogate (Hull 1990:155).

Although surrogates overwhelmingly cast their actions in a traditional light, couching the desire to become a surrogate in conservative and traditionally feminine terms, it is clear that in many respects surrogate motherhood represents a departure from traditional motherhood. It transforms private motherhood into public motherhood, and it provides women with remuneration for their reproductive work—work that has in American culture been done, as Schneider has noted, for "love" rather than for "money" (Schneider 1968). It is this aspect that has unintendedly become one of the primary foci of consideration in state legislatures throughout the United States. Of the 15 states that now have surrogacy laws in place, the "most common regulations, applicable in 11 states . . . are statutes voiding paid surrogacy contracts" (Andrews 1992:50). The overwhelming acceptance of the idea of unpaid or noncommercial surrogacy (both in the United States and in Britain) can be attributed to the belief that it "duplicates maternity in culturally the most self-less manner" (Strathern 1991:31).

But what is perhaps even more important, the corresponding rejection of paid or commercial surrogacy may also be said to result from a cultural resistance to conflating the symbolic value of the family with the world of work to which it has long been held in opposition. From a legal perspective, commercial surrogacy has been viewed largely by the courts as a matter of "merg[ing] the family with the world of business and commerce" (Dolgin 1993: 692), a prospect that presents a challenge to American cultural definitions of the family. . . .

Resistance in U. S. society to merging these two realms, the domestic and the public, may be traced to the entrenched belief that the

> private realm [is] where women are most in evidence, where natural functions like sex and bodily functions related to procreation take place, where the affective content of relations is primary and [that] a public realm [is] where men are most in evidence, where culture is produced, where one's efficiency at producing goods or services takes precedence. [Martin 1987:15–16]

With the introduction of the phenomenon of public motherhood in the form of surrogacy, however, the separation of family and work has been irrevocably challenged. Over time it became clear to me that many of the women who chose to become surrogate mothers did so as a way to transcend the limitations of their domestic roles as wives, mothers, and homemakers while concomitantly attesting to the importance of those roles and to the satisfaction they derived from them. That idea indeed accounted for some of their contradictory statements. Surrogates, who are for the most part from predominantly working-class backgrounds, have, for example, often been denied access to prestigious roles and other avenues for attaining status and power. Surrogacy thus provides them with confirmation that motherhood is important and socially valued.[3] Surrogacy also introduces them to a world filled with social interaction with people who are deeply appreciative of the work that they do, and in this way surrogates receive validation and are rewarded for their reproductive work through their participation in this new form of public motherhood.

Of all the surrogates' stated motivations, remuneration proved to be the most

problematic. On a symbolic level, remuneration detracts from the idealized cultural image of women/mothers as selfless, nurturant, and altruistic, an image that surrogates have no wish to alter. Then, too, if surrogates were to acknowledge money as adequate compensation for their reproductive work, they would lose the sense that theirs is a gift that transcends all monetary compensation. The fact that some surrogates had experienced difficult pregnancies and deliveries and were not thereby dissuaded from becoming surrogate mothers, coupled with their devaluation of remuneration and their tendency to characterize the child as a gift, suggested that current theories about surrogate motivations provided only a partial explanation for what was clearly a more complex phenomenon.

From the moment she places a telephone call to a surrogate mother program to the moment she delivers the child, the balance of power in a surrogate's personal life is altered radically. Her time can no longer be devoted exclusively to the care and nurture of her own family because she has entered into a legal and social contract to perform an important and economically rewarded task: helping an infertile couple to begin a family of their own. Unlike other types of employment, this activity cannot be regarded as unfeminine, selfish, or nonnurturant. As I have previously mentioned, the surrogate's husband must sign a consent form in which he agrees to abstain from sexual intercourse with his wife until a pregnancy has been confirmed. In so doing he agrees to relinquish both his sexual and procreative ties to his wife and thus is understood to be supporting his wife's decision to conceive and gestate another man's child (or another couple's child, in the case of gestational surrogacy). Once a surrogate enters a program, she also begins to recognize just how important having a child is to the commissioning couple. She sees with renewed clarity that no matter how much material success the couple has, their lives are emotionally impoverished because of their inability to have a child. In this way the surrogate's fertility serves as a leveling device for perceived, if unacknowledged, economic differences—and many surrogates begin to see themselves as altruistic or heroic figures who can rectify the imbalance in a couple's life.

Fathers, Adoptive Mothers, and Surrogate Mothers

Studies on surrogate motherhood have tended to characterize the couple's motivations as lacking in complexity; in other words, it is assumed that the primary motivation is to have a child that is biologically related to at least one member of the couple (in this case the father and, in the case of donor insemination, the mother) (Glover 1990). . . . Commissioning couples consistently articulate the belief that surrogacy is a superior alternative to adoption. Many couples have attempted to adopt, only to discover the shortage of healthy white infants and age limit criteria of adoption agencies: see Ragoné 1994. Surrogacy not only provides them with the highly desirable partial-genetic link (through the father), but it also permits them to meet and interact with the biological mother—something that is usually not possible with adoption. . . .

Although couples may be motivated initially by a desire to have a child that is biologically related to at least one of the partners, the fact that this can only be achieved by employing the services of a woman other than the wife introduces a host of dilemmas.

Fathers and adoptive mothers resolve the problems posed by surrogate motherhood through various and separate strategies. Their disparate concerns stem not only from the biogenetic relationship the father bears to the child and from the adoptive mother's lack of such a relationship, but also from the pressures of having to negotiate the landscape of this novel terrain. For the father the primary obstacle or

issue posed by surrogate motherhood is that a woman other than his wife will be the "mother" of his child. The following quotations from fathers illustrate the considerable degree of ambiguity created by surrogate motherhood. They also reveal the couples' shared assumptions about American kinship ideology and how it is that "biological elements have primarily symbolic significance" (Schneider 1972:45).

Tom and his wife, for example, had experienced 17 years of infertility. Initially opposed to surrogate motherhood out of concern that his wife would feel "left out," Tom described his early reactions: "Yes, the whole thing was at first strange. I thought to myself; here she [the surrogate] is carrying my baby. Isn't she supposed to be my wife?"

Ed, a 45-year-old college professor, described a similar sense of confusion: "I felt weird about another woman carrying my child, but as we all got to know one another it didn't seem weird. It seemed strangely comfortable after a while."

Richard, age 43, a computer engineer, described similar feelings of awkwardness about the child's biological tie to the surrogate:

> Seeing Jane [the surrogate] in him [his son], it's literally a part of herself she gave. That's fairly profound. I developed an appreciation of the magnitude of what she did and the inappropriateness of approaching this as a business relationship. It didn't seem like such a big thing initially for another woman to carry my baby, a little awkward in not knowing how to relate to her and not wanting to interfere with her relationship with her husband. But after Tommy was born I can see Jane in his appearance, and I had a feeling it was a strange thing we did not to have a relationship with Jane. But it's wearing off, and I'm not struck so much with: I've got a piece of Jane here.

Questions such as Tom's "Isn't she supposed to be my wife?" reflect the concern and confusion experienced by husbands, their ambivalence underscoring the continued symbolic centrality of sexual intercourse and procreation in American kinship, both of which continue to symbolize unity and love (Schneider 1968). The father's relationship to the surrogate, although strictly noncoital, is altered by the fact that it produces what was always, until the recent past, the product of a sexual union—namely, a child. Feelings of discomfort or "awkwardness," and concerns as to how to behave toward the surrogate and the surrogate's husband, stem from the idea that the father-surrogate relationship may be considered adultery by those unfamiliar with the particulars of the surrogate arrangement. For example, one program reported that a client arrived at the program office with the expectation that he would engage in sexual intercourse with the surrogate. One surrogate remarked on this ambivalence: "The general public thinks I went to bed with the father. They think I committed adultery!"

In addition to concerns about his relationship to the surrogate vis-à-vis the child, a father is aware that the child bears no genetic tie to his wife. The husband thus gains his inclusivity in the surrogate relationship through his biological contribution vis-à-vis the surrogate: he is both the genitor and pater; but it is the surrogate, not his wife, who is the genetrix. One of the primary strategies employed by both couples and surrogates is to deemphasize the husband's role precisely because it is the surrogate-father relationship that raises the specter of adultery or, more accurately, temporary polygandry and temporary polygyny. They also downplay the significance of his biological link to the child, focusing instead on the bond that develops between the adoptive and the surrogate mother.

The Surrogate and Adoptive Mother Bond

The adoptive mother attempts to resolve her lack of genetic relatedness to the child through what I have labeled her "mythic conception" of the child—that is, the notion that her desire to have a child is what first makes the surrogate arrangement a possibility. Cybil, an adoptive mother, explained the mythic conception in this way: "Ann is my baby; she was conceived in my heart before Lisa's [the surrogate's] body." Lucy, an adoptive mother, described the symbiotic relationship that developed between herself and her surrogate in a slightly different way: "She [the surrogate] represented that part of me that couldn't have a child."

The adoptive mother also experiences what can be described as a "pseudopregnancy" through which she experiences the state of pregnancy by proxy—as close to the experience as an infertile woman can be. As one surrogate said of this relationship, "I had a closeness with Sue [the adoptive mother] that you would have with your husband. She took Lamaze class and went to the delivery room with me." In fact, when geographical proximity permits, it is expected in the open programs that adoptive mothers will accompany surrogates to all medical appointments and birthing classes, in addition to attending the delivery of the child in the hospital (where the biological father and the surrogate's husband are also present whenever possible).

Together, the surrogate and the adoptive mother thus define reproduction as "women's business," often reiterating the idea that their relationship is a natural and exclusive one. As Celeste, a surrogate mother, pointed out: "The whole miracle of birth would be lost if she [the adoptive mother] wasn't there. If women don't experience the birth of their children being born they would be alienated and they would be breeders." Mary, a surrogate whose adoptive mother gave her a heart-shaped necklace to commemorate the birth of the child, said, "I feel a sisterhood to all women of the world. I am doing this for her, looking to see her holding the baby." Both of the adoptive mother's strategies, her mythic conception of the child and her pseudopregnancy, are—as these quotations demonstrate—greatly facilitated by the surrogate, who not only deemphasizes the importance of her physical pregnancy but also disavows the importance of her own biological link to the child. Celeste summed up the sentiment expressed by many surrogates when she stated, "She [the adoptive mother] was emotionally pregnant, and I was just *physically pregnant*" (emphasis added).

Without exception, when surrogates are asked whether they think of the child as their own, they say that they do not. Kay, a surrogate, age 35 and divorced with two children, explained her feelings in this way: "I never think of the child as mine. After I had the baby, the mother came into the room and held the baby. I couldn't relate that it had any part of me."

Mary, age 37, married with three children, similarly stated, "I don't think of the baby as my child. I donated an egg I wasn't going to be using." Jeannie, yet another surrogate, described herself as having no connection to the child: "I feel like a vehicle, just like a cow; it's their baby, it's his sperm."

The surrogate's ability to deemphasize her own biological link to the child is made possible in part by her focus upon the folk theory of procreation in which paternity is viewed as the "primary, essential and creative role" (Delaney 1986:495). Even though in the realm of scientific knowledge women have long been identified as cocreators, "in Europe and America, the knowledge has not been encompassed symbolically. Symbols change slowly and the two levels of discourse are hardly ever brought into conjunction" (Delaney 1986:509).

With the "dominant folk theory of procreation in the West," paternity has been conceptualized as the "power to create and engender life" (Delaney 1986:510), whereas maternity has come to mean "giving nurturance and giving birth" (Delaney 1986:495). Surrogates therefore emphasize the importance of nurturance and

consistently define that aspect of motherhood as a choice that one can elect to make or not make. This emphasis on nurturance is embraced readily by the surrogate and adoptive mother alike since "one of the central notions in the modern American construct of the family is that of nurturance" (Collier et al. 1982:34). In the United States nurturance until now has been considered "natural to women and [the] basis of their cultural authority" (Ginsburg 1987:629). Like other kinds of assisted reproduction, surrogate motherhood is understood to "fall into older cultural terrains, where women interpret their options in light of prior and contradictory meanings of pregnancy and childbearing" (Rapp 1990:41).

For this reason surrogates underplay their own biological contribution in order to bring to the fore the importance of the social, nurturant role played by the adoptive mother. The efforts of surrogates and adoptive mothers to separate social motherhood from biological motherhood can be seen to represent a reworking of the nature/culture dichotomy. A primary strategy an adoptive mother may employ in order to resolve her lack of genetic relatedness to the child is her use of the idea of intentionality, specifically of "conception in the heart"—that is, the idea that in the final analysis it is the adoptive mother's desire to have a child that brings the surrogate arrangement into being and ultimately results in the birth of a child. The surrogate thus devalues her own genetic/physical contribution while highlighting the pseudopregnancy of the adoptive mother and the importance of the latter's role as nurturer. In this way motherhood is reinterpreted as primarily an important social role in order to sidestep problematic aspects of the surrogate's biogenetic relationship to the child and the adoptive mother's lack of a biogenetic link. This focus upon intentionality and nurturance by both surrogates and adoptive mothers is reflected in the following statement by Andy, a 39-year-old surrogate, who is the divorced mother of two children and a full-time nurse:

> Parents are the ones who raise the child. I got that from my parents, who adopted children. My siblings were curious and my parents gave them the information they had and they never wanted to track down their biological parents. I don't think of the baby as mine; it is the *parents, the ones who raise the child,* that are important (emphasis added).

The adoptive mother and father of the child attempt to resolve the tensions inherent in the surrogate arrangement, in particular its rearrangement of boundaries through the blurring of the distinctions between pregnancy and motherhood, genetic relatedness and affective bonds, wife and mother, wife and husband, and wife and surrogate mother. The surrogate's role in achieving these goals is nevertheless essential. Through the process in which pregnancy and birth are defined as being exclusively women's business, the father's role is relegated to secondary status in the relational triangle. The surrogate plays a primary role in facilitating the adoptive mother's role as mother of the child, something that is made possible by her refusal to nurture the child to which she gives birth. In the interest of assisting this process the surrogate consistently devalues her biological contribution or genetic relationship to the child.

In this process of emphasizing the value of nurturance, surrogates describe motherhood as a role that one can adopt or refuse, and this concept of nurturance as choice is for them the single most important defining aspect of motherhood. Surrogates believe that, in the case of surrogacy, motherhood is comprised of two separable aspects: first, the biological process (insemination, pregnancy, and delivery); and second, the social process (nurturance). They reason that a woman can either choose to nurture—that is, to accept the role of social

mother—or choose not to nurture, thereby rejecting the role of social mother.

As we have seen, surrogates, couples, and surrogate mother programs work in concert to create a new idea of order and appropriate relations and boundaries by directing their attention to the sanctity of motherhood as it is illustrated in the surrogate and adoptive mother bond. The surrogate and adoptive mother work in unison, reinforcing one another's view that it is social rather than biological motherhood that ultimately creates a mother. Nurture, they reason together, is a far more important and central construct of motherhood than nature. The decision on the part of the surrogate not to nurture the child nullifies the value of biological motherhood, while the adoptive mother's choice to nurture activates or fully brings forth motherhood.

Because of the emphasis couples place on having a child that is biologically related to at least one partner, I was initially perplexed to learn that less than five percent of couples chose to have a paternity test performed once the child had been born (although this option is offered to every couple); surrogate contracts specifically state that the couple is under no obligation to accept the child until such a test has been performed. In view of the fact that couples spend between $40,000 and $45,000 in fees to have a child who is biologically related to them, such a lack of interest in the paternity test is initially perplexing. When asked about paternity testing, wives and husbands typically give responses such as these: "We knew she was ours from the minute we saw her," or "We decided that it really didn't matter; he was ours no matter what."

While these statements may initially appear to contradict the stated purpose of pursuing a partially biogenetic solution to childlessness, they can also be understood to fulfill two important purposes. From the wife's perspective, an element of doubt as to the child's paternity introduces a new variable that serves to equalize the issue of relatedness. The husband is of course aware that he has a decisive advantage over his wife in terms of his genetic relatedness to the child. Although paternal doubt is always present for males, in the case of surrogate motherhood paternal doubt is thereby culturally enhanced. Allowing paternal certainty to remain a mystery represents an attempt to redress symbolically the imbalance created between wife and husband through the surrogate arrangement. Before the advent of these reproductive technologies, the "figure of the mother provided a natural model for the social construction of the 'natural' facts" (Strathern 1991:5); motherhood was seen as a single, unified experience, combining both the social and biological aspects— unlike fatherhood, in which the father acquired a "double identity." With the separation of the social and biological elements, however, motherhood has, in the context of surrogacy, also acquired this double identity (Strathern 1991:4–5). In this way, surrogate motherhood thus produces the "maternal counterpart to the double identity of the father, certain in one mode and uncertain in another" (Strathern 1991:4).

All the participants in the surrogate motherhood triad work to downplay the importance of biological relatedness as it pertains to women. They tend to reinforce the idea of motherhood as nurturance so that the adoptive mother's inability to give birth or become a genetrix (both wife and mother) is of diminished importance. At the same time, the husband's relationship to the surrogate vis-à-vis the child, and his biological relationship to the child, is also deemphasized. The idea that the adoptive mother is a mother by virtue of her role as nurturer is frequently echoed by all parties concerned. In this sense motherhood, as it pertains to surrogacy, is redefined as a social role. This occludes the somewhat problematic issues of

the surrogate's biogenetic relationship to the child and the adoptive mother's lack of such a relationship.

Thus the decision not to have a paternity test performed provides additional reinforcement for the idea of parenthood as a social construct rather than a biological phenomenon. The importance of the bond that develops between the surrogate and the adoptive mother is twofold: it merges the adoptive mother (or mater) and the surrogate (or genetrix) into one by reinforcing and maintaining the unity of experience, erasing the boundaries that surrogacy creates; and, at the same time, it establishes and maintains new boundaries as they are needed between surrogate and father.

I have attempted here to show that surrogates' stated motivations for choosing surrogate motherhood represent only one aspect of a whole complex of motivations. While surrogates do, as they say, enjoy being pregnant, desire to help an infertile couple to start a family of their own, and value the compensation they receive, there are other equally good—if not more—compelling reasons that motivate this unique group of women to become surrogate mothers. Biological relatedness is both the initial motivation for and the ultimate goal of surrogacy, and it is also that facet of surrogacy that makes it most consistent with the biogenetic basis of American kinship ideology. Nevertheless, it must be deemphasized—even devalued—by all the participants in order to make surrogacy consistent with American cultural values about appropriate relations between wives and husbands. In addition to broadening the scope of our understanding about the motivations of the couples who choose to pursue a surrogate solution, I hope that this article has illuminated the complexity of the couples' decision-making process as well as their motivation.

[. . .]

In conclusion, it can be said that all the participants involved in the surrogacy process wish to attain traditional ends, and are therefore willing to set aside their reservations about the means by which parenthood is attained. Placing surrogacy inside tradition, they attempt to circumvent some of the more difficult issues raised by the surrogacy process. In this way, programs and participants pick and choose among American cultural values about family, parenthood, and reproduction, now choosing biological relatedness, now nurture, according to their needs.

NOTES

1. As of 1994, only seven of the original ten are now in existence. I have changed the names of programs, surrogates, couples, and directors in order to protect their identities.

2. One of the programs has, however, recently increased its rate to $15,000. Surrogates also receive an allowance for maternity clothing, remuneration for time lost from work (if they have employment outside of the home), and reimbursement for all babysitting fees incurred as a result of surrogate-related activities.

3. The quantifiable data reveal that surrogates are predominantly white, an average of 27 years of age, high school graduates, of Protestant or Catholic background, and married with an average of three children. Approximately 30 percent are full-time homemakers, and those surrogates who are employed outside the home tend to be employed in the service sector. A comparison of surrogate and couple statistics reveals pronounced differences in educational background, occupation, and income level. The average combined family income of commissioning couples is in excess of $100,000, as compared to $38,000 for married surrogates.

WORKS CITED

Annas, George. 1988. Fairy Tales Surrogate Mothers Tell. In *Surrogate Motherhood: Politics and Privacy.* Larry Gostin, ed. Pp. 43–55. Bloomington: Indiana University Press.

Andrews, Lori. 1984. *New Conceptions: A Consumer's Guide to the Newest Infertility Treatments.* New York: Ballantine.

———. 1992. Surrogacy Wars. *California Lawyer* 12(10):42–49.

Baber, Zaheer. 1991. Beyond the Structure/Agency Dualism: An Evaluation of Giddens' Theory of Structuration. *Sociological Inquiry* 61(2): 219–230

Browner, Carole. 1986. The Politics of Reproduction in a Mexican Village. *Signs* 11:710–724.

Cannell, Fenella. 1990. Concepts of Parenthood: The Warnock Report, the Gillick and Modern Myths. *American Ethnologist* 17:667–686.

Collier, Jane, Michelle Rosaldo, and Sylvia Yanagisako. 1982. Is There a Family? New Anthropological Views. In *Rethinking the Family: Some Feminist Questions.* Barrie Thorne and Marilyn Yalom, eds. Pp. 25–39. New York: Longman.

Delaney, Carol. 1986. The Meaning of Paternity and the Virgin Birth Debate. *Man* 24(3): 497–513.

———. 1991. *The Seed and the Soil: Gender and Cosmology in a Turkish Village Society.* Berkeley: University of California Press.

Dolgin, Janet. 1993. Just a Gene: Judicial Assumptions about Parenthood. *UCLA Law Review* 40(3).

Dworkin, Andrea. 1978. *Right-Wing Women.* New York: Perigee Books.

Ferree, Myra. 1984. Sacrifice, Satisfaction and Social Change: Employment and the Family. In *My Troubles Are Going to Have Trouble with Me.* Karen Sacks and Dorothy Remy, eds. Pp. 61–79. New Brunswick, NJ: Rutgers University Press.

Fox, Renée, and Judith Swazey. 1992. *Spare Parts: Organ Replacement in American Society.* Oxford: Oxford University Press.

Giddens, Anthony. 1984. *The Constitution of Society.* Berkeley: University of California Press.

Ginsburg, Faye. 1987. Procreation Stories: Reproduction, Nurturance and Procreation in Life Narratives of Abortion Activists. *American Ethnologist* 14(4):623–636.

———. 1989. *Contested Lives: The Abortion Debate in an American Community.* Berkeley: University of California Press.

Ginsburg, Faye, and Rayna Rapp. 1991. The Politics of Reproduction. *Annual Review of Anthropology* 20:311–343.

Glover, Jonathan. 1990. *Ethics of New Reproductive Technologies: The Glover Report to the European Commission.* DeKalb: Northern Illinois Press.

Gordon, Linda. 1988. *Heroes of Their Own Lives.* New York: Viking.

Gullestad, Marianne. 1992. *The Art of Social Relations.* Oslo, Norway: Scandinavian Press.

Hull, Richard. 1990. Gestational Surrogacy and Surrogate Motherhood. In *Ethical Issues in the New Reproductive Technologies.* Richard Hull, ed. Pp. 150–155. Belmont, CA: Wadsworth Publishers.

Leach, Edmund R. 1967. Virgin Birth. In *Proceedings of the Royal Anthropological Institute for 1960.* Pp. 39–49. London: RAI.

Martin, Emily. 1987. *The Woman in the Body: A Cultural Analysis of Reproduction.* Boston: Beacon Press.

Modell, Judith. 1989. Last Chance Babies: Interpretations of Parenthood in an In Vitro Fertilization Program. *Medical Anthropology Quarterly* 3(2):124–138.

Neuhaus, Robert. 1988. Renting Women, Buying Babies and Class Struggles. *Society* 25(3):8–10.

Newman, Lucile, ed. 1985. *Women's Medicine: A Cross-Cultural Study of Indigenous Fertility Regulations.* New Brunswick, NJ: Rutgers University Press.

Parker, Philip. 1983. Motivation of Surrogate Mothers: Initial Findings. American *Journal of Psychiatry* 140:117–119.

Ragoné, Helena. 1989. Proceedings from an information-gathering committee to the California State Legislature. Unpublished notes.

———. 1991. *Surrogate Motherhood in America.* Ph.D. dissertation, Brown University.

———. 1994. *Surrogate Motherhood: Conception in the Heart.* Boulder, CO, and Oxford: Westview Press/Basic Books.

Rapp, Rayna. 1978. Family and Class in Contemporary America: Notes toward an Understanding of Ideology. *Science and Society* 42(3): 278–300.

———. 1987. Moral Pioneers: Women, Men and Fetuses on a Frontier of Reproductive Technology. *Women and Health* 13(1/2):101–116.

———. 1988. Chromosomes and Communication: The Disclosure of Genetic Counseling. *Medical Anthropology Quarterly* 2:143–157.

———. 1990. Constructing Amniocentesis: Maternal and Medical Discourses. In *Uncertain Terms: Negotiating Gender in American Culture.* Faye Ginsburg and Anna Lowenhaupt Tsing, eds. Pp. 28–42. Boston: Beacon Press.

Rubin, Gayle. 1975. The Traffic in Woman: Notes on the Political Economy of Sex. In *Toward an Anthropology of Women.* Rayna Reiter, ed. Pp. 157–210. New York: Monthly Review Press.

Schneider, David. 1968. *American Kinship: A Cultural Accout.* Englewood Cliffs, NJ: Prentice Hall.

———. 1972. What Is Kinship All About? In *Kinship Studies in the Morgan Centennial Year.* Priscilla Reining, ed. Pp. 32–63. Washington, DC: Anthropological Society of Washington.

Scrimshaw, Susan. 1978. Infant Mortality and Behavior in the Regulation of Family Size. *Population Development Review* 4:383–403.

Simmel, Georg. 1978. *The Philosophy of Money.* London: Routledge and Kegan Paul.

Snowden, R. G. Mitchell, and E. Snowden. 1983. *Artificial Reproduction: A Social Investigation.* London: Allen and Unwin.

Spiro, Melford. 1968. Virgin Birth, Parthenogenesis, and Physiological Paternity: An Essay in Cultural Interpretation. *Man* (n.s.) 3:242–261.

Strathern, Marilyn. 1991. The Pursuit of Certainty: Investigating Kinship in the Late Twentieth Century. Paper presented at the 90th American Anthropological Association Annual Meeting, Chicago.

———. 1992a. *Reproducing the Future.* New York: Routledge.

———. 1992b. The Meaning of Assisted Kinship. In *Changing Human Reproduction.* Meg Stacey, ed. Pp. 148–169. London: Sage Publications.

———. 1992c. *After Nature: English Kinship in the Late Twentieth Century.* Cambridge: Cambridge University Press.

Titmuss, Richard. 1971. *The Gift Relationship: From Human Blood to Social Policy.* New York: Pantheon Books.

Zelizer, Vivian. 1985. *Pricing the Priceless Child.* New York: Basic Books.

THINKING ABOUT THE READING

According to Ragoné, what motivates these women to become surrogate mothers? Does it surprise you to learn that these women are not motivated primarily by economic gain? What does this article tell you about the connection between motherhood and work (especially what is considered appropriate women's work)? How does the characterization of surrogate motherhood enable these women to work and also see themselves as strongly feminine? How does this characterization facilitate the perpetuation of traditional parenting roles between the adoptive mother and father? Do you see any similarities or differences in the arrangements described in this article and those of lesbian or gay couples who seek sperm donors or surrogate mothers? What differences, if any, do you see between sperm donors and surrogate mothers? What do these differences tell us about the different ways we perceive motherhood and fatherhood, in general?

8
Constructing Difference
Social Deviance

According to most sociologists, deviance is not an inherent feature or personality trait. Instead, it is a consequence of a definitional process. Like beauty, it is in the eye of the beholder. Deviant labels can impede everyday social life by forming expectations in the minds of others. Some sociologists argue that the definition of deviance is a form of social control exerted by more powerful people and groups over less powerful ones.

Deviant labels are not only applied to people who engage in undesirable behaviors. In "Branded With Infamy: Inscriptions of Poverty and Class in America," Vivyan Adair describes the various ways in which poor women's bodies are marked as "unclean" or "unacceptable." These markings are the result of a life of poverty: lack of access to adequate health care, lack of proper nutrition and shelter, and a consequence of difficult and demanding physical labor. But more affluent people often come to view these women (and their children) not as victims of economic circumstances but as deviants who deserve to be disciplined, controlled, and punished.

The definitional process that results in the labeling of some people as deviant can occur at the institutional as well as the individual level. Powerful institutions are capable of creating a conception of deviance that the public comes to accept as truth. One such institution is the field of medicine. We usually think of medicine as a benevolent institution whose primary purpose is to help sick people get better. But in "Medicine as an Institution of Social Control," Peter Conrad and Joseph Schneider show how medical vocabularies and ideologies shape public perceptions of deviance. They show how various types of problematic behavior, previously considered crimes or sins, come to be seen as illnesses. We usually think of the individuals and organizations who make up the criminal justice system (police, courts, prisons) as the agents responsible for controlling deviance. But a medicalized view of deviance has given rise to a system of social control made up of physicians, psychiatrists, psychologists, counselors, and other specialists. The authors describe the important social implications of conceiving of deviance as a "disorder" that can and should be "treated" and "cured."

Branded With Infamy

Inscriptions of Poverty and Class in America

Vivyan Adair

(2002)

"My kids and I been chopped up and spit out just like when I was a kid. My rotten teeth, my kids' twisted feet. My son's dull skin and blank stare. My oldest girl's stooped posture and the way she can't look no one in the eye no more. This all says we got nothing and we deserve what we got. On the street good families look at us and see right away what they'd be if they don't follow the rules. They're scared too, real scared."

—Welfare recipient and activist, Olympia, Washington, 1998

I begin with the words of a poor, White, single mother of three. Although officially she has only a tenth-grade education, she expertly reads and articulates a complex theory of power, bodily inscription, and socialization that arose directly from material conditions of her own life. She sees what many far more "educated" scholars and citizens fail to recognize: that the bodies of poor women and children are produced and positioned as texts that facilitate the mandates of a . . . profoundly brutal and mean-spirited political regime. . . .

Over the past decade or so, a host of inspired feminist welfare scholars and activists have addressed and examined the relationship between state power and the lives of poor women and children. As important and insightful as these exposés are, with few exceptions, they do not get at the closed circuit that fuses together systems of power, the material conditions of poverty, and the bodily experiences that allow for the perpetuation—and indeed the justification—of these systems. They fail to consider what the speaker of my

opening passage recognized so astutely: that systems of power produce and patrol poverty through the reproduction of both social and bodily markers. . . .

. . . [In this article I employ the theory of Michel Foucault to describe how the body is] the product of historically specific power relations. Feminists have used this notion of social inscription to explain a range of bodily operations from cosmetic surgery (Brush 1998, Morgan 1991), prostitution (Bell 1994), and Anorexia Nervosa (Hopwood 1995, Bordo 1993) to motherhood (Chandler 1999, Smart 1992), race (Stoler 1995, Ford-Smith 1996), and cultural imperialism (Desmond 1991). As these analyses illustrate, Foucault allows us to consider and critique the body as it is invested with meaning and inserted into regimes of truth via the operations of power and knowledge. . . .

Foucault clarifies and expands on this process of bodily/social inscription in his early work. In "Nietzsche, Genealogy, History," he positions the physical body as virtual text, accounting for the fact that "the body is the inscribed surface of events that are traced by language and dissolved by ideas" (1977, 83). . . . For Foucault, the body and [power] are inseparable. In his logic, power constructs and holds bodies. . . .

In *Discipline and Punish* Foucault sets out to depict the genealogy of torture and discipline as it reflects a public display of power on the body of subjects in the 17th and 18th centuries. In graphic detail Foucault begins his book with the description of a criminal being tortured and then drawn and quartered in a public square. The crowds of good parents and their growing children watch and learn. The public spectacle works as a patrolling image, socializing and controlling bodies within the body politic. Eighteenth century torture "must mark the victim: it is intended, either by the scar it leaves on the body or by the spectacle that accompanies it, to brand the victim with infamy . . . it traces around or rather on the very body of the condemned man signs that cannot be effaced" (1984, 179). For Foucault, public exhibitions of punishment served as a socializing process, writing culture's codes and values on the minds and bodies of its subjects. In the process punishment . . . rearranged bodies.

. . . Foucault's point in *Discipline and Punish* is . . . that public exhibition and inscription have been replaced in contemporary society by a much more effective process of socialization and self-inscription. According to Foucault, today discipline has replaced torture as the privileged punishment, but the body continues to be written on. Discipline produces "subjected and practiced bodies, docile bodies" (1984, 182). We become subjects . . . of ideology, disciplining and inscribing our own bodies/minds in the process of becoming stable and singular subjects. . . . The body continues to be the site and operation of ideology. . . .

Indeed, while we are all marked discursively by ideology in Foucault's paradigm, in the United States today poor women and children of all races are multiply marked with signs of both discipline and punishment that cannot be erased or effaced. They are systematically produced through both 20th century forces of socialization and discipline and 18th century exhibitions of public mutilation. In addition to coming into being as disciplined and docile bodies, poor single welfare mothers and their children are physically inscribed, punished, and displayed as dangerous and pathological "other." It is important to note when considering the contemporary inscription of poverty as moral pathology etched onto the bodies of profoundly poor women and children, that these are more than metaphoric and self-patrolling marks of discipline. Rather on myriad levels—sexual, social, material and physical—poor women and their children, like the "deviants" publicly punished in Foucault's scenes of torture, are marked, mutilated, and made to bear and transmit signs in a public spectacle that brands the victim with infamy.

[. . .]

The (Not So) Hidden Injuries of Class

Recycled images of poor, welfare women permeate and shape our national consciousness.[1] Yet—as is so often the case—these images and narratives tell us more about the culture that spawned and embraced them than they do about the object of the culture's obsession. . . .

These productions orchestrate the story of poverty as one of moral and intellectual lack and of chaos, pathology, promiscuity, illogic, and sloth, juxtaposed always against the order, progress, and decency of "deserving" citizens. . . .

I am, and will probably always be, marked as a poor woman. I was raised by a poor, single, White mother who had to struggle to keep her four children fed, sheltered, and clothed by working at what seemed like an endless stream of minimum wage, exhausting, and demeaning jobs. As a child poverty was written onto and into my being at the level of private and public thought and body. At an early age my body bore witness to and emitted signs of the painful devaluation carved into my flesh; that same devaluation became integral to my being in the world. I came into being as disciplined body/mind while at the same time I was taught to read my abject body as the site of my own punishment and erasure. In this excess of meaning the space between private body and public sign was collapsed.

For many poor children this double exposure results in debilitating . . . shame and lack. As Carolyn Kay Steedman reminds us in *Landscape for a Good Woman,* the mental life of poor children flows from material deprivation. Steedman speaks of the "relentless laying down of guilt" she experienced as a poor child living in a world where identity was shaped through envy and unfulfilled desire and where her own body "told me stories of the terrible unfairness of things, of the subterranean culture of longing for that which one can never have" (1987, 8). For Steedman, public devaluation and punishment "demonstrated to us all the hierarchies of our illegality, the impropriety of our existence, our marginality within the social system" (1987, 9). Even as an adult she recalls that:

> . . . the baggage will never lighten for me or my sister. We were born, and had no choice in the matter; but we were social burdens, expensive, unworthy, never grateful enough. There was nothing we could do to pay back the debt of our existence. (1987, 19)

Indeed, poor children are often marked with bodily signs that cannot be forgotten or erased. Their bodies are physically inscribed as "other" and then read as pathological, dangerous, and undeserving. What I recall most

vividly about being a child in a profoundly poor family was that we were constantly hurt and ill, and because we could not afford medical care, small illnesses and accidents spiraled into more dangerous illnesses and complications that became both a part of who we were and written proof that we were of no value in the world.

In spite of my mother's heroic efforts, at an early age my brothers and sister and I were stooped, bore scars that never healed properly, and limped with feet mangled by ill-fitting, used Salvation Army shoes. When my sister's forehead was split open by a door slammed in frustration, my mother "pasted" the angry wound together on her own, leaving a mark of our inability to afford medical attention, of our lack, on her very forehead. When I suffered from a concussion, my mother simply put borrowed ice on my head and tried to keep me awake for a night. And when throughout elementary school we were sent to the office for mandatory and very public yearly checks, the school nurse sucked air through her teeth as she donned surgical gloves to check only the hair of poor children for lice.

We were read as unworthy, laughable, and often dangerous. Our school mates laughed at our "ugly shoes," our crooked and ill-serviced teeth, and the way we "stank," as teachers excoriated us for inability to concentrate in school, our "refusal" to come to class prepared with proper school supplies, and our unethical behavior when we tried to take more than our allocated share of "free lunch."[2] Whenever backpacks or library books came up missing, we were publicly interrogated and sent home to "think about" our offenses, often accompanied by notes that reminded my mother that as a poor single parent she should be working twice as hard to make up for the discipline that allegedly walked out the door with my father. When we sat glued to our seats, afraid to stand in front of the class in ragged and ill-fitting hand-me-downs, we were held up as examples of unprepared and uncooperative children. And when our grades reflected our otherness, they were used to justify even more elaborate punishment. . . .

Friends who were poor as children, and respondents to a survey I conducted in 1998,[3] tell similar stories of the branding they received at the hands of teachers, administrators, and peers. An African-American woman raised in Yesler Terrace, a public housing complex in Seattle, Washington, writes:

> Poor was all over our faces. My glasses were taped and too weak. My big brother had missing teeth. My mom was dull and ashy. It was like a story of how poor we were that anyone could see. My sister Evie's lip was bit by a dog and we just had dime store stuff to put on it. Her lip was a big scar. Then she never smiled and no one smiled at her cause she never smiled. Kids called her "Scarface." Teachers never smiled at her. The principle put her in detention all the time because she was mean and bad (they said).

And, a White woman in the Utica, New York, area remembers:

> We lived in dilapidated and unsafe housing that had fleas no matter how clean my mom tried to be. We had bites all over us. Living in our car between evictions was even worse— then we didn't have a bathroom so I got kidney problems that I never had doctor's help for. When my teachers wouldn't let me go to the bathroom every hour or so I would wet my pants in class. You can imagine what the kids did to me about that. And the teachers would refuse to let me go to the bathroom because they said I was willful.

Material deprivation is publicly written on the bodies of poor children in the world. In the United States poor families experience violent crime, hunger, lack of medical and dental care, utility shut-offs, the effects of living in unsafe housing and/or of being homeless, chronic

illness, and insufficient winter clothing (Lein and Edin 1996, 224–231). According to Jody Raphael of the Taylor Institute, poor women and their children are also at five times the risk of experiencing domestic violence (Raphael, 2000).

As children, our disheveled and broken bodies were produced and read as signs of our inferiority and undeservedness. As adults our mutilated bodies are read as signs of inner chaos, immaturity, and indecency as we are punished and then read as proof of need for further discipline and punishment. When my already bad teeth started to rot and I was out of my head with pain, my choices as an adult welfare recipient were to either let my teeth fall out or have them pulled out. In either case the culture would then read me as a "toothless illiterate," as a fearful joke. In order to pay my rent and to put shoes on my daughter's feet I sold blood at two or three different clinics on a monthly basis until I became so anemic that they refused to buy it from me. A neighbor of mine went back to the man who continued to beat her and her children after being denied welfare benefits, when she realized that she could not adequately feed, clothe, and house her family on her own minimum wage income. My good friend sold her ovum to a fertility clinic in a painful and potentially damaging process. Other friends exposed themselves to all manner of danger and disease by selling their bodies for sex in order to feed and clothe their babies.

Exhaustion also marks the bodies of poor women in indelible script. Rest becomes a privilege we simply cannot afford. After working full shifts each day, poor mothers trying to support themselves at minimum wage jobs continue to work to a point of exhaustion that is inscribed on their faces, their bodies, their posture, and their diminishing sense of self and value in the world. My former neighbor recently recalled:

I had to take connecting buses to bring and pick up my daughters at childcare after working on my feet all day. As soon as we arrived at home, we would head out again by bus to do laundry. Pick up groceries. Try to get to the food bank. Beg the electric company to not turn off our lights and heat again. Find free winter clothing. Sell my blood. I would be home at nine or ten o'clock at night. I was loaded down with one baby asleep and one crying. Carrying lots of heavy bags and ready to drop on my feet. I had bags under my eyes and no shampoo to wash my hair so I used soap. Anyway I had to stay up to wash diapers in the sink. Otherwise they wouldn't be dry when I left the house in the dark with my girls. In the morning I start all over again.

This bruised and lifeless body, hauling sniffling babies and bags of dirty laundry on the bus, was then read as a sign that she was a bad mother and a threat that needed to be disciplined and made to work even harder for her own good. Those who need the respite less go away for weekends, take drives in the woods, take their kids to the beach. Poor women without education are pushed into minimum wage jobs and have no money, no car, no time, no energy, and little support, as their bodies are made to display marks of their material deprivation as a socializing and patrolling force.

Ultimately, we come to recognize that our bodies are not our own; that they are rather public property. State mandated blood tests, interrogation of the most private aspects of our lives, the public humiliation of having to beg officials for food and medicine, and the loss of all right to privacy, teach us that our bodies are only useful as lessons, warnings, and signs of degradation that everyone loves to hate. In "From Welfare to Academe: Welfare Reform as College-Educated Welfare Mothers Know It," Sandy Smith-Madsen describes the erosion of her privacy as a poor welfare mother:

I was investigated. I was spied upon. A welfare investigator came into my home and after thoughtful deliberation, granted me permission to keep my belongings. . . . Like the witch hunts of old, if a neighbor reports you as a welfare queen, the guardians of the state's compelling interest come into your home and interrogate you. While they do not have the right to set your body ablaze on the public square, they can forever devastate heart and soul by snatching away children. Just like a police officer, they may use whatever they happen to see against you, including sexual orientation. Full-fledged citizens have the right to deny an officer entry into their home unless they possess a search warrant; welfare mothers fork over citizenship rights for the price of a welfare check. In Tennessee, constitutional rights go for a cash value of $185 per month for a family of three. (2000, 185)

Welfare reform policy is designed to publicly expose, humiliate, punish and display "deviant" welfare mothers. "Workfare" and "Learnfare"—two alleged successes of welfare reform—require that landlords, teachers, and employers be made explicitly aware of the second class status of these very public bodies. In Ohio, the Department of Human Services uses tax dollars to pay for advertisements on the side of Cleveland's RTA busses that show a "Welfare Queen" behind bars with a logo that proclaims "Crime does not pay. Welfare fraud is a crime" (Robinson 1999). In Michigan a pilot program mandating drug tests for all welfare recipients began on October 1, 1999. Recipients who refuse the test will lose their benefits immediately (Simon 1999). In Buffalo, New York, a County Executive proudly announced that his county will begin intensive investigation of all parents who refuse minimum wage jobs that are offered to them by the state. He warned: "We have many ways of investigating and exposing these errant parents who choose to exploit their children in this way" (Anderson 1999). And, welfare reform legislation enacted in 1996 as the Personal Responsibility and Work Opportunities Reconciliation Act (PRWORA), requires that poor mothers work full-time, earning minimum wage salaries with which they cannot support their children. Often denied medical, dental, and childcare benefits, and unable to provide their families with adequate food, heat, or clothing, through this legislation the state mandates child neglect and abuse. The crowds of good parents and their growing children watch and learn. . . .

Reading and Rewriting the Body . . .

The bodies of poor women and children, scarred and mutilated by state mandated material deprivation and public exhibition, work as spectacles, as patrolling images socializing and controlling bodies within the body politic. . . .

Spectacular cover stories of the "Welfare Queen" play and re-play in the national mind's eye, becoming a prescriptive lens through which the American public as a whole reads the individual dramas of the bodies of poor women and their place and value in the world. These dramas produce "normative" citizens as singular, stable, rational, ordered, and free. In this dichotomous, hierarchical frame the poor welfare mother is juxtaposed against a logic of "normative" subjectivity as the embodiment of disorder, disarray, and other-ness. Her broken and scarred body becomes proof of her inner pathology and chaos, suggesting the need for further punishment and discipline.

In contemporary narrative welfare women are imagined to be dangerous because they refuse to sacrifice their desires and fail to participate in legally sanctioned heterosexual relationships; theirs is read, as a result, as a selfish, "unnatural," and immature sexuality. In this script, the bodies of poor women are viewed as being dangerously beyond the control of men

and are as a result construed as the bearers of perverse desire. In this androcentric equation fathers become the sole bearers of order and of law, defending poor women and children against their own unchecked sexuality and lawlessness.

For Republican Senator [now Attorney General] John Ashcroft writing in *The St. Louis Dispatch,* the inner city is the site of "rampant illegitimacy" and a "space devoid of discipline" where all values are askew. For Ashcroft, what is insidious is not material poverty, but an entitlement system that has allowed "out-of-control" poor women to rupture traditional patriarchal authority, valuation, and boundaries (1995, A:23). Impoverished communities then become a site of chaos because without fathers they allegedly lack any organizing or patrolling principle. George Gilder agrees with Ashcroft when he writes in the conservative *American Spectator* that:

> The key problem of the welfare culture is not unemployed women and poor children. It is the women's skewed and traumatic relationships with men. In a reversal of the pattern of civilized societies, the women have the income and the ties to government authority and support. . . . This balance of power virtually prohibits marriage, which is everywhere based on the provider role of men, counterbalancing the sexual and domestic superiority of women. (1995, B:6)

For Gilder, the imprimatur of welfare women's sordid bodies unacceptably shifts the focus of the narrative from a male presence to a feminized absence.

In positioning welfare mothers as sexually chaotic, irrational, and unstable, their figures are temporarily immobilized and made to yield meaning as a space that must be brought under control and transformed through public displays of punishment. Poor single mothers and children who have been abandoned, have fled physical, sexual, and/or psychological abuse, or have in general refused to capitulate to male control within the home are mythologized as dangerous, pathological, out of control, and selfishly unable—or unwilling—to sacrifice their "naturally" unnatural desires. They are understood and punished as a danger to a culture resting on a foundation of inviolate male authority and absolute privilege in both public and private spheres.

William Raspberry disposes poor women as selfish and immature, when in "Ms. Smith Goes After Washington," he warrants that:

> . . . unfortunately [welfare] is paid to an unaccountable, accidental and unprepared parent who has chosen her head of household status as a personal form of satisfaction, while lacking the simple life skills and maturity to achieve love and job fulfillment from any other source. I submit that all of our other social ills—crime, drugs, violence, failing schools . . . are a direct result of the degradation of parenthood by emotionally immature recipients. (1995, A:19)

Raspberry goes on to assert that like poor children, poor mothers must be made visible reminders to the rest of the culture of the "poor choices" they have made. He claims that rather than "coddling" her, we have a responsibility to "shame her" and to use her failure to teach other young women that it is "morally wrong for unmarried women to bear children," as we "cast single motherhood as a selfish and immature act" (1995, A:19).

Continuous, multiple, and often seamless public inscription, punishing policy, and lives of unbearable material lack leave poor women and their children scarred, exhausted, and confused. As a result their bodies are imagined as an embodiment of decay and cultural dis-ease that threatens the health and progress of our nation. . . . In a 1995 *USA Today* article entitled "America at Risk: Can We Survive Without Moral Values?" for example, the inner city is portrayed as a "*dark*" realm of "*decay* rooted in the *loss* of values, the *death* of work ethics, and

the *deterioration* of families and communities." Allegedly here, "all morality has *rotted* due to a *breakdown* in gender discipline." This space of disorder and disease is marked with tropes of race and gender. It is also associated with the imagery of "communities of women *without* male leadership, cultural values and initiative [emphasis added]" (1995, C:3). In George Will's *Newsweek* editorial he proclaims that "*illogical* feminist and racial *anger* coupled with *misplaced* American emotion may be part or a cause of the *irresponsible* behavior *rampant* in poor neighborhoods." Will continues, proclaiming that here "mothers *lack* control over their children and have *selfishly* taught them to embrace a *pathological* ethos that values *self-need* and *self-expression* over self-control [emphasis added]" (1995, 23).

Poor women and children's bodies, publicly scarred and mutilated by material deprivation, are read as expressions of an essential lack of discipline and order. In response to this perception, journalist Ronald Brownstein of the *L.A. Times* proposed that the *Republican Contract with America* will "*restore* America to its path, *enforcing* social *order* and common *standards* of behavior, and replacing *stagnation* and *decay* with *movement* and *forward* thinking *energy* [emphasis added]" (1994, A:20). In these rhetorical fields poverty is . . . linked to lack of progress that would allegedly otherwise order, stabilize, and restore the culture. What emerges from these diatribes is the positioning of patriarchal, racist, capitalist, hierarchical, and heterosexist "order" and movement against the alleged stagnation and decay of the body of the "Welfare Queen."

Race is clearly written on the body of the poor single mother. The welfare mother, imagined as young, never married, and Black (contrary to statistical evidence[4]), is framed as dangerous and in need of punishment because she "naturally" emasculates her own men, refuses to service White men, and passes on—rather than appropriate codes of subservience and submission—a disruptive culture of resistance, survival, and "misplaced" pride to her children (Collins 1991). In stark contrast, widowed women with social security and divorced women with child support and alimony are imaged as White, legal, and propertied mothers whose value rests on their abilities to stay in their homes, care for their own children, and impart traditional cultural morals to their offspring, all for the betterment of the culture. In this narrative welfare mothers have only an "outlaw" culture to impart. Here the welfare mother is read as both the product and the producer of a culture of disease and disorder. These narratives imagine poor women as powerful contagion capable of, perhaps even lying in wait to infect their own children as raced, gendered, and classed agents of their "diseased" nature. In contemporary discourses of poverty racial tropes position poor women's bodies as dangerous sites of "naturalized chaos" and as potentially valuable economic commodities who refuse their proper role.

Gary McDougal in "The Missing Half of the Welfare Debate" furthers this image by referring to the "crab effect of poverty" through which mothers and friends of individuals striving to break free of economic dependency allegedly "pull them back down." McDougal affirms—again despite statistical evidence to the contrary—that the mothers of welfare recipients are most often themselves "generational welfare freeloaders lacking traditional values and family ties who can not, and will not, teach their children right from wrong." "These women" he asserts "would be better off doing any kind of labor regardless of how little it pays, just to get them out of the house, to break their cycles of degeneracy" (1996, A:16).

In this plenitude of images of evil mothers, the poor welfare mother threatens not just her own children, but all children. The Welfare Queen is made to signify moral aberration and economic drain; her figure becomes even more impacted once responsibility for the destruction of the "American Way of Life" is attributed to her. Ronald Brownstein reads her "spider web of dependency" as a "crisis of character development that leads to a morally bankrupt American ideology" (1994, A:6).

These representations position welfare mothers' bodies as sites of destruction and as catalysts for a culture of depravity and disobedience; in the process they produce a reading of the writing on the body of the poor woman that calls for further punishment and discipline. In New York City, "Workfare" programs force *lazy* poor women to take a job—"any job"—including working for the city wearing orange surplus prison uniforms picking up garbage on the highway and in parks for about $1.10 per hour (Dreier 1999). "Bridefare" programs in Wisconsin give added benefits to *licentious* welfare women who marry a man—"any man"—and publish a celebration of their "reform" in local newspapers (Dresand 1996). "Tidyfare" programs across the nation allow state workers to enter and inspect the homes of poor *slovenly* women so that they can monetarily sanction families whose homes are deemed to be appropriately tidied.[5] "Learnfare" programs in many states publicly expose and fine *undisciplined* mothers who for any reason have children who don't (or can't) attend school on a regular basis (Muir 1993). All of these welfare reform programs are designed to expose and publicly punish the *misfits* whose bodies are read as proof of their refusal or inability to capitulate to androcentric, capitalist, racist, and heterosexist values and mores.

The Power of Poor Women's Communal Resistance

Despite the rhetoric and policy that mark and mutilate our bodies, poor women survive. Hundreds of thousands of us are somehow good parents despite the systems that are designed to prohibit us from being so. We live on the unlivable and teach our children love, strength, and grace. We network, solve irresolvable dilemmas, and support each other and our families. If we somehow manage to find a decent pair of shoes, or save our food-stamps to buy our children a birthday cake, we are accused of being cheats or living too high. If our children suffer, it is read as proof of our inferiority and bad mothering; if they succeed we are suspect for being too pushy, for taking more than our share of free services, or for having too much free time to devote to them. Yet, as former welfare recipient Janet Diamond says in the introduction to *For Crying Out Loud:*

> In spite of public censure, welfare mothers graduate from school, get decent jobs, watch their children achieve, make good lives for themselves . . . welfare mothers continue to be my inspiration, not because they survive, but because they dare to dream. Because when you are a welfare recipient, laughter is an act of rebellion. (1986, 1)

. . . Because power is diffuse, heterogeneous, and contradictory, poor women struggle against the marks of their degradation. . . .

Poor women rebel by organizing for physical and emotional respite, and eventually for political power. My own resistance was born in the space between self-loathing and my love of and respect for poor women who were fighting together against oppression. In the throes of political activism (at first I was dragged blindly into such actions, ironically, in a protest that required, according to the organizer, just so many poor women's bodies) I became caught up in the contradiction between my body's meaning as despised public sign, and our shared sense of communal power, knowledge, authority, and beauty. Learning about labor movements, fighting for rent control, demanding fair treatment at the welfare office, sharing the costs, burdens,

and joys of raising children, forming good cooperatives, working with other poor women to go to college, and organizing for political change, became addictive and life affirming acts of resistance.

Communal affiliation among poor women is discouraged, indeed in many cases prohibited, by those with power over our lives. Welfare offices, for example, are designed to prevent poor women from talking together; uncomfortable plastic chairs are secured to the ground in arrangements that make it difficult to communicate, silence is maintained in waiting rooms, case workers are rotated so that they do not become too "attached" to their clients, and, reinforced by "Welfare Fraud" signs covering industrially painted walls, we are daily reminded not to trust anyone with the details of our lives for fear of further exposure and punishment. And so, like most poor women, I had remained isolated, ashamed, and convinced that I was alone in, and responsible for, my suffering.

Through shared activism we became increasingly aware of our individual bodies as sites of contestation and of our collective body as a site of resistance and as a source power.

Noemy Vides in "Together We Are Getting Freedom," reminds us that "by talking and writing about learned shame together, [poor women] pursue their own liberation" (305). Vides adds that it is through this process that she learned to challenge the dominant explanations that decreed her value in the world,

> provoking an awareness that the labels—ignorant peasant, abandoned woman, broken-English speaker, welfare cheat—have nothing to do with who one really is, but serve to keep women subjugated and divided. [This communal process] gives women tools to understand the uses of power; it emboldens us to move beyond the imposed shame that silences, to speak out and join together in a common liberatory struggle. (305)

In struggling together we contest the marks of our bodily inscription, disrupt the use of our bodies as public sign, change the conditions of our lives, and survive. In the process we come to understand that the shaping of our bodies is not coterminous with our beings or abilities as a whole. Contestation and the deployment of new truths cannot erase the marks of our poverty, but the process does transform the ways in which we are able to interrogate and critique our bodies and the systems that have branded them with infamy. As a result these signs are rendered fragile, unstable, and ultimately malleable.

NOTES

1. Throughout this paper I use the terms "welfare recipients," and "poor working women" interchangeably because as the recent *Urban Institute* study made clear, today these populations are, in fact, one and the same. (Loprest 1999)

2. As recently as 1995, in my daughter's public elementary school cafeteria, "free lunchers" (poor children who could not otherwise afford to eat lunch, including my daughter) were reminded with a large and colorful sign to "line up last."

3. The goal of my survey was to measure the impact of the 1996 welfare reform legislation on the lives of profoundly poor women and children in the United States. Early in 1998 I sent fifty questionnaires and narrative surveys to four groups of poor women on the West and the East coasts; thirty-nine were returned to me. I followed these surveys with forty-five minute interviews with twenty of the surveyed women.

4. In the two years directly preceding the passage of the PRWORA, as a part of sweeping welfare reform, in the United States the largest percentage of people on welfare were white (39%) and fewer than 10% were teen mothers. (1994. U.S. Department of Health and Human Services, "An Overview of Entitlement Programs")

5. *Tidyfare* programs additionally required that caseworkers inventory the belongings of AFDC recipients so that they could require them to "sell-down" their assets. In my own case, in 1994 a HUD inspector came into my home, counted my daughter's books, checked them against his list to see that as a nine year old she was only entitled to have twelve books, calculated what he perceived to be the value of the excess books, and then had my AFDC check reduced by that amount in the following month.

REFERENCES

Abramovitz, Mimi. 1989. *Regulating the lives of women, social welfare policy from colonial times to the present.* Boston: South End Press.

———. 2000. *Under attack, fighting back.* New York: Monthly Review Press.

Albelda, Randy. 1997. *Glass ceilings and bottomless pits: Women's work, women's poverty.* Boston: South End Press.

"America at risk; can we survive without moral values." 1995. *USA Today.* October, Sec. C: 3.

Amott, Teresa. 1993. *Caught in the crises: Women and the U.S. economy today.* New York: Monthly Review Press.

Anderson, Dale. 1999. "County to investigate some welfare recipients." *The Buffalo News.* August 18, Sec. B: 5.

Ashcroft, John. 1995. "Illegitimacy rampant." *The St. Louis Dispatch.* July 2, Sec. A: 23.

Bell, Shannon. 1994. *Reading, writing and rewriting the prostitute* body. Bloomington and Indianapolis: Indiana University Press.

Bordo, Susan, 1993. *Unbearable Weight: Feminism, western culture and the body.* Berkeley: University of California Press.

Brownstein, Ronald. 1994. "GOP welfare proposals more conservative." *Los Angeles Times,* May 20, Sec. A: 20.

———. 1994. "Latest welfare reform plan reflects liberals' priorities." *Los Angeles Times.* May 20, Sec. A: 6.

Chandler, Mielle. 1999. "Queering maternity." *Journal of the Association for Research on Mothering.* Vol. 1, no. 2, (21–32).

Collins, Patricia Hill. 2000. *Black feminist thought: Knowledge, consciousness, and the politics of empowerment.* New York: Routledge.

Crompton, Rosemary. 1986. *Gender and stratification.* New York: Polity Press.

Desmond, Jane. 1991. "Dancing out the difference; cultural imperialism and Ruth St. Denis's

Radna of 1906." *Signs.* Vol. 17, no. 1, Autumn, (28–49).

Diamond, Janet. 1986. *For crying out loud: Women and poverty in the United States.* Boston: Pilgrim Press.

Dreier, Peter. 1999. "Treat welfare recipients like workers." *Los Angeles Times.* August 29, Sec. M: 6.

Dresang, Joel. 1996. "Bridefare designer, reform beneficiary have role in governor's address." *Milwaukee Journal Sentinel.* August 14, Sec. 9.

Dujon, Diane and Ann Withorn. 1996. *For crying out loud: Women's poverty in the Unites States.* South End Press

Edin, Kathryn and Laura Lein. 1997. *Making ends meet: How single mothers survive welfare and low wage work.* Russell Sage Foundation.

Ford-Smith, Honor. 1995. "Making white ladies: Race, gender and the production of identity in late colonial Jamaica." *Resources for Feminist Research,* Vol. 23, no. 4, Winter, (55–67).

Foucault, Michel. 1984. Discipline and punish. In P. Rabinow (ed.) *The Foucault reader.* New York: Pantheon Books.

———. 1978. *The history of sexuality: An introduction.* Trans. R. Hurley. Harmondsworth: Penguin.

———. 1984. "Nietzsche, genealogy, history." In P. Rabinow (ed.) *The Foucault reader.* New York Pantheon Books.

———. 1980. *Power/knowledge: Selected interviews and other writings 1972–1977.* C. Gordon (ed.) Brighton: Harvester.

Funiciello, Theresa. 1998. "The brutality of bureaucracy." *Race, class and gender: An anthology,* 3rd ed. Eds. Margaret L. Andersen and Patricia Hill Collins. Belmont: Wadsworth Publishing Company, (377–381).

Gilder, George. 1995. "Welfare fraud today." *American Spectator.* September 5, Sec. B: 6.

Gordon, Linda. 1995. *Pitied, but not entitled: Single mothers and the history of welfare.* New York: Belknap Press, 1995.

Hooks, Bell. "Thinking about race, class, gender and ethics" 1999. Presentation at Hamilton College, Clinton, New York.

Hopwood, Catherine. 1995. "My discourse/ myself: therapy as possibility (for women who eat compulsively)." *Feminist Review.* No. 49, Spring, (66–82).

Langston, Donna. 1998. "Tired of playing monopoly?" In *Race, class and gender: An anthology,* 3rd ed. Eds. Margaret L. Andersen and Patricia Hill Collins. Belmont: Wadsworth Publishing Company, (126–136).

Lerman, Robert. 1995. "And for fathers?" *The Washington Post.* August 7, Sec. A: 19.

Loprest, Pamela. 1999. "Families who left welfare: who are they and how are they doing?" *The Urban Institute,* Washington, D.C. August, No. B-1.

McDougal, Gary. 1996. "The missing half of the welfare debate." *The Wall Street Journal.* September 6, Sec. A: 16 (W).

McNay, Lois. 1992. *Foucault and feminism: Power, gender and the self.* Boston: Northeastern University Press.

Mink, Gwendoly. 1998. *Welfare's end.* Cornell University Press.

———. 1996. *The wages of motherhood: Inequality in the welfare state 1917–1942,* Cornell University Press.

Morgan, Kathryn. 1991. "Women and the knife: Cosmetic surgery and the colonization of women's bodies." *Hypatia.* V6, No 3. Fall, (25–53).

Muir, Kate. 1993. "Runaway fathers at welfare's final frontier. *The Times.* Times Newspapers Limited. July 19, Sec. A: 2.

"An overview of entitlement programs." 1994. U.S. Department of Health and Human Services. Washington, DC: U.S. Government Printing Office.

Piven, Frances Fox and Richard Cloward. 1993. *Regulating the poor: The functions of public welfare.* New York: Vintage Books.

Raspberry, William. 1995. "Ms. Smith goes after Washington." *The Washington Post.* February 1, Sec. A: 19.

———. 1996. "Uplifting the human spirit." *The Washington Post.* August 8, Sec. A: 31.

Robinson, Valerie. 1999. "State's ad attacks the poor." *The Plain Dealer,* November 2, Sec. B: 8.

Sennett, Richard and Jonathan Cobb. 1972. *The hidden injuries of class.* New York: Vintage Books.

Sidel, Ruth. 1998. *Keeping women and children last: America's war on the poor.* New York: Penguin Books.

Simon, Stephanie. 1999. "Drug tests for welfare applicants." *Los Angeles Times.* December 18, Sec. A: 1. National Desk.

Smart, Carol. 1997. "Disruptive bodies and unruly sex: the regulation of reproduction and sexuality in the nineteenth century." *In Regulating womanhood: Historical essays on marriage, motherhood and sexuality.* Carol Smart, Ed. New York: Routledge, (7–32).

Smith-Madsen, Sandy. 2003. "From welfare to academe: Welfare reform as college-educated welfare mothers know it." *Reclaiming class: Women, poverty, and the promise of education in America.* Vivyan Adair and Sandra Dahlber, Eds. Philadelphia: Temple University Press, (160–186).

Steedman, Carolyn Kay. 1987. *Landscape for a good woman.* New Brunswick, N.J., Rutgers University Press.

Stoler, Ann Laura. 1995. *Race and the education of desire: Foucault's history of sexuality and the colonial order of things.* Durham: Duke University Press.

Sylvester, Kathleen. 1995. "Welfare debate." *The Washington Post.* September 3, Sec. E: 15.

Tanner, Michael. 1995. "Why welfare pays." *The Wall Street Journal.* September 28, Sec. A: 18 (W).

Vides, Noemy and Victoria Steinitz. 1996. "Together we are getting freedom." *For crying out loud.* Diane Dujon and Ann Withorn, Eds. Boston: South End Press, (295–306).

Will, George. 1995. "Welfare gate." *Newsweek.* February 5, Sec. 23.

THINKING ABOUT THE READING

When we think of people's bodies being labeled as deviant, we usually assume the bodies in question either deviate from cultural standards of shape and size or are marked by some noticeable physical handicap. However, Adair shows us that poor women's and children's bodies are tagged as deviant in ways that are just as profound and just as hard to erase. What does she mean when she says that the illnesses and accidents of youth became part of a visible reminder of who poor people are in the eyes of others? How do the public degradations suffered by poor people (for instance, having a school nurse wear surgical gloves to check only the hair of poor children for lice) reinforce their deviant status in society? Why do you think Adair continually evokes the images of "danger," "discipline," and "punishment" in describing the ways non-poor people perceive and respond to the physical appearance of poor people? Explain how focusing on the "deviance" of poor people deflects public attention away from the deviant acts committed by more affluent citizens. Do you see any connection between Adair's argument and the overrepresentation of poor people in prison?

Medicine as an Institution of Social Control

Peter Conrad and Joseph W. Schneider

(1992)

In our society we want to believe in medicine, as we want to believe in religion and our country; it wards off collective fears and reduces public anxieties (see Edelman, 1977). In significant ways medicine, especially psychiatry, has replaced religion as the most powerful extralegal institution of social control. Physicians have been endowed with some of the charisma of shamans. In the 20th century the medical model of deviance . . . ascended with the glitter of a rising star, expanding medicine's social control functions. . . .

Types of Medical Social Control

Medicine was first conceptualized as an agent of social control by Talcott Parsons (1951) in his seminal essay on the "sick role." . . . Elliot Freidson (1970a) and Irving Zola (1972) have elucidated the jurisdictional mandate the medical profession has over anything that can be labeled an illness, regardless of its ability to deal with it effectively. The boundaries of medicine are elastic and increasingly expansive (Ehrenreich & Ehrenreich, 1975), and some analysts have expressed concern at the increasing medicalization of life (Illich, 1976). Although medical social control has been conceptualized in several ways, including professional control of colleagues (Freidson, 1975) and control of the micropolitics of physician-patient interaction (Waitzkin & Stoeckle, 1976), the focus here is narrower. Our concern . . . is with the medical control of deviant behavior, an aspect of the

medicalization of deviance (Conrad, 1975; Pitts, 1968). Thus by medical social control we mean the ways in which medicine functions (wittingly or unwittingly) to secure adherence to social norms—specifically, by using medical means to minimize, eliminate, or normalize deviant behavior. This section illustrates and catalogues the broad range of medical controls of deviance and in so doing conceptualizes three major "ideal types" of medical social control.

On the most abstract level medical social control is the acceptance of a medical perspective as the dominant definition of certain phenomena. When medical perspectives of problems and their solutions become dominant, they diminish competing definitions. This is particularly true of problems related to bodily functioning and in areas where medical technology can demonstrate effectiveness (e.g., immunization, contraception, antibacterial drugs) and is increasingly the case for behavioral and social problems (Mechanic, 1973). This underlies the construction of medical norms (e.g., the definition of what is healthy) and the "enforcement" of both medical and social norms. Medical social control also includes medical advice, counsel, and information that are part of the general stock of knowledge: for example, a well-balanced diet is important, cigarette smoking causes cancer, being overweight increases health risks, exercising regularly is healthy, teeth should be brushed regularly. Such directives, even when unheeded, serve as road signs for desirable behavior. At a more concrete level, medical social control is enacted through professional medical intervention [and] treatment (although it may include some types of self-treatment such as self-medication or medically oriented self-help groups). This intervention aims at returning sick individuals to compliance with health norms and to their conventional social roles, adjusting them to new (e.g., impaired) roles, or, short or these, making individuals more comfortable with their condition (see Freidson, 1970a; Parsons, 1951). Medical social control of deviant behavior is usually a variant of medical intervention that seeks to eliminate, modify, isolate, or regulate behavior socially defined as deviant, with medical means and in the name of health.

Traditionally, psychiatry and public health have served as the clearest examples of medical control. Psychiatry's social control functions with mental illness, especially in terms of institutionalization, have been described clearly (e.g., Miller, K. S., 1976; Szasz, 1970). Recently it has been argued that psychotherapy, because it reinforces dominant values and adjusts people to their life situations, is an agent of social control and a supporter of the status quo (Halleck, 1971; Hurvitz, 1973). Public health's mandate, the control and elimination of conditions and diseases that are deemed a threat to the health of community, is more diffuse. It operates as a control agent by setting and enforcing certain "health" standards in the home, workplace, and community (e.g., food, water, sanitation) and by identifying, preventing, treating, and, if necessary, isolating persons with communicable diseases (Rosen, 1972). A clear example of the latter is the detection of venereal disease. Indeed, public health has exerted considerable coercive power in attempting to prevent the spread of infectious disease.

There are a number of types of medical control of deviance. The most common forms of medical social control include medicalizing deviant behavior—that is, defining the behavior

as an illness or a symptom of an illness or underlying disease—and subsequent direct medical intervention. This medical social control takes three general forms: medical technology, medical collaboration, and medical ideology.

Medical Technology

The growth of specialized medicine and the concomitant development of medical technology has produced an armamentarium of medical controls. Psychotechnologies, which include various forms of medical and behavioral technologies (Chorover, 1973), are the most common means of medical control of deviance. Since the emergence of phenothiazine medications in the early 1950s for the treatment and control of mental disorder, there has been a virtual explosion in the development and use of psychoactive medications to control behavioral deviance: tranquilizers such as chlordiazepoxide (Librium) and diazepam (Valium) for anxiety, nervousness, and general malaise; stimulant medications for hyperactive children; amphetamines for overeating and obesity; disulfiram (Antabuse) for alcoholism; methadone for heroin, and many others. These pharmaceutical discoveries, aggressively promoted by a highly profitable and powerful drug industry (Goddard, 1973), often become the treatment of choice for deviant behavior. They are easily administered under professional medical control, quite potent in their effects (i.e., controlling, modifying, and even eliminating behavior), and are generally less expensive than other medical treatments and controls (e.g., hospitalization, altering environments, long-term psychotherapy).

Psychosurgery, surgical procedures meant to correct certain "brain dysfunctions" presumed to cause deviant behavior, was developed in the early 1930s as prefrontal lobotomy, and has been used as a treatment for mental illness. But psychosurgery fell into disrepute in the early 1950s because the "side effects" (general passivity, difficulty with abstract thinking) were deemed too undesirable, and many patients remained institutionalized in spite of such treatments. Furthermore, new psychoactive medications were becoming available to control the mentally ill. By the middle 1950s, however, approximately 40,000 to 50,000 such operations were performed in the United States (Freeman, 1959). In the late 1960s a new and technologically more sophisticated variant of psychosurgery (including laser technology and brain implants) emerged and was heralded by some as a treatment for uncontrollable violent outbursts (Delgado, 1969; Mark & Ervin, 1970). Although psychosurgery for violence has been criticized from both within as well as outside the medical profession (Chorover, 1974b), and relatively few such operations have been performed, in 1976 a blue-ribbon national commission reporting to the Department of Health, Education and Welfare endorsed the use of psychosurgery as having "potential merit" and judged its risks "not excessive." This may encourage an increased use of this form of medical control.

Behavior modification, a psychotechnology based on B. F. Skinner's and other behaviorists' learning theories, has been adopted by some medical professionals as a treatment modality. A variety of types and variations of behavior modification exist (e.g., token economies, tier systems, positive reinforcement schedules, aversive conditioning). While they are not medical technologies per se, they have been used by physicians for the treatment of mental illness, mental retardation, homosexuality, violence, hyperactive children, autism, phobias, alcoholism, drug addiction, eating problems, and other disorders. An irony of the medical use of behavior modification is that behaviorism explicitly denies the medical model (that behavior is a symptom of illness) and adopts an environmental, albeit still individual, solution to the problem. This has not, however, hindered its adoption by medical professionals.

Human genetics is one of the most exciting and rapidly expanding areas of medical knowledge. Genetic screening and genetic counseling are becoming more commonplace. Genetic causes are proposed for such a variety of human problems as alcoholism, hyperactivity, learning disabilities, schizophrenia, manic depressive psychosis, homosexuality, and mental retardation. At this time, apart from specific genetic disorders such as pheylketonuria (PKU) and certain forms of retardation, genetic explanations tend to be general theories (i.e., at best positing "predispositions"), with only minimal empirical support, and are not at the level at which medical intervention occurs. The most well-publicized genetic theory of deviant behavior is that an XYY chromosome arrangement is a determinant factor in "criminal tendencies." Although this XYY research has been criticized severely (e.g., Fox, 1971), the controversy surrounding it may be a harbinger of things to come. Genetic anomalies may be discovered to have a correlation with deviant behavior and may become a causal explanation for this behavior. Medical control, in the form of genetic counseling (Sorenson, 1974), may discourage parents from having offspring with a high risk (e.g., 25%) of genetic impairment. Clearly the potentials for medical control go far beyond present use; one could imagine the possibility of licensing selected parents (with proper genes) to have children, and further manipulating gene arrangements to produce or eliminate certain traits.

Medical Collaboration

Medicine acts not only as an independent agent of social control (as above), but frequently medical collaboration with other authorities serves social control functions. Such collaboration includes roles as information provider, gatekeeper, institutional agent, and technician. These interdependent medical control functions highlight the extent to which medicine is interwoven in the fabric of society. Historically, medical personnel have reported information on gunshot wounds and venereal disease to state authorities. More recently this has included reporting "child abuse" to child welfare or law enforcement agencies (Pfohl, 1977).

The medical profession is the official designator of the "sick role." This imbues the physician with authority to define particular kinds of deviance as illness and exempt the patient from certain role obligations. These are general gatekeeping and social control tasks. In some instances the physician functions as a specific gatekeeper for special exemptions from conventional norms; here the exemptions are authorized because of illness, disease, or disability. A classic example is the so-called insanity defense in certain crime cases. Other more commonplace examples include competency to stand trial, medical deferment from the draft or a medical discharge from the military, requiring physicians' notes to legitimize missing an examination or excessive absences in school, and, before abortion was legalized, obtaining two psychiatrists' letters testifying to the therapeutic necessity of the abortion. Halleck (1971) has called this "the power of medical excuse." In a slightly different vein, but still forms of gatekeeping and medical excuse, are medical examinations for disability or workman's compensation benefits. Medical reports required for insurance coverage and employment or medical certification of an epileptic as seizure free to obtain a driver's license are also gatekeeping activities.

Physicians in total institutions have one of two roles. In some institutions, such as schools for the retarded or mental hospitals, they are usually the administrative authority; in others, such as in the military or prisons, they are employees of the administration. In total institutions, medicine's role as agent of social control (for the institution) is more apparent. In both the military and prisons, physicians have the power to confer the sick role and to offer medical excuses for deviance (see Daniels, 1969; Waitzkin & Waterman, 1974). For example, discharges and sick call are available medical designations for deviant behavior. Since physicians are both hired and paid by the institution, it is difficult for them to be fully an agent of the patient, engendering built-in role strains. An extreme example is in wartime when the physician's mandate is to return the soldier to combat duty as soon as possible. Under some circumstances physicians act as direct agents of control by prescribing medications to control unruly or disorderly inmates or to help a "neurotic" adjust to the conditions of a total institution. In such cases "captive professionals" (Daniels, 1969) are more likely to become the agent of the institution than the agent of the individual patient (Szasz, 1965; see also Menninger, 1967).

Under rather rare circumstances physicians may become "mere technicians," applying the sanctions of another authority who purchases their medical skills. An extreme example would be the behavior of the experimental and death physicians in Nazi Germany. A less heinous but nevertheless ominous example is provided by physicians who perform court-ordered sterilizations (Kittrie, 1971). . . . [Today, physicians administer] drugs as the "humanitarian" and painless executioners [in capital punishment cases.]

Medical Ideology

Medical ideology is a type of social control that involves defining a behavior or condition as an illness primarily because of the social and ideological benefits accrued by conceptualizing it in medical terms. These effects of medical ideology may benefit the individual, the dominant interests in the society, or both. They exist independently of any organic basis for illness or any available treatment. Howard Waitzkin and Barbara Waterman (1974) call one latent function of medicalization "secondary gain," arguing that assumption of the sick role can fulfill personality and individual needs (e.g., gaining nurturance or attention) or legitimize personal failure (Shuval & Antonovsky, 1973). One of the most important functions of the disease model of alcoholism and to a lesser extent drug addiction is the secondary gain of removing blame from, and constructing a shield against condemnation of, individuals for their deviant behavior, Alcoholics Anonymous, a nonmedical quasi-religious self-help organization, adopted a variant of the medical model of alcoholism independent of the medical profession. One suspects the secondary gain serves their purposes well.

Disease designations can support dominant social interests and institutions. A poignant example is prominent 19th-century New Orleans physician S. W. Cartwright's antebellum conceptualization of the disease drapetomania, a condition that affected only slaves. Its major symptom was running away from their masters (Cartwright, S. W., 1851). Medical conceptions and controls often support dominant social values and morality: the 19th-century Victorian conceptualization of the illness of and addiction to masturbation and the medical treatments developed to control this disease make chilling reading in the [21st century] (Comfort, 1967: Englehardt, 1974). The [former] Soviet labeling of political dissidents as mentally ill is another example of the manipulation of illness designations to support dominant political and social institutions (Conrad, 1977). These examples highlight the sociopolitical nature of illness designations in general (Zola, 1975).

In sum, medicine as an institution of social control has a number of faces. The three types of medical social control discussed here do not necessarily exist as discrete entities but

are found in combination with one another. For example, court-ordered sterilizations or medical prescribing of drugs to unruly nursing home patients combines both technological and collaborative aspects of medical control; legitimating disability status includes both ideological and collaborative aspects of medical control; and treating Soviet dissidents with drugs for their mental illness combines all three aspects of medical social control. It is clear that the enormous expansion of medicine in the past [70] years has increased the number of possible ways in which problems could be medicalized. In the next section we point out some of the consequences of this medicalization.

Social Consequences of Medicalizing Deviance

Jesse Pitts (1968), one of the first sociologists to give attention to the medicalization of deviance, suggests that "medicalization is one of the most effective means of social control and that it is destined to become the main mode of *formal* social control" (p. 391, emphasis in original). Although his bold prediction is far-reaching (and, in light of recent developments, perhaps a bit premature), his analysis . . . was curiously optimistic and uncritical of the effects and consequences of medicalization. Nonsociologists, especially psychiatric critic Thomas Szasz (1961, 1963, 1970, 1974) and legal scholar Nicholas Kittrie (1971), are much more critical in their evaluations of the ramifications of medicalization. Szasz's critiques are polemical and attack the medical, especially psychiatric, definitions and treatments for deviant behavior. Szasz's analyses, although pathbreaking, insightful, and suggestive, have not been presented in a particularly systematic form. Both he and Kittrie tend to focus on the effects of medicalization on individual civil liberties and judicial processes rather than on social consequences. Their writings, however, reveal that both are aware of sociological consequences.

In this section we discuss some of the more significant consequences and ramifications of defining deviant behavior as a medical problem. We must remind the reader that we are examining the *social* consequences of medicalizing deviance, which can be analyzed separately from the validity of medical definitions or diagnoses, the effectiveness of medical regimens, or their individual consequences. These variously "latent" consequences inhere in medicalization itself and occur *regardless* of how efficacious the particular medical treatment or social control mechanism. As will be apparent, our sociological analysis has left us skeptical of the social benefits of medical social control. We separate the consequences into the "brighter" and "darker" sides of medicalization. The "brighter" side will be presented first.

Brighter Side

The brighter side of medicalization includes the positive or beneficial qualities that are attributed to medicalization. We review briefly the accepted socially progressive aspects of medicalizing deviance. They are separated more for clarity of presentation than for any intrinsic separation in consequence.

First, medicalization is related to a longtime *humanitarian* trend in the conception and control of deviance. For example, alcoholism is no longer considered a sin or even a moral weakness; it is now a disease. Alcoholics are no longer arrested in many places for "public drunkenness"; they are now somehow "treated," if only to be dried out for a time. Medical treatment for the alcoholic can be seen as a more humanitarian means of social control. It is not retributive or punitive, but at least ideally, therapeutic. Troy Duster (1970, p. 10) suggests that medical definitions increase tolerance and compassion for human problems and they "have now been reinterpreted

in an almost nonmoral fashion." (We doubt this, but leave the morality issue for a later discussion.) Medicine and humanitarianism historically developed concurrently and, as some have observed, the use of medical language and evidence increases the prestige of human proposals and enhances their acceptance (Wootton, 1959; Zola, 1975). Medical definitions are imbued with the prestige of the medical profession and are considered the "scientific" and humane way of viewing a problem. . . . This is especially true if an apparently "successful" treatment for controlling the behavior is available, as with hyperkinesis.

Second, medicalization allows for the extension of the *sick role* to those labeled as deviants. . . . Many of the perceived benefits of the medicalization of deviance stem from the assignment of the sick role. Some have suggested that this is the most significant element of adopting the medical model of deviant behavior (Sigler & Osmond, 1974). By defining deviant behavior as an illness or a result of illness, one is absolved of responsibility for one's behavior. It diminishes or *removes blame* from the individual for deviant actions. Alcoholics are no longer held responsible for their uncontrolled drinking, and perhaps hyperactive children are no longer the classroom's "bad boys" but children with a medical disorder. There is some clear secondary gain here for the individual. The label "sick" is free of the moral opprobrium and implied culpability of "criminal" or "sinner." The designation of sickness also may reduce guilt for drinkers and their families and for hyperactive children and their parents. Similarly, it may result in reduced stigma for the deviant. It allows for the development of more acceptable accounts of deviance: a recent film depicted a child witnessing her father's helpless drunken stupor; her mother remarked, "It's okay. Daddy's just sick."

The sick role allows for the "conditional legitimization" of a certain amount of deviance, so long as the individual fulfills the obligation of the sick role. As Renée Fox (1977) notes:

> The fact that the exemptions of sickness have been extended to people with a widening arc of attitudes, experiences and behaviors in American society means primarily that what is regarded as "conditionally legitimated deviance" has increased. . . . So long as [the deviant] does not abandon himself to illness or eagerly embrace it, but works actively on his own or with medical professionals to improve his condition, he is considered to be responding appropriately, even admirably, to an unfortunate occurrence. Under these conditions, illness is accepted as legitimate deviance. (p. 15)

The deviant, in essence, is medically excused for the deviation. But, as Talcott Parsons (1972) has pointed out, "the conditional legitimization is bought at a 'price,' namely, the recognition that illness itself is an undesirable state, to be recovered from as expeditiously as possible" (p. 108). Thus the medical excuse for deviance is only valid when the patient-deviant accepts the medical perspective of the inherent undesirability of his or her sick behavior and submits to a subordinate relationship with an official agent of control (the physician) toward changing it. This, of course, negates any threat the deviant may pose to society's normative structure, for such deviants do not challenge the norm; by accepting deviance as sickness and social control as "treatment," the deviant underscores the validity of the violated norm.

Third, the medical model can be viewed as portraying an *optimistic* outcome for the deviant. Pitts (1968) notes, "the possibility that a patient may be exploited is somewhat minimized by therapeutic ideology, which creates an optimistic bias concerning the patient's fate" (p. 391). The therapeutic ideology, accepted in some form by all branches of medicine, suggests that a problem (e.g., deviant behavior) can be changed or alleviated

if only the proper treatment is discovered and administered. Defining deviant behavior as an illness may also mobilize hope in the individual patient that with proper treatment a "cure" is possible (Frank, J. 1974). Clearly this could have beneficial results and even become a self-fulfilling prophecy. Although the medical model is interpreted frequently as optimistic about individual change, under some circumstances it may lend itself to pessimistic interpretations. The attribution of physiological cause coupled with the lack of effective treatment engendered a somatic pessimism in the late 19th-century conception of madness. . . .

Fourth, medicalization lends the *prestige of the medical profession* to deviance designations and treatments. The medical profession is the most prestigious and dominant profession in American society (Freidson. 1970a). As just noted, medical definitions of deviance become imbued with the prestige of the medical profession and are construed to be the "scientific" way of viewing a problem. The medical mantle of science may serve to deflect definitional challenges. This is especially true if an apparently "successful" treatment for controlling the behavior is available. Medicalization places the problem in the hands of healing physicians. "The therapeutic value of professional dominance, from the patient's point of view, is that it becomes the *doctor's* problem" (Ehrenreich & Ehrenreich, 1975, p. 156, emphasis in original). Physicians are assumed to be beneficent and honorable. "The medical and paramedical professions," Pitts (1968) contends, "especially in the United States, are probably more immune to corruption than are the judicial and parajudicial professions and relatively immune to political pressure" (p. 391).

Fifth, medical social control is more *flexible* and often more *efficient* than judicial and legal controls. The impact of the flexibility of medicine is most profound on the "deviance of everyday life," since it allows "social pressures on deviance [to] increase without boxing the deviant into as rigid a category as 'criminal'" (Pitts, 1968, p. 391). Medical controls are adjustable to fit the needs of the individual patient, rather than being a response to the deviant act itself. It may be more efficient (and less expensive) to control opiate addiction with methadone maintenance than with long prison terms or mental hospitalization. The behavior of disruptive hyperactive children, who have been immune to all parental and teacher sanctions, may dramatically improve after treatment with medications. Medical controls circumvent complicated legal and judicial procedures and may be applied more informally. This can have a considerable effect on social control structures. For example, it has been noted that defining alcoholism as a disease would reduce arrest rates in some areas up to 50%.

In sum, the social benefits of medicalization include the creation of humanitarian and nonpunitive sanctions; the extension of the sick role to some deviants; a reduction of individual responsibility, blame, and possible stigma for deviance; an optimistic therapeutic ideology; care and treatment rendered by a prestigious medical profession; and the availability of a more flexible and often more efficient means of social control.

Darker Side

There is, however, another side to the medicalization of deviant behavior. Although it may often seem entirely humanitarian to conceptualize deviance as sickness as opposed to badness, it is not that simple. There is a "darker" side to the medicalization of deviance. In some senses these might be considered as the more clearly latent aspects of medicalization. In an earlier work Conrad (1975) elucidated four consequences of medicalizing deviance; building on that work, we expand our analysis to seven. Six are discussed here; the seventh is described separately in the next section.

Dislocation of responsibility. As we have seen, defining behavior as a medical problem removes or profoundly diminishes responsibility from the individual. Although affixing responsibility is always complex, medicalization produces confusion and ambiguity about who is responsible. Responsibility is separated from social action; it is located in the nether world of biophysiology or psyche. Although this takes the individual officially "off the hook," its excuse is only a partial one. The individual, the putative deviant, and the undesirable conduct are still associated. Aside from where such conduct is "seated," the sick deviant is the medium of its expression.

With the removal of responsibility also comes the lowering of status. A dual-class citizenship is created: those who are deemed responsible for their actions and those who are not. The not-completely-responsible sick are placed in a position of dependence on the fully responsible nonsick (Parsons, 1975, p. 108). Kittrie (1971, p. 347) notes in this regard that more than half the American population is no longer subject to the sanctions of criminal law. Such persons, among others, become true "second-class citizens."

Assumption of the moral neutrality of medicine. Cloaked in the mantle of science, medicine and medical practice are assumed to be objective and value free. But this profoundly misrepresents reality. The very nature of medical practice involves value judgment. To call something a disease is to deem it undesirable. Medicine is influenced by the moral order of society—witness the diagnosis and treatment of masturbation as a disease in Victorian times—yet medical language of disease and treatment is assumed to be morally neutral. It is not, and the very technological-scientific vocabulary of medicine that defines disease obfuscates this fact.

Defining deviance as disease allows behavior to keep its negative judgment, but medical language veils the political and moral nature of this decision in the guise of scientific fact. There was little public clamor for moral definitions of homosexuality as long as it remained defined an illness, but soon after the disease designation was removed, moral crusaders (e.g., Anita Bryant) launched public campaigns condemning the immorality of homosexuality. One only needs to scratch the surface of medical designations for deviant behavior to find overtly moral judgments.

Thus, as Zola (1975) points out, defining a problem as within medical jurisdiction

> is not morally neutral precisely because in establishing its relevance as a key dimension for action, the moral issue is prevented from being squarely faced and occasionally from even being raised. By the acceptance of a specific behavior as an undesirable state the issue becomes not whether to treat an individual problem but how and when. (p. 86)

Defining deviance as a medical phenomenon involves moral enterprise.

Domination of expert control. The medical profession is made up of experts; it has a monopoly on anything that can be conceptualized as an illness. Because of the way the medical profession is organized and the mandate it has from society, decisions related to medical diagnoses and treatment are controlled almost completely by medical professionals.

Conditions that enter the medical domain are not ipso facto medical problems, whether we speak of alcoholism, hyperactivity, or drug addiction. When a problem is defined as medical, it is removed from the public realm, where there can be discussion by ordinary people, and put on a plane where only medical people can discuss it. As Janice Reynolds (1973) succinctly states,

> The increasing acceptance, especially among the more educated segments of our populace,

of technical solutions—solutions administered by disinterested and morally neutral experts—results in the withdrawal of more and more areas of human experience from the realm of public discussion. For when drunkenness, juvenile delinquency, sub par performance and extreme political beliefs are seen as symptoms of an underlying illness or biological defect the merits and drawbacks of such behavior or beliefs need not be evaluated. (pp. 220–221)

The public may have their own conceptions of deviant behavior, but those of the experts are usually dominant. Medical definitions have a high likelihood for dominance and hegemony: they are often taken as the last scientific word. The language of medical experts increases mystification and decreases the accessibility of public debate.

Medical social control. Defining deviant behavior as a medical problem allows certain things to be done that could not otherwise be considered; for example, the body may be cut open or psychoactive medications given. As we elaborated above, this treatment can be a form of social control.

In regard to drug treatment, Henry Lennard (1971) observes: "Psychoactive drugs, especially those legally prescribed, tend to restrain individuals from behavior and experience that are not complementary with the requirements of the dominant value system" (p. 57). These forms of medical social control presume a prior definition of deviance as a medical problem. Psychosurgery on an individual prone to violent outbursts requires a diagnosis that something is wrong with his brain or nervous system. Similarly, prescribing drugs to restless, overactive, and disruptive schoolchildren requires a diagnosis of hyperkinesis. These forms of social control, what Stephan Chorover (1973) has called "psycho-technology," are powerful and often efficient means of controlling deviance. These relatively new and increasingly popular forms of medical control could not be used without the prior medicalization of deviant behavior. As is suggested from the discovery of hyperkineses and to a lesser extent the development of methadone treatment of opiate addiction, if a mechanism of medical social control seems useful, then the deviant behavior it modifies will be given a medical label or diagnosis. We imply no overt malevolence on the part of the medical profession; rather, it is part of a larger process, of which the medical profession is only a part. The larger process might be called the individualization of social problems.

Individualization of social problems. The medicalization of deviance is part of a larger phenomenon that is prevalent in our society: the individualization of social problems. We tend to look for causes and solutions to complex social problems in the individual rather than in the social system. William Ryan (1971a) has identified this process as "blaming the victim": seeing the causes of the problem in individuals (who are usually of low status) rather than as endemic to the society. We seek to change the "victim" rather than the society. The medical practice of diagnosing an illness in an individual lends itself to the individualization of social problems. Rather than seeing certain deviant behaviors as symptomatic of social conditions, the medical perspective focuses on the individual, diagnosing and treating the illness itself and generally ignoring the social situation.

Hyperkinesis serves as a good example of this. Both the school and parents are concerned with the child's behavior; the child is difficult at home and disruptive in school. No punishments or rewards seem consistently effective in modifying the behavior, and both parents and school are at their wits' end. A medical evaluation is suggested. The diagnosis of hyperkinetic behavior leads to prescribing stimulant medications. The child's behavior seems to become more socially

acceptable, reducing problems in school and home. Treatment is considered a medical success.

But there is an alternative perspective. By focusing on the symptoms and defining them as hyperkinesis, we ignore the possibility that the behavior is not an illness but an adaptation to a social situation. It diverts our attention from the family or school and from seriously entertaining the idea that the "problem" could be in the structure of the social system. By giving medications, we are essentially supporting the existing social and political arrangements in that it becomes a "symptom" of an individual disease rather than a possible "comment" on the nature of the present situation. Although the individualization of social problems aligns well with the individualistic ethic of American culture, medical intervention against deviance makes medicine a de facto agent of dominant social and political interests.

Depoliticization of deviant behavior. Depoliticization of deviant behavior is a result of both the process of medicalization and the individualization of social problems. Probably one of the clearest . . . examples of such depoliticization occurred when political dissidents in the [former] Soviet Union were declared mentally ill and confined to mental hospitals (Conrad, 1977). This strategy served to neutralize the meaning of political protest and dissent, rendering it (officially, at least) symptomatic of mental illness.

The medicalization of deviant behavior depoliticizes deviance in the same manner. By defining the overactive, restless, and disruptive child as hyperkinetic, we ignore the meaning of the behavior in the context of the social system. If we focused our analysis on the school system, we might see the child's behavior as a protest against some aspect of the school or classroom situation, rather than symptomatic of an individual neurological disorder. Similar examples could be drawn of the opiate addict in the ghetto, the alcoholic in the workplace, and others. Medicalizing deviant behavior precludes us from recognizing it as a possible international repudiation of existing political arrangements.

There are other related consequences of the medicalization of deviance beyond the six discussed. The medical ideal of early intervention may lead to early labeling and secondary deviance (see Lemert, 1972). The "medical decision rule," which approximates "when in doubt, treat," is nearly the converse of the legal dictum "innocent until proven guilty" and may unnecessarily enlarge the population of deviants (Scheff, 1963). Certain constitutional safeguards of the judicial system that protect individuals' rights are neutralized or by-passed by medicalization (Kittrie, 1971). Social control in the name of benevolence is at once insidious and difficult to confront. Although these are all significant, we wish to expand on still another consequence of considerable social importance, the exclusion of evil.

Exclusion of Evil

Evil has been excluded from the imagery of modern human problems. We are uncomfortable with notions of evil; we regard them as primitive and nonhumanitarian, as residues from a theological era. Medicalization contributes to the exclusion of concepts of evil in our society. Clearly medicalization is not the sole cause of exclusion of evil, but it shrouds conditions, events, and people and prevents them from being confronted as evil. The roots of the exclusion of evil are in the Enlightenment, the diminution of religious imagery of sin, the rise of determinist theories of human behavior, and the doctrine of cultural relativity. Social scientists as well have excluded the concept of evil from their analytic discourses (Wolff, 1969; for exceptions, see Becker, E., 1975, and Lyman, 1978).

Although we cannot here presume to identify the forms of evil in modern times, we would like to sensitize the reader to how medical definitions of deviance serve to further exclude evil from our view. It can be argued that regardless of what we construe as evil (e.g., destruction, pain, alienation, exploitation, oppression), there are at least two general types of evil: evil intent and evil consequence. Evil intent is similar to the legal concept mens rea, literally, "evil mind." Some evil is intended by a specific line of action. Evil consequence is, on the other hand, the result of action. No intent or motive to do evil is necessary for evil consequence to prevail; on the contrary, it often resembles the platitude "the road to hell is paved with good intentions." In either case medicalization dilutes or obstructs us from seeing evil. Sickness gives us a vocabulary of motive (Mills, 1940) that obliterates evil intent. And although it does not automatically render evil consequences good, the allegation that they were products of a "sick" mind or body relegates them to a status similar to that of "accidents."

For example, Hitler orchestrated the greatest mass genocide in modern history, yet some have reduced his motivation for the destruction of the Jews (and others) to a personal pathological condition. To them and to many of us, Hitler was sick. But this portrays the horror of the Holocaust as a product of individual pathology; as Thomas Szasz frequently points out, it prevents us from seeing and confronting man's inhumanity to man. Are Son of Sam, Charles Manson, the assassins of King and the Kennedys, the Richard Nixon of Watergate, Libya's Muammar Kaddafi, or the all-too-common child beater sick? Although many may well be troubled, we argue that there is little to be gained by deploying such a medical vocabulary of motives. It only hinders us from comprehending the human element in the decisions we make, the social structures we create, and the actions we take. Hannah Arendt (1963), in her exemplary study of the banality of evil, contends that Nazi war criminal Adolph Eichmann, rather than being sick, was "terribly, terrifyingly normal."

Susan Sontag (1978) has suggested that on a cultural level, we use the metaphor of illness to speak of various kinds of evil. Cancer, in particular, provides such a metaphor: we depict slums and pornography shops as "cancers" in our cities; J. Edgar Hoover's favorite metaphor for communism was "a cancer in our midst"; and Nixon's administration was deemed "cancerous," rotting from within. In our secular culture, where powerful religious connotations of sin and evil have been obscured, cancer (and for that matter, illness in general) is one of the few available images of unmitigated evil and wickedness. As Sontag (1978) observes:

> But how to be . . . [moral] in the late twentieth century? How, when . . . we have a sense of evil but no longer the religious or philosophical language to talk intelligently about evil. Trying to comprehend "radical" or "absolute" evil, we search for adequate metaphors. But the modern disease metaphors are all cheap shots. . . . Only in the most limited sense is any historical event or problem like an illness. It is invariably an encouragement to simplify what is complex. . . . (p. 85)

Thus we suggest that the medicalization of social problems detracts from our capability to see and confront the evils that face our world.

In sum, the "darker" side of the medicalization of deviance has profound consequences for the putative or alleged deviant and society. . . .

Medicalizing Deviance: A Final Note

The potential for medicalizing deviance has increased in the past few decades. The increasing dominance of the medical profession, the discovery of subtle physiological correlates of human behavior, and the creation of medical technologies (promoted by powerful pharmaceutical and medical technology industry interests) have advanced this trend. Although we remain skeptical of the overall social benefits of medicalization and are concerned about its "darker" side, it is much too simplistic to suggest a wholesale condemnation of medicalization. Offering alcoholics medical treatment in lieu of the drunk tank is undoubtedly a more humane response to deviance; methadone maintenance allows a select group of opiate addicts to make successful adaptations to society; some schoolchildren seem to benefit from stimulant medications for hyperkinesis; and the medical discovery of child abuse may well increase therapeutic intervention. Medicalization in general has reduced societal condemnation of deviants. But these benefits do not mean these conditions are in fact diseases or that the same results could not be achieved in another manner. And even in those instances of medical "success," the social consequences indicated . . . are still evident.

The most difficult consequence of medicalization for us to discuss is the exclusion of evil. In part this is because we are members of a culture that has largely eliminated evil from intellectual and public discourse. But our discomfort also stems from our ambivalence about what can meaningfully be construed as evil in our society. If we are excluding evil, what exactly are we excluding? We have no difficulty depicting such conditions as pain, violence, oppression, exploitation, and abject cruelty as evil. Social scientists of various stripes have been pointing to these evils and their consequences since the dawn of social science. It is also possible for us to conceive of "organizational evils" such as corporate price fixing, false advertising (or even all advertising), promoting life-threatening automobiles, or the wholesale drugging of nursing home patients to facilitate institutional management. We also have little trouble in seeing ideologies such as imperialism, chauvinism, and racial supremacy as evils. Our difficulty comes with seeing individuals as evil. While we would not adopt a Father-Flanagan-of-Boys-Town attitude of "there's no such thing as a bad boy," our own socialization and "liberal" assumptions as well as sociological perspective make it difficult for us to conceive of any individual as "evil." As sociologists we are more likely to see people as products of their psychological and social circumstances: there may be evil social structures, ideologies, or deeds, but not evil people. Yet when we confront a Hitler, an Idi Amin, or a Stalin of the forced labor camps, it is sometimes difficult to reach any other conclusion. We note this dilemma more as clarification of our stance than as a solution. There are both evils in society and people who are "victims" to those evils. Worthwhile social scientific goals include uncovering the evils, understanding and aiding the victims, and ultimately contributing to a more humane existence for all.

REFERENCES

Arendt, H. *Eichmann in Jerusalem*. New York: Viking Press, 1963.

Becker, E. *Escape from evil*. New York: The Free Press, 1975.

Cartwright, S. W. Report on the diseases and physical peculiarities of the negro race. *N.O. Med. Surg. J.*, 1851, *7*, 691–715.

Chorover, S. Big Brother and psychotechnology. *Psychol. Today*, 1973, *7*, 43–54 (Oct.).

Chorover, S. Psychosurgery: a neuropsychological perspective. *Boston U. Law Rev.*, 1974, *74*, 231–248 (March). (b)

Comfort, A. *The anxiety makers*. London: Thomas Nelson & Sons, 1967.

Conrad, P. The discovery of hyperkinesis: notes on the medicalization of deviant behavior. *Social Prob.*, 1975, *23*, 12–21 (Oct.).

Conrad, P. Soviet dissidents, ideological deviance, and mental hospitalization. Presented at Midwest Sociological Society Meetings, Minneapolis, 1977.

Daniels, A. K. The captive professional: bureaucratic limitation in the practice of military psychiatry. *J. Health Soc. Behav.*, 1969, *10*, 255–265 (Dec.).

Delgado, J. M. R. *Physical control of the mind: Toward a psychocivilized society*. New York: Harper & Row, Publishers, 1969.

Duster, T. *The legislation of morality*. New York: The Free Press, 1970.

Edelman, M. *Political language: Words that succeed and policies that fail*. New York: Academic Press, Inc., 1977.

Ehrenreich, B., & Ehrenreich, J. Medicine and social control. In B. R. Mandell (Ed.), *Welfare in America: Controlling the "dangerous" classes*. Englewood Cliffs, N.J.: Prentice-Hall, Inc., 1975.

Englehardt, H. T., Jr. The disease of masturbation: Values and the concept of disease. *Bull. Hist. Med.*, 1974, *48*, 234–248 (Summer).

Fox, Renée. The medicalization and demedicalization of American society. *Daedalus*, 1977, *106*, 9–22.

Fox, Richard G. The XYY offender: A modern myth? *J. Crimin. Law, Criminol., and Police Sci.*, 1971, *62* (1), 59–73.

Frank, J. *Persuasion and healing*. (Rev. ed.). New York: Schocken Books. Inc., 1974.

Freeman, W. Psychosurgery. In S. Arieti (Ed.), *American handbook of psychiatery* (Vol. 2). New York: Basic Books, Inc., 1959.

Freidson, E. *Profession of medicine*. New York: Harper & Row, Publishers Inc., 1970. (a)

Freidson, E. *Doctoring together*. New York: Elsevier North-Holland, Inc., 1975.

Goddard, J. The medical business. *Sci. Am.*, 1973, *229*, 161–168 (Sept.).

Halleck, S. L. *The politics of therapy*. New York: Science House, 1971.

Hurvitz, N. Psychotherapy as a means of social control. *J. Consult. Clin. Psychol.*, 1973, *40*, 232–239.

Illich, I. *Medical nemesis*. New York: Pantheon Books, Inc., 1976.

Kittrie, N. *The right to be different: Deviance and enforced therapy*. Baltimore: Johns Hopkins University Press, 1971. Copyright The Johns Hopkins Press, 1971.

Lemert, E. M. *Human deviance, social problems and social control* (2nd ed.). Englewood Cliffs, N.J.: Prentice-Hall, 1972.

Lennard, H. L., Esptein, L. J., Bernstein, A., & Ranson, D. C. *Mystification and drug misuse.* New York: Perennial Library, 1971.

Lyman, S. *The seven deadly sins: Society and evil.* New York: St. Martin's Press, Inc., 1978.

Mark, V., & Ervin, F. *Violence and the brain.* New York: Harper & Row Publishers, Inc., 1970.

Mechanic, D. Health and illness in technological societies. *Hastings Center Stud.* 1973, *1*(3), 7–18.

Menninger, W. C. *A psychiatrist for a troubled world.* B. H. Hall (Ed.), New York: Viking Press, 1967.

Miller, K. S. *Managing madness.* New York: The Free Press, 1976.

Mills, C. W. Situated actions and vocabularies of motive. *Am. Sociol. Rev.,* 1940, *6,* 904–913.

Parsons, T. *The social system.* New York: The Free Press, 1951.

Parsons, T. Definitions of illness and health in light of American values and social structure. In E. G. Jaco (Ed.), *Patients, physicians and illness.* (2nd ed.). New York: The Free Press, 1972.

Parsons, T. The sick role and the role of the physician reconsidered. *Health Society,* 1975 *53,* 257–278 (Summer).

Pfohl, S. J. The "discovery" of child abuse. *Social Prob.,* 1977, *24,* 310–323 (Feb.).

Pitts, J. Social control: The concepts. In D. Sills (Ed.), *International encyclopedia of social sciences.* (Vol. 14). New York: Macmillan Publishing Co., Inc., 1968.

Reynolds, J. M. The medical institution: The death and disease-producing appendage. In L. T. Reynolds & J. M. Henslin (Eds.), *American society: A critical analysis.* New York: David McKay Co., Inc., 1973.

Rosen, G. The evolution of social medicine. In H. E. Freeman, S. Levine, & L. Reeder (Eds.), *Handbook of medical sociology* (2nd ed.). Englewood Cliffs, N.J.: Prentice-Hall, Inc., 1972.

Ryan, W. *Blaming the victim.* New York: Vintage Books, 1971.

Scheff, T. J. Decision rules, types of errors, and their consequences in medical diagnosis. *Behav. Sci.,* 1963, *8,* 97–107.

Shuval, J. T., & Antonovsky, A. Illness: A mechanism for coping with failure. *Soc. Sci. Med.,* 1973, *7,* 259–265.

Sigler, M., & Osmond, H. *Models of madness, models of medicine.* New York: Macmillan Publishing Co., Inc., 1974.

Sontag, S. *Illness as metaphor.* New York: Farrar, Straus & Giroux, 1978.

Sorenson, J. Biomedical innovation, uncertainty, and doctor-patient interaction. *J. Health Soc. Behav.,* 1974, *15,* 366–374 (Dec.).

Szasz, T. *The myth of mental illness.* New York: Hoeber-Harper, 1961.

Szasz, T. *Law, liberty and psychiatry.* New York: Macmillan Publishing Co., Inc., 1963.

Szasz, T. Legal and moral aspects of homosexuality. In J. Marmor (Ed.), *Sexual inversion: The multiple roots of homosexuality.* New York: Basic Books, Inc., 1965.

Szasz, T. *The manufacture of madness,* New York: Harper & Row, Publishers, Inc., 1970.

Szasz, T. *Ceremonial chemistry.* New York: Anchor Books, 1974.

Waitzkin, H., & Stoeckle, J. Information control and the micropolitics of health care: Summary of an ongoing project. *Soc. Sci. Med.,* 1976, *10,* 263–276 (June).

Waitzkin, H. K., & Waterman, B. *The exploitation of illness in capitalist society.* Indianapolis: The Bobbs-Merrill Co., Inc., 1974.

Wolff, K. For a sociology of evil. *J. Soc. Issues,* 1969, *25,* 111–125.

Wootton, B. *Social science and social pathology.* London: George Allen & Unwin, 1959.

Zola, I. K. Medicine as an institution of social control. *Sociological Rev.,* 1972, *20,* 487–504.

Zola, I. K. In the name of health and illness: On some socio-political consequences of medical influence. *Soc. Sci. Med.,* 1975, *9,* 83–87.

THINKING ABOUT THE READING

How does medicine function as a means of social control? What do the authors mean when they say, "Evil has been excluded from the imagery of modern human problems"? Do you agree that perceiving troublesome behavior as an "illness" prevents us from confronting such behavior as evil? Why do you suppose we have such a profound desire to use the vocabulary of medicine to describe deviant behavior? Clearly some people are helped when their problematic behaviors are conceived as illnesses or disorders and they are prescribed drugs or some sort of surgical treatment. Do you think that Conrad and Schneider overstate the negative consequences of the medicalization of deviance?

PART III

Social Structure, Institutions, and Everyday Life

The Structure of Society

Organizations and Social Institutions

One of the great sociological paradoxes of our existence is that in a society that so fiercely extols the virtues of rugged individualism and personal accomplishment, we spend most of our lives under the influence of larger organizations and social institutions. From the nurturing environments of our churches and schools to the cold depersonalizations of massive bureaucracies, organizations and institutions are a fundamental part of our everyday lives.

One important organization in which you will eventually spend a great deal of your life (if you don't already) is your place of employment. Many people define themselves by their work. But just how much of our time and energy we should devote to our jobs is a matter of some debate and concern. In "The Overworked American," economist Juliet Schor demonstrates that Americans work more and have less leisure time than people in other developed countries. She feels that this phenomenon is not a result of Americans being hard workers but instead is a consequence of what she calls "the work-spend cycle." Americans have become accustomed to working longer hours so they can earn more money to spend on more things. She contrasts this situation with other countries in which the culture promotes a concept of working less and taking more leisure time.

No matter how powerful and influential they are, organizations are more than structures, rules, policies, goals, job descriptions, and standard operating procedures. Each organization, and each division within an organization, develops its own norms, values, and language. Furthermore, no matter how strict and unyielding a particular organization may appear to be, individuals within them are usually able to exert some control over their lives. Rarely is an organization what it appears to be on the surface.

In larger organizations, distinct cultures develop where similar meanings and perspectives are cultivated. As in society as a whole, however, distinct subcultures can develop. In "The Smile Factory," John Van Maanen examines the organizational culture of one of American society's most enduring icons: Disney theme parks. Disneyland and Disneyworld have a highly codified and strict set of conduct standards. Variations from tightly defined employee norms are not tolerated. You'd expect in such a place that employees would be a rather homogeneous group. However, Van Maanen discovers that beneath the surface of this self-proclaimed "Happiest Place on Earth" lies a mosaic of distinct groups that have created their own status system and that work hard to maintain the status boundaries between one another.

The Overworked American

Juliet B. Schor

(1991)

In the last twenty years the amount of time Americans have spent at their jobs has risen steadily. Each year the change is small, amounting to about nine hours, or slightly more than one additional day of work. In any given year, such a small increment has probably been imperceptible. But the accumulated increase over two decades is substantial. When surveyed, Americans report that they have only sixteen and a half hours of leisure a week, after the obligations of job and household are taken care of. Working hours are already longer than they were forty years ago. If present trends continue, . . . Americans will [soon] be spending as much time at their jobs as they did back in the 1920s.

The rise of worktime was unexpected. For nearly a hundred years, hours had been declining. When this decline abruptly ended in the late 1940s, it marked the beginning of a new era in worktime. But the change was barely noticed. Equally surprising, but also hardly recognized, has been the deviation from Western Europe. After progressing in tandem for nearly a century, the United States veered off into a trajectory of declining leisure, while in Europe work has been disappearing. Forty years later, the differences are large. U.S. manufacturing employees currently work 320 more hours—the equivalent of over two months—than their counterparts in . . . Germany or France.

The decline in American's leisure time is in sharp contrast to the potential provided by the growth of productivity. Productivity measures the goods and services that result from each hour worked. When productivity rises, a worker can either produce the current output in less time, or remain at work the same number of hours and produce more. Every time productivity increases, we are presented with the possibility of either more free time or more money. That's the productivity dividend.

Since 1948, productivity has failed to rise in only five years. The level of productivity of the U.S. worker has more than doubled. In other words, we could now produce our 1948 standard of living (measured in terms of marketed goods and services) in less than half the time it took in that year. We actually could have chosen the four-hour day. Or a working year of six months. Or, *every worker in the United States could now be taking every other year off from work—with pay.* Incredible as it may sound, this is just the simple arithmetic of productivity growth in operation.

But between 1948 and the present we did not use any of the productivity dividend to reduce hours. . . . [By] 1990, the average American owned and consumed more than twice as much as he or she did in 1948, but also had less free time.[1]

How did this happen? Why has leisure been such a conspicuous casualty of prosperity? In part, the answer lies in the difference between the markets for consumer products and free time. Consider the former, the legendary American market. It is a veritable consumer's paradise, offering a dazzling array of products varying in style, design, quality, price, and country of origin. The consumer is treated to GM versus Toyota, Kenmore versus GE, Sony, or Magnavox, the Apple versus the IBM. We've got Calvin Klein, Anne Klein, Liz Claiborne, and Levi-Strauss; McDonald's, Burger King, and Colonel Sanders. Marketing experts and advertisers spend vast sums of money to make these choices appealing—even irresistible. And they have been successful. In cross-country comparisons, Americans have been found to spend more time shopping than anyone else. They also spend a higher fraction of the money they earn. And with the explosion of consumer debt, many are now spending what they haven't earned.

After four decades of this shopping spree, the American standard of living embodies a level of material comfort unprecedented in human history. The American home is more spacious and luxurious than the dwellings of any other nation. Food is cheap and abundant. The typical family owns a fantastic array of household and consumer appliances: we have machines to wash our clothes and dishes, mow our lawns, and blow away our snow. . . .

On the other hand, the "market" for free time hardly even exists in America. With few exceptions, employers (the sellers) don't offer the chance to trade off income gains for a shorter work day or the occasional sabbatical. They just pass on income, in the form of annual pay raises or bonuses, or, if granting increased vacation or personal days, usually do so unilaterally. Employees rarely have the chance to exercise an actual choice about how they will spend their productivity dividend. The closest substitute for a "market in leisure" is the travel and other leisure industries that advertise products to occupy our free time. But this indirect effect has been weak, as consumers crowd increasingly expensive leisure spending into smaller periods of time. . . .

Sleep has become another casualty of modern life. According to sleep researchers, studies point to a "sleep deficit" among Americans, a majority of whom are currently getting between 60 and 90 minutes less a night than they should for optimum health and performance. The number of people showing up at sleep disorder clinics with serious problems has skyrocketed in the last decade. Shiftwork, long working hours, the growth of a global economy (with its attendant continent-hopping and twenty-four-hour business culture), and the accelerating pace of life have all contributed to sleep deprivation. If you need an alarm clock, the experts warn, you're probably sleeping too little.

The juggling act between job and family is another problem area. Half the population now says they have too little time for their families. The problem is particularly acute for women: in one study, half of all employed mothers reported it caused either "a lot" or an "extreme" level of stress. The same proportion feel that "when I'm at home I try to make up to my family for being away at work and as a result I rarely have any time for myself." This stress has placed tremendous burdens on marriages. Two-earner couples have less time together, which researchers have found reduces the happiness and satisfaction of a marriage. These couples often just don't have enough time to talk to each other. And growing numbers of husbands and wives are like ships passing in the night, working sequential schedules to manage their child care. Among young parents, the prevalence of at least one partner working outside regular daytime hours is now close to one half. But this "solution" is hardly a happy one. According to one parent: "I work 11–7 to accommodate my family—to eliminate the need for babysitters. However, the stress on myself is tremendous."[2] . . .

Time Squeeze: The Extra Month of Work

Time squeeze has become big news. . . . The première episode of Jane Pauley's television show, "Real Life," highlighted a single father whose computer job was so demanding that he found himself at 2:00 A.M. dragging his child into the office. A Boston-area documentary featured the fourteen- to sixteen-hour workdays of a growing army of moonlighters. CBS's "Forty-Eight Hours" warned of the accelerating pace of life for everyone from high-tech business executives (for whom there are only two types of people—"the quick and the dead") to assembly workers at Japanese-owned automobile factories (where a car comes by every sixty seconds). Employees at fast-food restaurants, who serve in twelve seconds, report that the horns start honking if the food hasn't arrived in fifteen. Nineteen-year-olds work seventy-hour weeks, children are "penciled" into their parents' schedules, and second-graders are given "half an hour a day to unwind" from the pressure to get good grades so they can get into a good college. By the beginning of the 1990s, the time squeeze had become a national focus of attention, appearing in almost all the nation's major media outlets. . . .

At cutting-edge corporations, which emphasize commitment, initiative, and flexibility, the time demands are often the greatest. "People who work for me should have phones in their bathrooms," says the CEO from one aggressive American company. Recent research on managerial habits reveals that work has become positively absorbing. When a deadline approached in one corporation, "people who had been working twelve-hour days and Saturdays started to come in on Sunday, and instead of leaving at midnight, they would stay a few more hours. Some did not go home at all, and others had to look at their watches to remember what day it was." The recent growth in small businesses has also contributed to overwork. When Dolores Kordek started a dental insurance company, her strategy for survival was to work harder than the competition. So the office was open from 7 A.M. to 10 P.M. 365 days a year. And she was virtually always in it.

This combination of retrenchment, economic competition, and innovative business management has raised hours substantially. One poll of senior executives found that weekly hours rose during the 1980s, and vacation time fell. Other surveys have yielded similar results. By the end of the decade, overwork at the upper echelons of the labor market had become endemic—and its scale was virtually unprecedented in living memory.

If the shortage of time had been confined to Wall Street or America's corporate boardrooms, it might have remained just a media curiosity. The number of people who work eighty hours a week and bring home—if they ever get there—a six-figure income is very small. But while the incomes of these rarefied individuals were out of reach, their schedules turned out to be downright common. As Wall Street waxed industrious, the longer schedules penetrated far down the corporate ladder, through middle management, into the secretarial pool, and even onto the factory floor itself.[3] Millions of ordinary Americans fell victim to the shortage of time. . . .

A twenty-eight-year-old Massachusetts factory worker explains the bind many fathers are in: "Either I can spend time with my family, or support them—not both." Overtime or a second job is financially compelling: "I can work 8–12 hours overtime a week at time and a half, and that's when the real money just starts to kick in. . . . If I don't work the OT my wife would have to work much longer hours to make up the difference, and our day care bill would double. . . . The trouble is, the little time I'm home I'm too tired to have any fun with them or be any real help around the house." Among white-collar employees the problem isn't paid overtime, but the regular hours. To get ahead, or even just to hold on to a position, long days may be virtually mandatory.

Overwork is also rampant among the nation's poorly paid workers. At $5, $6, or even $7 an hour, annual earnings before taxes and deductions range from $10,000 to $14,000. Soaring rents alone have been enough to put many of these low earners in financial jeopardy. For the more than one-third of all workers now earning hourly wages of $7 and below, the pressure to lengthen hours has been inexorable. Valerie Connor, a nursing-home worker in Hartford, explains that "you just can't make it on one job." She and many of her co-workers have been led to work two eight-hour shifts a day. According to an official of the Service Employees International Union in New England, nearly one-third of their nursing-home employees now hold two full-time jobs. Changes in the low end of the labor market have also played a role. There is less full-time, stable employment. "Twenty hours here, thirty hours there, and twenty hours here. That's what it takes to get a real paycheck," says Domenic Bozzotto, president of Boston's hotel and restaurant workers union, whose members are drowning in a sea of work. Two-job families? Those were the good old days, he says. "We've got four-job families." . . .

More People Working

The mythical American family of the 1950s and 1960s was comprised of five people, only one of whom "worked"—or at least did what society called work. Dad went off to his job every morning, while Mom and the three kids stayed at home. Of course, the 1950s-style family was never as common as popular memory has made it out to be. Even in the 1950s and 1960s, about one-fourth of wives with children held paying jobs. The nostalgia surrounding the family is especially inaccurate for African-American women, whose rates of job holding have historically been higher than whites'. Even so, in recent years, the steady growth of married women's participation in

the labor force has made the "working woman" the rule rather than the exception. By 1990, two-thirds of married American women were participating in the paid labor market. . . .

Female employment has justifiably received widespread attention: it is certainly the most significant development afoot. But the expansion of work effort in the American family is not occurring just among women. American youth are also working harder in a reversal of a long decline of teenage job holding, the result of increased schooling and economic prosperity. The likelihood that a teenager would hold a job began to rise in the mid-1960s, just as adult hours began their upward climb. By 1990, the labor force participation rate of teens had reached 53.7 percent, nearly 10 points higher than it had been twenty-five years earlier. . . .

Not only are more of the nation's young people working, but they are working longer hours. A 1989 nationwide sweep by government inspectors uncovered widescale abuses of child labor laws—violations of allowable hours, permissible activities, and ages of employment. Low-wage service sector establishments have been voracious in their appetite for teen labor, especially in regions with shortages of adult workers. In middle-class homes, much of this work is motivated by consumerism: teenagers buy clothes, music, even cars. Some observers are worried that the desire to make money has become a compulsion, with many young Americans now working full-time, in addition to full-time school. A New Hampshire study found that 85 percent of the state's tenth- to twelfth-graders hold jobs, and 45 percent of them work more than twenty hours a week. At 10 P.M. on a school night, Carolyn Collignon is just beginning hour eight on her shift at Friendly's restaurant. Teachers report that students are falling asleep in class, getting lower grades, and cannot pursue after-school activities. Robert Pimentel works five days a week at Wendy's to pay off loans on his car and a $5,600 motorcycle, the purchase of which he now describes as a "bad move." Pimentel averages "maybe six hours of sleep a night. If you consider school a job, which it pretty much is, I put in a long day." He wants to go to college, but his grades have suffered.

This is the picture in suburban America. In large urban centers, such as New York and Los Angeles, the problem is more serious. Inspectors have found nineteenth-century-style sweatshops where poor immigrants—young girls of twelve years and above—hold daytime jobs, missing out on school altogether. And a million to a million and a half migrant farmworker children—some as young as three and four years—are at work in the nation's fields. These families cannot survive without the effort of all their members. . . .

So what's pushing up hours? One factor is moonlighting—the practice of holding more than one job at a time. Moonlighting is now more prevalent than at any time during the three decades for which we have statistics. As of May 1989, more than seven million Americans, or slightly over 6 percent of those employed, officially reported having two or more jobs, with extremely high increases occurring among women. The real numbers are higher, perhaps twice as high—as tax evasion, illegal activities, and employer disapproval of second jobs make people reluctant to speak honestly. The main impetus behind this extra work is financial. Close to one-half of those polled say they hold two jobs in order to meet regular household expenses or pay off debts. . . .

A second factor, operating largely on weekly hours, is that Americans are working more overtime. After the recession of the early 1980s, many companies avoided costly rehiring of workers and, instead, scheduled extra overtime. Among manufacturing employees, paid overtime hours rose substantially after the recession and, by the end of 1987, accounted

for the equivalent of an additional five weeks of work per year. One automobile worker noted, "You have to work the hours, because a few months later they'll lay you off for a model changeover and you'll need the extra money when you're out of work. It never rains but it pours—either there's more than you can stand, or there isn't enough." While many welcome the chance to earn premium wages, the added effort can be onerous. Older workers are often compelled to stretch themselves, because many companies calculate pension benefits only on recent earnings. A fifty-nine-year-old male worker explains:

> Just at the point in my life where I was hoping I could ease up a little bit on the job and with the overtime, I find that I have to work harder than ever. If I'm going to have enough money when I retire, I have to put in five good years now with a lot of overtime because that is what they will base my pension on. With all the overtime I have to work to build my pension, I hope I live long enough to collect it.

(Apparently he didn't—he was diagnosed with incurable cancer not long after this interview.)

The Shrinking Vacation

One of the most notable developments of the 1980s [and 1990s] is that paid time off is actually shrinking. European workers have been gaining vacation time—minimum allotments are now in the range of four to five weeks in many countries—but Americans are losing it. In the last decade, U.S. workers have gotten *less* paid time off—on the order of three and a half fewer days each year of vacation time, holidays, sick pay, and other paid absences. . . .

Part of the shrinkage has been caused by the economic squeeze many companies faced in the 1980s [and 1990s]. Cost-cutting measures often included reductions in vacations and holidays. DuPont reduced its top vacation allotment from seven to four weeks and eliminated three holidays a year. Personnel departments also tightened up on benefits such as sick leave and bereavement time. As employees became more fearful about job loss, they spent less time away from the workplace. Days lost to illness fell dramatically. So did unpaid absences—which declined for the first time since 1973.

The other factor reducing vacations has been the restructuring of the labor market. Companies have turned to more "casual" workforces—firing long-term employees and signing on consultants, part-timers, or temporaries. Early retirements among senior workers also reduced vacation time. Because the length of vacations in this country is based on duration of employment, these changes have all contributed to lowering the amount of time off people actually receive. The growth of service sector occupations, where the duration of employment tends to be shortest, has also been a factor. . . .

Involuntary Leisure: Underemployment and Unemployment

There is at least one group of Americans for whom time squeeze is not a problem. These are the millions who cannot get enough work or who cannot get any at all. They have plenty of "leisure" but can hardly enjoy it. One of the great ironies of our present situation is that overwork for the majority has been accompanied by the growth of enforced idleness for the minority. The proportion of the labor force who cannot work as many hours as they would like has more than doubled in the last twenty years. Just as surely as our economic system is "underproducing" leisure for some, it is "overproducing" it for others.

Declining industries provide poignant illustrations of the coexistence of long hours and unemployment. The manufacturing sector lost over a million jobs in the 1980s. At the same time (from 1980 to 1987), overtime hours rose by fifty per year. Many of those on permanent layoff watch their former coworkers put in steady overtime, week after week, year after year. Outside manufacturing, unemployment also rose steadily. At the height of each business expansion (1969, 1973, 1979, and 1987), the proportion of the labor force without a job was higher—rising from only 3.4 percent in 1969 to almost twice that—6.1 percent—in 1987.

Enforced idleness is not just confined to those who have been laid off. Underemployment is also growing. The fraction of the labor force working part-time but desiring full-time work increased more than seven times . . . [to] almost 17 percent. . . .

The trend toward underemployment and unemployment signals a disturbing failure of the labor market: the U.S. economy is increasingly unable to provide work for its population. It is all the more noticeable that growing idleness is occurring at a time when those who are fully employed are at their workplaces for ever longer hours. Like long hours, the growth of unemployment stems from the basic structure of the economy. Capitalist systems such as our own do not operate in order to provide employment. Their guiding principle is the pursuit of profitability. If profitability results in high employment, that is a happy coincidence for those who want jobs. If it does not, bottom-line oriented companies will not take it upon themselves to hire those their plans have left behind. . . . Full employment typically occurs only when government commits itself to the task. . . .

. . . Employers have strong incentives to keep hours long. And these incentives have been instrumental in raising hours and keeping them high. In retrospect, the reformers underestimated the obstacles within capitalism itself to solving both the nation's shortage of jobs and its shortage of time.

The Insidious Cycle of Work-and-Spend

Shop 'Til You Drop

We live in what may be the most con-sumer-oriented society in history. Americans spend three to four times as many hours a year shopping as their counterparts in Western European countries. Once a purely utilitarian chore, shopping has been elevated to the status of a national passion.

Shopping has become a leisure activity in its own right. Going to the mall is a common Friday or Saturday night's entertainment, not only for the teens who seem to live in them, but also for adults. Shopping is also the most popular weekday evening "out-of-home enter-tainment." And malls are everywhere. Four bil-lion square feet of our total land area has been converted into shopping centers, or about 16 square feet for every American man, woman, and child. Actually, shopping is no longer con-fined to stores or malls but is permeating the entire geography. Any phone line is a conduit to thousands of products. Most homes are vir-tual retail outlets, with cable shopping chan-nels, mail-order catalogues, toll-free numbers, and computer hookups. We can shop during lunch hour, from the office. We can shop while traveling, from the car. We can even shop in the airport, where video monitors have been installed for immediate on-screen purchasing.

Some of the country's most popular leisure activities have been turned into extended shopping expeditions. National parks, music concerts, and art museums are now acquisition opportunities. When the South Street Seaport Museum in New York City opened in the early 1980s as a combina-tion museum-shopping center, its director explained the commercialization as a bow to reality: "The fact is that shopping is the chief cultural activity in the United States." Americans used to visit Europe to see the sights or meet the people. Now "Born to Shop" guides are replacing Fodor and Baedeker, com-plete with walking tours from Ferragamo to Fendi. Even island paradises, where we go "to get away from it all," are not immune: witness titles such as *Shopping in Exciting Australia and Papua New Guinea.*

Debt has been an important part of the shopping frenzy. Buying is easier when there's no requirement to pay immediately, and credit cards have seduced many people beyond their means: "I wanted to be able to pick up the tab for ten people, or take a cab when I wanted. I thought that part of being an adult was being able to go to a restaurant, look at the menu, and go in if you like the food, not because you're looking at the prices." This young man quickly found himself with $18,000 of credit card debt, and realized that he and his wife "could have gone to Europe last year on [the] interest alone." For some people, shopping has become an addiction, like alcohol or drugs. "Enabled" by plastic, compulsive shoppers spend money they don't have on items they absolutely "can't" do without and never use. The lucky ones find their way to self-help groups like Debtors Anonymous and Shopaholics Limited. And for every serious compulsive shopper, there are many more with mild habits. Linda Weltner was lucky enough to keep her addiction within manageable financial bounds, but still her "mindless shopping" grew into a "troubling preoccupation . . . which was impoverishing [her] life." . . .

The Pitfalls of Consumerism

The consumerism that took root in the 1920s was premised on the idea of *dis*satisfac-tion. As much as one has, it is never enough. The implicit mentality is that the next pur-chase will yield happiness, and then the next. In the words of the baby-boom writer, Katy Butler, it was the new couch, the quieter street, and the vacation cottage. Yet happiness turned out to be elusive. Today's luxuries became tomorrow's necessities, no longer appreciated. When the Joneses also got a new couch or a second home, these acquisitions were no longer quite as satisfying. Consumerism turned out to be full of pitfalls—a vicious pattern of wanting and spending which failed to deliver on its promises.

The inability of the consumerist life style to create durable satisfaction can be seen in the syndrome of "keeping up with the Joneses." This competition is based on the fact that it is not the absolute level of consumption that matters, but how much one consumes relative to one's peers. The great English economist John Maynard Keynes made this distinction over fifty years ago: "[Needs] fall into two classes—those which are absolute in the sense that we feel them whatever the situation of our fellow human beings may be, and those which are relative only in that their satisfaction lifts us above, makes us feel superior to, our fellows." Since then, economists have invented a variety of terms for "keeping up with the Joneses": "relative income or consumption," "positional goods," or "local status." A brand-new Toyota Corolla may be a luxury and status symbol in a lower-middle-class town, but it appears paltry next to the BMWs and Mercedes that fill the driveways of the fancy suburb. A 10-percent raise sounds great until you find that your co-workers all got 12 percent. The cellular phone, fur coat, or _____ (fill in the blank) gives a lot of satisfaction only before everyone else has one. In the words of one . . . investment banker: "You tend to live up to your income level. You see it in relation to the people of your category. They're living in a certain way and you want to live in that way. You keep up with other people of your situation who have also leveraged themselves."

Over time, keeping up with the Joneses becomes a real trap—because the Joneses also keep up with you. If everyone's income goes up by 10 percent, then relative positions don't change at all. No satisfaction is gained. The more of our happiness we derive from comparisons with others, the less additional welfare we get from general increases in income—which is probably why happiness has failed to keep pace with economic growth. This dynamic may be only partly conscious. We may not even be aware that we are competing with the Joneses, or experience it as a competition. It may be as simple as the fact that exposure to their latest "life-style upgrade" plants the seed in our own mind that we must have it, too—whether it be a European vacation, this year's fashion statement, or piano lessons for the children.

In the choice between income and leisure, the quest for relative standing has biased us toward income. That's because status comparisons have been mostly around commodities—cars, clothing, houses, even second houses. If Mrs. Jones works long hours, she will be able to buy the second home, the designer dresses, or the fancier car. If her neighbor Mrs. Smith opts for more free time instead, her two-car garage and walk-in closet will be half empty. As long as the competition is more oriented to visible commodities, the tendency will be for both women to prefer income to time off. But once they both spend the income, they're back to where they started. Neither is *relatively* better off. If free time is less of a "relative" good than other commodities, then true welfare could be gained by having more of it, and worrying less about what the Joneses are buying.

It's not easy to get off the income treadmill and into a new, more leisured life style. Mrs. Smith won't do it on her own, because it'll set her back in comparison to Mrs. Jones. And Mrs. Jones is just like Mrs. Smith. . . . We also know their employers won't initiate a shift to more leisure, because they prefer employees to work long hours.

A second vicious cycle arises from the fact that the satisfactions gained from consumption are often short-lived. For many, consumption can be habit forming. Like drug addicts who develop a tolerance, consumers need additional hits to maintain any given level of satisfaction. The switch from black and white to color television was a real improvement when it occurred. But soon viewers became habituated to color. Going back to black and white would have reduced well-being, but having color may not have yielded a permanently higher level of satisfaction. Telephones are another example. Rotary dialing was a major improvement. Then came touch-tone, which made us impatient with rotaries. Now numbers are preprogrammed and some people begin to find any dialing a chore.

Our lives are filled with goods to which we have become so habituated that we take them for granted. Indoor plumbing was once a great luxury—and still is in much of the world. Now it is so ingrained in our life style that we don't give it a second thought. The same holds true for all but the newest household appliances—stoves, refrigerators, and vacuum cleaners are just part of the landscape. We may pay great attention to the kind of automobile we drive, but the fact of having a car is something adults grew accustomed to long ago. . . .

. . . The consumption traps I have described are just the flip side of the bias toward long hours embedded in the production system. We are not merely caught in a pattern of spend-and-spend—the problem identified by many critics of consumer culture. The whole story is that we work, and spend, and work and spend some more.

Causes of the Work-and-Spend Cycle

The irony in all the consuming Americans do is that, when asked, they reject materialist values. The Gallup Poll recently asked respondents to choose what was most important to them—family life, betterment of society, physical health, a strict moral code, and so on. Among

a list of nine, the materialist option—"having a nice home, car and other belongings"—ranked *last*. In a second survey, respondents ranked "having nice things" twenty-sixth in a list of twenty-eight. . . . Over two-thirds of the population says it would "welcome less emphasis on money." Yet behavior is often contrary to these stated values. Millions of working parents see their children or spouses far less than they should or would like to. "Working" mothers complain they have no time for themselves. Volunteer work is on the decline, presumably because people have little time for it. Employed Americans spend long hours at jobs that are adversely affecting their health—through injury, occupationally induced diseases, and stress. My explanation for this paradoxical behavior is that people are operating under a powerful set of constraints: they are trapped by the cycle of work-and-spend.

Work-and-spend is driven by productivity growth. Whether the annual increment is 3 percent, as it was for much of the postwar period, or less, as it has been in recent years, growth in productivity provides the chance either to raise income or to reduce working hours. This is where the cycle begins, with the employer's reaction to the choice between "time and money." Usually a company does not offer this choice to its employees but unilaterally decides to maintain existing hours and give a pay increase instead. As we have seen, for forty years, only a negligible portion of productivity increase has been channeled into free time. Using productivity to raise incomes has become the firmly entrenched "default option." . . .

Once a pay increase is granted, it sets off the consumption cycles I have described. The additional income will be spent. . . . The employee will become habituated to this spending and incorporate it into his or her usual standard of living. Gaining free time by *reducing* income becomes undesirable, both because of relative comparisons (Joneses versus Smiths) and habit formation. The next year, when another increase in productivity occurs, the process starts again. The company offers income, which the employee spends and becomes accustomed to. This interpretation is consistent with the history of the last half-century. Annual productivity growth has made possible higher incomes or more free time. Repeatedly, the bulk of the productivity increase has been channeled into the former. Consumption has kept pace. . . .

The Social Nature of Work-and-Spend

Part of the power of the work-and-spend cycle is its social pervasiveness. Although individuals are the proximate decision makers, their actions are influenced and constrained by social norms and conventions. The social character of the cycle of work-and-spend means that individuals have a hard time breaking out of it on their own. This is part of why, despite evidence of growing desires for less demanding jobs and disillusionment with "work-and-spend," hours are still rising.

To see the difficulties individuals have in deviating from the status quo, consider what would happen to an ordinary couple who have grown tired of the rat race. John and Jane Doe, like nearly half of all Americans, want more time to spend with their children and each other. What will happen if they both decide to reduce their hours by half and are willing to live on half their usual earnings?

The transition will be most abrupt for John. Few men work part-time, with the exception of teens, students, and some seniors. Among males aged twenty-five to forty-four, virtually none . . . voluntarily choose part-time schedules. Most report that they are not able to reduce their hours of work at all. And of those who do have the freedom to work fewer hours, it is likely that only a small percentage can reduce hours by as much as half. Unless John has truly unusual talents, his employer will probably refuse to sanction a change to part-time work. Chances are he'll have to find a new job.

Given the paucity of part-time jobs for men, John's choices will be limited. It will be almost impossible to secure a position in a managerial, professional, or administrative capacity. Most part-time jobs are in the service sector. When he does land a job, his pay will fall far short of what he earned in full-time work. The median hourly wage rate among male workers is about $10.50, with weekly earnings of $450. As a part-time worker paid by the hour, his median wage will be about $4, or $80 a week. He will also lose many of the benefits that went with his full-time job. Only 15 percent of part-time workers are given health insurance.[4] The total income loss John will suffer is likely to exceed 80 percent. Under these conditions, part-time work hardly seems feasible.

The social nature of John's choice is revealed by the drama of his attempt to go against the grain. Since few adult men choose part-time work, there is almost none to be had. The social convention of full-time work gives the individual little choice about it. Those who contemplate a shift to part-time will be deterred by the economic penalty. There may even be many who would prefer shorter hours, but they will exert very little influence on the actual choices available, because their desires are latent. Exit from existing jobs—one channel for influencing the market—is not available, because they cannot find part-time jobs to exit to. Unless people begin to speak up and collectively demand that employers provide alternatives, they will probably remain trapped in full-time work.

Jane's switch to part-time will be less traumatic. She will find more job possibilities, because more women work part-time. Her earnings loss will be less, because women are already discriminated against in full-time work. . . . If Jane can get health insurance through John's employment, part-time work may be feasible. But a great deal depends on his earnings and benefits. Even under the best of assumptions, Jane will have to forgo a wide variety of occupations, including most of those with the best pay and working conditions. She will most likely be relegated to the bottom part of the female labor market—the service, sales, and clerical jobs where the majority of women part-timers reside. Social convention and the economic incentives it creates will reproduce inequalities of gender. Despite their original intentions, Jane, rather than John, will end up in part-time employment.

These are the obstacles on the labor market side—low wages, few benefits, and severe limitations on choice of occupations. The dominance of full-time jobs also has effects on the consumption side. Imagine that Jane and John still want to cut back their hours, even under the adverse circumstances I have described. Their income will now be very low, and they will be forced to economize greatly on their purchases. This will affect their ability to fit in socially. As half-time workers, they will find many social occasions too expensive (lunches and dinners out, movies). At first, friends will be understanding, but eventually the clash in lifestyles will create a social gap. Their children will have social difficulties if they don't have access to common after-school activities or the latest toys and clothes. They'll drop off the birthday party circuit because they can't afford to bring gifts. We can even see these pressures with full-time workers, as parents take on extra employment to live up to neighborhood standards. After her divorce Celeste Henderson worked two jobs to give her children the things their schoolmates had. Ms. Henderson's daughter says her mother "saved her the embarrassment of looking poor to the other children."[5] For a family with only part-time workers, the inability to consume in the manner of their peers is likely to lead to some social alienation. Unless they have a community of others in similar circumstances, dropping down will include an element of dropping out. Many Americans, especially those with children, are not willing to risk such a fate.

Even with careful budgeting, a couple like the Does may have trouble procuring the basics (housing, food, and clothing), because the U.S. standard of living is geared to at least one full-time income and, increasingly, to two. Rents will be high relative to the Does' income. In part, this is because of price increases in the last decade. But there is also a more fundamental impediment. As I have argued, contemporary houses and apartments are large and luxurious. They have indoor plumbing, central heating, stoves, and refrigerators. They have expensive features such as closets, garages, and individual bedrooms. In our society, housing must conform to legal and social conventions that define the acceptable standard of housing. The difficulty is that the social norm prevailing in the housing market is matched to a full-time income (or incomes). It is not only that the cost of living is high these days. It is also that bare-bones housing, affordable on only half a salary, is rare. Even if the Does were willing to go without closets, garages, and central heating in order to save money, they would be hard-pressed to find such a dwelling.

This problem is common to many goods and services. In an economy where nearly everyone works full-time, manufacturers cater to the purchasing power of the full-time income. There is a limited market for products that are desired only by those with half an income. A whole range of cheap products are not even available. Only the better-quality goods will be demanded, and hence only they will be produced. We can see this phenomenon in the continual upscaling of products. We've gone from blender to Cuisinart, from polyester to cotton, from one-speed Schwinn to fancy trail bike. Remember the things that were available forty years ago but have disappeared? The semiautomatic washing machine. The hand-driven coffee grinder. The rotary dial telephone. For those who are skeptical about this point, consider the markets of poor countries. In India, one can find very cheap, low-quality clothing—at a fraction of the price of the least expensive items in the United States. Semiautomatic washers and stripped-down cars are the norm. On a world scale, the American consumer market is very upscale, which means that Americans need an upscale income to participate in it.

The strength of social norms does not mean that the nature of work cannot be changed. Part-time employment *could* become a viable option for larger numbers of people. But the existence of social norms suggests that change will not come about . . . [without] intervention on a social level—from government, unions, professional associations, and other collective organizations. . . .

[Although] most Americans may find it hard to understand that such changes are in their interest, many who have made them are confident that getting off the consumer treadmill yields a deeper and truer sense of well-being. When Linda Weltner, a former shopping addict, stopped buying, she didn't "suffer pangs of self-denial" but felt "filled to the brim." Her life has become far richer. And not only will we help ourselves. Forswearing a bankrupting consumerist path, the new consumer of the twenty-first century will be in a far better position to address issues of global inequality and move us off our current collision course with nature. But to do these things, we must be open to major changes in how we run our businesses, households, and the connections between them. And we must organize ourselves to make those changes happen—in spite of all-too-certain opposition from those who benefit from the status quo. . . .

NOTES

1. These are from my calculations of total working hours per capita and per labor force from the National Income and Product Accounts. Between 1948 and 1969, per-capita hours rose from 1,069 to 1,124, or 55 hours. Annual hours per labor force participant fell slightly—from 1,968 to 1,944 hours. . . .

On a per-person basis, gross national product went from $9,060 in 1948 to $19,900 at the end of 1988 (measured in constant 1988 dollars). See *ERP* [Economic Report of the President], 1989 ed., 308, table B–1 and 344, table B–32.

2. MassMutual Family Values Study. (Washington, D.C.: Mellman & Lazarus, 1989), 3, on families and time.

Diane S. Burden and Bradley Googins, *Boston University Balancing Job and Homelife Study* (Boston University: mimeo, 1987), 26, on women and stress.

"When I'm at home," from Harris, *Inside America*, 95.

Paul Williams Kingston and Steven L. Nock, "Time Together Among Dual-Earner Couples," *American Sociological Review*, 52 (June 1987): 391–400. See also Arlie Hochschild, *The Second Shift: Working Parents and the Revolution at Home* (New York: Viking Penguin, 1989).

Harriet Presser, "Shift Work and Child Care Among Young Dual-Earner American Parents," *Journal of Marriage and the Family* 50, 1 (February 1988): 133–48. This figure is for couples in which the wife works full time. Among part-timers, the proportion is over one-half.

Quote from Parents United for Child Care (PUCC) survey comments, mimeo, Boston, Massachusetts, 1989.

3. See Amanda Bennett, *The Death of the Organization Man* (New York: William Morrow, 1990), and Rosabeth Moss Kanter's *When Giants Learn to Dance* (New York: Simon & Schuster, 1989), chap. 10, p. 275, for evidence from case-study research on individual companies.

4. Median wage rate from Mishel and Frankel, *Working America*, 79, table 3.6.

Eighty percent of part-timers are paid by the hour. Earl F. Mellor and Steven E. Haugen, "Hourly Paid Workers: Who They Are and What They Earn," *Monthly Labor Review* (February 1986): 21–22, tables 1 and 2.

Health insurance data pertain to those who work 19 or fewer hours a week. Diane S. Rothberg and Barbara Ensor Cook, *Employee Benefits for Part-Timers,* 2nd ed. (McLean, Va.: Association of Part-Time Professionals, 1987), 6, table 4. Among workers at 20 to 29 hours, 49 percent have medical benefits.

5. Quoted in Peter T. Kilborn, "For Many Women, One Job Just Isn't Enough," *New York Times,* 15 February 1990.

REFERENCES

Bennett, Amanda. *The Death of the Organization Man.* New York: William Morrow, 1990.

Burden, Diane S., and Googins, Bradley. *Boston University Balancing Job and Homelife Study.* Boston University, 1987, Mimeographed.

Economic Report of the President. Washington, D.C.: Government Printing Office, 1989 and 1991.

Harris, Louis. *Inside America.* New York: Vintage, 1987.

Hochschild, Arlie. *The Second Shift: Working Parents and the Revolution at Home.* New York: Viking Penguin, 1989.

Kanter, Rosabeth Moss. *When Giants Learn to Dance: Mastering the Challenge of Strategy, Management and Careers in the 1990s.* New York: Simon & Schuster, 1989.

Kilborn, Peter T. "For Many Women, One Job Isn't Enough." *New York Times,* 15 February 1990.

Kingston, Paul Williams, and Nock, Steven L. "Time Together Among Dual-Earner Couples." *American Sociological Review* 52 (June 1987): 391–400.

MassMutual Family Values Study. Washington, D.C.: Mellman & Lazarus, 1989.

Mellor, Earl F., and Haugen, Steven E. "Hourly Paid Workers: Who They Are and What They Earn." *Monthly Labor Review* 109 (February 1986): 20–26.

Mishel, Lawrence, and Frankel, David M. *The State of Working America.* Armonk, N.Y.: M. E. Sharpe, 1990–91 Edition.

Parents United for Child Care (PUCC). Survey comments, Boston, Massachusetts, 1989. Mimeographed.

Presser, Harriet. "Shift Work and Child Care Among Young Dual-Earner American Parents." *Journal of Marriage and the Family* 50 (February 1988): 133–48.

Rothberg, Dianne S., and Cook, Barbara Ensor. *Employee Benefits for Part-Timers.* McLean, Va.: Association of Part-Time Professionals, 1987.

THINKING ABOUT THE READING

Schor argues that American workers are working longer hours because they want more money to buy things. Why is the trend toward working longer hours among U.S. workers so different from the trend among western European workers of wanting more leisure time? What role do other social institutions play in perpetuating this trend? Schor originally wrote this piece more than 10 years ago. Do you think the situation she describes (increasing work hours coupled with decreasing leisure time) has gotten better, worse, or stayed the same in the past decade? (You may use your own work experiences to help answer this question.) Is this condition something that individuals can remedy on their own or is it something that requires societal-level changes carried out by corporations or by the government?

The Smile Factory

Work at Disneyland

John Van Maanen

(1991)

Part of Walt Disney Enterprises includes the theme park Disneyland. In its pioneering form in Anaheim, California, this amusement center has been a consistent money maker since the gates were first opened in 1955. Apart from its sociological charm, it has, of late, become something of an exemplar for culture vultures and has been held up for public acclaim in several best-selling publications as one of America's top companies. . . . To outsiders, the cheerful demeanor of its employees, the seemingly inexhaustible repeat business it generates from its customers, the immaculate condition of park grounds, and, more generally, the intricate physical and social order of the business itself appear wondrous.

Disneyland as the self-proclaimed "Happiest Place on Earth" certainly occupies an enviable position in the amusement and entertainment worlds as well as the commercial world in general. Its product, it seems, is emotion—"laughter and well-being." Insiders are not bashful about promoting the product. Bill Ross, a Disneyland executive, summarizes the corporate position nicely by noting that "although we focus our attention on profit and loss, day-in and day-out we cannot lose sight of the fact that this is a feeling business and we make our profits from that."

The "feeling business" does not operate, however, by management decree alone. Whatever services Disneyland executives believe they are providing to the 60 to 70 thousand visitors per day that flow through the park during its peak summer season, employees at the bottom of the organization are the ones who most provide them. The work-a-day practices that employees adopt to amplify or dampen customer spirits are therefore a core concern of this feeling business. The happiness trade is an interactional one. It rests partly on the symbolic resources put into place by history and park design but it also rests on an animated workforce that is more or less eager to greet the guests, pack the trams, push the buttons, deliver the food, dump the garbage, clean the streets, and, in general, marshal the will to meet and perhaps exceed customer expectations. False moves, rude words, careless disregard, detected insincerity, or a sleepy and bored presence can all undermine the enterprise and ruin a sale. The smile factory has its rules.

Author's Note: This paper has been cobbled together using three-penny nails of other writings. Parts come from a paper presented to the American Anthropological Association Annual Meetings in Washington D.C. on November 16, 1989 called "Whistle While You Work." Other parts come from J. Van Maanen and G. Kunda, 1989. "Real feelings: Emotional expressions and organization culture." In B. Staw & L. L. Cummings (Eds.), *Research in Organization Behavior* (Vol. 11, pp. 43–103). Greenwich, CT: JAI Press. In coming to this version, I've had a good deal of help from my friends Steve Barley, Nicole Biggart, Michael Owen Jones, Rosanna Hertz, Gideon Kunda, Joanne Martin, Maria Lydia Spinelli, Bob Sutton, and Bob Thomas.

It's a Small World

. . . This rendition is of course abbreviated and selective. I focus primarily on such matters as the stock appearance (vanilla), status order (rigid), and social life (full), and swiftly learned codes of conduct (formal and informal) that are associated with Disneyland ride operators. These employees comprise the largest category of hourly workers on the payroll. During the summer months, they number close to four thousand and run the 60-odd rides and attractions in the park.

They are also a well-screened bunch. There is—among insiders and outsiders alike—a rather fixed view about the social attributes carried by the standard-make Disneyland ride operator. Single, white males and females in their early twenties, without facial blemish, of above average height and below average weight, with straight teeth, conservative grooming standards, and a chin-up, shoulder-back posture radiating the sort of good health suggestive of a recent history in sports are typical of these social identifiers. There are representative minorities on the payroll but because ethnic displays are sternly discouraged by management, minority employees are rather close copies of the standard model Disneylander, albeit in different colors.

This Disneyland look is often a source of some amusement to employees who delight in pointing out that even the patron saint, Walt himself, could not be hired today without shaving off his trademark pencil-thin mustache. But, to get a job in Disneyland and keep it means conforming to a rather exacting set of appearance rules. These rules are put forth in a handbook on the Disney image in which readers learn, for example, that facial hair or long hair is banned for men as are aviator glasses and earrings and that women must not tease their hair, wear fancy jewelry, or apply more than a modest dab of makeup. Both men and women are to look neat and prim, keep their uniforms fresh, polish their shoes, and maintain an upbeat countenance and light dignity to complement their appearance—no low spirits or cornball raffishness at Disneyland.

The legendary "people skills" of park employees, so often mentioned in Disneyland publicity and training materials, do not amount to very much according to ride operators. Most tasks require little interaction with customers and are physically designed to practically insure that is the case. The contact that does occur typically is fleeting and swift, a matter usually of only a few seconds. In the rare event sustained interaction with customers might be required, employees are taught to deflect potential exchanges to area supervisors or security. A Training Manual offers the proper procedure: "On misunderstandings, guests should be told to call City Hall. . . . In everything from damaged cameras to physical injuries, don't discuss anything with guests . . . there will always be one of us nearby." Employees learn quickly that security is hidden but everywhere. On Main Street security cops are Keystone Kops; in Frontierland, they are Town Marshalls; on Tom Sawyer's Island, they are Cavalry Officers, and so on.

Occasionally, what employees call "line talk" or "crowd control" is required of them to explain delays, answer direct questions, or provide directions that go beyond the endless stream of recorded messages coming from virtually every nook and cranny of the park. Because such tasks are so simple, consisting of little more than keeping the crowd informed and moving, it is perhaps obvious why management considers the sharp appearance and wide smile of employees so vital to park operations. There is little more they could ask of ride operators whose main interactive tasks with visitors consist of being, in their own terms, "information booths," "line signs," "pretty props," "shepherds," and "talking statues."

A few employees do go out of their way to initiate contact with Disneyland customers but, as a rule, most do not and consider those who do to be a bit odd. In general, one need do little more than exercise common courtesy while looking reasonably alert and pleasant. Interactive skills that are advanced by the job have less to do with making customers feel warm and welcome than they do with keeping each other amused and happy. This is, of course, a more complex matter.

Employees bring to the job personal badges of status that are of more than passing interest to peers. In rough order, these include: good looks, college affiliation, career aspirations, past achievements, age (directly related to status up to about age 23 or 24 and inversely related thereafter), and assorted other idiosyncratic matters. Nested closely alongside these imported status badges are organizational ones that are also of concern and value to employees.

Where one works in the park carries much social weight. Postings are consequential because the ride and area a person is assigned provide rewards and benefits beyond those of wages. In-the-park stature for ride operators turns partly on whether or not unique skills are required. Disneyland neatly complements labor market theorizing on this dimension because employees with the most differentiated skills find themselves at the top of the internal status ladder, thus making their loyalties to the organization more predictable.

Ride operators, as a large but distinctly middle-class group of hourly employees on the floor of the organization, compete for status not only with each other but also with other employee groupings whose members are hired for the season from the same applicant pool. A loose approximation of the rank ordering among these groups can be constructed as follows:

1. The upper-class prestigious Disneyland Ambassadors and Tour Guides (bilingual young women in charge of ushering—some say rushing—little bands of tourists through the park);

2. Ride operators performing coveted "skilled work" such as live narrations or tricky transportation tasks like those who symbolically control customer access to the park and drive the costly entry vehicles (such as the antique trains, horse-drawn carriages, and Monorail);

3. All other ride operators;

4. The proletarian Sweepers (keepers of the concrete grounds);

5. The sub-prole or peasant status Food and Concession workers (whose park sobriquets reflect their lowly social worth—"pancake ladies," "peanut pushers," "coke blokes," "suds divers," and the seemingly irreplaceable "soda jerks").

Pay differentials are slight among these employee groups. The collective status adheres, as it does internally for ride operators, to assignment or functional distinctions. As the rank order suggests, most employee status goes to those who work jobs that require higher degrees of special skill, [offer] relative freedom from constant and direct supervision, and provide the opportunity to organize and direct customer desires and behavior rather than to merely respond to them as spontaneously expressed.

The basis for sorting individuals into these various broad bands of job categories is often unknown to employees—a sort of deep, dark secret of the casting directors in personnel. When prospective employees are interviewed, they interview for "a job at Disneyland," not a specific one. Personnel decides what particular job they will eventually occupy. Personal contacts are considered by employees as crucial in this job-assignment process as they are in the hiring decision. Some employees, especially those who wind up in the lower ranking jobs, are quite disappointed with their assignments as is the case when, for example, a would-be Adventureland guide is posted to a New Orleans Square restaurant as a pot scrubber. Although many of the outside acquaintances of our pot scrubber may know only that he works at Disneyland, rest assured, insiders will know immediately where he works and judge him accordingly.

Uniforms are crucial in this regard for they provide instant communication about the social merits or demerits of the wearer within the little world of Disneyland workers. Uniforms also correspond to a wider status ranking that casts a significant shadow on employees of all types. Male ride operators on the Autopia wear, for example, untailored jump-suits similar to pit mechanics and consequently generate about as much respect from peers as the grease-stained outfits worn by pump jockeys generate from real motorists in gas stations. The ill-fitting and homogeneous "whites" worn by Sweepers signify lowly institutional work tinged, perhaps, with a reminder of hospital orderlies rather than street cleanup crews. On the other hand, for males, the crisp, officer-like Monorail operator stands alongside the swashbuckling Pirate of the Caribbean, the casual cowpoke of Big Thunder Mountain, or the smartly vested Riverboat pilot as carriers of valued symbols in and outside the park. Employees lust for these higher status positions and the rights to small advantages such uniforms provide. A lively internal labor market exists wherein there is much scheming for the more prestigious assignments.

For women, a similar market exists although the perceived "sexiness" of uniforms, rather than social rank, seems to play a larger role. To wit, the rather heated antagonisms that developed years ago when the ride "It's a Small World" first opened and began outfitting the ride operators with what were felt to be the shortest skirts and most revealing blouses in

the park. Tour Guides, who traditionally headed the fashion vanguard at Disneyland in their above-the-knee kilts, knee socks, tailored vests, black English hats, and smart riding crops were apparently appalled at being upstaged by their social inferiors and lobbied actively (and, judging by the results, successfully) to lower the skirts, raise the necklines, and generally remake their Small World rivals.

Important, also, to ride operators are the break schedules followed on the various rides. The more the better. Work teams develop inventive ways to increase the number of "time-outs" they take during the work day. Most rides are organized on a rotational basis (e.g., the operator moving from a break, to queue monitor, to turnstile overseer, to unit loader, to traffic controller, to driver, and, again, to a break). The number of break men or women on a rotation (or ride) varies by the number of employees on duty and by the number of units on line. Supervisors, foremen, and operators also vary as to what they regard as appropriate break standards (and, more importantly, as to the value of the many situational factors that can enter the calculation of break rituals—crowd size, condition of ride, accidents, breakdowns, heat, operator absences, special occasions, and so forth). Self-monitoring teams with sleepy supervisors and lax (or savvy) foremen can sometimes manage a shift comprised of 15 minutes on and 45 minutes off each hour. They are envied by others, and rides that have such a potential are eyed hungrily by others who feel trapped by their more rigid (and observed) circumstances.

Movement across jobs is not encouraged by park management, but some does occur (mostly within an area and job category). Employees claim that a sort of "once a sweeper, always a sweeper" rule obtains but all know of at least a few exceptions to prove the rule. The exceptions offer some (not much) hope for those working at the social margins of the park and perhaps keep them on the job longer than might otherwise be expected. Dishwashers can dream of becoming Pirates, and with persistence and a little help from their friends, such dreams just might come true next season (or the next).

These examples are precious, perhaps, but they are also important. There is an intricate pecking order among very similar categories of employees. Attributes of reward and status tend to cluster, and there is intense concern about the cluster to which one belongs (or would like to belong). To a degree, form follows function in Disneyland because the jobs requiring the most abilities and offering the most interest also offer the most status and social reward. Interaction patterns reflect and sustain this order. Few Ambassadors or Tour Guides, for instance, will stoop to speak at length with Sweepers who speak mostly among themselves or to Food workers. Ride operators, between the poles, line up in ways referred to above with only ride proximity (i.e., sharing a break area) representing a potentially significant intervening variable in the interaction calculation. . . .

Paid employment at Disneyland begins with the much renowned University of Disneyland whose faculty runs a day-long orientation program (Traditions I) as part of a 40-hour apprenticeship program, most of which takes place on the rides. In the classroom, however, newly hired ride operators are given a very thorough introduction to matters of managerial concern and are tested on their absorption of famous Disneyland fact, lore, and procedure. Employee demeanor is governed, for example, by three rules:

First, we practice the friendly smile.

Second, we use only friendly and courteous phrases.

Third, we are not stuffy—the only Misters in Disneyland are Mr. Toad and Mr. Smee.

Employees learn too that the Disneyland culture is officially defined. The employee handbook put it in this format:

Dis-ney Cor-po-rate Cul-ture (diz'ne kor'pr'it kul'cher) *n* 1. Of or pertaining to the Disney organization, as *a:* the philosophy underlying all business decisions; *b:* the commitment of top leadership and management to that philosophy; *c:* the actions taken by individual cast members that reinforce the image.

Language is also a central feature of university life, and new employees are schooled in its proper use. Customers at Disneyland are, for instance, never referred to as such, they are "guests." There are no rides at Disneyland, only "attractions." Disneyland itself is a "Park," not an amusement center, and it is divided into "back-stage," "on-stage," and "staging" regions. Law enforcement personnel hired by the park are not policemen, but "security hosts." Employees do not wear uniforms but check out fresh "costumes" each working day from "wardrobe." And, of course, there are no accidents at Disneyland, only "incidents." . . .

The university curriculum also anticipates probable questions ride operators may someday face from customers, and they are taught the approved public response. A sample:

Question (posed by trainer): What do you tell a guest who requests a rain check?

Answer (in three parts): We don't offer rain checks at Disneyland because (1) the main attractions are all indoors; (2) we would go broke if we offered passes; and (3) sunny days would be too crowded if we gave passes.

Shrewd trainees readily note that such an answer blissfully disregards the fact that waiting areas of Disneyland are mostly outdoors and that there are no subways in the park to carry guests from land to land. Nor do they miss the economic assumption concerning the apparent frequency of Southern California rains. They discuss such matters together, of course, but rarely raise them in the training classroom. In most respects, these are recruits who easily take the role of good student.

Classes are organized and designed by professional Disneyland trainers who also instruct a well-screened group of representative hourly employees straight from park operations on the approved newcomer training methods and materials. New-hires seldom see professional trainers in class but are brought on board by enthusiastic peers who concentrate on those aspects of park procedure thought highly general matters to be learned by all employees. Particular skill training (and "reality shock") is reserved for the second wave of socialization occurring on the rides themselves as operators are taught, for example, how and when to send a mock bobsled caroming down the track or, more delicately, the proper ways to stuff an obese adult customer into the midst of children riding the Monkey car on the Casey Jones Circus Train or, most problematically, what exactly to tell an irate customer standing in the rain who, in no uncertain terms, wants his or her money back and wants it back now.

During orientation, considerable concern is placed on particular values the Disney organization considers central to its operations. These values range from the "customer is king" verities to the more or less unique kind, of which "everyone is a child at heart when at Disneyland" is a decent example. This latter piety is one few employees fail to recognize as also attaching to everyone's mind as well after a few months of work experience. Elaborate checklists of appearance standards are learned and gone over in the classroom and great efforts are spent trying to bring employee emotional responses in line with such standards. Employees are told repeatedly that if they are happy and cheerful at work, so, too, will the guests at play. Inspirational films,

hearty pep talks, family imagery, and exemplars of corporate performance are all representative of the strong symbolic stuff of these training rites. . . .

Yet, like employees everywhere, there is a limit to which such overt company propaganda can be effective. Students and trainers both seem to agree on where the line is drawn, for there is much satirical banter, mischievous winking, and playful exaggeration in the classroom. As young seasonal employees note, it is difficult to take seriously an organization that provides its retirees "Golden Ears" instead of gold watches after 20 or more years of service. All newcomers are aware that the label "Disneyland" has both an unserious and artificial connotation and that a full embrace of the Disneyland role would be as deviant as its full rejection. It does seem, however, because of the corporate imagery, the recruiting and selection devices, the goodwill trainees hold toward the organization at entry, the peer-based employment context, and the smooth fit with real student calendars, the job is considered by most ride operators to be a good one. The University of Disneyland, it appears, graduates students with a modest amount of pride and a considerable amount of fact and faith firmly ingrained as important things to know (if not always accept).

Matters become more interesting as new hires move into the various realms of Disneyland enterprise. There are real customers "out there" and employees soon learn that these good folks do not always measure up to the typically well mannered and grateful guest of the training classroom. Moreover, ride operators may find it difficult to utter the prescribed "Welcome Voyager" (or its equivalent) when it is to be given to the 20-thousandth human being passing through the Space Mountain turnstile on a crowded day in July. Other difficulties present themselves as well, but operators learn that there are others on-stage to assist or thwart them.

Employees learn quickly that supervisors and, to a lesser degree, foremen are not only on the premises to help them, but also to catch them when they slip over or brazenly violate set procedures or park policies. Because most rides are tightly designed to eliminate human judgment and minimize operational disasters, much of the supervisory monitoring is directed at activities ride operators consider trivial: taking too long a break; not wearing parts of one's official uniform such as a hat, standard-issue belt, or correct shoes; rushing the ride (although more frequent violations seem to be detected for the provision of longer-than-usual rides for lucky customers); fraternizing with guests beyond the call of duty; talking back to quarrelsome or sometimes merely querisome customers; and so forth. All are matters covered quite explicitly in the codebooks ride operators are to be familiar with, and violations of such codes are often subject to instant and harsh discipline. The firing of what to supervisors are "malcontents," "trouble-makers," "bumblers," "attitude problems," or simply "jerks" is a frequent occasion at Disneyland, and among part-timers, who are most subject to degradation and being fired, the threat is omnipresent. There are few workers who have not witnessed firsthand the rapid disappearance of a co-worker for offenses they would regard as "Mickey Mouse." Moreover, there are few employees who themselves have not violated a good number of operational and demeanor standards and anticipate, with just cause, the violation of more in the future.

In part, because of the punitive and what are widely held to be capricious supervisory practices in the park, foremen and ride operators are usually drawn close and shield one another from suspicious area supervisors. Throughout the year, each land is assigned a number of area supervisors who, dressed alike in short-sleeved white shirts and ties with walkie-talkies hitched to their belts, wander about their territories on the lookout for deviations from park procedures (and other signs of disorder). Occasionally, higher level supervisors pose in "plainclothes" and ghost-ride the various attractions just to be sure everything is up to snuff. Some area supervisors are well-known among park employees for the variety of surreptitious techniques they employ when going about their monitoring duties. Blind observation posts are legendary, almost sacred, sites within the park ("This is where Old Man Weston hangs out. He can see Dumbo, Storybook, the Carousel, and the Tea Cups from here"). Supervisors in Tomorrowland are, for example, famous for their penchant of hiding in the bushes above the submarine caves, timing the arrivals and departures of the supposedly fully loaded boats making the $8^{1}/_{2}$ minute cruise under the polar icecaps. That they might also catch a submarine captain furtively enjoying a cigarette (or worse) while inside the conning tower (his upper body out of view of the crowd on the vessel) might just make a supervisor's day—and unmake the employee's. In short, supervisors, if not foremen, are regarded by ride operators as sneaks and tricksters out to get them and representative of the dark side of park life. Their presence is, of course, an orchestrated one and does more than merely watch over the ride operators. It also draws operators together as cohesive little units who must look out for one another while they work (and shirk). . . .

Employees are also subject to what might be regarded as remote controls. These stem not from supervisors or peers but from thousands of paying guests who parade daily through the park. The public, for the most part, wants Disneyland employees to play only the roles for which they are hired and costumed. If, for instance, Judy of the Jets is feeling tired, grouchy, or bored, few customers want to know about it. Disneyland employees are expected to be sunny and helpful; and the job, with its limited opportunities for sustained interaction, is designed to support such a stance. Thus, if a ride operator's behavior drifts noticeably away from the norm, customers are sure to point it out—"Why aren't you smiling?" "What's wrong with you?" "Having a bad day?" "Did Goofy step on your foot?" Ride operators learn swiftly from the constant hints, glances, glares, and tactful (and tactless) cues sent by their audience what their role in the park is to be, and as long as they keep to it, there will be no objections from those passing by.

> I can remember being out on the river looking at the people on the Mark Twain looking down on the people in the Keel Boats who are looking up at them. I'd come by on my raft and they'd all turn and stare at me. If I gave them a little wave and a grin, they'd all wave back and smile; all ten thousand of them. I always wondered what would happen if I gave them the finger? (Ex-ride operator, 1988)

Ride operators also learn how different categories of customers respond to them and the parts they are playing on-stage. For example, infants and small children are generally timid, if not frightened, in their presence. School-age children are somewhat curious, aware that the operator is at work playing a role but sometimes in awe of the role itself. Nonetheless, these children can be quite critical of any flaw in the operator's performance. Teenagers, especially males in groups, present problems because they sometimes go to great lengths to embarrass, challenge, ridicule, or outwit an operator. Adults are generally appreciative and approving of an operator's conduct provided it meets their rather minimal standards, but they sometimes overreact to the part an operator is playing (positively) if accompanied by small children. . . .

The point here is that ride operators learn what the public (or, at least, their idealized version of the public) expects of their role and find it easier to conform to such expectations than not. Moreover, they discover that when they are bright and lively others respond to them in like ways. This . . . balancing of the emotional exchange is such that ride operators come to expect good treatment. They assume, with good cause, that most people will react to their little waves and smiles with some affection and perhaps joy. When they do not, it can ruin a ride operator's day.

With this interaction formula in mind, it is perhaps less difficult to see why ride operators detest and scorn the ill-mannered or unruly guest. At times, these grumpy, careless, or otherwise unresponsive characters insult the very role the operators play and have come to appreciate—"You can't treat the Captain of the USS Nautilus like that!" Such out-of-line visitors offer breaks from routine, some amusement, consternation, or the occasional job challenge that occurs when remedies are deemed necessary to restore employee and role dignity.

By and large, however, the people-processing tasks of ride operators pass good naturedly and smoothly, with operators hardly noticing much more than the bodies passing in front of view (special bodies, however, merit special attention as when crew members on the subs gather to assist a young lady in a revealing outfit on board and then linger over the hatch to admire the view as she descends the steep steps to take her seat on the boat). Yet, sometimes, more than a body becomes visible, as happens when customers overstep their roles and challenge employee authority, insult an operator, or otherwise disrupt the routines of the job. In the process, guests become "doofuses," "ducks," and "assholes" (just three of many derisive terms used by ride operators to label those customers they believe to have gone beyond the pale). Normally, these characters are brought to the attention of park security officers, ride foremen, or area supervisors who, in turn, decide how they are to be disciplined (usually expulsion from the park).

Occasionally, however, the alleged slight is too personal or simply too extraordinary for a ride operator to let it pass unnoticed or merely inform others and allow them to decide what, if anything, is to be done. Restoration of one's respect is called for, and routine practices have been developed for these circumstances. For example, common remedies include: the "seatbelt squeeze," a small token of appreciation given to a deviant customer consisting of the rapid cinching-up of a required seatbelt such that the passenger is doubled-over at the point of departure and left gasping for the duration of the trip; the "break-toss," an acrobatic gesture of the Autopia trade whereby operators jump on the outside of a norm violator's car, stealthily unhitching the safety belt, then slamming on the brakes, bringing the car to an almost instant stop while the driver flies on the hood of the car (or beyond); the "seatbelt slap," an equally distinguished (if primitive) gesture by which an offending customer receives a sharp, quick snap of a hard plastic belt across the face (or other parts of the body) when entering or exiting a seat-belted ride; the "break-up-the-party" gambit, a queuing device put to use in officious fashion whereby bothersome pairs are separated at the last minute into different units, thus forcing on them the pain of strange companions for the duration of a ride through the Haunted Mansion or a ramble on Mr. Toad's Wild Ride; the "hatch-cover ploy," a much beloved practice of Submarine pilots who, in collusion with mates on the loading dock, are able to drench offensive guests with water as their units pass under a waterfall; and, lastly, the rather ignoble variants of the "Sorry-I-didn't-see-your-hand" tactic, a savage move designed to crunch a particularly irksome customer's hand (foot, finger, arm, leg, etc.) by bringing a piece of Disneyland property to bear on the appendage, such as the door of a Thunder Mountain railroad car or the starboard side of a Jungle Cruise boat. This latter remedy is, most often, a "near miss" designed to startle the little criminals of Disneyland.

All of these unofficial procedures (and many more) are learned on the job. Although they are used sparingly, they are used. Occasions of use provide a continual stream of sweet revenge talk to enliven and enrich colleague conversation at break time or after work. Too much, of course, can be made of these subversive practices and the rhetoric that surrounds their use. Ride operators are quite aware that there are limits beyond which they dare not pass. If they are caught, they know that restoration of corporate pride will be swift and clean.

In general, Disneyland employees are remarkable for their forbearance and polite good manners even under trying conditions. They are taught, and some come to believe, for a while at least, that they are really "on-stage" at work. And, as noted, surveillance by supervisory personnel certainly fades in light of the unceasing glances an employee receives from the paying guests who tromp daily through the park in the summer. Disneyland employees know well that they are part of the product being sold and learn to check their more discriminating manners in favor of the generalized countenance of a cheerful lad or lassie whose enthusiasm and dedication is obvious to all.

At times, the emotional resources of employees appear awesome. When the going gets tough and the park is jammed, the nerves of all employees are frayed and sorely tested by the crowd, din, sweltering sun, and eyeburning smog. Customers wait in what employees call "bullpens" (and park officials call "reception areas") for up to several hours for a 3½ minute ride that operators are sometimes hell-bent on cutting to 2½ minutes. Surely a monument to the human ability to suppress feelings has been created when both users and providers alike can maintain their composure and seeming regard for one another when in such a fix.

It is in this domain where corporate culture and the order it helps to sustain must be given its due. Perhaps the depth of a culture is visible only when its members are under the gun. The orderliness—a good part of the Disney formula for financial success—is an accomplishment based not only on physical design and elaborate procedures, but also on the low-level, part-time employees who, in the final analysis, must be willing, even eager, to keep the show afloat. The ease with which employees glide into their kindly and smiling roles is, in large measure, a feat of social engineering. Disneyland does not pay well; its supervision is arbitrary and skin-close; its working conditions are chaotic; its jobs require minimal amounts of intelligence or judgment; and asks a kind of sacrifice and loyalty of its employees that is almost fanatical. Yet, it attracts a particularly able workforce whose personal backgrounds suggest abilities far exceeding those required of a Disneyland traffic cop, people stuffer, queue or line manager, and button pusher. As I have suggested, not all of Disneyland is covered by the culture put forth by management. There are numerous pockets of resistance and various degrees of autonomy maintained by employees. Nonetheless, adherence and support for the organization are remarkable. And, like swallows returning to Capistrano, many part-timers look forward to their migration back to the park for several seasons.

The Disney Way

Four features alluded to in this unofficial guide to Disneyland seem to account for a good deal of the social order that obtains within the park. First, socialization, although costly, is of a most selective, collective, intensive,

serial, sequential, and closed sort. These tactics are notable for their penetration into the private spheres of individual thought and feeling. . . . Incoming identities are not so much dismantled as they are set aside as employees are schooled in the use of new identities of the situational sort. Many of these are symbolically powerful and, for some, laden with social approval. It is hardly surprising that some of the more problematic positions in terms of turnover during the summer occur in the food and concession domains where employees apparently find little to identify with on the job. Cowpokes on Big Thunder Mountain, Jet Pilots, Storybook Princesses, Tour Guides, Space Cadets, Jungle Boat Skippers, or Southern Belles of New Orleans Square have less difficulty on this score. Disneyland, by design, bestows identity through a process carefully set up to strip away the job relevance of other sources of identity and learned response and replace them with others of organizational relevance. It works.

Second, this is a work culture whose designers have left little room for individual experimentation. Supervisors, as apparent in their focused wandering and attentive looks, keep very close tabs on what is going on at any moment in all the lands. Every bush, rock, and tree in Disneyland is numbered and checked continually as to the part it is playing in the park. So too are employees. Discretion of a personal sort is quite limited while employees are "on-stage." Even "back-stage" and certain "off-stage" domains have their corporate monitors. Employees are indeed aware that their "off-stage" life beyond the picnics, parties, and softball games is subject to some scrutiny, for police checks are made on potential and current employees. Nor do all employees discount the rumors that park officials make periodic inquiries on their own as to a person's habits concerning sex and drugs. Moreover, the sheer number of rules and regulations is striking, thus making the grounds for dismissal a matter of multiple choice for supervisors who discover a target for the use of such grounds. The feeling of being watched is, unsurprisingly, a rather prevalent complaint among Disneyland people, and it is one that employees must live with if they are to remain at Disneyland.

Third, emotional management occurs in the park in a number of quite distinct ways. From the instructors at the university who beseech recruits to "wish every guest a pleasant good day," to the foremen who plead with their charges to, "say thank you when you herd them through the gate," to the impish customer who seductively licks her lips and asks, "what does Tom Sawyer want for Christmas?" appearance, demeanor, and etiquette have special meanings at Disneyland. Because these are prized personal attributes over which we normally feel in control, making them commodities can be unnerving. Much self-monitoring is involved, of course, but even here self-management has an organizational side. Consider ride operators who may complain of being "too tired to smile" but, at the same time, feel a little guilty for uttering such a confession. Ride operators who have worked an early morning shift on the Matterhorn (or other popular rides) tell of a queasy feeling they get when the park is opened for business and they suddenly feel the ground begin to shake under their feet and hear the low thunder of the hordes of customers coming at them, oblivious of civil restraint and the small children who might be among them. Consider, too, the discomforting pressures of being "on-stage" all day and the cumulative annoyance of having adults ask permission to leave a line to go to the bathroom, whether the water in the lagoon is real, where the well-marked entrances might be, where Walt Disney's cryogenic tomb is to be found, or—the real clincher—whether or not one is "really real."

The mere fact that so much operator discourse concerns the handling of bothersome guests suggests that these little emotional disturbances have costs. There are, for instance, times in all employee careers when they put themselves on "automatic pilot," "go robot," "can't feel a thing," "lapse into a dream," "go into a trance," or otherwise "check out" while still on duty. Despite a crafty supervisor's (or curious visitor's) attempt to measure the glimmer in an employee's eye, this sort of willed emotional numbness is common to many of the "on-stage" Disneyland personnel. Much of this numbness is, of course, beyond the knowledge of supervisors and guests because most employees have little trouble appearing as if they are present even when they are not. It is, in a sense, a passive form of resistance that suggests there still is a sacred preserve of individuality left among employees in the park.

Finally, taking these three points together, it seems that even when people are trained, paid, and told to be nice, it is hard for them to do so all of the time. But, when efforts to be nice have succeeded to the degree that is true of Disneyland, it appears as a rather towering (if not always admirable) achievement. It works at the collective level by virtue of elaborate direction. Employees—at all ranks—are stage-managed by higher ranking employees who, having come through themselves, hire, train, and closely supervise those who have replaced them below. Expression rules are laid out in corporate manuals. Employee time-outs intensify work experience. Social exchanges are forced into narrow bands of interacting groups. Training and retraining programs are continual. Hiding places are few. Although little sore spots and irritations remain for each individual, it is difficult to imagine work roles being more defined (and accepted) than those at Disneyland. Here, it seems, is a work culture worthy of the name.

THINKING ABOUT THE READING

What is the significance of the title, "The Smile Factory"? What, exactly, is the factory-made product that Disney sells in its theme parks? How does the Disney organizational culture shape the lives of employees? Disney is frequently criticized for its strict—some would say oppressive—employee rules and regulations. But would it be possible to run a "smile factory" with a more relaxed code of conduct where employees could regularly make their own decisions and act as they pleased? Explain. Disney theme parks abroad (in Japan and France, for instance) have not been nearly as successful as Disneyland and Disneyworld. Why has it been so difficult to export the "feeling business" to other countries? Consider also how Van Maanen describes the ways in which employees define the social rank of different positions within Disneyland. Describe an organizational situation you've been in where such a ranking of members occurred. What were the criteria upon which such rankings were made?

The Architecture of Stratification

Social Class and Inequality

nequality is woven into the fabric of all societies through a structured system of *social stratification.* Social stratification is a ranking of entire groups of people that perpetuates unequal rewards and life chances in society. The structural-functionalist explanation of stratification is that the stability of society depends on all social positions being filled—that is, there are people around to do all the jobs that need to be done. Higher rewards, such as prestige and large salaries, are afforded to the most important positions, thereby ensuring that the most qualified individuals will occupy the highest positions. In contrast, conflict theory argues that stratification reflects an unequal distribution of power in society and is a primary source of conflict and tension.

Social class is the primary means of stratification in American society. Contemporary sociologists are likely to define one's class standing as a combination of income, wealth, occupational prestige, and educational attainment. It is tempting to see class differences as simply the result of an economic stratification system that exists at a level above the individual. Although inequality is created and maintained by larger social institutions, however, it is often felt most forcefully and is reinforced most effectively in the chain of interactions that take place in our day-to-day lives.

In "Software Entrepreneurship Among the Urban Poor," Alice Amsden and Jon Collins Clark examine the subtle but powerful ways stratification conveys advantages on some at the expense of others. They pose the deceptively simple question: If Bill Gates was poor and black would he be as successful as he is? In the process of answering their own question, they identify what they consider to be the factors necessary to become a successful entrepreneur: "gumption," connections, financial backing, and so on. Notice that none of these factors have anything to do with actual skill.

It is impossible to fully examine the American stratification system without addressing the plight of those at the bottom. Despite the much publicized economic recovery of the late 1990s, poverty continues to be a large and, in many cases, deadly social problem. The face of American poverty has changed somewhat over the past several decades. The economic status of single mothers and their children has deteriorated while that of people over age 65 has improved somewhat.

What hasn't changed is the ever-widening gap between the rich and the poor. Poverty persists because in a free-market and competitive society it serves economic and social functions. In addition, poverty receives institutional "support" in the form of segmented labor markets and inadequate educational systems. The ideology of competitive individualism—that to succeed in life all one has to do is work hard and win in competition with others—creates a belief that poor people are to blame for their own suffering. So although the problem of poverty remains serious, public attitudes toward poverty and poor people are frequently indifferent or even hostile. Furthermore, important social institutions can perpetuate the problem. In "Savage Inequalities in America's Schools," Jonathan Kozol provides a troubling portrait of inequality in the American educational system by comparing the school experiences of children in two very different cities. Although the children of destitute East St. Louis, Illinois, and affluent Rye, New York, are citizens of the same country, they live in two very different worlds. Kozol draws compelling contrasts between the broken-down classrooms, outdated textbooks, and faulty plumbing in East St. Louis and the sparkling new auditoriums and up-to-date computers in Rye. These vastly different educational experiences make it difficult to sustain the myth that all children, no matter where they live, are competing in a fair race for society's resources.

Software Entrepreneurship Among the Urban Poor
Could Bill Gates Have Succeeded If He Were Black? . . .
Or Impoverished?

Alice H. Amsden and Jon Collins Clark

(2000)

Introduction:
The Gumption Factor

The computer software industry is a bastion of entrepreneurship in the late twentieth century. Drug dealing aside, it is one of the few industries associated with the "third industrial revolution" in which the individual entrepreneur can become a multimillionaire overnight.[1] The best example is Bill Gates, whose entrepreneurship and ten-digit financial fortune [were] the subject of admiration and awe in at least three popular books in print in the 1990s.

The software industry has been identified as a fertile field for aspiring modern-day Horatio Algers because of its perceived low start-up requirements and barriers to entry. Take, for instance, the following citation from a contemporary conference on the subject of entrepreneurship: "The microcomputer software industry is both a throwback to the classic cottage industry of entrepreneurship and at the same time a leading edge of the new wave of technological entrepreneurship. Like the cottage industry of old, the barriers to entry are modest in the extreme. An investment of a few hundred dollars in hardware; a corner in a room; combined with commitment and hard work can, in most cases, produce a product, and in a few cases, a business" (Teach, Tarpley and Schwartz 1985, p. 546).

This supposed ease of entry for entrepreneurs into software production presumes that even society's most disadvantaged can reap potential gains in this industry. Because barriers to entry are supposedly so low, individuals from the ranks of the urban poor can make it as computer software entrepreneurs alongside individuals from the ranks of the wealthy and privileged. All that is needed is imagination, perseverance, and painstaking effort—"gumption" for short.

We have sought to examine the validity of this proposition. It is intriguing because entrepreneurship is an enchanted and extraordinary talent that seems to emerge from unexpected soils—impoverished youth, as in the case of Andrew Carnegie and Henry Ford, and especially the cultures of persecuted minority groups, as in the Jews, French Huguenots, Indians in East Africa, Chinese in Southeast Asia, and so forth. If entrepreneurship can blossom in these inhospitable climes, then why not in the software industry among the urban poor in American cities, which are typically rife with persecuted minorities?

By entrepreneurship we mean a process whereby an individual or group of individuals perceive a new profit-making opportunity, coordinate and mobilize the resources necessary to implement the original idea, and then monitor the implementation procedures necessary to ensure the efficient execution of plans. . . .

Certainly entrepreneurship is rare and inspired, and more of an art than a science. Nevertheless, from data on who has innovated in the American software industry, it appears that entrepreneurship is not nearly as quirky as once believed. As we hope to show:

1. American software entrepreneurs tend to have standard characteristics: a very large portion of them are white, male, and extremely well educated. They may all have gumption, but the gumption factor *alone* works in only a very small number of cases (the details of which are in any event unclear).

2. Entry barriers into the software industry may be low in terms of physical capital but are high in terms of human capital, which is generally a key difference between the second and third industrial revolutions. "Human capital" refers to education and work experience. Also important for success is "social capital," or the contacts and networks that facilitate business interactions (Putnam 1993).

3. The category of "entrepreneur" in the United States—which we proxy statistically with certain subcategories of "self-employed"— includes a large number of African Americans. Being black and being an entrepreneur (even in software) are not mutually exclusive, although blacks tend to have a lower incidence of entrepreneurship than whites for reasons that are discussed later in this [article].

4. We infer from this that what restrains entrepreneurship in industries like software in American inner cities is not race but rather *poverty,* with characteristics of low education and an absence of influential business contacts that are antagonistic to those required for entry into the new high-tech information sectors.

5. Quick fixes—like the dumping of computers into inner-city schools—may encourage

the necessary tinkering with hardware that seems to flow in the veins of software engineers. But such gestures are far from sufficient to ensure even a small steady stream of inner-city entrepreneurial talent. Even before that flow can start to trickle, imbalances must first be addressed in the state of education in general, computer education in particular, job training and job availability, and other factors that currently serve to make real levels of human capital so disparate among different economic classes in the United States.

Entrepreneurship and the Software Industry

Who Are Entrepreneurs?

To understand software entrepreneurship, it is instructive to have some background information on the demographics of entrepreneurs in general. Most research concentrates on the category of the "self-employed" rather than of the "entrepreneur" because no data are available directly on the latter. These two populations overlap considerably, but they are by no means identical (see Reynolds 1995 and Becker 1984). Some self-employed are not entrepreneurs and some entrepreneurs are not self-employed.[2]

The ranks of the self-employed contain many independent professionals who by most definitions including ours, would not be considered entrepreneurs. "More than half of all dentists, veterinarians, optometrists, podiatrists, and other health diagnosing technicians, authors, painters, and sculptors, auctioneers, street and door-to-door sales workers, barbers, child-care workers, and farm operators and managers were self employed in 1983" (Becker 1984, p. 17). Given the heterogeneity of this classification, inferences about entrepreneurs drawn from this population must be taken gingerly.

Research shows that the self-employed are disproportionately represented by native-born white males. Put another way, the self-employment rates among both women and minorities are significantly lower than those among white men. Among minorities, rates of self-employment are lowest among African Americans, somewhat higher among Hispanics, and in the case of Asian Americans, almost equal to that of native-born whites (Aronson 1991; Reynolds 1995; Butler 1991). Just why this has been the case has been the cause for much debate and will be discussed in further detail later in this [article].

The self-employed are generally older and have some work experience. "The probability of being self-employed increases with labor market experience" (Evans and Leighton 1989, p. 532). In other words, most self-employed are not high school dropouts, college dropouts, or even recent high school or college graduates; they are former employees with real job experience. . . . On average, the self-employed are better educated than the population at large. This holds true even when controlling for the "professional" contingent among the self-employed—that is, independent lawyers, doctors, and so on (see Evans and Leighton 1989 and Light 1995). This suggests a quality about entrepreneurs that tends to make them better educated, all else being equal. . . .

Software Entrepreneurship

Fortunately, some specific research has been conducted on the demographic profile of software entrepreneurs themselves (Teach, Tarpley and Schwartz 1986). Perhaps the most important insight gained is that most software entrepreneurs *are extremely well educated.* A whopping 86 percent of the software entrepreneurs analyzed in one sample (approximately two hundred software firms) had at least a college degree, and 47 percent held advanced degrees (Teach, Tarpley and Schwartz 1985).

Another study in 1987 found similar results among a sample of over two hundred high-tech firms (Goslin 1987). This entry qualification of high educational credentials appears to have accelerated over time. A follow-up study to the 1987 study provided evidence of " . . . the virtual disappearance of the 'computer jock' without a college degree" (Teach et al. 1987, p. 465).

Software entrepreneurs also usually have some work experience prior to opening their own businesses. The Haug 1991 study of the software industry in Washington state found that only 3 percent of software company founders launched their companies directly out of high school or college. Approximately 86 percent had previously held some position in industry working for another firm, and a majority (approximately 57 percent) had been employed by a software company. In the Teach, Tarpley and Schwartz 1985 study, less than 2 percent reported that their current position was their first position. Over 40 percent had worked as employees in the software industry.

Research confirms the notion that *physical capital requirements for software entrepreneurs are relatively low.* Initial capitalization levels of the firms in the Teach, Tarpley and Schwartz 1985 study were relatively small. Roughly 50 percent reported initial capitalization levels of $10,000 or less. A follow-up investigation in 1986 found that over 75 percent of firms were initially capitalized exclusively with the personal funds of the principals (Teach, Tarpley and Schwartz 1986).

The Haug 1991 study found that approximately 83 percent of software companies were initially capitalized through the personal funds of the principals and/or their families and friends. In the Goslin 1987 study, 71 percent of firms were capitalized exclusively with the personal funds of the principals. These findings are consistent with those of Light (1995) and others who have found that physical capital requirements for *all* entrepreneurs, regardless

Table 1   Composition of the Urban Poor

	Persistently poor (8 or more years, 1974–1983)	Poor in 1979	Total U.S. urban population
Ethnicity			
Black	66%	51%	21%
White	34%	49%	79%
Education Among Heads of Household			
K–8 grades	49%	29%	12%
9–11 grades	29%	27%	17%
12 grades	18%	32%	33%
13 or more	4%	11%	38%

Source: Survey Research Center, 1984, *User Guide to the Panel Study of Income Dynamics,* University of Michigan, Ann Arbor, as adapted from Adams et al. 1988.

of industry, tend to be relatively lower than one might expect. . . .

Finally, software entrepreneurs appear to be predominantly male. Only 15 percent of those in the Teach, Tarpley and Schwartz 1985 sample were women. This proportion is significantly lower than the number of women found among the self-employed as a whole, most estimates of which range between 30 and 40 percent (Becker 1984 and Reynolds 1995).

The Urban Poor: Software Entrepreneurs-in-Waiting

Urban Poor

The urban poor have become of greater interest to policymakers and social scientists alike because they represent an increasing proportion of the total poor in the United States (Sandefur 1988). The steady increase in the "spatial concentration" of poverty in American inner cities has led us to consider ways of addressing poverty particularly in these geographical centers. . . .

Poverty in U.S. urban centers often has a dual nature. Two kinds of poor are present in the inner city at any given time: first there are

the transient poor (poor at a given moment but not likely to be so in the near future), and second are the "persistent poor" (those who have been and are likely to remain in a state of poverty) (Adams et al. 1988). We are mostly concerned with the persistent poor—not with those who are transiently poor on the basis of their reported income in a given year.[3]

As can be seen in Table 1, the urban poor are mostly black. Notice that 66 percent of the *persistent* poor were black, whereas the corresponding number of blacks in the urban population as a whole was only 21 percent. Perhaps most significantly for the purposes of this study, the urban poor as described in Table 1 are poorly educated. Among the persistently poor, 78 percent of the heads of the house-hold did not graduate from high school. Only 4 percent had even one year of schooling beyond high school.

As a final note, it is important to recognize that the urban poor are often unemployed or out of the labor force altogether. The correlation between poverty and unemployment is widely acknowledged and is possibly becoming stronger (Wilson 1996). . . . For our purposes, it is important to be aware that those living in poverty, because they are often unemployed, are likely to have no recent job experience in any industry whatsoever. . . .

Urban Poor and Software Entrepreneurs: How Do They Match Up?

Now that we have two basic demographic portraits, of software entrepreneurs and of the urban poor, the question is how they match up. We know that software entrepreneurs are, on average, white, male, college-educated professionals with some job experience, often in the field of computers. Among the urban poor, we know that they are, on average, black, have not graduated from high school, and are often currently unemployed or out of the workforce altogether. Many are also female heads of households.[4] Clearly, these two groups do not seem to overlap very much.

Nevertheless, the set of general demographic characteristics among the urban poor that we have provided here does not altogether preclude the existence of entrepreneurship in urban areas. There are, in fact, urban entrepreneurs. Rates of entrepreneurship in the inner city, however, fall significantly below those in the country as a whole. . . .

Race and Entrepreneurship

Thus far the evidence does not suggest that skin color is a prerequisite for success in entrepreneurial endeavors, whatever their nature. It is true that rates of self-employment among blacks and Hispanics have lagged behind those of nonminorities . . . and there has been considerable debate as to the cause of this disparity. Much of the variation in rates of self-employment is *not* explained by independent variables such as education, age, and income (Butler 1991 and Light 1995).

Instead, some have argued that cultural differences among ethnic groups have been the greatest source of differing rates of self-employment (Light 1995). But other factors

must also be considered. For instance, it may be that racial discrimination on the demand side may influence the decision of minorities to become self-employed. The more (perceived) discrimination, the greater the risk of failure and, therefore, the higher the opportunity costs of investing in entrepreneurship. . . . Others have suggested that a lack of past experience in business and a consequent underdevelopment of social and business networks for some ethnic groups is a crucial contributing factor (Fratoe 1988).

But despite variations in the proportions of those who are self-employed among different ethnic groups, there is still a substantial number of self-employed who are from minority groups. Moreover, concrete evidence suggests that their characteristics and experiences are remarkably similar to those of the nonminority self-employed. . . . Bates' 1987 study of the self-employed found that among those whose self-employment income was *below* average, the characteristics and earnings in minorities and nonminorities were almost identical. The results of this study are provided in Table 2.

As can be seen in the table, the same commonalties cannot be said to be true among those with *above* average earnings. In the high-earner category, nonminorities appear to have earned approximately 20 percent more than their minority counterparts. Most of this disparity in earnings, however, can be accounted for by differences in three independent variables: age, education, and sex (Bates 1987). . . .

Research . . . shows that the qualities that make high-earning entrepreneurs among minorities are the same qualities that make high-earning entrepreneurs among nonminorities; namely, among both demographic groups, those with higher levels of education and with some working experience earn more than those with less education and experience (all else being equal) (Bates 1987; Fratoe 1988; Hisrich and Brush 1986).

Table 2   Mean Traits of Above Average Versus Below Average Earners of Self-Employment Income

	Low earners		High earners	
	Minorities	*Nonminorities*	*Minorities*	*Nonminorities*
Age	43.5	44.5	43.1	44.7
Education	10.9	12.3	12.1	13.4
Proportion female	0.322	0.337	0.133	0.091
1979 self-employment income	$4,446	$4,447	$22,689	$27,199
1979 income from all sources	$7,028	$8,878	$25,792	$31,676
1979 household income	$17,710	$20,211	$34,297	$38,263
No. of observations	13,845	3414	7119	1805

Source: 1980 Census of Population Public Use Samples as cited in Bates 1987.

Note: High earners are those earning self-employment income above the sample mean of $10,640. Low earners fall below the mean. Data exclude doctors and lawyers; nonfarm agricultural industries are included. Self-employment earnings include nonfarm earnings only.

Thus, as a step toward answering the question we posed in the title of this chapter—Could Bill Gates have succeeded were he black (or a member of another minority)?—our answer is yes, he could have succeeded, *all else being equal.* Nevertheless, all else is typically not equal. The incidence of poverty is significantly higher among most minorities than in the population at large. As we show in the following section, it is the pathology of poverty, including low levels of human and social capital, that is most inimical to entrepreneurship.

What Does It Take?

Human and Social Capital

Even though race may not be a determining factor in the success of prospective entrepreneurs, evidence strongly suggests that both human and social capital are critical ingredients of success. As mentioned in the previous section, successful minority entrepreneurs have the same characteristics as nonminority entrepreneurs: they are well educated and usually have relevant job experience. In other words, they have higher levels of human capital. They also have higher levels of social capital, in part as

a result of their better education and richer job experience.

Research concerning the importance of formal education in the success of entrepreneurs has been extensive and conclusive. Study after study indicates that successful entrepreneurs have above-average levels of education. . . . We have every reason to believe, then, that formal schooling is becoming increasingly important as a determinant of high self-employed earnings, just as it is in the labor force at large. . . .

More specifically, advanced business degrees and entrepreneurial-specific training seem to serve as important assets to entrepreneurs in general, including those in software. One study of software venture teams found that those that contained at least one member with an advanced business degree were more successful than those that did not (Teach, Tarpley and Schwartz 1985). Specific courses that targeted potential entrepreneurs and taught them the practical know-how needed to start their own businesses have also been shown to be effective (Balkin 1989; Price 1991; Rush et al. 1987).

Not only an advanced degree but a college degree in any discipline seems to contribute to entrepreneurial success. The nature of that degree, if not in business, would most likely depend on the nature of the entrepreneur's intended industry. For instance, the Teach, Tarpley and Schwartz (1985) study of software entrepreneurs found that a majority of the respondents had undergraduate degrees in a technical field (engineering, math, science, or computer science). Another quarter of respondents, however, had degrees in liberal arts or humanities. This suggests that beyond the specific nature of the degree, there are other benefits that a college degree can provide to the potential entrepreneur.

One such potential benefit is the opportunity it can provide for the degree holder to gain relevant job experience and make social contacts. This is especially true when one considers what we already know about the importance to entrepreneurs of having previous job experience.

Another potential benefit of a college degree is the membership it can provide graduates in instrumental peer networks. A great deal of research has been done on the importance of social connections for entrepreneurial success. Researchers have found that higher levels of social capital contribute to an increased probability of entrepreneurial success (Fratoe 1988); for instance, peer networks have been shown to contribute to the development of marketing and subcontracting among new firms (Holt 1987 and Rush et al. 1987). It is this development of social capital no less than human capital that has contributed to entrepreneurial success among those with undergraduate and graduate degrees.

Computer Education and Software Entrepreneurship

Given the abundant evidence that successful entrepreneurship, whether in software or other endeavors, is strongly associated with high levels of education, the hypothesis of low

entry barriers into the software industry requires serious revision. Barriers in the form of physical capital may be relatively low, but those in the form of human and social capital appear substantial. Thus, even though the eccentric individual with megadoses of gumption may succeed as an entrepreneur whatever his or her background, population groups with low levels of human and social capital are unlikely *on average* to pioneer new, legitimate business ventures, small or large.

Nevertheless, the cherished American ideal that anyone with gumption can make it as an entrepreneur lives on with respect to information technology. Consequently, there has been a vigorous attempt on the part of government and business to blanket the inner cities with computers and computer-related crash courses, the hardware and software supposedly needed for anyone with a dream to become a software entrepreneur. The increased proliferation of computers throughout American public schools has thus rekindled the old American dream of equal opportunity. Nevertheless, a closer look at the nature of computer education in poor urban schools shows why this dream is seriously out of focus.

It is true that in recent years much has been done to increase the number of computers in poor urban schools. Initiatives have been launched by large private corporations such as AT&T, Microsoft, and Xerox to place computers and develop computer networks in public schools (U.S. Department of Education 1996). Local private companies have complemented these initiatives by donating their outdated computers. Meanwhile, the federal government has begun to pay more attention to the importance of computer education, a visible example being [former] President Clinton's . . . campaign promise to "put a computer in every classroom" and to link these computers on the Internet. Nevertheless, the impact these developments have had on the overall quality of computer education among the poor remains suspect for the following reasons.

First, although the absolute number of computers in poorer schools has increased, it still appears to fall short of the number in more wealthy classrooms. Picciano's 1991 study comparing computer education in schools in Westchester County, New York, with those in New York City found that the ratio of computers to students was more than twice as high in Westchester. Another study found similar degrees of imbalance in the computer-to-student ratio between suburban and urban districts (Quality Education Data 1991). Thus, although it may be true that some effort has been made to address the discrepancy in access to computers in poor and rich schools, serious imbalances persist.

Perhaps even more important, researchers have found that there are significant differences in how computers are used in school districts with different income levels. According to Owens (1995, p. 84), "urban schools with predominantly minority students have been found typically to use computers for tutorial and rote drill-and-practice programs, while suburban schools with students from higher-income families have generally been found to use computers for problem solving and programming." In eighth-grade mathematics classes, "urban teachers reported that they were more likely than suburban and rural teachers to use computers for remedial purposes" (Owens 1995, p. 90). Thus, there is reason to believe that the overall quality of computer education in inner-city schools suffers compared with that of suburban schools; the nature of "literacy" is different.

Alongside the inequities in computer education that exist in the nation's schools, one must further consider the inequities that characterize young people's access to computers at home. . . . Access to computers at home as well as at school is an important condition for the nurturing of software entrepreneurship. A 1994 national survey found that the degree of technology used in the home was largely dependent on income: "college graduates and families with high incomes were more likely to own several types of electronic technology" (Black Child Advocate 1995, p. 3).

Young people who have exposure to creative uses for computers, and continued access to and experience with computers in their own homes, are far more likely to tinker in creating software than those who do not. These and other inequities in asset endowments put the poor at a distinct disadvantage in fulfilling any entrepreneurial dreams with respect to information technology.

Conclusion

The urban poor are not likely on average to become software entrepreneurs for many of the same reasons they are not likely to become brain surgeons, investment bankers, or CEOs of Fortune 500 companies—they simply do not have the requisite educational and social capital. . . . Although [these are] not the only factor[s] inhibiting the development of high-earning entrepreneurs in the inner city, to our minds . . . [they are] primary . . . in light of the technological requirements of the third industrial revolution through which the U.S. and other advanced economies are now passing. Were education, training, and job experience brought up to par, then policymakers could begin to address other entry barriers to small-firm entrepreneurship, such as access to finance capital.[5] But these other barriers will remain moot as long as the urban poor remain insufficiently skilled to take the first step on the long road to successful entrepreneurship—the mere conception of a novel product or process that sufficient numbers of people with high enough levels of income are willing and able to buy.

Thus, even though Bill Gates may be the *un*characteristic software entrepreneur in having dropped out of college (Harvard no less), he is typical insofar as he enjoyed membership in a privileged American economic and social elite. The odds that he would have succeeded had his social world been that of the urban ghetto may be predicted to be infinitesimally small.

All this puts an enormous burden on education to bootstrap the poor. We would suggest, however, that although better education in poor neighborhoods may increase the number of successful entrepreneurs, it is insufficient for a technomodernization of the American inner city itself. This may be illustrated briefly by drawing an analogy between poor people in rich countries and poor countries in the world economy. After World War II a large number of extremely poor underdeveloped countries attempted to industrialize. Most failed because they started from a capital base (physical, human, and social) that was too low to allow them to compete in world markets. But a few enjoyed spectacular success, in particular South Korea and Taiwan, which were very poor initially but which had exceptionally equal income distributions (a result of land reform) and unusually high levels of education (in part as a consequence of the geopolitics underlying American foreign aid allocation). What is noteworthy about South Korea and Taiwan, however, is that initially their high investments in education resulted not in rapid domestic economic growth but in a "brain drain"—the educated migrated abroad to high-wage countries and only returned home once endogenous growth had begun—by a variety of complex and controversial means, although none of these means involved the exploitation of high technology. The industries in which South Korea and Taiwan (and Japan before it) prospered involved first low- and then mid-technology, such as steel, industrial chemicals, and later automobiles (Hikino and Amsden 1994).

So, too, we would suggest, better education of the poor will initially result in their migration out of the inner city, and not necessarily in an immediate improvement in living standards of the inner city proper. What remains unclear—and controversial—is how the inner city itself is to be modernized, and what role high technology, specifically information technology, will play in that process.

NOTES

1. The "third industrial revolution" is associated with innovations in electronics, communications, chemicals, and pharmaceuticals, including biotechnology, which is also friendly toward the small entrepreneur (Chandler Jr. and Hikino 1997).

2. "Downsizing" in large American corporations appears to have swelled the ranks of the "self-employed" in the form of a burgeoning number of underemployed "consultants."

3. We are concerned with the persistent poor in order to understand the entrepreneurship among the most disadvantaged. . . .

4. Roughly 70 percent of a sample of poor urban households were found to be headed by females (Adams et al. 1988).

5. Teach, Tarpley and Schwartz (1985) found that a large percentage of software entrepreneurs borrowed large sums of money from friends and family. How many among the urban poor could do so?

REFERENCES

Adams, T., G. Duncan, and W. Rogers. 1988. "The Persistence of Urban Poverty." In *Quiet Riots,* edited by F. Harris and R. Wilkins pp. 78–99. New York: Pantheon Books.

Aronson, R. L. 1991. *Self-Employment: A Labor Market Perspective.* Ithaca: NY: ILR Press.

Balkin, S. 1989. *Self Employment for Low-Income People.* New York: Praeger.

Bates, T. 1987. "Self-Employed Minorities: Traits and Trends." *Social Science Quarterly* 68: 539–551.

Becker, E. 1984. "Self-Employed Workers: An Update to 1983." *Monthly Labor Review* 107(7): 14–18.

Butler, J. S. C. H. 1991. "Ethnicity and Entrepreneurship in America: Toward an Explanation of Racial and Ethnic Group Variations in Self-Employment." *Sociological Perspectives* 34(1): 79–94.

Chandler Jr., A. D., and T. Hikino. 1997. The Large Industrial Enterprise and the Dynamics of Modern Economic Growth. In *Big Business and the Wealth of Nations,* edited by A. D. Chandler Jr., F. Amatori, and T. Hikino. Cambridge: Cambridge University Press.

Danziger, S. P. G. 1987. "Continuing Black Poverty: Earnings Inequality, the Spatial Concentration of Poverty, and the Underclass." *American Economic Review* 77(2): 211–215.

Evans, D., and B. Jovanovic. 1989. "An Estimated Model of Entrepreneurial Choice Under Liquidity Constraints." *Journal of Political Economy* 97(4): 808–827.

Evans, D., and L. Leighton. 1989. "Some Empirical Aspects of Entrepreneurship." *American Economic Review* 79(3): 519–535.

Field, A., and C. Harris. 1986. "Software: The Growing Gets Rough." *Business Week:* (March 24): 128–134.

Fratoe, F. 1988. "Social Capital in Black Business Owners." *Development of Black Political Economy* 16(4): 33–50.

Glade, W. P. 1967. "Approaches to a Theory of Entrepreneurship Formation." *Explorations in Entrepreneurial History* 5(3).

Goslin, L. N. 1987. "Characteristics of Successful High-Tech Start-Up Firms." In *Frontiers of Entrepreneurship Research,* edited by N. Churchill, B. Kirchoff, W. Krasner, and K. Vesper. Wellesley, MA: Babson College.

Harbison, F. H. 1956. "Entrepreneurial Organization as a Factor in Economic Development." *Quarterly Journal of Economics* 70(3).

Haug, P. 1991. "Regional Formation of High-Technology Service Industries: The Software Industry in Washington State." *Environment and Planning A* 23: 869–884.

Hikino, T., and A. H. Amsden 1994. "Staying Behind, Stumbling Back, Sneaking Up, Soaring Ahead: Late Industrialization in Historical Perspective." In *Convergence of Productivity: Cross-National Studies and Historical Evidence,* edited by W. J. Baumol, R. R. Nelson and E. N. Wolff, pp. 285–315. New York: Oxford University Press.

Hisrich, R., and C. Brush. 1986. "Characteristics of the Minority Entrepreneur." *Journal of Small Business Management* 24(4): 1–8.

Holt, D. 1987. "Network, Support Systems: How Communities Can Encourage Entrepreneurship." In *Frontiers of Entrepreneurship Research,* edited by N. Churchill, R. Kirchoff, W. Krasner, and K. Vespero. Wellesley, MA: Babson College.

Juliussen, K., and E. Juliussen. 1993. *The 1993 Computer Industry Almanac.* Austin: The Reference Press Inc.

Lichter, D. 1988. "Racial Differences in Underemployment in American Cities." *American Journal of Sociology* 93(4): 771–792.

Light, I. C. R. 1995. *Race, Ethnicity, and Entrepreneurship in Urban America.* New York: Aldine De Gruyter.

Marris, P. 1968. "The Social Barriers to African Entrepreneurship." *Journal of Development Studies* 5(1).

Merges, R. P. 1996. "A Comparative Look at Intellectual Property Rights and the Software Industry." In *The International Computer Software Industry,* edited by D. Mowery, pp. 272–303. New York: Oxford University Press.

Owens, E. H. W. 1995. "Differences Among Urban, Suburban, and Rural Schools on Technology Access and Use in Eighth-Grade Mathematics Classrooms." *Journal of Educational Technology Systems* 24(1): 83–92.

"Parents Must Ensure That Children Have Access to Information Technologies." 1995. *Black Child Advocate* (Summer): 3–7.

Picciano, A. 1991. "Computers, City and Suburb: A Study of New York City and Westchester County Public Schools." *The Urban Review* 23(3): 191–203.

Price, C. D. F., 1991. "Four Year Study of Colorado Entrepreneurship with Minority and Women Business Owners." In *Frontiers of Entrepreneurship Research,* edited by W. Bygrave. Wellesley, MA: Babson College.

Putnam, R. D. 1993. *Making Democracy Work: Civic Traditions in Modern Italy.* Princeton, NJ: Princeton University Press.

Quality Education Data. 1991. Microcomputer Uses in Schools: A 1990–91 Q.E.D. Update. Denver.

Reynolds, P. 1995. "Who Starts New Firms? Linear Additive Versus Interaction Based Models." In *Frontiers of Entrepreneurship Research.* W. Bygrave. Wellesley, MA: Babson College.

Rush, B. et al. 1987. "The Use of Peer Networks in the Start-Up Process." *Frontiers of Entrepreneurship Research.* N. Churchill, B. Kirchoff, W. Krasner, and K. Vespero. Wellesley, MA: Babson College.

Sandefur, G. D. M. T., ed. 1988. *Divided Opportunities: Minorities, Poverty, and Social Policy.* New York: Plenum Press.

Teach, R., F. Tarpley, and R. Schwartz. 1985. "Who Are the Microcomputer Software Entrepreneurs?" In *Frontiers of Entrepreneurship Research.* B. Kirchoff. Wellesley, MA: Babson College.

Teach, R., F. Tarpley, R. Schwartz, and D. Brawley. 1987. "Maturation in the Microcomputers Software Industry: Venture Teams and Their Firms." In *Frontiers of Entrepreneurship Research,* 1987. N. Churchill, B. Kirchoff, W. Krasner, and K. Vesper. Wellesley, MA: Babson College.

U.S. Department of Education. 1996. "Private Companies Already Offering Computer Aid to Schools." *Department of Education Reports* 17(9): 5–8.

Wilson, W. J. 1987. *The Truly Disadvantaged.* Chicago: University of Chicago Press.

Wilson, W. J. 1996. *When Work Disappears: The World of the New Urban Poor.* New York: Random House.

THINKING ABOUT THE READING

What do the authors mean when they say that entry barriers into the software industry are low in physical capital but high in human and social capital? If a person doesn't have access to higher education and social networks, but has a lot of drive and "gumption," what sorts of other money-making activities might he or she be inclined to get into? Amsden and Clark point out that high levels of education are strongly associated with successful entrepreneurship. But there is a perception today that many young people are foregoing higher education and moving instead into high-paying jobs in the dot com industries. Given the data Amsden and Clark present, what sorts of jobs are these young people likely to have? Why do the authors feel that providing poor, inner-city people with computers and computer instruction is not sufficient to correct imbalances in software entrepreneurship? If they're correct, how would you go about increasing entrepreneurship among the urban poor? Use this article to discuss how stratification provides those at the top with important, nonmonetary social advantages.

Savage Inequalities in America's Schools

Life on the Mississippi—East St. Louis, Illinois

Jonathan Kozol

(1991)

"East of anywhere," writes a reporter for the *St. Louis Post-Dispatch,* "often evokes the other side of the tracks. But, for a first-time visitor suddenly deposited on its eerily empty streets, East St. Louis might suggest another world." The city, which is 98 percent black, has no obstetric services, no regular trash collection, and few jobs. Nearly a third of its families live on less than $7,500 a year; 75 percent of its population lives on welfare of some form. The U.S. Department of Housing and Urban Development describes it as "the most distressed small city in America."

Only three of the 13 buildings on Missouri Avenue, one of the city's major thoroughfares, are occupied. A 13-story office building, tallest in the city, has been boarded up. Outside, on the sidewalk, a pile of garbage fills a ten-foot crater.

The city, which by night and day is clouded by the fumes that pour from vents and smokestacks at the Pfizer and Monsanto chemical plants, has one of the highest rates of child asthma in America.

It is, according to a teacher at the University of Southern Illinois, "a repository for a nonwhite population that is now regarded as expendable." The *Post-Dispatch* describes it as "America's Soweto."

Fiscal shortages have forced the layoff of 1,170 of the city's 1,400 employees in the past 12 years. The city, which is often unable to buy heating fuel or toilet paper for the city hall, recently announced that it might have to cashier all but 10 percent of the remaining work force of 230. In 1989 the mayor announced that he might need to sell the city hall and all six fire stations to raise needed cash. Last year the plan had to be scrapped after the city lost its city hall in a court judgment to a creditor. East St. Louis is mortgaged into the next century but has the highest property-tax rate in the state.

Since October 1987, when the city's garbage pickups ceased, the backyards of residents have been employed as dump sites. In the spring of 1988 a policeman tells a visitor that 40 plastic bags of trash are waiting for removal from the backyard of his mother's house. Public health officials are concerned the garbage will attract a plague of flies and rodents in the summer. The policeman speaks of "rats as big as puppies" in his mother's yard. They are known to the residents, he says, as "bull rats." Many people have no cars or funds to cart the trash and simply burn it in their yards. The odor of smoke from burning garbage, says the *Post-Dispatch,* "has become one of the scents of spring" in East St. Louis.

Railroad tracks still used to transport hazardous chemicals run through the city. "Always present," says the *Post-Dispatch,* "is the threat of chemical spills. . . . The wail of sirens warning residents to evacuate after a spill is common." The most recent spill, the paper says, "was at the Monsanto Company plant. . . . Nearly 300 gallons of phosphorous trichloride spilled when a railroad tank was overfilled. About 450 residents were taken to St. Mary's Hospital. . . . The frequency of the emergencies has caused Monsanto to have a 'standing account' at St. Mary's." . . .

The dangers of exposure to raw sewage, which backs up repeatedly into the homes of residents in East St. Louis, were first noticed, in the spring of 1989, at a public housing project, Villa Griffin. Raw sewage, says the *Post-Dispatch,* overflowed into a playground just behind the housing project, which is home to 187 children, "forming an oozing lake of . . . tainted water." Two schoolgirls, we are told, "experienced hair loss since raw sewage flowed into their homes."

While local physicians are not certain whether loss of hair is caused by the raw sewage, they have issued warnings that exposure to raw sewage can provoke a cholera or hepatitis outbreak. A St. Louis health official voices her dismay that children live with waste in their backyards. "The development of working sewage systems made cities livable a hundred years ago," she notes. "Sewage systems separate us from the Third World."

The sewage, which is flowing from collapsed pipes and dysfunctional pumping stations, has also flooded basements all over the city. The city's vacuum truck, which uses water and suction to unclog the city's sewers, cannot be used because it needs $5,000 in repairs. Even when it works, it sometimes can't be used because there isn't money to hire drivers. A single engineer now does the work that 14 others did before they were laid off. By April the pool of overflow behind the Villa Griffin project has expanded into a lagoon of sewage. Two million gallons of raw sewage lie outside the children's homes. . . .

The Daughters of Charity, whose works of mercy are well known in the Third World, operate a mission at the Villa Griffin homes. On an afternoon in early spring of 1990, Sister Julia Huiskamp meets me on King Boulevard and drives me to the Griffin homes.

As we ride past blocks and blocks of skeletal structures, some of which are still inhabited, she slows the car repeatedly at railroad crossings. A seemingly endless railroad train rolls past us to the right. On the left: a blackened lot where garbage has been burning. Next to the burning garbage is a row of 12 white cabins, charred by fire. Next: a lot that holds a heap of auto tires and a mountain of tin cans. More burnt houses. More trash fires. The train moves almost imperceptibly across the flatness of the land.

Fifty years old, and wearing a blue suit, white blouse, and blue head-cover, Sister Julia points to the nicest house in sight. The sign on the front reads MOTEL. "It's a whorehouse," Sister Julia says.

When she slows the car beside a group of teen-age boys, one of them steps out toward the car, then backs away as she is recognized.

The 99 units of the Villa Griffin homes—two-story structures, brick on the first floor, yellow wood above—form one border of a recessed park and playground that were filled with fecal matter last year when the sewage mains exploded. The sewage is gone now and the grass is very green and looks inviting. When nine-year-old Serena and her seven-year-old brother take me for a walk, however, I discover that our shoes sink into what is still a sewage marsh. An inch-deep residue of fouled water still remains.

Serena's brother is a handsome, joyous little boy, but troublingly thin. Three other children join us as we walk along the marsh: Smokey, who is nine years old but cannot yet tell time; Mickey, who is seven; and a tiny child with a ponytail and big brown eyes who talks a constant stream of words that I can't always understand.

"Hush, Little Sister," says Serena. I ask for her name, but "Little Sister" is the only name the children seem to know.

"There go my cousins," Smokey says, pointing to two teen-age girls above us on the hill.

The day is warm, although we're only in the second week of March; several dogs and cats are playing by the edges of the marsh. "It's a lot of squirrels here," says Smokey. "There go one!"

"This here squirrel is a friend of mine," says Little Sister.

None of the children can tell me the approximate time that school begins. One says five o'clock. One says six. Another says that school begins at noon.

When I ask what song they sing after the flag pledge, one says "Jingle Bells."

Smokey cannot decide if he is in the second or third grade.

Seven-year-old Mickey sucks his thumb during the walk.

The children regale me with a chilling story as we stand beside the marsh. Smokey says his sister was raped and murdered and then dumped behind his school. Other children add more details: Smokey's sister was 11 years old. She was beaten with a brick until she died. The murder was committed by a man who knew her mother.

The narrative begins when, without warning, Smokey says, "My sister has got killed."

"She was my best friend," Serena says.

"They had beat her in the head and raped her," Smokey says.

"She was hollering out loud," says Little Sister.

I ask them when it happened. Smokey says, "Last year." Serena then corrects him and she says, "Last week."

"It scared me because I had to cry," says Little Sister.

"The police arrested one man but they didn't catch the other," Smokey says.

Serena says, "He was some kin to her."

But Smokey objects, "He weren't no kin to me. He was my momma's friend."

"Her face was busted," Little Sister says.

Serena describes this sequence of events: "They told her go behind the school. They'll give her a quarter if she do. Then they knock her down and told her not to tell what they had did."

I ask, "Why did they kill her?"

"They was scared that she would tell," Serena says.

"One is in jail," says Smokey. "They can't find the other."

"Instead of raping little bitty children, they should find themselves a wife," says Little Sister.

"I hope," Serena says, "her spirit will come back and get that man."

"And *kill* that man," says Little Sister.

"Give her another chance to live," Serena says.

"My teacher came to the funeral," says Smokey.

"When a little child dies, my momma say a star go straight to Heaven," says Serena.

"My grandma was murdered," Mickey says out of the blue. "Somebody shot two bullets in her head."

I ask him, "Is she really dead?"

"She dead all right," says Mickey. "She was layin' there, just dead."

"I love my friends," Serena says. "I don't care if they no kin to me. I care for them. I hope his mother have another baby. Name her for my friend that's dead."

"I have a cat with three legs," Smokey says.

"Snakes hate rabbits," Mickey says, again for no apparent reason.

"Cats hate fishes," Little Sister says.

"It's a lot of hate," says Smokey.

Later, at the mission, Sister Julia tells me this: "The Jefferson School, which they attend, is a decrepit hulk. Next to it is a modern school, erected two years ago, which was to have replaced the one that they attend. But the construction was not done correctly. The roof is too heavy for the walls, and the entire structure has begun to sink. It can't be occupied. Smokey's sister was raped and murdered and dumped between the old school and the new one."

As the children drift back to their homes for supper, Sister Julia stands outside with me and talks about the health concerns that trouble people in the neighborhood. In the setting sun, the voices of the children fill the evening air. Nourished by the sewage marsh, a field of wild daffodils is blooming. Standing here, you wouldn't think that anything was wrong. The street is calm. The poison in the soil can't be seen. The sewage is invisible and only makes the grass a little greener. Bikes thrown down by children lie outside their kitchen doors. It could be an ordinary twilight in a small suburban town.

Night comes on and Sister Julia goes inside to telephone a cab. In another hour, the St. Louis taxis will not come into the neighborhood. . . .

East St. Louis—which the local press refers to as "an inner city without an outer city"—has some of the sickest children in America. Of 66 cities in Illinois, East St. Louis ranks first in fetal death, first in premature birth, and third in infant death. Among the negative factors listed by the city's health director are the sewage running in the streets, air that has been fouled by the local plants, the high lead levels noted in the soil, poverty, lack of education, crime, dilapidated housing, insufficient health care, unemployment. Hospital care is deficient too. There is no place to have a baby in East St. Louis. The maternity ward at the city's Catholic hospital, a 100-year-old structure, was shut down some years ago. The only other hospital in town was forced by lack of funds to close in 1990. The closest obstetrics service open to the women here is seven miles away. The infant death rate is still rising.

As in New York City's poorest neighborhoods, dental problems also plague the children here. Although dental problems don't command the instant fears associated with low birth weight, fetal death or cholera, they do have the consequence of wearing down the stamina of children and defeating their ambitions. Bleeding gums, impacted teeth and rotting teeth are routine matters for the children I have interviewed in the South Bronx. Children get used to feeling constant pain. They go to sleep with it. They go to school with it. Sometimes their teachers are alarmed and try to get them to a clinic. But it's all so slow and heavily encumbered with red tape and waiting lists and missing, lost or canceled welfare cards, that dental care is often long delayed. Children live for months with pain that grown-ups would find unendurable. The gradual attrition of accepted pain erodes their energy and aspiration. I have seen children in New York with teeth that look like brownish, broken sticks. I have also seen teenagers who were missing half their teeth. But, to me, most shocking is to see a child with an abscess that has been inflamed for weeks and that he has simply lived with and accepts as part of the routine of life. Many teachers in the urban schools have seen this. It is almost commonplace.

Compounding these problems is the poor nutrition of the children here—average daily food expenditure in East St. Louis is $2.40 for one child—and the underimmunization of young children. Of every 100 children recently surveyed in East St. Louis, 55 were incompletely immunized for polio, diphtheria, measles and whooping cough. In this context, health officials look with all the more uneasiness at those lagoons of sewage outside public housing.

On top of all else is the very high risk of death by homicide in East St. Louis. In a recent year in which three cities in the state of roughly the same size as East St. Louis had an average of four homicides apiece, there were 54 homicides in East St. Louis. But it is the heat of summer that officials here particularly dread. The heat that breeds the insects bearing polio or hepatitis in raw sewage also heightens asthma and frustration and reduces patience. "The heat," says a man in public housing, "can bring out the beast. . . ."

The fear of violence is very real in East St. Louis. The CEO of one of the large companies out on the edge of town has developed an "evacuation plan" for his employees. State troopers are routinely sent to East St. Louis to put down disturbances that the police cannot control. If the misery of this community explodes someday in a real riot (it has happened in the past), residents believe that state and federal law-enforcement agencies will have no hesitation in applying massive force to keep the violence contained. . . .

The problems of the streets in urban areas, as teachers often note, frequently spill over into public schools. In the public schools of East St. Louis this is literally the case.

"Martin Luther King Junior High School," notes the *Post-Dispatch* in a story published in the early spring of 1989, "was evacuated Friday afternoon after sewage flowed into the kitchen. . . . The kitchen was closed and students were sent home." On Monday, the paper continues, "East St. Louis Senior High School was awash in sewage for the second time this year." The school had to be shut because of "fumes and backed-up toilets." Sewage flowed into the basement, through the floor, then up into the kitchen and the students' bathrooms. The backup, we read, "occurred in the food preparation areas."

School is resumed the following morning at the high school, but a few days later the overflow recurs. This time the entire system is affected, since the meals distributed to every student in the city are prepared in the two schools that have been flooded. School is called off for all 16,500 students in the district. The sewage backup, caused by the failure of two pumping stations, forces officials at the high school to shut down the furnaces.

At Martin Luther King, the parking lot and gym are also flooded. "It's a disaster," says a legislator. "The streets are underwater; gaseous fumes are being emitted from the pipes under the schools," she says, "making people ill."

In the same week, the schools announce the layoff of 280 teachers, 166 cooks and cafeteria workers, 25 teacher aides, 16 custodians and 18 painters, electricians, engineers and plumbers. The president of the teachers' union says the cuts, which will bring the size of kindergarten and primary classes up to 30 students, and the size of fourth to twelfth grade classes up to 35, will have "an unimaginable impact" on the students. "If you have a high school teacher with five classes each day and between 150 and 175 students . . . , it's going to have a devastating effect." The school system, it is also noted, has been using more than 70 "permanent substitute teachers," who are paid only $10,000 yearly, as a way of saving money.

Governor Thompson, however, tells the press that he will not pour money into East St. Louis to solve long-term problems. East St. Louis residents, he says, must help themselves. "There is money in the community," the governor insists. "It's just not being spent for what it should be spent for."

The governor, while acknowledging that East St. Louis faces economic problems, nonetheless refers dismissively to those who live in East St. Louis. "What in the community," he asks, "is being done right?" He takes the opportunity of a visit to the area to announce a fiscal grant for sewer improvement to a relatively wealthy town nearby.

In East St. Louis, meanwhile, teachers are running out of chalk and paper, and their paychecks are arriving two weeks late. The city warns its teachers to expect a cut of half their pay until the fiscal crisis has been eased.

The threatened teacher layoffs are mandated by the Illinois Board of Education, which, because of the city's fiscal crisis, has been given supervisory control of the school budget. Two weeks later the state superintendent partially relents. In a tone very different from that of the governor, he notes that East St. Louis does not have the means to solve its education problems on its own. "There is no natural way," he says, that "East St. Louis can bring itself out of this situation." Several cuts will be required in any case—one quarter of the system's teachers, 75 teacher aides, and several dozen others will be given notice—but, the state board notes, sports and music programs will not be affected.

East St. Louis, says the chairman of the state board, "is simply the worst possible place I can imagine to have a child brought up. . . . The community is in desperate circumstances." Sports and music, he observes, are, for many children here, "the only avenues of success." Sadly enough, no matter how it ratifies the stereotype, this is the truth; and there is a poignant aspect to the fact that, even with class size soaring and one quarter of the system's teachers being given their dismissal, the state board of education demonstrates its genuine but skewed compassion by attempting to leave sports and music untouched by the overall austerity.

Even sports facilities, however, are degrading by comparison with those found and expected at most high schools in America. The football field at East St. Louis High is missing almost everything—including goalposts. There are a couple of metal pipes—no crossbar, just the pipes. Bob Shannon, the football coach, who has to use his personal funds to purchase footballs and has had to cut and rake the football field himself, has dreams of having goalposts someday. He'd also like to let his students have new uniforms. The ones they wear are nine years old and held together somehow by a patchwork of repairs. Keeping them clean is a problem, too. The school cannot afford a washing machine. The uniforms are carted to a corner laundromat with fifteen dollars' worth of quarters. . . .

In the wing of the school that holds vocational classes, a damp, unpleasant odor fills the halls. The school has a machine shop, which cannot be used for lack of staff, and a woodworking shop. The only shop that's occupied this morning is the auto-body class. A man with long blond hair and wearing a white sweat suit swings a paddle to get children in their chairs. "What we need the most is new equipment," he reports. "I have equipment for alignment, for example, but we don't have money to install it. We also need a better form of egress. We bring the cars in through two other classes." Computerized equipment used in most repair shops, he reports, is far beyond the high school's budget. It looks like a very old gas station in an isolated rural town. . . .

The science labs at East St. Louis High are 30 to 50 years outdated. John McMillan, a soft-spoken man, teaches physics at the school. He shows me his lab. The six lab stations in the room have empty holes where pipes were once attached. "It would be great if we had water," says McMillan. . . .

Leaving the chemistry labs, I pass a double-sized classroom in which roughly 60 kids are sitting fairly still but doing nothing. "This is supervised study hall," a teacher tells me in the corridor. But when we step inside, he finds there is no teacher. "The teacher must be out today," he says.

Irl Solomon's history classes, which I visit next, have been described by journalists who cover East St. Louis as the highlight of the school. Solomon, a man of 54 whose reddish hair is turning white, has taught in urban schools for almost 30 years. A graduate of Brandeis University in 1961, he entered law school but was drawn away by a concern with civil rights. "After one semester, I decided that the law was not for me. I said, 'Go and find the toughest place there is to teach. See if you like it.' I'm still here. . . .'"

Teachers like Mr. Solomon, working in low-income districts such as East St. Louis, often tell me that they feel cut off from educational developments in modern public schools. "Well, it's amazing," Solomon says. "I have done without so much so long that, if I were assigned to a suburban school, I'm not sure I'd recognize what they are doing. We are utterly cut off."

"Very little education in the school would be considered academic in the suburbs. Maybe 10 to 15 percent of students are in truly academic programs. Of the 55 percent who graduate, 20 percent may go to four-year colleges: something like 10 percent of any entering class. Another 10 to 20 percent may get some other kind of higher education. An equal number join the military. . . ."

"Sometimes I get worried that I'm starting to burn out. Still, I hate to miss a day. The department frequently can't find a substitute to come here, and my kids don't like me to be absent."

Solomon's advanced class, which soon comes into the room, includes some lively students with strong views.

"I don't go to physics class, because my lab has no equipment," says one student. "The typewriters in my typing class don't work. The women's toilets. . . ." She makes a sour face. "I'll be honest," she says. "I just don't use the toilets. If I do, I come back into class and I feel dirty."

"I wanted to study Latin," says another student. "But we don't have Latin in this school."

"We lost our only Latin teacher," Solomon says.

A girl in a white jersey with the message DO THE RIGHT THING on the front raises her hand. "You visit other schools," she says. "Do you think the children in this school are getting what we'd get in a nice section of St. Louis?"

I note that we are in a different state and city.

"Are we citizens of East St. Louis or America?" she asks. . . .

Clark Junior High School is regarded as the top school in the city. I visit, in part, at the request of school officials, who would like me to see education in the city at its very best. Even here, however, there is a disturbing sense that one has entered a backwater of America.

"We spend the entire eighth grade year preparing for the state exams," a teacher tells me in a top-ranked English class. The teacher seems devoted to the children, but three students sitting near me sleep through the entire period. The teacher rouses one of them, a girl in the seat next to me, but the student promptly lays her head back on her crossed arms and is soon asleep again. Four of the 14 ceiling lights are broken. The corridor outside the room is filled with voices. Outside the window, where I see no schoolyard, is an empty lot.

In a mathematics class of 30 children packed into a space that might be adequate for 15 kids, there is one white student. The first white student I have seen in East St. Louis, she is polishing her nails with bright red polish. A tiny black girl next to her is writing with a one-inch pencil stub.

In a seventh grade social studies class, the only book that bears some relevance to black concerns—its title is *The American Negro*—bears a publication date of 1967. The teacher invites me to ask the class some questions. Uncertain where to start, I ask the students what they've learned about the civil rights campaigns of recent decades.

A 14-year-old girl with short black curly hair says this: "Every year in February we are told to read the same old speech of Martin Luther King. We read it every year. 'I have a dream.' . . . It does begin to seem—what is the word?" She hesitates and then she finds the word: "perfunctory."

I ask her what she means.

"We have a school in East St. Louis named for Dr. King," she says. "The school is full of sewer water and the doors are locked with chains. Every student in that school is black. It's like a terrible joke on history."

It startles me to hear her words, but I am startled even more to think how seldom any press reporter has observed the irony of naming segregated schools for Martin Luther King. Children reach the heart of these hypocrisies much quicker than the grown-ups and the experts do.

Public Education in New York

The train ride from Grand Central Station to suburban Rye, New York, takes 35 to 40 minutes. The high school is a short ride from the station. Built of handsome gray stone and set in a landscaped campus, it resembles a New England prep school. On a day in early June of 1990, I enter the school and am directed by a student to the office.

The principal, a relaxed, unhurried man who, unlike many urban principals, seems gratified to have me visit in his school, takes me in to see the auditorium, which, he says, was recently restored with private charitable funds ($400,000) raised by parents. The crenellated ceiling, which is white and spotless, and the polished dark-wood paneling contrast with the collapsing structure of the auditorium at Morris High. The principal strikes his fist against the balcony: "They made this place extremely solid." Through a window, one can see the spreading branches of a beech tree in the central courtyard of the school.

In a student lounge, a dozen seniors are relaxing on a carpeted floor that is constructed with a number of tiers so that, as the principal explains, "they can stretch out and be comfortable while reading."

The library is wood-paneled, like the auditorium. Students, all of whom are white, are seated at private carrels, of which there are approximately 40. Some are doing homework; others are looking through the *New York Times*. Every student that I see during my visit to the school is white or Asian, though I later learn there are a number of Hispanic students and that 1 or 2 percent of students in the school are black.

According to the principal, the school has 96 computers for 546 children. The typical student, he says, studies a foreign language

for four or five years, beginning in the junior high school, and a second foreign language (Latin is available) for two years. Of 140 seniors, 92 are now enrolled in AP classes. Maximum teacher salary will soon reach $70,000. Per-pupil funding is above $12,000 at the time I visit.

The students I meet include eleventh and twelfth graders. The teacher tells me that the class is reading Robert Coles, Studs Terkel, Alice Walker. He tells me I will find them more than willing to engage me in debate, and this turns out to be correct. Primed for my visit, it appears, they arrow in directly on the dual questions of equality and race.

Three general positions soon emerge and seem to be accepted widely. The first is that the fiscal inequalities "do matter very much" in shaping what a school can offer ("That is obvious," one student says) and that any loss of funds in Rye, as a potential consequence of future equalizing, would be damaging to many things the town regards as quite essential.

The second position is that racial integration—for example, by the busing of black children from the city or a nonwhite suburb to this school—would meet with strong resistance, and the reason would not simply be the fear that certain standards might decline. The reason, several students say straightforwardly, is "racial" or, as others say it, "out-and-out racism" on the part of adults.

The third position voiced by many students, but not all, is that equity is basically a goal to be desired and should be pursued for moral reasons, but "will probably make no major difference" since poor children "still would lack the motivation" and "would probably fail in any case because of other problems."

At this point, I ask if they can truly say "it wouldn't make a difference" since it's never been attempted. Several students then seem to rethink their views and say that "it might work, but it would have to start with preschool and the elementary grades" and "it might be 20 years before we'd see a difference."

At this stage in the discussion, several students speak with some real feeling of the present inequalities, which, they say, are "obviously unfair," and one student goes a little further and proposes that "we need to change a lot more than the schools." Another says she'd favor racial integration "by whatever means—including busing—even if my parents disapprove." But a contradictory opinion also is expressed with a good deal of fervor and is stated by one student in a rather biting voice: "I don't see why we should do it. How could it be of benefit to us?"

Throughout the discussion, whatever the views the children voice, there is a degree of unreality about the whole exchange. The children are lucid and their language is well chosen and their arguments well made, but there is a sense that they are dealing with an issue that does not feel very vivid, and that nothing that we say about it to each other really matters since it's "just a theoretical discussion." To a certain degree, the skillfulness and cleverness that they display seem to derive precisely from this sense of unreality. Questions of unfairness feel more like a geometric problem than a matter of humanity or conscience. A few of the students do break through the note of unreality, but, when they do, they cease to be so agile in their use of words and speak more awkwardly. Ethical challenges seem to threaten their effectiveness. There is the sense that they were skating over ice and that the issues we addressed were safely frozen underneath. When they stop to look beneath the ice they start to stumble. The verbal competence they have acquired here may have been gained by building walls around some regions of the heart.

"I don't think that busing students from their ghetto to a different school would do much good," one student says. "You can take them out of the environment, but you can't take the environment out of *them*. If someone grows up in the South Bronx, he's not going to be prone to learn." His name is Max and he has short black hair and speaks with confidence. "Busing didn't work when it was tried," he says. I ask him how he knows this and he says he saw a television movie about Boston.

"I agree that it's unfair the way it is," another student says. "We have AP courses and they don't. Our classes are much smaller." But, she says, "putting them in schools like ours is not the answer. Why not put some AP classes into *their* school? Fix the roof and paint the halls so it will not be so depressing."

The students know the term "separate but equal," but seem unaware of its historical associations. "Keep them where they are but make it equal," says a girl in the front row.

A student named Jennifer, whose manner of speech is somewhat less refined and polished than that of the others, tells me that her parents came here from New York. "My family is originally from the Bronx. Schools are hell there. That's one reason that we moved. I don't think it's our responsibility to pay our taxes to provide for *them*. I mean, my parents used to live there and they wanted to get out. There's no point in coming to a place like this, where schools are good, and then your taxes go back to the place where you began."

I bait her a bit: "Do you mean that, now that you are not in hell, you have no feeling for the people that you left behind?"

"It has to be the people in the area who want an education. If your parents just don't care, it won't do any good to spend a lot of money. Someone else can't want a good life for you. You have got to want it for yourself." Then she adds, however, "I agree that everyone should have a chance at taking the same courses. . . ."

I ask her if she'd think it fair to pay more taxes so that this was possible.

"I don't see how that benefits me," she says.

It occurs to me how hard it would have been for anyone to make that kind of statement, even in the wealthiest suburban school, in 1968. Her classmates would have been unsettled by the voicing of such undisguised self-interest. Here in Rye, in 1990, she can say this with impunity. She's an interesting girl and I reluctantly admire her for being so straightforward.

Max raises a different point. "I'm not convinced," he says, "that AP courses would be valued in the Bronx. Not everyone is going to go to college."

Jennifer picks up on this and carries it a little further. "The point," she says, "is that you cannot give an equal chance to every single person. If you did it, you'd be changing the whole economic system. Let's be honest. If you equalize the money, someone's got to be shortchanged. I don't doubt that children in the Bronx are getting a bad deal. But do we want *everyone* to get a mediocre education?"

"The other point," says Max, "is that you need to match the money that you spend to whether children in the school can profit from it. We get twice as much as kids in the South Bronx, but our school is *more* than twice as good and that's because of who is here. Money isn't the whole story. . . ."

"In New York," says Jennifer, "rich people put their kids in private school. If we equalize between New York and Rye, you would see the same thing happen here. People would pull out their kids. Some people do it now. So it would happen a lot more."

An eleventh grader shakes her head at this. "Poor children need more money. It's as simple as that," she says. "Money comes from taxes. If we have it, we should pay it."

It is at this point that a boy named David picks up on a statement made before. "Someone said just now that this is not our obligation, our responsibility. I don't think that that's the question. I don't think you'd do it, pay more taxes or whatever, out of obligation. You would

do it just because . . . it is unfair the way it is." He falters on these words and looks a bit embarrassed. Unlike many of the other students who have spoken, he is somewhat hesitant and seems to choke up on his words. "Well, it's easy for me to be sitting here and say I'd spend my parents' money. I'm not working. I don't earn the money. I don't need to be conservative until I do. I can be as open-minded and unrealistic as I want to be. You can be a liberal until you have a mortgage."

I ask him what he'd likely say if he were ten years older. "Hopefully," he says, "my values would remain the same. But I know that having money does affect you. This, at least, is what they tell me."

Spurred perhaps by David's words, another student says, "The biggest tax that people pay is to the federal government. Why not take some money from the budget that we spend on armaments and use it for the children in these urban schools?"

A well-dressed student with a healthy tan, however, says that using federal taxes for the poor "would be like giving charity," and "charitable things have never worked. . . . Charity will not instill the poor with self-respect."

Max returns to something that he said before: "The environment is everything. It's going to take something more than money." He goes on to speak of inefficiency and of alleged corruption in the New York City schools. "Some years ago the chancellor was caught in borrowing $100,000 from the schools. I am told that he did not intend to pay it back. These things happen too much in New York. Why should we pour money in, when they are wasting what they have?"

I ask him, "Have we *any* obligations to poor people?"

"I don't think the burden is on us," says Jennifer again. "Taxing the rich to help the poor—we'd be getting nothing out of it. I don't understand how it would make a better educational experience for me."

"A child's in school only six hours in a day," says Max. "You've got to deal with what is happening at home. If his father's in the streets, his mother's using crack ... how is money going to make a difference?"

David dismisses this and tells me, "Here's what we should do. Put more money into preschool, kindergarten, elementary years. Pay college kids to tutor inner-city children. Get rid of the property tax, which is too uneven, and use income taxes to support these schools. Pay teachers more to work in places like the Bronx. It has to come from taxes. Pay them extra to go into the worst schools. You could forgive their college loans to make it worth their while."

"Give the children Head Start classes," says another student. "If they need more buildings, give them extra money so they wouldn't need to be so crowded."

"It has got to come from taxes," David says again.

"I'm against busing," Max repeats, although this subject hasn't been brought up by anybody else in a long while.

"When people talk this way," says David, "they are saying, actually—" He stops and starts again: "They're saying that black kids will never learn. Even if you spend more in New York. Even if you bring them here to Rye. So what it means is—you are writing people off. You're just dismissing them. . . ."

"I'd like it if we had black students in this school," the girl beside him says.

"It seems rather odd," says David when the hour is up, "that we were sitting in an AP class discussing whether poor kids in the Bronx deserve to get an AP class. We are in a powerful position."

THINKING ABOUT THE READING

What do you suppose would happen if a student from a place like East St. Louis were to attend a school in a place like Rye? Or vice versa? At one point in the reading, one of the students from Rye says, "You can take them [that is, poor, underprivileged students] out of the environment, but you can't take the environment out of them." Do you agree or disagree with that assessment of the problem of unequal education? Do you think this is a common attitude in American society? Does it enhance or impede progress regarding inequality in this country?

The Architecture of Inequality

Race and Ethnicity

The history of race in American society is an ambivalent one. Our famous sayings about equality conflict with the experiences of most racial and ethnic minorities: oppression, violence, and exploitation. Opportunities for life, liberty, and the pursuit of happiness have always been distributed along racial and ethnic lines. U.S. society is built on the assumption that different immigrant groups will ultimately assimilate, changing their way of life to conform to that of the dominant culture. But the increasing diversity of the population has shaped people's ideas about what it means to be an American and has influenced our relationships with one another and with our social institutions.

Racial inequality is both a personal and structural phenomenon. On the one hand, it is lodged in individual prejudice and discrimination. On the other hand, it resides in our language, collective beliefs, and important social institutions. This latter manifestation of racism is more difficult to detect than personal racism, hence it is more difficult to stop. Because such racism exists at a level above personal attitudes, it will not disappear simply by reducing people's prejudices.

It has been said that white people in the United States have the luxury of "having no color." When someone is described with no mention of race, the default assumption is that he or she is white. In other words, "white" is used far less often as a modifying adjective than "Black," "Asian," or "Latino." As a result, "whiteness" is rarely questioned or examined as a racial category. Only recently have scholars begun to explore the origins and characteristics of whiteness. Contemporary scholars suggest that "whiteness" became an increasingly large cultural and ethnic category, in part, by assimilating ethnically distinct immigrant groups such as the Irish and Italians. Karen Brodkin, an anthropologist, examines this issue in "How the Jews Became White Folks." She points out that perceptions of being Jewish and being white vary by generation. She traces these generational shifts and connects the increasing perception of whiteness among Jews to economic and political factors such as increasing suburbanization and changing political and economic opportunities. Following this article is a brief questionnaire designed to elicit reflections on what whiteness is and how it is recognized culturally, politically and economically.

Maxine Thompson and Verna Keith explore the complex nuances of "blackness" in "The Blacker the Berry." They examine the highly emotional issue of skin color prejudice *within* the African-American community and the different effects such prejudice has for men and women. They analyzed the responses of a sample of over 2,000 African

Americans to questions on the National Survey of Black Americans to draw conclusions about how gender and skin tone combine to influence evaluations of self-worth and self-competence among African Americans.

In "Counting Native Americans" John Anner raises several critical questions regarding the underrepresentation of native people in the U.S. census. Anner points out that the census is a significant source of political and economic information. Lack of recognition, therefore, also has significant cultural implications. The miscounting of Native Americans reflects U.S. ambivalence and exclusion regarding the presence of the continent's first peoples.

How the Jews Became White Folks

Karen Brodkin

(1998)

This article is about the ways our racial-ethnic backgrounds—American Jewishness in particular—contribute to the making of social identity in the United States. We fashion identities in the context of a wider conversation about American nationhood—to whom it belongs and what belonging means. Race and ethnicity, class, gender, and sexuality have been staple ingredients of this conversation. They are salient aspects of social being from which economic practices, political policies, and popular discourses create "Americans." Because all these facets of social being have such significant meanings on a national scale, they also have significant consequences for the life chances of individuals and groups, which is why they are such important parts of our social and political identities.

I focus on American Jews partly for personal reasons and partly because the history of Jews in the United States is a history of racial change that provides useful insights on race in America. Prevailing classifications at a particular time have sometimes assigned us to the white race, and at other times have created an off-white race for Jews to inhabit. Those changes in our racial assignment have shaped the ways in which American Jews who grew up in different eras have constructed their ethnoracial identities. Those changes give us a kind of double vision that comes from racial middleness: of an experience of marginality vis-à-vis whiteness, and an experience of whiteness and belonging vis-à-vis blackness.

Historical changes in Jews' racial assignment make for different constructions of Jewish political selves within the same family. Consequently, we may experience our racial selves in multiple ways, even within our own families. One of my teenage pranks showed me the differences between my parents' racial experience and mine. As a child, I spent summer vacations at a lake in Vermont in a bungalow colony of Jewish families whose adult members were mostly New York City public school teachers. Late one summer night, a group of us tied up all the rowboats that belonged to our group of families out in the middle of the lake. We looked forward to parental surprise when they woke up, but we weren't prepared for their genuine alarm: This could only be an anti-Semitic act by angry Yankees. What did it portend for our group? We were surprised on two counts: that the adults didn't assume we had done it, since we were always playing practical jokes, and that they thought our Jewishness mattered to Vermont Yankees.

[. . .]

In relation to Vermonters and other mainstream white folks, my parents and grandparents lived in a time when Jews were not white. They expected that particular racial assignment to shape their relationship with such people. This was the larger context within which they formed their sense of Jewish ethnoracial identity.

It is important to make a conceptual distinction between ethnoracial assignment and ethnoracial identity. Assignment is about popularly held classifications and their deployment by those with national power to make them matter economically, politically, and socially to the individuals classified. We construct ethnoracial identities ourselves, but we do it within the context of ethnoracial assignment.

However, even though ethnoracial assignment and ethnoracial identity are conceptually distinct, they are also deeply interrelated. The Jewish world of my childhood was a product of the community that anti-Semitism produced, and my Jewish identity has its roots there. However, because my racial assignment differed from that of my parents, so too did the ethnoracial content of my Jewish identity. Different generations in my family have different ethnoracial identities. My sons, who did not grow up in a Jewish milieu, tell me they don't really think of themselves as Jewish but rather as generic whites. When I asked my parents, Sylvia and Jack Brodkin, what they thought of that, they both gave me a funny look. "We're Jewish," was my father's answer, to which my mother added that, yes, she supposed that was white, but Jewish was how she saw herself. I see myself as both—white and Jewish.

[. . .]

Although my parents' Jewishness was formed in a community context organized to cope with times when Jews weren't white, most of my childhood coincided with America's philo-Semitic 1950s, where Jews were a wonderful kind of white folks. We lived where Jews had not been allowed to live a few generations earlier, and we interacted easily with people whose families had been white for a very long time. So, while my parents taught me their Jewishness-as-not-quite-white, they also wanted our family to adjust to Jews' new postwar, racially white place.

This meant we all had to learn the ways of whiteness. Shortly after we moved to Valley Stream, perhaps to help me figure it out, my parents bought me a storybook, *The Happy Family,* where life began in the kitchen and stopped at the borders of the lawn, where Mom, Dad, the kids, and the dog were relentlessly cheerful, and where no one ever raised their voices except to laugh. It was my favorite, and I desperately wanted my family to look like the one in the book. When I became an adolescent, my goal in life became to have a pageboy hairstyle and to own a camel-hair coat, like the pictures in *Seventeen* magazine. I thought of storybook and magazine people as "the blond people," a species for whom life naturally came easily, who inherited happiness as a birthright, and I wanted my family to be like that, to be "normal." Maybe then I'd be normal too. My childhood divide was between everyone I knew and the blond people, between most of the real people I knew, whether in the suburbs or in the city, and the mythical, "normal" America of the then-primitive but still quite effective mass media—radio, magazines, and the new TV.

Still, to be Jewish, to have Jewishness as a central part of my political identity, meant being a little different. At the very least it meant being part of a Jewish social and work world that I shared with my parents. True, this community differed from the Jewish community of my parents' youth, but it also differed from my suburban community of school and neighborhood, not to mention from that of the mythical blond people. Trying to be "normal," that is, white, and Jewish presented a double bind. Neither was satisfactory by itself, and it seemed to me that each commented negatively on the other: to be "normal" meant to reject the Jewishness of my family and our circle, as well as a more congenial kind of girlhood; to be Jewish meant to be a voluntary outsider at school. I wanted to embrace my family *and* to be an insider. At the time, it seemed that I had a choice and that I had to choose; one couldn't be both at the same time and in the same place.

[. . .]

Euroraces

The late nineteenth century and early decades of the twentieth saw a steady stream of warnings by scientists, policymakers, and the popular press that "mongrelization" of the Nordic or Anglo-Saxon race—the real Americans—by inferior European races (as well as by inferior non-European ones) was destroying the fabric of the nation.

—Kenneth Roberts,
"Why Europe Leaves Home"

I continue to be surprised when I read books that indicate that America once regarded its immigrant European workers as something other than white, as biologically different. My parents are not surprised; they expect anti-Semitism to be part of the fabric of daily life, much as I expect racism to be part of it. They came of age in the Jewish world of the 1920s and 1930s, at the peak of anti-Semitism in America. They are rightly proud of their upward mobility and think of themselves as pulling themselves up by their own bootstraps. I grew up during the 1950s in the Euro-ethnic New York suburb of Valley Stream, where Jews were simply one kind of white folks and where ethnicity meant little more to my generation than food and family heritage. Part of my ethnic heritage was the belief that Jews were smart and that our success was due to our own efforts and abilities, reinforced by a culture that valued sticking together, hard work, education, and deferred gratification.

[. . .]

It is certainly true that the United States has a history of anti-Semitism and of beliefs that Jews are members of an inferior race. But Jews were hardly alone. American anti-Semitism was part of a broader pattern of late-nineteenth-century racism against all southern and eastern European immigrants, as well as against Asian immigrants, not to mention African Americans, Native Americans, and Mexicans. These views justified all sorts of discriminatory treatment, including closing the doors, between 1882 and 1927, to immigration from Europe and Asia. This picture changed radically after World War II. Suddenly, the same folks who had promoted nativism and xenophobia were eager to believe that the Euro-origin people whom they had deported, reviled as members of inferior races, and prevented from immigrating only a few years earlier, were now model middle-class white suburban citizens.

It was not an educational epiphany that made those in power change their hearts, their minds, and our race. Instead, it was the biggest and best affirmative action program in the history of our nation, and it was for Euromales. That is not how it was billed, but it is the way it worked out in practice. I tell this story to show the institutional nature of racism and the centrality of state policies to creating and changing races. Here, those policies reconfigured the category of whiteness to include European immigrants. There are similarities and differences in the ways each of the European immigrant groups became "whitened." I tell the story in a way that links anti-Semitism to other varieties of anti-European racism because this highlights what Jews shared with other Euro-immigrants.

The U.S. "discovery" that Europe was divided into inferior and superior races began with the racialization of the Irish in the mid-nineteenth century and flowered in response to the great waves of immigration from southern and eastern Europe that began in the late nineteenth century. Before that time, European immigrants—including Jews—had been largely assimilated into the white population. However, the 23 million European immigrants who came to work in U.S. cities in the waves of migration after 1880 were too many and too concentrated to absorb. Since immigrants and their children made up more than 70 percent of the population of most of the country's largest cities, by the 1890s urban American had taken on a distinctly southern and eastern European immigrant flavor. Like the Irish in Boston and New York, their urban concentrations in dilapidated neighborhoods put them cheek by jowl next to the rising elites and the middle class with whom they shared public space and to whom their working-class ethnic communities were particularly visible.

The Red Scare of 1919 clearly linked anti-immigrant with anti-working-class sentiment—to the extent that the Seattle general strike by largely native-born workers was blamed on foreign agitators. The Red Scare was fueled by an economic depression, a massive postwar wave of strikes, the Russian Revolution, and another influx of postwar immigration. Strikers in the steel and garment industries in New York and New England were mainly new immigrants. "As part of a fierce counteroffensive, employers inflamed the historic identification of class conflict with immigrant radicalism." Anticommunism and anti-immigrant sentiment came together in the Palmer raids and deportation of immigrant working-class activists. There was real fear of revolution. One of President Wilson's aides feared it was "the first appearance of the soviet in this country."

Not surprisingly, the belief in European races took root most deeply among the wealthy, U.S.-born Protestant elite, who feared a hostile and seemingly inassimilable working class. By the end of the nineteenth century, Senator Henry Cabot Lodge pressed Congress to cut off immigration to the United States; Theodore Roosevelt raised the alarm of "race suicide" and took Anglo-Saxon women to task for allowing "native" stock to be outbred by inferior immigrants. In the early twentieth century, these fears gained a great deal of social legitimacy thanks to the efforts of an influential network of aristocrats and scientists who developed theories of eugenics—breeding for a "better" humanity—and scientific racism.

[...]

By the 1920s, scientific racism sanctified the notion that real Americans were white and that real whites came from northwest Europe. Racism by white workers in the West fueled laws excluding and expelling the Chinese in 1882. Widespread racism led to closing the immigration door to virtually all Asians and most Europeans between 1924 and 1927, and to deportation of Mexicans during the Great Depression.

Racism in general, and anti-Semitism in particular, flourished in higher education. Jews were the first of the Euro-immigrant groups to enter college in significant numbers, so it was not surprising that they faced the brunt of discrimination there. The Protestant elite complained that Jews were unwashed, uncouth, unrefined, loud, and pushy. Harvard University President A. Lawrence Lowell, who was also a vice president of the Immigration Restriction League, was open about his opposition to Jews at Harvard. The Seven Sister schools had a reputation for "flagrant discrimination." M. Carey Thomas, Bryn Mawr president, may have been some kind of feminist, but she was also an admirer of scientific racism and an advocate of immigration restriction. She "blocked both the admission of black students and the promotion of Jewish instructors."

Jews are justifiably proud of the academic skills that gained them access to the most elite schools of the nation despite the prejudices of their gatekeepers. However, it is well to remember that they had no serious competition from their Protestant classmates. This is because college was not about academic pursuits. It was about social connection—through its clubs, sports and other activities, as well as in the friendships one was expected to forge with other children of elites. From this, the real purpose of the college experience, Jews remained largely excluded.

[. . .]

Whitening Euro-Ethnics

By the time I was an adolescent, Jews were just as white as the next white person. Until I was eight, I was a Jew in a world of Jews. Everyone on Avenue Z in Sheepshead Bay was Jewish. I spent my days playing and going to school on three blocks of Avenue Z, and visiting my grandparents in the nearby Jewish neighborhoods of Brighton Beach and Coney Island. There were plenty of Italians in my neighborhood, but they lived around the corner. They were a kind of Jew, but on the margins of my social horizons. Portuguese were even more distant, at the end of the bus ride, at Sheepshead Bay. The *shul*, or temple, was on Avenue Z, and I begged my father to take me like all the other fathers took their kids, but religion wasn't part of my family's Judaism. Just how Jewish my neighborhood was hit me in first grade, when I was one of two kids to go to school on Rosh Hashanah. My teacher was shocked—she was Jewish too—and I was embarrassed to tears when she sent me home. I was never again sent to school on Jewish holidays. We left that world in 1949 when we moved to Valley Stream, Long Island, which was Protestant and Republican and even had farms until Irish, Italian, and Jewish ex-urbanites like us gave it a more suburban and Democratic flavor.

Neither religion nor ethnicity separated us at school or in the neighborhood. Except temporarily. During my elementary school years, I remember a fair number of dirt-bomb (a good suburban weapon) wars on the block. Periodically, one of the Catholic boys would accuse me or my brother of killing his god, to which we'd reply, "Did not," and start lobbing dirt bombs. Sometimes he'd get his friends from Catholic school and I'd get mine from

public school kids on the block, some of whom were Catholic. Hostilities didn't last for more than a couple of hours and punctuated an otherwise friendly relationship. They ended by our junior high years, when other things became more important. Jews, Catholics and Protestants, Italians, Irish, Poles, "English" (I don't remember hearing WASP as a kid), were mixed up on the block and in school. We thought of ourselves as middle class and very enlightened because our ethnic backgrounds seemed so irrelevant to high school culture. We didn't see race (we thought), and racism was not part of our peer consciousness. Nor were the immigrant or working-class histories of our families.

As with most chicken-and-egg problems, it is hard to know which came first. Did Jews and other Euro-ethnics become white because they became middle-class? That is, did money whiten? Or did being incorporated into an expanded version of whiteness open up the economic doors to middle-class status? Clearly, both tendencies were at work.

Some of the changes set in motion during the war against fascism led to a more inclusive version of whiteness. Anti-Semitism and anti-European racism lost respectability. The 1940 Census no longer distinguished native whites of native parentage from those, like my parents, of immigrant parentage, so Euro-immigrants and their children were more securely white by submersion in an expanded notion of whiteness.

Theories of nurture and culture replaced theories of nature and biology. Instead of dirty and dangerous races that would destroy American democracy, immigrants became ethnic groups whose children had successfully assimilated into the mainstream and risen to the middle class. In this new myth, Euro-ethnic suburbs like mine became the measure of American democracy's victory over racism. Jewish mobility became a new Horatio Alger story. In time and with hard work, every ethnic group would get a piece of the pie, and the United States would be a nation with equal opportunity for all its people to become part of a prosperous middle-class majority. And it seemed that Euro-ethnic immigrants and their children were delighted to join middle America.

[. . .]

Although changing views on who was white made it easier for Euro-ethnics to become middle class, economic prosperity also played a very powerful role in the whitening process. The economic mobility of Jews and other Euro-ethnics derived ultimately from America's postwar economic prosperity and its enormously expanded need for professional, technical, and managerial labor, as well as on government assistance in providing it.

The United States emerged from the war with the strongest economy in the world. Real wages rose between 1946 and 1960, increasing buying power a hefty 22 percent and giving most Americans some discretionary income. American manufacturing, banking, and business services were increasingly dominated by large corporations, and these grew into multinational corporations. Their organizational centers lay in big, new urban headquarters that demanded growing numbers of clerical, technical, and managerial workers. The postwar period was a historic moment for real class mobility and for the affluence we have erroneously come to believe was the American norm. It was a time when the old white and the newly white masses became middle class.

[. . .]

Education and Occupation

It is important to remember that, prior to the war, a college degree was still very much a "mark of the upper class," that colleges were largely finishing schools for Protestant elites. Before the postwar boom, schools could not begin to accommodate the American masses. Even in New York City before the 1930s, neither the public schools nor City College had room for more than a tiny fraction of potential immigrant students.

Not so after the war. The almost 8 million GIs who took advantage of their educational benefits under the GI Bill caused "the greatest wave of college building in American history." White male GIs were able to take advantage of their educational benefits for college and technical training, so they were particularly well positioned to seize the opportunities provided by the new demands for professional, managerial, and technical labor.

[. . .]

Just how valuable a college education was for white men's occupational mobility can be seen in who benefited from the metamorphosis of California's Santa Clara Valley into Silicon Valley. Formerly an agricultural region, in the 1950s it became the scene of explosive growth in the semiconductor electronics industry.

[. . .]

Postwar expansion made college accessible to Euromales in general and to Jews in particular. My generation's "Think what you could have been!" answer to our parents became our reality as quotas and old occupational barriers fell and new fields opened up to Jews. The most striking result was a sharp decline in Jewish small businesses and a skyrocketing increase in Jewish professionals. For example, as quotas in medical schools fell, the numbers of Jewish M.D.'s shot up. If Boston is any indication, just over 1 percent of all Jewish men before the war were doctors, but 16 percent of the postwar generation became M.D.'s. A similar Jewish mass movement took place into college and university faculties, especially in "new and expanding fields in the social and natural sciences."

Although these Jewish college professors tended to be sons of businessmen and professionals, the postwar boom saw the first large-scale class mobility among Jewish men. Sons of working-class Jews now went to college and became professionals themselves.

[...]

Even more significantly, the postwar boom transformed America's class structure—or at least its status structure—so that the middle class expanded to encompass most of the population. Before the war, most Jews, like most other Americans, were part of the working class, defined in terms of occupation, education, and income. Already upwardly mobile before the war relative to other immigrants, Jews floated high on this rising economic tide, and most of them entered the middle class. The children of other immigrants did too. Still, even the high tide missed some Jews. As late as 1973, some 15 percent of New York's Jews were poor or near poor, and in the 1960s, almost 25 percent of employed Jewish men remained manual workers.

The reason I refer to educational and occupational GI benefits as affirmative action programs for white males is because they were decidedly not extended to African Americans or to women of any race. Theoretically they were available to all veterans; in practice women and black veterans did not get anywhere near their share. Women's Army and Air Force units were initially organized as auxiliaries, hence not part of the military. When that status was changed, in July 1943, only those who re-enlisted in the armed forces were eligible for veterans' benefits. Many women thought they were simply being demobilized and returned home. The majority remained and were ultimately eligible for veterans' benefits. But there was little counseling, and a social climate that discouraged women's careers and independence cut down on women's knowledge and sense of entitlement. The Veterans Administration kept no statistics on the number of women who used their GI benefits.

The barriers that almost completely shut African American GIs out of their benefits were even more formidable. Black GIs anticipated starting new lives, just like their white counterparts. Over 43 percent hoped to return to school, and most expected to relocate, to find better jobs in new lines of work. The exodus from the South toward the North and West was particularly large. So it was not a question of any lack of ambition on the part of African American GIs. White male privilege was shaped against the backdrop of wartime racism and postwar sexism.

During and after the war, there was an upsurge in white racist violence against black servicemen, in public schools, and by the Ku Klux Klan. It spread to California and New York. The number of lynchings rose during the war, and in 1943 there were antiblack race riots in several large northern cities. Although there was a wartime labor shortage, black people were discriminated against when it came to well-paid defense industry jobs and housing. In 1946, white riots against African Americans occurred across the South and in Chicago and Philadelphia.

Gains made as a result of the wartime civil rights movement, especially in defense-related employment, were lost with peace-time conversion, as black workers were the first to be fired, often in violation of seniority.

[...]

Black GIs faced discrimination in the educational system as well. Despite the end of restrictions on Jews and other Euro-ethnics, African Americans were not welcome in white colleges. Black colleges were overcrowded, but the combination of segregation and prejudice made for few alternatives. About 20,000 black veterans attended college by 1947, most in black colleges, but almost as many, 15,000, could not gain entry. Predictably, the disproportionately few African Americans who did gain access to their educational benefits were able, like their white counterparts, to become doctors and engineers, and to enter the black middle class.

Suburbanization

In 1949, ensconced in Valley Stream, I watched potato farms turn into Levittown and Idlewild (later Kennedy) airport. This was the major spectator sport in our first years on Long Island. A typical weekend would bring various aunts, uncles, and cousins out from the city. After a huge meal, we'd pile into the car—itself a novelty—to look at the bulldozed acres and comment on the matchbox construction. During the week, my mother and I would look at the houses going up within walking distance.

Bill Levitt built a basic, 900–1,000 square foot, somewhat expandable house for a lower-middle-class and working-class market on Long Island, and later in Pennsylvania and New Jersey. Levittown started out as 2,000 units of rental housing at $60 a month, designed to meet the low-income housing needs of returning war vets, many of whom, like my Aunt Evie and Uncle Julie, were living in Quonset huts. By May 1947, Levitt and Sons had acquired enough land in Hempstead Township on Long Island to build 4,000 houses, and by the next February, he had built 6,000 units and named the development after himself. After 1948, federal financing for the construction of rental housing tightened, and Levitt switched to building houses for sale. By 1951, Levittown was a development of some 15,000 families.

At the beginning of World War II, about one-third of all American families owned their houses. That percentage doubled in twenty years. Most Levittowners looked just like my family. They came from New York City or Long Island; about 17 percent were military, from nearby Mitchell Field; Levittown was their first

house, and almost everyone was married. Three-quarters of the 1947 inhabitants were white collar, but by 1950 more blue-collar families had moved in, so that by 1951, "barely half" of the new residents were white collar, and by 1960 their occupational profile was somewhat more working class than for Nassau County as a whole. By this time too, almost one-third of Levittown's people were either foreign-born or, like my parents, first-generation U.S.-born.

The Federal Housing Administration (FHA) was key to buyers and builders alike. Thanks to the FHA, suburbia was open to more than GIs. People like us would never have been in the market for houses without FHA and Veterans Administration (VA) low-down-payment, low-interest, long-term loans to young buyers. Most suburbs were built by "merchant builders," large-scale entrepreneurs like Levitt, who obtained their own direct FHA and VA loans. In the view of one major builder, "[w]ithout FHA and VA loans merchant building would not have happened."

[. . .]

In residential life, as in jobs and education, federal programs and GI benefits were crucial for mass entry into a middle-class, home-owning suburban lifestyle. Together they raised the American standard of living to a middle-class one.

It was in housing policy that the federal government's racism reached its high point. . . .

The FHA believed in racial segregation. Throughout its history, it publicly and actively promoted restrictive covenants. Before the war, these forbade sales to Jews and Catholics as well as to African Americans. The deed to my house in Detroit had such a covenant, which theoretically prevented it from being sold to Jews or African Americans. Even after the Supreme

Court outlawed restrictive covenants in 1948, the FHA continued to encourage builders to write them in against African Americans. FHA underwriting manuals openly insisted on racially homogenous neighborhoods, and their loans were made only in white neighborhoods. . . .

With the federal government behind them, virtually all developers refused to sell to African Americans. Palo Alto and Levittown, like most suburbs as late as 1960, were virtually all white. Out of 15,741 houses and 65,276 people, averaging 4.2 people per house, only 220 Levittowners, or 52 households, were "nonwhite." In 1958, Levitt announced publicly, at a press conference held to open his New Jersey development, that he would not sell to black buyers. This caused a furor because the state of New Jersey (but not the U.S. government) prohibited discrimination in federally subsidized housing. Levitt was sued and fought it. There had been a white riot in his Pennsylvania development when a black family moved in a few years earlier. In New Jersey, he was ultimately persuaded by township ministers to integrate. West Coast builder Joe Eichler had a policy of selling to any African American who could afford to buy. But his son pointed out that his father's clientele in more affluent Palo Alto was less likely to feel threatened. They liked to think of themselves as liberal, which was relatively easy to do because there were relatively few African Americans in the Bay area, and fewer still could afford homes in Palo Alto.

The result of these policies was that African Americans were totally shut out of the suburban boom.

[. . .]

Urban renewal was the other side of the process by which Jewish and other working-class Euro-immigrants became middle class.

It was the push to suburbia's seductive pull. The fortunate white survivors of urban renewal headed disproportionately for suburbia, where they could partake of prosperity and the good life. There was a reason for its attraction. It was often cheaper to buy in the suburbs than to rent in the city. Even Euro-ethnics and families who would be considered working class, based on their occupations, were able to buy into the emerging white suburban lifestyle. And as Levittown indicates, they did so in increasing numbers, so that by 1966 half of all workers and 75 percent of those under forty nationwide lived in suburbs. They too were considered middle-class.

[. . .]

Conclusion

The myth that Jews pulled themselves up by their own bootstraps ignores the fact that it took federal programs to create the conditions whereby the abilities of Jews and other European immigrants could be recognized and rewarded rather than denigrated and denied. The GI Bill and FHA and VA mortgages, even though they were advertised as open to all, functioned as a set of racial privileges. They were privileges because they were extended to white GIs but not to black GIs. Such privileges were forms of affirmative action that allowed Jews and other Euro-American men to become suburban homeowners and to get the training that allowed them—but much less so women vets or war workers—to become professionals, technicians, salesmen, and managers in a growing economy. Jews and other white ethnics' upward mobility was due to programs that allowed us to float on a rising economic tide. . . .

Those racially skewed gains have been passed across the generations, so that racial inequality seems to maintain itself "naturally," even after legal segregation ended. Today, I own a house in Venice, California, like the one in which I grew up in Valley Stream, and my brother until recently owned a house in Palo Alto much like an Eichler house. Both of us are where we are thanks largely to the postwar benefits our parents received and passed on to us, and to the educational benefits we received in the 1960s as a result of affluence and the social agitation that developed from the black Freedom Movement. I have white, African American, and Asian American colleagues whose parents received fewer or none of America's postwar benefits and who expect never to own a house despite their considerable academic achievements. Some of these colleagues who are a few years younger than I also carry staggering debts for their education, which they expect to have to repay for the rest of their lives.

Conventional wisdom has it that the United States has always been an affluent land of opportunity. But the truth is that affluence has been the exception and that real upward mobility has required massive affirmative action programs. The myth of affluence persists today long after the industrial boom, and the public policies that supported good union contracts and real employment opportunities for (almost) all are gone. It is increasingly clear that the affluent period between 1940 and 1970 or 1975 was an aberrant one for America's white working class. The Jewish ethnic wisdom I grew up with, that we pulled ourselves up by our own bootstraps, by sticking together, by being damned

smart, leaves out an important part of the truth: that not all Jews made it, and that those who did had a great deal of help from the federal government.

Today, in a shrinking economy, where downward mobility is the norm, the children and grandchildren of the postwar beneficiaries of the economic boom have some precious advantages. For example, having parents who own their own homes or who have decent retirement benefits can make a real difference in a young person's ability to take on huge college loans or to come up with a down payment for a house. Even this simple inheritance helps perpetuate the gap between whites and people of color. Sure, Jews needed ability, but that was never enough for more than a few to make it. The same applies today. Whatever advantages I bequeath them, my sons will never have their parents' or grandparents' experience of life on a rising economic tide. . . .

Public policies like the anti-immigrant Proposition 187 and anti-affirmative action Proposition 209 in California, the abolition of affirmative action policies at the University of California, and media demonization of African Americans and Central American immigrants as lazy welfare cheats encourage feelings of white entitlement to middle-class privilege. But our children's and grandchildren's realities are that they are downwardly mobile relative to their grandparents, not because people of color are getting the good jobs by affirmative action but because the good jobs and prosperity in general are ceasing to exist.

THINKING ABOUT THE READING

What does this article tell us about the social construction of race? According to Brodkin, what are some of the social and economic factors that contribute to racial assignment? Consider other ethnic groups who have become white over time? How might their experiences differ from that of Jews? What are some of the cultural, political, and economic features associated with whiteness? Why are these features more often associated with being a "typical American" than as a racial or ethnic category? What does it mean to say that whiteness is the "default" racial category in the United States? When you are talking about people you have encountered how often do you mark them as white (e.g., "that white professor. . .")? Some sociologists have suggested that increased focus on race has led many white people to focus on their particular ethnic background (e.g., German or Irish). One author calls this a form of "ethnic accessorizing." What do you think of this concept? How might the experiences of white ethnic groups such as Norwegian American or Italian American be different than those of more marked racial groups? In places like Hawaii, whites comprise a minority of the population. Do you think this minority presence has the same cultural, political, and economic implications experienced by ethnic and racial minority populations in the continental United States. The following questionnaire from *The Hungry Mind Review* invites you to explore the meaning of whiteness.

Questionnaire: On Whiteness

From the *Hungry Mind Review*

(1998)

1. How do you list your race on the census?

2. How would you describe your racial background if you could use twenty-five words?

3. Should white people think of themselves as a race?

4. List five stereotypes about white people. Which if any, do you agree with?

5. List five stereotypes about Latinos, Asians. Blacks. Which if any, do you agree with?

6. Name some racial epithets that get directed exclusively at white people. How do they rate against those directed at nonwhites? Why?

7. When you hear the words "American citizen" whom do you visualize?

8. How would you define "American culture"?

9. Do you believe there is a common, if unarticulated, ideology of whiteness in this country and, if so, how would you describe it?

10. What five items would be essential components in a white culture center?

11. What ten items would be essential components in an American culture center?

12. If you perceive white people as enjoying a distinct series of privileges, what are some appropriate ways for whites to respond to this privilege?

13. In what ways have you used the color of your skin to your advantage?

14. In what ways has the color of your skin been a burden to you?

15. Before Europeans came to North America, did any people consider themselves white?

16. What are some ways you've seen your own attitudes toward race, and "whiteness" change in recent times, and how have those shifts in attitude been reflected in the choices you make in your personal life?

17. Do you believe that the study of white culture is merely another means for white people to "get credit"?

18. To whom would you turn for information about whiteness? Why?

19. Do you believe political leaders can have any effect in generating a nationwide conversation about race? How, specifically?

20. When are you white?

21. Can whites be black?

22. Which of the following are white: Arabs, Jews, Indians, Icelanders, Greeks? Why?

23. Is anyone really white?

The Blacker the Berry

Gender, Skin Tone, Self-Esteem, and Self-Efficacy

Maxine S. Thompson and Verna M. Keith

(2001)

She should have been a boy, then color of skin wouldn't have mattered so much, for wasn't her mother always saying that a Black boy could get along, but that a Black girl would never know anything but sorrow and disappointment? But she wasn't a boy; she was a girl, and color did matter, mattered so much that she would rather have missed receiving her high school diploma than have to sit as she now sat, the only odd and conspicuous figure on the auditorium platform of the Boise high school. . . .

Get a diploma?—What did it mean to her? College?—Perhaps. A job?—Perhaps again. She was going to have a high school diploma, but it would mean nothing to her whatsoever.

—Thurman 1929, 4–5

Wallace Thurman (1929) speaking through the voice of the main character, Emma Lou Morgan, in his novel, "The Blacker the Berry," about skin color bias within the African American community, asserts that the disadvantages and emotional pain of being "dark skinned" are greater for women than men and that skin color, not achievement, determines identity and attitudes about the self. Thurman's work describes social relationships among African Americans that were shaped by their experiences in the white community during slavery and its aftermath. In the African American community, skin color, an ascribed status attribute, played an integral role in determining class distinctions. Mulattoes, African Americans with white progenitors, led a more privileged existence when compared with their Black counterparts, and in areas of the Deep South (i.e., most notably Louisiana and South Carolina), mulattoes served as a buffer class between whites and Blacks (Russell, Wilson, and Hall 1992). In the *Black Bourgeoisie*, Frazier (1957) describes affluent organized clubs within the Black community called "blue vein" societies. To be accepted into these clubs, skin tone was required to be lighter than a "paper bag" or light enough for visibility of "blue veins" (Okazawa Rey, Robinson, and Ward 1987). Preferential treatment given by both Black and white cultures to African Americans with light skin have conveyed to many Blacks that if they conformed to the white, majority standard of beauty, their lives would be more rewarding (Bond and Cash 1992; Gatewood 1988).

Although Thurman's novel was written in 1929, the issue of *colorism* (Okazawa Rey, Robinson, and Ward 1987), intraracial discrimination based on skin color, continues to divide and shape life experiences within the African American community. The status advantages afforded to persons of light complexion continue despite the political preference for dark skin tones in the Black awareness movement during the 1960s. No longer an unspoken taboo, color prejudice within the African American community has been a "hot" topic of talk shows, novels, and movies and an issue in a court case on discrimination in the workplace (Russell, Wilson, and Hall 1992). In addition to discussions within lay communities, research scholars have had considerable interest in the importance of skin color. At the structural levels, studies have noted that skin color is an important determinant of educational and occupational attainment: Lighter skinned Blacks complete more years of schooling, have more prestigious jobs, and earn more than darker skinned Blacks (Hughes and Hertel 1990; Keith and Herring 1991). In fact, one study notes that the effect of skin color on earnings of "lighter" and "darker" Blacks is as great as the effect of race on the earnings of whites and all Blacks (Hughes and Hertel 1990). The most impressive research on skin tone effects is studies on skin tone and blood pressure. Using a reflectometer to measure skin color, research has shown that dark skin tone is associated with high blood pressure in African Americans with low socioeconomic status (Klag et al. 1991; Tryoler and James 1978). And at the social-psychological level, studies find that skin color is related to feelings of self-worth and attractiveness, self-control, satisfaction, and quality of life (Bond and Cash 1992; Boyd Franklin 1991; Cash and Duncan 1984; Chambers et al. 1994; Neal and Wilson 1989; Okazawa Rey, Robinson, and Ward 1987).

It is important to note that skin color is highly correlated with other phenotypic features—eye color, hair texture, broadness of nose, and fullness of lips. Along with light skin, blue and green eyes, European-shaped noses, and straight as opposed to "kinky" hair are all accorded higher status both within and beyond the African American community. Colorism embodies preference and desire for both light skin as well as these other attendant features. Hair, eye color, and facial features function along with color in complex ways to shape opportunities, norms regarding attractiveness, self-concept, and overall body image. Yet, it is color that has received the most attention in research on African Americans.[1] The reasons for this emphasis are not clear, although one can speculate that it is due to the fact that color is the most visible physical feature and is also the feature that is most enduring and difficult to change. As Russell, Wilson, and Hall (1992) pointed out, hair can be straightened with chemicals, eye color can be changed with contact lenses, and a broad nose can be altered with cosmetic surgery. Bleaching skin to a lighter tone, however, seldom meets with success (Okazawa Rey, Robinson, and Ward 1987). Ethnographic research also suggests that the research focus on skin color is somewhat justified. For example, it played the central role in determining membership in the affluent African American clubs.

Although colorism affects attitudes about the self for both men and women, it appears that these effects are stronger for women than men. In early studies, dark-skinned women were seen as occupying the bottom rungs of the social ladder, least marriageable, having the fewest options for higher education and career advancement, and as more color conscious than their male counterparts (Parrish 1944; Warner, Junker, and Adams 1941). There is very little empirical research on the relationship between gender, skin color, and self-concept development. In this article, we evaluate the relative importance of skin color to feelings about the self for men and women within the African American community. . . .

. . . Using an adult sample of respondents who are representative of the national population, we examine[d] the relationship of skin tone to self-concept development. . . . More important, we examine[d] the way in which gender socially constructs the impact of skin tone on self-concept development. . . .

The Sample

Data for this study come from the National Survey of Black Americans (NSBA) (Jackson and Gurin 1987). . . . Only self-identified Black American citizens were eligible for the study. Face-to-face interviews were carried out by trained Black interviewers, yielding a sample of 2,107 respondents. The response rate was approximately 69 percent. For the most part, the NSBA is representative of the national Black population enumerated in the 1980 census, with the exception of a slight overrepresentation of women and older Blacks and a small under-representation of southerners (Jackson, Tucker, and Gurin 1987). . . . [Using these data we were able to study the relationship between skin tone, gender, and self-evaluation. (For a description of the methods and results, see the complete article.)]

Skin Tone and Gender

Issues of skin color and physical attractiveness are closely linked and because expectations of physical attractiveness are applied more heavily to women across all cultures, stereotypes of attractiveness and color preference are more profound for Black women (Warner, Junker, and Adams 1941). In the clinical literature (Boyd Franklin 1991; Grier and Cobbs 1968; Neal and Wilson 1989; Okazawa Rey, Robinson, and Ward 1987), issues of racial identity, skin color, and attractiveness were central concerns of women. The "what is beautiful is good" stereotype creates a "halo" effect for light-skinned persons. The positive glow generated by physical attractiveness includes a host of desirable personality traits. Included in these positive judgments are beliefs that

attractive people would be significantly more intelligent, kind, confident, interesting, sexy, assertive, poised, modest, and successful, and they appear to have higher self-esteem and self-worth (Dion, Berscheid, and Walster 1972). When complexion is the indicator of attractiveness, similar stereotypic attributes are found. There is evidence that gender difference in response to the importance of skin color to attractiveness appears during childhood. Girls as young as six are twice as likely as boys to be sensitive to the social importance of skin color (Porter 1971; Russell, Wilson, and Hall 1992, 68). In a study of facial features, skin color, and attractiveness, Neal (cited in Neal and Wilson 1989, 328) found that

> unattractive women were perceived as having darker skin tones than attractive women and that women with more Caucasoid features were perceived as more attractive to the opposite sex, more successful in their love lives and their careers than women with Negroid features.

Frequent exposure to negative evaluations can undermine a woman's sense of self. "A dark skinned Black woman who feels herself unattractive, however, may think that she has nothing to offer society no matter how intelligent or inventive she is" (Russell, Wilson, and Hall 1992, 42).

Several explanations are proffered for gender differences in self-esteem among Blacks. One is that women are socialized to attend to evaluations of others and are vulnerable to negative appraisals. Women seek to validate their selves through appraisal from others more than men do. And the media has encouraged greater negative self-appraisals for dark-skinned women. A second explanation is that colorism and its associated stressors are not the same for dark-skinned men and women. For men, stereotypes associated with perceived dangerousness, criminality, and competence are associated with dark skin tone, while for women the issue is attractiveness (Russell, Wilson, and Hall 1992, 38). Educational attainment is a vehicle by which men might overcome skin color bias, but changes in physical features are difficult to accomplish. Third, women may react more strongly to skin color bias because they feel less control of their lives. Research studies show that women and persons of low status tend to feel fatalistic (Pearlin and Schooler 1978; Turner and Noh 1983) and to react more intensely than comparable others to stressors (Kessler and McLeod 1984; Pearlin and Johnson 1977; Thoits 1982, 1984; Turner and Noh 1983). This suggests a triple jeopardy situation: black women face problems of racism and sexism, and when these two negative status positions—being Black and being female—combine with colorism, a triple threat lowers self-esteem and feelings of competence among dark Black women.

Skin Tone and Self-Evaluation

William James (1890) conceived of the self as an integrating social product consisting of various constituent parts (i.e., the physical, social, and spiritual selves). Body image, the aspect of the self that we recognize first, is one of the major components of the self and remains important throughout life. One can assume that if one's bodily attributes are judged positively, the impact on one's self is positive. Likewise, if society devalues certain physical attributes, negative feelings about the self are likely to ensue. Body image is influenced by a number of factors including skin color, size, and shape. In our society, dark-skinned men and women are raised to believe that "light" skin is preferred. They see very light-skinned Blacks having successful experiences in advertisements, in magazines, in professional positions, and so forth. They are led to believe that "light" skin is the key to popularity, professional status, and a desirable marriage. Russell, Wilson, and Hall (1992) argue that the African

American gay and lesbian community is also affected by colorism because a light-skinned or even white mate confers status. Whether heterosexual, gay, or lesbian, colorism may lead to negative self-evaluations among African Americans with dark skin.

Self-evaluations are seen as having two dimensions, one reflecting the person's moral worth and the other reflecting the individual's competency or agency (Gecas 1989). The former refers to self-esteem and indicates how we feel about ourselves. The latter refers to self-efficacy and indicates our belief in the ability to control our own fate. These are two different dimensions in that people can feel that they are good and useful but also feel that what happens to them is due to luck or forces outside themselves.

Self-esteem and skin tone. Self-esteem consists of feeling good, liking yourself, and being liked and treated well. Self-esteem is influenced both by the social comparisons we make of ourselves with others and by the reactions that other people have toward us (i.e., reflected appraisals). The self-concept depends also on the attributes of others who are available for comparison. Self-evaluation theory emphasizes the importance of consonant environmental context for personal comparisons; that is, Blacks will compare themselves with other Blacks in their community. Consonant environmental context assumes that significant others will provide affirmation of one's identity and that similarity between oneself and others shapes the self. Thus, a sense of personal connectedness to other African Americans is most important for fostering and reinforcing positive self-evaluations. This explains why the personal self-esteem of Blacks, despite their lower status position, was as high as that of whites (Porter and Washington 1989, 345; Rosenberg and Simmons 1971).[2] It does not explain the possible influence of colorism on self-esteem within the African American community. Evidence suggests that conflictual and dissonant racial environments have negative effects on self-esteem, especially within the working class (Porter and Washington 1989, 346; Verna and Runion 1985). The heterogeneity of skin tone hues and colorism create a dissonant racial environment and become a source of negative self-evaluation.

Self-efficacy and skin tone. Self-efficacy, as defined by Bandura (1977, 1982), is the belief that one can master situations and control events. Performance influences self-efficacy such that when faced with a failure, individuals with high self-efficacy generally believe that extra effort or persistence will lead to success (Bandura 1982). However, if failure is related to some stable personal characteristic such as "dark skin color" or social constraints such as blocked opportunities resulting from mainstreaming practices in the workplace, then one is likely to be discouraged by failure and to feel less efficacious than his or her lighter counterparts. In fact, Pearlin and colleagues (1981) argue that stressors that seem to be associated with inadequacy of one's efforts or lack of success are implicated in a diminished sense of self. Problems or hardships "to which people can see no end, those that seem to become fixtures of their existence" pose the most sustained affront to a sense of mastery and self-worth (Pearlin et al. 1981, 345). For Bandura, however, individual agency plays a role in sustaining the self. Individuals actively engage in activities that are congenial with a positive sense of self. Self-efficacy results not primarily from beliefs or attitudes about performance but from undertaking challenges and succeeding. Thus, darker skinned Blacks who experience success in their everyday world (e.g., work, education, etc.) will feel more confident and empowered.

Following the literature, we predict a strong relationship between skin tone and self-esteem and self-efficacy, but the mechanisms are different for the two dimensions. The effect of skin tone on self-efficacy will be partially mediated by occupation and income. The effect will be direct for self-esteem. That is, the direct effect will be stronger for self-esteem than for self-efficacy. Furthermore, we expect a stronger relationship between skin tone and self-esteem for women than men because women's self-esteem is conditioned by the appraisals of others, and the media have encouraged negative appraisals for dark-skinned women.

Discussion [of the Study]

The data in this study indicate that gender—mediated by socioeconomic status variables such as education, occupation, and income—socially constructs the importance of skin color evaluations of self-esteem and self-efficacy. Self-efficacy results not primarily from beliefs or attitudes about performance but rather reflects an individual's competency or agency from undertaking challenges and succeeding at overcoming them. Self-esteem consists of feeling good about oneself and being liked and treated favorably by others. However, the effect of skin color on these two domains of self is different for women and men. Skin color is an important predictor of perceived efficacy for Black men but not Black women. And skin color predicts self-esteem for Black women but not Black men. This pattern conforms to traditional gendered expectations (Hill Collins 1990, 79–80). The traditional definitions of masculinity demand men specialize in achievement outside the home, dominate in interpersonal relationships, and remain rational and self-contained. Women, in contrast, are expected to seek affirmation from others, to be warm and nurturing. Thus, consistent with gendered characteristics of men and women, skin color is important in self-domains that are central to masculinity (i.e., competence) and femininity (i.e., affirmation of the self).[3]

Turning our attention to the association between skin color and self-concept for Black men, the association between skin color and self-efficacy increases significantly as skin color lightens. And this is independent of the strong positive contribution of education—and ultimately socioeconomic status—to feelings of competence of men. We think that the effect of skin tone on self-efficacy is the result of widespread negative stereotyping and fear associated with dark-skinned men that pervade the larger society and operates independent of social class. Correspondingly, employers view darker African American men as violent, uncooperative, dishonest, and unstable (Kirschenman and Neckerman, 1998). As a consequence, employers exclude "darker" African American men from employment and thus block their access to rewards and resources.

Evidence from research on the relationship between skin tone and achievement supports our interpretation. The literature on achievement and skin tone shows that lighter skinned Blacks are economically better off than darker skinned persons (Hughes and Hertel 1990; Keith and Herring 1991). Hughes and Hertal (1990), using the NSBA data, present findings that show that for every dollar a light-skinned African American earns, the darker skinned person earns 72 cents. Thus, it seems colorism is operative within the workplace. Lighter skinned persons are probably better able to predict what will happen to them and what doors will open and remain open, thus leading to a higher sense of control over their environment. Our data support this finding and add additional information on how that process might work, at least in the lives of Black men. Perhaps employers are looking to hire African American men who will assimilate into the work environment, who do not alienate their clients (Kirschenman and Neckerman 1998), and who are nonthreatening. One consequence of mainstreaming the workplace is

that darker skinned Black men have fewer opportunities to demonstrate competence in the breadwinner role. It is no accident that our inner cities where unemployment is highest are filled with darker skinned persons, especially men (Russell, Wilson, and Hall 1992, 38). During adolescence, lighter skinned boys discover that they have better job prospects, appear less threatening to whites, and have a clearer sense of who they are and their competency (Russell, Wilson, and Hall 1992, 67). In contrast, darker skinned African American men may feel powerless and less able to affect change through the "normal" channels available to light-skinned African American men (who are able to achieve a more prestigious socioeconomic status).

While skin color is an important predictor of self-efficacy for African American men, it is more important as a predictor of self-esteem for African American women. These data confirm much of the anecdotal information from clinical studies of clients in psychotherapy that found that dark-skinned Black women have problems with self-worth and confidence. Our findings suggest that this pattern is not limited to experiences of women who are in therapy but that colorism is part of the everyday reality of black women. Black women expect to be judged by their skin tone. No doubt messages from peers, the media, and family show a preference for lighter skin tones. Several studies cited in the literature review point out that Black women of all ages tend to prefer lighter skin tones and believe that lighter hues are perceived as most attractive by their Black male counterparts (Bond and Cash 1992; Chambers et al. 1994; Porter 1971; T. L. Robinson and Ward 1995).

Evidence from personal accounts reported by St. John and Feagin (1998, 75) in research on the impact of racism in the everyday lives of Black women supports this interpretation. One young woman describes her father's efforts to shape her expectations about the meaning of beauty in our society and where Black women entered this equation.

> Beauty, beauty standards in this country, a big thing with me. It's a big gripe, because I went through a lot of personal anguish over that, being Black and being female, it's a real big thing with me, because it took a lot for me to find a sense of self...in this white-male-dominated society. And just how beauty standards are so warped because like my daddy always tell me, "white is right." The whiter you are, somehow the better you are, and if you look white, well hell, you've got your ticket, and anything you want, too.

Nevertheless, the relationship between skin color and self-esteem among African American women is moderated by socioeconomic status. For example, there is no correlation between skin color and self-esteem among women who have a more privileged socioeconomic status. Consequently, women who are darker and "successful" evaluate themselves just as positively as women of a lighter color. On the other hand, the relationship between skin color and self-esteem is stronger for African American women from the less privileged socioeconomic sectors. In other words, darker skinned women with the lowest incomes display the lowest levels of self-esteem, but self-esteem increases as their skin color lightens. Why does skin color have such importance for self-regard in the context of low income or poverty? Low income shapes self-esteem because it provides fewer opportunities for rewarding experiences or affirming relationships. In addition, there are more negative attributes associated with behaviors of individuals from less privileged socioeconomic status than with those of a more prestigious one. For example, the derisive comment "ghetto chick" is often used to describe the behaviors, dress, communication and interaction styles of women from low-income groups. Combine stereotypes of classism and colorism,

and you have a mixture that fosters an undesirable if not malignant context for self-esteem development. An important finding of this research is that skin color and income determine self-worth for Black women and especially that these factors can work together. Dark skin and low income produce Black women with very low self-esteem. Accordingly, [our study] help[s] refine [the] understanding of gendered racism and of "triple oppression" involving race, gender, and class that places women of color in a subordinate social and economic position relative to men of color and the larger white population as well (Segura 1986). More important, the data suggest that darker skinned African American women actually experience a "quadruple" oppression originating in the convergence of social inequalities based on gender, class, race, and color. . . . We noted the absence of an interaction effect between skin tone and education, and we can only speculate on the explanation for this nonfinding. Perhaps education does not have the same implications for self-esteem as income because it is a less visible symbol of success. Financial success affords one the ability to purchase consumer items that tell others, even at a distance, that an individual is successful. These visible symbols include the place where we live, the kind of car we drive, and the kind of clothing that we wear. Educational attainment is not as easily grasped, especially in distant social interactions—passing on the street, walking in the park, or attending a concert event. In other words, for a dark-skinned African American woman, her M.A. or Ph.D. may be largely unknown outside her immediate friends, family, and coworkers. Her Lexus or Mercedes, however, is visible to the world and is generally accorded a great deal of prestige.

Finally, the data indicate that self-esteem increases as skin color becomes lighter among African American women who are judged as having "low and average levels of attractiveness."

There is no relationship between skin color and self-esteem for women who are judged "highly attractive," just as there is no correlation between skin color and self-esteem for women of higher socioeconomic status. That physical attractiveness influenced feelings of self-worth for Black women is not surprising. Women have traditionally been concerned with appearance, regardless of ethnicity. Indeed, the pursuit and preoccupation with beauty are central features of female sex-role socialization. Our findings suggest that women who are judged "unattractive" are more vulnerable to color bias than those judged attractive.

NOTES

1. Skin color bias has also been investigated among Latino groups, although more emphasis has been placed on the combination of both color and European phenotype facial characteristics. Studies of Mexican Americans have documented that those with lighter skin and European features attain more schooling (Telles and Murguia 1990) and generally have higher socioeconomic status (Acre, Murguia, and Frisbie 1987) than those of darker complexion with more Indian features. Similar findings have been reported for Puerto Ricans (Rodriguez 1989), a population with African admixture.

2. Self-concept theory argued that the experience of social inequality would foster lower self-concept of persons in lower status positions compared with their higher status counterparts. However, when comparing the self-concept of African American schoolboys and schoolgirls, Rosenberg and Simmons (1971) found that their self-feelings were as high and in some instances higher than those of white schoolchildren. This "unexpected" finding was explained by strong ties and bonds within the African American community as opposed to identifying with the larger community.

3. These findings also reflect the dual nature of colorism as it pertains to Black women. Colorism is an aspect of racism that results in anti-Black discrimination in the wider society and, owing to historical patterns, also occurs within the Black community. The finding that the effects of skin tone on self-efficacy become nonsignificant when

socioeconomic status variables are added suggests that the interracial discrimination aspect of colorism is more operational for Black women's self-efficacy via access to jobs and income. The finding that the effect of skin tone is more central to Black women's self-esteem indicates that colorism within the Black community is the more central mechanism. Self-esteem is derived from family, friends, and close associates.

REFERENCES

Acre, Carlos, Edward Murguia, and W. P. Frisbie, 1987. Phenotype and life chances among Chicanos. *Hispanic Journal of Behavioral Sciences* 9(1): 19–32.

Aiken, Leona S., and Stephen G. West. 1991. *Multiple regression: Testing and interpreting interactions.* Newbury Park, CA: Sage.

Bachman, J. G., and Johnson. 1978. *The monitoring the future project: Design and procedures.* Ann Arbor: University of Michigan, Institute for Social Research.

Bandura, A. 1977. Self efficacy: Towards a unifying theory of behavioral change. *Psychological Review* 84: 191–215.

———. 1982. Self efficacy mechanism in human agency. *American Psychologist* 37: 122–47.

Bond, S., and T. F. Cash. 1992. Black beauty: Skin color and body images among African-American college women. *Journal of Applied Social Psychology* 22 (11): 874–88.

Boyd Franklin, N. 1991. Recurrent themes in the treatment of African-American women in group psychotherapy. *Women and Therapy.* 11 (2): 25–40.

Cash, T. S., and N. C. Duncan. 1984. Physical attractiveness stereotyping among Black American college students. *Journal of Social Psychology* 1:71–77.

Chambers, J. W., T. Clark, L. Dantzler, and J. A. Baldwin. 1994. Perceived attractiveness, facial features, and African self-consciousness. *Journal of Black Psychology* 20 (3): 305–24.

Dion, K., E. Berscheid, and E. Walster. 1972. What is beautiful is good. *Journal of Personality and Social Psychology* 24:285–90.

Frazier, E. Franklin. 1957. *Black bourgeoise: The rise of the new middle class.* New York: Free Press.

Freeman, H. E., J. M. Ross, S. Armor, and R. F. Pettigrew. 1966. Color gradation and attitudes among middle class income Negroes. *American Sociological Review* 31: 365–74.

Gatewood, W. B. 1988. Aristocrat of color: South and North and the Black elite, 1880–1920. *Journal of Southern History* 54: 3–19.

Gecas, Viktor. 1989. The social psychology of self-efficacy. *Annual Review of Sociology* 15: 291–316.

Grier, W., and P. Cobbs. 1968. *Black rage.* New York: Basic Books.

Hill Collins, Patricia. 1990. *Black feminist thought: Knowledge, consciousness, and the politics of empowerment.* Boston: Unwin Hyman.

Hughes, M., and B. R. Hertel. 1990 The significance of color remains: A study of life chances, mate selection, and ethnic consciousness among Black Americans. *Social Forces* 68(4): 1105–20.

Hughes, Michael, and David H. Demo. 1989. Self perceptions of Black Americans: Self-esteem and personal efficacy. *American Journal of Sociology* 95: 132–59.

Jackson, J., and G. Gurin. 1987. *National survey of Black Americans, 1979–1980* (machine-readable codebook). Ann Arbor: University of Michigan, Inter-University Consortium for Political and Social Research.

Jackson, J. S., B. Tucker, and G. Gurin. 1987. *National survey of Black Americans 1979–1980* (MRDF). Ann Arbor, MI: Institute for Social Research.

James, W. 1890. *The principles of psychology.* New York: Smith.

Keith, V. M., and C. Herring. 1991. Skin tone and stratification in the Black community. *American Journal of Sociology* 97 (3): 760–78.

Kessler, R. C., and J. D. McLeod. 1984. Sex differences in vulnerability to undesirable life events. *American Sociological Review* 49: 620–31.

Kirschenman, J., and K. M. Neckerman. 1998. We'd love to hire them, but . . . In *The meaning of race for employers in working American: Continuity, conflict, and change,* edited by Amy S. Wharton. Mountain View, CA: Mayfield.

Klag, Michael, Paul Whelton, Josef Coresh, Clarence Grim, and Lewis Kuller. 1991. The association of skin color with blood pressure in U.S. Blacks with low socioeconomic status. *Journal of the American Medical Association* 65(5): 599–602.

Miller, Herman P. 1964. *Rich man, poor man.* New York: Corwell.

Neal, A., and M. Wilson. 1989. The role of skin color and features in the Black community: Implications for Black women in therapy. *Clinical Psychology Review* 9 (3): 323–33.

Okazawa Rey, Margo, Tracy Robinson, and Janie V. Ward. 1987. *Black women and the politics of skin color and hair.* New York: Haworth.

Parrish, Charles. 1944. The significance of skin color in the Negro community. Ph.D. diss., University of Chicago.

Pearlin, L. I., and J. S. Johnson. 1977. Marital status, life strains, and depression. *American Sociological Review* 42: 704–15.

Pearlin, L. I., M. A. Liberman, E. G. Meneghan, and J. T. Mullan. 1981. The stress process. *Journal of Health and Social Behavior* 22 (December): 337–56.

Pearlin, L. I., and C., Schooler. 1978. The structure of coping. *Journal of Health and Social Behavior* 19: 2–21.

Porter, J. 1971. *Black child, white child: The development of racial attitudes.* Cambridge, MA: Harvard University Press.

Porter, J. R., and R. E. Washington. 1989. Developments in research on black identity and self esteem: 1979–88. *Review of International Psychology and Sociology* 2:341–53.

Ransford, E. H. 1970. Skin color, life chances and anti-white attitudes. *Social Problems* 18: 164–78.

Robinson, J. P., and P. R. Shaver. 1969. *Measures of social psychological attitudes.* Ann Arbor: University of Michigan, Institute of Social Research.

Robinson, T. L., and J. V. Ward. 1995. African American adolescents and skin color. *Journal of Black Psychology* 21 (3): 256–74.

Rodriguez, Clara. 1989. *Puerto Ricans: Born in the USA.* Boston: Unwin Hyman.

Rosenberg, M. 1979. *Conceiving the self.* New York: Basic Books.

Rosenberg, M., and R. Simmons. 1971. *Black and white self-esteem: The urban school child.* Washington, DC: American Sociological Association.

Russell, Kathy, Midge Wilson, and Ronald Hall. 1992. *The color complex: The politics of skin color among African Americans.* New York: Harcourt Brace Jovanovich.

Segura, Denise. 1986. Chicanas and triple oppression in the labor force. In *Chicana voices: Intersections of class, race, and gender,* edited by Teresa Cordova and the National Association of Chicana Studies Editorial Committee. Austin, TX: Center for Mexican American Studies.

St. John, Y., and J. R. Reagin. 1998. *Double burden: Black women and everyday racism.* New York: M. E. Sharpe.

Telles, Edward E., and Edward Murguia. 1990. Phenotypic discrimination and income differences among Mexican Americans. *Social Science Quarterly* 71 (4): 682–95.

Thoits, Peggy A. 1982. Life stress, social support, and psychological vulnerability: Epidemiological considerations. *Journal of Community Psychology* 10: 341–62.

———. 1984. Explaining distributions of psychological vulnerability: Lack of social support in the face of life stress. *Social Forces* 63: 452–81.

Thurman, Wallace. 1929. *The blacker the berry: A novel of Negro life.* New York: Macmillan.

Tryoler, H. A., and S. A. James. 1978. Blood pressure and skin color. *American Journal of Public Health* 58: 1170–72.

Turner, R. J., and S. Noh. 1983. Class and psychological vulnerability among women: The significance of social support and personal control. *Journal of Health and Social Behavior* 24: 2–15.

Udry, J. R., K. E. Baumann, and C. Chase. 1969. Skin color, status, and mate selection. *American Journal of Sociology* 76: 722–33.

Verna. G., and K. Runion. 1985. The effects of contextual dissonance on the self concept of youth from high vs. low socially valued group. *Journal of Social Psychology* 125: 449–58.

Warner, W. L., B. H. Junker, and W. A. Adams. 1941. *Color and human nature.* Washington, DC: American Council on Education.

Wright, B. 1976. *The dissent of the governed: Alienation and democracy in America.* New York: Academic Press.

THINKING ABOUT THE READING

Describe the different effects skin tone has on black men and women. How can you explain the gender differences in the relationship between skin tone and self-esteem and between skin tone and self-efficacy? What role does socioeconomic status play in mediating these relationships? What are the long-term economic and political consequences of skin color bias? Thompson and Keith state that *colorism*—intraracial discrimination based on skin color—still divides and shapes the lives of African Americans. How does this skin color bias within the African-American community compare to the prejudice and discrimination blacks are subjected to by non-blacks? Is there comparable *within-group* prejudice among other races? If so, how does it compare to what Thompson and Keith describe? If not, why is such prejudice unique to the African-American community?

Counting Native Americans

John Anner

(1991)

"Statistical genocide," says Dr. Susan Lobo, who works with the Intertribal Friendship House in Oakland, California, "relates to the ways in which figures and statistics are used to determine programs and set policies." The most important source of these figures and statistics is the once-a-decade national census. Census figures are used to determine, among other things, who gets what in terms of federal funding and congressional representation. If you are not counted by the census, then, in the eyes of government agencies, you don't count. In fact, you don't exist at all.

For Native Americans, the last U.S. census—which science writer James Gleick says "seems certain to stand as a bleak landmark in the annals of arithmetic"—deserves the name "statistical genocide." It has made a lot of people vanish, for the most part people of color. Native Americans, however, claim that their communities are undercounted much more than other races or ethnicities, and the process has made them all but invisible in urban America. "Demography," writes University of California at Davis Professor Jack Forbes, "for Native Americans, has always pointed towards a struggle against disappearance, or, more precisely, against being forced to vanish!"

As census officials readily admit, the national count always misses people of color more often than whites, due to mistrust of agents of the federal government, cultural and language communication problems, and so on. Depending on the area and ethnic group in question, this undercount is variously estimated at three to fifteen percent. Whites are generally undercounted by approximately one percent, according to the Census Bureau. Some Native American leaders, however, feel that their urban constituencies are undercounted by as much as 60 percent. And in some ways, an accurate count is even more important to Native Americans than it is to other people of color, for reasons having to do with federal recognition of various tribes and new proposals regarding how Bureau of Indian Affairs (BIA) money is allocated.

Despite the magnitude of the problem and the importance of the outcome, however, the 1990 U.S. Census will be tabulated without much attention to Native American objections to the way it was conducted, or protests about the severity of the undercount. In part, this has to do with size of the census project; it is difficult to change the overall direction of a massive bureaucracy that at its height employed some 350,000 workers in 487 field offices around the country. As Ramona Wilson, coordinator of the Urban Indian Child Resource Center said in an interview, "the census machinery is very rigid. Populations are put into the machinery and have to accommodate themselves to it, rather than the machinery accommodating itself to people."

The census is also an undertaking involving the abilities of a horde of statisticians and other "number-crunchers" who are not trained to be aware of cultural biases, and whose general attitude is, according to Lobo, "don't worry, we have sophisticated techniques—which you wouldn't understand—for correcting any problems." But the Native American community also failed to mobilize around the census in a way that could have changed the outcome, which reflects a lack of political clout on the national level and a scarcity of organizing in the local arena. In part, this failure to mobilize around the census is due to the barriers to organizing a community that lives dispersed, and is composed of numerous tribes that speak different languages and have different cultures. As explained below, the census undercounts Native Americans in part because they generally do not live in clustered residential communities. This same geographical scattering makes it more difficult to use traditional community organizing techniques with Native Americans. . . .

Survival Tactics

Native Americans, according to Lobo, are loathe to get involved with the federal government on any level, especially one that involves being counted—which brings back memories of being registered in federal programs that relocated and dispossessed Indian people from their traditional lands. "For Indian people," said Lobo, "being invisible is a survival tactic that has proved its worth in the past." Thus, although the benefits of being counted by the census were clear to many organizers and service providers, on the whole there was little enthusiasm on the part of their Native American constituency. Lobo also said that, for many Native American organizations, the census was a "new issue" around which they had not yet learned to organize effectively.

According to the organizations contacted for this article, there are three main changes they would like to see the Census Bureau make to better count Native Americans:

1. Change the way the census questions are worded to make it easier to self-identify as Native American;

2. Change the way the census is conducted in some areas to account for the dispersed living patterns of Native Americans;

3. Hire more outreach workers to work in Native American communities (there were only two for all of California in 1990).

Oakland, California, was one of several sites chosen around the country in which to do "post-enumeration surveys" (PES) to determine why certain populations were missed by census counters. (According to John Reader, Western Regional Census Director, the Census Bureau always does these surveys, and has until July 15, 1991, to decide if it wants to adjust the census figures based on the results of the PES.) The Bureau hired Dr. Susan Lobo and the Inter-tribal Friendship House to do follow-up, in-depth interviews with 100 Native American families to determine what characteristics Native Americans have that cause them to be undercounted by the census.

Census Cover-Up

Framing the question in this way, says Lobo, automatically puts the blame for being missed on the people, not on the Census Bureau. "The more we got into the project," Lobo said in an interview, "the more we realized that . . . this study was something they created to cover their tracks. The real reason for the undercount is problems with the census process itself, not because people move too much or because they don't have recognizable housing."

Despite their sophisticated statistical techniques, according to Lobo, the census count is based on flawed assumptions about urban Native Americans, who now make up over half of all Native Americans in the U.S. The most important of these is the premise that all people of color live in homogeneous residential communities, i.e., that Latinos will tend to live near other Latinos, Asians near other Asians from similar geographic background, etc. This is important because in areas where large percentages of mailed-out census forms are not sent back—estimated at over 50% in many communities of color—census takes must go door-to-door to count people. If people are not home or refuse to answer the door, census takers must resort to "last resort information," i.e., asking the neighbors for information about others who live nearby. If no information is available, a residence is "coded as previously coded household"; in other words entered exactly as the prior household from which information was obtained.

This approach can work fairly well in ethnically homogeneous neighborhoods. For Native Americans, however, it is fundamentally flawed. Native Americans tend not to live in clustered residential communities, as do other people of color. Using the "coded as previously coded household" technique will thus miss many Native Americans. In addition, "a lot of Indian people will keep a real low profile," says Lobo, and when people are asked for the ethnic background of Native American neighbors they are likely to guess that they are Latino or Filipino, rather than American Indian.

"I think the real reason why Indian people are so undercounted is due to the insensitivity and ignorance of the census people," Lobo said, "at one point, after explaining again why census assumptions about people living in congregated communities does not hold for Indian people, one of the census officials in Washington told me 'well, your information does not fit in with our profile of immigrant communities!'"

Lobo also found that once census information is collected, it is then coded in ways that can discriminate against people who don't fit the Census Bureau's assumptions. The census computer is programmed to reject census forms that indicate, for example, that the person who filled it out is 175 years old, or is an 11-year-old widow. According to one story, the census coding system was at one point set to reject any form that indicated that the person was American Indian, lived in a high-income urban area and had an educational degree of Master's level or better. The census officials were apparently more ready to believe that the person in question accidently marked "American Indian" than that a Native American could reach such levels.

Luckily, this particular example of census bias was dropped following strenuous objections from a sociologist who happened to be in the room when the question was being discussed. Since the coding process is not made public, however, it is difficult to determine what other kinds of programmed bias might exist in the census computers.

Lobo and Inter-tribal Friendship House eventually decided that the census evaluation they were being asked to perform was rigged from the start, and they removed themselves from the study.

The census numbers—whether accurate or inaccurate—are important on a number of different levels. The *New York Times* reports that more than 400 programs covering everything from transportation to health and housing are funded based on census figures. Every single person counted in the census is worth between $125 and $400 in federal aid to cities, making an undercount a matter of intense concern to city officials, social service organizations, and community groups in an era of rapidly declining federal assistance and constantly rising needs.

Political influence is also a function of census statistics. Congressional and state legislative apportionment are both determined by census figures. A study conducted by the Joint Center for Political Studies, for example, indicates that three seats currently held by African-American Democrats (Reps. George Crockett and John

Conyers of Michigan and William Gray of Philadelphia) may be lost when congressional districts are redrawn based on the 1990 census.

Latino political leaders also claim that significant numbers of people in their communities were missed by census enumerators; the *Guardian* cites congressional testimony by representatives from Texas who dispute figures showing declines in the population of Latino neighborhoods, and steep rises in the populations of mostly white suburbs. Asian political leaders have also complained bitterly about being undercounted; by some estimates Asian communities lost $50 to $110 million in federal revenue over the past ten years based on a 4 to 6 percent undercount in the 1980 census.

Being undercounted, for all people of color, means losing out both on government funding for various programs and on political representation, but for Native Americans there are two other potentially serious repercussions. First, there are a number of new proposals being floated in Congress that would allocate Bureau of Indian Affairs (BIA) money to Native American tribes to administer. Called "New Federalism" by proponents, it would decentralize the funding allocation process. Both total money allocated and the proportions that are allocated to each tribe will be determined by census figures.

Second, in order to get access to BIA funding in the first place (and to get access to a number of other federal programs), a tribe has to be officially recognized by the federal government. When a tribe applies for recognition, census figures are often used as a determining factor. If only a small number can be identified from census figures, the chances of being recognized are correspondingly small.

Fighting Tooth and Nail

Despite how important the census figures are to Native Americans, and regardless of the extent of the undercount, there is little that can be done now to change the census figures. The census will give its final collected statistics to the White House on December 15. "At this point," Sally Gallego, director of the Consortium of Indian Nations (CUIN) told the *Trendsletter,* "there is really no recourse." Wilson of the Indian Education Center concurs: "The best we can hope for is that this experience will make [the census process] easier and better the next time."

However, it is likely that much could have been done earlier on to improve the way the census was conducted. Asians, for example, who were upset with the way the census questions were set up in the 1980 census, have a relatively strong presence in Congress, and were willing "to fight tooth and nail" (according to an article in *Asian Week*) to get the Census Bureau to add extra categories to the 1990 census to better define and count the Asian community. After strong pressure by Rep. Robert Matsui (D. California) and others, the Census Bureau added nine Asian subgroups to the census questionnaire. Clearly, the way the census is written and conducted is susceptible to pressure.

In fact, as Forbes makes clear in his writing, the process of making up the census questions carrying out the count is based first and foremost on political considerations. For example, people originally from Latin America, Puerto Rico, and Cuba can only classify themselves as Latino; the category of "Native American" is limited only to North Americans, despite the fact that the majority of Latin Americans are partially or wholly Native American. This is done, suggests Forbes, to subordinate Native American cultures and reduce their political presence—as well as to limit the numbers of people qualifying for federal assistance. A stronger national political presence may have given Native Americans the ability to influence the way the questionnaire is structured; it remains for Native Americans to build the constituency and alliances and develop the tactics necessary for that presence.

Political Leverage Needed

Like the census itself, the post-enumeration survey can also be "adjusted" (with sufficient political leverage). According to Reader, the PES does not include urban Native Americans as a category that could be adjusted. By contrast, *Asian Week* reported that "[i]n response to months of pressure from Asian American groups, the U.S. Census Bureau announced October 18 that it would make a special count of Asians and Pacific Islanders in its post-enumeration survey (PES)" to see how many the original census may have missed. Urban Native Americans, therefore, will be the only category of "minority population" not specifically counted by the PES.

Census officials told the *Trendsletter* that this is more a scientific problem than a political one, and that Native Americans lack sufficient numbers to make a statistically significant sample size, but it seems odd that the census should be so sure of how many there are before counting them. Most observers familiar with the census process readily agree that the whole operation is, in fact, highly political, rather than based on any purely scientific considerations.

On the local level, it is up to cities to sue the Census Bureau if they feel their populations were undercounted. While in many cities Native Americans did participate in so-called "full-count committees," Native American leaders admit that in general their communities had little visibility or political presence. Gallegos, for example, said that CUIN did not attempt to put constant pressure on city governments to recognize the extent of the Native American undercount. Organized local political pressure could conceivably have forced cities to sue the Census Bureau on behalf of their undercounted Native American populations. At best, says Wilson, Native Americans might get an official acknowledgement that the count is inaccurate (census officials contacted by the *Trendsletter* said this was unlikely). If the Census Bureau is forced to issue such a statement, however, it would at least give Native Americans room to argue that other methods need to be used to determine how their people's needs are met when questions of federal funding arise.

REFERENCES

"Census Outrage: Counting Asians As Caucasians," *Asian Week*, 7/6/90.

"Census Relents. Will Do Asian Survey," *Asian Week*, 10/26/90.

"Census Shows City 'Depopulation,'" *Guardian*, 10/10/90.

"Census Takers Recall Resistance and Lies in New York City Tally," *New York Times*, 9/3/90.

"Director Defends Census. Challenging Cities on the Uncounted," *New York Times*, 9/12/90.

Forbes, Jack. "Undercounting Native Americans" (unpublished study).

Gleick, James. "The Census That Doesn't Add Up," *This World*, 7/22/90.

"Many Cities Expected to Challenge Census," *San Francisco Chronicle*, 8/3/90.

"Matsui: Census Pits Asians against Blacks and Latinos," *Asian Week*, 9/14/90.

THINKING ABOUT THE READING

What are some of the cultural, economic and political consequences of being officially miscounted? Can you think of some other examples of the failure to acknowledge the presence of Native Americans in this U.S? This article is based on the 1990 Census. Changes were made to the 2000 Census, the most important being the ability to select more than one racial/ethnic category on the questionnaire. How do you think this change will affect the concerns raised by Anner?

The Architecture of Inequality

Sex and Gender

Along with racial and class inequality, sexual inequality—and the struggle against it—has been a fundamental part of the historical development of our national identity. Along the way it has influenced the lives and dreams of individual people, shaped popular culture, and created or maintained social institutions. Gender is a major criterion for the distribution of important economic, political, and educational resources in most societies. Sexual inequality is perpetuated by a dominant cultural ideology that devalues women on the basis of presumed biological differences between men and women. This ideology overlooks the equally important role of social forces in determining male and female behavior.

Like the article, "The Blacker the Berry . . ." in the previous chapter, Bart Landry explores the intersections of race and gender in "Black Women and a New Definition of Womanhood." Landry examines the difficulties black women have faced throughout history in being seen by others as virtuous and moral. This article provides a fascinating picture of women's struggle for equality from the perspective of black women, a group that is often ignored and marginalized in discussions of the women's movement. Although much of the article focuses on black women's activism in the 19th century, it provides important insight into the intersection of race and gender today.

Another persistent source of gender difference and inequality is sexual socialization. In "What is Wanting? Gender, Equality, and Desire," Judith Levine examines the distinct ideals teenage boys and girls are taught about sexuality. These ideals result in different expectations regarding sexual behavior that are misleading and harmful and contribute to persistent gender inequalities. Boys, for example, are taught that they should constantly desire women and sex—the more the better. Girls are taught that the only acceptable expression of sexual desire is in connection with "true" love and romance. These distinctive ideals alienate boys and girls from one another and from the development of a healthy and socially responsible understanding of desire.

Institutional sexism exists in the law, in the family (in terms of such things as the domestic division of labor), and in economics. Not only are social institutions sexist, in that women are systematically segregated, exploited, and excluded, they are also gendered. Institutions themselves are structured along gender lines so that traits associated with success are usually stereotypically male characteristics: tough-mindedness, rationality, assertiveness, competitiveness, and so forth.

Women have made significant advances politically, economically, educationally, and socially over the past decades. The traditional obstacles to advancement continue to fall. Women have entered the labor force in unprecedented numbers. Yet despite their growing presence in the labor force and their entry into historically male occupations, rarely do women work alongside men or perform the same tasks and functions.

Jobs within an occupation still tend to be divided into "men's work" and "women's work." Such sex segregation has serious consequences for women in the form of blocked advancement and lower salaries. But looking at sex segregation on the job as something that happens only to women gives us an incomplete picture of the situation. It is just as important to examine what keeps men out of "female" jobs as it is to examine what keeps women out of "male" jobs. The proportion of women in male jobs has increased over the past several decades, but the proportion of men in female jobs has remained virtually unchanged. In "Still a Man's World," Christine Williams looks at the experiences of male nurses, social workers, elementary school teachers, and librarians. She finds that although these men do feel somewhat stigmatized by their nontraditional career choices, they still enjoy significant gender advantages.

Black Women and a New Definition of Womanhood

Bart Landry

(2000)

A popular novel of 1852 chirped that the white heroine, Eoline, "with her fair hair, and celestial blue eyes bending over the harp . . . really seemed 'little lower than the angels,' and an aureola of purity and piety appeared to beam around her brow."[1] By contrast, in another popular antebellum novel, *Maum Guinea and Her Plantation Children* (1861), black women are excluded from the category of true womanhood without debate: "The idea of modesty and virtue in a Louisiana colored-girl might well be ridiculed; as a general thing, she has neither."[2] Decades later, in 1902, a commentator for the popular magazine *The Independent* noted, "I sometimes hear of a virtuous Negro woman, but the idea is absolutely inconceivable to me. . . . I cannot imagine such a creature as a virtuous Negro woman."[3] Another writer, reflecting early-twentieth-century white male stereotypes of black and white women, remarked that, like white women, "Black women had the brains of a child, [and] the passions of a woman" but, unlike white women, were "steeped in centuries of ignorance and savagery, and wrapped about with immoral vices."[4]

Faced with the prevailing views of white society that placed them outside the boundaries of true womanhood, black women had no choice but to defend their virtue. Middle-class black women led this defense, communicating their response in words and in the actions of their daily lives. In doing so they went well beyond defending their own virtue to espouse a broader conception of womanhood that anticipated modern views by more than half a century. Their vision of womanhood combined the public and the private spheres and eventually took for granted a role for women as paid workers outside the home. More than merely an abstract vision, it was a philosophy of womanhood embodied in the lives of countless middle-class black women in both the late nineteenth and the early twentieth centuries.

Virtue Defended

Although black women were seen as devoid of all four of the cardinal virtues of true womanhood—piety, purity, submissiveness, and domesticity—white attention centered on purity. As Hazel Carby suggests, this stemmed in part from the role assigned to black women in the plantation economy. She argues that "two very different but interdependent codes of sexuality operated in the antebellum South, producing opposite definitions of motherhood and womanhood for white and black women which coalesce in the figures of the slave and the mistress."[5] In this scheme, white mistresses gave birth to heirs, slave women to property. A slave woman who attempted to preserve her virtue or sexual autonomy was a threat to the plantation economy. In the words of Harriet Jacobs's slave narrative, *Incidents in the Life of a Slave Girl* (1861), it was "deemed a crime in her [the slave woman] to wish to be virtuous."[6]

Linda Brent, the pseudonym Jacobs used to portray her own life, was an ex-slave struggling to survive economically and protect herself and her daughter from sexual exploitation. In telling her story, she recounts the difficulty all black women faced in practicing the virtues of true womanhood. The contrasting contexts of black and white women's lives called for different, even opposite, responses. While submissiveness and passivity brought protection to the white mistress, these characteristics merely exposed black women to sexual and economic exploitation. Black women, therefore, had to develop strength rather than glory in fragility, and had to be active and assertive rather than passive and submissive.

Though "conventional principles of morality were rendered impossible by the conditions of the slave," as Jacobs argued,[7] Linda Brent embodied the virtues required by black women to survive with dignity in a hostile environment. It was a world in which "Freedom replaced and transcended purity."[8] In the conventional sentimental novels of the period, white heroines who lost their purity chose death or went mad. Black women saw death as an alternative to slavery. "As I passed the wreck of the old meeting house," Linda Brent mused, "where, before Nat Turner's time, the slaves had been allowed to meet for worship, I seemed to hear my father's voice come from it, bidding me not to tarry till I reached freedom or the grave."[9] Painfully aware of her inability to meet the standards of conventional white womanhood ("I do not sit with my children in a home of my own. I still long for a hearthstone of my own, however humble."[10]), Linda Brent nevertheless represented a fundamental challenge to this ideology and the beginnings of an alternative, broader definition of womanhood, one that incorporated resourcefulness and independence.

Three decades later, in the 1890s, black women found reasons to defend their moral integrity with new urgency against attacks from all sides. Views such as those in *The Independent* noted earlier were given respectability by a report of the Slater Fund, a foundation that supported welfare projects for blacks in this period. The foundation asserted without argument, "The negro women of the South are subject to temptations . . . which come to them from the days of their race enslavement. . . . To meet such temptations the negro woman can only offer the resistance of a low moral standard, an inheritance from the system of slavery, made still lower from a lifelong residence in a one-room cabin."[11]

At the 1893 World Columbian Exposition in Chicago, where black women were effectively barred from the exhibits on the achievements of American women, the few black women allowed to address a women's convention there felt compelled to publicly challenge these views. One speaker, Fannie Barrier Williams, shocked her audience by her forthrightness. "I regret the necessity of speaking of the moral question of our women," but "the morality of our home life has been commented on so disparagingly and meanly that we are placed in the unfortunate position of being defenders of our name."[12] She went on to emphasize that black women continued to be the victims of sexual harassment by white men and chided her white female audience for failing to protect their black sisters. In the same vein, black activist and educator Anna Julia Cooper told the audience that it was not a question of "temptations" as much as it was "the painful, patient, and silent toil of mothers to gain title to the bodies of their daughters."[13] Williams was later to write on the same theme. "It is a significant and shameful fact that I am constantly in receipt of letters from the still unprotected women in the South, begging me to find employment for their daughters . . . to save them from going into the homes of the

South as servants as there is nothing to save them from dishonor and degradation."[14] Another black male writer was moved to reveal in *The Independent:* "I know of more than one colored woman who was openly importuned by White women to become the mistress of their husbands, on the ground that they, the white wives, were afraid that, if their husbands did not associate with colored women they would certainly do so with outside white women. . . . And the white wives, for reasons which ought to be perfectly obvious, preferred to have all their husbands do wrong with colored women in order to keep their husbands *straight!*"[15] The attacks on black women's virtue came to a head with a letter written by James Jacks, president of the Missouri Press Association, in which he alleged, "The Negroes in this country were wholly devoid of morality, the women were prostitutes and all were natural thieves and liars."[16] These remarks, coming from such a prominent individual, drew an immediate reaction from black women throughout the country. The most visible was Josephine St. Pierre Ruffin's invitation to black club women to a national convention in Boston in 1895; one hundred women from ten states came to Boston in response. In a memorable address to representatives of some twenty clubs, Ruffin directly attacked the scurrilous accusations:

> Now for the sake of the thousands of self-sacrificing young women teaching and preaching in lonely southern backwoods, for the noble army of mothers who gave birth to these girls, mothers whose intelligence is only limited by their opportunity to get at books, for the cultured women who have carried off the honors at school here and often abroad, for the sake of our own dignity, the dignity of our race and the future good name of our children, it is "meet, right and our bounden duty" to stand forth and declare ourselves and our principles, to teach an ignorant and suspicious world that our aims and interests are identical with those

of all good, aspiring women. Too long have we been silent under unjust and unholy charges. . . . It is to break this silence, not by noisy protestations of what we are not, but by a dignified showing of what we are and hope to become, that we are impelled to take this step, to make of this gathering an object lesson to the world.[17]

At the end of three days of meetings, the National Federation of Afro-American Women was founded, uniting thirty-six black women's clubs in twelve states.[18] The following year, the National Federation merged with the National League of Colored Women to form the National Association of Colored Women (NACW).

Racial Uplift: In Defense of the Black Community

While the catalyst for these national organizations was in part the felt need of black women to defend themselves against moral attacks by whites, they soon went beyond this narrow goal. Twenty years after its founding, the NACW had grown to fifty thousand members in twenty-eight federations and more than one thousand clubs.[19] The founding of these organizations represented a steady movement by middle-class black women to assume more active roles in the community. Historian Deborah Gray White argues that black club women "insisted that only black women could save the black race," a position that inspired them to pursue an almost feverish pace of activities.[20]

These clubs, however, were not the first attempts by black women to participate actively in their communities. Since the late 1700s black women had been active in mutual-aid societies in the North, and in the 1830s northern black women organized anti-slavery societies. In 1880 Mary Ann Shadd Cary and six other women founded the Colored Women's Progressive Franchise Association in

Washington, D.C. Among its stated goals were equal rights for women, including the vote, and the even broader feminist objective of taking "an aggressive stand against the assumption that men only begin and conduct industrial and other things."[21] Giving expression to this goal were a growing number of black women professionals, including the first female physicians to practice in the South.[22] By the turn of the twentieth century, the National Business League, founded by Booker T. Washington, could report that there were "160 Black female physicians, seven dentists, ten lawyers, 164 ministers, assorted journalists, writers, artists, 1,185 musicians and teachers of music, and 13,525 school instructors."[23]

Black women's activism was spurred by the urgency of the struggle for equality, which had led to a greater acceptance of black female involvement in the abolitionist movement. At a time when patriarchal notions of women's domestic role dominated, historian Paula Giddings asserts, "There is no question that there was greater acceptance among Black men of women in activist roles than there was in the broader society."[24] This is not to say that all black men accepted women as equals or the activist roles that many were taking. But when faced with resistance, black women often *demanded* acceptance of their involvement. In 1849, for example, at a black convention in Ohio, "Black women, led by Jane P. Merritt, threatened to boycott the meetings if they were not given a more substantial voice in the proceedings."[25]

In the postbellum period black women continued their struggle for an equal voice in activities for racial uplift in both secular and religious organizations. Historian Evelyn Brooks Higginbotham has offered a detailed account of the successful struggle of black women in the Baptist Church during the late nineteenth century to win acceptance of independent organizations led by themselves.[26] These women's organizations then played a significant role not only in missionary activities, but also in general racial uplift activities in both rural and urban areas.[27] . . .

Black Women and the Suffrage Movement

In their struggle for their own rights, black women moved into the political fray and eagerly joined the movement for passage of a constitutional amendment giving women the right to vote. Unlike white women suffragists, who focused exclusively on the benefits of the vote for their sex, black women saw the franchise as a means of improving the condition of the black community generally. For them, race and gender issues were inseparable. As historian Rosalyn Terborg-Penn emphasizes, black feminists believed that by "increasing the black electorate" they "would not only uplift the women of the race, but help the children and the men as well."[28]

Prominent black women leaders as well as national and regional organizations threw their support behind the suffrage movement. At least twenty black suffrage organizations were founded, and black women participated in rallies and demonstrations and gave public speeches.[29] Ironically, they often found themselves battling white women suffragists as well as men. Southern white women opposed including black women under a federal suffrage as a matter of principle. Northern white women suffragists, eager to retain the support of southern white women, leaned toward accepting a wording of the amendment that would have allowed the southern states to determine their own position on giving black women the vote, a move that would have certainly led to their exclusion.[30]

After the Nineteenth Amendment was ratified in 1920 in its original form, black women braved formidable obstacles in registering to vote. All across the South white registrars used "subterfuge and trickery" to hinder them from registering, including a "grandmother clause" in North Carolina, literacy tests in Virginia, and a $300 poll tax in Columbia, South Carolina. In Columbia, black women "waited up to twelve hours to register" while white women were registered first.[31] In their struggle to register, black women appealed to the NAACP, signed affidavits against registrars who disqualified them, and finally asked for assistance from national white women suffrage leaders. They were especially disappointed in this last attempt. After fighting side by side with white women suffragists for passage of the Nineteenth Amendment, they were rebuffed by the National Woman's Party leadership with the argument that theirs was a race rather than a women's rights issue.[32] Thus, white women continued to separate issues of race and sex that black women saw as inseparable.

Challenging the Primacy of Domesticity

A conflicting conception of the relationship between gender and race issues was not the only major difference in the approaches of black and white women to their roles in the family and society. For most white women, their domestic roles as wives and mothers remained primary. In the late nineteenth century, as they began increasingly to argue for acceptance of their involvement on behalf of child-labor reform and growing urban problems, white women often defended these activities as extensions of their housekeeping role. Historian Barbara Harris comments, "The [white women] pioneers in women's education, who probably did more than anyone else in this period to effect change in the female sphere, advocated education for women and their entrance into the teaching profession on the basis of the values proclaimed by the cult of true womanhood. In a similar way, females defended their careers as authors

and their involvement in charitable, religious, temperance, and moral reform societies."[33] Paula Giddings notes that in this way white women were able "to become more active outside the home while still preserving the probity of 'true womanhood.'"[34] From the birth of white feminism at the Seneca Falls Convention in 1848, white feminists had a difficult time advancing their goals. Their numbers were few and their members often divided over the propriety of challenging the cult of domesticity. . . .

In the late nineteenth century the cult of domesticity remained primary even for white women graduates of progressive women's colleges such as Vassar, Smith, and Wellesley. For them, no less than for those with only a high-school education, "A Woman's Kingdom" was "a well-ordered home."[35] In a student essay, one Vassar student answered her rhetorical question, "Has the educated woman a duty towards the kitchen?" by emphasizing that the kitchen was "exactly where the college woman belonged" for "the orderly, disciplined, independent graduate is the woman best prepared to manage the home, in which lies the salvation of the world."[36] This essay reflects the dilemma faced by these young white women graduates. They found little support in white society to combine marriage and career. In *Beyond Her Sphere* historian Barbara Harris comments, "To a degree that is hard for us to appreciate, a [white] woman had to make a choice: she either married and had children, or she remained single and had a career. . . . Yet, after their exhilarating years at college, many women were far too committed to the pursuit of knowledge or the practical application of their education to retreat willingly to the narrow confines of Victorian domesticity. And so, in surprising numbers, they chose the other alternative and rejected marriage."[37] Historian Carl Degler estimates that in 1900 25 percent of white women college graduates and 50 percent of those receiving Ph.D.s remained single. Graduates of elite women's colleges in the East were even less likely to marry: 45 and 57 percent, respectively, of Bryn Mawr and Wellesley graduates between 1889 and 1909. While the increasing numbers of white women receiving college degrees did contribute to the ranks of activists, this did not result in a frontal attack on the cult of domesticity. In fact, a number of prominent feminists such as Angelina Grimké and Antoinette Brown Blackwell "disappeared from the ranks of feminist leaders after their marriage," and Alice Freeman Palmer, the president of Wellesley College, resigned after her marriage in 1887 to Herbert Palmer, a philosophy professor at Harvard.[38] Society sanctioned only three courses for the middle-class white woman in the Progressive period: "marriage, charity work or teaching."[39] Marriage and motherhood stood as the highest calling. If there were no economic need for them to work, single women were encouraged to do volunteer charity work. For those who needed an independent income, teaching was the only acceptable occupation.

Historian John Rousmaniere suggests that the white college-educated women involved in the early settlement house movement saw themselves as fulfilling the "service norm" so prominent among middle-class women of the day. At the same time, he argues, it was their sense of uniqueness as college-educated women and their felt isolation upon returning home that led them to this form of service. The settlement houses, located as they were in white immigrant, working-class slums, catered to these women's sense of noblesse oblige; they derived a sense of accomplishment from providing an example of genteel middle-class virtues to the poor. Yet the settlement houses also played into a sense of adventure, leading one resident to write, "We feel that we know life for the first time."[40] For all their felt uniqueness, however, with some notable exceptions these women's lives usually offered no fundamental challenge to the basic assumptions of true womanhood. Residency in settlement

houses was for the most part of short duration, and most volunteers eventually embraced their true roles of wife and mother without significant outside involvement. The exceptions were women like Jane Addams, Florence Kelley, Julia Lathrop, and Grace Abbott, who became major figures in the public sphere. Although their lives disputed the doctrine of white women's confinement to the private sphere, the challenge was limited in that most of them did not themselves combine the two spheres of marriage and a public life. Although Florence Kelley was a divorced mother, she nevertheless upheld "the American tradition that men support their families, their wives throughout life," and bemoaned the "retrograde movement" against man as the breadwinner.[41]

Most college-educated black middle-class women also felt a unique sense of mission. They accepted Lucy Laney's 1899 challenge to lift up their race and saw themselves walking in the footsteps of black women activists and feminists of previous generations. But their efforts were not simply "charity work"; their focus was on "racial uplift" on behalf of themselves as well as of the economically less fortunate members of their race.[42] The black women's club movement, in contrast to the white women's, tended to concern themselves from the beginning with the "social and legal problems that confronted both black women and men."[43] While there was certainly some elitism in the NACW's motto, "Lifting as We Climb," these activists were always conscious that they shared a common experience of exploitation and discrimination with the masses and could not completely retreat to the safe haven of their middle-class homes.[44] On the way to meetings they shared the black experience of riding in segregated cars or of being ejected if they tried to do otherwise, as Ida B. Wells did in 1884.[45] Unlike white women for whom, as black feminist Frances Ellen Watkins Harper had emphasized in 1869, "the priorities in the struggle for human rights were sex, not race,"[46] black women could not separate these twin sources of their oppression. They understood that, together with their working-class sisters, they were assumed by whites to have "low animalistic urges." Their exclusion from the category of true womanhood was no less complete than for their less educated black sisters.

It is not surprising, therefore, that the most independent and radical of black female activists led the way in challenging the icons of true womanhood, including on occasion motherhood and marriage. Not only did they chafe under their exclusion from true womanhood, they viewed its tenents as strictures to their efforts on behalf of racial uplift and their own freedom and integrity as women. In 1894 *The Woman's Era* (a black women's magazine) set forth the heretical opinion that "not all women are intended for mothers. Some of us have not the temperament for family life. . . . Clubs will make women think seriously of their future lives, and not make girls think their only alternative is to marry."[47] Anna Julia Cooper, one of the most dynamic women of the period, who had been married and widowed, added that a woman was not "compelled to look to sexual love as the one sensation capable of giving tone and relish, movement and vim to the life she leads. Her horizon is extended."[48] Elsewhere Cooper advised black women that if they married they should seek egalitarian relationships. "The question is not now with the woman 'How shall I so cramp, stunt, and simplify and nullify myself as to make me eligible to the honor of being swallowed up into some little man?' but the problem . . . rests with the man as to how he can so develop . . . to reach the ideal of a generation of women who demand the noblest, grandest and best achievements of which he is capable."[49]

. . . Black activists were far more likely to combine marriage and activism than white activists. . . . Historian Linda Gordon found this to be the case in her study of sixty-nine black and seventy-six white activists in national welfare reform between 1890 and 1945. Only 34 percent of the white activists had ever been married, compared to 85 percent of the black activists. Most of these women (83 percent of blacks and 86 percent of whites) were college educated.[50] She also found that "The white women [reformers], with few exceptions, tended to view married women's economic dependence on men as desirable, and their employment as a misfortune. . . ."[51] On the other hand, although there were exceptions, Gordon writes, " . . . most black women activists projected a favorable view of working women and women's professional aspirations."[52] Nor could it be claimed that these black activists worked out of necessity, since the majority were married to prominent men "who could support them."[53]

Witness Ida B. Wells-Barnett (married to the publisher of Chicago's leading black newspaper) in 1896, her six-month-old son in tow, stumping from city to city making political speeches on behalf of the Illinois Women's State Central Committee. And Mary Church Terrell dismissing the opinion of those who suggested that studying higher mathematics would make her unappealing as a marriage partner with a curt, "I'd take a chance and run the risk."[54] She did eventually marry and raised a daughter and an adopted child. Her husband, Robert Terrell, a Harvard graduate, was a school principal, a lawyer, and eventually a municipal court judge in Washington, D.C. A biographer later wrote of Mary Terrell's life, "But absorbing as motherhood was, it never became a full-time occupation."[55] While this could also be said of Stanton, perhaps what most distinguished black from white feminists and activists was the larger number of the former who unequivocally challenged domesticity and the greater receptivity they found for their views in the black community. As a result, while the cult of domesticity remained dominant in the white community at the turn of the twentieth century, it did not hold sway within the black community.

Rejection of the Public/Private Dichotomy

Black women of the nineteenth and early twentieth centuries saw their efforts on behalf of the black community as necessary for their own survival, rather than as noblesse oblige. "Self preservation," wrote Mary Church Terrell in 1902, "demands that [black women] go among the lowly, illiterate and even the vicious, to whom they are bound by ties of race and sex . . . to reclaim them."[56] These women rejected the confinement to the private sphere mandated by the cult of domesticity. They felt women could enter the public sphere without detriment to the home. As historian Elsa Barkley Brown has emphasized, black women believed that "Only a strong and unified community made up of both women and men could wield the power necessary to allow black people to shape their own lives. Therefore, only when women were able to exercise their full strength would the community be at its full strength. . . ."[57]

In her study of black communities in Illinois during the late Victorian era (1880–1910), historian Shirley Carlson contrasts the black and white communities' expectations of the "ideal woman" at that time:

> The black community's appreciation for and development of the feminine intellect contrasted sharply with the views of the larger society. In the latter, intelligence was regarded as a masculine quality that would "defeminize" women. The ideal white woman, being married, confined herself almost exclusively to the private domain of the household. She was demure, perhaps even self-effacing. She often deferred to her husband's presumably superior judgment, rather than formulating her own

views and vocally expressing them, as black women often did. A woman in the larger society might skillfully manipulate her husband for her own purposes, but she was not supposed to confront or challenge him directly. Black women were often direct, and frequently won community approval for this quality, especially when such a characteristic was directed toward achieving racial uplift. Further, even after her marriage, a black woman might remain in the public domain, possibly in paid employment. The ideal black woman's domain, then, was both the private and public spheres. She was wife and mother, but she could also assume other roles such as schoolteacher, social activist, or businesswoman, among others. And she was intelligent.[58]

In their struggle for an expansion of roles beyond the domestic sphere, black women sometimes had to contend with opposition from within the black community, especially from men, as well as with the larger society's definition of women's proper role. When Ida Wells-Barnett was elected financial secretary of the Afro-American Council, the *Colored American* newspaper suggested that a man should hold the position. While recognizing that "She is a woman of unusual mental powers," the newspaper argued that "the proprieties would have been observed by giving her an assignment more in keeping with the popular idea of women's work and which would not interfere so disastrously with her domestic duties."[59]

Feminist Maggie Lena Walker, the first woman in the nation (and the first African American, male or female) to establish and head a bank and founder of the Richmond Council of Colored Women in Virginia, also met with male opposition in her efforts for racial uplift and expanded women's roles. She too opposed these limitations to the domestic sphere, contending, "Men should not be so pessimistic and down on women's clubs. They don't seek to destroy the home or disgrace the race."[60] The Woman's Union, a Richmond female insurance company founded in 1898, took as its motto, "The Hand That Rocks the Cradle Rules the World." As Brown has clarified, however, "unlike nineteenth-century white women's rendering of that expression to signify the limitation of woman's influence to that which she had by virtue of rearing her sons, the idea as these women conceived it transcended the separation of private and public spheres and spoke to the idea that women, while not abandoning their roles as wives and mothers, could also move into economic and political activities in ways that would support rather than conflict with family and community."[61]

Although many black males, like most white males, opposed the expansion of black women's roles, many other black males supported women's activism and even criticized their brethren for their opposition. Echoing Maggie Walker's sentiments, T. Thomas Fortune wrote, "The race could not succeed nor build strong citizens, until we have a race of women competent to do more than hear a brood of negative men."[62] Support for women's suffrage was especially strong among black males. . . . Black men saw women's suffrage as advancing the political empowerment of the race. For black women, suffrage promised to be a potent weapon in their fight for their rights, for education and jobs.[63]

A Threefold Commitment

An expanded role for black women did not end at the ballot box or in activities promoting racial uplift. Black middle-class women demanded a place for themselves in the paid labor force. Theirs was a threefold commitment to family, career, and social movements. According to historian Rosalyn Terborg-Penn, "most black feminists and leaders had been wives and mothers who worked yet found time not only to struggle for the

good of their sex, but for their race." Such a threefold commitment "was not common among white women."[64]

In her study of eighty African American women throughout the country who worked in "the feminized professions" (such as teaching) between the 1880s and the 1950s, historian Stephanie Shaw comments on the way they were socialized to lives dedicated to home, work, and community. When these women were children, she indicates, "the model of womanhood held before [them] was one of achievement in *both* public and private spheres. Parents cast domesticity as a complement rather than a contradiction to success in public arenas."[65] Later, in her discussion of one woman whose husband opposed her desire to work outside the home, Shaw observes, "It seems, then, that Henry Riddick subscribed to an old tradition (which was becoming less and less influential in general, and which *had never been a real tradition among most black families*) wherein the wife of a 'good' husband did not need to work for pay."[66]

An analysis of the lives of 108 of the first generation of black clubwomen bears this out. "The career-oriented clubwomen, comments Paula Giddings, "seemed to have no ambivalence concerning their right to work, whether necessity dictated it or not."[67] According to Giddings, three-quarters of these 108 early clubwomen were married, and almost three-quarters worked outside the home, while one-quarter had children.

A number of these clubwomen and other black women activists not only had careers but also spoke forcefully about the importance of work, demonstrating surprisingly progressive attitudes with a very modern ring. "The old doctrine that a man marries a woman to support her," quipped Walker, "is pretty nearly thread-bare to-day."[68] "Every dollar a woman makes," she declared in a 1912 speech to the Federation of Colored Women's Clubs, "some man gets the direct benefit of same. Every woman was by Divine Providence created for some man; not for some man to marry, take home and support, but for the purpose of using her powers, ability, health and strength, to forward the financial . . . success of the partnership into which she may go, if she will. . . ."[69] Being married with three sons and an adopted daughter did not in any way dampen her commitment to gender equality and an expanded role for wives.

Such views were not new. In a pamphlet entitled *The Awakening of the Afro-American Woman*, written in 1897 to celebrate the earlier founding of the National Association of Colored Women, Victoria Earle Matthews referred to black women as "co-breadwinners in their families."[70] Almost twenty years earlier, in 1878, feminist writer and activist Frances Ellen Harper sounded a similar theme of equality when she insisted, "The women as a class are quite equal to the men in energy and executive ability." She went on to recount instances of black women managing small and large farms in the postbellum period.[71]

It is clear that in the process of racial uplift work, black middle-class women also included membership in the labor force as part of their identity. They were well ahead of their time in realizing that their membership in the paid labor force was critical to achieving true equality with men. For this reason, the National Association of Wage Earners insisted that all black women should be able to support themselves.[72] . . .

. . . A number of women began their fight for careers when still very young and continued this battle throughout their lives. Braving the opposition of family and friends, Terrell dared to earn an A.B. degree in mathematics from Oberlin, even though "It was held by most people that women were unfitted to do their work in the home if they studied Latin, Greek and higher mathematics." Upon graduation, she defied her father's furious objection to her employment and took a teaching job at

Wilberforce College. For her act of rebellion she was "disinherited" by her irate father, who "refused to write to me for a year."[73] But Terrell enjoyed the full support of her husband, Robert.

In 1963 in *The Feminine Mystique*, Betty Friedan wrote, "I never knew a woman, when I was growing up, who used her mind, played her own part in the world, and also loved, and had children."[74] Her experience, however, was only of white middle-class women. In fact, many black middle-class women did fit this description, and Friedan's lack of acquaintance with these women attests to the deep chasm that has historically separated the worlds of black and white women. As W. E. B. Du Bois commented as early as 1924, "Negro women more than the women of any other group in America are the protagonists in the fight for an economically independent womanhood in modern countries. . . . The matter of economic independence is, of course, the central fact in the struggle of women for equality."[75]

Defining Black Womanhood

In the late 1930s when Mary McLeod Bethune, the acknowledged leader of black women at the time and an adviser to President Franklin Roosevelt on matters affecting the black community, referred to herself as the representative of "Negro womanhood" and asserted that black women had "room in their lives to be wives and mothers as well as to have careers," she was not announcing a new idea.[76] As Terborg-Penn emphasizes:

> . . . most black feminists and leaders had been wives and mothers who worked yet found time not only to struggle for the good of their sex, but for their race. Until the 1970s, however, this threefold commitment—to family and to career and to one or more social movements— was not common among white women. The key to the uniqueness among black feminists of this period appears to be their link with the

past. The generation of the woman suffrage era had learned from their late nineteenth-century foremothers in the black women's club movement, just as the generation of the post World War I era had learned and accepted the experiences of the preceding generation. Theirs was a sense of continuity, a sense of group consciousness that transcended class.[77]

This "sense of continuity" with past generations of black women was clearly articulated in 1917 by Mary Talbert, president of the NACW. Launching an NACW campaign to save the home of the late Frederick Douglass, she said, "We realize today is the psychological moment for us women to show our true worth and prove the Negro women of today measure up to those sainted women of our race, who passed through the fire of slavery and its galling remembrances."[78] Talbert certainly lived up to her words, going on to direct the NAACP's antilynching campaign and becoming the first woman to receive the NAACP's Spingarn Medal for her achievements.

What then is the expanded definition of true womanhood found in these black middle-class women's words and embodied in their lives? First, they tended to define womanhood in an inclusive rather than exclusive sense. Within white society, true womanhood was defined so narrowly that it excluded all but a small minority of white upper- and upper-middle-class women with husbands who were able to support them economically. Immigrant women and poor women—of any color—did not fit this definition. Nor did black women as a whole, regardless of class, because they were all seen as lacking an essential characteristic of true womanhood—virtue. For black women, however, true womanhood transcended class and race boundaries. Anna Julia Cooper called for "reverence for woman as woman regardless of rank, wealth, or culture."[79] Unlike white women, black women refused to isolate gender issues from other forms of oppression such as race and nationality, including the struggles of

colonized nations of Africa and other parts of the world. Women's issues, they suggested, were tied to issues of oppression, whatever form that oppression might assume.

As discussed above, black women organized to defend their virtue against the vicious attacks of white society. They pointed out—Fannie Barrier Williams and Ida B. Wells-Barnett forcefully among them—that the real culprits were white males who continued to harass and prey upon them with the tacit support of white women. At times they also chastised black males for failing to protect them. Black women obviously saw themselves as virtuous, both individually and as a group. Yet, apart from defending themselves against these attacks, black women did not dwell upon virtue in defining womanhood. theirs was not the sexless purity forced on white women by white males who placed their women on pedestals while seeking out black women for their pleasure. . . .

The traditional white ideology of true womanhood separated the active world of men from the passive world of women. As we have seen, women's activities were confined to the home, where their greatest achievement was maintaining their own virtue and decorum and rearing future generations of male leaders. Although elite black women did not reject their domestic roles as such, many expanded permissible public activities beyond charity work to encompass employment and participation in social progress. They founded such organizations as the Atlanta Congress of Colored Women, which historian Erlene Stetson claims was the first grassroots women's movement organized "for social and political good."[80]

The tendency of black women to define womanhood inclusively and to see their roles extending beyond the boundaries of the home led them naturally to include other characteristics in their vision. One of these was intellectual equality. While the "true" woman was portrayed as submissive ("conscious of inferiority, and therefore grateful for support"),[81] according to literary scholar Hazel Carby, black women such as Anna Julia Cooper argued for a "partnership with husbands on a plane of intellectual equality."[82] Such equality could not exist without the pursuit of education, particularly higher education, and participation in the labor force. Cooper, like many other black women, saw men's opposition to higher education for women as an attempt to make them conform to a narrow view of women as "sexual objects for exchange in the marriage market."[83] Education for women at all levels became a preoccupation for many black feminists and activists. Not a few—like Anna Cooper, Mary L. Europe, and Estelle Pinckney Webster—devoted their entire lives to promoting it, especially among young girls. Womanhood, as conceived by black women, was compatible with—indeed, required—intellectual equality. In this they were supported by the black community. While expansion of educational opportunities for women was a preoccupation of white feminists in the nineteenth century, as I noted above, a college education tended to create a dilemma in the lives of white women who found little community support for combining marriage and career. In contrast, as Shirley Carlson emphasizes, "The black community did not regard intelligence and femininity as conflicting values, as the larger society did. That society often expressed the fear that intelligent women would develop masculine characteristics—a thickening waist, a diminution of breasts and hips, and finally, even the growth of facial hair. Blacks seemed to have had no such trepidations, or at least they were willing to have their women take these risks."[84]

In addition to women's rights to an education, Cooper, Walker, Alexander, Terrell, the leaders of the National Association of Wage Earners, and countless other black feminists and activists insisted on their right to work outside the home. They dared to continue very active lives after marriage. Middle-class black women's insistence on the right to pursue careers paralleled their view that a true woman could move in both the private and the public spheres and that marriage did not require submissiveness or subordination. In fact, as Shirley Carlson has observed in her study of black women in Illinois in the late Victorian period, many activist black women "continued to be identified by their maiden names—usually as their middle names or as part of their hyphenated surnames—indicating that their own identities were not subsumed in their husbands."[85]

While the views of black women on womanhood were all unusual for their time, their insistence on the right of all women—including wives and mothers—to work outside the home was the most revolutionary. In their view the need for paid work was not merely a response to economic circumstances, but the fulfillment of women's right to self-actualization. Middle-class black women like Ida B. Wells-Barnett, Margaret Washington, and Mary Church Terrell, married to men who were well able to support them, continued to pursue careers throughout their lives, and some did so even as they reared children. These women were far ahead of their time, foreshadowing societal changes that would not occur within the white community for several generations. . . .

Rather than accepting white society's views of paid work outside the home as deviant, therefore, black women fashioned a competing ideology of womanhood—one that supported the needs of an oppressed black community and their own desire for gender equality. Middle-class black women, especially, often supported by the black community, developed a consciousness of themselves as persons who were competent and capable of being influential. They believed in higher education as a means of sharpening their talents, and in a sexist world that looked on men as superior, they dared to see themselves as equals both in and out of marriage.

This new ideology of womanhood came to have a profound impact on the conception of black families and gender roles. Black women's insistence on their role as co-breadwinners clearly foreshadows today's dual-career and dual-worker families. Since our conception of the family is inseparably tied to our views of women's and men's roles, the broader definition of womanhood advocated by black women was also an argument against the traditional family. The cult of domesticity was anchored in a patriarchal notion of women as subordinate to men in both the family and the larger society. The broader definition of womanhood championed by black middle-class women struck a blow for an expansion of women's rights in society and a more egalitarian position in the home, making for a far more progressive system among blacks at this time than among whites.

NOTES

1. Quoted in Hazel V. Carby, *Reconstructing Womanhood: The Emergence of the Afro-American Woman Novelist* (New York: Oxford University Press, 1987), p. 26.

2. Ibid.

3. Quoted in Paula Giddings, *When and Where I Enter: The Impact of Black Women and Race and Sex in America* (New York: Bantam Books, 1985), p. 82.

4. Ibid., p. 82.

5. Carby, *Reconstructing Womanhood*, p. 20.

6. Harriet Jacobs, *Incidents in the Life of a Slave Girl*, L. Baria Child, ed. (1861; paperback reprint, New York: Harcourt Brace Jovanovich, 1973), p. 29.

7. Carby, *Reconstructing Womanhood*, pp. 58–59.

8. Ibid., p. 60.

9. Jacobs, *Incidents in the Life of a Slave Girl*, p. 93.

10. Ibid., p. 207.

11. Quoted in Giddings, *When and Where I Enter*, p. 82.

12. Ibid., p. 86.

13. Ibid., p. 87.

14. Ibid., pp. 86–87.

15. Ibid., p. 87.

16. Quoted in Sharon Harley, "Black Women in a Southern City: Washington, D.C., 1890–1920," pp. 59–78 in Joanne V. Hawks and Shiela L. Skemp, eds., *Sex, Race, and the Role of Women in the South* (Jackson, Miss.: University Press of Mississippi, 1983), p. 72.

17. Eleanor Flexner, *Century of Struggle: The Woman's Rights Movement in the United States* (Cambridge: Harvard University Press, 1959), p. 194.

18. Giddings, *When and Where I Enter*, p. 93.

19. Ibid., p. 95. For a discussion of elitism in the "uplift" movement and organizations, see Kevin K. Gains, *Uplifting the Race: Black Leadership, Politics, and Culture in the Twentieth Century* (Chapel Hill, N.C.: University of North Carolina Press, 1996). Black reformers, enlightened as they were, could not entirely escape being influenced by Social Darwinist currents of the times.

20. Deborah Gray White, *Too Heavy a Load: Black Women in Defense of Themselves, 1894–1994* (New York: W. W. Norton & Company, 1999), p. 36.

21. Quoted in Giddings, *When and Where I Enter*, p. 75.

22. Ibid.

23. Ibid.

24. Ibid., p. 59.

25. Ibid.

26. Evelyn Brooks Higginbotham, *Righteous Discontent: The Women's Movement in the Black Baptist Church, 1880–1920* (Cambridge: Harvard University Press, 1993).

27. Ibid., p. 20.

28. Rosalyn Terborg-Penn, "Discontented Black Feminists: Prelude and Postscript to the Passage of the Nineteenth Amendment," pp. 261–278 in Lois Scharf and Joan M. Jensen, eds., *Decades of Discontent: The Woman's Movement, 1920–1940* (Westport, Conn.: Greenwood Press, 1983), p. 264.

29. Ibid., p. 261.

30. Ibid., p. 264.

31. Ibid., p. 266.

32. Ibid., pp. 266–267.

33. Barbara J. Harris, *Beyond Her Sphere: Women and the Professions in American History* (Westport, Conn.: Greenwood Press, 1978), pp. 85–86.

34. Giddings, *When and Where I Enter*, p. 81.

35. John P. Rousmaniere, "Cultural Hybrid in the Slums: The College Woman and the Settlement House, 1889–1984," *American Quarterly* 22 (Spring 1970): p. 56.

36. Ibid., p. 55.

37. Barbara J. Harris, *Beyond Her Sphere*, pp. 101–102.

38. Ibid., pp. 101–102.

39. Rousmaniere, "Cultural Hybrid in the Slums," p. 56.

40. Ibid., p. 61.

41. Quoted in Linda Gordon, "Black and White Visions of Welfare: Women's Welfare Activism, 1890–1945," *Journal of American History* 78 (September 1991): 583.

42. Giddings, *When and Where I Enter*, p. 97.

43. Estelle Freedman, "Separatism as Strategy: Female Institution Building and American Feminism, 1870–1930," pp. 445–462 in Nancy F. Cott, ed., *Women Together: Organizational Life* (New Providence, RI: K. G. Saur, 1994), p. 450; Nancy Forderhase, "'Limited Only by Earth and Sky': The Louisville Woman's Club and Progressive Reform, 1900–1910," pp. 365–381 in Cott, ed. *Women Together: Organizational Life* (New Providence, RI: K. G. Saur, 1994); . . . Mary Dell Brady, "Kansas Federation of Colored Women's Clubs, 1900–1930," pp. 382–408 in Nancy F. Cott, *Women Together*.

44. Higginbotham, *Righteous Discontent*, pp. 206–207.

45. Giddings, *When and Where I Enter*, p. 22.

46. Terborg-Penn, "Discontented Black Feminists," p. 267.

47. Giddings, *When and Where I Enter*, p. 108.

48. Ibid., pp. 108–109.

49. Ibid., p. 113.

50. Linda Gordon, "Black and Whites Visions of Welfare," p. 583.

51. Ibid., p. 582.

52. Ibid., p. 585.

53. Ibid., pp. 568–69.

54. Ibid., p. 109.

55. Quoted in Giddings, ibid., p. 110.

56. Ibid., p. 97.

57. Elsa Barkley Brown, "Womanist Consciousness: Maggie Lena Walker and the Independent Order of Saint Luke," *Journal of Women in Culture and Society* 14, no. 3 (1989): 188.

58. Shirley J. Carlson, "Black Ideals of Womanhood in the Late Victorian Era," *Journal of Negro History* 77, no. 2 (Spring 1992): 62. Carlson notes that these black women of the late Victorian era also observed the proprieties of Victorian womanhood in their deportment and appearance but combined them with the expectations of the black community for intelligence, education, and active involvement in racial uplift.

59. Giddings, *When and Where I Enter*, pp. 110–111.

60. Brown, "Womanist Consciousness," p. 180.

61. Ibid., p. 178.

62. Quoted in Giddings, *When and Where I Enter*, p. 117.

63. See Rosalyn Terborg-Penn, *African American Women in the Struggle for the Vote, 1850–1920* (Bloomington, Ind.: Indiana University Press, 1998).

64. Rosalyn Terborg-Penn, "Discontented Black Feminists," p. 274.

65. Stephanie J. Shaw, *What a Woman Ought to Be and to Do: Black Professional Women Workers During the Jim Crow Era* (Chicago: University of Chicago Press, 1996), p. 29. Shaw details the efforts of family and community to socialize these women for both personal achievement and community service. The sacrifices some families made included sending them to private schools and sometimes relocating the entire family near a desired school.

66. Ibid., p. 126. Italics added.

67. Giddings, *When and Where I Enter*, p. 108.

68. Brown, "Womanist Consciousness," p. 622.

69. Ibid., p. 623.

70. Carby, *Reconstructing Womanhood*, p. 117.

71. Quoted in Giddings, *When and Where I Enter*, p. 72.

72. Brown, "Womanist Consciousness," p. 182.

73. Quoted in Giddings, *Where and When I Enter*, p. 109.

74. Betty Friedan, *The Feminine Mystique* (New York: Dell, 1963), p. 68.

75. Quoted in Giddings, *Where and When I Enter*, p. 197.

76. Quoted in Terborg-Penn, "Discontented Black Feminists," p. 274.

77. Ibid., p. 274.

78. Quoted in Giddings, *Where and When I Enter*, p. 138.

79. Quoted in Carby, *Reconstructing Womanhood,* p. 98.

80. Erlene Stetson, "Black Feminism in Indiana, 1893–1933," *Phylon* 44 (December 1983): 294.

81. Quoted in Barbara Welter, "The Cult of True Womanhood: 1820–1860," p. 318.

82. Carby, *Reconstructing Womanhood,* p. 100.

83. Ibid., p. 99.

84. Carlson, "Black Ideals of Womanhood in the Late Victorian Era," p. 69. This view is supported by historian Evelyn Brooks Higginbotham's analysis of schools for blacks established by northern Baptists in the postbellum period, schools that encouraged the attendance of both girls and boys. Although, as Higginbotham observes, northern Baptists founded these schools in part to spread white middle-class values among blacks, blacks nevertheless came to see higher education as an instrument of their own liberation (*Righteous Discontent,* p. 20).

85. Ibid., p. 67.

THINKING ABOUT THE READING

How were the needs of black women during the 19th century movement for gender equality different from those of white women? How did their lives differ with regard to the importance of marriage, motherhood, and employment? What does Landry mean when he says that for these women, "race and gender are inseparable"? What was the significance of the "clubs" for these black women? How does this article change what you previously thought about the contemporary women's movement?

What Is Wanting?

Gender, Equality, and Desire

Judith Levine

(2002)

There is a powerful norm of heterosexuality, and a powerful double standard. Girls focus largely on appearance and boyfriends, boys focus on machismo and sexual gains. To deviate is not accepted.

—Laurie Mandel, Dowling College,
on suburban middle schools (1999)

Gender starts cutting down kids' experiential options early: a pre-school teacher told me the boys in her class refuse to use the red crayon because "red is a girl's color." By middle or junior high school, the gender codes have been cast in steel, enforced both by the "hidden gender curricula" of school programs and by the "feeling rules" kept in check by both adults and other children (Thorne 1997; Connell 1995). Kids, especially during the jangled early- and midadolescent years, are urgently concerned with what sociologist Gary Fine calls "impression management," the personal effort to control and monitor what other people think of you. For the vast majority of young people, social survival is a matter of conformity. And one of the safest survival strategies is to toe the line of gender, assiduously acting the part assigned to the body you're in and steering clear of people who don't.

In school, perhaps more than at home (which is why parents are sometimes appalled when they catch their kids unawares among their friends), both masculinity and femininity are narrow balancing beams, easy to tumble off.

Girls must appear amenable to sex but not too amenable. If a girl is standoffish or proud, she is a "bitch." But if she talks too dirty or behaves too lasciviously, she's a "slut" or a "ho." A boy who does the latter is admired as a "player."

If he does the latter toward girls, that is. Because if a boy is shy or insufficiently enthusiastic about, say, discussing the size of a classmate's breasts, he can find himself ostracized as a "faggot." Masculinity is policed chiefly by boys against other boys, and homophobia is its billy club. "Anything that is feminine, boys learn to reject—sensitivity, empathy, vulnerability," said Deborah Rakowsky, a guidance counselor in a suburban middle school. But this is not just a phenomenon of lockstep suburban conformity. Carol Kapuscik, the mother of a seventeen-year-old male skateboarding fanatic named Max, described how her son participated in casual gay-bashing, even though he had grown up in the sexually iconoclastic Lower East Side of New York, with many gay and lesbian family friends and neighbors (the waitresses at the corner restaurant are drag queens). "Everything they denigrate is 'faggot,'" said Carol. "That's a 'faggot' movie, 'faggot' pants, a 'faggot' video game. I've even heard them refer to certain foods as 'faggot.'" She did not think her son uses the term against other boys but said, "Even though they throw the word around like it was nothing, when a kid is called a faggot, it really has the power to sting."

No wonder few gay or lesbian kids have the wherewithal to be "out" in junior high or high school. As a straight boy who graduated from high school in rural Vermont told me, "Everybody called everybody 'faggot' or 'queer.' But there were no gay people at school." I imagine his second observation was wrong.

The Australian sociologist Bob Connell has pointed out that masculine and feminine styles differ from school to school and among social classes, races, or ethnic groups. Michael Reichert, a Pennsylvania sociologist whose work on boys has taken him both to Philadelphia housing projects and to an elite suburban boys' prep school, noted, for instance, that a working-class boy might assert his dominance by beating up another kid, whereas an upper-class boy would do the deed verbally, with sarcasm (verbal "dissing," of course, is a high art of hip-hop as well) (Reichert 1997).

Teens even stick to gender roles when they dissemble about sex. "Three times more junior high school boys than girls say they have had sex, at an earlier age and with more partners. What does this mean?" asked sociologist Mike Males. "Are a few girls really getting around? Are boys having sex with aliens? Each other? (Alexander et al. 1993). (In his incredulity that the last could happen, Males isn't unlike the kids he's talking about.) Another study found that when kids lied, boys tended to state falsely that they had had sex, whereas girls said they were virgins. (Newcomer and Udry 1988).

What may be most consistent about gender norms is the degree of their totalitarianism. A child, said Connell, does have the option to "collude, resist, or conform" when faced with the prevailing gender codes. If he resists, he may reap the benefits of pride, integrity, and a certain liberation. But he will also pay a price. As sociologist Laurie Mandel put it, "To deviate is not accepted."

None of this is good for kids—or for sex. For while young people are doing their damnedest to avoid rocking the boat of gender, there's evidence that gender is sinking the ship, with girls and boys clinging to the gunwales as it goes down. Interestingly, it's not just gendered behavior (what cultural theories call the *performance* of gender) but even gendered *thought* that narrows the sexual experience, to individual's detriment. Research shows that strong belief in the ideologies of masculinity and femininity makes for bad and unsafe sexual relations. Joseph Pleck, a research psychologist at the University of Illinois at Champaign-Urbana and one the founders of the pro-feminist men's movement, discovered that young men who subscribe to traditional ideologies of masculinity (for example, who agree strongly that men should be sure of themselves or that men are always ready for sex) are less likely to use condoms. Evidence of dating violence between teenagers is spotty but troubling. Although a certain number of young couples report relationships of frequent mutual violence, girls are much more likely to be the victims than the instigators or perpetrators; they report, along with extreme physical injury, emotional hurt and persistent fear following the incidents ("Fact Sheet" n.d.). Extreme masculine identity, including the sort that is socially rewarded, has also been linked with violence. In 1986, the FBI found that college football and basketball players, the masculine elite, were reported to the police for sexual assault 38 percent more often than the average male student. Members of prestigious fraternities were also disproportionately involved in sexual violence against women (Lefkowitz 1998, pp. 278–279).

Nor does femininity stand girls in good stead for taking care of themselves sexually.

According to Deborah Tolman, a senior research fellow at the Wellesley College Center for Research on Women, "Feminine ideology is associated with diminished sexual health." The more concerned a girl is with looking pretty and behaving tractably, the more likely she is to bend to peer pressure from older guys, to have sex while high on drugs, and to take sexual risks such as unprotected intercourse. The "rejection of conventional feminine ideology," on the other hand, "is associated with more agency," said Tolman. The less "girly" a girl is, the more she'll take hold of her own sexual destiny, having sex when, with whom, and in what ways she wants.

Gendered sexuality goes far deeper than social attitudes or behavior. It shapes our very fantasies, which are the wellspring of desire, not only what we believe we should want, but also what, in our hearts and groins, we do want: the silent, menacing male stranger; the reserved but sexually yielding, then voracious, girl next door. Without alternatives to these ingrained fantasies (and again, particularly in the hyperconformist adolescent years) these caricatured desires can impede the process of discovering and accepting the idiosyncracies of what a person might really want in sex and of finding emotional fulfillment in relationships.

[. . .]

What Girls Can Learn

Desire resides in the body

"How do I know when I want to have sex?" Melissa, the thirteen-year-old daughter of a Washington, D.C., union officer asked her mother. "When you want it so much that you feel you can't not have it," the mother, Andrea Ely, answered. She went on to say that you could always have sex in the future, but once you'd had it, it would change the way you felt about the other person and you could not

undo what you had done or unfeel what you felt. Consider your decision, she was saying. It will have emotional consequences. But she was also telling her daughter that the call of the body, if strong enough, was worth listening to—that desire is worth taking seriously.

For some girls, like some Deborah Tolman interviewed, the signals of desire are palpable and recognizable. These girls describe feelings of great urgency and "unmistakable intensity," Tolman wrote (Tolman 1994, p. 255). "The feelings are so strong inside you that they're just like ready to burst," one girl said. Said another. "My body says yes yes yes yes" (but her mind, no no no). Teen girls' desire can have almost flulike symptoms, reported guidance counselor Rakowsky, laughing and shaking her head. "They tell me it makes their stomach hurt, it makes them sleepy, it gives them a headache."

But desire doesn't always speak clearly. Listening requires interpretation. And, sadly, many girls tell us that they don't know if they're feeling sexual desire or pleasure at all.

Writer and former sex educator Sharon Thompson believes it is imperative for girls to learn to identify and analyze desire, because it fuels much-needed female independence. "Here's a young girl and she's feeling excited. She might be excited just in general, about the idea of becoming involved with someone or some kind of person, about being in her body at that time of life." Whatever the feelings, she told me, "it's really important for girls to recognize and expect that feeling and understand there is a sexual component of that feeling. To sit back quietly in their bodies and their minds, and get a sense of all the factors and become at ease with it."

Masturbation, said Thompson, is the first step toward understanding, and owning, one's desire. "One of the things that masturbation teaches is that much of what you feel is your own body. So many girls elide all the feelings that have in a relationship with one person.

They don't recognize that a large part of those feelings are really there already, and they can have those feelings without that person. A girl can realize, 'Oh, I had something before this [relationship].' That [realization] is good and sustaining. It can carry someone through romantic disappointment," as well as help a girl extricate herself from an abusive or destructive, but sexually compelling, relationship.

I asked Thompson if girls should be taught, through books and films or conversations with adults or each other, how to name and classify the sensations of arousal. "It's essential," she said. "A large number of girls have those feelings and have no idea what they are. They only suspect they have to do with sex." When arousal occurs, "they go into a sort of trance state and absent themselves from themselves; they have no idea what happens next. They've been educated to believe they won't have those feelings, and it sends them into this hysteria. If only there was some foreknowledge about the feelings and a permission to have them, they could be recognized, and they could make decisions to protect themselves." Thompson tells educators to take advantage of the feminine culture of "girltalk," the intense, minutely detailed, and endless conversations among girls about love and romance—but rarely, specifically, about sex. "Girls will spend hours and hours discussing what everyone wore," she said, "but does anyone ever ask, 'And did your vagina get wet?' Now *that*," she said, laughing, "would be a useful conversation!"

Crucial to getting that useful conversation going between girls is the explicit message from adults that girls *do* desire and that their feelings can be just as pressing as boys.' The writer Mary Kay Blakely was the dean at a Catholic school in the 1970s where the headmaster each year gave a lecture on sex. "He'd have two glasses on the podium," she recounted. "He'd drop an aspirin into one, and it would just sit there. He'd say, 'This is how girls feel about sex.'" Into the other, the headmaster, a priest, would drop an Alka-Seltzer, to illustrate boys' sexuality. "After that, I'd have a stream of desperate girls in my office," said Blakely. "They'd tell me, 'I'm the Alka-Seltzer, not the aspirin! Is there something wrong with me?'" Blakely assured them that, no there was nothing wrong with them. In fact, she implied, they were lucky to have those effervescent feelings, and encouraged them to come back and talk more when they were thinking about how to express them.

Fantasy is a way of exploring transgressive desire

As a child, the dancer and poet Flora Martin, daughter of permissive but not libertine parents, had heard little but positive, accurate things about sex. But of course she had no way of knowing what it was really like. So she imagined the parts she knew about, in the imagery of her own childish experience. "I thought intercourse must be great," said Flora, who was thirty-three when we talked. "To have part of another person inside of you, that seemed so . . . comforting. Like being hugged from the inside."

She also had an active, early fantasy life. "When I was about seven, I would lie in my bed and have fantasies about growing up and getting to live on my own. In my favorite one, I had a big apartment with one room. The room was empty except for two things: a huge bed with thousands of pillows and beautiful covers on it, and a refrigerator filled with ice cream and cake. My idea of being a grown up was that you could have sex and eat ice cream and cake all the time."

To me, this fantasy seemed so luscious, but also so *wholesome*, befitting the product of the sensual but eminently sane and upright family I knew. Then I learned from her younger sister that Flora's thoughts ran afoul of one of the Martin family's values. If the Martins held both food and sexuality in high regard, they were snobs about the former. In their house, overindulgence in food was looked upon with disapproval, and store-bought sweets were beneath contempt. For Flora, the cake and ice cream—not the sex!—supplied what the sex therapist Jack Morin calls one of the "corner stones" of eroticized desire: the violation of prohibitions (Morin 1995, 83–85). In a family atmosphere of sexual openness and liberty, which nonetheless transmitted a sense of boundaries, this daughter was reaching toward what sex can be at its best: a permissible transgression, a forbidden but guiltless pleasure.

A girl can be both a "sex object" and a sexual subject

"My main problem has to do with women being seen as sex objects," Linda Bailey, a nurse, told me and a group of mothers who had gotten together in a Berkeley, California, living room to talk about sex and child raising. "I still have a really hard time with the idea that Olivia might be flitting from one relationship to another sexually, because to me somehow that seems like she would be viewing herself as a sexual object, as opposed to being a whole person. . . . I don't know how she will reconcile being tough and feisty and independent with all the sexy stuff about being a girl." Bailey said that even at five, her daughter was learning at school that girls are (or should be) beautiful, first and foremost.

Can a girl care about beauty and also be tough and feisty? Can she be a "sex object" and also a "whole person"? Unlike many other feminists, Sharon Thompson doesn't worry too much about girls who primp and vamp. "They are trying on differ-ent ways to be an adult woman," she said of the problem of "objectification." "It's almost an extension of dress-up. It's not necessarily [developmentally] definitive or bad. When you try on acting sexual, at least it's an admission, a taking possession of a sexual

self." Of course, she'd like to see a much wider range of what it is to be sexy in American culture, including lesbian styles, butch, femme, fat, thin, and in between, and so would I. "It's a misfortune that we don't like the styles of being sexual that are most prevalent in our culture," she said, meaning "we" feminists. "But when you put on one of those images, it doesn't mean you can now pretend you don't have a mind. You can still possess other parts of yourself."

Patricia Villas, forty-one, is the Peruvian American mother of a boy and two girls and a food service manager. She lives not far from Linda Bailey (but on the other side of the tracks) in Oakland. She says she's worried about her thirteen-year-old daughter, Moira, who is beginning to hate her body because she is plump. Villas is trying to help her daughter eat more healthily rather than diet or become obsessed with her size. Unlike Bailey, Villas is more concerned that her daughter will find her own body insufficiently sexy instead of overly so. In talking with Moira, she emphasizes the positive value of female sexual subjectivity over the dangers of masculine sexual objectification. Villas believes that knowing herself sexually will help Moira make the right decisions. "I wanted to have sex as a teenager. . . . I want Moira to understand how I learned about my body, what it feels like. I masturbated, I fantasized, and I had sex with boys. Sex is learning about yourself, in the same way as learning about all the other things you like. . . . I told her about the clit. I pointed it out: there it is. I tell her, 'You demand that [satisfaction]. You have needs. You have them fulfilled. And you have pride, you have dignity. You make the choices.'"

Desire alone does not guarantee sexual satisfaction

We are all trained to think that sexual pleasure goes without saying—and that everyone knows sex is pleasurable. That's why so many people feel there's something wrong with them when sex doesn't "work."

But girls don't always have a pleasurable experience of sex. And too many begin to suspect that it isn't what it's cracked up to be and that there's not much you can do about it except lower your expectations. "It's not love, it's not even a relationship. It's not really always, like, fun. It's just something that you do," a fifteen-year-old suburban girl said of "hooking up," which means anything from light petting to anal or vaginal intercourse. Emotional detachment such as she describes isn't the only cause of adolescent sexual ennui, though. Pleasure isn't automatic, even when affection and desire are plentiful. "It hurt, but it was beautiful," was a common description of first intercourse among girls Thompson interviewed in researching her book *Going All the Way*.

Asked what messages young people need to hear about sex, California sex and marriage therapist Marty Klein told me: "Sex shouldn't hurt. If it hurts, you're doing it wrong." But how do you get from "sex shouldn't hurt" to doing it "right"? The answer: Young people need to learn that desire isn't enough, love isn't enough. Sexual desire is cultivated, and technique is learned.

"This is the thing I am trying to do differently," said Sally Keirnan, one cool California afternoon in late August 1997, when we talked with her friend and longtime business partner, Terry Rorty, about raising their daughters, River Keirnan, fourteen, and Heather Rorty, thirteen. "I grew up in Boulder, with liberal parents. My mother talked to me about the mechanics of sex—the penis goes in the vagina, you know—but she didn't talk about pleasure. She did say, 'You'll like it when you get there.' But I couldn't imagine anything pleasant about it." Sally pushed her blond hair behind her ears and continued: "The other thing my mother never

told me anything about was that there was movement, or ejaculation."

The two women, both in their forties, live in a wealthy Bay Area suburb, where they run an import-export business. Recently, they had taken their girls out to a special dinner, during which they imparted some of their experience, wisdom, pleasures, and doubts about sex, love, and desire. Sally had one "main message": "It's isn't like there's just the act, and you know what to do. It's a matter of discovery. I told them about masturbation. That it's good to do, that I was ashamed and felt bad, but that I did it [anyway] throughout my teenage years." Much later she learned "that it is part of that discovery process. It took me fifteen years to learn to experiment, to figure out what worked for me."

Terry, sturdy and tall where Sally is petite, told River and Heather about the first time she had intercourse. "I had waited until my boyfriend's twenty-first birthday. The thing was, I was in love. But it was awful and painful anyway. I broke out into hives. We had no idea how to do it."

Still, Terry convinced Sally that detailing the techniques of how to do it would be too mortifying for the girls to hear from their mothers, especially in a restaurant. ("My daughter dies of embarrassment if your hair is parted the wrong way," noted Terry.) So while Sally refrained from her intended hip-thrust demonstration, she did mention "movement" during intercourse. The reaction: "They both chuckled, as if they knew that already," said Sally. In spite of the girls' feints of sophistication, said Terry, "we could tell they were sopping it up," and the girls had since come back to their mothers with questions.

At the restaurant, however, they employed every time-honored teenage tactic of deflecting embarrassment. "River's demeanor was like benevolently listening to two old aunts," said Terry. "Heather had a straw up her nose."

Even if the desire for a storybook romance is likely to be disappointed, the desire for sex that accompanies such fantasies is neither wrong nor harmful

"Most early" (meaning high school) "sexual experience in our culture is harmful to girls," declares clinical psychologist Mary Pipher in her best-selling *Reviving Ophelia: Saving the Selves of Adolescent Girls* (1994, p. 208). In a kind of feminine Peter Pan story of the Little Lost Girls (and also an iteration of work by Harvard social psychologist Carol Gilligan, who saw a decline in female self-confidence starting at around the age of eleven), Pipher argues that girls have an authentic core, which is the flat-chested, soccer-playing preadolescent self. Once inside the adolescent body, inside American culture, however, all the piss and vinegar of that "true self" drain out, leaving girls vulnerable to depression and self-destruction, in need of rescue. The premise of *Ophelia* also underlies much popular advice about and for girls: that sex gets in the way of what they want and need in order to grow up happy and healthy.

There is no disputing that American girls must struggle with all their might to feel good about themselves once they start having women's bodies. But sexuality is both a blessing and a curse in that fight for self-love. In her book, Pipher paints it as a near-unremitting curse, describing the girls who engage in sex as "casualties."

"Lizzie," seventeen, strays from her steady high school boyfriend and loses her virginity to an older, more worldly male counselor at camp. When Boyfriend Number One finds out, he enlists his (and her former) friends in taunting and ostracizing Lizzie. Meanwhile, attention from her summertime lover fades. Lizzie is wrecked, but after a while, she recovers. She returns to her studies and finds solace in solitude and her loyal friendships. She starts dating again, this time "stop[ping] short of intercourse" because, according to Pipher, "she wasn't ready to handle the pain that followed losing a lover (pp. 205–213)."

But Lizzie did handle the pain, quite well. And it's hard to say, as Pipher reflexively does, that it was sex that hurt Lizzie. The lion's share of her grief was inflicted by her fickle, conformist, and sexist so-called friends. She may have been temporarily gun shy after her disappointment, but, as Pipher admits, she had also learned "to take care of herself and withstand disapproval" and "to take responsibility for sexual decisions."

What else might she have learned? Something useful about sex itself from the devilish camp counselor (who was, after all, a more practiced lover than she)? The beginnings of discerning what felt good to her, what made her comfortable enough to receive pleasure, or what might give pleasure to another person? If, according to her therapist, Pipher (and to the canon of advice literature), sex was the trauma and semichastity the recovery, then she had to repudiate anything positive about the sex she'd had with this young man in order for her to heal.

Thompson thinks this orthodoxy is backward, and I agree. Girls, she says, are far more likely to be ruined by love than by sex. A better lesson for Lizzy might have been to moderate her romantic expectations the next time. Then she might be able to glean self-esteem and enjoyment from the sex and emotional closeness of the relationship. Teen romances end, says Thompson; that is their nature. If sex educators and therapists could drop the bias that long-term commitment is the highest goal and the only context for sexual expression, they might be able to help youngsters (especially girls, who are more burdened by romantic illusion) relish such relationships, protect themselves while they last, and bounce back when they are over.

Love and lust are not the same thing, and love doesn't always make sex good

Because girls receive so many messages that what they really want is love (and thus interpret the urge for sex as love), adults who care about girls "should make knowing about and understanding girls' sexual desire central, rather than bury the possibility of girls' sexual desire and agency under relational wishes," writes Deborah Tolman (Tolman 1994, p. 251).

The problem is, of course, that sexual desire is not buried under relational wishes only in theory or only by adults. To many girls much of the time, love and lust feel mixed together, inextricable. That's how they feel to many grown women, too, which makes educating their daughters a tough job.

"I understood love as the thing I always was trying for," said Terry Rorty. "I did not understand sex [well enough for it to be] a super way to have love and express love." Twenty-five years after her first sexual experience, which was sexually unsatisfying in spite of deep love, Terry still finds it difficult and painful to sort out love and sex. In fact, she said, she and Sally had been planning the "girls' dinner" for two years, but they kept putting it off. "And really," said Terry, "the reason was that I was waiting to have something intelligent that would be worthy of a mother telling a daughter—and I felt stupid." Her eyes filled with tears. "I still feel stupid." Like many women, Terry struggles between the pull of romance and a solid sense of herself as a sexual agent. When I asked about desire, she admitted, "I don't know if I know when or what or who I desire, really, even now."

She continued: "I realized that after all these [sexual] stripes, I don't feel I have a comprehensive, empowering conversation to have with my daughter. And that was a source of grief. I think what I am upset about is that I am afraid that my daughter is already programmed to make all the mistakes I made,

defining herself in terms of a man's love." She went on, with difficulty. "I am still compelled by romance. What do I know about the distinction between sex and love? I can't find a distinction. It's troublesome. It ends me up not very happy a lot of the time."

Sally watched Terry tenderly, then said, "I think that's your ultimate goal: that the combination of the two is the best." Terry glanced back doubtfully. Then, after a while, a look of tentative triumph crossed the planes of her wide Irish face. "We wanted to give the girls a little about what to expect, to tell them some things that were useful. Sally saying it takes some time to get sex right. And me saying love was worth it, but loving someone doesn't always make sex good."

What Boys Can Learn

Boys, it is assumed, are brimming with desire. And, from my vantage point at the back of the auditorium of a residential facility for delinquent boys, during an eighth- and ninth-grade sex-ed class, that certainly looked true. The instructor was a talented young Planned Parenthood educator named Matthew Buscemi, who specializes in working with boys. The curriculum for the day was fairly standard: information about the female reproductive system, the menstrual cycle, pregnancy, and at the end, a film on childbirth. But alongside the official discourse, an unofficial one, a discourse of desire, was asserting itself. . . .

Striving for maximal comfort, Buscemi joked, elicited participation from the shyer kids ("What do you start getting on your face when you reach puberty?" I heard him ask a class of sixth-graders and their fathers in another town, another evening. A tentative reply from a boy at the back: "Acme?"). He answered all questions without scolding or moralizing.

In a reform school, where every minute is regimented, such license, coupled with the subject at hand, stirred nervousness that kept threatening to erupt into wildness. The minute Buscemi took out his poster-board diagrams, the wiry kid wriggling in the metal chair beside me was supplementing the lesson with his own supposedly firsthand knowledge, just audible enough for his neighbors to hear. After a while, his zeal grew too great for this private performance, and when Buscemi mentioned the vagina, the boy shot up his hand and shouted, "That's the pussy, right?"

"Right, the vagina is the pussy," answered Buscemi evenly, clearing up possible confusion and maintaining his free-floating control.

With this and a patter of similar questions, the boy was surely challenging Buscemi's authority (finally it earned him a threat of expulsion from the room by one of the regular teachers). He was also playing out the perennial conflict in the sex-ed classroom between the teacher's agenda to transmit necessary, nonerotic information and students yearning for "carnal knowledge." He was dirtying up the sanitized clinical discourse with the recognizable cadences of the street.

But he was also expressing something positive about the masculine relationship to sex (one that, I might add, is often held against boys): its enthusiasm. With each remark, this boy scored a round of sniggers from his peers, along with their own comments, a mixture of appreciation and aggression ("Ooh, I'd like to get my dick in . . ."). But signs of another kind of ambivalence toward women and their bodies also emerged. During the section on pregnancy, a student inquired with touching concern about whether intercourse hurts a pregnant woman or her fetus. Then, during a short, explicit film on childbirth, virtually the whole possible spectrum of thirteen- and fourteen-year-old masculine responses to the female body came pouring out, First, the boys jeered as the couples gazed into each other's eyes and talked about love and babies. Then they whooped with amazement and relish as

the camera focused on a woman's spread, naked crotch, which looked indistinguishable from a pornographic pussy. The whoops quickly turned to howls of disgust, or maybe terror, when that pussy transmogrified to an educational, reproductive vagina and the baby's bloody head emerged, followed by a gooey plop of afterbirth. The cozy family scenes that concluded the film brought mostly groans and chortling, as if the boys were either exhausted from the intensity of the foregoing or ashamed to reveal they were moved. I had noticed a few watching the birth raptly, entranced.

Boys learn that they should want sex, always be ready for it, and also be "good" at it. They learn early to pay attention to their sexual parts and to name at least the grossest manifestation of arousal (hang around any group of male seven-year-olds and you're sure to pick up the word *boner* or its local equivalent). But adults give them almost no clue about the potentialities of their own bodies, much less women's or other men's, and even fewer strategies for sorting out the mélange of curiosity, ardor, awkwardness, fear, and awe they feel. As I witnessed at the Long Island school, those feelings too often devolve into thin bravado and sexist cant.

Boys' desire education, then would be different from girls.' Simply put, the emphasis might fall on the other side of the love-lust divide.

Boys are more than hormone-pumping bodies

While boys feel permission to experience their sexual bodies, they may hardly be closer to knowing the full range of that experience than girls are. From the get-go, they are expected always to want sex. "There is a pressure all around boys to commodify sex. Sex is an 'it,' a thing to get," said Tolman, when we spoke at the early stages of her long-term study of boys' feelings about sexuality and masculinity. She suggested that these demands require a kind of alienation not only from feelings but from the body as well. "Boys are considered all body. But if we really try to understand what their experience is, I would bet they are observing sexuality in a profoundly dissociative way. They are watching, not feeling. I don't think boys are having incredibly wonderful sexual pleasure, even though they are supposed to. They may have orgasms more than girls. And coming is pleasure. But performance is such a big part of it, too. That stinks for women and for men."

Helping boys to connect feelings with sexual performance may contribute to sexual equality, implies Harvard psychologist William Pollack in *Real Boys: Rescuing Our Sons from the Myths of Boyhood.* Rather than charge girls with resisting and boys with refraining from sex, we should recognize that boys are not "sexual machines" any more than girls are sexual doormats, says Pollack (Pollack 1998, pp. 150–151).

A girl can be both a sexual object and a sexual subject. So can a boy

Boys' apparent sexual voracity is not really sexual, Pollack implies. It is a cover for boys' fear of sexual humiliation: "Their behavior is a compromise between a desire for connection and the fears of rejection, additionally fueled by unconscious shameful fears of early abandonment" (Pollack 1998, p. 151). Well, maybe. Maybe sometimes.

The achievement of equality does not require that we desexualize boys as we have girls. The masculine self-recognition of sexuality is something to be celebrated. Rather, the message to boys about their own as well as girls' sexuality should be that it is as variable as the people in whom it resides, and that any individual girl can be expected sometimes to want sex with a particular person, and sometimes not to. Placing girls on a pedestal of purity is not the same as respect. It only perpetuates the division of the female population into

virgins and whores, a division upheld with dreary diligence by our nation's schoolchildren. The task for boys is to listen and discern a partner's clues. (These lessons apply equally to a male partner, if that is the boy's choice. The difference is, other boys don't arrive with a veil of mystery around them.) Boys can also expect girls to listen to them. In this way, neither gender is cast as the permanent aggressor or resister, expert or innocent.

We have evidence that this is already happening and that practice in listening bears fruit over time. A heartening study of sexual consent conducted by Charlene Muehlenhard and Susan Hickman at the University of Kansas psychology department showed that while college women and men often make their willingness to have sex known in different ways, they almost universally understand the cues from a partner of the other sex. And—good riddance to bad myths—"a direct refusal (saying 'no') was not perceived as representative of sexual consent by either women or men," Muehlenhard wrote me. "They seemed to agree that 'no' meant 'no'" (Hickman and Muehlenhard 1996).

This is surely good news. The next task is for boys to hear yes and, even more complex, the expressions of desire between absolute no and absolute yes.

"Dirty talk" need not be derogatory

Because boys feel permission to "talk dirty" and girls do not, boys own sexual slang, at least in the coed public. Taught that girls' sexuality is both hotly desirable and repulsive and that their own sexuality must be dominant and cool, boys (and men) deploy "obscene" language simultaneously to express desire and to deny the intensity of that desire by communicating contempt for the girl (or woman) who inspires it. Similar ambivalence may play into the use of feminized obscenities, such as *bitch* or *pussy,* to insult boys deemed insufficiently masculine or cool. Suspecting that for young men dirty talk is mostly a way of strutting and a vocabulary of hostility, most teachers confronting the word pussy would criticize and prohibit its use.

Yet in the privacy of their bedrooms, these very same teachers, male or female, might utter the same word with passion, humor, and affection. Sexual language, formal or slang, attains meaning in context. "To me, the word *slut* is a compliment," said therapist Klein. "It simply means a woman who likes sex and isn't ashamed of it."

The point is not to strip boys' vocabularies of "obscenity" but to broaden the meanings they can assign to the erotic vernacular. This can be accomplished only if the context in which that language is used—sex and relationships—becomes more egalitarian, a far harder, longer-term project than expurgating "bad words" from the language. In the meantime, perhaps teachers should not jump to conclusion about the intent behind the use of any given word. By translating *pussy* to *vagina*, without further comment, Matt Buscemi may have succeeded in transmitting the message that sexual slang can be used neutrally.

Sex causes vulnerability. And vulnerability has its benefits in sex

Being tough and casual about sex may protect boys from deep hurt, but it also insulates them from deep satisfaction. The process of opening oneself begins with desire. Of course, boys long for love and for particular love objects, and when they're being honest most admit to fewer hits than misses in their pursuit. Of his first (and in his opinion long-overdue) sexual experience in the early 1960s, a male friend told me, "Oh, I had been thinking a lot about breasts for years—*years*. But it never occurred to me in my wildest imagination that I'd ever have *access* to them." This masculine anxiety that one will be completely excluded from the possibility of gratifying desire has hardly disappeared in the allegedly promiscuous 2000s.

Still, as long as boys are expected to cultivate and express an attitude of "What the hell, why not?" whenever sexual opportunity knocks, they may miss out on learning discernment about what they really want and, in the process, dull the sexual experiences they do have. Wanting more, or wanting something or someone specific, means having more to lose. But potentially, more may also be gained. The vulnerability entailed in true desire has its benefits.

"We like to retell the story of Thetis and Achilles," said Niki Fedele, a therapist who, along with colleague Cate Dooley, heads the Mother-Son Project at Wellesley College's Jean Baker Miller Training Institute, in Massachusetts. In the myth, the mother Thetis dips her son Achilles into the River Styx to render him invincible as a warrior. But she grasps him by the heel, and it is Achilles' heel that Paris's arrow finally finds, fatally wounding the hero.

The classical interpretation of the myth is to blame Thetis for Achilles' downfall: mother-love makes a man weak, not strong; it is accountable, indeed, for his fatal flaw. But Fedele and Dooley apply a feminist spin. "She gave her son a gift," Fedele explained to a group of mothers in a Saturday workshop about raising sons. "She allowed him to be human. We say, let boys have vulnerability and become fully human."

Whereas Fedele and Dooley assign the nurturing of boys' tenderness to mothers, fathers can certainly do it too. Mauricio Vela, a Salvadoran American youth worker in San Francisco, worried about the pressure on his junior high school sons to be macho. As an antidote, he offered the example of a sweet and soft, though strong, man. "I kiss my boys and hug them all the time. I try to tell them I love them as much as I can." And he tells them in, quite literally, a tender language. "I speak Spanish to my sons because there is more *cariño* in it." *Cariño* means "loving care," literally, "dearness."

Emily Feinstein, a sculptor who drives her beat-up Toyota pick-up truck around the boroughs of New York City to teach conflict resolution to middle schoolers, sees their toughness more as a ruse than a deep-seated personal reality. Its origins, especially in the poorer boys she works with, she says, are social and political. "I see these incredibly tender-hearted people who want to make a difference, who want to love each other, and who are systematically taught not to show that," said Feinstein. "They are constantly being put down by the school and the culture. They don't want to be vulnerable to what's coming at them . . . [and] if you don't want to feel criticized, belittled, and humiliated, you take on this posture that nothing matters to you." Adults, she says, often mistake a pose of not-caring for cynicism and universal disdain. She believes the opposite is true. "They feel too much, there's no room to show that, so the posture says, 'Nothing is going to get to me.' They have certain things they care about passionately, where [all the need for belonging and appreciation] has gotten lodged. Clothes, music, hair: these things are desperately important to them. It's where they get to show they want to be loved."

One of Feinstein's main exercises in the classroom is the open expression of caring for friends—what she calls "put-ups," the antonym of "put-downs." Homophobia stands foursquare in the path of boys' showing their affection to each other. But she persists, and the put-ups get closer to the intended mark. "At first, the boys will think and think and say something like, 'You play sports good.'" Eventually, though, they begin to use the exercise not only to assess another person positively but also to acknowledge a *relationship*. "More and more, they'll say things like 'You've helped me with math. You've been a good friend.'" Feinstein thinks the homophobic restraints on masculine affection might also thwart boys' playfulness and tenderness in heterosexual sex—and that learning to express closeness openly could do the opposite.

Tolman echoes this contention, more explicitly about sex. "Boys are given so few tools to be conscious of connection between sex and love—that they, too, are involved with that connection." Still, she is hopeful. "I've just got to believe that it's a human thing to be profoundly connected to another person. And that is part of what we get in sexuality."

Not-knowing isn't unmanly. It can unlock the clues to desire

"If the average male has difficulty asking directions while driving, you can imagine how hard it is to set aside his bravado and ego to ask about sex," commented Alwyn Cohall, director of the Harlem Health Promotion Center at the Columbia University School of Public Health, at a Planned Parenthood conference in the late 1990s (Cohall 1998).

Months later, in a conversation in a minuscule office at the Columbia Presbyterian Hospital Young Men's Clinic, Cohall's colleague Bruce Armstrong agreed. "There's so little talking among us," said the physician, sighing. That's an understatement. A survey in the mid-1990s of sexually experienced teens found that only a third had talked with their partner about contraception and 40 percent had talked about safe sex, but of those, one in five waited until after the fact to have that discussion (Kaiser Family Foundation 1998). "We hardly ever get an opportunity to hear from each other in a tension-free atmosphere," said Armstrong. Apparently, in bed at the moment of sexual intercourse is not a tension-free atmosphere for lots of teens.

The clinic, which Armstrong directs, provides that atmosphere. "One of the things that's really fabulous about our clinic is that when guys want to talk to a woman about their bodies, our female staff is here for them to do that. They want to know what a woman's orgasm feels like, what does it feel like to have a baby." He paused to talk to one of the interns who help staff the clinic, a young Pakistani American woman, then returned to our conversations. "These are not especially 'sensitive' guys. They're your typical macho-looking, baggy-pants-wearing guys from Washington Heights and North Harlem," the mostly Dominican and African American low-income section of upper Manhattan that the hospital serves. He paused in appreciation of the young men he refers to as "our fellas." "But they ask such piercing questions."

These young men, it seems, have found few adults to talk frankly with them about sex, least of all their families. As I've noted, families who are willing and able are few. But they exist. For one such family, the bottom line is creating an atmosphere where it is okay not to know. That family is the extraordinary ménage that raises Jeremy Pergolese, who was eleven when I met his parents. In two separate, single-sex-couple households, Jeremy's mother, Carol, and her partner, Beth Stein, coparent Jeremy along with their friends (and now legal coguardians) Jed Marks and his partner, David Booth. Three of the four parents are engaged in sex-related professions: Carol and Jed are employed by the same reproductive-health clinic, and David is a psychotherapist and professor of human sexuality. Because of the unconventionality of their family and the fact that they are lesbians and gay men, these mothers and fathers have found it necessary, and more or less natural, to raise an emotionally expressive, sexually informed boy. The ground rule, said Jed: "Whatever he asks, we tell him the truth. And we also tell him stuff he doesn't ask."

What does he ask? "I heard that you can have sex with more than two people at the same time. How do you do that?" (Jed's answer: "Picture three men, six hands, three penises. Jeremy goes, 'Ohhh, I get it.'") Other, more oblique queries have revealed Jeremy's anxieties about his fathers' sexuality. "Dad, do you have AIDS?" he asked Jed in a pizzeria when he was seven. "It was the first time he'd ever brought up our gayness on his own," said

Jed, explaining his theory of why this was the first such question: Jeremy had learned to associate gay sex with condoms, which his dads keep out in the open, so that the boy can handle them and consider them a normal part of life. But at school the only thing Jeremy had learned about condoms was that they prevented AIDS. And he'd learned from his friends that gay men got AIDS. Although Jed was surprised and saddened that he and David had missed getting the message across earlier and that Jeremy had had to wonder and worry, the father assured his son that both he and his partner were healthy.

In a midtown restaurant, Carol told me that Jeremy's family offered him ideas of how to live and love in a more conventional sense, too. "In our two homes, he sees two radically different models," she explained. "Beth and I are really domesticated. Over there [at Jed and David's], there's freedom and independence. Jeremy doesn't want me to break up with Beth. He thinks a couple is normal." She is thankful to "the guys" for being so explicit about sex, which she feels shyer about discussing. But, she added, "I'd rather he be ready for the emotional part. What if the girl falls in love? Or if you do? Do you just want to do it, or is it in the context of an ongoing relationship? The brutal fact is, he is not going to wait until he is ready. Most people start having sex when they aren't ready."

Simply being the son of parents rehearses a boy in the comedy and tragedy of loving, Carol thinks. "All the power, love, and fear—the elements that go into making things sexy later—these are there with parents." Saying this, her face softened, like a woman thinking of her lover or like a mother, of her son. "It's a weird setup, but we must be doing something right. Or maybe we're just lucky. Jeremy is a laughy, huggy, kissy, funny, interesting kid. He is not afraid to feel."

David gives Carol and Beth and Jed and himself more credit than this nod to accident.

He had parents, too, he reminded me, and didn't end up as open to the range of feelings as Jeremy appears to be. A parent's accessibility to being asked any questions about sex is about much more than sex, David insisted. "If a child learns it is not okay to ask about sex, that translates into 'Don't ask about other not-okay stuff that may come up,'" he said. "It goes way beyond sex. It allows open communication about what is known and what is not known. The child learns that it is okay not to know, to lose, face, to be puzzled, to have ambivalent feelings."

Growing up in homes where marginalized desire is "normal" while attending school where it isn't, Jeremy may already be more comfortable with ambivalence and conflict than most children are. ("Your father's gay," a kid jeered at him on the playground. "Yeah, I know," he replied. "So what?") Because he has witnessed a variety of sexual styles and expressions among his parents' friends, and because he may or may not follow sexually in his fathers' footsteps, he is learning that desire is unpredictable, personal, protean, and broad in possibility.

Gender provides fixed points of reference and defenses against ambiguity and the unknown sexual future. It's not hard to understand why most kids cling to the strictly conformist styles of masculinity and femininity. Challenging the certainties of gender may discomfit young people in the short term, but it can enrich their lives for the duration. Comfort with the unknown may be the most important ally in the interrogation of desire and in its fulfillment throughout a lifetime.

REFERENCES

Alexander, Cheryl S., et al. 1993. "Consistency of Adolescents' Self-Report of Sexual Behavior in a Longitudinal Study," *Journal of Youth and Adolescence 22*: 455–71.

Cohall, Alwyn, speaking at a Planned Parenthood of New York conference, "Adolescent Sexual Health: New Data and Implications for Services and Programs," October 26, 1998.

Connell, R. W. 1995. *Masculinities: Knowledge, Power, and Social Change.* Los Angeles: University of California Press.

"Fact Sheet: Dating Violence Among Adolescents," Advocates for Youth (accessed at www.advocatesforyouth.org), Washington, D.C., n.d.

Hickman, Susan E. and Muehlenhard, Charleen L. "By the Semi-Mystical Appearance of a Condom: How Young Women and Men Communicate Sexual Consent," paper presented at the annual meeting of the Society for the Scientific Study of Sex, Houston, Texas, November 1996.

Kaiser Family Foundation, "National Survey of Teens on Dating, Intimacy, and Sexual Experiences," reported by SIECUS, *SHOP Talk Bulletin 2* (April 17, 1998).

Lefkowitz, Bernard. 1998. *Our Guys.* New York: Vintage Books, 278–79.

Morin, Jack. 1995. *The Erotic Mind.* New York: Harper Collins, 83–85.

Newcomer, Susan and Udry, J. Richard. 1988. "Adolescents' Honesty in a Survey of Sexual Behavior," *Journal of Adolescent Research 1,* no. 3/4: 419–23.

Pipher, Mary. 1994. *Reviving Ophelia: Saving the Selves of Adolescent Girls.* New York: Ballantine Books.

Pollack, William. 1998. *Real Boys: Rescuing Our Sons from the Myths of Boyhood.* New York: Random House, 150–51.

Reichert, Michael. 1997. "On Behalf of Boys," *Independent School Magazine.* Spring.

Thorne, Barrie. 1997. *Gender Play: Girls and Boys in School.* New Brunswick, N.J.: Rutgers University Press.

Tolman, Deborah. 1994. "Daring to Desire: Culture and the Bodies of Adolescent Girls." In *Sexual Cultures and the Construction of Adolescent Identities,* ed. Janice M. Irvine. Philadelphia: Temple University Press.

THINKING ABOUT THE READING

How is the experience of adolescence different for boys and girls? How do the sexual messages and expectations girls are provided as they're growing up leave them feeling ashamed and vulnerable? What consequences do cultural sexual pressures have for boys? Why does the author think girls are more likely to be ruined by cultural ideals of love and romance than by sex? Do you think the author's view of sexual cultures reflects your own experiences during adolescence? What would a healthy and responsible sexual education look like? Would it be different for boys and girls?

Still a Man's World

Men Who Do "Women's Work"

Christine L. Williams

(1995)

Gendered Jobs and Gendered Workers

A 1959 article in *Library Journal* entitled "The Male Librarian—An Anomaly?" begins this way:

> My friends keep trying to get me out of the library. . . . Library work is fine, they agree, but they smile and shake their heads benevolently and charitably, as if it were unnecessary to add that it is one of the dullest, most poorly paid, unrewarding, off-beat activities any man could be consigned to. If you have a heart condition, if you're physically handicapped in other ways, well, such a job is a blessing. And for women there's no question library work is fine; there are some wonderful women in libraries and we all ought to be thankful to them. But let's face it, no healthy man of normal intelligence should go into it.[1]

Male librarians still face this treatment today, as do other men who work in predominantly female occupations. In 1990, my local newspaper featured a story entitled "Men Still Avoiding Women's Work" that described my research on men in nursing, librarianship, teaching, and social work. Soon afterwards, a humor columnist for the same paper wrote a spoof on the story that he titled, "Most Men Avoid Women's Work Because It Is Usually So Boring."[2] The columnist poked fun at hairdressing, librarianship, nursing, and babysitting—in his view, all "lousy" jobs requiring low intelligence and a high tolerance for boredom. Evidently people still wonder why any "healthy man of normal intelligence" would willingly work in a "woman's occupation."

In fact, not very many men do work in these fields, although their numbers are growing. In 1990, over 500,000 men were employed in these four occupations, constituting approximately 6 percent of all registered nurses, 15 percent of all elementary school teachers, 17 percent of all librarians, and 32 percent of all social workers. These percentages have fluctuated in recent years: As Table 1 indicates, librarianship and social work have undergone slight declines in the proportions of men since 1975; teaching has remained somewhat stable; while nursing has experienced noticeable gains. The number of men in nursing actually doubled between 1980 and 1990; however, their overall proportional representation remains very low.

Very little is known about these men who "cross over" into these nontraditional occupations. While numerous books have been written about women entering male-dominated occupations, few have asked why men are underrepresented in traditionally female jobs.[3] The underlying assumption in most research on gender and work is that, given a free choice, both men and women would work in predominantly male occupations, as they are generally

Table 1   Men in the "Women's Professions": Number (in thousands) and Distribution of Men Employed in the Occupations, Selected Years

Profession	1975	1980	1990
Registered Nurses			
Number of men	28	46	92
% men	3.0	3.5	5.5
Elementary Teachers[a]			
Number of men	194	225	223
% men	14.6	16.3	14.8
Librarians			
Number of men	34	27	32
% men	18.9	14.8	16.7
Social Workers			
Number of men	116	134	179
% men	39.2	35.0	21.8

Sources: U.S. Department of Labor, Bureau of Labor Statistics, *Employment and Earnings* 38 no. 1 (January 1991), Table 22 (employed civilians by detailed occupation), p. 185; vol. 28, no. 1 (January 1981), Table 23 (employed persons by detailed occupation), p. 180; vol. 22, no. 7 (January 1976), Table 2 (employed persons by detailed occupation), p. 11.

[a]Excludes kindergarten teachers.

better paying and more prestigious than predominantly female occupations. The few men who willingly "cross over" must be, as the 1959 article suggests, "anomalies."

Popular culture reinforces the belief that these men are "anomalies." Men are rarely portrayed working in these occupations, and when they are, they are represented in extremely stereotypical ways. For example, in the 1990 movie *Kindergarten Cop,* muscle-man Arnold Schwarzenegger played a detective forced to work undercover as a kindergarten teacher; the otherwise competent Schwarzenegger was completely overwhelmed by the five-year-old children in his class. . . .

[I] challenge these stereotypes about men who do "women's work" through case studies of men in four predominantly female occupations: nursing, elementary school teaching, librarianship, and social work. I show that men maintain their masculinity in these occupations, despite the popular stereotypes. Moreover, male power and privilege is preserved and reproduced in these occupations through a complex interplay between gendered expectations embedded in organizations, and the gendered interests workers bring with them to their jobs. Each of these occupations is "still a man's world" even though mostly women work in them.

I selected these four professions as case studies of men who do "women's work" for a variety of reasons. First, because they are so strongly associated with women and femininity in our popular culture, these professions highlight and perhaps even exaggerate the barriers and advantages men face when entering predominantly female environments. Second, they each require extended periods of educational training and apprenticeship, requiring individuals in these occupations to be at least somewhat committed to their work (unlike those employed in, say, clerical or domestic work). Therefore I thought they would be reflective about their decisions to join these "nontraditional" occupations, making them

Table 2   Median Weekly Earnings of Full-Time Professional Workers, by Sex, and Ratio of Female: Male Earnings, 1990

Occupation	Both	Men	Women	Ratio
Registered Nurses	608	616	608	.99
Elementary Teachers	519	575	513	.89
Librarians	489	—*	479	—
Social Workers	445	483	427	.88
Engineers	814	822	736	.90
Physicians	892	978	802	.82
College Teachers	747	808	620	.77
Lawyers	1,045	1,178	875	.74

Source: U.S. Department of Labor, Bureau of Labor Statistics, Employment and Earnings 38, no. 1 (January 1991), Table 56, p. 223.

*The Labor Department does not report income averages for base sample sizes consisting of fewer than 50,000 individuals.

"acute observers" and, hence, ideal informants about the sort of social and psychological processes I am interested in describing.[4] Third, these occupations vary a great deal in the proportion of men working in them. Although my aim was not to engage in between-group comparisons, I believed that the proportions of men in a work setting would strongly influence the degree to which they felt accepted and satisfied with their jobs.[5]

I traveled across the United States conducting in-depth interviews with seventy-six men and twenty-three women who work in nursing, teaching, librarianship, and social work. Like the people employed in these professions generally, those in my sample were predominantly white (90 percent). Their ages ranged from twenty to sixty-six, and the average age was thirty-eight. I interviewed women as well as men to gauge their feelings and reactions to men's entry into "their" professions. Respondents were intentionally selected to represent a wide range of specialties and levels of education and experience. I interviewed students in professional schools, "front line" practitioners, administrators, and retirees, asking them about their motivations to enter these professions, their on-the-job experiences, and their opinions about men's status and prospects in these fields. . . .

Riding the Glass Escalator

Men earn more money than women in every occupation—even in predominantly female jobs (with the possible exceptions of fashion modeling and prostitution).[6] Table 2 shows that men outearn women in teaching, librarianship, and social work; their salaries in nursing are virtually identical. The ratios between women's and men's earnings in these occupations are higher than those found in the "male" professions, where women earn 74 to 90 percent of men's salaries. That there is a wage gap at all in predominantly female professions, however, attests to asymmetries in the workplace experiences of male and female tokens. These salary figures indicate that the men who do "women's work" fare as well as, and often better than, the women who work in these fields. . . .

Hiring Decisions

Contrary to the experience of many women in the male-dominated professions, many of the men and women I spoke to indicated that there is a *preference* for hiring men in these four occupations. A Texas librarian at a junior high school said that his school district "would hire a male over a female":

[CW: Why do you think that is?]

Because there are so few, and the . . . ones that they do have, the library directors seem to really . . . think they're doing great jobs. I don't know, maybe they just feel they're being progressive or something, [but] I have had a real sense that they really appreciate having a male, particularly at the junior high. . . . As I said, when seven of us lost our jobs from the high schools and were redistributed, there were only four positions at junior high, and I got one of them. Three of the librarians, some who had been here longer than I had with the school district, were put down in elementary school as librarians. And I definitely think that being male made a difference in my being moved to the junior high rather than an elementary school.

Many of the men perceived their token status as males in predominantly female occupations as an *advantage* in hiring and promotions. When I asked an Arizona teacher whether his specialty (elementary special education) was an unusual area for men compared to other areas within education, he said,

Much more so. I am extremely marketable in special education. That's not why I got into the field. But I am extremely marketable because I am a man.

. . . Sometimes the preference for men in these occupations is institutionalized. One man landed his first job in teaching before he earned the appropriate credential "because I was a wrestler and they wanted a wrestling coach." A female math teacher similarly told of her inability to find a full-time teaching position because the schools she applied to reserved the math jobs for people (presumably men) who could double as coaches. . . .

. . . Some men described being "tracked" into practice areas within their professions which were considered more legitimate for men. For example, one Texas man described how he was pushed into administration and planning in social work, even though "I'm not interested in writing policy; I'm much more interested in research and clinical stuff." A nurse who is interested in pursuing graduate study in family and child health in Boston said he was dissuaded from entering the program specialty in favor of a concentration in "adult nursing." And a kindergarten teacher described his difficulty finding a job in his specialty after graduation: "I was recruited immediately to start getting into a track to become an administrator. And it was men who recruited me. It was men that ran the system at that time, especially in Los Angeles."

This tracking may bar men from the most female-identified specialties within these professions. But men are effectively being "kicked upstairs" in the process. Those specialties considered more legitimate practice areas for men also tend to be the most prestigious, and better-paying specialties as well. For example, men in nursing are overrepresented in critical care and psychiatric specialties, which tend to be higher paying than the others.[7] The highest paying and most prestigious library types are the academic libraries (where men are 35 percent of librarians) and the special libraries which are typically associated with businesses or other private organizations (where men constitute 20 percent of librarians).[8]

A distinguished kindergarten teacher, who had been voted citywide "Teacher of the Year," described the informal pressures he faced to advance in his field. He told me that even though people were pleased to see him in the classroom, "there's been some encouragement to think about administration, and there's been some encouragement to think about teaching at the university level or something like that, or a supervisory-type position."

The effect of this "tracking" is the opposite of that experienced by women in male-dominated occupations. Researchers have reported that many women encounter "glass ceilings" in their efforts to scale organizational and professional hierarchies. That is, they reach invisible barriers to promotion in their careers, caused mainly by the sexist attitudes of men in the highest positions.[9] In contrast to this "glass ceiling," many of the men I interviewed seem to encounter a "glass escalator." Often, despite their intentions, they face invisible pressures to move up in their professions. Like being on a moving escalator, they have to work to stay in place. . . .

Supervisors and Colleagues: The Working Environment

. . . Respondents in this study were asked about their relationships with supervisors and female colleagues to ascertain whether men also experienced "poisoned" work environments when entering nontraditional occupations.

A major difference in the experience of men and women in nontraditional occupations is that men are far more likely to be supervised by a member of their own sex. In each of the four professions I studied, men are overrepresented in administrative and managerial capacities, or, as in the case of nursing, the organizational hierarchy is governed by men. For example, 15 percent of all elementary school teachers are men, but men make up over 80 percent of all elementary school principals and 96 percent of all public school superintendents and assistant superintendents.[10] Likewise, over 40 percent of all male social workers hold administrative or managerial positions, compared to 30 percent of all female social workers.[11] And 50 percent of male librarians hold administrative positions, compared to 30 percent of female librarians, and the majority of deans and directors

of major university and public libraries are men.[12] Thus, unlike women who enter "male fields," the men in these professions often work under the direct supervision of other men.

Many of the men interviewed reported that they had good rapport with their male supervisors. It was not uncommon in education, for example, for the male principal to informally socialize with the male staff, as a Texas special education teacher describes:

> Occasionally I've had a principal who would regard me as "the other man on the campus" and "it's us against them," you know? I mean, nothing really that extreme, except that some male principals feel like there's nobody there to talk to except the other man. So I've been in that position.

These personal ties can have important consequences for men's careers. For example, one California nurse, whose performance was judged marginal by his nursing superiors, was transferred to the emergency room staff (a prestigious promotion) due to his personal friendship with the physician in charge. And a Massachusetts teacher acknowledged that his principal's personal interest in him landed him his current job:

> [CW: You had mentioned that your principal had sort of spotted you at your previous job and had wanted to bring you here [to this school]. Do you think that has anything to do with the fact that you're a man, aside from your skills as a teacher?]
>
> Yes, I would say in that particular case, that was part of it. . . . We have certain things in common, certain interests that really lined up.
>
> [CW: Vis-à-vis teaching?]
>
> Well, more extraneous things—running specifically, and music. And we just seemed to get along real well right off the bat. It is just kind of a guy thing; we just liked each other. . . .

Interviewees did not report many instances of male supervisors discriminating against them, or refusing to accept them because they were male. Indeed, these men were much more likely to report that their male bosses discriminated against the *females* in their professions. . . .

Of course, not all the men who work in these occupations are supervised by men. Many of the men interviewed who had female bosses also reported high levels of acceptance—although the level of intimacy they achieved with women did not seem as great as with other men. But in some cases, men reported feeling shut-out from decision making when the higher administration was constituted entirely by women. I asked this Arizona librarian whether men in the library profession were discriminated against hiring because of their sex:

> Professionally speaking, people go to considerable lengths to keep that kind of thing out of their [hiring] deliberations. Personally, is another matter. It's pretty common around here to talk about the "old girl network." This is one of the few libraries that I've had any intimate knowledge of which is actually controlled by women. . . . Most of the department heads and upper level administrators are women. And there's an "old girl network" that works just like the "old boy network," except that the important conferences take place in the women's room rather than on the golf course. But the political mechanism is the same, the exclusion of the other sex from decision making is the same. The reasons are the same. It's somewhat discouraging. . . .

Although I did not interview many supervisors, I did include twenty-three women in my sample to ascertain their perspectives about the presence of men in their professions. All of the women I interviewed claimed to be supportive of their male colleagues, but some conveyed ambivalence. For example, a social work professor said she would like to see more men enter the social work profession, particularly in the clinical specialty (where they are underrepresented). She said she would favor affirmative action hiring guidelines for men in the profession, and yet, she resented the fact that her department hired "another white male" during a recent search. I confronted her about this apparent ambivalence:

> [CW: I find it very interesting that, on the one hand, you sort of perceive this preference and perhaps even sexism with regard to how men are evaluated and how they achieve higher positions within the profession, yet, on the other hand, you would be encouraging of more men to enter the field. Is that contradictory to you, or . . . ?]
>
> Yeah, it's contradictory. . . .

Men's reception by their female colleagues is thus somewhat mixed. It appears that women are generally eager to see men enter "their" occupations, and the women I interviewed claimed they were supportive of their male peers. Indeed, several men agreed with this social worker that their female colleagues had facilitated their careers in various ways (including college mentorship). At the same time, however, women often resent the apparent ease with which men seem to advance within these professions, sensing that men at the higher levels receive preferential treatment, and thus close off advancement opportunities for women.

But this ambivalence does not seem to translate into the "poisoned" work environment described by many women who work in male-dominated occupations. Among the male interviewees, there were no accounts of sexual harassment (indeed, one man claimed this was a disappointment to him!) However, women do treat their male colleagues differently on occasion. It is not uncommon in nursing, for example, for men to be called upon to help catheterize male patients, or to lift especially heavy patients. Some librarians also said that women asked them to lift and move heavy boxes of books because they were men. . . .

Another stereotype confronting men, in nursing and social work in particular, is the expectation that they are better able than women to handle aggressive individuals and diffuse violent situations. An Arizona social worker who was the first male caseworker in a rural district, described this preference for men:

> They welcomed a man, particularly in child welfare. Sometimes you have to go into some tough parts of towns and cities, and they felt it was nice to have a man around to accompany them or be present when they were dealing with a difficult client. Or just doing things that males can do. I always felt very welcomed.

But this special treatment bothered some respondents: Getting assigned all the violent patients or discipline problems can make for difficult and unpleasant working conditions. Nurses, for example, described how they were called upon to subdue violent patients. A traveling psychiatric nurse I interviewed in Texas told how his female colleagues gave him "plenty of opportunities" to use his wrestling skills. . . .

But many men claimed that this differential treatment did not distress them. In fact, several said they liked being appreciated for the special traits and abilities (such as strength) they could contribute to their professions.

Furthermore, women's special treatment of men sometimes enhanced—rather than detracted from—the men's work environments. One Texas librarian said he felt "more comfortable working with women than men" because "I think it has something to do with control. Maybe it's that women will let me take control more than men will." Several men reported that their female colleagues often cast them into leadership roles. . . .

The interviews suggest that the working environment encountered by "nontraditional" male workers is quite unlike that faced by women who work in traditionally male fields. Because it is not uncommon for men in predominantly female professions to be supervised by other men, they tend to have closer rapport and more intimate social relationships with people in management. These ties can facilitate men's careers by smoothing the way for future promotions. Relationships with female supervisors were also described for the most part in positive terms, although in some cases, men perceived an "old girls'" network in place that excluded them from decision making. But in sharp contrast to the reports of women in nontraditional occupations, men in these fields did not complain of feeling discriminated against because they were men. If anything, they felt that being male was an asset that enhanced their career prospects.

Those men interviewed for this study also described congenial workplaces, and a very high level of acceptance from their female colleagues. The sentiment was echoed by women I spoke to who said that they were pleased to see more men enter "their" professions. Some women, however, did express resentment over the "fast-tracking" that their male colleagues seem to experience. But this ambivalence did not translate into a hostile work environment for men: Women generally included men in their informal social events and, in some ways, even facilitated men's careers. By casting men into leadership roles, presuming they were more knowledgeable and qualified, or relying on them to perform certain critical tasks, women unwittingly contributed to the "glass escalator effect" facing men who do "women's work."

Relationships With Clients

Workers in these service-oriented occupations come into frequent contact with the public during the course of their work day. Nurses treat patients; social workers usually have client case loads; librarians serve patrons; and teachers are in constant contact with children, and often with parents as well. Many of those interviewed claimed that the clients they served had different expectations of men and women in these occupations, and often treated them differently.

People react with surprise and often disbelief when they encounter a man in nursing, elementary school teaching, and, to a lesser extent, librarianship. (Usually people have no clear expectations about the sex of social workers.) The stereotypes men face are often negative. For example, according to this Massachusetts nurse, it is frequently assumed that male nurses are gay:

> Fortunately, I carry one thing with me that protects me from [the stereotype that male nurses are gay], and the one thing I carry with me is a wedding ring, and it makes a big difference. The perfect example was conversations before I was married. . . . [People would ask], "Oh, do you have a girlfriend?" Or you'd hear patients asking questions along that idea, and they were simply implying, "Why is this guy in nursing? Is it because he's gay and he's a pervert?" And I'm not associating the two by any means, but this is the thought process.

. . . It is not uncommon for both gay and straight men in these occupations to encounter people who believe that they are "gay 'til proven otherwise," as one nurse put it. In fact, there are many gay men employed in these occupations. But gender stereotypes are at least as responsible for this general belief as any "empirical" assessment of men's sexual lifestyles. To the degree that men in these professions are perceived as not "measuring up" to the supposedly more challenging occupational roles and standards demanded of "real" men, they are immediately suspected of being effeminate— "like women"—and thus, homosexual.

An equally prevalent sexual stereotype about men in these occupations is that they are potentially dangerous and abusive. Several men described special rules they followed to guard against the widespread presumption of sexual abuse. For example, nurses were sometimes required to have a female "chaperone" present when performing certain procedures or working with specific populations. This psychiatric nurse described a former workplace:

> I worked on a floor for the criminally insane. Pretty threatening work. So you have to have a certain number of females on the floor just to balance out. Because there were female patients on the floor too. And you didn't want to be accused of rape or any sex crimes.

Teachers and librarians described the steps they took to protect themselves from suspicions of sexual impropriety. A kindergarten teacher said:

> I know that I'm careful about how I respond to students. I'm careful in a number of ways—in my physical interaction with students. It's mainly to reassure parents. . . . For example, a little girl was very affectionate, very anxious to give me a hug. She'll just throw herself at me. I need to tell her very carefully: "Sonia, you need to tell me when you want to hug me." That way I can come down, crouch down. Because you don't want a child giving you a hug on your hip. You just don't want to do that. So I'm very careful about body position.

. . . Although negative stereotypes about men who do "women's work" can push men out of specific jobs, their effects can actually benefit men. Instead of being a source of negative discrimination, these prejudices can add to the "glass escalator effect" by pressuring men to move *out* of the most feminine-identified areas and *up* to those regarded as more legitimate for men.

The public's reactions to men working in these occupations, however, are by no means always negative. Several men and women reported that people often assume that men in these occupations are more competent than women, or that they bring special skills and expertise to their professional practice. For example, a female academic librarian told me that patrons usually address their questions to the male reference librarian when there is a choice between asking a male or a female. A male clinical social worker in private practice claimed that both men and women generally preferred male psychotherapists. And several male nurses told me that people often assume that they are physicians and direct their medical inquiries to them instead of to the female nurses.[13]

The presumption that men are more competent than women is another difference in the experience of token men and women. Women who work in nontraditional occupations are often suspected of being incompetent, unable to survive the pressures of "men's work." As a consequence, these women often report feeling compelled to prove themselves and, as the saying goes, "work twice as hard as men to be considered half as good." To the degree that men are assumed to be competent and in control, they may have to be twice as incompetent to be considered half as bad. One man claimed that "if you're a mediocre male teacher, you're considered a better teacher than if you're a female and a mediocre teacher. I think there's that prejudice there." . . .

There are different standards and assumptions about men's competence that follow them into nontraditional occupations. In contrast, women in both traditional and nontraditional occupations must contend with the presumption that they are neither competent nor qualified. . . .

The reasons that clients give for preferring or rejecting men reflect the complexity of our society's stereotypes about masculinity and femininity. Masculinity is often associated with competence and mastery, in contrast to femininity, which is often associated with instrumental incompetence. Because of these stereotypes, men are perceived as being stricter disciplinarians and stronger than women, and thus better able to handle violent or potentially violent situations. . . .

Conclusion

Both men and women who work in nontraditional occupations encounter discrimination, but the forms and the consequences of this discrimination are very different for the two groups. Unlike "nontraditional" women workers, most of the discrimination and prejudice facing men in the "female" professions comes from clients. For the most part, the men and women I interviewed believed that men are given fair—if not preferential—treatment in hiring and promotion decisions, are accepted by their supervisors and colleagues, and are well-integrated into the workplace subculture. Indeed, there seem to be subtle mechanisms in place that enhance men's positions in these professions—a phenomenon I refer to as a "glass escalator effect."

Men encounter their most "mixed" reception in their dealings with clients, who often react negatively to male nurses, teachers, and to a lesser extent, librarians. Many people assume that the men are sexually suspect if they are employed in these "feminine" occupations either because they do or they do not conform to stereotypical masculine characteristics.

Dealing with the stress of these negative stereotypes can be overwhelming, and it probably pushes some men out of these occupations.[14] The challenge facing the men who stay in these fields is to accentuate their positive contribution to what our society defines as essentially "women's work." . . .

NOTES

1. Allan Angoff, "The Male Librarian—An Anomaly?" *Library Journal*, February 15, 1959, p. 553.

2. *Austin-American Statesman,* January 16, 1990; response by John Kelso, January 18, 1990.

3. Some of the most important studies of women in male-dominated occupations are: Rosabeth Moss Kanter, *Men and Women of the Corporation* (New York: Basic Books, 1977); Susan Martin, *Breaking and Entering: Policewomen on Patrol* (Berkeley: University of California Press, 1980); Cynthia Fuchs Epstein, *Women in Law* (New York: Basic Books, 1981); Kay Deaux and Joseph Ullman, *Women of Steel* (New York: Praeger, 1983); Judith Hicks Stiehm, *Arms and the Enlisted Woman* (Philadelphia: Temple University Press, 1989); Jerry Jacobs, *Revolving Doors: Sex Segregation and Women's Careers* (Stanford: Stanford University Press, 1989); Barbara Reskin and Patricia Roos, *Job Queues, Gender Queues: Explaining Women's Inroads into Male Occupations* (Philadelphia: Temple University Press, 1990).

Among the few books that do examine men's status in predominantly female occupations are Carol Tropp Schreiber, *Changing Places: Men and Women in Transitional Occupations* (Cambridge: MIT Press, 1979); Christine L. Williams, *Gender Differences at Work: Women and Men in Nontraditional Occupations* (Berkeley: University of California Press, 1989); and Christine L. Williams, ed., *Doing "Women's Work": Men in Nontraditional Occupations* (Newbury Park, CA: Sage Publications, 1993).

4. In an influential essay on methodological principles, Herbert Blumer counseled sociologists to "sedulously seek participants in the sphere of life who are acute observers and who are well informed. One such person is worth a hundred others who are merely unobservant participants." See "The Methodological Position of Symbolic Interactionism," in *Symbolic Interactionism: Perspective and Method* (Berkeley: University of California Press, 1969), p. 41.

5. The overall proportions in the population do not necessarily represent the experiences of individuals in my sample. Some nurses, for example, worked in groups that were composed almost entirely of men, while some social workers had the experience of being the only man in their group. The overall statistics provide a general guide, but relying on them exclusively can distort the actual experiences of individuals in the workplace. The statistics available for research on occupational sex segregation are not specific enough to measure internal divisions among workers. Research that uses firm-level data finds a far greater degree of segregation than research that uses national data. See William T. Bielby and James N. Baron, "A Woman's Place Is with Other Women: Sex Segregation within Organizations," in *Sex Segregation in the Workplace: Trends, Explanations, Remedies,* ed. Barbara Reskin (Washington, D.C.: National Academy Press, 1984), pp. 27–55.

6. Catharine MacKinnon, *Feminism Unmodified* (Cambridge: Harvard University Press, 1987), pp. 24–25.

7. Howard S. Rowland, *The Nurse's Almanac,* 2d ed. (Rockville, MD: Aspen Systems Corp., 1984), p. 153; John W. Wright, *The American Almanac of Jobs and Salaries,* 2d ed. (New York: Avon, 1984), p. 639.

8. King Research, Inc., *Library Human Resources: A Study of Supply and Demand* (Chicago: American Library Association, 1983), p. 41.

9. See, for example, Sue J. M. Freeman, *Managing Lives: Corporate Women and Social Change* (Amherst: University of Massachusetts Press, 1990).

10. Patricia A. Schmuck, "Women School Employees in the United States," in *Women Educators: Employees of Schools in Western Countries* (Albany: State University of New York Press, 1987), p. 85; James W. Grimm and Robert N. Stern, "Sex Roles and Internal Labor Market Structures: The Female Semi-Professions," *Social Problems* 21(1974): 690–705.

11. David A. Hardcastle and Arthur J. Katz, *Employment and Unemployment in Social Work: A Study of NASW Members* (Washington, D.C.: NASW, 1979), p. 41; Reginold O. York, H. Carl Henley and Dorothy N. Gamble, "Sexual Discrimination in Social Work: Is It Salary or Advancement?" *Social Work* 32 (1987): 336–340; Grimm and Stern, "Sex Roles and Internal Labor Market Structures."

12. Leigh Estabrook, "Women's Work in the Library/Information Sector," in *My Troubles Are Going to Have Trouble with Me,* ed. Karen Brodkin Sacks and Dorothy Remy (New Brunswick, NJ: Rutgers University Press, 1984), p. 165.

13. Liliane Floge and D. M. Merrill found a similar phenomenon in their study of male nurses. See "Tokenism Reconsidered: Male Nurses and Female Physicians in a Hospital Setting," Social Forces 64 (1986): 931–932.

14. Jim Allan makes this argument in "Male Elementary Teachers: Experiences and Perspectives," in *Doing "Women's Work": Men in Nontraditional Occupations,* ed. Christine L. Williams (Newbury Park, CA: Sage Publications, 1993), pp. 113–127.

THINKING ABOUT THE READING

Compare the discrimination men experience in traditionally female occupations to that experienced by women in traditionally male occupations. What is the "glass escalator effect"? In what ways can the glass escalator actually be harmful to men? What do you suppose might happen to the structure of the American labor force if men did in fact begin to enter predominantly female occupations in the same proportion as women entering predominantly male occupations?

The Global Dynamics of Population

Demographic Trends

In the past several chapters we have examined the various interrelated sources of social stratification. Race, class, and gender continue to determine access to cultural, economic, and political opportunities. Yet another source of inequality that we don't think much about but that has enormous local, national, and global significance is the changing size and shape of the human population. Globally, population imbalances between richer and poorer societies underlie most if not all of the other important forces for change that are taking place today. Poor, developing countries are expanding rapidly, while the populations in wealthy, developed countries have either stabilized or, in some cases, declined. When the population of a country grows rapidly, the age structure is increasingly dominated by young people. In slow-growth countries with low birthrates and high life expectancy, the population is much older.

Often overlooked in our quest to identify the structural factors that shape our everyday experiences are the effects of our *birth cohort*. Birth cohorts are more than just a collection of individuals born within a few years of each other; they are distinctive generations tied together by historical events, national and global population trends, and large-scale societal changes.

In "From Sweatshop to Hip-Hop," Ryan Pintado-Vertner describes the relationship between the economic needs of multinational corporations and the tastes and styles of youth of color. These youth have long been ignored by the fashion industry. Today, however, they are at the heart of multi-billion-dollar marketing campaigns. Pintado-Vertner asks why there is now such keen interest in this cohort and what the broader social consequences of such interest will be.

As social and demographic conditions in poor, developing countries grow worse, pressures to migrate increase, creating a variety of cultural, political, and economic fears in countries experiencing high levels of immigration. Immigration—both legal and illegal—has become one of the most contentious political issues in the United States today. While politicians debate proposed immigration restrictions, people from all corners of the globe continue to come to this country looking for a better life. In "Border Blues: Mexican Immigration and Mexican-American Identity," Farai Chideya describes life on the U.S.–Mexico border from the perspective of both border patrol agents and the immigrants themselves. Chideya points out that conflict over illegal immigration is not between the United States and Mexico, but between the various visions of what Mexican immigration means to the United States. Although some people decry the waves of illegal immigration as a burden and a scourge on society, others profit from the cheap labor that illegal immigrants provide.

It is also important to remember that the movement of people between countries has set the groundwork for inequality and stratification that extend beyond national borders. Third-world laborers have become a crucial part of the global economic marketplace and an important foreign resource for multinational corporations. Low-skilled jobs are frequently exported to developing countries that have cheaper labor costs. On the surface, it would appear that such an arrangement benefits all involved: The multinational corporations benefit from higher profits, the developing countries benefit from higher rates of employment, the workers themselves benefit from earning a wage that would have otherwise been unavailable to them, and consumers in wealthy countries benefit from less expensive products.

But most of us are unaware of and unconcerned with the harsh conditions under which our most coveted products are made. William Greider, in "These Dark Satanic Mills," discusses the exploitative potential of relying on third-world factories. He uses a particular tragedy, the 1993 industrial fire at the Kader Industrial Toy Company in Thailand, to illustrate how global economics create and sustain international inequality. Greider shows us the complex paradox of the global marketplace: While foreign manufacturing facilities free factory workers from certain poverty, they also ensnare the workers in new and sometimes lethal forms of domination.

From Sweatshop to Hip-Hop

Ryan Pintado-Vertner

(2002)

India Arie is smiling down at you from a Gap billboard. A half-mile later, it is progressive hip-hop crew Black Eyed Peas looking fresh in Levi's Silver Tab jeans. Rewind two years, and it was Mos Def and Talib Kweli, then De La Soul. Rewind 10 years, and hip-hop was absent in the mainstream fashion industry. The billboards would have featured thin, slightly curved white female models who refused to smile.

Ten years ago, when Gap Inc. and Levi Strauss & Company gazed into the future of their clothing empires, youth of color were an irrelevant demographic. The fashion power-houses believed that hip-hop was an annoyingly violent fad that would pass through like a bullet. They gambled against hip-hop. And so far, they have lost millions. Today their futures look very different. Both companies have become lightning rods for bad news. Gap stock, once flying high and helping its Republican founder Don Fisher buy political clout in San Francisco, was degraded to junk status by Moody's in February after 21 months of non-stop losses. In the same month, CARMA, a media analysis firm, announced that among U.S. retailers, Gap had received the second-worst media coverage in the world, second only to bankrupt K-Mart.

Meanwhile, Levi Strauss & Company has been losing profits—and laying off workers—in what seems to be an irreversible downhill slide in U.S. sales. It has recycled executives like tin cans, dumped marketing agencies left and right, gone IPO and then reversed course back to private stockholdings—all in an effort to stop losing money. When announcing their bad news to investors, both companies focus on business details like profitability per square footage of retail real estate, or they talk generally about the need for more competitive fashion designs, or, like everyone, they blame September 11.

Neither Gap nor Levi's confesses to the deeper irony of their situation. Both companies are suffering from a loss of cool—the fashion industry's equivalent of cardiac arrest. Where did cool go? It shifted to the very people who were dismissed by fashion insiders as "sociopaths" in the 1980s and early 1990s. They are the kids shooting hoops in concrete jungles, the break-dancers taking over high school hallways, the American-born children of exploited garment workers. The kind of people who rarely made it into fashion billboards. Today, coolness lives among youth of color and their beloved hip-hop. And now, if they are to survive the new millennium, Gap and Levi's must take that coolness back.

Garment Exploits

The difference between this reality and what the companies anticipated is enormous. Levi's predicted a cheaper, globalized workforce, and began closing U.S. factories and relocating those jobs to countries like Costa Rica and China. In the 1980s alone Levi's closed 58 plants, putting 10,400 people out of work and moving about half of its production overseas. Gap did the same thing, subcontracting with 3,600 factories in 50 countries by 2001. As a result, Gap and Levi's, like others in the industry, are the focus of dozens of anti-sweatshop campaigns internationally, which have revealed terrible labor conditions in the garment factories sewing their clothing. Both companies have been sued by garment workers in Saipan, a U.S. territory in the Pacific. The suit alleges that the factories, sewing clothes for a who's-who of fashion companies, including Tommy Hilfiger, Calvin Klein, Target and the Limited, practiced indentured servitude. Witness, a human rights organization, says that in Saipan, "14 hour shifts, payless paydays and lock-downs are routine."

In 1990, Levi Strauss & Company closed a factory in San Antonio, laid off more than thousand workers, gave them horrible severance packages, and then moved the jobs to Costa Rica. Jason Morteo understands all of this. He is a 17-year-old Chicano lyricist, beat junkie, and grafitti writer in San Antonio. On Wednesday nights, he can be found at Bruno's, a local restaurant, battling other mcees in the freestyle competition. ("I would have won first place, except the other dude started beat-boxing on me.") He has a front row seat for what Levi's and other clothing companies are trying to do with hip-hop and garment workers. "For me, I find it so ironic that Levi's, of all companies, is going to try to make a profit off of hip-hop culture, on top of that Latin hip-hop culture, when there's so many people here they exploit so much," he says. "And the companies do their best to keep that out of the media."

Defining Cool

To bury this negative publicity, both Gap and Levi's spend hundreds of millions of dollars on marketing, showering us with images of cool. For years, those images, alternately flashy and sexy and subdued, were, above all, white.

The formula seemed unbeatable: white models + brown workers = mega-profits. Gap became the largest clothing company in the world. Levi's held its own, struggling at times, but still flexing its iconic muscle. Youth of color continued to be invisible, except in so far as they worked at garment factories abroad. (Levi's code of conduct allows 15-year-old laborers to work 60 hours per week in its factories.) In its marketing, Gap focused on selling khakis to the predominately white professional class and their children, and Levi's left the power of its name on auto-pilot, selling denim to teenagers in department stores.

Then, after hip-hop awoke in the 1990s, reality slapped them right in the face. They finally got the hint, and the shift is evident on television commercials and billboards across the country. Since 1997, Gap ads have featured L.L. Cool J, Missy Elliot, and RUN DMC. Last season, Gap's commercials featured deejaying, one of the least celebrated elements of hip-hop. DJs Shortkut and Rob Swift cut it up with Shannyn Sossamon, an up and coming L.A. deejay. More recently, Lisa "Left Eye" Lopes and Shaggy sang in the "Give A Little" television ads, along with India Arie and Macy Gray. Levi's focused its attention on progressive artists. It sponsored a Lauryn Hill concert tour. It promoted Mos Def and Talib Kweli before Mos Def's career sky-rocketed. Most recently it has scooped up Black Eyed Peas.

But, like most of the fashion industry, Gap and Levi's were more than a decade late on hip-hop. "Within a few years, well before 'Yo! MTV Raps,' it was clear that this was a massive movement that would influence everything from fashion to automobiles to lifestyle," says Irma Zandl of Zandl Group, a New York-based marketing and trend consultant whose clients include Gap. "Hip-hop culture has gradually enveloped mainstream youth culture not only in the suburbs but also throughout the world."

Why the lag? It certainly was not for lack of opportunity. Hip-hop has long been one of the most fashion-conscious cultural phenomena in America. In the 1980s, its most popular artists defined themselves with signature products. RUN DMC wrote a hit song called "My Adidas" that transformed the shoe into a cult classic. To this day, people rock the Adidas that RUN DMC made famous. L.L. Cool J did the same thing with Kangol hats. The list of fashion breakthroughs stretched on through the years: biker shorts, Daisy Dukes, huge clock necklaces, African medallions, fat gold chains, sportswear.

The brand consciousness reflects one basic truth about hip-hop: it emerged from despair. Black and brown youth, trapped in fire-blown ghettos across the United States, used rap lyrics to imagine an antidote to their desperation. They watched as the so-called free market created two very different worlds. In one, their own, emptiness reigned: empty pockets, empty blocks, empty promises. In the other, every edifice, every healthy child, every manicured lawn was a testament to the euphoric, distracting power of capitalism.

Presented with this dual world, some rap musicians became activists. Others simply proclaimed that the clear antidote to poverty was wealth. These artists came to define popular rap culture. They wore thick gold chains, leather outfits, fur coats and eventually Tommy Hilfiger, Gucci, Donna Karan—symbols of their success. In the rap culture they created, wealth and fame could erase any stigma, even the oldest, most basic manifestation of American racism: the idea that blackness is ugly. Murdered rapper Notorious B.I.G., who grew up poor in Brooklyn, once rapped about himself:

> Heart throb, never/
> Black and ugly as ever/
> However/
> I stay COOGI down to the socks

COOGI, a luxury Australian knitwear label, sells clothes for more money than most poor people make in a week. The company, which never capitalized on its hip-hop potential, is now teetering on the financial edge.

Crashing the Party

Still, despite the clear evidence, it took the mostly white fashion world another decade to notice that hip-hop, perhaps more than any other cultural phenomenon in contemporary America, is a gold mine of mind-boggling proportions. Two things seemed to block its vision. One was racism. Rap triggered virtually every racial stereotype possible in the white imagination. The race-fueled controversy surrounding hip-hop in its first decade was phenomenal. Unable to move beyond this visceral disgust, and still enamored of America's basic whiteness, the fashion industry stayed away. Its second blindspot was mass marketing. Companies like Levi's and Gap marketed to enormous young audiences—from 10-year-olds to young professionals. To cover such territory, companies would shoot for the most common denominators in their marketing strategies. They chose themes and images that attracted the largest proportion of their audience—middle-income white Americans.

But economists and marketers noticed that the middle was shrinking. Economic policy during the 1970s and 1980s created more wealth and more poverty, while reducing the size of the middle class. Race demographics also shifted dramatically, especially in certain geographic regions, as people of color make up an increased percentage of the total population. Suddenly, the old marketing strategy—aiming for the all-purpose middle—no longer worked. In 1997 a market research firm called Roper Starch released a report suggesting ways to market to the "Two Americas." The new approach was known as two-tier marketing. Many companies, from banks to fashion labels, created multiple marketing strategies for the same products: one strategy targeted the wealthy, the other targeted the poor. For Gap, this meant adding the high-priced Banana Republic label and the discount Old Navy brand—three versions of essentially the same product.

Once companies learned to divide their enormous markets into smaller pieces, it became easier for them to recognize the value of hip-hop. Marketers learned to use hip-hop strategically, while using other approaches for other niches—often all in the same marketing campaign. But beyond two-tier marketing strategies, trend-spotters like Zandl Group and Teenage Research Unlimited pointed to the real bottomline with hip-hop and marketing: white kids with "purchasing power" were listening to it. They warned that if apparel companies like Levi's and Gap underestimated the impact of hip-hop on young consumers—not just on youth of color, but all youth—they would "suffer dearly," as Irma Zandl put it. "Even today, as rock reasserts itself, hip hop beats and hip hop flava are dominant."

Tommy Hilfiger listened to the oracles. Tommy, one of the companies trying to settle with the Saipan workers, was among the first mainstream fashion icons to cash in on the hip-hop strategy. Its traditional marketing strategy relied on heavy doses of American patriotism, sharp-jawed white men, and New England atmosphere to compete with companies like Polo and Calvin Klein for the men's apparel market. But then one day hip-hop headz discovered the brand, and Tommy was suddenly, almost effortlessly, the epitome of cool. Without fully abandoning its traditional marketing approach, the company cultivated its hip-hop audience on the down-low with strategies like giving rappers free shopping sprees—and even clothing a hip-hop Santa ornament for the White House Christmas tree. Snoop Doggy Dogg performed on "Saturday Night Live" in 1994 wearing all Tommy gear, and Tommy sales increased $90 million that year, according to industry estimates. On the strength of hip-hop listeners, the company's sales shot past a billion dollars a year, making it the blockbuster label of the 1990s. Tommy got so phat that it even tried to buy its competitor Calvin Klein—the gangster rapper challenging the preppy white model to a fight.

Rumor swirled around Tommy's rise to power, as some communities of color were suspicious of the company's real interest in them. For years, urban legend reported various versions of the same story: that Tommy Hilfiger, the man himself, told the press (or, as I heard the rumor years ago, told Oprah Winfrey) that he was disgusted by all these hip-hoppers wearing his clothes, because he was not designing clothes with such people in mind. Regardless of whether the rumor was true, it spoke to the basic irony of hip-hop and fashion marketing. In a white-dominated industry obsessed by coolness, the underdog has become the undisputed champion of cool.

And Gap and Levi's are suffering for it.

Though no one believes they will collapse into bankruptcy like K-Mart, many think Gap and Levi's waited too long to join the hip-hop parade. Gap itself refuses to acknowledge that hip-hop has played any role in its current doldrums. Likewise, it denies any strategic reason for using hip hop artists in its marketing, and claims no direct interest in youth of color. Gap spokeswoman Rebeccah Weiss puts it this way:

> We chose DJs Shortkut and Rob Swift, as well as India Arie, because they are talented, we like their music, and most importantly, they express unique personal style. We cast them along with many other types of musicians in order to reach out to many different audiences.

Levi Strauss & Company, on the other hand, has been more blunt. "Many white teens identify with black culture, which they find powerful and attractive," Marian Salzman, founding director of TBWA Chiat/Day, Levi's former marketing agency, told a journalist in 1996. "A typical gangsta rap listener is a

14-year-old white boy from the suburbs. An in-your-face attitude is a marketing hook that screams authentic." This was a startling shift for a company that was an icon of white American culture. The century-old denim pants were the blue jean of choice for the Industrial Age and the Wild West. By the 1970s, Levi's had been marketed by James Dean, Marilyn Monroe, Elvis Presley and Bob Dylan.

Basking in all of this white nostalgia, Levi Strauss & Company was looking the wrong way when black and brown youth turned the fashion world on its head. "It has suffered dearly," says Zandl. "Its popularity amongst teen boys has gone from 28 percent in '94 to 4 percent in 2001–a whopping 86 percent decline." In 1996, Levi's began its hunt for black culture by launching a television advertising campaign featuring young black kids scaring the shit out of Wall Street professionals, asking in the tag line, "Do you fear me?" The controversial campaign flopped, but has been followed by many others, including the most recent Black Eyed Peas billboard.

This trend infuriates Esperanza Garza, an organizer with Fuerza Unida, which works with women and youth affected by Levi's plant closures in San Antonio. But she really hit the roof when she saw Levi's mega-popular Super Bowl commercial this year: a young Latino, wearing Levi's and a tank top, was break-dancing down the street in Mexico City, listening to Spanish-language hip-hop group Control Machete (of Amores Perros fame). The featured break-dancer was 21-year-old Johnny Cervin, a Mexican-American hip-hopper from Los Angeles.

"They are trying to sell to us now. We are the new market. They can't fool us. We know who they are," Garza says. While the company courts black and brown youth, she says, it continues to exploit their parents here and abroad. Levi Strauss is closing its two remaining factories in San Antonio in April and "negotiating contracts that are worse than severance agreements in 1999."

Jason Morteo puts it this way. "It's disappointing as a hip-hop artist, and as a Latin American, that I know something so wrong is done to my people, but people are starting to go out and buy these clothes," he says. "People are so deceived, they don't know the full truth about what this company has done."

THINKING ABOUT THE READING

Why has the fashion industry suddenly started paying attention to youth of color as a potentially lucrative market? What are some of the implications of this focus for the representation of hip-hop culture? When multinational companies begin to recognize cultural subgroups and incorporate these images into their advertising, who ultimately controls the images that the world sees? What kind of distinctiveness will these cultural groups be able to retain as they become part of this global marketing process? Do you see these processes as a good thing or as problematic—or both?

Border Blues

Mexican Immigration and Mexican-American Identity

Farai Chideya

(1999)

The land around El Paso, Texas, is an imposing desert scene painted in tones of ochre and red clay—stark mountains, vast sky, arid plains. It's so far west that it's the only major Texas city in the mountain, rather than the central, time zone. Atop a nearby mountain is the massive Christo Rey—an imposing figure of Jesus hewn out of tons of stone. It seems like a peaceful vista, but this land is the staging ground for a colossal clash of cultures—the meeting of Mexico and the United States at the border. The biggest clash is not between Mexico and the United States per se, but between many competing visions of what Mexican immigration means to the United States. Mexican immigration has been decried as an "illegal alien invasion," an erosion of American's job base, even the beginnings of a plot to return the Southwest to Mexican hands. And sometimes Mexican Americans themselves are perceived with suspicion, in the belief their allegiance is pledged to Mexico, not the United States.

What's the reality behind these perceptions? And what's life on the border like? . . . I've spent virtually my whole life living on the East Coast, where the Latino communities are dominated by Puerto Ricans, Dominicans, Cubans. I groove to Latin hip-hop and Afro-Cuban sounds, but I hadn't heard much Mexican-American music like ranchero and Tejano. I know a good plate of *pernil* when I eat

one, but I couldn't tell you from *tortas*. And I've heard more opinions over whether Puerto Rico should become independent than I've heard firsthand accounts of life on the border. In other words, when I came to El Paso I was starting at ground zero. Why did I choose El Paso? Well, first, this border city has been the site of a well-publicized crackdown on illegal immigration. Second, it's been deeply impacted by government policies like NAFTA. But third, and most important to me, El Paso is not majority Anglo but 70 percent Latino and Mexican American, a place where there are bound to be differences of opinion between members of the Latino community.

I head for El Paso in the summer of 1996, a time when the federal government is debating whether to bar the children of undocumented immigrants from going to schools and whether to tighten limits on even legal immigration. The measures are championed by Senator and presidential candidate Bob Dole. A bill that would have clamped down on legal immigration also withered on the vine. It is the continuation of a vigorous ongoing national debate over immigration. Three years before, the newly installed Clinton administration had pushed for and ultimately passed the hotly contested North American Free Trade Agreement. Proponents said NAFTA would stimulate U.S.-Mexican trade, putting dollars into America's economy. Opponents argued it would cost thousands of U.S. jobs when plants relocated to take advantage of Mexican workers who earn as little as five dollars per day. Then, in November of 1994, California voters passed Proposition 187, a referendum designed to deny all public services—health care, welfare, even elementary and secondary education—to illegal immigrants. Sixty-three percent of white Californians voted for Proposition 187, while 69 percent of Latinos voted against it. Before 187 could be implemented, opponents challenged its constitutionality and sent the issue to the courts.

Like California, Texas is just under 30 percent Latino. But the state's governor and senators, all of them Republicans, didn't follow California's lead and try to impose new laws on illegal immigration. Instead, they voiced objections to anti-immigrant legislation. Public opinion, culture, and commerce all played a role. Polls show that most Texas residents still view immigration as a boon, not a burden, while the opposite is true in California. Texas draws identity from the Mexican border, whether it's the heritage of many of its citizens, historical events like the Alamo, or the hallmarks of everyday life, like food. (The term "Tex-Mex" says it all.) And an analysis by *The Economist* points to more tangible commodities. In 1995, Texas exported $24 billion in goods to Mexico, its leading trading partner. Mexico was only California's fourth trading partner, with $7 billion in goods.

But while trade with Mexico has been good for Texas in general, the NAFTA free trade treaty has hit El Paso's economy hard. The city already has an unemployment rate double the national average. Now plants that used to pay workers five dollars an hour in El Paso can pay them five dollars a day just across the border in Juarez— and not pay duty on the goods shipped back to the United States. Among the issues I want to explore here in El Paso are not just questions of Mexican-American identity—how they see themselves—but also how they see their (real or distant) cousins across the border. Do the residents of El Paso look upon the Mexicans as brothers, economic competitors—or a bit of both?

One of the first people I meet in El Paso gives me a hint of the differences in opinion about border issues. Nora is chic, almost out of place in the grungy alternative bar we're both sitting in, with high cheekbones, light skin, and curly black hair cut in a bob. "I hate to say it, but I agree with him," she says. "They need to learn English." The "him" Nora is talking about is a black city councilman who chewed out a citizen who addressed a town hall meeting in Spanish. The "they"—an implicit "they"—are recent Mexican immigrants. Nora, who used to model in New York and now works in the local clothing industry, takes the councilman's side. But some local cartoonists lampooned the politician's outrage, and many residents wrote letters of protest to the newspaper.

Many El Paso residents are from first- or second-generation immigrant families, people who remember life in Mexico and have direct family ties across the border. But it's a mistake to think that they encompass all of El Paso's Latinos. A large proportion of El Paso families, like Nora's, are *Tejano*, a term which means that her forebears have lived in Texas for generations—i.e., even before it was part of the United States. (As many Tejanos like to say, "We didn't cross the border. The border crossed us.") The unique Tex-Mex culture of the Tejanos gave rise to one of the biggest Latina singing sensations, Selena, whose premature death in 1995 woke America up to the size of the Latino community. And one lesson America has yet to learn about the Latino community is how many different cultural and political perspectives there are—even within a single group, like Mexican Americans.

Those different perspectives come into direct conflict when it comes to an issue as controversial as the border. I focused on two groups of people familiar with El Paso: the enforcers who try to keep people out, and the border crossers desperate to stay in America.

The Enforcers

Melissa Lucio gets the radio call at noon on a scorching summer day. An electric sensor just inside the U.S. border's been tripped; agents are looking around but they haven't found anyone yet. She heads for the sensor's coordinates and pulls up alongside a couple of agents. They're beating the bushes around a splotch of water halfway between a pond and a puddle. After a minute, a guy about thirty-five years old steps out of a thicket with a resigned look on his face and a satchel slung over his shoulder. A Mexican worker who's crossed illegally into the States, he also happens to be wearing an OFFICIAL U.S. TAXPAYER baseball cap. When I laughingly point this out to Melissa, she goes me one better. "We had a guy who walked in with a Border Patrol hat the other day. We asked him where he got it and he said he found it on the bank of the river. The officer's name was still written on the inside—he'd lost it over a year ago."

Melissa's just one of the thousands of U.S. Border Patrol agents charged with the thankless (and some would say impossible) task of keeping illegal immigrants out of America and catching them once they come in. A Mexican-American El Paso native, she's also the wife of another Mexican-American Border Patrol agent. Just thirty years old, she's also the mother of five sons. With her thick black hair pulled back in a neat French braid, her brown uniform replete with two-way radio and gun, Melissa rides the Texas–Mexico–New Mexico border tracking and detaining border crossers. Sometimes she gets help from the electronic signals of hidden sensors, but much of the time she relies on her own eyes, scanning the horizon and bending toward the earth to interpret "signs"—the scant marks and footprints in the dry earth which she reads for vital clues

of time and direction. The day is hot and clear. Recent rains have made it easier to track signs—and have also put desert flowers into bloom. Melissa's comments as she navigates the covered-cab truck around bumps and gullies are punctuated with interjections about the wildlife—"Beautiful bird!" "Really cool lizard!" "Check out that jackrabbit!" But her ear is always tuned to the radio, and she's tough when she has to be. If her truck gets stuck, she breaks off branches and digs it out; if a suspect in a vehicle takes off into a residential area, she pursues and radios the local police. As we traverse highways, dirt roads, and long stretches of pristine desert, we don't run into any other female agents out in the field.

The man Melissa has just picked up doesn't protest when she puts him in the covered back area of the truck. In fact, he reaches into his satchel, pulls out a newspaper, and starts to read. At my request, she asks him where he was going and what he was going to do.

"*¿Para dónde vas?*" she asks.

"*Para Coronodo,*" he answers.

Coronado is an affluent area, replete with a country club, where he was headed to cut yards. "He was actually closer to the east side of Juarez," Melissa translates, "and I asked him why he didn't cross over there. And he said there's a lot of *cholos* [bandits] stealing and robbing in that area. He says it's easier to cross over here. He says he doesn't come often, but every once in a while when he needs money."

One stereotype of illegal immigrants is that they're a bunch of welfare cheats. But this crosser, and most of the ones that Melissa picks up, are coming in strictly to work—sometimes to stay for the day and go back that night. The economics are clear cut. The starting wage in the *maquiladoras,* or twin plants—so named because they're owned by U.S. corporations who maintain both Mexican factories and their "twins" across the border—is about five dollars a day. The wages for yard work are far, far higher. "If they have their own tools, they could make sixty bucks a day," Melissa says. "If not, it could be thirty or forty." In other words, one day per week of work in the United States earns more than an entire week's labor in Mexico. Of course, there'd be no point crossing the border if U.S. employers weren't willing, even eager, to give undocumented workers jobs. If a border crosser makes it in every day, the payoff is good even relative to U.S. workers. "If you think about minimum wage, four sixty per hour with taxes taken out, [the border crossers] are going to make more," she says. "Even the Mexican police officers, some of them make four hundred dollars per month if they're lucky."

I ask Melissa if the people she picks up ever give her flack for being Mexican American and picking up Mexicans. "I've only had one person say, 'Don't you think you're being mean?'" she says. "And I say, if you had a job, you would do it to the best of your ability, right? They say 'Yeah.'"—she draws the word out to give it a dubious inflection. "And I say that's just what I'm doing. I've got five children. I want to maintain my household. And they understand."

"Like this education issue," she continues. "Let's say you educate them, and then what? They're illegal in the United States so they can't obtain work. Or let's say they become legal, then they're going to be competing against my children or me for a job that could have very well been mine." She's no fan of NAFTA, which she believes has knocked the wind out of an already weakened local economy. "Not a month goes by that you don't hear about a local company that's up and relocating to Mexico," she says. "It may be a good law, but not for the people who live paycheck to paycheck."

We drop our passenger off at the Paso Del Norte processing station, a short-term holding area that seems appropriately located in the middle of nowhere. Inside the plain building is a bullpen of officers at their desks, surrounded by large cells where individuals are sorted by gender, age, and area of origin. Locals—people from Juarez and nearby border areas—are the easiest to process and return. People from the interior of Mexico, farther south, are interviewed by Mexican officials and given bus fare home. And last of all are detainees from Central America, some of whom have traveled hundreds upon hundreds of miles from Honduras and points south, only to be caught on the final leg of their journey. There are men and women, old and young—really young. One of the kids in the pen, who flashes me an impish grin when I check him out, looks about twelve.

"Oh, we get kids who are eight, nine, ten. I ask them, 'Your Mom, doesn't she worry about you?' And some of their parents do, but they really run wild. If they know a lady at a bakery [in the United States] will give them sweetbreads, stuff like that, they'll come. Some of them have friends they come to goof off with. This is what they do. This is recreation."

By the time they're sixteen—which is the age of the next border crosser we pick up—they're usually crossing to work. The teenager has tan skin and hair bleached nearly blond by the sun; he's carrying yard tools.

"*¿Con qué te posito entro los Estados Unidos?*" Melissa asks.

"*Trabajo.*"

"*¿Qué clase trabajo?*"

"*En yardas,*" he answers. He was headed to Coronado as well.

An Economic Judgment

Melissa Lucio is not only a Border Patrol agent, but a mother and a taxpayer as well. She believes the influx of illegal immigrants could curtail her children's chances at prosperity. "When people talk about immigration issues as being racial," she says, "you have Hispanics as well as Anglos as well as other ethnic groups that will say the same thing: 'We need to be strong on immigration issues.' Why should my tax dollars and my anything be funding someone else?"

Melissa's family immigrated from Mexico a couple of generations ago. "My grandma jokes that I'm going to send her back over the border," Melissa says. She had what she describes as a typical, happy coming of age in El Paso. She met her first love, Rick, who's also Mexican American, in high school, and married him right after she graduated. Like several members of both of their families, Rick went into law enforcement, joining the Border Patrol. Melissa dreamed about the same thing for ten years before she decided to take the plunge. "I had thought about going to college and to the FBI behavioral science department, to pursue some forensics. But the more and more children I started having, I just started to see that dream being pushed further and further away," she says.

Melissa found out the Border Patrol was hiring when Rick told her about a career day he was coordinating—but he tried to discourage her from trying out. It was an arduous process. First she had to take a written test to get admitted to the academy. Then she had to get in shape. After seven years of bearing and raising five sons (Daniel, David, Derek, Dario, and Andrew—"we ran out of Ds," she says), she was two hundred and twenty pounds. She quit her job and lost forty before going into the academy, and another ten once she was there. When it came time for the induction ceremony, she received her badge from an officer who'd specially requested the honor—her husband. "As he's pinning me he whispers in my ear, 'Oh Melissa, I never thought you would make it. You've never made me so proud.'" She beams. "It was absolutely great. It was amazing."

Now Melissa works just past the El Paso line in the Christo Rey area of New Mexico. Standing atop the hill that supports the huge statue of Christ, you can see Mexico, New Mexico, and Texas in panorama. You can also see the latest attempts to keep the border

clamped down. Along the length of the border, construction crews are putting up an immense fence designed to eventually cover the entire U.S.-Mexico line. But Melissa for one is skeptical it will stop the crossings. "They'll just have to walk a little further," she says, to where mesas break the fence line.

Her division, which contains forty to sixty agents per day depending on scheduling, picks up about a hundred and fifty people per day, a thousand per week. It's labor-intensive work, particularly given the nature of the terrain. The El Paso Border Patrol region gained prominence in 1991 when Silvestre Reyes, the chief at the time, implemented a policy he called Operation Hold the Line. Instead of chasing border crossers after they walked over train tracks or through the Rio Grande (at the Juarez-El Paso border, the river is little more than a trickle in a concrete culvert), Reyes posted agents in vehicles along large stretches of the border. Their presence dropped the number of crossers at that juncture from eight thousand a day to virtually zero. But that meant more Mexicans who wanted to come to Texas chose to go through the New Mexico mountains. "You can't do that here. You'd have to have a ton of agents to watch every side of every hill. We have to be mobile," Melissa says.

It seems like an awful lot of work for each agent on an eight-hour shift to pick up the equivalent of three border jumpers a day. But the political stakes are far higher than those numbers would suggest. Tensions about immigration characterize the turn of this century as deeply as they marked the turn of the last one. But instead of Italians, Irish, and Jews who received a lukewarm welcome disembarking at Ellis Island in the late 1800s and early 1900s, Mexican Americans crossing into the border for points as far flung as New York and the Midwest are the immigrants under scrutiny today. According to the Immigration and Naturalization Service, in 1995 eighty-six thousand Mexicans emigrated to the United

States legally, to work, study, or join their families. They were the largest single group of U.S. immigrants, and joined approximately 6 million Mexican immigrants living legally in the United States. (All told, there are over 30 million Latinos living in the United States.) U.S. officials estimate there are more than 5 million illegal immigrants in the United States, 54 percent of them Mexicans, most of whom also came to work or go to school. While some agents are used as human scare-crows, keeping would-be border crossers out, Melissa's job is mainly to track and capture the people who do make it through.

The pickups don't always go smoothly. Some of the border crossers have passed out and nearly died from heat stroke or dehydra-tion as they're being taken in; other times agents just find the bodies. (One agent tells me a gruesome, perhaps apocryphal tale of find-ing a body whose eyes had literally popped out of the scorched head.) Sometimes people resist or carry weapons. The agents also have to watch out for *cholos*—gang members who can come from either side of the border, and who often prey on those crossing the border to work. In a Wild West twist, some of the *cholos* rob trains passing through the region. "A ban-dit will board the trains out West and pilfer through first, and say, 'The Nike tennis shoes are here.' Then they have their buddies, twenty or thirty or forty guys, shunt the track so the little computer tells the train to stop. As soon as it stops, these guys start throwing the stuff down. They don't care if the nine hundred ninety-nine dollar television cracks open because the good ones will land somewhere and they will grab it and sell it. Or on the other hand, in the next two weeks you'll arrest a bunch of people that are all wearing brand new Nike tennis shoes."

Sometimes they prey on the individuals working along the border fence line. As our day together draws to a close, Melissa gets a radio call from one of the men erecting the new fence. He's worried because four men are approaching and he's alone. "Ten-four. Horse patrol and myself will thirteen over there and check it out." Melissa radios back. As we approach, two men on powerful horses gallop parallel, about twenty yards away. "I'm on the list for horseback," Melissa says. "I think it's so cool." She surveys the situation as we approach. "These guys are definitely up to no good." I ask how she can tell. "They don't have any bags, which means they're not crossing. They don't have any water and they're just hanging around with no attempt to go north." They might have wanted to get their hands on some of the construction supplies, she figures.

Every eight weeks Melissa and the other agents change shift—days, evenings, overnights (which start at midnight). Now she's working days and her husband is working evenings, making it easy for him to take the kids to and from school. They try to avoid both doing the evening shift, "because we've noticed that our kids' grades drop."

To help out, Rick and Melissa have hired a live-in housekeeper, which is a drama in and of itself. "I advertised for a housekeeper two years ago, [and] the first thing off the bat was, 'Are you a U.S. citizen or a legal resi-dent? If not, I work for immigration and I can't hire you.' And half the people would hang up. A quarter of the people would say, 'I'm a border crosser,' but they were not per-mitted to work. The lady we hired, she's late forties, great with the kids, teaching the kids Spanish, and she's a legal resident, so it worked out really, really, well."

"So what's funny, a neighbor came up and said, 'Do you realize your house is under sur-veillance?' I was like 'Excuse me?'" One day, when both husband and wife were gone, an agent came to the home and asked their house-keeper for documents. Neighbors came out to watch, and she waved right back at them to say "I'm still here because I'm legal," Melissa says. The couple learned why the Immigration and

Naturalization Service suspected them when they talked the matter over with their chief. A neighbor had phoned in with an elaborate tale how the housekeeper, supposedly illegal, had begged up and down the street for work and found it with the Lucios. "It's just someone being vindictive. I thought, that is really terrible," Melissa says. "At the time we lived in the Coronado Country Club area. They were really unhappy about Hold the Line because their maids couldn't come in illegally." As we head back into the station, I think again about the economics of the illegal immigration debate. The reality is that for every undocumented immigrant who finds low-wage work in America, there is somebody willing to hire that person. And some of the same people benefiting from below-market labor loudly decry illegal immigration at the same time.

The Politics of the Border

America likes to think its immigration laws are tough. And while they're arguably harsh on people who cross the border, most penalties on the businesses that hire illegal immigrants are modest. And people like the border crossers Melissa Lucio picked up often don't work for "businesses" at all, but everyday U.S. citizens who usually suspect the person they've hired to cut their lawn or babysit their kids doesn't hold a green card. America decries the waves of illegal immigration. But some Americans on the border and throughout the United States profit from the cheap labor these immigrants provide.

The economics of the border are full of conflict and duplicity, people who profit, people who lose, and people who lie about which camp they're in. Most important, the economics are deeply intertwined. Downtown El Paso, an unremarkable collection of modest office buildings and low-priced shops, is tethered by a bridge to downtown Juarez, Mexico. The Mexicans who cross the bridge come to work,

visit, and shop. The Anglos going the other way often buy cheap groceries and pharmaceuticals (you can purchase Valium and Prozac without a prescription there), and college students hit the bars, where the words "drinking age" are meaningless. What happens when the Border Patrol cracks down on illegal crossings? Many downtown El Paso businessmen say their shops suffer, deprived of the day workers that used to buy clothes and consumer goods.

Many Mexican residents of Juarez aren't happy about the increasingly fortified border, either. El Paso and Juarez are separated by an unimpressive trickle of water that, amazingly enough, is part of the mighty Rio Grande river. A cement aqueduct, fenced on both sides, contains the water and separates the people. Painted on the concrete are signs decrying the border fortifications:

One reads OJO MIGRA (eyes are painted into the *o*'s) ¡¡YA BASTA!!

Another says: POR CADA ILEGAL QUE NOS MALTRATEN EN LOS ESTADOS UNIDOS DE N.A. VAMOS A MALTRATAR UN VISITANTE GAVACHO. BIENVENIDOS LOS PAISANOS.

Their translations: "Look, Immigration—enough already!" and "For every illegal they mistreat in the United States, we are going to mistreat a visiting gringo. Welcome, countrymen."

It sounds like a bit of useless bravado, the "welcome, countrymen" sign. But the history of the Southwest is the history of what Mexico founded and America fought to win—not particularly fairly, either. Writes biographer Hugh Pearson:

> In 1845, hewing to the strictures of Manifest Destiny we annexed the Republic of Texas, which had been part of Mexico. Its American settlers decided to introduce slavery into the territory, which was illegal in Mexico. Then, as gratitude for the Mexican government's inviting them to settle the territory and because they wanted to keep their slaves, they fought

for independence. As former President and Gen. Ulysses S. Grant wrote in his memoirs, "The occupation, separation and annexation were, from the inception of the movement to its final consummation, a conspiracy to acquire territory out of which slave states might be formed for the American union."

After accepting the Texas republic's petition to be annexed by the United States, a dispute between the United States and Mexico ensued, regarding where the exact boundary of Texas lay. Mexican and U.S. patrols clashed somewhere along the disputed territory and the United States declared war on Mexico. In the process of fighting the war, U.S. troops captured from Mexico what is now New Mexico and what the Mexicans called Upper California. As conditions for surrender, Mexico was forced to cede all of the captured territory north of the Rio Grande River, and an agreed upon jagged imaginary line that now separates California, Arizona and New Mexico from Mexico. So today, Mexicans crossing into U.S. California are treated as illegal aliens if they don't go through the proper channels for entering territory that was originally theirs.

I didn't learn any of this in high school, and I'd wager that many Americans don't know it today. What happened doesn't change the fact that America has the right to control its borders, but it does cast into sharper relief the interconnectedness of these two nations. Texas was birthed from Mexico. But—defying the stereotypes that pervade much of the news coverage about the border—many Mexican Americans are now the ones guarding the border.

Silvestre Reyes headed the Border Patrol for the entire El Paso region. After gaining recognition for starting Operation Hold the Line, Reyes resigned in November 1995 in order to run for a seat in the U.S. Congress, hoping the "sleeping giant" of Mexican-American political clout [would] work in his favor. (In November 1996, he won that seat.)

I meet the solid, handsome fifty-year-old in the offices where he's running his campaign with the help of his twenty-five-year-old daughter. Even in his civilian clothes, he's got the demeanor of a law enforcement officer. Reyes grew up in a small farming town where his high school graduating class was made up of just twenty-six students. When he was a child, he served as a lookout against *la migra*—the Border Patrol—in the fields where Mexicans worked. He served in Vietnam, then worked as a Border Patrol agent for over twenty-five years. He believes that people's opinions about the border don't have anything to do with ethnic loyalty, but quality of life. "Hispanics, like every ethnic group in the country, have an expectation to be safe and secure in their neighborhoods," he says. "A Hispanic no more than anybody else appreciates undocumented people flowing through their backyards, creating a chaotic situation."

Still, Reyes says he'd like to find a way to benefit both Mexicans and Americans at the same time. "Mexican citizens don't want to come up here," he says. "They would rather stay home. But they stay home, they starve. We've got forces down in Mexico that want jobs, and people up here that want them to come up here. But the whole problem is, let's find a system that does it legally."

Despite its adverse effect on the El Paso economy, Reyes supports NAFTA as a way of increasing employment opportunities in Mexico. If things don't get better there, he reasons, illegal immigration will never stop. "Mexico has a surplus of manpower. I think 60 percent of Mexican citizens are under the age of twenty, if I remember my statistics right," he says. The problem with NAFTA in the short term is that it's relied on minimum-wage jobs, jobs that are the first to be transferred to the other side of the border. "In El Paso, we have a minimum-wage mentality. When they graduate, kids want to go someplace else. They don't want to stay here and work for four thirty-five or five fifteen or whatever the [minimum] wage finally ends up to be when they can go to Dallas, L.A., Denver, Chicago and participate in high-paying, high-tech kinds of jobs. Anybody with any kind of ambition knows that in order to make it, you've got to leave here."

One policy he doesn't support is California's Proposition 187, which voters passed in 1994 in an effort, among other things, to prevent illegal immigrants from receiving government medical care or public education. Reyes calls the measure "illegal and unconstitutional," and rejects the calls of national politicians like former Senator Bob Dole to replicate it. "Should we amend the Constitution in order to deny children born in this country their citizenships? I think we're crazy," he says. "What's gonna keep someone from going back retroactively and saying, 'You know, your father was born to illegal parents back in 1924. Therefore he was illegal, therefore you're illegal.'" (Such logic recalls a joke by Mexican-American comedian Paul Rodriguez, who says he supports making deportations for illegal immigration retroactive and shipping the Anglos back home.) The idea of barring education to undocumented children is "insanity running amok. The way that people enslave whole segments of our society is by keeping them ignorant. . . . To me it doesn't matter whether it's black or Hispanics or Chinese or whites or who it is. I think it's just wrong for any country to guarantee a subculture of ignorance. And that's what you're doing when you don't educate the kids."

The wording of California's Proposition 187 was also openly militaristic, reading:

> WE CAN STOP ILLEGAL ALIENS. If the citizens and the taxpayers of our state wait for the politicians in Washington and Sacramento to stop the incredible flow of ILLEGAL ALIENS, California will be in economic and social bankruptcy. We have to act and ACT NOW! On our ballot, Proposition 187 will be the first giant stride in ultimately ending the ILLEGAL ALIEN invasion.

Some advocates say the border has already become militarized, infringing upon the rights of citizens and legal immigrants. El Paso's Border Rights Coalition says that in 1995, half of the individuals who complained to their group about mistreatment by the Border Patrol, Immigration and Naturalization Service, and U.S. Customs were U.S. citizens, not legal or illegal immigrants. The group helped students at El Paso's Bowie High School file a class action suit. They alleged that Border Patrol agents were routinely harassing individuals on and near campus—in one case, arresting a group of students, U.S. citizens, who were driving to school. Today, the Border Patrol is operating under a settlement that requires they meet higher standards before detaining individuals, and limits searches at schools and churches.

Of course, the ultimate military-style solution would be to create a physical wall between Mexico and the United States. Reyes strongly disagrees with such a plan. "That's impractical, you know. The Berlin wall didn't seal, and that was using mines and barbed wire and guards and concrete, and all of that, and still people got out of there," he says. Yet as Reyes and I talk, construction on just such a wall is happening along the border near El Paso. While I'm out with Melissa Lucio, she shows me the early stages of the construction site. It's impossible to cover the whole border, of course. But by 1998, several miles of what Reyes calls the "impractical" solution stand completed.

The Border Crossers

A Family Full of Contradictions

Gilberto, an eighteen-year-old undocumented immigrant from Chihuahua, has few marketable skills but one strong advantage on his side. He has family legally in the United States who are willing to help him. Gilberto is the brother-in-law of a naturalized U.S. citizen who emigrated from Hong Kong. Chiu, who went to college in the United States, met his wife Lorena, in a Juarez nightclub. Now they have two children, baby Jenny Anna and Andy, who turned three the day after I spoke with them. Both attend the University of Texas at El Paso, and they earn a living by running a home care facility for the elderly.

Gilberto helps out with the home care, meaning he's guaranteed a job as well as a place to stay far from the eyes of the Border Patrol. Like virtually all illegal immigrants, he's an unskilled laborer. Like many Mexicans, he finished the "secondario" level of schooling at fifteen and then started working. His first job was in a junk-yard—hot, heavy work for very little money. Still, like a teenager, he used the remaining money he had to party rather than save. Asked if he's worried *la migra* will find him—something they did once before, as he was out and about—he shakes his head confidently, "No."

Chiu and Lorena's generous brick house is nestled in a pristine, upper-middle-class enclave undergoing rapid development. Bold and self-assured, Chiu strongly opposes illegal immigration, a position it's hard not to think deeply about when you see Gilberto sitting sheepishly on the other side of the table. "My brother-in-law, he's an illegal alien. He come and go whenever he wants. When you're talking about Hold the Line, it's only to make the government look good," Chiu scolds. "Washington, D.C., will furnish a lot of money for this project because it's very successful— you catch ten billion illegal aliens. Oh great job!" he sneers. "Now they have this Hold the Line thing, OK, and then they say, 'Nobody coming across.' But in the reality it's not true. In Mexico, if the people over there are making three to five dollars a day and if they cannot support their kids, do you think they would just sit there and die?"

Gilberto isn't in the dire straits many border crossers are. In fact, he originally entered not to stay but to fulfill teenage longings. "All the boys, they have the same dream: you know, they wanted to come and get some money and

buy a truck, a nice truck," his sister Lorena translates, "and then go back to Mexico and spend one or two months or whatever on the money they saved up. Then after that, they come back to the United States again and work and get some more money. That's the way they think." Now Gilberto's changed his mind. He wants to stay in the United States and become a nurse. "It's very important to learn to speak English, otherwise there's no way to find a job—well, maybe in El Paso a very low job. But I want to go further," he says. He's enrolled in a local high school, where his legal status proved no problem. "As a matter of fact, they are not allowed to ask you whether you have papers or not or whether you have a Social Security number or not, because if they do that they have violated federal law," Chiu says. "So they have to let him register although he's an illegal alien." In a clear example of how self-interest overrides politics, Chiu says that he's happy his brother-in-law can be enrolled, but that he is opposed to educating undocumented children. "When they do that they are inviting illegal immigrants to come to school here, you see. I would say no illegal immigrants to go to school in this country for free."

Neither Mexican nor American

A pensive seventeen-year-old named Diana finds herself in the opposite situation from Gilberto: with her near-perfect English and years of schooling in the United States, she seems culturally American, but this undocu-mented immigrant has no one to advocate for her or protect her. She's been caught between two worlds most of her life. Four years ago, Diana crossed into the United States at the Juarez–El Paso bridge that symbolizes the border so well. Now she's a senior at Fremont High School in Oakland, California. . . . Before crossing the Rio Grande, she spent her junior high school years near Durango, Mexico. And before that, from the ages of two until nine, she lived in the United States—attending American schools, playing with American toys, speaking both English and Spanish. Without a green card or citizenship, but with a keen understanding of American culture and her precarious position in it, she is neither fully American nor fully Mexican.

Diana remembers the day her family crossed over from Juarez to El Paso. "We used a raft to get across. It was really sunny that day. People were on the bridge watching us. They were like 'Oh look!'" she says. "I remember I saw this man with a little boy in his arms pointing at us." Once they got to El Paso, her family tried to blend in with the rest of the crowds in the downtown shopping area. "We crossed the street right in front of a Border Patrol car," Diana remembers. "The car stopped so we could cross the street! My Mom was praying and I was like, 'Mom, they're not going to do anything to us now.' They didn't."

While her experience in crossing the Rio Grande was a common one until recently, Diana's reasons for going back and forth between the United States and Mexico are personal and complex. Like most families who cross over from Mexico, Diana's came to work and make a better life for their children. Her father has a green card, so he was able to live and work legally; but he brought Diana, her mother, and Diana's older brother into the country without papers. Diana's father began drinking too much, and after living in the United States for several years, he decided to move the family back to Mexico and pull himself together. But there's little work near Durango, so he ended up going back to the United States to earn a living (taking Diana's teenage brother along with him) and sending money to the family back home. It was only once her father had stopped drinking that he decided to reunite the family, arranging for a "coyote"—or someone who smuggles people across the border—to bring Diana and the rest of the family north through Mexico, on a raft over the Rio Grande, and by truck out of Texas.

Diana was too young to remember the first time she crossed the border. She was only two years old, and friends of the family who had papers for their own toddler smuggled her in as their child. "People told me I kept saying, 'I want my mother.' They needed me to be quiet," she says. From two on, Diana lived in Chico, California, as a normal Mexican-American kid—almost. When I ask her if she knew she was an "illegal immigrant," she says, "That question really bothered me and came into my head in, I think, the second grade. Most of my friends would go to Mexico on their summer vacations to see their grandparents, and I would ask, 'Why aren't we going to Mexico?' My mother would say, 'We can't.' Then," she continues, "one time in school I said, 'Um, I'm illegal.' And my teacher said, 'Honey, don't say that out loud. You could get your parents in a lot of trouble.' That's when I started feeling a little inferior to other kids."

Sometimes she still does. "Not because of who I am but because of what I can't do," she says, quietly breaking into tears. One thing she can't do is apply to college, even though she's a solid student. Without legal residence papers, she has little hope of attending school or getting anything but the most menial of jobs. Her older brother tried enrolling in college, but after they repeatedly asked him for a Social Security number, he simply left. Now he plays in a band. "I want to get a green card so I can work, so I can go to school, so I don't need to worry about getting deported and everything. But we have to pay a lawyer seven hundred dollars for each person applying for the green card," money her struggling family doesn't have. After she gets a green card, she wants to become a citizen "because I would like to be heard in this country. I would like to vote and be part of the process."

The most wrenching part of her experience is that Diana knows she could have been a legal resident by now. In 1987, she says, "we could have gotten our papers through the National Amnesty Program," a one-shot chance for illegal immigrants to declare themselves to officials in exchange for a green card. "My mother applied for us, but my Dad [who was drinking] felt that if we went back to Mexico, everything would be for the best." She remembers the day they left the United States. "I had to leave all my friends and the things I had. We left everything: the furniture, my toys, my Barbies. I had to practically leave my life there."

Yet Diana credits the time she spent in Mexico with helping her reconnect with her heritage. She became close with her grandmother, was in the Mexican equivalent of junior ROTC, and won dramatic speaking contests, reciting poetry. "In Mexico, I always wanted to be the one with the best grades—always wanted to be the center of attention," she says. "Maybe because I believed in myself and what I did," she says. That sense of confidence is lacking in Diana today. But if she had stayed in Mexico, it would have been difficult for her to continue her education considering how little money her family had. Most of the girls Diana knew stopped going to school at fourteen or fifteen, got married to a farmer or laborer, and started a family.

So, in one sense, Diana feels she was lucky to return to the United States. But when she first arrived, she had a difficult time readjusting. She returned in time for ninth grade, which in Oakland at the time was still a part of junior high school. Teachers put her in an English as a second language program, probably because her shyness inhibited her from talking much. "It wasn't very helpful," she says. Luckily, as soon as one of her teachers found out how good Diana's English really was, Diana was moved into the regular track.

But Diana was dealing not only with educational displacement but ethnic culture shock. "In the ninth grade, there was only my Mexican friends . . . and we felt a little inferior to the rest." In her opinion, the Mexican kids broke

down into two cliques: the "Mexican Mexicans," or hard-working immigrants, and the "little gangsters," or tough, Americanized teens. She hung out with the former—until tenth grade, when she went to Fremont and joined the Media Academy. There she made friends of several races. "When I got to Fremont there was African Americans, Asians, and Mexicans and everybody hangs out together and it was cool," she says.

What is heartbreaking to Diana today is that, though she loves school, she has little hope of continuing her education. She remembers a time that her teacher was leading them through an exercise in filling out college applications. "Everybody was like: 'Oh, I want to go to this place and I wanna go such and such and oh, my grades are good and everything.' My teacher was like, 'Aren't you going to fill out your applications?' And I was like, 'What for?'" Another girl in the class asked the question Diana was desperate to, but just couldn't. "What if you're not a legal resident?" Her teacher said to leave the Social Security number slot blank, but Diana says, dejected, "I didn't want to continue it."

The passage of Proposition 187 during Diana's junior year made the issues seem even more overwhelming. "I felt, Oh God, here goes another barrier. I'm trying to get over these little things and now here comes this big one." She's already experienced difficulty getting services. When she had a bad tooth, she went to the local clinic. They told her they could no longer help her if she didn't have a Social Security number. "My mom was like, 'We'll pay,' but no, she's like, 'We're sorry and everything is frozen until we get more orders.'"

As we drive through Oakland, she points out the tiny repair shop her father runs, nestled in an alley off of the East Fourteenth Street corridor. Her house, on a block of modest but well-kept homes with front and backyards, is filled with worn-out used furniture. Her mother, a warm, friendly woman who speaks little English, sits in the kitchen feeding an infant she babysits for extra cash. Her three younger siblings—adorable mischievous imps—run in and out of the house with their friends. Her youngest brother, who's five, doesn't have legal status, but her two middle siblings, both in elementary school, are U.S. citizens because they were born while her family was living in Chico. In California alone there are hundreds of thousands of families with mixed legal status (where some family members have green cards or citizenship and others have neither). Diana tries not to, but sometimes she resents the freedom that her two siblings have for being citizens. To her, their futures seem open, boundless; her own seems closed.

Still, "Regardless of all the barriers that are put between you and other people, America *is* the Land of Opportunity," says Diana. "No matter where you go, you will never find another place where even when you're not legal you can still get a job that pays you. There's no other place like it. In Mexico you can't even get a job. You depend on the crops on your land and live on what grows. There's nowhere for you to go, no McDonald's for you to hang out at. To me, it's better in America."

Mexicanizing America?

The unspoken fear that underlies much of our policy about the border is that an influx of immigrants will "Mexicanize" America. But my journey through El Paso illustrates the complex culture of Mexican Americans, and just how unfounded the fears about "Mexicanization" are. Those living on the U.S.-Mexican border face some difficult political and economic questions: whether Americans can compete with the low-wage workers in Mexico; whether Washington lawmakers can truly understand the issues facing Americans on the border; and, for Mexican Americans in particular, whether they should feel some connection to the problems facing Mexicans, or simply focus on their own issues. The influence of Mexican culture on America's should be seen as part of a continuum. Just as every immigration wave has shaped this country, so will the rise of the Latino population. In a best-case scenario, border towns like El Paso would help foster a rich appreciation for Mexican culture as *part* of American-style diversity. Silvestre Reyes describes his hopes for the next generation as quite literally out of this world. "You hope that someday you get to the point where *Star Trek* is today," he says. "That someday it doesn't matter who you are or what you look like or what your name is, but the important thing is that you're working in harmony."

THINKING ABOUT THE READING

Describe the various ways that illegal Mexican immigrants to the United States are victimized. Faced with the sorts of dangers mentioned in this article as well as the hostility of Border Patrol agents, why do you think people are still willing to take the risk and enter this country illegally? Do you consider illegal immigration to be a serious social problem? Do you think that tightening the border and increasing Border Patrol surveillance will ever reduce illegal immigration? If not, how would you go about reducing it? How do the Border Patrol agents' perceptions and attitudes affect your beliefs about illegal immigration? How would you now characterize the agents themselves? Why does Chideya think that the fear that illegal immigrants will "Mexicanize" the United States is unfounded?

These Dark Satanic Mills

William Greider

(1997)

... If the question were put now to everyone, everywhere—do you wish to become a citizen of the world?—it is safe to assume that most people in most places would answer, no, they wish to remain who they are. With very few exceptions, people think of themselves as belonging to a place, a citizen of France or Malaysia, of Boston or Tokyo or Warsaw, loyally bound to native culture, sovereign nation. The Chinese who aspire to get gloriously rich, as Deng instructed, do not intend to become Japanese or Americans. Americans may like to think of themselves as the world's leader, but not as citizens of "one world."

The deepest social meaning of the global industrial revolution is that people no longer have free choice in this matter of identity. Ready or not, they are already of the world. As producers or consumers, as workers or merchants or investors, they are now bound to distant others through the complex strands of commerce and finance reorganizing the globe as a unified marketplace. The prosperity of South Carolina or Scotland is deeply linked to Stuttgart's or Kuala Lumpur's. The true social values of Californians or Swedes will be determined by what is tolerated in the factories of Thailand or Bangladesh. The energies and brutalities of China will influence community anxieties in Seattle or Toulouse or Nagoya.

... Unless one intends to withdraw from modern industrial life, there is no place to hide from the others. Major portions of the earth, to be sure, remain on the periphery of the system, impoverished bystanders still waiting to be included in the action. But the patterns of global interconnectedness are already the dominant reality. Commerce has leapt beyond social consciousness and, in doing so, opened up challenging new vistas for the human potential. Most people, it seems fair to say, are not yet prepared to face the implications. ...

The process of industrialization has never been pretty in its primitive stages. Americans or Europeans who draw back in horror at the present brutalities in Asia or Latin America should understand that they are glimpsing repetitions of what happened in their own national histories, practices that were forbidden as inhumane in their own countries only after long political struggle. To make that historical point complicates the moral responses, but does not extinguish the social question.

The other realm, of course, is the wealthy nation where the established social structure is under assault, both from market forces depressing wages and employment and from the political initiatives to dismantle the welfare state. The governments' obligations to social equity were erected during the upheavals of the last century to ameliorate the harsher edges of unfettered capitalism; now they are in question again. The economic pressures to shrink or withdraw public benefits are relentless, yet no one has explained how wealthy industrial nations will maintain the social peace by deepening their inequalities.

A standard response to all these social concerns is the reassuring argument that market forces will eventually correct them—if no one interferes. The new wealth of industrialization, it is said, will lead naturally to middle-class democracy in the poorer countries and the barbarisms will eventually be eradicated. In the older societies, it is assumed that technology will create new realms of work that in time replace the lost employment, restore living wages and spread the prosperity widely again. People need only be patient with the future and not interrupt the revolution.

The global system has more or less been proceeding on these assumptions for at least a generation and one may observe that the unfolding reality has so far gravely disappointed these expectations. Nor does the free-market argument conform with the actual history of how democratic development or social equity was advanced over the last two centuries, neither of which emerged anywhere without titanic political struggles. A more pointed contradiction is the hypocrisy of those who make these arguments. If multinational enterprises truly expect greater human freedom and social equity to emerge from the marketplace, then why do they expend so much political energy to prevent these conditions from developing?

In any case, the theoretical arguments about the future do not satisfy the moral question that exists concretely at present. If one benefits tangibly from the exploitation of others who are weak, is one morally implicated in their predicament? Or are basic rights of human existence confined to those civilized societies wealthy enough to afford them? Everyone's values are defined by what they will tolerate when it is done to others. Everyone's sense of virtue is degraded by the present reality. . . .

Two centuries ago, when the English industrial revolution dawned with its fantastic invention and productive energies, the prophetic poet William Blake drew back in moral revulsion. Amid the explosion of new wealth, human destruction was spread over England—peasant families displaced from their lands, paupers and poorhouses crowded into London slums, children sent to labor at the belching ironworks or textile looms. Blake

delivered a thunderous rebuke to the pious Christians of the English aristocracy with these immortal lines:

> And was Jerusalem builded here
> Among these dark Satanic mills?

Blake's "dark Satanic mills" have returned now and are flourishing again, accompanied by the same question.[1]

On May 10, 1993, the worst industrial fire in the history of capitalism occurred at a toy factory on the outskirts of Bangkok and was reported on page 25 of the *Washington Post*. The *Financial Times* of London, which styles itself as the daily newspaper of the global economy, ran a brief item on page 6. The *Wall Street Journal* followed a day late with an account on page 11. The *New York Times* also put the story inside, but printed a dramatic photo on its front page: rows of small shrouded bodies on bamboo pallets—dozens of them—lined along the damp pavement, while dazed rescue workers stood awkwardly among the corpses. In the background, one could see the collapsed, smoldering structure of a mammoth factory where the Kader Industrial Toy Company of Thailand had employed three thousand workers manufacturing stuffed toys and plastic dolls, playthings destined for American children.[2]

The official count was 188 dead, 469 injured, but the actual toll was undoubtedly higher since the four-story buildings had collapsed swiftly in the intense heat and many bodies were incinerated. Some of the missing were never found; others fled home to their villages. All but fourteen of the dead were women, most of them young, some as young as thirteen years old. Hundreds of the workers had been trapped on upper floors of the burning building, forced to jump from third- or fourth-floor windows, since the main exit doors were kept locked by the managers, and the narrow stairways became clotted with trampled bodies or collapsed.

When I visited Bangkok about nine months later, physical evidence of the disaster was gone—the site scraped clean by bulldozers—and Kader was already resuming production at a new toy factory, built far from the city in a rural province of northeastern Thailand. When I talked with Thai labor leaders and civic activists, people who had rallied to the cause of the fire victims, some of them were under the impression that a worldwide boycott of Kader products was under way, organized by conscience-stricken Americans and Europeans. I had to inform them that the civilized world had barely noticed their tragedy.

As news accounts pointed out, the Kader fire surpassed what was previously the worst industrial fire in history—the Triangle Shirtwaist Company fire of 1911—when 146 young immigrant women died in similar circumstances at a garment factory on the Lower East Side of Manhattan. The Triangle Shirtwaist fire became a pivotal event in American politics, a public scandal that provoked citizen reform movements and energized the labor organizing that built the International Ladies Garment Workers Union and other unions. The fire in Thailand did not produce meaningful political responses or even shame among consumers. The indifference of the leading newspapers merely reflected the tastes of their readers, who might be moved by human suffering in their own communities but were inured to news of recurring calamities in distant places. A fire in Bangkok was like a typhoon in Bangladesh, an earthquake in Turkey.

The Kader fire might have been more meaningful for Americans if they could have seen the thousands of soot-stained dolls that spilled from the wreckage, macabre litter scattered among the dead. Bugs Bunny, Bart Simpson and the Muppets. Big Bird and other *Sesame Street* dolls. Playskool "Water Pets."

Santa Claus. What the initial news accounts did not mention was that Kader's Thai factory produced most of its toys for American companies—Toys "R" Us, Fisher-Price, Hasbro, Tyco, Arco, Kenner, Gund and J. C. Penney—as well as stuffed dolls, slippers and souvenirs for Europe.[3]

Globalized civilization has uncovered an odd parochialism in the American character: Americans worried obsessively over the everyday safety of their children, and the U.S. government's regulators diligently policed the design of toys to avoid injury to young innocents. Yet neither citizens nor government took any interest in the brutal and dangerous conditions imposed on the people who manufactured those same toys, many of whom were mere adolescent children themselves. Indeed, the government position, both in Washington and Bangkok, assumed that there was no social obligation connecting consumers with workers, at least none that governments could enforce without disrupting free trade or invading the sovereignty of other nations.

The toy industry, not surprisingly, felt the same. Hasbro Industries, maker of Playskool, subsequently told the *Boston Globe* that it would no longer do business with Kader, but, in general, the U.S. companies shrugged off responsibility. Kader, a major toy manufacturer based in Hong Kong, "is extremely reputable, not sleaze bags," David Miller, president of the Toy Manufacturers of America, assured *USA Today*. "The responsibility for those factories," Miller told ABC News, "is in the hands of those who are there and managing the factory."[4]

The grisly details of what occurred revealed the casual irresponsibility of both companies and governments. The Kader factory compound consisted of four interconnected, four-story industrial barns on a three-acre lot on Buddhamondhol VI Road in the Sampran district west of Bangkok. It was one among Thailand's thriving new industrial zones for garments, textiles, electronics and toys. More than 50,000 people, most of them migrants from the Thai countryside, worked in the district at 7,500 large and small firms. Thailand's economic boom was based on places such as this, and Bangkok was almost choking on its own fantastic growth, dizzily erecting luxury hotels and office towers.

The fire started late on a Monday afternoon on the ground floor in the first building and spread rapidly upward, jumping to two adjoining buildings, all three of which swiftly collapsed. Investigators noted afterwards that the structures had been cheaply built, without concrete reinforcement, so steel girders and stairways crumpled easily in the heat. Thai law required that in such a large factory, fire-escape stairways must be sixteen to thirty-three feet wide, but Kader's were a mere four and a half feet. Main doors were locked and many windows barred to prevent pilfering by the employees. Flammable raw materials—fabric, stuffing, animal fibers—were stacked everywhere, on walkways and next to electrical boxes. Neither safety drills nor fire alarms and sprinkler systems had been provided.

Let some of the survivors describe what happened.

A young woman named Lampan Taptim: "There was the sound of yelling about a fire. I tried to leave the section but my supervisor told me to get back to work. My sister who worked on the fourth floor with me pulled me away and insisted we try to get out. We tried to go down the stairs and got to the second floor; we found that the stairs had already caved in. There was a lot of yelling and confusion. . . . In desperation, I went back up to the windows and went back and forth, looking down below. The smoke was thick and I picked the best place to jump in a pile of boxes. My sister jumped, too. She died."

A young woman named Cheng: "There is no way out [people were shouting], the security guard has locked the main door out! It was horrifying. I thought I would die. I took off my gold ring and kept it in my pocket and put on my name tag so that my body could be identifiable. I had to decide to die in the fire or from jumping down from a three stories' height." As the walls collapsed around her, Cheng clung to a pipe and fell downward with it, landing on a pile of dead bodies, injured but alive.

An older woman named La-iad Nadanguen: "Four or five pregnant women jumped before me. They died before my eyes." Her own daughter jumped from the top floor and broke both hips.

Chauweewan Mekpan, who was five months pregnant: "I thought that if I jumped, at least my parents would see my remains, but if I stayed, nothing would be left of me." Though her back was severely injured, she and her unborn child miraculously survived.

An older textile worker named Vilaiwa Satieti, who sewed shirts and pants at a neighboring factory, described to me the carnage she encountered: "I got off work about five and passed by Kader and saw many dead bodies lying around, uncovered. Some of them I knew. I tried to help the workers who had jumped from the factory. They had broken legs and broken arms and broken heads. We tried to keep them alive until they got to the hospital, that's all you could do. Oh, they were teenagers, fifteen to twenty years, no more than that, and so many of them, so many."

This was not the first serious fire at Kader's factory, but the third or fourth. "I heard somebody yelling 'fire, fire,'" Tumthong Podhirun testified, " . . . but I did not take it seriously because it has happened before. Soon I smelled smoke and very quickly it billowed inside the place. I headed for the back door but it was locked. . . . Finally, I had no choice but to join the others and jumped out of the window. I saw many of my friends lying dead on the ground beside me."[5]

In the aftermath of the tragedy, some Bangkok activists circulated an old snapshot of two smiling peasant girls standing arm in arm beside a thicket of palm trees. One of them, Praphai Prayonghorm, died in the 1993 fire at Kader. Her friend, Kammoin Konmanee, had died in the 1989 fire. Some of the Kader workers insisted afterwards that their factory had been haunted by ghosts, that it was built on the site of an old graveyard, disturbing the dead. The folklore expressed raw poetic truth: the fire in Bangkok eerily resembled the now-forgotten details of the Triangle Shirtwaist disaster eighty years before. Perhaps the "ghosts" that some workers felt present were young women from New York who had died in 1911.

Similar tragedies, large and small, were now commonplace across developing Asia and elsewhere. Two months after Kader, another fire at a Bangkok shirt factory killed ten women. Three months after Kader, a six-story hotel collapsed and killed 133 people, injuring 351. The embarrassed minister of industry ordered special inspections of 244 large factories in the Bangkok region and found that 60 percent of them had basic violations similar to Kader's. Thai industry was growing explosively—12 to 15 percent a year—but workplace injuries and illnesses were growing even faster, from 37,000 victims in 1987 to more than 150,000 by 1992 and an estimated 200,000 by 1994.

In China, six months after Kader, eighty-four women died and dozens of others were severely burned at another toy factory fire in the burgeoning industrial zone at Shenzhen. At Dongguan, a Hong Kong–owned raincoat factory burned in 1991, killing more than eighty people (Kader Industries also had a factory at Dongguan where two fires have been reported since 1990). In late 1993, some sixty women died at the Taiwanese-owned Gaofu textile plant in Fuzhou Province, many of them smothered in their dormitory beds by toxic fumes from burning textiles. In 1994, a shoe factory fire killed ten persons at Jiangmen; a textile factory fire killed thirty-eight and injured 160 at the Qianshan industrial zone.[6]

"Why must these tragedies repeat themselves again and again?" the *People's Daily* in Beijing asked. The official *Economic Daily* complained: "The way some of these foreign investors ignore international practice, ignore our own national rules, act completely lawlessly and immorally and lust after wealth is enough to make one's hair stand on end."[7]

America was itself no longer insulated from such brutalities. When a chicken-processing factory at Hamlet, North Carolina, caught fire in 1991, the exit doors there were also locked and twenty-five people died. A garment factory discovered by labor investigators in El Monte, California, held seventy-two Thai immigrants in virtual peonage, working eighteen hours a day in "sub-human conditions." One could not lament the deaths, harsh working conditions, child labor and subminimum wages in Thailand or across Asia and Central America without also recognizing that similar conditions have reappeared in the United States for roughly the same reasons.

Sweatshops, mainly in the garment industry, scandalized Los Angeles, New York and Dallas. The grim, foul assembly lines of the poultry-processing industry were spread across the rural South; the *Wall Street Journal's* Tony Horwitz won a Pulitzer Prize for his harrowing description of this low-wage work. "In general," the U.S. Government Accounting Office reported in 1994, "the description of today's sweatshops differs little from that at the turn of the century."[8]

That was the real mystery: Why did global commerce, with all of its supposed modernity and wondrous technologies, restore the old barbarisms that had long ago been forbidden by law? If the information age has enabled multinational corporations to manage production and marketing spread across continents, why were their managers unable—or unwilling—to organize such mundane matters as fire prevention?

The short answer, of course, was profits, but the deeper answer was about power: Firms behaved this way because they could, because nobody would stop them. When law and social values retreated before the power of markets, then capitalism's natural drive to maximize returns had no internal governor to check its social behavior. When one enterprise took the low road to gain advantage, others would follow.

The toy fire in Bangkok provided a dramatic illustration for the much broader, less visible forms of human exploitation that were flourishing in the global system, including the widespread use of children in manufacturing, even forced labor camps in China or Burma. These matters were not a buried secret. Indeed, American television has aggressively exposed the "dark Satanic mills" with dramatic reports. ABCs *20/20* broadcast correspondent Lynn Sherr's devastating account of the Kader fire; CNN ran disturbing footage. Mike Wallace of CBS's *60 Minutes* exposed the prison labor exploited in China. NBC's *Dateline* did a piece on Wal-Mart's grim production in Bangladesh. CBS's *Street Stories* toured the shoe factories of Indonesia.

The baffling quality about modern communications was that its images could take us to people in remote corners of the world vividly and instantly, but these images have not as yet created genuine community with them. In terms of human consciousness, the "global village" was still only a picture on the TV screen.

Public opinion, moreover, absorbed contradictory messages about the global reality that were difficult to sort out. The opening stages of industrialization presented, as always, a great paradox: the process was profoundly liberating for millions, freeing them from material scarcity and limited life choices, while it also ensnared other millions in brutal new forms of domination. Both aspects were true, but there was no scale on which these opposing consequences could be easily balanced, since the good and ill

effects were not usually apportioned among the same people. Some human beings were set free, while other lives were turned into cheap and expendable commodities.

Workers at Kader, for instance, earned about 100 baht a day for sewing and assembling dolls, the official minimum wage of $4, but the constant stream of new entrants meant that many at the factory actually worked for much less—only $2 or $3 a day—during a required "probationary" period of three to six months that was often extended much longer by the managers. Only one hundred of the three thousand workers at Kader were legally designated employees; the rest were "contract workers" without permanent rights and benefits, the same employment system now popularized in the United States.

"Lint, fabric, dust and animal hair filled the air on the production floor," the International Confederation of Free Trade Unions based in Brussels observed in its investigative report. "Noise, heat, congestion and fumes from various sources were reported by many. Dust control was nonexistent; protective equipment inadequate. Inhaling the dust created respiratory problems and contact with it caused skin diseases." A factory clinic dispensed antihistamines or other drugs and referred the more serious symptoms to outside hospitals. Workers paid for the medication themselves and were reimbursed, up to $6, only if they had contributed 10 baht a month to the company's health fund.

A common response to such facts, even from many sensitive people, was: yes, that was terrible, but wouldn't those workers be even worse off if civil standards were imposed on their employers since they might lose their jobs as a result? This was the same economic rationale offered by American manufacturers a century before to explain why American children must work in the coal mines and textile mills. U.S. industry had survived somehow (and, in fact, flourished) when child labor and the other malpractices were eventually prohibited by social reforms. Furthermore, it was not coincidence that industry always assigned the harshest conditions and lowest pay to the weakest members of a society—women, children, uprooted migrants. Whether the factory was in Thailand or the United States or Mexico's *maquiladora* zone, people who were already quite powerless were less likely to resist, less able to demand decency from their employers.

Nor did these enterprises necessarily consist of small, struggling firms that could not afford to treat their workers better. Small sweatshops, it was true, were numerous in Thailand, and I saw some myself in a working-class neighborhood of Bangkok. Behind iron grillwork, children who looked to be ten to twelve years old squatted on the cement floors of the open-air shops, assembling suitcases, sewing raincoats, packing T-shirts. Across the street, a swarm of adolescents in blue smocks ate dinner at long tables outside a two-story building, then trooped back upstairs to the sewing machines.

Kader Holding Company, Ltd., however, was neither small nor struggling. It was a powerhouse of the global toy industry—headquartered in Hong Kong, incorporated in Bermuda, owned by a wealthy Hong Kong Chinese family named Ting that got its start after World War II making plastic goods and flashlights under procurement contracts from the U.S. military. Now Kader controlled a global maze of factories and interlocking subsidiaries in eight countries, from China and Thailand to Britain and the United States, where it owned Bachmann toys.[9]

After the fire Thai union members, intellectuals and middle-class activists from social rights organizations (the groups known in developing countries as nongovernmental organizations, or NGOs) formed the Committee to Support Kader Workers and began demanding justice from the employer. They sent a delegation to Hong Kong to confront Kader officials and investigate the complex corporate linkages of the enterprise. What they discovered was that Kader's partner in the Bangkok toy factory was actually a fabulously wealthy Thai family, the Chearavanonts, ethnic Chinese merchants who own the Charoen Pokphand Group, Thailand's own leading multinational corporation.

The CP Group owns farms, feed mills, real estate, air-conditioning and motorcycle factories, food-franchise chains—two hundred companies worldwide, several of them listed on the New York Stock Exchange. The patriarch and chairman, Dhanin Chearavanont, was said by *Fortune* magazine to be the seventy-fifth richest man in the world, with personal assets of $2.6 billion (or 65 billion baht, as the *Bangkok Post* put it). Like the other emerging "Chinese multinationals," the Pokphand Group operates through the informal networks of kinfolk and ethnic contacts spread around the world by the Chinese diaspora, while it also participates in the more rigorous accounting systems of Western economies.

In the mother country, China, the conglomerate nurtured political-business alliances and has become the largest outside investor in new factories and joint ventures. In the United States, it maintained superb political connections. The Chearavanonts co-sponsored a much-heralded visit to Bangkok by ex-president George [H. W.] Bush, who delivered a speech before Thai business leaders in early 1994, eight months after the Kader fire. The price tag for Bush's appearance, according to the Bangkok press, was $400,000 (equivalent to one month's payroll for all three thousand workers at Kader). The day after Bush's appearance, the Chearavanonts hosted a banquet for a leading entrepreneur from China—Deng Xiaoping's daughter.[10]

The Pokphand Group at first denied any connection to the Kader fire, but reformers and local reporters dug out the facts of the family's involvement. Dhanin Chearavanont himself owned 11 percent of Honbo Investment Company and with relatives and corporate directors held majority control. Honbo, in turn, owned half of KCP Toys (KCP stood for Kader Charoen Pokphand), which, in turn, owned 80 percent of Kader Industrial (Thailand) Company. Armed with these facts, three hundred workers from the destroyed factory marched on the Pokphand Group's corporate tower on Silom Road, where they staged a gentle sit-down demonstration in the lobby, demanding just compensation for the victims.[11]

In the context of Thai society and politics, the workers' demonstration against Pokphand was itself extraordinary, like peasants confronting the nobility. Under continuing pressures from the support group, the company agreed to pay much larger compensation for victims and their families—$12,000 for each death, a trivial amount in American terms but more than double the Thai standard. "When we worked on Kader," said Professor Voravidh Charoenloet, an economist at Chulalongkorn University, "the government and local entrepreneurs and factory owners didn't want us to challenge these people; even the police tried to obstruct us from making an issue. We were accused of trying to destroy the country's reputation."

The settlement, in fact, required the Thai activists to halt their agitation and fall silent. "Once the extra compensation was paid," Voravidh explained, "we were forced to stop. One of the demands by the government was that everything should stop. Our organization had to accept it. We wanted to link with the international organizations and have a great boycott, but we had to cease."

The global boycott, he assumed, was going forward anyway because he knew that international labor groups like the ICFTU and the AFL-CIO had investigated the Kader fire and issued stinging denunciations. I told him that aside from organized labor, the rest of the world remained indifferent. There was no boycott of Kader toys in America. The professor slumped in his chair and was silent, a twisted expression on his face.

"I feel very bad," Voravidh said at last. "Maybe we should not have accepted it. But when we came away, we felt that was what we could accomplish. The people wanted more. There must be something more."

In the larger context, this tragedy was not explained by the arrogant power of one wealthy family or the elusive complexities of interlocking corporations. The Kader fire was ordained and organized by the free market itself. The toy industry—much like textiles and garments, shoes, electronics assembly and other low-wage sectors—existed (and thrived) by exploiting a crude ladder of desperate competition among the poorest nations. Its factories regularly hopped to new locations where wages were even lower, where the governments would be even more tolerant of abusive practices. The contract work assigned to foreign firms, including thousands of small sweatshops, fitted neatly into the systems of far-flung production of major brand names and distanced the capital owners from personal responsibility. The "virtual corporation" celebrated by some business futurists already existed in these sectors and, indeed, was now being emulated in some ways by advanced manufacturing—cars, aircraft, computers.

Over the last generation, toy manufacturers and others have moved around the Asian rim in search of the bottom-rung conditions: from Hong Kong, Korea and Taiwan to Thailand and Indonesia, from there to China, Vietnam and Bangladesh, perhaps on next to Burma, Nepal or Cambodia. Since the world had a nearly inexhaustible supply of poor people and suppliant governments, the market would keep driving in search of lower rungs; no one could say where the bottom was located. Industrial conditions were not getting better, as conventional theory assured the innocent consumers, but in many sectors were getting much worse. In America, the U.S. diplomatic opening to Vietnam was celebrated as progressive politics. In Southeast Asia, it merely opened another trapdoor beneath wages and working conditions.

A country like Thailand was caught in the middle: if it conscientiously tried to improve, it would pay a huge price. When Thai unions lobbied to win improvements in minimum-wage standards, textile plants began leaving for Vietnam and elsewhere or even importing cheaper "guest workers" from Burma. When China opened its fast-growing industrial zones in Shenzhen, Dongguan and other locations, the new competition had direct consequences on the factory floors of Bangkok.

Kader, according to the ICFTU, opened two new factories in Shekou and Dongguan where young people were working fourteen-hour days, seven days a week, to fill the U.S. Christmas orders for Mickey Mouse and other American dolls. Why should a company worry about sprinkler systems or fire escapes for a dusty factory in Bangkok when it could hire brand-new workers in China for only $20 a month, one fifth of the labor cost in Thailand?

The ICFTU report described the market forces: "The lower cost of production of toys in China changes the investment climate for countries like Thailand. Thailand competes with China to attract investment capital for local toy production. With this development, Thailand has become sadly lax in enforcing its own legislation. It turns a blind eye to health violations, thus allowing factory owners to ignore safety standards. Since China entered the picture, accidents in Thailand have nearly tripled."

The Thai minister of industry, Sanan Kachornprasart, described the market reality more succinctly: "If we punish them, who will want to invest here?" Thai authorities subsequently filed charges against three Kader factory managers, but none against the company itself nor, of course, the Chearavanont family.[12]

In the aftermath, a deputy managing director of Kader Industrial, Pichet Laokasem, entered a Buddhist monastery "to make merit for the fire victims," *The Nation* of Bangkok reported. Pichet told reporters he would serve as a monk until he felt better emotionally. "Most of the families affected by the fire lost only a loved one," he explained. "I lost nearly two hundred of my workers all at once."

The fire in Bangkok reflected the amorality of the marketplace when it has been freed of social obligations. But the tragedy also mocked the moral claims of three great religions, whose adherents were all implicated. Thais built splendid golden temples exalting Buddha, who taught them to put spiritual being before material wealth. Chinese claimed to have acquired superior social values, reverence for family and community, derived from the teachings of Confucius. Americans bought the toys from Asia to celebrate the birth of Jesus Christ. Their shared complicity was another of the strange convergences made possible by global commerce. . . .

In the modern industrial world, only the ignorant can pretend to self-righteousness since only the primitive are truly innocent. No advanced society has reached that lofty stage without enduring barbaric consequences and despoliation along the way; no one who enjoys the uses of electricity or the internal combustion engine may claim to oppose industrialization for others without indulging in imperious hypocrisy.

Americans, one may recall, built their early national infrastructure and organized large-scale agriculture with slave labor. The developing American nation swept native populations from their ancient lands and drained the swampy prairies to grow grain. It burned forests to make farmland, decimated wildlife, dammed the wild rivers and displaced people who were in the way. It assigned the dirtiest, most dangerous work to immigrants and children. It eventually granted political rights to all, but grudgingly and only after great conflicts, including a terrible civil war.

The actual history of nations is useful to remember when trying to form judgments about the new world. Asian leaders regularly remind Americans and Europeans of exactly how the richest nation-states became wealthy and observe further that, despite their great wealth, those countries have not perfected social relations among rich and poor, weak and powerful. The maldistribution of incomes is worsening in America, too, not yet as extreme as Thailand's, but worse than many less fortunate nations.

Hypocrisies run the other way, too, however. The fashionable pose among some leaders in developing Asia is to lecture the West on its decadent ways and hold up "Asian values" as morally superior, as well as more productive. If their cultural claims sound plausible at a distance, they seem less noble, even duplicitous up close. The Asian societies' supposed reverence for family, for instance, is expressed in the "dark Satanic mills" where the women and children are sent to work. "Family" and "social order" are often mere euphemisms for hierarchy and domination. A system that depends upon rigid control from above or the rank exploitation of weaker groups is not about values, but about power. Nothing distinctive about that. Human societies have struggled to overcome those conditions for centuries.

My point is that any prospect of developing a common global social consciousness will inevitably force people to reexamine themselves first and come to terms with the contradictions and hypocrisies in their own national histories. Americans, in particular, are not especially equipped for that exercise. A distinguished historian, Lawrence Goodwyn of Duke University, once said to me in frustration: You cannot teach American history to American students. You can teach the iconic version, he said, that portrays America as beautiful and unblemished or you can teach a radical version that demonizes the country. But American culture does not equip young people to deal with the "irreconcilable conflicts" embedded in their own history, the past that does not yield to patriotic moralisms. "Race is the most obvious example of what I mean," he said.

Coming to terms with one's own history ought not only to induce a degree of humility toward others and their struggles, but also to clarify what one really believes about human society. No one can undo the past, but that does not relieve people of the burden of making judgments about the living present or facing up to its moral implications. If the global system has truly created a unified marketplace, then every worker, every consumer, every society is already connected to the other. The responsibility exists and invoking history is not an excuse to hide from the new social questions.

Just as Americans cannot claim a higher morality while benefiting from inhumane exploitation, neither can developing countries pretend to become modern "one world" producers and expect exemption from the world's social values. Neither can the global enterprises. The future asks: Can capitalism itself be altered and reformed? Or is the world doomed to keep renewing these inhumanities in the name of economic progress?

The proposition that human dignity is indivisible does not suppose that everyone will become equal or alike or perfectly content in his or her circumstances. It does insist that certain well-understood social principles exist internationally which are enforceable and ought to be the price of admission in the global system. The idea is very simple: every person—man, woman and child—regardless of where he or she exists in time and place or on the chain of economic development, is entitled to respect as an individual being.

For many in the world, life itself is all that they possess; an economic program that deprives them of life's precious possibilities is not only unjust, but also utterly unnecessary. Peasants may not become kings, but they are entitled to be treated with decent regard for their sentient and moral beings, not as cheap commodities. Newly industrialized nations cannot change social patterns overnight, any more than the advanced economies did before them, but they can demonstrate that they are changing.

This proposition is invasive, no question, and will disturb the economic and political arrangements within many societies. But every nation has a sovereign choice in this matter, the sort of choice made in the marketplace every day. If Thailand or China resents the intrusion of global social standards, it does not have to sell its toys to America. And Americans do not have to buy them. If Singapore rejects the idea of basic rights for women, then women in America or Europe may reject Singapore—and multinational firms that profit from the subordination of women. If people do not assert these values in global trade, then their own convictions will be steadily coarsened.

In Bangkok, when I asked Professor Voravidh to step back from Thailand's problems and suggest a broader remedy, he thought for a long time and then said: "We need cooperation among nations because the multinational corporations can shift from one country to another. If they don't like Thailand, they move to Vietnam or China. Right now, we are all competing and the world is getting worse. We need a GATT on labor conditions and on the minimum wage, we need a standard on the minimum conditions for work and a higher standard for children."

The most direct approach, as Voravidh suggested, is an international agreement to incorporate such standards in the terms of trade, with penalties and incentives, even temporary embargoes, that will impose social obligations on the global system, the firms and countries. Most of the leading governments, including the United States, have long claimed to support this idea—a so-called social clause for GATT—but the practical reality is that they do not. Aside from rhetoric, when their negotiators are at the table, they always yield readily to objections from the multinational corporations and developing nations. Both the firms and the governing elites of poor countries have a strong incentive to block the proposition since both profit from a free-running system that exploits the weak. A countering force has to come from concerned citizens. Governments refuse to act, but voters and consumers are not impotent, and, in the meantime, they can begin the political campaign by purposefully targeting the producers—boycotting especially the well-known brand names that depend upon lovable images for their sales. Americans will not stop buying toys at Christmas, but they might single out one or two American toy companies for Yuletide boycotts, based on their scandalous relations with Kader and other manufacturers. Boycotts are difficult to organize and sustain, but every one of the consumer-goods companies is exquisitely vulnerable.

In India, the South Asian Coalition on Child Servitude, led by Kailash Satyarthi, has created a promising model for how to connect the social obligations of consumers and workers. Indian carpet makers are notorious for using small children at their looms—bonded children like Thailand's bonded prostitutes—and have always claimed economic necessity. India is a poor nation and the work gives wage income to extremely poor families, they insist. But these children will never escape poverty if they are deprived of schooling, the compulsory education promised by law.

The reformers created a "no child labor" label that certifies the rugs were made under honorable conditions and they persuaded major importers in Germany to insist upon the label. The exporters in India, in turn, have to allow regular citizen inspections of their workplaces to win the label for their rugs. Since this consumer-led certification system began, the carpet industry's use of children has fallen dramatically. A Textile Ministry official in New Delhi said: "The government is now contemplating the total eradication of child labor in the next few years."[13]

Toys, shoes, electronics, garments—many consumer sectors are vulnerable to similar approaches, though obviously the scope of manufacturing is too diverse and complex for consumers to police it. Governments have to act collectively. If a worldwide agreement is impossible to achieve, then groups of governments can form their own preferential trading systems, introducing social standards that reverse the incentives for developing countries and for capital choosing new locations for production.

The crucial point illustrated by Thailand's predicament is that global social standards will help the poorer countries escape their economic trap. Until a floor is built beneath the market's social behavior, there is no way that a small developing country like Thailand can hope to overcome the downward pull of competition from other, poorer nations. It must debase its citizens to hold on to what it has achieved. The path to improvement is blocked by the economics of an irresponsible marketplace.

Setting standards will undoubtedly slow down the easy movement of capital—and close down the most scandalous operations— but that is not a harmful consequence for people in struggling nations that aspire to industrial prosperity or for a global economy burdened with surpluses and inadequate consumption. When global capital makes a commitment to a developing economy, it ought not to acquire the power to blackmail that nation in perpetuity. Supported by global rules, those nations can begin to improve conditions and stabilize their own social development. At least they would have a chance to avoid the great class conflicts that others have experienced.

In the meantime, the very least that citizens can demand of their own government is that it no longer use public money to finance the brutal upheavals or environmental despoliation that have flowed from large-scale projects of the World Bank and other lending agencies. The social distress in the cities begins in the countryside, and the wealthy nations have often financed it in the name of aiding development. The World Bank repeatedly proclaims its new commitment to strategies that address the development ideas of indigenous peoples and halt the destruction of natural systems. But social critics and the people I encountered in Thailand and elsewhere have not seen much evidence of real change.

The terms of trade are usually thought of as commercial agreements, but they are also an implicit statement of moral values. In its present terms, the global system values property over human life. When a nation like China steals the property of capital, pirating copyrights, films or technology, other governments will take action to stop it and be willing to impose sanctions and penalty tariffs on the offending nation's trade. When human lives are stolen in the "dark Satanic mills," nothing happens to the offenders since, according to the free market's sense of conscience, there is no crime.

NOTES

1. William Blake's immortal lines are from "Milton," one of his "prophetic books" written between 1804 and 1808. *The Portable Blake*, Alfred Kazin, editor (New York: Penguin Books, 1976).

2. *Washington Post, Financial Times* and *New York Times*, May 12, 1993, and *Wall Street Journal*, May 13, 1993.

3. The U.S. contract clients for Kader's Bangkok factory were cited by the International Confederation of Free Trade Unions headquartered in Brussels in its investigatory report, "From the Ashes: A Toy Factory Fire in Thailand," December 1994. In the aftermath, the ICFTU and some non-governmental organizations attempted to mount an "international toy campaign" and a few sporadic demonstrations occurred in Hong Kong and London, but there never was a general boycott of the industry or any of its individual companies. The labor federation met with associations of British and American toy manufacturers and urged them to adopt a "code of conduct" that might discourage the abuses. The proposed codes were inadequate, the ICFTU acknowledged, but it was optimistic about their general adoption by the international industry.

4. Mitchell Zuckoff of the *Boston Globe* produced a powerful series of stories on labor conditions in developing Asia and reported Hasbro's reaction to the Kader fire, July 10, 1994. David Miller was quoted in *USA Today*, May 13, 1993, and on ABC News *20/20*, July 30, 1993.

5. The first-person descriptions of the Kader fire are but a small sampling from survivors' horrifying accounts, collected by investigators and reporters at the scene. My account of the disaster is especially indebted to the investigative report by the International Confederation of Free Trade Unions; Bangkok's English-language newspapers, the *Post* and *The Nation;* the Asia Monitor Resource Center of Hong Kong; and Lynn Sherr's devastating report on ABCs *20/20,* July 30, 1993. Lampan Taptim and Tumthong Podhirun, "From the Ashes," ICFTU, December 1994; Cheng: *Asian Labour Update,* Asia Monitor Resource Center, Hong Kong, July 1993; La-iad Nads-nguen: *The Nation,* Bangkok, May 12, 1993; and Chaweewan Mekpan: *20/20.*

6. Details on Thailand's worker injuries and the litany of fires in China are from the ICFTU report and other labor bulletins, as well as interviews in Bangkok.

7. The *People's Daily* and *Economic Daily* were quoted by Andrew Quinn of Reuters in *The Daily Citizen* of Washington, DC, January 18, 1994.

8. Tony Horwitz described chicken-processing employment as the second fastest growing manufacturing job in America: *Wall Street Journal,* December 1, 1994. U.S. sweatshops were reviewed in "Garment Industry: Efforts to Address the Prevalence and Conditions of Sweatshops," U.S. Government Accounting Office, November 1994.

9. Corporate details on Kader are from the ICFTU and the Asia Monitor Resource Center's *Asian Labour Update,* July 1993.

10. Dhanin Chearavanont's wealth: *Bangkok Post,* June 15, 1993; Pokphand Group ventures in China and elsewhere: *Far Eastern Economic Review,* October 21, 1993; George Bush's appearance in Bangkok: *Bangkok Post,* January 22, 1994. The dinner for Deng's daughter, Deng Nan, was reported in *The Nation,* Bangkok, January 28, 1994.

11. The complex structure of ownership was used to deflect corporate responsibility. Kader's Kenneth Ting protested after the fire that his family's firm owned only a 40 percent stake in the Thai factory, but people blamed them "because we have our name on it. That's the whole problem." The lesson, he said, was to "never lend your name or logo to any company if you don't have managing control in the company." That lesson, of course, contradicted the basic structure of how the global toy industry was organized: *Bangkok Post,* May 17, 1993. The chain of ownership was reported in several places, including *The Nation* of Bangkok, May 28, 1993. Details of the Kader workers' sit-in: *Bangkok Post,* July 13, 1993.

12. Sanan was quoted in the *Bangkok Post,* May 29, 1993.

13. The New Delhi–based campaign against child labor in the carpet industry is admittedly limited to a narrow market and expensive product, but its essential value is demonstrating how retailers and their customers can be connected to a distant factory floor. See, for instance, Hugh Williamson, "Stamp of Approval," *Far Eastern Economic Review,* February 2, 1995, and N. Vasuk Rao in the *Journal of Commerce,* March 1, 1995

THINKING ABOUT THE READING

Greider argues that the tragedy of the Kader industrial fire cannot be explained simply by focusing on greedy families and multinational corporations. Instead, he blames global economics and the organization of the international toy industry. He writes, "The Kader fire was ordained and organized by the free market itself." What do you suppose he means by this? Given the enormous economic pressures that this and other multinational industries operate under, are such tragedies inevitable? Why have attempts to improve the working conditions in Third World factories been so ineffective?

14 Architects of Change

Reconstructing Society

Throughout this book you've seen examples of how society is socially constructed and how these social constructions, in turn, affect the lives of individuals. It's hard not to feel a little helpless when discussing the control that culture, massive bureaucratic organizations, social institutions, systems of social stratification and global population trends have over our individual lives. However, social change is as much a part of society as social stability. Whether at the personal, cultural, or institutional level, change is the preeminent feature of modern societies.

Religious institutions are often intertwined with movements for widespread social change. Sometimes the religious ideology that underlies a particular movement is one that emphasizes peace and justice. The civil rights movement of the 1950s and the anti-war movement of the 1960s are two such examples. Other times, however, the supportive religious ideology of a movement can be used to deny civil rights and even incite violence. In his article, "Popular Christianity and Political Extremism in the United States," James Aho describes the relationship between Christianity and violent rightwing extremism. Every American generation, he argues, has experienced movements built on religiously inspired hatred. Today, however, these movements have been able to take advantage of sophisticated weapons and communications technology, making them especially lethal.

In the end, the nature of society, from its large institutions to its small, unspoken rules of everyday life, can be understood only by examining what people do and think. Individuals, acting collectively, can shape institutions, influence government policy, and alter the course of society. It's easy to forget that social movements consist of flesh-and-blood individuals acting together for a cause they believe in. In "Challenging Power," Celene Krauss examines the process by which white, working-class women with very traditional ideas about women's role in the family became community activists in toxic waste protests. She shows how these women became politicized not by the broader ideology of the environmentalist movement but by the direct health threats toxic waste posed to their children.

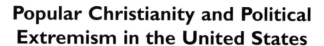

Popular Christianity and Political Extremism in the United States

James Aho

(1996)

December 8, 1984. In a shootout on Puget Sound, Washington, involving several hundred federal and local law enforcement officials, the leader of a terrorist group compromised of self-proclaimed Christian soldiers is killed, ending a crime spree involving multi-state robberies, armored car heists, arson attacks, three murders, and a teenage suicide.

—Flynn and Gerhardt 1989

Christmas Eve, 1985. A "Christian patriot soldier" in Seattle trying to save America by eliminating the Jewish-Communist leader of the so-called one-world conspiracy, murders an innocent family of four, including two pre-teen children.

—Aho 1994: 35–49

August 1992. In northern Idaho, three persons are killed and two others critically injured in the course of a stand-off between federal marshals, ATF officers, the FBI, and a white separatist Christian family seeking refuge from the "Time of Tribulations" prophesied in the Book of Revelations.

—Aho 1994: 50–65

Three isolated incidents, twelve dead bodies, scores of young men imprisoned, shattered families, millions of dollars in litigation fees and investigation expenses. Why? What can sociology tell us about the causes of these events that they might be averted in the future? In particular, insofar as Christianity figures so prominently in these stories, what role has this religion played in them? Has Christianity been a cause of right-wing extremism in the United States? Or has it been an excuse for extremism occasioned by other factors? Or is the association between right-wing extremism and Christianity merely anecdotal and incidental? Our object is to address these questions.

Extremism Defined

The word "extremism" is used rhetorically in everyday political discourse to disparage and undermine one's opponents. In this sense, it refers essentially to anyone who disagrees with me politically. In this chapter, however, "extremism" will refer exclusively to particular kinds of behaviors, namely, to non-democratic actions, regardless of their ideology—that is, regardless of whether we agree with the ideas behind them or not (Lipset and Raab 1970: 4–17). Thus, extremism includes: (1) efforts to deny civil rights to certain people, including their right to express unpopular views, their right to due process at law, to own property, etc.; (2) thwarting attempts by others to organize in opposition to us, to run for office, or vote; (3) not playing according to legal constitutional rules of political fairness: using personal smears like "Communist Jew-fag" and "nigger lover" in place of rational discussion; and above all, settling differences by vandalizing or destroying the property or life of one's opponents. The test is not the end as such, but the means employed to achieve it.

Cycles of American Right-Wing Extremism

In this [article] we are concerned with the most rabid right-wing extremists, those who have threatened or succeeded in injuring and killing their opponents. We are interested, furthermore, only in such activities as are connected at least indirectly to Christianity. By no means is this limitation of focus intended to suggest that American Christians are characteristically more violent than their non-Christian neighbors. Nor are we arguing that American Christians engage only in right-wing activities. We are focusing on Christianity and on rightist extremism because in America today this connection has become newsworthy and because it is sociologically problematic.

American political history has long been acquainted with Christian-oriented rightist extremism. As early as the 1790s, for example, Federalist Party activists, inspired partly by Presbyterian and Congregationalist preachers, took-up arms against a mythical anti-Christian cabal known as the Illuminati—Illuminati = bringers of light = Lucifer, the devil.

The most notable result of anti-Illuminatism was what became popularly known as the "Reign of Terror": passage of the Alien and Sedition acts (1798). These required federal registration of recent immigrants to America from Ireland and France, reputed to be the homes of Illuminatism, lengthened the

time of naturalization to become a citizen from five to fourteen years, restricted "subversive" speech and newspapers—that is, outlets advocating liberal Jeffersonian or what were known then as "republican" sentiments—and permitted the deportation of "alien enemies" without trial.

The alleged designs of the Illuminati were detailed in a three hundred-page book entitled *Proofs of a Conspiracy Against All the Religions and Governments of Europe Carried on in the Secret Meetings of . . . Illuminati* (Robison 1967 [1798]). Over two hundred years later *Proofs of a Conspiracy* continues to serve as a sourcebook for right-wing extremist commentary on American social issues. Its basic themes are: (1) *manichaenism:* that the world is divided into the warring principles of absolute good and evil; (2) *populism:* that the citizenry naturally would be inclined to ally with the powers of good, but have become indolent, immoral, and uninformed of the present danger to themselves; (3) *conspiracy:* that this is because the forces of evil have enacted a scheme using educators, newspapers, music, and intoxicants to weaken the people's will and intelligence; (4) *anti-modernism:* that the results of the conspiracy are the very laws and institutions celebrated by the unthinking masses as "progressive": representative government, the separation of church and State, the extension of suffrage to the propertyless, free public education, public-health measures, etc.; and (5) *apocalypticism:* that the results of what liberals call social progress are increased crime rates, insubordination to "natural" authorities (such as royal families and property-owning Anglo-Saxon males), loss of faith, and the decline of common decency—in short, the end of the world.

Approximately every thirty years America has experienced decade-long popular resurrections of these five themes. While the titles of the alleged evil-doers in each era have been adjusted to meet changing circumstances, their program is said to have remained the same. They constitute a diabolic *Plot Against Christianity* (Dilling 1952). In the 1830s, the cabal was said to be comprised of the leaders of Masonic lodges: in the 1890s, they were accused of being Papists and Jesuits; in the 1920s, they were the Hidden Hand; in the 1950s, the Insiders or Force X; and today they are known as Rockefellerian "one-world" Trilateralists or Bilderbergers.

Several parallels are observable in these periods of American right-wing resurgence. First, while occasionally they have evolved into democratically-organized political parties holding conventions that nominate slates of candidates to run for office—the American Party, the Anti-Masonic Party, the People's Party, the Prohibition Party—more often, they have become secret societies in their own right, with arcane passwords, handshakes, and vestments, plotting campaigns of counter-resistance behind closed doors. That is, they come to mirror the fantasies against which they have taken up arms. Indeed, it is this ironic fact that typically occasions the public ridicule and undoing of these groups. The most notable examples are the Know Nothings, so-called because under interrogation they were directed to deny knowledge of the organization; the Ku Klux Klan, which during the 1920s had several million members; the Order of the Star Spangled Banner, which flourished during the 1890s; the Black Legion of Michigan, circa 1930; the Minutemen of the late 1960s; and most recently, the *Bruders Schweigen,* Secret Brotherhood, or as it is more widely known, The Order.

Secondly, the thirty-year cycle noted above evidently has no connection with economic booms and busts. While the hysteria of the 1890s took place during a nation-wide depression, McCarthyism exploded on the scene during the most prosperous era in American history. On close view, American right-wing extremism is more often associated

with economic good times than with bad, the 1920s, the 1830s, and the 1980s being prime examples. On the contrary, the cycle seems to have more to do with the length of a modern generation than with any other factor.

Third, and most important for our purposes, Christian preachers have played pivotal roles in all American right-wing hysterias. The presence of Dan Gayman, James Ellison, and Bertrand Comparet spear-heading movements to preserve America from decline today continues a tradition going back to Jedidiah Morse nearly two centuries ago, continuing through Samuel D. Burchard, Billy Sunday, G. L. K. Smith, and Fred Schwarz's Christian Anti-Communist Crusade.

In the nineteenth century, the honorary title "Christian patriot" was restricted to white males with Protestant credentials. By the 1930s, however, Catholic ideologues, like the anti-Semitic radio priest Father Coughlin, had come to assume leadership positions in the movement. Today, somewhat uneasily, Mormons are included in the fold. The Ku Klux Klan, once rabidly anti-Catholic and misogynist, now encourages Catholic recruits and even allows females into its regular organization, instead of requiring them to form auxiliary groups.

Christianity: A Cause of Political Extremism?

The upper Rocky Mountain region is the heartland of American right-wing extremism in our time. Montana, Idaho, Oregon, and Washington have the highest per capita rates of extremist groups of any area in the entire country (Aho 1994: 152–153). Research on the members of these groups show that they are virtually identical to the surrounding population in all respects but one (Aho 1991: 135–163)—they are not less formally educated than the surrounding population. Furthermore, as indicated by their rates of geographic mobility, marital stability, occupational choice, and conventional political participation, they are no more estranged from their local communities than those with whom they live. And finally, their social status seems no more threatened than that of their more moderate neighbors. Indeed, there exists anecdotal evidence that American right-wing extremists today are drawn from the more favored, upwardly-mobile sectors of society. They are college-educated, professional suburbanites residing in the rapidly-growing, prosperous Western states (Simpson 1983).

In other words, the standard sociological theories of right-wing extremism—theories holding, respectively, that extremists are typically undereducated, if not stupid, transient and alienated from ordinary channels of belonging, and suffer inordinately from status insecurity—find little empirical support. Additionally, the popular psychological notion that right-wing extremists are more neurotic than the general population, perhaps paranoid to the point of psychosis, can not be confirmed. None of the right-wing political murderers whose psychiatric records this author has accessed have been medically certified as insane (Aho 1991: 68–82; Aho 1994: 46–49). If this is true for right-wing murderers, it probably also holds for extremists who have not taken the lives of others.

The single way in which right-wing extremists *do* differ from their immediate neighbors is seen in their religious biographies. Those with Christian backgrounds generally, and Presbyterians, Baptists and members of independent fundamentalist Protestant groups specifically, all are overrepresented among intermountain radical patriots (Aho 1991: 164–182). Although it concerns a somewhat different population, this finding is consistent with surveys of the religious affiliations of Americans with conservative voting and attitudinal patterns (Lipset and Raab 1970: 229–232, 359–361, 387–392, 433–437, 448–452; Shupe and Stacey 1983; Wilcox 1992).

Correlations do not prove causality. Merely because American extremists are members of certain denominations and sects does not permit the conclusion that these religious groups compel their members to extremism. In the first place, the vast majority of independent fundamentalists, Baptists, and Presbyterians are not political extremists, even if they are inclined generally to support conservative causes. Secondly, it is conceivable that violently-predisposed individuals are attracted to particular religions because of what they hear from the pulpit; and what they hear channels their *already* violent inclinations in political directions.

Today, a man named Gary Yarbrough, gaunt-faced and red-bearded, languishes in federal prison because of his participation in the *Bruders Schweigen*. Although he was recruited into terrorism from the Church of Jesus Christian—Aryan Nations—it was not the church itself that made him violent, at least not in a simplistic way. On the contrary, Yarbrough was the offspring of a notorious Pima, Arizona, family that one reporter (Ring 1985) describes as "very volatile—very anti-police, anti-social, anti-everybody." Charges against its various members have ranged from burglary and robbery to witness-intimidation.

Lloyd, Steve, and Gary Yarbrough are sons of a family of drifters. Red, the father, works as an itinerant builder and miner. Rusty, his wife, tends bar and waitresses. Child rearing, such as it was, is said to have been "severely heavy handed." Nor was much love lost between the parents. Fist fights were common and once Rusty stabbed Red so badly he was hospitalized. Not surprisingly, "the boys did not get very good schooling." Still, mother vehemently defends her boys. One night, she jumped over a bar to attack an overly inquisitive detective concerning their whereabouts.

After a spree of drugs, vandalism, and thievery, Gary, like his brothers, eventually found himself behind bars at the Arizona State

Prison. It was there that he was contacted, first by letter and later personally, by the Aryan Nations prison ministry in Idaho. He was the kind of man the church was searching for: malleable, fearless, sentimental, tough. Immediately upon release, Yarbrough moved with his wife and daughter to Idaho to be close to church headquarters. He finally found his calling: working with like-minded souls in the name of Christ to protect God's chosen people, the white race, from mongrelization.

Yarbrough purchased the requisite dark blue twill trousers, postman's shirt, Nazi pins, Sam Browne holster-belt, and 9 mm. semi-automatic pistol. The pastor of the church assigned him to head the security detail. At annual church conventions, he helped conduct rifle training. But Yarbrough was a man of action; he soon became bored with the routine of guarding the compound against aliens who never arrived. He met others in the congregation who shared his impatience. Together in a farm building, deep in the woods, over the napping figure of one of the member's infant children, they founded the *Bruders Schweigen,* swearing together an oath to war against what they called ZOG—Zionist Occupation Government (Flynn and Gerhardt 1989).

The point is not that every extremist is a violent personality searching to legitimize criminality with religion. Instead, the example illustrates the subtle ways in which religious belief, practice, and organization all play upon individual psychology to produce persons prepared to violate others in the name of principle. Let us look at each of these factors separately, understanding that in reality they intermesh in complicated, sometimes contradictory ways that can only be touched upon here.

Belief

American right-wing politics has appropriated from popular Christianity several tenets: the concept of unredeemable human depravity, the idea of America as a specially chosen people, covenant theology and the right to revolt, the belief in a national mission, millennialism, and anti-Semitism. Each of these in its own way has inspired rightist extremism.

The New Israel

The notion of America as the new Israel, for example, is the primary axiom of a fast-growing religiously-based form of radical politics known as Identity Christianity. Idaho's Aryan Nations Church is simply the most well-known Identity congregation. The adjective "identity" refers to its insistence that Anglo-Saxons are in truth the Israelites. They are "Isaac's-sons"—the Saxons—and hence the Bible is *their* historical record, not that of the Jews (Barkun 1994). The idea is that after its exile to what today is northern Iran around seven hundred B.C., the Israelites migrated over the Caucasus mountains—hence their racial type, "caucasian"—and settled in various European countries. Several of these allegedly still contain mementos of their origins: the nation of Denmark is said to be comprised of descendants from the tribe of Dan; the German-speaking Jutland, from the tribe of Judah; Catalonia, Scotland, from the tribe of Gad.

Covenant Theology

Identity Christianity is not orthodox Christianity. Nevertheless, the notion of America as an especially favored people, or as Ronald Reagan once said, quoting Puritan founders, a "city on a hill," the New Jerusalem, is widely shared by Americans. Reagan and most conservatives, of course, consider the linkage between America and Israel largely symbolic. Many right-wing extremists, however, view the relationship literally as an historical fact and for them, just as the ancient Israelites entered into a covenant with the Lord, America has done the same. According to radical patriots America's covenant is what they call the "organic Constitution." This refers to the original articles of the Constitution plus the first ten amendments, the Bill of Rights. Other amendments, especially the 16th establishing a federal income tax, are considered to have questionable legal status because allegedly they were not passed according to constitutional strictures.

The most extreme patriots deny the constitutionality of the 13th, 14th, and 15th amendments—those outlawing slavery and guaranteeing free men civil and political rights as full American citizens. Their argument is that the organic Constitution was written by white men exclusively for themselves and their blood descendents (Preamble 1986). Non-caucasians residing in America are considered "guest peoples" with no constitutional rights. Their continued residency in this country is entirely contingent upon the pleasure of their hosts, the Anglo-Saxon citizenry. According to some, it is now time for the property of these guests to be confiscated and they themselves exiled to their places of origin (Pace 1985).

All right-wing extremists insist that if America adheres to the edicts of the organic Constitution, she, like Israel before her, shall be favored among the world's nations. Her harvests shall be bountiful, her communities secure, her children obedient to the voices of their parents, and her armies undefeated. But if she falters in her faith, behaving in ways that contravene the sacred compact, then calamities, both natural and human-made, shall follow. This is the explanation for the widespread conviction among extremists today for America's decline in the world. In short, the federal government has established agencies and laws contrary to America's divine compact: these include the Internal Revenue Service; the Federal Reserve System; the Bureau of Alcohol, Tobacco and Firearms; the Forest Service; the Bureau of Land Management; Social Security; Medicare and Medicaid; the Environmental Protection Agency; Housing and Urban Development; and the official apparatus enforcing civil rights for "so-called" minorities.

Essentially, American right-wing extremists view the entire executive branch of the United States government as little more than "jack-booted Nazi thugs," to borrow a phrase from the National Rifle Association fund-raising letter: a threat to freedom of religion, the right to carry weapons, freedom of speech, and the right to have one's property secure from illegal search and seizure.

Clumsy federal-agency assaults, first on the Weaver family in northern Idaho in 1992, then on the Branch Davidian sect in Waco, Texas, in 1993, followed by passage of the assault weapons ban in 1994, are viewed as indicators that the organic Constitution presently is imperiled. This has been the immediate impetus for the appearance throughout rural and Western America of armed militias since the summer of 1994. The terrorists who bombed a federal building in Oklahoma City in the spring of 1995, killing one hundred sixty-eight, were associated with militias headquartered in Michigan and Arizona. One month after the bombing, the national director of the United States Militia Association warned that after the current government falls, homosexuals, abortionists, rapists, "unfaithful politicians," and any criminal not rehabilitated in seven years will be executed. Tax evaders will no longer be treated as felons; instead they will lose their library privileges (Sherwood 1995).

Millennialism

Leading to both the Waco and Weaver incidents was a belief on the victims' parts that world apocalypse is imminent. The Branch Davidians split from the Seventh-Day Adventists in 1935 but share with the mother church its own millenarian convictions. The Weavers received their apocalypticism from *The Late Great Planet Earth* by fundamentalist lay preacher Hal Lindsey (1970), a book that has enjoyed a wide reading on the Christian right.

Both the Davidians and the Weavers were imbued with the idea that the thousand-year-reign of Christ would be preceded by a final battle between the forces of light and darkness. To this end both had deployed elaborate arsenals to protect themselves from the anticipated invasion of "Babylonish troops." These, they feared, would be comprised of agents from the various federal bureaucracies mentioned above, together with UN troops stationed on America's borders awaiting orders from Trilateralists. Ever alert to "signs" of the impending invasion, both fired at federal officers who had come upon their property; and both ended up precipitating their own martyrdom. Far from quelling millenarian fervor, however, the two tragedies were immediately seized upon by extremists as further evidence of the approaching End Times.

Millenarianism is not unique to Christianity, nor to Western religions; furthermore, millenarianism culminating in violence is not new—in part because one psychological effect of end-time prophesying is a devaluation of worldly things, including property, honors, and human life. At the end of the first Christian millennium (A.D. 1000) as itinerant prophets were announcing the Second Coming, their followers were taking-up arms to prepare the way, and uncounted numbers died (Cohn 1967). It should not surprise observers if, as the second millennium draws to a close and promises of Christ's imminent return increase in frequency, more and more armed cults flee to the mountains, there to prepare for the final conflagration.

Anti-Semitism

Many post-Holocaust Christian and Jewish scholars alike recognize that a pervasive anti-Judaism can be read from the pages of the New Testament, especially in focusing on the role attributed to Jews in Jesus' crucifixion. Rosemary Ruether, for example, argues that anti-Judaism constitutes the "left-hand of Christianity," its archetypal negation (Ruether 1979). Although pre-Christian Greece and Rome were also critical of Jews for alleged disloyalty, anti-Semitism reached unparalleled heights in Christian theology, sometimes relegating Jews to the status of Satan's spawn, the human embodiments of Evil itself.

During the Roman Catholic era, this association became embellished with frightening myths and images. Jews—pictured as feces-eating swine and rats—were accused of murdering Christian children on high feast days, using their blood to make unleavened bread, and poisoning wells. Added to these legends were charges during the capitalist era that Jews control international banking and by means of usury have brought simple, kind-hearted Christians into financial ruin (Hay 1981 [1950]). All of this was incorporated into popular Protestant culture through, among other vehicles, Martin Luther's diatribe, *On the Jews and Their Lies,* a pamphlet that still experiences brisk sales from patriotic bookstores. This is one possible reason for a survey finding by Charles Glock and Rodney Stark that created a minor scandal in the late 1960s. Rigidly orthodox American Christians, they found, displayed far higher levels of Jew-hatred than other Christians, regardless of their education, occupation, race, or income (Glock and Stark 1966).

In the last thirty years there has been "a sharp decline" in anti-Semitic prejudice in America, according to Glock (1993: 68). Mainline churches have played some role in this decline by facilitating Christian-Jewish dialogue, de-emphasizing offensive scriptural passages, and ending missions directed at Jews. Nevertheless, ancient anti-Jewish calumnies continue to be raised by leaders of the groups that are the focus of interest in this [article].

Far from being a product of neurotic syndromes like the so-called Authoritarian (or fascist) Personality, the Jew-hatred of many right-wing extremists today is directly traceable to what they have absorbed from these preachments, sometimes as children.

Human Depravity

> *There is none righteous, no not one; . . . there is none that doeth the good, no, no one. Their throat is an open sepulchre. With their tongues they have used deceit; the poison of asps in under their lips. In these words of the apostle Paul, John Calvin says God inveighs not against particular individuals, but against all mankind. "Let it be admitted, then, that men . . . are . . . corrupt . . . by a depravity of nature"* (Calvin 1966: 34–36; see Romans 3:11–24).

One of the fundamentals of Calvinist theology, appropriated into popular American Christianity, is this: a transcendent and sovereign God resides in the heavens, relative to whom the earth and its human inhabitants are utterly, hopelessly fallen. True, Calvin only developed a line of thought already anticipated in Genesis and amplified repeatedly over the centuries. However, with a lawyer's penetrating logic, Calvin brought this tradition to its most stark, pessimistic articulation. It is this belief that accompanied the Pilgrims in their venture across the Atlantic, eventually rooting itself in the American psyche.

From its beginnings, a particular version of the doctrine of human depravity has figured prominently in American right-wing extremist discourse. It has served as the basis of its perennial misogyny, shared by both men and women. The female, being supposedly less rational and more passive, is said to be closer to earth's evil. Too, the theology of world devaluation is the likely inspiration for the right-wing's gossipy preoccupation with the body's appetites and the "perilous eroticism of emotion," for its prudish fulminations against music, dance, drink, and dress, and for its homophobia. Here, too, is found legitimation for the right-wing's vitriol against Satanist ouiji boards, "Dungeons and Dragons," and New Age witchcrafters with their horoscopes and aroma-therapies, and most recently, against "pagan-earth-worshippers" and "tree hugging idolaters" (environmentalists). In standing tall to "Satan's Kids" and their cravenness, certain neo-Calvinists in Baptist, Presbyterian, and fundamentalist clothing accomplish their own purity and sanctification.

Conspiratorialism

According to Calvin, earthquakes, pestilence, famine, and plague should pose no challenge to faith in God. We petty, self-absorbed creatures have no right to question sovereign reason. But even in Calvin's time, and more frequently later, many Christians have persisted in asking: if God is truly all-powerful, all-knowing, and all-good, then how is evil possible? Why do innocents suffer? One perennial, quasi-theological response is conspiratorialism. In short, there are AIDS epidemics, murderous holocausts, rampant poverty, and floods because counter-poised to God there exists a second hidden force of nearly equal power and omniscience: the Devil and His human consorters—Jews, Jesuits, Hidden Hands, Insiders, Masons, and Bilderbergers.

By conspiratorialism, we are not referring to documented cases of people secretly scheming to destroy co-workers, steal elections, or run competitors out of business. Conspiracies are a common feature of group life. Instead, we mean the attempt to explain the entirety of human history by means of a cosmic Conspiracy, such as that promulgated in the infamous *Protocols of the Learned Elders of Zion*. This purports to account for all modern institutions by attributing them to the designs of twelve or thirteen—one representing each of the tribes of Israel—Jewish elders (Aho 1994, 68–82). *The Protocols* enjoys immense and endless popularity on the right; and has generated numerous spin-offs: *The International Jew, None Dare Call It Conspiracy,* and the *Mystery of [Jewish] Iniquity,* to name three.

To posit the existence of an evil divinity is heresy in orthodox Christianity. But, theological objections aside, it is difficult indeed for some believers to resist the temptation of intellectual certitude conspiratorialism affords. This certainty derives from the fact that conspiratorialism in the cosmic sense can not be falsified. Every historical event can, and often is, taken as further verification of conspiracies. If newspapers report a case of government corruption, this is evidence of government conspiracy; if they do not, this is evidence of news media complicity in the conspiracy. If the media deny involvement in a cover-up, this is still further proof of their guilt; if they admit to having sat on the story, this is surely an admission of what is already known.

Practice

Christianity means more than adhering to a particular doctrine. To be Christian is to live righteously. God-fearing righteousness may either be understood as a *sign* of one's salvation, as in orthodox Christianity or, as in Mormonism, a way to *earn* eternal life in the celestial heavens.

Nor is it sufficient for the faithful merely to display righteousness in their personal lives and businesses, by being honest, hardworking, and reliable. Many Christians also are obligated to witness to, or labor toward, salvation in the political arena; to work with others to remake this charnel-house world after the will of God; to help establish God's kingdom on earth. Occasionally this means becoming involved in liberal causes—abolitionism, civil rights, the peace and ecological movements;

often it has entailed supporting causes on the right. In either case it may require that one publicly stand up to evil. For, as Saint Paul said, to love God is to hate what is contrary to God.

Such a mentality may lead to "holy war," the organized effort to eliminate human fetishes of evil (Aho 1994: 23–34). For some, in cleansing the world of putrefaction their identity as Christian is recognized, it is re-known. This is not to argue that holy war is unique to Christianity, or that all Christians participate in holy wars. Most Christians are satisfied to renew their faith through the rites of Christmas, Easter, baptism, marriage, or mass. Furthermore, those who *do* speak of holy war often use it metaphorically to describe a private spiritual battle against temptation, as in "I am a soldier of Christ, therefore I am not permitted to fight" (Sandford 1966). Lastly, even holy war in the political sense does not necessarily imply the use of violence. Although they sometimes have danced tantalizingly close to extremism (in the sense defined earlier), neither Pat Robertson nor Jerry Falwell, for example, have advocated non-democratic means in their "wars" to avert America's decline.

Let us examine the notion of Christian holy war more closely. The sixteenth-century father of Protestant reform, Martin Luther, repudiated the concept of holy war, arguing that there exist two realms: holiness, which is the responsibility of the Church, and warfare, which falls under the State's authority (Luther 1974). Mixing these realms, he says, perverts the former while unnecessarily hamstringing the latter. This does not mean that Christians may forswear warfare, according to Luther. In his infinite wisdom, God has ordained princes to quell civil unrest and protect nations from invasion. Luther's exhortations to German officials that they spare no means in putting down peasant revolts are well known. Indeed, few theologians have "so highly praised the virtues of the State as Luther," says Ernst Troeltsch. Nevertheless, State violence is at best "sinful power to punish sin" for Luther. It is not a sacred instrument (Troeltsch 1960: 539–544, 656–677). To this day, Lutherans generally are less responsive to calls for holy wars than many other Christians.

John Calvin, on the other hand, rejected Luther's proposal to separate church from State. Instead, his goal was to establish a Christocracy in Geneva along Roman Catholic lines, and to attain this goal through force, if need be, as Catholicism had done. Calvin says that not only is violence to establish God's rule on earth permitted, it is commanded. "Good brother, we must bend unto all means that give furtherance to the holy cause" (Walzer 1965: 17, 38, 68–87, 90–91, 100–109; see Troeltsch 1960: 599–601, 651–652, 921–922 n. 399). This notion profoundly influenced Oliver Cromwell and his English revolutionary army known as the Ironsides, so named because of its righteously cold brutality (Solt 1971). And it was the Calvinist ethic, not that of Luther, that was imported to America by the Puritans, informing the politics of Presbyterians and Congregationalists—the immediate heirs of Calvinism—as well as some Methodists and many Baptists. Hence, it is not surprising that those raised in these denominations are often overrepresented in samples of "saints" on armed crusades to save the world for Christ.

Seminal to the so-called pedagogic or educational function of holy war are two requirements. First, the enemy against whom the saint fights must be portrayed in terms appropriate to his status as a fetish of evil. Second, the campaign against him must be equal to his diabolism. It must be terrifying, bloodthirsty, uncompromising.

"Prepare War!" was issued by the now defunct Covenant, Sword and the Arm of the Lord, a fundamentalist Christian paramilitary commune headquartered in Missouri. A raid on the compound in the late 1980s uncovered one of the largest private arms caches ever in American history. Evidently, this arsenal was to be used to combat what the pamphlet calls "Negro-beasts of the field . . . who eat the flesh of men. . . . This cannibalistic fervor shall cause them to eat the dead *and* the living during" the time of Tribulations, prophesied in The Book of Revelation (CSA n.d.: 19). The weapons were also to be directed against "Sodomite homosexuals waiting in their lusts to rape," "Seed-of-Satan Jews, who are today sacrificing people in darkness," and "do-gooders who've fought for the 'rights' of these groups" (CSA n.d.: 19). When the Lord God has delivered these enemies into our hands, warns the pamphlet quoting the Old Testament, "thou shalt save alive nothing that breatheth: but thou shalt utterly destroy them" (CSA n.d.: 20; see Deuteronomy 20: 10–18).

The 1990s saw a series of State-level initiatives seeking to deny homosexuals civil rights. Although most of these failed by narrow margins, one in Colorado was passed (later to be adjudged unconstitutional), due largely to the efforts of a consortium of fundamentalist Christian churches. One of the most influential of these was the Laporte, Colorado, Church of Christ, America's largest Identity congregation (more on Identity Christianity below). Acknowledging that the title of their pamphlet "Death Penalty for Homosexuals" would bring upon them the wrath of liberals, its authors insist that "such slanderous tactics" will not deter the anti-homosexual campaign. "For truth will ultimately prevail, no matter how many truth-bearers are stoned." And what precisely is this truth? It is that the Lord Himself has declared that "if a man also lie with mankind, as he lieth with a woman, both of them have committed an abomination: they shall surely be put to death; their blood shall be upon them" (Peters 1992: i; see Leviticus 20:13).

Like "Prepare War!," "Death Penalty for Homosexuals" is not satisfied merely to cite biblical references. To justify the extremity of its attack, it must paint the homosexual in luridly terrifying colors. Finding and citing a quote from the most extreme of radical gay activists, their pamphlet warns (CSA n.d.: 19):

> [They] shall sodomize [our] sons. . . . [They] shall seduce them in [our] schools, . . . in [our] locker rooms, . . . in [our] army bunkhouses . . . wherever men are with men together. [Our] sons shall become [their] minions and do [their] bidding. . . . All laws banning homosexual activity will be revoked. Instead, legislation shall be passed which engenders love between men. . . . [They] shall stage plays in which man openly caresses man. . . . The museums of the world will be filled only with paintings of . . . naked lads. . . . Love between men [will become] fashionable and de rigueur. [They] will eliminate heterosexual liaisons. . . . There will be no compromises. . . . Those who oppose [them] will be exiled. [They] shall raise vast private armies . . . to defeat [us]. . . . The family unit . . . will be abolished. . . . All churches who condemn [them] will be closed . . . . The society to emerge will be governed by . . . gay poets . . . . Any heterosexual man will be barred from . . . influence. All males who insist on remaining . . . heterosexual will be tried in homosexual courts of justice."

What should Christians do in the face of this looming specter, asks the pamphlet? "We, today, can and should have God's Law concerning Homosexuality and its judgment of the death penalty." For "they which commit such things," says the apostle Paul, "are worthy of death" (CSA n.d.: 15; see Romans 1:27–32). Extremism fans the flames of extremism.

Organization

Contrary to popular thinking, people rarely join right-wing groups because they have a prior belief in doctrines such as those enumerated above. Rather, they come to believe because they have first joined. That is, people first affiliate with right-wing activists and only then begin altering their intellectual outlooks to sustain and strengthen these ties. The original ties may develop from their jobs, among neighbors, among prison acquaintances, or through romantic relationships.

Take the case of Cindy Cutler, who was last seen teaching music at the Aryan Nations Church academy (Mauer, 1980). Reflecting on the previous decade she could well wonder at how far she had come in such a short time.

Cindy had been raised Baptist. "I was with the Jesus Christ thing, that Jesus was my savior and God was love. We'd go to the beach up to a perfect stranger and say, 'Are you saved?'" Such was the serene existence of an uncommonly pretty thrice born-again teenager then residing in San Diego—until she met Gary Cutler, a Navy man stationed nearby. Gary was fourteen years Cindy's senior and seemed the "good Christian man" she had been looking for when they met one Sunday at Baptist services.

Gary and Cindy were already dating when he discovered Identity Christianity. Brought up as a Mormon, he had left the church when it began granting priesthood powers to Black members during the 1970s. After several years searching for a new religious home, Gary claims to have first heard the Identity message one evening while randomly spinning the radio dial. An Identity preacher was extolling the white race as God's chosen people. Gary says the sermon gave him "new found pride."

In the meantime, Cindy's fondness for Gary was growing. The only problem was his espousal of Identity beliefs. As part of her faith, Cindy had learned that Jews, not Anglo-Saxons, were from Israel, and that Jesus was Jewish. Both of these notions were in conflict with what Gary was now saying. Perhaps, Cindy feared, she and Gary were incompatible after all. How could she ever find intellectual consensus with her fiance?

Gary and Cindy routinely spent time together in Bible study. One evening Cindy saw the light. She had already learned from church that Jews were supposedly "Christ killers." It was this information that enabled her to overcome what she calls her prideful resistance to Identity. The occasion of her conversion was this passage:

"My sheep know me and hear my voice, and follow me" (John 10: 27). "That's how I got into Identity," she later said. "I questioned how they [the Jews] could be God's chosen people if they hate my Christ." Having discovered a shared theological ground upon which to stand, Gary and Cindy could now marry.

The point of this story is the sociological truth that the way in which some people become right-wing extremists is indistinguishable from the way others become vegetarians, peace activists, or members of mainline churches (Lofland and Stark 1965; Aho 1991: 185–211). *Their affiliations are mediated by significant others already in the movement.* It is from these others that they first learn of the cause; sometimes it is through the loaning of a pamphlet or videotape; occasionally it takes the form of an invitation to a meeting or workshop. As the relationship with the other tightens, the recruit's viewpoint begins to change. At this stage old friends, family members, and cohorts, observing the recruit spending inordinate time with "those new people," begin their interrogations: "What's up with you, man?" In answer, the new recruit typically voices shocking things: bizarre theologies, conspiracy theories, manichaeistic worldviews. Either because of conscious "disowning" or unconscious avoidance, the recruit finds the old ties loosening, and as they unbind, the "stupidity" and "backwardness" of prior acquaintances becomes increasingly evident.

Pushed away from old relationships and simultaneously pulled into the waiting arms of new friends, lovers, and comrades, the recruit is absorbed into the movement. Announcements of full conversion to extremism follow. To display commitment to the cause, further steps may be deemed necessary: pulling one's children out of public schools where "secular humanism" is taught; working for radical political candidates to stop America's "moral decline"; refusing to support ZOG with taxes; renouncing one's citizenship and throwing away social security card and driver's license; moving to a rugged wilderness to await the End Times. Occasionally it means donning camouflage, taking up high-powered weaponry, and confronting the "forces of satan" themselves.

There are two implications to this sociology of recruitment. First and most obviously, involvement in social networks is crucial to being mobilized into right-wing activism. Hence, contrary to the claims of the estrangement theory of extremism mentioned above, those who are truly isolated from their local communities are the last and least likely to become extremists themselves. My research (Aho 1991, 1994) suggests that among the most important of these community ties is membership in independent fundamentalist, Baptist, or Presbyterian congregations.

Secondly, being situated in particular networks is largely a matter of chance. None of us choose our parents. Few choose their co-workers, fellow congregants, or neighbors, and even friendships and marriages are restricted to those available to us by the happenstance of our geography and times. What this means is that almost any person could find themselves in a Christian patriot communications network that would position them for recruitment into right-wing extremism.

As we have already pointed out, American right-wing extremists are neither educationally nor psychologically different from the general population. Nor are they any more status insecure than other Americans. What makes them different is how they are socially positioned. This positioning includes their religious affiliation. Some people find themselves in churches that expose them to the right-wing world. This increases the likelihood of their becoming right-wingers.

Conclusion

Throughout American history, a particular style of Christianity has nurtured right-wing extremism. Espousing doctrines like human depravity, white America as God's elect people, conspiratorialism, Jews as Christ killers, covenant theology and the right to revolt, and millennialism, this brand of Christianity is partly rooted in orthodox Calvinism and in the theologically questionable fantasies of popular imagination. Whatever its source, repeatedly during the last two centuries, its doctrines have served to prepare believers cognitively to assume hostile attitudes toward "un-Christian"—hence un-American—individuals, groups, and institutional practices.

This style of Christianity has also given impetus to hatred and violence through its advocacy of armed crusades against evil. Most of all, however, the cults, sects, and denominations wherein this style flourishes have served as mobilization centers for recruitment into right-wing causes. From the time of America's inception, right-wing political leaders in search of supporters have successfully enlisted clergymen who preach these principles to bring their congregations into the fold in "wars" to save America for Christ.

It is a mistake to think that modern Americans are more bigoted and racist than their ancestors were. Every American generation has experienced right-wing extremism, even that occasionally erupting into vigilante violence of the sort witnessed daily on the news today. What is different in our time is the sophistication and availability of communications and weapons technology. Today, mobilizations to right-wing causes has been infinitely enhanced by the availability of personal computer systems capable of storing and retrieving information on millions of potential recruits. Mobilization has also been facilitated by cheap shortwave radio and cable-television access, the telephone tree, desktop publishing, and readily available studio-quality recorders. Small coteries of extremists can now activate supporters across immense distances at the touch of a button. Add to this the modern

instrumentality for maiming and killing available to the average American citizen: military-style assault weaponry easily convertible into fully automatic machine guns, powerful explosives manufacturable from substances like diesel oil and fertilizer, harmless in themselves, hence purchasable over-the-counter. Anti-tank and aircraft weapons, together with assault vehicles, have also been uncovered recently in private-arms caches in the Western states.

Because of these technological changes, religious and political leaders today have a greater responsibility to speak and write with care regarding those with whom they disagree. Specifically, they must control the temptation to demonize their opponents, lest, in their declarations of war they bring unforeseen destruction not only on their enemies, but on themselves.

REFERENCES

Aho, J. 1991. *The Politics of Righteousness: Idaho Christian Patriotism.* Seattle: University of Washington Press.

———. 1994. *This Thing of Darkness: A Sociology of the Enemy.* Seattle: University of Washington Press.

Barkun, M. 1994. *Religion and the Racist Right: The Origins of the Christian Identity Movement.* Chapel Hill: North Carolina University Press.

Calvin J. 1966. *On God and Man.* F. W. Strothmann (ed.). New York: Ungar.

Cohn, N. 1967. *The Pursuit of the Millennium.* New York: Oxford University Press.

CSA. n.d. "Prepare War!" Pontiac, Missouri: CSA Bookstore.

Dilling, E. 1952. *The Plot Against Christianity.* n.p.

Flynn, K. and G. Gerhardt. 1989. *The Silent Brotherhood: Inside America's Racist Underground.* New York: Free Press.

Glock, C. 1993. "The Churches and Social Change in Twentieth-Century America." *Annals of the American Academy of Political and Social Science.* 527: 67–83.

Glock, C. and R. Stark. 1966. *Christian Beliefs and Anti-Semitism.* New York: Harper & Row.

Hay, M. 1981 (1950). *The Roots of Christian Anti-Semitism.* New York: Anti-Defamation League of B'nai B'rith.

Lindsey, H. 1970. *The Late Great Planet Earth.* Grand Rapids: Zondervan.

Lipset, S. M. and E. Raab. 1970. *The Politics of Unreason: Right-Wing Extremism in America, 1790–1970.* New York: Harper & Row.

Lofland, J. and R. Stark. 1965. "Becoming a World-Saver: A Theory of Conversation to a Deviant Perspective." *American Sociological Review* 30: 862–875.

Luther, M. 1974. *Luther: Selected Political Writings,* J. M. Porter, ed. Philadelphia: Fortress Press.

Mannheim, K. 1952. "The Problem of Generations," in *Essays in the Sociology of Knowledge.* London: Routledge and Kegan Paul.

Mauer, D. 1980. "Couple Finds Answers in Butler's Teachings." *Idaho Statesman.* Sept. 14.

Nisbet, R. 1953. *The Quest for Community.* New York: Harper and Brothers.

Pace, J. O. 1985. Amendment to the Constitution. Los Angeles: Johnson, Pace, Simmons and Fennel.

Peters, P. 1992. *Death Penalty for Homosexuals.* LaPorte, Colorado: Scriptures for America.

Preamble. 1986. "Preamble to the United States Constitution: Who Are the Posterity?" Oregon City, Oregon: Republic vs. Democracy Redress.

Ring, R. H. 1985. "The Yarbrough's." *The Denver Post.* Jan. 6.

Robison, J. 1967 (1798). *Proofs of a Conspiracy. . . .* Los Angeles: Western Islands.

Ruether, R. 1979. *Faith and Fratricide: The Theological Roots of Anti-Semitism.* New York: Seabury.

Sandford, F. W. 1966. *The Art of War for the Christian Soldier.* Amherst, New Hampshire: Kingdom Press.

Schlesinger, A. 1986. *The Cycles of American History.* Boston: Houghton Mifflin.

Sherwood, "Commander" S. 1995. Quoted in *Idaho State Journal.* May 21.

Shupe, A. and W. Stacey. 1983. "The Moral Majority Constituency," in *The New Christian Right,* R. Liebman and R. Wuthnow, eds. New York: Aldine.

Simpson, J. 1983. "Moral Issues and Status Politics," in *The New Christian Right,* R. Liebman and R. Wuthnow, eds. New York: Aldine.

Solt, L. 1971. *Saints in Arms: Puritanism and Democracy in Cromwell's Army.* New York: AMS Press.

Stark, R. and William Bainbridge. 1985. The *Future of Religion: Secularization, Revival and Cult Formation.* Berkeley: University of California Press.

Stouffer, S. A. 1966. *Communism, Conformity and Civil* Liberties. New York: John Wiley.

Troeltsch, E. 1960. *Social Teachings of the Christian Churches.* Trans. by O. Wyon. New York: Harper & Row.

Walzer, M. 1965. *The Revolution of the Saints.* Cambridge, MA: Harvard University Press.

Wilcox, C. 1992. *God's Warriors: The Christian Right in Twentieth Century America.* Baltimore, MD: Johns Hopkins University Press.

THINKING ABOUT THE READING

Describe the religious doctrines that typically characterize right-wing extremist groups in the United States. Compare the groups that Aho describes to the so-called Islamic extremist groups that became the focus of national attention after the attacks of September 11, 2001. How are they alike? How do they differ? After reading Aho's article, do you think that Christianity is a cause of right-wing extremism? If not, how can you account for the religiously inspired rhetoric of such movements? If so, what responsibility do "less extreme" churches have in suppressing extremist groups? In a more general sense, what role do you think religious institutions ought to play in movements for political and social change?

Challenging Power

Toxic Waste Protests and the Politicization of White, Working-Class Women

Celene Krauss

(1998)

Over the past two decades, toxic waste disposal has been a central focus of women's grassroots environmental activism. Women of diverse racial, ethnic, and class backgrounds have assumed the leadership of community environmental struggles around toxic waste issues (Krauss 1993). Out of their experience of protest, these women have constructed ideologies of environmental justice that reveal broader issues of inequality underlying environmental hazards (Bullard 1990, 1994). Environmental justice does not exist as an abstract concept prior to these women's activism. It grows out of the concrete, immediate, everyday experience of struggles around issues of survival. As women become involved in toxic waste issues, they go through a politicizing process that is mediated by their experiences of class, race, and ethnicity (Krauss 1993).

Among the earliest community activists in toxic waste protests were white, working-class women. This [article] examines the process by which these women became politicized through grassroots protest activities in the 1980s, which led to their analyses of environmental justice, and in many instances to their leadership in regional and national toxic waste coalitions. These women would seem unlikely candidates for becoming involved in political protest. They came out of a culture that shares a strong belief in the existing political system, and in which traditional women's roles center around the private arena of family. Although financial necessity may have led them into the workplace, the primary roles from which they derived meaning, identity, and satisfaction are those of mothering and taking care of family. Yet, as we shall see, the threat that toxic wastes posed to family health and community survival disrupted the taken-for-granted fabric of their lives, politicizing women who had never viewed themselves as activists. . . .

This [article] shows how white, working-class women's involvement in toxic waste issues has wider implications for social change. . . . These women . . . fought to close down toxic waste dump sites, to prevent the siting of hazardous waste incinerators, to oppose companies' waste-disposal policies, to push for recycling projects, and so on. Their voices show us . . . that their single-issue community protests led them through a process of politicization and their broader analysis of inequities of class and gender in the public arena and in the family. Propelled into the public arena in defense of their children, they ultimately challenged government, corporations, experts, husbands, and their own insecurities as working-class women. Their analysis of environmental justice and inequality led them to form coalitions with labor and people of color around environmental issues. These women's traditional beliefs about motherhood, family, and democracy served a crucial function in this politicizing process. While they framed their analyses in terms of traditional constructions of gender and the state, they actively reinterpreted these constructions into an oppostitional ideology, which became a resource of resistance and a source of power in the public arena.

Subjective Dimensions of Grassroots Activism

In most sociological analysis of social movements, the subjective dimension of protest has often been ignored or viewed as private and individualistic. . . . [Contemporary theories] show us how experience is not merely a personal, individualistic concept: it is social. People's experiences reflect where they fit into the social hierarchy. . . . Thus, white, working-class women interpret their experience of toxic waste problems within the context of their particular cultural history, arriving at a critique that reflects broader issues of class and gender. . . .

. . . This article focuses on the subjective process by which white, working-class women involved in toxic waste protests construct an oppositional consciousness out of their everyday lives, experiences, and identities. As these women became involved in the public arena, they confronted a world of power normally hidden from them. This forced them to re-examine their assumptions about private and public power and to develop a broad reconceptualization of gender, family, and government.

The experience of protest is central to this process and can reshape traditional beliefs and values (see Thompson 1963). My analysis reveals the contradictory ways in which traditional culture mediates white, working-class women's subjective experience and interpretation of structural inequality. Their protests are framed in terms of dominant ideologies of

motherhood, family, and a deep faith in the democratic system. Their experience also reveals how dominant ideologies are appropriated and reconstructed as an instrument of their politicization and a legitimating ideology used to justify resistance. For example, as the political economy of growth displaces environmental problems into their communities, threatening the survival of children and family and creating everyday crises, government toxic waste policies are seen to violate their traditional belief that a democratic government will protect their families. Ideologies of motherhood and democracy become political resources which these women use to initiate and justify their resistance, their increasing politicization, and their fight for a genuine democracy.

Methodological Considerations

My analysis is based on the oral and written voices of white, working-class women involved in toxic waste protests. Sources include individual interviews, as well as conference presentations, pamphlets, books, and other written materials that have emerged from this movement. Interviews were conducted with a snowball sample of twenty white, working-class women who were leaders in grassroots protest activities against toxic waste landfills and incinerators during the 1980s. These women ranged in age from twenty-five to forty; all but one had young children at the time of their protest. They were drawn from a cross section of the country, representing urban, suburban, and rural areas. None of them had been politically active before the protest; many of them, however, have continued to be active in subsequent community movements, often becoming leaders in statewide and national coalitions around environmental and social justice issues. I established contact with these women through networking at activist conferences. Open-ended interviews were conducted between May 1989, and December 1991, and lasted from two to four hours. The interview was designed to generate a history of these women's activist experiences, information about changes in political beliefs, and insights into their perceptions of their roles as women, mothers, and wives.

Interviews were also conducted with Lois Gibbs and four other organizers for the Citizens Clearinghouse for Hazardous Wastes (CCHW). CCHW is a nation-wide organization created by Gibbs, who is best known for her successful campaign to relocate families in Love Canal, New York. Over the past two decades, this organization has functioned as a key resource for community groups fighting around toxic waste issues in the United States. Its leadership and staff are composed primarily of women, and the organization played a key role in shaping the ideology of working-class women's environmental activism in the 1980s.

My scholarly interest in working-class women's community activism grew out of my own involvement as a community activist and organizer in the 1970s. This decade marked the period of my own politicization as a white, middle-class woman working with women from many different racial-ethnic backgrounds as they challenged corporate and governmental policies that were destroying urban, working-class neighborhoods. My subsequent academic research has focused on the community protests of working-class women, who are often forgotten in our understanding of movements for social change. My experiences within the environmental movement helped guide my research and deepen my analysis. Through the issue of toxic waste protests, I have examined different facets of working-class women's community activism, most recently the ways in which consciousness and agency are mediated by different experiences of race and ethnicity (Krauss 1993).

The Process of Politicization

Women identify the toxic waste movement as a women's movement, composed primarily of mothers. As one woman who fought against an incinerator in Arizona and subsequently worked on other anti-incinerator campaigns throughout the state stressed: "Women are the backbone of the grassroots groups, they are the ones who stick with it, the ones who won't back off." Because mothers are traditionally responsible for the health of their children, they are more likely than others within their communities to begin to make the link between toxic waste and their children's ill health. And in communities around the United States, it was women who began to uncover numerous toxin-related health problems: multiple miscarriages, birth defects, cancer, neurological symptoms, and so on. Given the placement of toxic waste facilities in working-class and low-income communities and communities of color, it is not surprising that women from these groups have played a particularly important role in fighting against environmental hazards.

White, working-class women's involvement in toxic waste issues is complicated by the political reality that they, like most people, are excluded from the policy-making process. For the most part, corporate and governmental disposal policies with far-reaching social and political consequences are made without the knowledge of community residents. People may unknowingly live near (or even on top of) a toxic waste dump, or they may assume that the facility is well regulated by the government. Consequently, residents are often faced with a number of problems of seemingly indeterminate origin, and the information withheld from them may make them unwitting contributors to the ill health of their children.

The discovery of a toxic waste problem and the threat it poses to family sets in motion a process of critical questioning about the relationship between women's private work as mothers and the public arena of politics. The narratives of the women involved in toxic waste protests focus on political transformation, on the process of "becoming" an activist. Prior to their discovery of the link between their family's health and toxic waste, few of these women had been politically active. They saw their primary work in terms of the "private" sphere of motherhood and family. But the realization that toxic waste issues threatened their families thrust them into the public arena in defense of this private sphere. According to Penny Newman:

> We woke up one day to discover that our families were being damaged by toxic contamination, a situation in which we had little, if any, input. It wasn't a situation in which we chose to become involved, rather we did it because we had to . . . it was a matter of our survival. (Newman 1991, 8)

Lois Gibbs offered a similar account of her involvement in Love Canal:

> When my mother asked me what I wanted to do when I grew up, I said I wanted to have six children and be a homemaker. . . . I moved into Love Canal and I bought the American Dream: a house, two children, a husband, and HBO. And then something happened to me and that was Love Canal. I got involved because my son Michael had epilepsy . . . and my daughter Melissa developed a rare blood disease and almost died because of something someone else did. . . . I never thought of myself as an activist or an organizer. I was a housewife, a mother, but all of a sudden it was my family, my children, and my neighbors. . . .

It was through their role as mothers that many of these women began to suspect a connection between the invisible hazard posed by toxic wastes and their children's ill health, and this was their first step toward political activism. At Love Canal, for example, Lois Gibbs's fight to expose toxic waste hazards was triggered by the link she made between her son's seizures and the toxic waste dump site. After reading about toxic hazards in a local newspaper, she thought about her son and then surveyed her neighbors to find that they had similar health problems. In Woburn, Massachusetts, Ann Anderson found that other neighborhood children were, like her son, being treated for leukemia, and she began to wonder if this was an unusually high incidence of the disease. In Denver, mothers comparing stories at Tupperware parties were led to question the unusually large number of sick and dying children in their community. These women's practical activity as mothers and their extended networks of family and community led them to make the connection between toxic waste and sick children—a discovery process rooted in what Sara Ruddick (1989) has called the everyday practice of mothering, in which, through their informal networks, mothers compare notes and experiences, developing a shared body of personal, empirical knowledge.

Upon making the link between their family's ill health and toxic wastes, the women's first response was to go to the government, a response that reflects a deeply held faith in democracy embedded in their working-class culture. They assumed that the government would protect the health and welfare of their children. Gibbs (1982, 12) reports:

> I grew up in a blue-collar community, I was very patriotic, into democracy . . . I believed in government. . . . I believed that if you had a complaint, you went to the right person in government. If there was a way to solve the problem, they would be glad to do it.

An Alabama activist who fought to prevent the siting of an incinerator describes a similar response:

> We just started educating ourselves and gathering information about the problems of incineration. We didn't think our elected officials knew. Surely, if they knew that there was already a toxic waste dump in our county, they would stop it.

In case after case, however, these women described facing a government that was indifferent, if not antagonistic, to their concerns. At Love Canal, local officials claimed that the toxic waste pollution was insignificant, the equivalent of smoking just three cigarettes a day. In South Brunswick, New Jersey, governmental officials argued that living with pollution was the price of a better way of life. In Jacksonville, Arkansas, women were told that the dangers associated with dioxin emitted from a hazardous waste incinerator were exaggerated, no worse than "eating two or three tablespoons of peanut butter over a thirty-year period." Also in Arkansas, a woman who linked her ill health to a fire at a military site that produced agent orange was told by doctors that she was going through a "change of life." In Stringfellow, California, eight hundred thousand gallons of toxic chemical waste pumped into the community flowed directly behind the elementary school and into the playground. Children played in contaminated puddles yet officials withheld information from their parents because "they didn't want to panic the public."

Government's dismissal of their concerns about the health of their families and communities challenged these white, working-class women's democratic assumptions and opened a window on a world of power whose working they had not before questioned. Government explanations starkly contradicted the personal, empirical evidence which the women discovered as mothers, the everyday knowledge that their children and their neighbors' children were ill. Indeed, a recurring theme in the narratives of these women is the transformation of their beliefs about government. Their politicization is rooted in a deep sense of violation, hurt, and betrayal from finding out their government will not protect their families. Echoes of this disillusionment are heard from women throughout the country. In the CCHW publication *Empowering Women* (1989, 31) one activist noted:

> All our lives we are taught to believe certain things about ourselves as women, about democracy and justice, and about people in positions of authority. Once we become involved with toxic waste problems, we need to confront some our old beliefs and change the way we view things.

Lois Gibbs summed up this feeling when she stated:

> There is something about discovering that democracy isn't democracy as we know it. When you lose faith in your government, it's like finding out your mother was fooling around on your father. I was very upset. It almost broke my heart because I really believed in the system. I still believe in the system, only now I believe that democracy is of the people and by the people, that people have to move it, it ain't gonna move by itself.

These women's loss of faith in "democracy" as they had understood it led them to develop a more autonomous and critical stance. Their investigation shifted to a political critique of the undemocratic nature of government itself, making the link between government inaction and corporate power, and discovering that government places corporate interests and profit ahead of the health needs of families and communities. At Love Canal, residents found that local government's refusal to acknowledge the scope of the toxic waste danger was related to plans of Hooker Chemical, the polluting industry, for a multi-million dollar downtown development project. In Woburn, Massachusetts, government officials feared that awareness of the health hazard posed by a dump would limit their plans for real-estate development. In communities throughout the United States, women came to see that government policies supported waste companies' preference of incineration over recycling because incineration was more profitable.

Ultimately, their involvement in toxic waste protests led these women to develop a perspective on environmental justice rooted in issues of class and a critique of the corporate state. They argued that government's claims—to be democratic, to act on behalf of the public interest, to hold the family sacrosanct—are false. One woman who fought an incinerator in Arizona recalled:

> I believed in government. When I heard EPA, I thought, "Ooh, that was so big." Now I wouldn't believe them if they said it was sunny outside. I have a list of the revolving door of the EPA. Most of them come from Browning Ferris or Waste Management, the companies that plan landfills and incinerators.

As one activist in Alabama related:

> I was politically naive. I was real surprised because I live in an area that's like the Bible belt of the South. Now I think the God of the United States is really economic development, and that has got to change.

Another activist emphasized:

> We take on government and polluters. . . . We are up against the largest corporations in the United States. They have lots of money to lobby, pay off, bribe, cajole, and influence. They threaten us. Yet we challenge them with the only things we have—people and the truth. We learn that our government is not out to protect our rights. To protect our families we are now forced to picket, protest and shout. (Zeff et al. 1989, 31)

In the process of protest, these women were also forced to examine their assumptions about the family as a private haven, separate from the public arena, which would however be protected by the policies and actions of government should the need arise. The issue of toxic waste shows the many ways in which government allows this haven to be invaded by polluted water, hazardous chemicals, and other conditions that threaten the everyday life of the family. Ultimately, these women arrived at a concept of environmental injustice rooted in the inequities of power that displace the costs of toxic waste unequally onto their communities. The result was a critical political stance that contributed to the militancy of their activism. Highly traditional values of democracy and motherhood remained central to their lives: they justified their resistance as mothers protecting their children and working to make the promise of democracy real. Women's politicization around toxic waste protests led them to transform their traditional beliefs into resources of opposition which enabled them to enter the public arena and challenge its legitimacy, breaking down the public/private distinction.

Appropriating Power in the Public Arena

Toxic waste issues and their threat to family and community prompted white, working-class women to redefine their roles as mothers. Their work of mothering came to extend beyond taking care of the children, husband, and housework; they saw the necessity of preserving the family by entering the public arena. In so doing, they discovered and overcame a more subtle process of intimidation, which limited their participation in the public sphere.

As these women became involved in toxic waste issues, they came into conflict with a public world where policy makers are traditionally white, male, and middle class. The Citizen's Clearinghouse for Hazardous Waste, in the summary of its 1989 conference on women and organizing, noted:

> Seventy to eighty percent of local leaders are women. They are women leaders in a community run by men. Because of this, many of the obstacles that these women face as leaders stem from the conflicts between their traditional female role in the community and their new role as leader: conflicts with male officials and

authorities who have not yet adjusted to these persistent, vocal, head-strong women challenging the system. . . . Women are frequently ignored by male politicians, male government officials and male corporate spokesmen.

Entering the public arena meant overcoming internal and external barriers to participation, shaped by gender and class. White, working-class women's reconstructed definition of motherhood became a resource for this process, and their narratives reveal several aspects of this transformation.

For these women, entering the public arena around toxic waste issues was often extremely stressful. Many of them were initially shy and intimidated, as simple actions such as speaking at a meeting opened up wider issues about authority, and experiences of gender and class combined to heighten their sense of inadequacy. Many of these women describe, for example, that their high-school education left them feeling ill-equipped to challenge "experts," whose legitimacy, in which they had traditionally believed, was based on advanced degrees and specialized knowledge.

One woman who fought to stop the siting of an incinerator in her community in Arizona recalled: "I used to cry if I had to speak at a PTA meeting. I was so frightened." An activist in Alabama described her experience in fighting the siting of an incinerator in her community:

> I was a woman . . . an assistant Sunday School teacher. . . . In the South, women are taught not to be aggressive, we're supposed to be hospitable and charitable and friendly. We don't protest, we don't challenge authority. So it was kind of difficult for me to get involved. I was afraid to speak. And all of a sudden everything became controversial. . . . I think a lot of it had to do with not knowing what I was. . . . The more I began to know, the better I was . . . the more empowered.

Male officials further exacerbated this intimidation by ignoring the women, by

criticizing them for being overemotional, and by delegitimizing their authority by labeling them "hysterical housewives"—a label used widely, regardless of the professional status of the woman. In so doing, they revealed an antipathy to emotionality, a quality valued in the private sphere of family and motherhood but scorned in the public arena as irrational and inappropriate to "objective" discourse.

On several levels, the debate around toxic waste issues was framed by policy makers in such a way as to exclude women's participation, values, and expression. Women's concerns about their children were trivialized by being placed against a claim that the wider community benefits from growth and progress. Information was withheld from them. Discourse was framed as rational, technical, and scientific, using the testimony of "experts" to discredit the everyday empirical knowledge of the women. Even such details as seating arrangements reflected traditional power relations and reinforced the women's internalization of those relations.

These objective and subjective barriers to participation derived from a traditional definition of women's roles based on the separation of the public and private arenas. Yet it is out of these women's political redefinition of the traditional role of mother that they found the resources to overcome these constraints, ultimately becoming self-confident and assertive. They used the resources of their own experience to alter the power relations they had discovered in the public arena.

The traditional role of mother, of protector of the family and community, served to empower these activists on a number of levels. From the beginning, their view of this role provided the motivation for women to take risks in defense of their families and overcome their fears of participating in the public sphere. A woman who fought the siting of an incinerator in Arkansas described this power:

I was afraid to hurt anyone's feelings or step on anyone's toes. But I'm protective and aggressive, especially where my children are concerned. That's what brought it out of me. A mother protecting my kids. It appalled me that money could be more important than the health of my children.

A mother in New Jersey described overcoming her fear in dealing with male governmental officials at public hearings, "When I look at a male government official, I remember that he was once a little boy, born of a woman like me, and then I feel more powerful." In talking about Love Canal, Lois Gibbs showed the power of motherhood to carry women into activities alien to their experience:

> When it came to Love Canal, we never thought about ourselves as protestors. We carried signs, we barricaded, we blocked the gates, we were arrested. We thought of it as parents protecting our children. In retrospect, of course, we were protesting. I think if it had occurred to us we wouldn't have done it.

In these ways, they appropriated the power they felt in the private arena as a source of empowerment in the public sphere. "We're insecure challenging the authority of trained experts," notes Gibbs, "but we also have a title of authority, 'mother.'"

Working-class women's experiences as organizers of family life served as a further source of empowerment. Lois Gibbs noted that women organized at Love Canal by constantly analyzing how they would handle a situation in the family, and then translating that analysis into political action. For example, Gibbs explained:

> If our child wanted a pair of jeans, who would they go to? Well they would go to their father since their father had the money—that meant we should go to Governor Carey.

Gibbs drew on her own experience to develop organizing conferences that helped working-class women learn to translate their skills as family organizers into the political arena.

> I decided as a housewife and mother much of what I learned to keep the household running smoothly were skills that translated very well into this new thing called organizing. I also decided that this training in running a home was one of the key reasons why so many of the best leaders in the toxic movement—in fact, the overwhelming majority—are women, and specifically women who are housewives and mothers. (Zeff 1989, 177)

Of her work with the CCHW, Gibbs stated:

> In our own organization we're drawing out these experiences for women. So we say, what do you mean you're not an organizer? Are you a homemaker—then God damn it you can organize and you don't know it. So, for example, when we say you need to plan long-term and short-term goals, women may say, I don't know how to do that. . . . We say, what do you mean you don't know how to do that? Let's talk about something in the household—you plan meals for five, seven, fourteen days—you think about what you want for today and what you're going to eat on Sunday—that is short-term and long-term goals.

Movement language like "plug up the toilet," the expression for waste reduction, helped women to reinterpret toxic waste issues in the framework of their everyday experience. "If one does not produce the mess in the first place, one will not have to clean it up later," may sound like a maternal warning, but the expression's use in the toxic waste context implies a radical economic critique, calling for a change in the production processes of industry itself.

As women came to understand that government is not an objective, neutral mediator for the public good, they discovered that "logic" and "objectivity" are tools used by the government to obscure its bias in favor of industry, and motherhood became a strategy to counter public power by framing the terms of the debate. The labels of "hysterical housewives" or "emotional women," used by policy makers to delegitimize the women's authority, became a language of critique and empowerment, one which exposed the limits of the public arena's ability to address the importance of family, health, and community. These labels were appropriated as the women saw that their emotionalism, a valued trait in the private sphere, could be transformed into a powerful weapon in the public arena.

> What's really so bad about showing your feelings? Emotions and intellect are not conflicting traits. In fact, emotions may well be the quality that makes women so effective in the movement. . . . They help us speak the truth.

Finally, through toxic waste protests, women discovered the power they wield as mothers to bring moral issues to the public, exposing the contradictions of a society that purports to value motherhood and family, yet creates social policies that undermine these values:

> We bring the authority of mother—who can condemn mothers? . . . It is a tool we have. Our crying brings the moral issues to the table. And when the public sees our children it brings a concrete, moral dimension to our experience. . . . They are not an abstract statistic.

White, working-class women's stories of their involvement in grassroots toxic waste protests reveal their transformations of initial shyness and intimidation into the self-confidence to challenge the existing system. In reconceptualizing their traditional roles as mothers, these women discovered a new strength. As one activist from Arizona says of herself, "Now I like myself better. I am more assertive and aggressive." These women's role in the private world of family ultimately became a source of personal strength, empirical knowledge, and political strategy in the public sphere. It was a resource of political critique and empowerment which the women appropriated and used as they struggled to protect their families.

Overcoming Obstacles to Participation: Gender Conflicts in the Family

In order to succeed in their fights against toxic wastes in their homes and communities, these women confronted and overcame obstacles not only in the public sphere, but also within the family itself, as their entry into the public arena disrupted both the power relationships and the highly traditional gender roles within the family. Divorce and separation were the manifestations of the crises these disruptions induced. All of the women I interviewed had been married when they first became active in the toxic waste movement. By the time of my interviews with them, more than half were divorced.

A central theme of these women's narratives is the tension created in their marriages by participation in toxic waste protests. This aspect of struggle, so particular to women's lives, is an especially hidden dimension of white, working-class women's activism. Noted one activist from New York:

> People are always talking to us about forming coalitions, but look at all we must deal with beyond the specific issue, the flack that comes with it, the insecurity of your husband that you have outgrown him. Or how do you deal with your children's anger, when they say you love the fight more than me. In a blue-collar community that is very important.

For the most part, white, working-class women's acceptance of a traditional gendered division of labor has also led them to take for granted the power relations within the family.

Penny Newman, who was the West Coast Director of CCHW, reflected on the beginnings of her community involvement:

> I had been married just a couple of years. My husband is a fireman. They have very strict ideas of what family life is in which the woman does not work, you stay at home. . . . I was so insecure, so shy, that when I finally got to join an organization, a woman's club, . . . it would take me two weeks to build up the courage to ask my husband to watch the kids that night. I would really plan out my life a month ahead of time just to build in these little hints that there is a meeting coming up in two weeks, will you be available. Now, if he didn't want to do it, or had other plans, I didn't go to the meeting. (Zeff 1989, 183)

Involvement in toxic waste issues created a conflict between these traditional assumptions and women's concerns about protecting their children, and this conflict made visible the power relations within the family. The CCHW publication *Empowering Women* (1989, 33) noted that:

> Women's involvement in grassroots activism may change their views about the world and their relations with their husbands. Some husbands are actively supportive. Some take no stand: "Go ahead and do what you want. Just make sure you have dinner on the table and my shirts washed." Others forbid time away from the family.

Many of these women struggled to develop coping strategies to defuse conflict and accommodate traditional gender-based power relations in the family. The strategies included involving husbands in protest activities and minimizing their own leadership roles. As Lois Gibbs commented: "If you bring a spouse in, if you can make them part of your growth, then the marriage is more likely to survive, but that is real hard to do sometimes." Will Collette, a former director at CCHW,

relates the ways in which he has observed women avoiding acknowledged leadership roles. He described this encounter with women involved in a toxic waste protest in New York:

> I was sitting around a kitchen table with several women who were leading a protest. And they were complaining about how Lou and Joe did not do their homework and weren't able to handle reports and so on. I asked them why they were officers and the women were doing all the work. They said, "That's what the guys like, it keeps them in and gives us a little peace at home."

In a similar vein, Collette recalled working with an activist from Texas to plan a large public hearing. Upon arriving at the meeting, he discovered that she was sitting in the back, while he was placed on the dais along with the male leadership, which had had no part in the planning process.

As the women became more active in the public arena, traditional assumptions about gender roles created further conflict in their marriages. Women who became visible community leaders experienced the greatest tension. In some cases, the husbands were held responsible for their wives' activities, since they were supposed to be able to "control" their wives. For example, a woman who fought against an incinerator in Arkansas related.

> When the mayor saw my husband, he wanted to know why he couldn't keep his pretty little wife's mouth shut. As I became more active and more outspoken, our marriage became rockier. My husband asked me to tone it down, which I didn't do.

In other cases, women's morals were often called into question by husbands or other community members. Collette relates the experience of an activist in North Dakota who was rumored to be having an affair. The basis for the rumor, as Collette describes, was that "an uppity woman has got to be promiscuous if she dares to organize. In this case, she was at a late-night meeting in another town, and she slept over, so of course she had to have had sex."

Toxic waste issues thus set the stage for tremendous conflict between these women and their husbands. Men saw their roles as providers threatened: the homes they had bought may have become valueless; their jobs may have been at risk; they were asked by their wives to take on housework and child care. Meanwhile, their wives' public activities increasingly challenged traditional views of gender roles. For the women, their husbands' negative response to their entry into the public sphere contradicted an assumption in the family that both husband and wife were equally concerned with the well-being of the children. In talking about Love Canal, Gibbs explained:

> The husband in a blue-collar community is saying, get your ass home and cook me dinner, it's either me or the issue, make your choice. The woman says: How can I make a choice, you're telling me choose between the health of my children and your fucking dinner, how do I deal with that?

When women were asked to choose between their children and their husbands' needs, they began to see the ways in which the children had to be their primary concern.

At times this conflict resulted in more equal power relations within the marriages, a direction that CCHW tried to encourage by organizing family stress workshops. By and large, however, the families of activist women did not tolerate this stress well. Furthermore, as the women began openly to contest traditional power relations in the family, many found that their marriages could not withstand the challenges. As one activist from Arkansas described:

I thought [my husband] didn't care enough about our children to continue to expose them to this danger. I begged him to move. He wouldn't. So I moved my kids out of town to live with my mom.

All twenty women interviewed for this article were active leaders around toxic waste issues in their communities, but only two described the importance of their husband's continuing support. One white woman who formed an interracial coalition in Alabama credited her husband's support in sustaining her resolve:

> I've had death threats. I was scared my husband would lose his job, afraid that somebody's going to kill me. If it weren't for my husband's support, I don't think I could get through all this.

In contrast, most of these activists described the ongoing conflict within their marriages, which often resulted in their abandoning their traditional role in the family, a process filled with inner turmoil. One woman described that turmoil as follows:

> I had doubts about what I was doing, especially when my marriage was getting real rocky. I thought of getting out of [the protest]. I sat down and talked to God many, many times. I asked him to lead me in the right direction because I knew my marriage was failing and I found it hard leaving my kids when I had to go to meetings. I had to struggle to feel that I was doing the right thing. I said a prayer and went on.

Reflecting on the strength she felt as a mother, which empowered her to challenge her government and leave her marriage, she continued:

> It's an amazing ordeal. You always know you would protect your children. But it's amazing to find out how far you will go to protect your own kids.

The disruption of the traditional family often reflected positive changes in women's empowerment. Women grew through the protest; they became stronger and more self-confident. In some cases they found new marriages with men who respected them as strong individuals. Children also came to see their mothers as outspoken and confident.

Thus, for these women, the particularistic issue of toxic waste made visible oppression not only in the public sphere, but also in the family itself. As the traditional organization of family life was disrupted, inequities in underlying power relations were revealed. In order to succeed in fighting a toxic waste issue, these women had also to engage in another level of struggle as they reconceptualized their traditional role in family life in order to carry out their responsibilities as mothers.

Conclusion

The narratives of white, working-class women involved in toxic waste protests in the 1980s reveal the ways in which their subjective, particular experiences led them to analyses that extended beyond the particularistic issue to wider questions of power. Their broader environmental critique grew out of the concrete, immediate, everyday experience of struggling around survival issues. In the process of environmental protest, these women became engaged with specific governmental and corporate institutions and they were forced to reflect on the contradictions of their family life. To win a policy issue, they had to go through a process of developing an oppositional or critical consciousness which informed the direction of their actions and challenged the power of traditional policy makers. The contradiction between a government that claimed to act on behalf of the family and the actual environmental policies and actions of that government were unmasked. The inequities of power between

white, working-class women and middle-class, male public officials were made visible. The reproduction within the family of traditional power relationships was also revealed. In the process of protest these women uncovered and confronted a world of political power shaped by gender and class. This enabled them to act politically around environmental issues, and in some measure to challenge the social relationships of power, inside and outside the home.

Ideologies of motherhood played a central role in the politicizing of white, working-class women around toxic waste issues. Their resistance grew out of an acceptance of a sexual division of labor that assigns to women responsibility for "sustaining the lives of their children and, in a broader sense, their families, including husband, relatives, elders and community." . . .

The analysis of white, working-class women's politicization through toxic waste protests reveals the contradictory role played by dominant ideologies about mothering and democracy in the shaping of these women's oppositional consciousness. The analysis these women developed was not a rejection of these ideologies. Rather, it was a reinterpretation, which became a source of power in the public arena. Their beliefs provided the initial impetus for involvement in toxic waste protests, and became a rich source of empowerment as they appropriated and reshaped traditional ideologies and meanings into an ideology of resistance. . . .

REFERENCES

Bullard, Robert D. 1990. *Dumping in Dixie: Race, Class and Environmental Quality*. Boulder, CO: Westview Press.

Bullard, Robert D. 1994. *Communities of Color and Environmental Justice*. San Francisco: Sierra Club Books.

Citizen's Clearing House for Hazardous Wastes. 1989. *Empowering Women*. Washington, DC: Author.

Krauss, Celene. 1993. "Women and Toxic Waste Protests: Race, Class and Gender as Resources of Resistance." *Qualitative Sociology* 16(3):247–262.

Newman, Penny. 1991. "Women and the Environment in the United States of America." Paper presented at the Conference of Women and the Environment, Bangladore, India.

Ruddick, Sara. 1989. *Maternal Thinking: Towards a Politics of Peace.* New York: Ballantine Books.

Thompson, E. P. 1963. *The Making of the English Working Class.* New York: Pantheon Books.

Zeff, Robin Lee. 1989. "Not in My Backyard/Not in Anyone's Backyard: A Folklorist Examination of the American Grassroots Movement for Environmental Justice." Ph.D. dissertation, Indiana University.

THINKING ABOUT THE READING

Krauss describes how ordinary women became mobilized to construct a movement for social change when they felt their children's health was being threatened. Did their traditional beliefs about motherhood and family help or hinder their involvement in this protest movement? What effect did their participation have on their own families? Why do the women Krauss interviewed identify the toxic waste movement as a women's movement? Why don't men seem to be equally concerned about these health issues? How did the relative powerlessness of their working-class status shape the women's perspective on environmental justice?

Credits

Chapter 1

"Becoming a Marihuana User" by Howard S. Becker. *The American Journal of Sociology*, 59:235-242. Reprinted by permission of The University of Chicago Press.

Chapter 2

"The My Lai Massacre: A Military Crime of Obedience," by Herbert Kelman and V. Lee Hamilton. In *Crimes of Obedience* (pp.1–20), edited by Herbert Kelman and V. Lee Hamilton. © 1989 by Yale University Press. Reprinted by permission.

Speaking of Sadness: Depression, Disconnection, and the Meanings of Illness by David A. Karp (pp. 3-11, 165-185). © 1996 by Oxford University Press, Inc. Used by permission of Oxford University Press, Inc.

Chapter 3

Excerpts from "The Crack Attack: Politics and Media in the Crack Scare" from *Crack in America: Demon Drugs and Social Justice* (pp. 18–51), edited by Craig Reinarman and Harry G. Levine. Berkeley: University of California Press. Copyright © 1997 by the Regents of the University of California. Reprinted by permission.

"Researching Dealers and Smugglers" by Patricia A. Adler, excerpts from *Construction of Deviance: Social Power, Context, and Interaction (with InfoTrac), Fourth Edition*, by P.A. Adler and P. Adler. © 2003. Reprinted with permission of Wadsworth, a division of Thomson Learning (www.thomsonrights.com).

Chapter 4

"Body Ritual among the Nacirema" by Horace Miner. *American Anthropologist* 58:3, June 1956, pp. 503–507.

Excerpts from "The Melting Pot," from *The Spirit Catches You and You Fall Down: A Hmong Child, Her American Doctors, and the Collision of Two Cultures* (pp. 181-209), by Anne Fadiman. Copyright 1997 by Anne Fadiman. Reprinted by permission of Farrar, Straus, and Giroux, LLC.

Chapter 5

"Life as the Maid's Daughter: An Exploration of the Everyday Boundaries of Race, Class, and Gender" by Mary Romero, from *Feminisms in the Academy* by Mary Romero, Abigail J. Stewart, and Donna Stanton (eds.) (pp. 157–179). Copyright © 1995. Used by permission of The University of Michigan Press.

"Sisyphus in a Wheelchair: Men with Physical Disabilities Confront Gender Domination," from *Coming to Terms With Disability*, by Thomas J. Gerschick." © 1998. Pp. 289-212 in J. O'Brien and J. Howard (eds). *Everyday Inequalities: Critical Inquiries* (pp. 189-211). London: Basil Blackwell. Copyright © Blackwell Publishers Ltd., 1998. Editorial introduction and arrangement copyright © Jodi O'Brien and Judith A. Howard, 1998. Used by permission.

Chapter 6

"Frederick the Great or Frederick's of Hollywood? The Accomplishment of Gender Among Women in the Military" by Melissa S. Herbert, in *Everyday Inequalities: Critical Inquiries* (pp. 157-187), edited by Jodi O'Brien and Judith A. Howard. © 1998. Copyright © Blackwell Publishers Ltd., 1998. Editorial introduction and arrangement copyright © Jodi O'Brien and Judith A. Howard, 1998. Used by permission.

"Suspended Identity: Transformation in a Maximum Security Prison" by Thomas J. Schmid and Richard S. Jones. *Symbolic Interaction, 14*(4):415-432. © 1991 by JAI Press, Inc. Reprinted by permission of the University of California Press.

"Webcam Women: Life on Your Screen" by Donald Snyder, in *Web Studies: Rewiring Media Studies for the Digital Age* (pp. 68-73), edited by D. Gauntlett. © 2000 by David Gauntlett. Reprinted by permission of Hodder Arnold.

Chapter 7

Excerpt from *No Place Like Home* by Christopher Carrington. Copyright © 1999. Used by permission of the University of Chicago Press.

"Chasing the Blood Tie: Surrogate Mothers, Adoptive Mothers, and Fathers" Helena Ragoné. 1996. *American Ethnologist, 23*:2. Reprinted by permission of the American Anthropological Association. Not for sale or further reproduction.

Chapter 8

"Branded With Infamy: Inscriptions of Poverty and Class in America" by Vivyan Adair. *Signs* 27(2):451-472 (2002). Used by permission of the University of Chicago Press.

"Medicine as an Institution of Social Control," by Peter Conrad and Joseph W. Schneider. In *Deviance and Medicalization: From Badness to Sickness,* by Peter Conrad and Joseph W. Schneider. Copyright 1992 by Temple University Press and the authors. Used by permission of Temple University Press and the authors; all rights reserved.

Chapter 9

"The Overworked American" by Juliet Schor. Republished with permission of Perseus Books Group, from *Overworked American: The Unexpected Decline of Leisure* by Juliet Schor, Copyright © 1991; permission conveyed through Copyright Clearance Center, Inc.

"The Smile Factory: Work at Disneyland," by John Van Maanen, from *Reframing Organizational Culture,* edited by Peter Frost. Copyright © 1991. Reprinted by permission of Sage Publications, Inc.

Chapter 10

"Software Entrepreneurship Among the Urban Poor: Could Bill Gates Have Succeeded If He Were Black? Or Impoverished?" by Alice H. Amsden and Jon Collins Clark, from *High Technology and Low-Income Communities: Prospects for the Positive Use of Advanced Information Technology,* edited by Donald A. Schon, Bish Sanyal, and William J. Mitchell. Copyright © 2000. Used by permission of The MIT Press.

From *Savage Inequalities* by Jonathan Kozol, copyright © 1991 by Jonathan Kozol. Used by permission of Crown Publishers, a division of Random House, Inc.

Chapter 11

Chapter 12

Chapter 13

Chapter 14